ORGANIZATIONAL BEHAVIOR

WILEY SERIES IN MANAGEMENT

For further information on these and additional Wiley business titles visit the Wiley home page at http://www.wiley.com/college.html.

ORGANIZATIONAL BEHAVIOR

SIXTH EDITION

JOHN R. SCHERMERHORN, JR.
Ohio University

JAMES G. HUNT
Texas Tech University

RICHARD N. OSBORN
Wayne State University

JOHN WILEY & SONS, INC.

New York   Chichester   Brisbane   Toronto   Singapore

Acquisitions Editors	Petra Sellers, Ellen Ford
Developmental Editor	Rachel Nelson
Cover Photo	Dave Lawrence/The Stock Market
Cover Design	Madelyn Lesure
Text Design	Laura Ierardi/LCI Design
OB Workbook Design	Kenny Beck/Kenny Beck Design
Illustrators	Radiant Illustration and Design
	Hudson River Studio
Production Editor	Tony VenGraitis
Outside Production Management	Suzanne Ingrao at Ingrao Associates
Senior Marketing Manager	Karen Allman
Manufacturing Manager	Mark Cirillo
Copy Editor	Lindsay Ardwin
Photo Researcher	Hilary Newman
Illustration Coordinator	Rosa Bryant
Photo Research Associate	Elaine Paoloni
Program Assistant	Pui Szeto

This book was set in Century Old Style by Ruttle, Shaw & Wetherill, Inc. and printed and bound by Von Hoffmann Press. The cover was printed by Lehigh Press. Color separations were handled by Lehigh Press Colortronics.

Recognizing the importance of preserving what has been written, it is a policy of John Wiley & Sons, Inc. to have books of enduring value published in the United States printed on acid-free paper, and we exert our best efforts to that end.

The paper in this book was manufactured by a mill whose forest management programs include sustained yield harvesting of its timberlands. Sustained yield harvesting principles ensure that the number of trees cut each year does not exceed the amount of new growth.

Library of Congress Cataloging-in-Publication Data

Schermerhorn, John R.
    Organizational behavior / John R. Schermerhorn, Jr., James G.
  Hunt, Richard N. Osborn. — 6th ed.
        p.   cm.
    Rev. ed. of: Managing organizational behavior, 4th ed. c1991.
    Includes bibliographical references and index.
    ISBN 0-471-15416-4 (cloth : alk. paper)
    1. Organizational behavior. 2. Management. I. Schermerhorn,
John R. Managing organizational behavior. II. Hunt, James G.,
1932–   . III. Osborn, Richard. IV. Title.
HD58.7.S34   1997
658—dc20   96-35434
                                                                CIP

Printed in the United States of America.

10 9 8 7 6 5 4 3 2

CONTRIBUTORS

▼ CASES FOR CRITICAL THINKING

Barry R. Armandi, *State University of New York,* Forrest F. Aven, *University of Houston, Downtown,* Kim Cameron, *Brigham Young University,* Daniel S. Cochran, *Mississippi State University,* Anne C. Cowden, *California State University, Sacramento,* Bernardo M. Ferdman, *California School of Professional Psychology,* Placido L. Gallegos, *Southwest Communications Resources, Inc. and the Kaleel Jamison Consulting Group. Inc.,* Tony A. Gregory, *Private Consultant,* Ellen Ernst Kossek, *Michigan State University,* Ronald P. Lewis, *IBM Consulting Group,* Barbara McCain, *Oklahoma City University,* Mary McGarry, *Empire State College,* Aneil Mishra, *Pennsylvania State University,* Karen Mishra, *Pennsylvania State University,* William T. Neese, *Troy State University,* Marc Osborn, *Arizona Chamber of Commerce,* V. Jean Ramsey, *Texas Southern University,* Franklin Ramsoomair, *Wilfrid Laurier University,* John Seeger, *Bentley College.*

▼ EXPERIENTIAL EXERCISES AND SELF-ASSESSMENT INVENTORIES

Barry R. Armandi, *State University of New York, Old Westbury,* Ariel Fishman, *The Wharton School, University of Pennsylvania,* D.T. Hall, *Boston University,* F.S. Hall, *University of New Hampshire,* Conrad N. Jackson, *MPC, Inc.,* Mary Khalili, *Oklahoma City University,* Robert Ledman, *Morehouse College,* Paul Lyons, *Frostburg State University,* J. Marcus Maier, *Chapman University,* Michael R. Manning, *New Mexico State University,* Barbara McCain, *Oklahoma City University,* Annie McKee, *The Wharton School, University of Pennsylvania,* Bonnie McNeely, *Murray State University,* Alfonso Mountouri, *Saybrook Institute,* Ronald E. Purser, *Loyola University of Chicago,* W. Alan Randolph, *University of Baltimore,* Paula J. Schmidt, *New Mexico State University,* Susan Schor, *Pace University,* Timothy T. Serey, *Northern Kentucky University,* Barbara Walker, *Diversity Consultant,* Paula S. Weber, *New Mexico Highlands University,* Janet W. Wohlberg, *President, Hands-On Learning, Inc.,* Susan Rawson Zacur, *University of Baltimore.*

ABOUT THE AUTHORS

D R. JOHN R. SCHERMERHORN, JR., is the Charles G. O'Bleness Professor of Management in the College of Business Administration at Ohio University. He earned a Ph.D. in organizational behavior from Northwestern University, after receiving an M.B.A. (with distinction) from New York University, and a B.S. from the State University of New York at Buffalo. He was on-site Coordinator of Ohio University E.M.B.A. and M.B.A. programs in Malaysia and has served as Visiting Professor of Management at the Chinese University of Hong Kong as well as Visiting Scholar at Liaoning University in China and the Technical University of Wroclaw in Poland. Dr. Schermerhorn has won awards for teaching excellence at Tulane University, the University of Vermont, and Ohio University, where he has been named a University Professor, the university's leading award for undergraduate teaching. He is the author and coauthor of over 50 journal articles, book chapters, and proceedings. His other Wiley books include *Management* (Wiley, Fifth Edition, 1996), *Management and Organizational Behavior Essentials* (Wiley, 1996), and *Basic Organizational Behavior* (Wiley, 1995).

D R. JAMES G. (JERRY) HUNT is the Paul Whitfield Horn Professor of Management, Professor of Health Organization Management, Director, Program in Leadership, Institute for Management and Leadership Research, and department chair of Management, Texas Tech University. He received his Ph.D. and Master's degrees from the University of Illinois, after completing a B.S. (with honors) at Michigan Technological University. Dr. Hunt has coauthored an Organization Theory text and *Basic Organizational Behavior* (John Wiley & Sons, 1995) and has authored or coauthored three leadership monographs. He founded the Leadership Symposia Series and coedited the eight volumes based on the series. He has presented or published nearly 200 articles, papers, and book chapters, and his most recent books are *Leadership: A New Synthesis*, published by Sage, and *Strategic Leadership: A Multiorganizational-Level Perspective*, published by Quorum. The former was a finalist for the Academy of Management's 1993 Terry Distinguished Book Award. Recently, Dr. Hunt received the Distinguished Service Award from the Academy of Management and the Barnie E. Rushing. Jr. Distinguished Researcher Award from Texas Tech University for his long-term contributions to management research and scholarship.

D R. RICHARD N. OSBORN is Professor of Management and Organizational Sciences in the School of Business Administration, Wayne State University. He has received teaching awards at Southern Illinois University at Carbondale and Wayne State University, and he has also taught at Monash University (Australia), Tulane University, and the University of Washington. With over 100 publications, Dr. Osborn is a leading authority on international alliances in tech-

nology-intensive industries and is a member of the editorial boards of the *Academy of Management Journal*, *Technology Studies*, and *Journal of High Technology Management*. He is very active in the Academy of Management, having served as divisional program chair and president, and he is currently the Academy representative for the International Federation of Scholarly Associations of Management. Dr. Osborn's research has been sponsored by the Department of Defense, Ford Motor Company, National Science Foundation, Nissan, and the Nuclear Regulatory Commission, among others. In addition to teaching, Dr. Osborn spent a number of years in private industry, including a position as a senior research scientist with the Battelle Memorial Institute in Seattle, where he worked on improving the safety of commercial nuclear power.

PREFACE

The study of organizational behavior is essential for anyone who plans to become a part of the modern workplace. It doesn't matter whether an individual career unfolds in the arena of business, government, education, or public service. It *does* matter that the individual is prepared for a career that is highly uncertain, bound for continuous change, and affected by the forces and challenges of high technology. The goal of this book is to help today's students become leaders of tomorrow's organizations. The twenty-first century is before us, and its character belongs to the students reading this book. What they do as managers will not only shape the contributions of the institutions of developed societies but also fundamentally alter lives around the globe.

Just as borderlines are disappearing in the global economy, functional lines are disappearing within organizations. One has only to read the business and management media—from the pages of *The Wall Street Journal, Fortune, Business Week, The Economist,* and other periodicals and local newspapers—to find reports on all the current developments in organizations and management. The notion of continuous change is also evident in the hallway conversations and informal networks in which professional managers meet to share approaches and discuss problems and opportunities with one another.

As educators, we make up an important component of a new era—one in which the old ways and standards just aren't good enough anymore. We live and work in a society that expects high performance and high quality-of-work-life to go hand in hand; that considers ethics and social responsibility paramount measures of individual and organizational performance; whose workforces are increasingly rich in demographic and cultural diversity; and in which the imprint of a global economy and the internationalization of daily life are pervasive themes.

The sixth edition of *Organizational Behavior* was revised with these realities in mind. The book has been substantially redesigned and redeveloped from the foundations set by its predecessors, five editions of *Managing Organizational Behavior.* Our recommitment to organizational behavior and the central role of OB in the learning environment is best communicated by the simpler and more direct new title — *Organizational Behavior, Sixth Edition.* You will find that this latest edition offers similar content to its predecessors but in a trimmer, reorganized, updated, and completely redesigned format to better serve the needs of students who must face the challenges of tomorrow's workplace, not yesterday's. This revision was guided by the feedback we received through a series of focus groups with both students and instructors in the United States and Canada. We have written this book for students who want to understand the discipline of OB in full awareness of its practical value and importance to their future careers. And we have written this book to meet the needs of instructors who want to give their students a solid introduction to the discipline with a strong emphasis and a com-

mitment to its practical application. *Organizational Behavior, Sixth Edition* is our contribution to the study of this dynamic and increasingly relevant discipline.

John R. Schermerhorn, Jr.
Ohio University

James G. (Jerry) Hunt
Texas Tech University

Richard N. Osborn
Seattle, Washington

ABOUT THIS BOOK

Organizational Behavior, Sixth Edition brings to its readers the solid and complete content core of prior editions, along with many revisions, updates, and enhancements that reflect today's dynamic times. The book covers the discipline in an orderly progression, but allows for parts and/or chapters to be used out of sequence at the instructor's prerogative. We do strongly suggest, however, that the two opening chapters in Part 1: The Environment—Chapter 1, "Organizational Behavior and the New Workplace," and Chapter 2, "International Dimensions of Organizational Behavior"—be used in sequence to set the context for a course. This frames the study of organizational behavior in the environment of the newly emerging workplace and the rapid internationalization of work and careers.

Parts 2, 3, 4, and 5 offer the basic building blocks for understanding OB—the study of individuals, groups, organizations, and processes, respectively. In each of these parts, readers will find chapters offering solid coverage of the basic theories and concepts of organizational behavior, along with many examples and guidelines emphasizing their practical application in management.

▼ CHANGES AND UPDATES

In addition to the foundations provided in preceding editions, *Organizational Behavior, Sixth Edition* offers new and expanded coverage of the following topics.

- *Chapter 1: Organizational Behavior and the New Workplace*—Changes in the workplace, life-long learning, ethical behavior, social responsibility, quality of working life
- *Chapter 2: International Dimensions of Organizational Behavior*—Regional economic alliances, values and national cultures, cultural differences, expatriate work, global organizational learning
- *Chapter 3: Diversity and Individual Differences*—Workforce diversity, demographic differences, personality differences, valuing and managing diversity
- *Chapter 4: Perception and Attribution*—Perception as an influence in organizational behavior, attribution theory and implications
- *Chapter 5: Motivation*—Motivation across cultures, motivation and job satisfaction
- *Chapter 6: Performance Management and Rewards*—Human resource management, career planning and development, performance evaluation, reward systems
- *Chapter 7: Learning and Reinforcement*—Social learning and behavioral self-management
- *Chapter 8: Job Design, Goal Setting, and Work Arrangements*—Technology and job design, process reengineering, goal setting and MBO, alternative work schedules

- *Chapter 9: The Nature of Groups*—Group contributions to organizations, foundations of group effectiveness, group dynamics and decision making
- *Chapter 10: Teamwork and Workgroup Design*—High-performance teams, team building, employee involvement groups, self-managing teams, virtual teams
- *Chapter 11: Basic Attributes of Organizations*—Organizational goals, control systems, alternative structures
- *Chapter 12: Organizational Design and Learning*—Contingency influences of size, technology, environment, and strategy; organizational learning
- *Chapter 13: Organizational Culture*—Values and organizational culture, sub-cultures, culture building through organizational development
- *Chapter 14: Power and Politics*—Gaining and using power, empowerment, understanding and dealing with organizational politics
- *Chapter 15: Leadership*—Behavioral and contingency theory updates, attribution theory and the new leadership, leadership and high-performance teams
- *Chapter 16: Communication*—Effective communication, technology and communication, the electronic office, cultural differences
- *Chapter 17: Decision Making*—Decision-making models, judgmental heuristics, participation, ethics, cultural differences
- *Chapter 18: Conflict and Negotiation*—Constructive conflict, conflict management, integrative negotiation
- *Chapter 19: Change, Innovation, and Stress*—Continuous change, strategies of change, innovation processes, stress management
- *Supplementary Module: Research Foundations of OB*—Research designs, working with data, ethical considerations

▼ PEDAGOGICAL FEATURES

As always, a primary goal in writing this book is to create a textbook that appeals to the student reader, while still offering solid content. Through market research surveys and focus groups with students and professors, we learned what features worked best from previous editions, what could be improved, and what could be added to accomplish this goal both effectively and efficiently. The participants in the focus groups in particular were quite forthcoming about their likes and dislikes. With a number of textbooks laid out before them, they told us what worked for them and what didn't. The outcome is the following list of pedagogical elements that appear in every chapter of *Organizational Behavior, Sixth Edition.*

- *Chapter-opening Photo Essays* Each chapter opens with a "best practices" vignette that is linked to the chapter content. These real-world examples show how people can make a difference in the way organizations operate and offer a visionary stimulus to start students on a voyage of discovery as they examine the content that follows. Internet web site addresses of many of the companies are included in these essays.
- *Study Questions* Following the opening vignette, the chapter focuses the reader's attention through a set of boxed study questions that are tied to both the major headings of the chapter and the concluding summary.

- *Embedded Boxes* Throughout the chapter, embedded boxes are used to further illustrate best practices applications. These boxes have been substantially reduced in length from the previous edition, providing more concise and relevant examples without disrupting the flow of the text. *Diversity, Quality, Ethics and Social Responsibility,* and *Global* issues are the themes of these visual examples.

- New to this edition, *annotated margin photos* add variety to the content without breaking up the flow of text. These annotated margin photos provide additional current real-world examples of OB in practice. Many include the company's web site address so that the student can peruse additional information about the company on the Internet.

- The Effective Manager boxes that appeared in the margins of the fifth edition have been moved into the text as *Take A Note* memos. These practical tips and applications have been streamlined and embedded in the text discussion, offering useful action guidelines on a number of relevant topics.

- The list of key terms that appear in the *running glossary* of the previous edition has been minimized to avoid complicating the presentation. Only the most important and relevant concepts are boldfaced and defined in the margin as key terms, reducing the jargon and the need to memorize terminology. All of the boldfaced key terms and additional italicized important terms are included in a comprehensive *glossary* at the end of the book, providing one-stop definitions of all the terms introduced in the book.

- The use of lists has been minimized in this edition as well; where they are used, *margin list identifiers* call them out for the reader's attention.

- At the end of each chapter, the reader finds a complete *Chapter Study Guide,* a total learning instrument that meets the student's needs. This feature includes three components that help students consolidate their learning and prepare for quizzes and examinations. A *bullet-list summary* is tied back to the chapter-opening study questions. A *list of key terms*, with page references, links them back to the boldfaced terms in the text and their margin definitions. A chapter *self-test* serves as a built-in study guide, offering multiple-choice, true–false, short response, and applications essay questions. Specifically added at the request of students, the format of the self-tests reflects the types of questions students will be expected to answer on in-class exams. Answers to all of the self-test questions, including the applications essays, are available in the back of the book.

▼ THE ORGANIZATIONAL BEHAVIOR WORKBOOK

Numerous *case studies for critical thinking, experiential exercises,* and *self-assessment inventories* have been contributed by a number of professors of Organizational Behavior throughout the United States and Canada and assembled in a new section of the book, *The Organizational Behavior Workbook.* This selection represents a collection of both tried-and-true and unique cases, exercises, and assessments that have been used in classrooms throughout North America. We have brought them to you in one self-contained section of this book to help you enrich your class sessions. Rather than tie this vast portfolio of choices to specific chapters, we have offered a matrix of choices for you to select from. Most importantly, we have gathered these from colleagues who are known for their innovative teaching. Among the case studies included in *The Organizational Behavior Workbook* are some adapted from those published by the North American Case Research Association and the Western Business School of London, Ontario. The exercises and assessments provide a mix of group and individual activities for classroom use.

New *Internet exercises* have been developed to match the content of each chapter of the text. These exercises ask students to call up the web site of a company, search for relevant information related to the chapter content, and answer thought-provoking questions. The student can access these exercises by clicking on the Wiley homepage at http://www.wiley.com/college.html. This feature is updated regularly, ensuring that your students are as up-to-date as others in understanding this vast electronic information resource.

▼ SUPPORT PACKAGE

Organizational Behavior, Sixth Edition is supported by a comprehensive learning package that assists the instructor in creating a motivating and enthusiastic environment.

- Written by Franklin Ramsoomair of Wilfrid Laurier University, the *Instructor's Resource Guide* is a comprehensive guide to building a system of customized instruction. The guide provides a general philosophy of the text, selected issues in teaching an Organizational Behavior course, sample course outlines, sample assignments, notes on the use of cases, group assignments, videos, and a teaching guide for each chapter. In addition, each chapter of the text is broken down into an outline and synopsis, additional resources, teaching tips, questions for class discussion, and additional examples. Answers to all end-of-book cases, exercises, and assessments are also included.
- A comprehensive *Test Bank* is available, consisting of over 2500 multiple-choice, true–false, and essay questions, categorized by page number and type of questions (factual or applied). Hrach Bedrosian of New York University and the Educational Testing Service carefully reviewed every question of the fifth edition, providing insight as to which questions to keep, revise, and replace, to ensure that the new test bank is both valid and reliable. The test bank was authored by Abdul Aziz of the College of Charleston and Robb Bay of Community College of Southern Nevada and is also available in a computerized version for IBM compatible computers.
- Over 100 full-color *transparency acetates* are available consisting of all text art and additional key concepts. A series of electronic *Power Point transparencies* serves as a powerful lecture aid to reinforce the principles introduced in the text visually and graphically. Instructors are also able to add their own material to the presentation or modify existing material to meet their needs.
- A comprehensive *Video Package* offers an audiovisual supplement that ties directly to the core topics of the text and brings to life real-world examples of organizational behavior in practice. The *Wiley Nightly Business Report* video

contains segments from the highly respected *Nightly Business Report*, which have been selected for their applicability to organizational behavior principles and for their reinforcement of key concepts in the text. Each of the segments is approximately 3 to 5 minutes long and can be used to introduce topics to the students, enhance lecture material, and provide real-world context for related concepts. An additional *integrating video case on AT&T* has been developed by Ann Cowden of California State University, Sacramento. Culled from *Nightly Business Report* segments, the video spans the entire period from the breakup of the Bell System in 1984 to AT&T's latest plan to spin off into three independent companies, laying off thousands of workers in the process. The series corresponds to the five parts of the texts, focusing on such major topics as teamwork, empowerment, competitive pressures, and downsizing.

- An *Organizational Behavior Workbook Supplement* is available, providing additional cases and experiential exercises to supplement those found in the text.
- Key instructor's supplements, including all text art, are available on one CD ROM disk, *CD ROM Lecture Support.* An easy-to-follow instruction guide describes how to access the various components.
- *The Wiley Custom Publishing System* is a database of selected Wiley management textbooks and trade titles, complete with exercises, figures, and illustrations. If you cannot find the right text that exactly matches your course needs, the Custom Publishing System allows you to draw upon Wiley's management resources to create your own classic text by browsing through the database of titles, selecting the materials you want, by chapter, from as many books as you like, adding your own original material, if you like. Wiley will pull together the material for you, establish a unique ISBN for your custom textbook, and deliver the finished product to the bookstore.

ACKNOWLEDGMENTS

Organizational Behavior, Sixth Edition benefits from insights provided by a dedicated group of management educators from around the globe who carefully read and critiqued draft chapters of this edition. We are pleased to express our appreciation to the following colleagues for their contributions to this new edition.

Steve Axley
Western Illinois University

Roger A. Dean
Washington & Lee University

Theresa Feener
Northern Alberta Institute of Technology

Robert Giambatista
University of Wisconsin

Stephen Gourlay
Kingston University

Peter Gustavson
Linkoping University

Kristi Harrison
Centennial College

Howard Kahn
Heriot-Watt University, Edinburgh

Beverly Linnell
Southern Alberta Institute of Technology

Michael London
The Wharton School, University of Pennsylvania

Franklin Ramsoomair
Wilfrid Laurier University

R. Murray Sharp
British Columbia Institute of Technology

Pat Sniderman
Ryerson Polytechnic University

Bobbie Williams
Georgia Southern University

Barry Wright
Queen's University

We also thank those reviewers who contributed to the success of previous editions, setting the groundwork for this sixth edition:

Merle Ace
Chi Anyansi-Archibong
Terry Armstrong
Leanne Atwater
Richard Babcock
Robert Barbato
Richard Barrett
Nancy Bartell
Anna Bavetta
Bonnie Betters-Reed
Gerald Biberman
Mauritz Blonder
Dale Blount
G. B. Bohn
Joseph F. Byrnes
Gene E. Burton
Daniel R. Cillis
Paul Collins
Deborah Crown
Delf Dodge

Dennis Duchon
Michael Dumler
Ken Eastman
Dalmar Fisher
J. Benjamin Forbes
Cynthia V. Fukami
Normandie Gaitley
Daniel Ganster
Joe Garcia
Manton Gibbs
Eugene Gomolka
Barbara Goodman
Frederick Greene
Richard Grover
Bengt Gustafsson
Don Hantula
William Hart
Nell Hartley
Neil J. Humphreys
David Hunt

Eugene Hunt
Harriet Kandelman
Paul N. Keaton
Peter Kreiner
Donald Lantham
Kathy Lippert
Carol Lucchesi
David Luther
Lorna Martin
Douglas McCabe
James McFillen
Charles Milton
Herff L. Moore
David Morean
Sandra Morgan
Paula Morrow
Richard Mowday
Linda Neider
Dennis Pappas
Edward B. Parks

Robert F. Pearse
Lawrence Peters
Joseph Porac
Samuel Rabinowitz
Charles L. Roegiers
Steven Ross
Michael Rush
Richard J. Sebastian
Anson Seers
Allen N. Shub

Dayle Smith
Walter W. Smock
Ritch L. Sorenson
Shanthi Srinivas
Paul L. Starkey
Sharon Tucker
Ted Valvoda
Joyce Vincelette
David Vollrath
W. Fran Waller

Charles Wankel
Fred A. Ware, Jr.
Andrea F. Warfield
Harry Waters, Jr.
Joseph W. Weiss
Deborah Wells
Barry L. Wisdom
Wayne Wormley
Raymond Zammuto

Efforts to extend *Organizational Behavior, Sixth Edition* in new directions have benefited greatly from those educators whose works are represented in *The Organizational Behavior Workbook*, a major new feature of this text. These colleagues are identified in the workbook with their contributions, and we greatly appreciate the range of innovative pedagogical options they help provide users of this book. We would also like to acknowledge Theresa Feener and her student, Karly Merwin, of Northern Alberta Institute of Technology, for their valuable work collecting and suggesting articles on Canadian companies to include in this edition. They provided a valuable resource of company examples, many of which appear in this book. We would also like to thank Franklin Ramsoomair of Wilfrid Laurier University for developing the Internet exercises that are available through the Wiley homepage.

We are grateful for all the hard work of the supplements authors who worked to develop the comprehensive ancillary package described above. In particular, we thank Franklin Ramsoomair, this time for authoring the Instructor's Resource Guide; Abdul Aziz, of College of Charleston, and Robb Bay, of Community College of Southern Nevada for developing the test bank, and Hrach Bedrosian of New York University and the ETS for providing developmental input into the test questions; Ann Cowden of California State University, Sacramento for developing the *Nightly Business Report AT&T* video series; and Marian Provenzano for her work in assembling the Wiley Custom Publishing System.

As always, the support staff at John Wiley & Sons was most helpful in the various stages of developing and producing this edition. Our editors, Petra Sellers and Ellen Ford, applied the very best of OB to build a committed high-performance team to work with us on the book. We thank them for maintaining the quest for quality and timeliness—in all aspects of the book's content and design. Rachel Nelson's dedicated efforts as developmental editor both led and supported us in exploring new directions throughout the project. Maddy Lesure was the creative force behind the new design, while Hilary Newman's special talent as photo researcher resulted in the beautiful use of photography that enhances this edition. We also thank Suzanne Ingrao of Ingrao Associates and Tony VenGraitis of Wiley for their excellent production assistance, Lindsay Ardwin for copyediting, Rosa Bryant for overseeing the illustration program, Mark Cirillo for supervising the manufacturing of the book, and Andrea Bryant for managing the development of the supplements package. Ellen Ford's extra efforts in developing *The Organizational Behavior Workbook* are also greatly appreciated. Thank you everyone!!

BRIEF CONTENTS

CONTENTS

THE ORGANIZATIONAL BEHAVIOR
WORKBOOK   427

ORGANIZATIONAL BEHAVIOR AND THE NEW WORKPLACE

When Lynda Chavez-Thompson won election to become the first executive vice president of the AFL-CIO, she broke the "glass ceiling." She is the first woman or Latina to hold such a high office in the 110-year history of this labor organization, representing more than 13 million workers. The organization needs her, say such outside observers as Professor Thomas A. Kochan of the Massachusetts Institute of Technology, who considers the appointment "essential" to the AFL-CIO's future success. The American labor movement has been struggling to offset declining union membership. Among the bright spots in this otherwise gloomy picture is growth in minority representation of women, African Americans, and Latino Americans. Chavez-Thompson believes she is there to help expand union penetration in these growth markets, saying: "I'm a woman and I'm tan and I'm from Texas. I represent the America that organized labor has tended to overlook." Still, she has to carve out legitimacy in an organization whose leadership has been dominated by white males. Not everyone is on her side, and questions have been raised about her experience and possible tokenism in her appointment. But Chavez-Thompson is confident and committed. With many years of union organizing behind her, she seems well prepared for the task. This daughter of a Mexican-American sharecropper isn't backing down to criticisms. "I've walked, talked, and won everything a labor leader has needed to do to protect her workers," she says. As she tackles her new job, Lynda Chavez-Thompson serves as a role model for others. (http://www.cornell.edu/othersites/index/Employee/AFL Org Inst.html)[1]

This book is about people at work in new and highly demanding settings. It is about people who seek career fulfillment in challenging times dominated by issues of productivity, quality, diversity, and competitive advantage. And it is about workers who experience *future shock,* the discomfort of continual and uncertain change.[2] No one understands this message better than Lynda Chavez-Thompson. She and others like her recognize that jobs today are complicated by unprecedented complications and opportunities. We live and work in an age of global competition, new technologies, shifting demographics, and changing social values. We work in organizations that seek ever-higher performance while implementing new technologies, streamlining employment, and simplifying systems and processes. We also work in organizations challenged by declines in workforce loyalty, even as they seek to increase employee involvement and foster more integrated cross-functional thinking.

Chapter 1 introduces the field of organizational behavior as a useful knowledge base for today's dynamic environment. As you read the chapter, keep in mind these key questions.

- ◉ Why is organizational behavior important in the new workplace?
- ◉ How do we learn about organizational behavior?
- ◉ What are organizations like as work settings?
- ◉ What is the nature of managerial work?
- ◉ How do ethics influence human behavior in organizations?

ORGANIZATIONAL BEHAVIOR TODAY

Progressive workplaces today—and most certainly the typical workplaces of tomorrow—have different features and ways of operating from those of the past. The workplace is changing, and it will continue to do so. A magazine article describes the situation this way: "Call it whatever you like—reengineering, restructuring, transformation, flattening, downsizing, rightsizing, a quest for global competitiveness —it's real, it's radical, and it's arriving every day at a company near you."[3] Speaking to everyone whose careers will unfold in such settings, the article points out that ". . . the revolution feels something like this: scary, guilty, painful, liberating, disorienting, exhilarating, empowering, frustrating, fulfilling, confusing, challenging. In other words, it feels very much like chaos."

SEARS ROEBUCK & Co.

Sears, Roebuck & Co. sets a model for employing the disabled. "The bulk of our accommodations are common sense and any company should be able to provide them," says a spokesperson. The firm finds that many changes can be made at little or no cost.[6]

▼ WHAT IS ORGANIZATIONAL BEHAVIOR?

Formally defined, **organizational behavior** (OB for short) is the study of individuals and groups in organizations. It is a body of knowledge that has special implications for people at work in all types of settings. Learning about OB will help you develop a better work-related understanding about yourself and other people; it can expand your potential for career success in the dynamic, shifting, complex, and challenging *new* workplaces of today...and tomorrow.

▼ CHANGES IN THE WORKFORCE

One important watchword of the day is **workforce diversity**—the presence of differences based upon gender, race and ethnicity, age, and able-bodiedness.[4] Success in the new workplace increasingly requires a set of skills for working successfully with a broad mix of people from different racial and ethnic backgrounds, of different ages and genders, and of different domestic and national cultures. The theme of *valuing diversity* is prominent. This refers to managing and working with others in full respect for their individual differences. Interpersonal sensitivity and understanding are indispensable to valuing diversity. The job title of "diversity manager" is already appearing on many organizational charts; the job holder is expected to lead the push to make the workplace truly open to the talents of persons of all demographic backgrounds.[5]

But even with the emphasis on valuing diversity, all is not equal in the workplace. In still too many situations, a **glass ceiling** exists as a hidden barrier limiting the career advancement of women and minorities. For example, women hold fewer than 5 percent of senior executive jobs in corporate America; overall, they earn about 5 to 15 percent less than men in similar jobs. Unemployment rates for African Americans often double those of whites, and they earn only about two thirds as much as whites.[7] In Canada, native aboriginals earn an average of 14,000 to 17,000 Canadian dollars per year less than whites, regardless of their credentials and gender.[8] Even though almost one half of Canada's chartered accountants are female, they trail men in partnership admissions at the largest account-

Organizational behavior is the study of individuals and groups in organizations.

Workforce diversity involves differences based on gender, race and ethnicity, age, and able-bodiedness.

The **glass ceiling** is a hidden barrier limiting advancement of women and minorities in organizations.

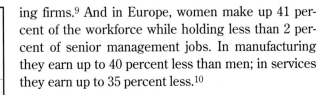

ing firms.[9] And in Europe, women make up 41 percent of the workforce while holding less than 2 percent of senior management jobs. In manufacturing they earn up to 40 percent less than men; in services they earn up to 35 percent less.[10]

> ### ▼ CHANGES IN CUSTOMER EXPECTATIONS

Only those organizations that deliver what customers want in terms of quality, service, and cost will prosper in today's highly competitive environments. This is the age of **total quality management** (TQM)—management dedicated to ensuring that an organization and all of its members are committed to high quality, continuous improvement, and customer satisfaction. *"Quality"* in this sense means that customers' needs are met and that all tasks are done right the first time. Indeed, the term *total service management* is increasingly being used to emphasize the customer commmitment that underlies true total quality management. An important hallmark of total quality or total service management is the notion of **continuous improvement**—the belief that anything and everything done in the workplace should be continually evaluated by asking two questions: (1) Is this necessary? and (2) If so, can it be done better?

Of course, one of the risks is that any quality program will be considered a magical cure for whatever ails an organization. Indeed, consultants report that some firms actually waste money pursuing quality improvement strategies that don't work.[11] This typically happens when the approaches lack important long-term and organizational support; the programs are left to succeed on the basis of well-publicized slogans alone. Unless the values and beliefs shared among organization members reflect a true commitment to quality operations and outcomes, neither TQM nor any program like it will work—at least not as well as expected.

Some companies approach TQM as though it's a magic formula. They say a few words, make some gestures, and—poof—little happens. But at Honeywell UK of Newhouse, Scotland, TQM principles are applied to every aspect of its business. Internal and external customers are interviewed to identify problems; managers are trained to support quality. The firm has increased production speed, reduced inventory, freed up storage space, and slashed overhead costs. Response time has improved so that inventory turns over 36 times a year. There is no business problem Honeywell can't tackle, as long as employees embrace empowerment and TQM goals. Indeed, employees generate so many ideas for continuous improvement that the company faces a new and unique challenge—how to prioritize all the ideas.[12]

GLOBAL

Take A Note 1.1

HOW TO MAKE DIVERSITY STICK

· Focus on getting the best talent
· Develop career plans for all employees
· Provide career mentoring by diversity cohorts
· Promote minorities to responsible positions
· Hold managers accountable for diversity goals
· Build diversity into senior management

Total quality management is a total commitment to high-quality results, continuous improvement, and meeting customer needs.

Continuous improvement is the belief that anything and everything done in the workplace should be continually improved.

▼ CHANGES IN ORGANIZATIONS

The 1990s may well be remembered as the decade that fundamentally changed the way people work.[13] We have experienced the stresses of downsizing and restructuring; we have gained sensitivity to the peaks and valleys of changing economic times; and we have witnessed the advent of the internet with its impact on both people and organizations. Truly progressive organizations, however, are doing much more than simply cutting employees and adding technology to reduce the scale of operations in the quest for productivity. They are changing the very essence of the way things are done.

One of the latest developments in the fast-paced world of organizational change is **process reengineering**. Formally defined, this involves rethinking and radically redesigning business processes to stimulate innovation and change and improve critical performance measures such as cost, quality, service, and speed.[14] Organizations are asked to "start over"— to forget how things were done in the past and to ask only how they should be done to best meet critical performance measures. Answers to these questions are used to redesign activities and workflows to give better value to both internal and external customers.

Also consistent with the newer values is the **upside-down pyramid** view of organizations, as shown in Figure 1.1. This figure focuses attention on total quality service to customers and clients by placing them at the top of the upside-down pyramid. It requires that workers operate in ways that directly affect customers and clients; it requires that supervisors and middle managers do things that directly support the workers; it requires that top managers clarify the organizational mission and objectives, set strategies, and make adequate resources available.[15]

New technology has made possible the **virtual corporation**, one that exists only as a temporary network or alliance of otherwise independent companies jointly pursuing a particular business interest.[16] Members of a typical virtual corporation consist of independent suppliers, customers, and even competitors, who link up with the latest electronic information technologies and share such things as skills, costs, and access to global markets.[17] They work together in shifting pools of alliances that are formed, utilized, and disbanded with ease, all in quick response to business opportunities.

The changing organizational environment has led British scholar and consultant Charles Handy to describe the career implications of what he calls the *shamrock organization*.[18] A shamrock, the Irish national emblem, has three leaves per stem. Each leaf represents a different group of people. The first leaf is a core group of workers made up of permanent, full-time employees with critical skills, who follow standard career paths. This is a relatively small group, perhaps those who remain after major downsizing of a more traditional organization. The second leaf is a group of outside operators who are engaged contractually by the core group to perform a variety of jobs essential to the daily functioning of the organization. Many of these jobs would be performed by full-time staff in a more traditional organization. The third leaf is a group of part-timers who can be hired temporarily by the core group as the needs of the business grow and who can just

Process reengineering is the total rethinking and redesign of organizational processes to improve performance and innovation.

The **upside-down pyramid** puts customers first and views the job of managers as supporting customer service workers.

A **virtual corporation** is a temporary network or alliance of otherwise independent companies pursuing a joint business interest.

MIT's CENTER FOR COORDINATION SCIENCE

Researchers at MIT's Center for Coordination Science study the "wired economy," where internet and other computer networks are changing organizations. The language of electronic communication enables people to work free of geographical and time constraints.

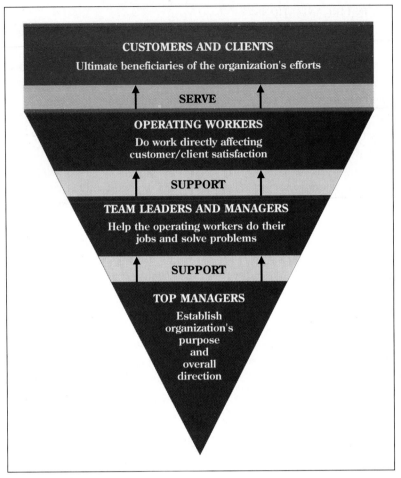

■   FIGURE 1.1
The "upside-down pyramid" view of organizations and management.

as easily be let go when business falls. Today's college graduates must be prepared to succeed in the second and third leaves, not just the first.

▼ CHANGES IN MANAGERS

Managers are formally responsible for supporting the work efforts of other people.

In all organizations, **managers** perform jobs that involve directly supporting the work efforts of others. Being a manager is a unique challenge that carries distinct responsibilities. People are key resources of organizations; the performance of individuals, working alone and in groups, is the basic building block of organizational success. Accordingly, it is the job of the manager to help other people get important things done in a timely, high-quality, and personally satisfying way. In the new workplace, this will be accomplished by more "helping" and "supporting" than the traditional "directing" and "controlling." Indeed, the word "manager" is increasingly more being replaced in the new workplace by "coordinator," "coach," or "team leader."[19]

LEARNING ABOUT ORGANIZATIONAL BEHAVIOR ◀

The winds of change have brought with them a challenging and multifaceted new workplace. They have also brought a clear emphasis on the importance of **organizational learning**—the process of acquiring knowledge and utilizing information to adapt successfully to changing circumstances.[20] Organizations must be able to change continuously and positively in today's challenging times; they must commit to searching continuously for new ideas and opportunities for improvement. The same applies to each of us as individual members of organizations and society. We too must strive for continuous personal and professional development to keep pace with a dynamic and complex environment.

> **Organizational learning** is the process of acquiring knowledge and using information to adapt to changing circumstances.

▼ LIFE-LONG AND EXPERIENTIAL LEARNING

Together, the many topics presented in this book offer a meaningful study of organizational behavior and its managerial implications in organizations small and large. As you read, these words of management consultant Tom Peters are worth remembering. "Students: Remember that (1) education is the *only* ticket to success and (2) it doesn't stop with the last certificate you pick up. Education is the 'big game' in the globally interdependent economy."[22]

Now is a good time to recognize that the important TQM notion of continuous improvement applies equally well to your career development. Through *life-long learning* you can and must learn from day-to-day work experiences, conversations with colleagues and friends, counseling and advice from mentors, success models, training seminars and workshops, and the information available in the popular press and mass media. In your OB course, you may also be encouraged to participate actively in *experiential learning* activities. This process involves an actual or simulated work experience and subsequent reflection, followed by both theory building to explain what has taken place and the testing of new behaviors at the next opportunity.[23] *The Organizational Behavior Workbook* included in this book contains many opportunities for you, both individually and as part of student study groups, to analyze cases, participate in experiential exercises, and complete self-assessment inventories to experience the active learning process.

✳ **DISNEY**
*http://www.z.
disney.com/*

More than tourists visit Disney World's Magic Kingdom. Corporate visitors come also, to study how Disney excels in employee selection, training, support, and benefits. Says a South African visitor: "If we can get that kind of atmosphere at our company, the productivity will go up."[21]

▼ SCIENTIFIC FOUNDATIONS OF ORGANIZATIONAL BEHAVIOR

By the dawn of the twentieth century, consultants and scholars were giving increased attention to the systematic study of management. Although most attention was initially on physical working conditions, principles of administration, and industrial engineering principles, by the 1940s the focus broadened to include the essential human factor. This gave impetus to research dealing with individual attitudes, group dynamics, and the working relationships between managers and their subordinates. Eventually, the discipline of organizational behavior emerged as a broader and encompassing approach. Today, it continues to evolve as a discipline devoted to scientific understanding of individuals and groups in organizations, and of the performance implications of organizational structures, systems, and processes.[24]

From these roots, organizational behavior has developed four special characteristics. First, *OB is an interdisciplinary body of knowledge* with strong ties to the behavioral sciences—psychology, sociology, and anthropology—as well as to allied social sciences, such as economics and political science. Organizational behavior is unique, however, in its devotion to applying and integrating these diverse insights toward a better understanding of human behavior in organizations.

Second, and as explained further in the module "Research Foundations of Organizational Behavior" at the end of this book, *OB uses scientific methods* to develop and empirically test generalizations about behavior in organizations. Figure 1.2 describes the research methodologies commonly used to generate insights into organizational behavior. In all cases, scientific thinking is important to OB researchers and scholars for these reasons: (1) the process of data collection is controlled and systematic; (2) proposed explanations are carefully tested; and (3) only explanations that can be scientifically verified are accepted.

Third, the research in *OB focuses on applications* and seeks relevancy in answering practical questions relating to human behavior in organizations. For example, the outcome or dependent variables of most interest to OB researchers include such things as task performance, job satisfaction, absenteeism, and turnover.

Fourth, *OB uses contingency thinking* in its search for ways to improve upon these outcomes. Rather than assume that there is one "best" or universal way to manage people and organizations, OB recognizes that management practices must be tailored to fit the exact nature of each situation. Using a **contingency ap-**

■ FIGURE 1.2
Research methods in organizational behavior.

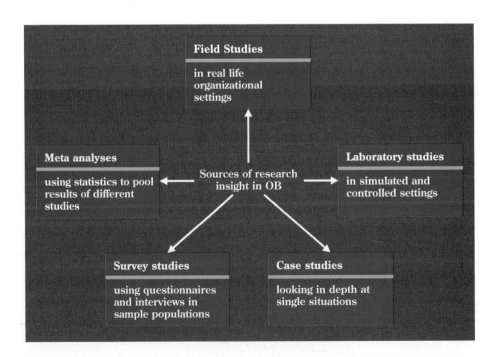

proach, researchers try to identify how different situations can best be understood and handled. As discussed in Chapter 2, for example, culture affects how management theories and concepts apply in different countries.[25] What works well in one culture may not work as well in another. Other important contingency variables addressed in this book include environment, technology, structure, and people.

> The **contingency approach** seeks ways to meet the needs of different management situations.

THE NATURE OF ORGANIZATIONS

The study of OB must be framed in the context of organizations as work settings. Formally defined, an **organization** is a collection of people working together in a division of labor to achieve a common purpose. This definition describes a wide variety of clubs, voluntary organizations, and religious bodies, as well as entities such as businesses, schools, hospitals, government agencies, and the like. The insights and applications of OB apply to all of these.

> **Organizations** are collections of people working together in a division of labor to achieve a common purpose.

▼ PURPOSE AND MISSION

The purpose of organizations may be simply stated as to produce goods or services for society. Nonprofit organizations produce services with public benefits, such as health care, education, judicial processing, and highway maintenance. Large and small for-profit businesses produce consumer goods and services such as automobiles, banking, travel, gourmet dining, and accommodations. Formal *mission statements* are increasingly used to focus the attention of members on the core purpose and specific domain in which organizations intend to operate.[26]

▼ ORGANIZATIONS AS OPEN SYSTEMS

A well-functioning organization accomplishes its purpose with the benefits of *synergy,* the creation of a whole that is greater than the sum of its parts. To achieve this, organizations ultimately depend on the activities and collective efforts of many people—their employees or members. People are the indispensable **human resources** of organizations—the individuals and groups whose performance contributions advance mission accomplishment. They use *material resources,* including technology, information, physical equipment and facilities, raw materials, and money, to produce finished goods or services that are, it is hoped, of value to society at large.

> **Human resources** are the people who do the work that helps organizations fulfill their missions.

Many OB scholars view organizations from the perspective shown in Figure 1.3. As **open systems**, organizations obtain human resources and material resource inputs from the environment and transform them into product outputs in the form of finished goods and/or services. If everything works right, the environment values these outputs and creates a continuing demand for them, thus allowing the organization to survive and prosper over the long run. Things can and

> **Open systems** transform human and material resource inputs into finished goods and services.

■ FIGURE 1.3
How an organization operates as an open system.

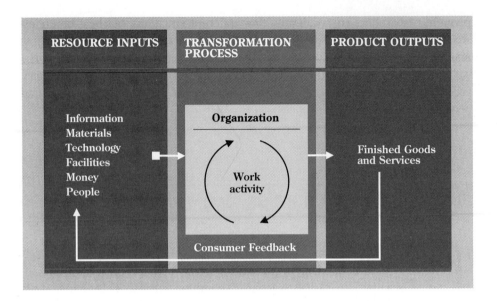

do go wrong, of course. If an organization's goods or services are unpopular, it will sooner or later have difficulty obtaining resource inputs. In the extreme case, it will be forced out of existence.

THE NATURE OF MANAGERIAL WORK

✳ BEN & JERRY'S
http://www.benjerry. com/

Ben & Jerry's Homemade, Inc., states its mission as:
To make, distribute and sell the finest quality, all-natural ice cream and related products in a wide variety of innovative flavors made from Vermont dairy products.[27]

A manager is responsible for work that is largely accomplished through the efforts of one or more other people. Traditionally identified in organization charts as a manager's subordinates or direct reports, these "other people" in the new workplace are increasingly known as team members or work associates. Managers whose traditional job titles include supervisor, department head, general manager, and president may now also be called team leaders, coordinators, and project directors, among other possibilities.

Regardless of the exact title held, any manager's job in any organization is busy and demanding, as the results of continuing research on managerial work show.[28] *Managers work long hours.* A work week of at least 50 hours is typical; up to 90 hours is not unheard of. The length of the work week tends to increase as one advances to higher managerial levels; heads of organizations often work the longest hours. *Managers are busy people.* Their work is intense and involves doing many different things on any given work day. The busy day of a manager includes at least 20 or 30 separate incidents or episodes in an 8-hour period for chief executives and up to 200 at supervisory levels. *Managers are often interrupted.* Their work is fragmented and variable. Interruptions are frequent, and many tasks must be completed quickly. *Managers work mostly with other people.* In fact, they spend little time working alone. Time spent with others includes working with bosses, peers, subordinates, subordinates of their subordinates, as well as outsiders, such as customers, suppliers, and the like. *Managers are communicators.* In general, managers spend a lot of time getting, giving, and processing information. Their work is often face-to-face verbal communication that takes place during formal and informal meetings. Higher level managers typically spend more time in scheduled meetings than do lower level managers.

▼ THE MANAGEMENT PROCESS

An *effective manager* is one whose organizational unit, group, or team consistently achieves high levels of goal accomplishment by a capable and enthusiastic workforce. This definition focuses attention on two key results in a manager's daily work. The first is *task performance*—the quality and quantity of the work produced or the services provided by the work unit as a whole. The second is *job satisfaction*—how people feel about their work and the work setting. Just as a valuable machine should not be allowed to break down for lack of proper maintenance, the valuable contributions of the human resource should never be lost for lack of proper care. Accordingly, OB directs a manager's attention to such matters as job satisfaction, job involvement, and organizational commitment, as well as measures of actual task performance.

Effective managers create opportunities for individuals and groups to make high-performance contributions in organizations and to experience satisfaction in the process. They do this, in part, by becoming skilled at these four *functions of management:*

Planning—setting performance objectives and identifying the actions needed to achieve them.

Organizing—dividing up tasks and arranging resources to acccomplish the important work.

Leading—creating enthusiasm for others to work hard to accomplish tasks successfully.

Controlling— monitoring performance and taking corrective action as necessary.

▼ MANAGERIAL ROLES AND NETWORKS

In a classic study of managerial behavior, Henry Mintzberg identified three major categories of roles or activities that managers must be prepared to perform on a daily basis. As shown in Figure 1.4, the manager's *interpersonal roles* involve working directly with other people. They include hosting and attending official ceremonies (figurehead), creating enthusiasm and serving people's needs (leader), and maintaining contacts with important people and groups (liaison). The *informational roles* involve exchanging information with other people. They include seeking out relevant information (monitor), sharing relevant information with insiders (disseminator), and sharing relevant information with outsiders (spokesperson). The *decisional roles* involve making decisions that affect other people. They include seeking out problems to solve and opportunities to explore

Planning sets objectives and identifies the actions needed to achieve them.

Organizing divides up tasks and arranges resources to acccomplish them.

■ Four functions of management

Leading creates enthusiasm to work hard to accomplish tasks successfully.

Controlling monitors performance and takes any needed corrective action.

■ FIGURE 1.4
Ten roles of effective managers.

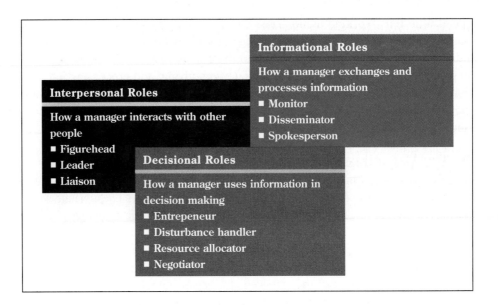

(entrepreneur), helping to resolve conflicts (disturbance handler), allocating resources to various uses (resource allocator), and negotiating with other parties (negotiator).

Essential to these roles and all managerial work is the importance of establishing and maintaining good interpersonal relationships with a wide variety of people, both inside and outside the organization. The nature of these interpersonal networks is illustrated by this description from John Kotter's book *The General Managers*.[29]

> B. J. Sparksman had a good working relationship with his four bosses and a close mentor–protege relationship with one of them. He had cordial to good relations with his peers, some of whom were friends and all of whom were aware of this track record. . . . He also had a good working relationship with many of the subordinates of his peers (hundreds of people) based mostly on his reputation. B. J. had a close and strong working relationship with all but one of his main direct reports because they respected him, because he was the boss, and the fact that he tried to treat them fairly and with respect. Outside the firm, B. J. maintained fairly strong relationships with dozens of top people in firms that were important clients for his organization. . . . He also had relationships with dozens of other important people in the local community.

This passage describes a manager who gets his job done through a complex set of interpersonal networks, many that fall outside the formal chain of command. Inside the organization, Sparksman's networks included both vertical relationships with a variety of superiors and subordinates and lateral relationships with peers. His networks also included relationships with many outsiders, such as customers and suppliers. More specifically, managers should be able to develop, maintain, and work well within *task networks*—of specific job-related contacts, *career networks*—of career guidance and opportunity resources, and *social networks*—of trustworthy friends and peers.[30] These networks are increasingly recognized as an important aspect of managerial work.[31]

▼ MANAGERIAL SKILLS AND COMPETENCIES

Certain skills are required to achieve managerial success in a dynamic environment. A *skill* is an ability to translate knowledge into action that results in desired performance. Robert Katz divides the essential managerial skills into three categories: technical, human, and conceptual.[32]

A **technical skill** is an ability to perform specialized tasks. Such ability derives from knowledge or expertise gained from education or experience. This skill involves proficiency at using select methods, processes, and procedures to accomplish tasks. Examples include the work of accountants, engineers, and attorneys, whose technical skills are acquired through formal education. Most jobs have some technical skill components. Some require preparatory education, whereas others foster skills through specific training and on-the-job experience.

> **Technical skill** is an ability to perform specialized tasks.

A **human skill** is the ability to work well with other people. It emerges as a spirit of trust, enthusiasm, and genuine involvement in interpersonal relationships. A person with good human skills will have a high degree of self-awareness and a capacity for understanding or empathizing with the feelings of others. This skill is clearly essential to the manager's "networking" responsibilities described earlier.

> **Human skill** is the ability to work well with other people.

All good managers are able to view the organization or situation as a whole and to solve problems to the benefit of everyone concerned. This ability to analyze and solve complex problems is a **conceptual skill**. It draws heavily on one's mental capacities to identify problems and opportunities, to gather and interpret relevant information, and to make good problem-solving decisions that serve the organization's purpose.

> **Conceptual skill** is the ability to analyze and solve complex problems.

According to Katz, the relative importance of these essential skills varies across levels of management. Technical skills are shown to be more important at lower management levels, where supervisors must deal with concrete problems. Broader, more ambiguous, and longer term decisions dominate the manager's concerns at higher levels; thus, conceptual skills are more important at these levels. Importantly, the human skills—which are at the core of organizational behavior applications—are consistently important across all managerial levels.

ETHICS AND ORGANIZATIONAL BEHAVIOR

The word "ethics" often appears in the news these days. Formally defined, **ethical behavior** is behavior that is accepted as morally "good" and "right," as opposed to "bad" or "wrong," in a particular setting. Is it ethical, for example, to pay a bribe to obtain a business contract in a foreign country? Is it ethical to withhold information that might discourage a job candidate from joining your organization? Is it ethical to ask someone to take a job you know will not be good

> **Ethical behavior** is morally accepted as "good" and "right" as opposed to "bad" and "wrong."

for his or her career progress? The list of questions can go on and on, but an important point remains: The public is increasingly demanding that government officials, managers, workers, and the organizations they represent all act in accordance with high ethical and moral standards.

▼ WAYS OF THINKING ABOUT ETHICAL BEHAVIOR

Ethical behavior conforms not only to the dictates of law but also to a broader moral code that is common to society as a whole. Just exactly what moral code governs a person's choices, however, is a subject of debate. Over the years, philosophers such as John Stuart Mill, John Locke, and Thomas Jefferson have identified at least four ways of thinking about ethical behavior.

The *utilitarian view* considers ethical behavior to be that which delivers the greatest good to the greatest number of people. Those who subscribe to the results-oriented utilitarian logic assess the moral aspects of their decisions in terms of the consequences they create. From such a perspective, it may be ethical to close a factory in one town in order to keep the parent corporation profitable and operating in several other towns.

The *individualism view* considers ethical behavior to be that which is best for an individual's long-term self-interests. In principle, at least, someone who acts unethically in the short run—such as by denying a qualified minority employee a promotion—should *not* succeed in the long run because the short-run action will not be tolerated. Thus, if everyone operated with long-term self-interest in mind, their short-run actions would be ethical.

The *moral-rights view* considers ethical behavior to be that which respects fundamental rights shared by all human beings. This view is tied very closely to the principle of basic human rights, such as those of life, liberty, and fair treatment by law. In an organization, this principle is reflected in such issues as rights to privacy, due process, and freedom of speech. Ethical behavior does not violate any of these fundamental human rights.

The *justice view* considers ethical behavior to be that which is fair and impartial in its treatment of people. It is based on the concept of equitable treatment for all concerned. In OB, two issues are particularly important to the justice view of ethical behavior.[33] The first is **procedural justice**—the degree to which the rules and procedures specified by policies are properly followed in all cases under which they are applied. In a sexual harassment case, for example, this may mean that required hearings are held for every case submitted for administrative review. The second is **distributive justice**—the degree to which all people are treated the same under a policy, regardless of race, ethnicity, gender, age, or any other demographic characteristic. In a sexual harassment case, this might mean that a complaint filed by a man against a woman would receive the same hearing as one filed by a woman against a man.

▼ ETHICAL DILEMMAS IN THE WORKPLACE

An **ethical dilemma** is a situation in which a person must decide whether or not to do something that, although benefiting them or the organization, or both, may be considered unethical. It is difficult to predict exactly what ethical dilemmas

Procedural justice is the degree to which policies and procedures are properly followed in all cases to which they apply.

Distributive justice is the degree to which all people are treated the same under a policy regardless of individual differences.

An **ethical dilemma** requires a person to choose among actions that offer possible benefits while also violating ethical standards.

you will someday face. However, research suggests that people at work often encounter such dilemmas in their relationships with superiors, subordinates, customers, competitors, suppliers, and regulators. Common issues underlying the dilemmas involve honesty in communications and contracts, gifts and entertainment, kickbacks, pricing practices, and employee terminations.[34] It might be helpful to anticipate having to deal with such possibilities. For example, how would you handle a request by your boss not to identify an important weakness in a product you are selling unless asked by the customer? Would you "pad" your expense account to cover the cost of a gift you purchased for an important client? Would you give a positive letter of recommendation to a poorly performing employee, in the hopes that he or she will take another job outside of your work unit?

More and more organizations are offering ethics training programs that teach and reinforce the preceding framework for handling ethical dilemmas.[35] In addition, the training helps participants learn how to identify and deal with common rationalizations that may be used to help justify actual or potential misconduct. These are:[36]

- Pretending the behavior is not really unethical or illegal.
- Excusing the behavior by saying it's really in the organization's or your best interest.
- Assuming the behavior is okay because no one else is expected to find out about it.
- Presuming your superiors will support and protect you if anything should go wrong.

> ■ Ways to rationalize unethical behavior

> *Take A Note 1.2*
>
> HOW TO DEAL WITH ETHICAL DILEMMAS
>
> 1. Recognize and clarify the dilemma.
> 2. Get all the possible facts.
> 3. List all of your options.
> 4. Test each option by asking: Is it legal? Is it right? Is it beneficial?
> 5. Make your decision.
> 6. Double check your decision by asking: How will I feel if my family finds out?   How will I feel if this is printed in the newspaper?"
> 7. Then, and only then, take action.

▼ ORGANIZATIONAL SOCIAL RESPONSIBILITY

Closely related to the ethics of workplace behavior is **social responsibility**—the obligation of organizations to behave in ethical and moral ways as institutions of the broader society. This concept suggests that members must ensure that their ethical frameworks extend to the organization as a whole. Managers in particular, take the lead in committing the organization to actions that are consistent with both the quest for high productivity and the objective of corporate social responsibility. Unfortunately, it doesn't always turn out this way. Some years ago, in a notorious case of organizational wrongdoing, two Beech-nut senior executives were sentenced to jail for their roles in a scandal involving the sale of adulterated apple juice for infants. Labeled "100% fruit juice," the juice turned out to be a blend of chemical ingredients. This case, like many others, came to public awareness because of a *whistleblower*—someone within the organization who exposes the wrongdoings of others in order to preserve high ethical standards.[37]

> **Social responsibility** is the obligation of organizations to behave in ethical and moral ways.

ETHICS AND
SOCIAL RESPONSIBILITY

Social responsibility counts at Home Depot, the popular do-it-yourself home improvement retailer. The company helps build the communities in which it operates and employs a corporate Director of Community Affairs. "Team De-

pot," an organized volunteer force, was developed in 1992 to promote volunteer activities within the local communities the stores serve. The company donates more than $8 million annually to community and charitable programs and is a leader in "green marketing"—offering products that are environmentally friendly. For all this and more, Home Depot received the Superior Community Involvement Award from *Business Ethics* magazine.[38]

▼ QUALITY OF WORKING LIFE

A central element in any commitment to workplace ethics and social responsibility involves the treatment of an organization's workforce. All organizations should be managed for performance success. But they must also be managed for satisfaction by and among the persons doing the work.

> **Quality of work life**, or QWL, indicates the overall quality of human experiences in the workplace.

The term **quality of work life**, or QWL, is prominent in OB as an indicator of the overall quality of human experience in the workplace. It expresses a special way of thinking about people, their work, and the organizations in which their careers are fulfilled. It is also a clear reminder that high performance can and should be accomplished by high levels of job satisfaction. A commitment to QWL can be considered a core value of OB. Among the many concepts and theories discussed in this book, for example, the foundations for QWL are reflected in such hallmarks of managerial excellence as: *participation*—involving people from all levels of responsibility in decision making; *trust*—redesigning jobs, systems, and structures to give people more freedom at work; *reward*—creating reward systems that are fair, relevant, and contingent on work performance; and *responsiveness*—making the work setting more pleasant and able to serve individual needs.[39] In many ways, the study of organizational behavior is a search for practical ideas on how to best help organizations achieve high-performance outcomes while always offering their members truly high quality of work life environments.

▶ CHAPTER 1 STUDY GUIDE

SUMMARY

Why is organizational behavior important in the new workplace?

- Organizational behavior is the study of individuals and groups in organizations.
- Dramatic changes in today's organizations signal the emergence of a new workplace

of workforce diversity, customer service, and high-performance systems, structures, and practices.

- Valuing diversity and respecting differences is a key theme in organizations whose workforces are increasingly diverse in terms of gender, race and ethnicity, age, and able-bodiedness.
- Total quality management, with its commitment to high quality, continous improvement, and customer focus, is also central to the new workplace.
- Process reengineering, the upside-down pyramid, and virtual corporations are among the developments in organizations experiencing continuing pressures for change.
- Managers in the new workplace are expected to play new roles, requiring them to act more like "coaches" and "facilitators" than the traditional "bosses" and "controllers" of the past.

How do we learn about organizational behavior?

- Organizational learning is the process of acquiring knowledge and utilizing information to adapt successfully to changing circumstances.
- Learning about organizational behavior involves more than just reading a textbook; it also involves a commitment to continuous learning from experience.
- OB has many historical roots and has emerged as an applied discipline based on scientific methods.
- OB uses a contingency approach, recognizing that management practices must be tailored to fit the exact nature of each situation.

What are organizations like as work settings?

- An organization is a collection of people working together in a division of labor for a common purpose—to produce goods or services for society.
- Organizations need materials—such as technology, capital, and raw materials, as well as human resources—the people who do the required work.
- As open systems, organizations interact with their environments to obtain resources that are transformed into product outputs, which are then returned to the environment for consumption.

What is the nature of managerial work?

- A manager is anyone in an organization to whom one or more persons report directly.
- An effective manager is one whose work unit, team, or group accomplishes high levels of performance that are sustainable over the long term by enthusiastic workers.
- The four functions of management are (1) planning to set directions, (2) organizing to assemble resources and systems, (3) leading to create workforce enthusiasm, and (4) controlling to ensure desired results.
- Daily managerial work involves long hours, intense activity, and frequent interruptions.
- Managers fulfill a variety of interpersonal, informational, and decisional roles while working with networks of people both inside and outside of the organization.
- Managerial performance is based on a combination of essential technical, human, and conceptual skills.

How do ethics influence human behavior in organizations?

- Ethical behavior is that which is accepted as morally "good" and "right" instead of "bad" or "wrong."
- Ways of thinking about on ethical behavior include the individualism, utilitarian, moral rights, and justice views.
- The workplace is a source of possible ethical dilemmas in which people may be asked to do or are tempted to do things that violate ethical standards.
- Organizational social responsibility is the obligation of organizations as a whole to act in ethical ways.
- The insights of OB can help build and maintain work environments that offer their members a high quality of work life.

KEY TERMS

Conceptual skill (p. 13)

Contingency approach (p. 9)

Continuous improvement (p. 4)

Controlling (p. 11)

Distributive justice (p. 14)

Ethical behavior (p. 13)

Ethical dilemma (p. 14)

Glass ceiling (p. 3)

Human resources (p. 9)

Human skill (p. 13)

Leading (p. 11)

Manager (p. 6)

Open system (p. 9)

Organization (p. 9)

Organizational behavior (p. 3)

Organizational learning (p. 7)

Organizing (p. 11)

Planning (p. 11)

Procedural justice (p. 14)

Process reengineering (p. 5)

Quality of work life (p.16)

Social responsibility (p. 15)

Technical skill (p. 13)

Total quality management (p. 4)

Upside-down pyramid (p. 5)

Virtual corporation (p. 5)

Workforce diversity (p. 3)

SELF-TEST 1

▼ MULTIPLE CHOICE

1. The term "workforce diversity" refers to differences in race, age, gender, ethnicity, and _____ among people at work. (a) social status (b) personal wealth (c) able-bodiedness (d) political preference

2. Formally defined, TQM is management dedicated to ensuring that an organization operates with a total commitment to high quality, _____, and meeting customer needs. (a) low cost (b) high quantity (c) job satisfaction (d) continuous improvement

3. The main focus of process reengineering is _____. (a) how things were done in the past (b) how things should be done in the future (c) reducing labor costs (d) raising capital

4. An organization made up of core permanent workers, independent contractors, and part-time or temporary workers is called a _____ by Handy. (a) shamrock organization (b) network organization (c) virtual organization (d) restructured organization

5. Which statement about OB is most correct? (a) OB seeks "one-best-way" solutions to management problems. (b) OB is a unique science that has little relationship to other scientific disciplines. (c) OB is focused on using knowledge for practical applications. (d) OB is so modern that it has no historical roots.

6. In the open systems view of organizations, technology, information, and money, are among the _____. (a) products (b) services (c) inputs (d) outputs
7. The management function of _____ is concerned with creating enthusiasm for hard work. (a) planning (b) organizing (c) staffing (d) leading
8. Justifying ethical behavior based on the principle of the greatest good for the most people is an example of the _____ view. (a) utilitarian (b) individualism (c) moral rights (d) justice
9. When someone excuses unethical behavior by pointing out that it is really in the organization's best interest, they are _____. (a) doing the right thing for themselves (b) doing the right thing for society (c) rationalizing the unethical conduct (d) following the rule of procedural justice
10. When facing an ethical dilemma, final action should be taken only after _____. (a) recognizing the dilemma (b) checking whether or not the action will be legal (c) making sure no one will find out if the action is wrong (d) double checking to make sure that you are personally comfortable with the decision.

▼ TRUE–FALSE

11. Organizational behavior is defined as the study of how organizations behave in different countries. T F
12. The term "total service management" is often used to emphasize the customer commitment underlying true TQM. T F
13. Organizational learning is a process of acquiring knowledge and using information to adapt to changing circumstances. T F
14. The external environment is not very important to organizations viewed as open systems. T F
15. When a president holds frequent meetings with a task force to stay informed about its progress, she is fulfilling the planning function of management. T F
16. Technical skills are probably the most important skills for top-level managers. T F
17. Kotter's view of managerial work suggests that important agendas are implemented through interpersonal networks. T F
18. A team leader who gives a friend special preference under a vacation leave policy is violating distributive justice. T F
19. A whistleblower is someone who exposes unethical behavior in organizations. T F
20. Research suggests that organizational superiors are the causes of many ethical dilemmas faced by people at work. T F

▼ SHORT RESPONSE

21. What does "valuing diversity" mean in the workplace?
22. What is an effective manager?
23. How would Henry Mintzberg describe a typical executive workday?
24. Why is QWL an issue of organizational social responsibility?

▼ APPLICATIONS ESSAY

25. Petra Nelson is the new owner of a small, upscale clothing store in a college town. She wants to operate her store as an "upside-down organizational pyramid." Just what does this mean in terms of the way Petra will manage, and the way she will expect her department heads and salespersons to operate?

2

INTERNATIONAL DIMENSIONS OF ORGANIZATIONAL BEHAVIOR

When Wal-Mart, Home Depot, and other aggressive retailers moved into Canada, the local stalwart, Canadian Tire, was sent on the run. Many observers believed the firm would not survive the intense competition. But along came a smart new CEO, Stephen Bachand.

With two decades of experience in hardware retailing—in the United States, interestingly enough—Bachand spearheaded major changes in the firm's logistics, product mix, store design, office management, and customer service. He made home office executives and support staff spend time working in the retail stores to get a better sense of the business. Says Bachand: "Why is that? Because we're in the retail business." Bachand personally meets with dealers and encourages communication. "When we tell those at the head office things, they listen and respond," a dealer says. And respond they must, according to Bachand. "When you have a good idea," he points out, "customers see, but so do competitors. I'm never satisfied. You've got to be fleet of foot."

The turnaround at Canadian Tire is not complete, but the firm's performance is improving at a time when Wal-Mart and others are struggling for success in Canada. A better understanding of the culture might help. Whereas the American retailers push their "everyday low prices" strategy, which is popular at home, Bachand and Canadian Tire haven't followed suit. "The thing that's clear," he says, "is that Canadians like to shop where they know that the price is right." Watch out, Wal-Mart; a Canadian Tire store may soon show up in your home town of Bensonville, Arkansas. (http://www.cyberplex.com/hrl)[1]

S tephen Bachand learned first-hand one of the foremost lessons of doing business in international markets—you've got to understand the local culture. All around the world, people like Bachand, working in large and small businesses alike, are facing the many challenges and opportunities associated with business competition in an increasingly complex and "borderless" world.[2] The ability to respect differences and value diversity is an important key to success in managing organizational behavior across cultures. Today's organizations need managers with global awareness and cultural sensitivity. This doesn't mean that they all must work in foreign lands. But it does mean that they are aware of how international events may affect the wellbeing of organizations, they know how to deal with people from other countries and cultures, and they can learn quickly from management practices around the world. This chapter will help you to understand the important international dimensions of organizational behavior.

This chapter will broaden your understanding of people and organizations operating in a global economy. As you read Chapter 2, keep in mind these key questions:

 What is the international context of organizational behavior?

- What is culture?
- How does the international dimension affect people at work?
- What is a global view on organizational learning?

►

ORGANIZATIONAL BEHAVIOR AND THE INTERNATIONAL CONTEXT

Ⓗ ow it will end remains to be seen, but the present decade has been one of massive social and political changes. We have witnessed the reunification of Germany and the arrival of democracy in former Eastern Bloc nations; we continue to watch with concern as republics of the former Soviet Union struggle to deal with freedom. We applauded the advent of nonracial democracy in South Africa and were appalled at ethnic violence in Rwanda. The United Nations' fiftieth birthday was spoiled by its difficulties in dealing with war-torn Bosnia.

Amidst all this, a worldwide force continues to mature and reign supreme. This is the age of the **global economy** with its complex networks of competition, resource supplies, and product markets transcending national boundaries and circling the globe.[3] No one can fail to notice its impact on organizations, their managers and workers, and our everyday lives. Consider these potential career implications: (1) You may someday work overseas in the foreign operation of a domestic firm; (2) you may someday work overseas as an expatriate employee of a foreign firm; and (3) you may someday work as a domestic employee of a foreign firm operating in your country. The field of organizational behavior recognizes these global realities.

> The **global economy** involves worldwide interdependence of resource suppliers, product markets, and business competition.

▼ A GLOBAL ECONOMY

Our awareness of the global economy has been heightened by the rapid growth of information technology and electronic communications. The international news brings the entire world into our homes and our thoughts daily. An explosion of opportunities on the internet and worldwide web allows us to share and gather information from global sources easily, at relatively low cost, and right from our desktop personal computers. And, always, the transnational movement of products, trends, values, and innovations continues to change lifestyles at a rapid pace. At the same time that valuable skills and investments move from country to country, cultural diversity among the populations increases. Immigration is having profound implications for many nations. Today's employers deal more and more with a truly *multicultural workforce,* one that draws workers from nontraditional labor sources and from ethnic backgrounds representing all corners of the globe.[4]

Domestic self-sufficiency is no longer enough for nations or businesses. Of the 100 largest corporations, the majority are headquarted outside of North America. Of the top 10 global firms in terms of sales revenues, 6 are Japanese, led by Mitsubishi; three are American, led by General Motors at number 5; Royal/Dutch Shell represents Europe at number 10. Of the world's 10 largest banks, 9 are Japanese.[5] Companies that wish to compete successfully in world markets need to recognize this global economy and develop international links.[6]

Business investments travel the trade routes of the world. Canadian businesses have their sights set on the United States, with some $65 billion already invested there. An international consortium headed by Bombardier will build Amtrak's new high-speed train. The Japanese have ownership stakes in over 1500 U.S. factories, employing over 350,000 people.[8] The famous Harrod's, a British department store, is owned by Egyptians. In the town of Winyard, England, Queen Elizabeth helped dedicate a new £400+ million electronics plant owned by the Korean conglomerate Samsung.[9] In Scotland with its low taxes, excellent infrastructure, and skilled workers, high technology firms like IBM have invested some S4.5+ billion in what is now being called "Silicon Glen."[10]

International suppliers play growing roles in the operations of many industries. The U.S. automobile industry, for example, imports Japanese, Mexican, and Brazilian engines; utilizes German instruments and British electronics; and employs Italian designers. Advances in technology make it possible for people to work for foreign employers without ever leaving their home countries. The Irish government's investments to upgrade the country's telephone systems, for example, attracted the attention of the California-based software firm Quarterdeck. If you call Quarterdeck's "800" number in the United States to report a problem, you may be served by a phone-answering operation in Dublin; calls are simply rerouted by special phone lines to the Ireland office with its staff of multilingual programmers.[11]

✳ MOTOROLA
http://www. motorola.com/

Computer programming and equipment design for the global giant Motorola is done around the world. The company has design centers in China, India, Singapore, Hong Kong, Taiwan, and Australia and will soon have one in South America.[7]

▼ REGIONAL ECONOMIC ALLIANCES

News headlines often address free trade versus protectionism, and other issues relating to open borders and economic globalization.[12] Most countries have signed the *General Agreement on Trade and Tariffs* (GATT) and have agreed to cooperate in reducing trade barriers and restrictions. However, within this global umbrella for trade another force of great magnitude and importance exists—the rise of regional economic alliances.

Events of the last decade have seen the formation of a "new Europe:" the *European Union* (EU), with its goal of political, economic, and monetary union among member countries. The EU presently numbers 15 members, has agreed in principle to accession talks with 9 more countries, and is projected to have 25 or more members someday. Among the nations of western Europe and Scandinavia, only Norway and Switzerland are not members.[13]

Within the EU, businesses from member countries have access to a market of some 400 million customers. Agreements to eliminate border controls and trade barriers, create uniform technical product standards, open government procurement contracts, and unify financial regulations, are all designed to bring economic benefit to the region. Longer-term and more controversial issues relate to handling accession applications from potential new members, selecting the first countries for economic and monetary union, and more generally handling the politics of a multi-national alliance.

The *North American Free Trade Agreement* (NAFTA) links the economies and customer markets of Canada, the United States, and Mexico in freer trade. Praised for uniting in trade a region with more potential customers than the European Union, NAFTA continues to face controversies. Forces within American politics, for example, complain about job losses to Mexico, where businesses don't have to operate with the same standards; in Canada, some worry about economic domination by U.S. manufacturers; in Mexico, pressures of economic adjustment have caused monetary devaluation and domestic discontent.

Looking to the future, Chile has been admitted as a NAFTA partner, and other countries of the Americas may soon follow. Some business and government leaders even speak of an all-encompassing Free Trade Agreement for the Americas (FTAA) by 2005. The Caribbean Community (CARICOM) presently seeks to negotiate free trade agreements with Latin American countries; the Andean Pact (linking Venezuela, Colombia, Ecuador, Peru, and Bolivia) and Mercosur (linking Brazil, Paraguay, Uruguay, and Argentina) are active in South America.[14]

Turning to Asia, the *Asian Pacific Economic Cooperation Forum* (APEC) is a framework for bringing about joint economic development among countries of the Asia–Pacific basin. A region known for its power in the world economy, Asia is the home of many world-class competitors in global business. Japan's economic power is an ever-evident force, as is the economic might of China. But, there is more to Asia than these two countries alone. The "Tigers" also include Hong Kong, Taiwan, Singapore, and South Korea; Malaysia, Thailand, and Indonesia are homes to some of the world's fastest growing economies; India, with its huge population, is an economy on the move and is recognized as a world-class supplier of software expertise.

As the global economy continues to develop, other regions of the world will likely form alliances and join existing ones. Africa, led by developments in post-Apartheid South Africa, is an important example. The late U.S. Secretary of Commerce, Ron Brown, once commented during a trade mission: "The trade and investment opportunities emerging in the new South Africa represent enormous potential for African-American entrepreneurs."[15]

One indicator of the importance of business globalization is the quality management term *ISO 9000*. It stands for quality standards that have been set by the International Standards Organization (ISO) in Geneva, Switzerland, as a universal framework for quality assurance in the EU. ISO 9000 certification is a must for European companies; importantly, its quality standards have been endorsed by more than 50 countries, including the United States, Canada, and Mexico. The certification is fast becoming a goal for companies around the world who want to do business in Europe and/or acquire reputations as total quality "world-class" manufacturers.

A **global manager** has the international awareness and cultural sensitivity needed to work well across national borders.

▼ GLOBAL MANAGERS

The search is on for a new breed of manager—the **global manager**, someone who knows how to conduct business across borders.[16] Often multilingual, the global manager thinks with a world view; appreciates diverse beliefs, values, behaviors, and practices; and is able to map strategy accordingly. If you fit this description, or soon will, get ready. Corporate recruiters are scrambling to find people with these skills and interests.

The global dimension in business and management is pervasive, but there are many barriers to overcome. Even high performers with proven technical skills at home may find that their styles and attitudes just don't work well overseas. Experienced international managers indicate that a "global mindset" of cultural adaptability, patience, flexibility, and tolerance are indispensable.[17] The failure rate for Americans in overseas assignments runs as high as 25 percent[18]; a recent study criticizes British and German companies for giving inadequate preparation to staff sent abroad.[19]

Take A Note 2.2

ATTRIBUTES OF THE "GLOBAL MANAGER"

- Adapts well to different business environments.
- Respects different beliefs, values, practices.
- Solves problems quickly in new circumstances.
- Communicates well with people from different cultures.
- Speaks more than one language.
- Understands different government and political systems.
- Conveys respect and enthusiasm when dealing with others.
- Possesses high technical expertise for a job.

 At The University of Michigan, executives from various nations come together to study worldwide management. In a 5-week course called the Global Leadership Program, participants learn from an Int'del team of world class educators and engage in cutting edge cross-cultural team exercises and projects. The program is designed to develop participants' awareness of the complications and challenges associated with global management. Participants are grouped into six-person teams. Each team develops strategic plans for doing business in foreign countries. Team members even go together on special 2-week regional business assessment visits to the target countries. They then share the key learning of top management from the industries studied in the program.[20]

 GOING GLOBAL

WHAT IS CULTURE? ◀

The word "culture" is frequently used in OB—in connection with the concept of organizational or corporate culture, in connection with the growing interest in workforce diversity, and with respect to broad differences among peo-

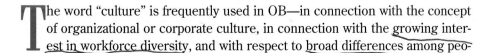

> **Culture** is the learned and shared ways of thinking and acting among a group of people or society.

ple around the world. Specialists tend to agree that **culture** is the learned, shared way of doing things in a particular society —the ways in which its members eat, dress, greet and treat one another, teach their children, solve everyday problems, and so on.[21] We are not born with a culture; we are born into a society that teaches us its culture. And because a culture is shared by people, it helps to define the boundaries between different groups.

▼ POPULAR DIMENSIONS OF CULTURE

The popular dimensions of culture are those things that are most apparent to the individual traveling abroad. They include language, time orientation, use of space, and religion.

Language   Perhaps the most conspicuous aspect of culture—and certainly the one the traveler notices first—is language. There are over 3000 languages in the world. Some are spoken by only a handful of people, whereas others, such as English, Spanish, and Chinese, are spoken by millions. Some countries, such as France and Malaysia, have one official language; others, such as Canada, Switzerland, and India, have more than one; and, still others, like the United States, have none.

The vocabulary and structure of a language reflect the history of a society and can also reveal how members relate to the environment.[22] Arabic, for example, has many different words for the camel, its parts, and related equipment. As you might expect, English is very poor in its ability to describe camels. The fact that many people apparently speak the same language, such as English, doesn't mean that they share the same culture or that every word carries the same meaning. A "truck" in Chicago is a "lorry" in London; "hydro" in Calgary is "electric power" in Boston. And, whereas grocery shoppers in the American Midwest put "pop" in their "sacks," East Coast shoppers put "soda" in their "bags."

> In **low-context cultures** messages are expressed mainly by the spoken and written word.

> In **high-context cultures** words convey only part of a message, while the rest of the message must be inferred from body language and additional contextual cues.

The anthropologist Edward T. Hall notes important differences in the ways language is used in different cultures.[23] Members of **low-context cultures** are very explicit in using the spoken and written word. In these cultures, such as those of Australia, Canada, and United States, the message is largely conveyed by the words someone uses. Members of **high-context cultures**, by contrast, use words to convey only part of the message. The rest must be inferred or interpreted from the "context" that includes body language, the physical setting, and past relationships—all of which add meaning to what is being said. Many Asian and Middle Eastern cultures are considered low context, according to Hall.

High

> In a **polychronic culture** people tend to do more than one thing at a time.

Time Orientation   Hall also uses time orientation to classify cultures.[24] In **polychronic cultures** people hold a traditional view of time that may be described as a "circle." This suggests repetition in the sense that time "goes around and around," and that one will have another chance to pass the same way again. If an opportunity is lost today—no problem, it may return again tomorrow. Polychronic cultures tend to emphasize the present, and members tend to do more than one thing at a time.[25] An important business or government official in a

Mediterranean country, for example, may have a large reception area outside his or her office. Visitors wait in this area and may transact business with the official and others who move in and out and around the room conferring as they go.

Members of **monochronic cultures** view time more as a "straight line." The past is gone; the present is here briefly; and the future is almost upon us. In monochronic cultures time is measured precisely. People appreciate schedules and appointments and talk about "saving" and "wasting" time; long-range goals become important, and planning is a way of managing the future. In contrast to the Mediterranean official, for example, a British manager will typically allot a certain amount of time to deal with a business visitor. During this time the visitor receives his or her complete attention. Only after one visitor leaves, will another one be received.

Use of Space Personal space is the "bubble" that surrounds us, and its preferred size tends to vary from one culture to another.[26] When others invade or close in on our personal space, we tend to feel uncomfortable. Then again, if people are too far away, communication becomes difficult. Arabs and South Americans seem more comfortable talking at closer distances than do North Americans; Asians seem to prefer even greater distances. When a Saudi moves close to speak with a visiting Canadian executive, the visitor may back away to keep more distance between them. But the same Canadian may approach a Malaysian too closely when doing business in Kuala Lumpur, causing her or his host to back away. Cross-cultural misunderstandings due to natural tendencies to manage personal space are quite common.

In some cultures, often polychronic ones, space is organized in such a way that many activities can be carried out simultaneously. Spanish and Italian towns are organized around central squares (plazas or piazzas), whereas American towns are structured linearly along the traditional "Main Street." Similar cultural influences are seen in the layout of work space. Americans, who seem to prefer individual offices, may have difficulty adjusting to Japanese employers who prefer open floor plans.

Religion Religion is also a major element of culture and can be one of its more visible manifestations. The influence of religion often prescribes rituals, holy days, and foods that can be eaten. Codes of ethics and moral behavior often have their roots in religious beliefs. The influence of religion on economic matters can also be significant.[27] In the Middle East, one finds interest-free "Islamic" banks that operate on principles set forth in the Koran; in Malaysia, business dinners are scheduled after 8:00 p.m. so that Muslim guests can first attend to their evening prayer.

▼ VALUES AND NATIONAL CULTURES

Cultures vary in their underlying patterns of values and attitudes. The way people think about such matters as achievement, wealth and material gain, risk and change, may influence how they approach work and their relationships with orga-

In a **monochronic culture** people tend to do one thing at a time.

nizations. A framework developed by Geert Hofstede, a Dutch scholar and consultant, offers one approach for understanding value differences across national cultures.[28] The five dimensions of national culture in his framework can be described as follows:[29]

■ Hofstede's dimensions of national cultures

Power distance is the willingness of a culture to accept status and power differences among its members.

Uncertainty avoidance is the cultural tendency to be uncomfortable with uncertainty and risk in everyday life.

Individualism–collectivism is the tendency of a culture's members to emphasize individual self-interests or group relationships.

Masculinity–femininity is the degree to which a society values so-called masculine or feminine traits.

Long-term–short-term orientation is the degree to which a culture emphasizes long-term or short-term thinking.

❶ **Power distance** is the willingness of a culture to accept status and power differences among its members. It reflects the degree to which people are likely to respect hierarchy and rank in organizations. Indonesia is considered a high-power distance culture, whereas the Netherlands is considered a relatively low-power distance culture.

❷ **Uncertainty avoidance** is a cultural tendency toward discomfort with risk and ambiguity. It reflects the degree to which people are likely to prefer structured or unstructured organizational situations. France is considered a high-uncertainty avoidance culture, whereas Hong Kong is considered a low-uncertainty avoidance culture.

❸ **Individualism–collectivism** is the tendency of a culture to emphasize individual versus group interests. It reflects the degree to which people are likely to prefer working as individuals or working together in groups. The United States is a highly individualistic culture, whereas Sweden is a more highly collectivist one.

❹ **Masculinity–femininity** is the tendency of a culture to value stereotypical masculine or feminine traits. It reflects the degree to which organizations emphasize competitive and achievement-oriented goal behavior versus more sensitivity and concerns for relationships. Japan is considered a very masculine culture, whereas the Netherlands is considered a more feminine culture.

❺ **Long-term short-term orientation** is the tendency of a culture to emphasize values associated with the future, such as thrift and persistence, versus values that focus largely on the present. It reflects the degree to which people and organizations adopt long term or short term performance horizons. South Korea is high on long-term orientation, whereas the United States is more short term oriented.

Hofstede's framework originated with a study of 116,000 employees of a multinational corporation operating in more than 40 countries. As a result of this analysis, he initially identified the four dimensions of power distance, uncertainty avoidance, individualism-collectivism, and masculinity-femininity. Later he added the fifth value dimension of long-term short-term orientation, based on research using the Chinese Values Survey developed by cross-cultural psychologist Michael Bond and his colleagues.[30] Hofstede and Bond discuss with respect to *Confucian dynamism,* with its emphasis on persistence, the ordering or relationships, thrift, a sense of shame, personal steadiness, reciprocity, protecting "face," and respect for tradition. Naturally, these influences are strong in Asian cultures. In fact, Hofstede and Bond argue that the long-term value and influence of Confucian dynamism may help account for recent economic successes by many East and Southeast Asian nations.[31]

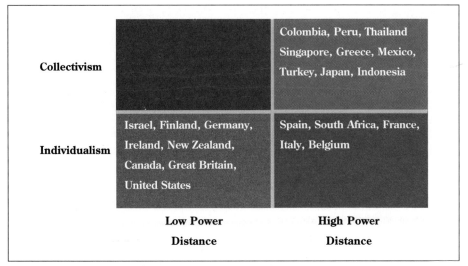

	Low Power Distance	High Power Distance
Collectivism		Colombia, Peru, Thailand Singapore, Greece, Mexico, Turkey, Japan, Indonesia
Individualism	Israel, Finland, Germany, Ireland, New Zealand, Canada, Great Britain, United States	Spain, South Africa, France, Italy, Belgium

■ FIGURE 2.1

Sample country clusters on Hofstede's dimensions of individualism-collectivism and power distance. [Source: Developed from Geert Hofstede, *Culture's Consequences* (Beverly Hills, CA: Sage Publications, 1980).]

When using Hofstede's framework, it is important to remember that the dimensions are interrelated and not independent.[32] National cultures may best be understood in terms of cluster maps or collages that combine multiple dimensions. For example, Figure 2.1 shows a sample grouping of countries based on individualism-collectivism and power distance. Note that high power distance and collectivism are often found together, as are low power distance and individualism. Whereas high collectivism may lead us to expect a work team in Indonesia to operate consensually, the high power distance may cause the consensus to be heavily influenced by the desires of a formal leader. A similar team operating in more individualist and low power distance Great Britain or America might make decisions with more open debate, including expressions of disagreement with a leader's stated preferences.

▼ UNDERSTANDING CULTURAL DIFFERENCES

The starting point for dealing well with people from different cultures is to first understand your own culture. We are usually unaware of our own culture until we come into contact with a very different one. Knowing your own culture helps guard against two problems that arise too frequently in international dealings. One is the danger of *parochialism*—assuming that the ways of your culture are the *only* ways of doing things. The other is the danger of *ethnocentrism*—assuming that the ways of your culture are the *best* ways of doing things.[33] It is parochial for a traveling American businesswoman to insist that all of her business contacts speak English; it is ethnocentric for her to think that anyone who dines with a spoon rather than a knife and fork lacks proper table manners.

Canada, USA, Ireland	Universalism vs. Particularism	Indonesia, China, Venezuela
USA, Hungary, Russia	Individualism vs. Collectivism	Thailand, Japan, Mexico
Indonesia, Germany, Japan	Neutral vs. Affective	Italy, France, USA
Spain, Poland, USA	Specific vs. Diffuse	India, Great Britain, Egypt
Australia, Canada, Norway	Achievement vs. Ascription	Philippines, Pakistan, Brazil
Great Britain, Belgium, USA	Sequential vs. Synchronic	Malaysia, Venezuela, France

■ FIGURE 2.2

Sample country clusters on Trompenaars' framework for understanding cultural differences. [Source: Developed from Fons Trompenaars, *Riding the Waves of Culture* (London: Nicholas Brealey Publishing, 1993).]

A framework recently developed by Fons Trompenaars offers another starting point for better understanding, and, hopefully, dealing with, cultural differences.[34] Working from a data bank of 14,993 respondents from 47 national cultures, he suggests that cultures vary in the way their members solve problems of three major types: (1) relationships with people, (2) attitudes toward time, and (3) attitudes toward the environment. Figure 2.2 shows where selected countries might fall on his set of cultural dimensions.

Trompenaars identifies five major ways in which cultures may differ on how their members handle *relationships with people*. The orientations are:

■ How cultures handle relationships with people

❶ *Universalism versus particularism*—relative emphasis on rules and consistency or relationships and flexibility.
❷ *Individualism versus collectivism*—relative emphasis on individual freedom and responsibility or group interests and consensus.
❸ *Neutral versus affective*—relative emphasis on objectivity and detachment or on emotion and expressed feelings.
❹ *Specific versus diffuse*—relative emphasis on focused, narrow involvement or involvement with the whole person.
❺ *Achievement versus prescription*—relative emphasis on performance-based, earned status or ascribed status.

In respect to problems based on *attitudes toward time*, Trompenaars distinguishes between cultures with *sequential versus synchronic* orientations. Time in a sequential view is a passing series of events; in a synchronic view, it consists of an interrelated past, present, and future. In respect to problems based on *attitudes toward the environment*, he contrasts how different cultures may relate to nature in *inner-directed versus outer-directed* ways. Members of an inner-directed culture tend to view themselves separate from nature and believe they can control it. Those in an outer-directed culture view themselves as part of nature and believe they must go along with it.

MULTICULTURAL PERSPECTIVES ON PEOPLE AT WORK

The term *international management* applies in organizations whose activities span more than one country; the term *international organizational behavior* refers to the study of individuals and groups in organizations that operate internationally and with multicultural workforces.[35] OB scholars increasingly try to use the cultural frameworks just discussed to better understand how management and organizational practices vary around the world.

▼ MULTINATIONAL EMPLOYERS

Usually a firm enters the international market on a small scale—by exporting one of its products, for example. As the international side of the business grows, a position or department responsible for export sales is usually created. With further international growth the firm may form *joint ventures* by investing with a foreign partner or set up wholly owned subsidiaries abroad. As the number of joint ventures and foreign subsidiaries grows, a headquarters group or international division often is assembled to manage the firm's international operations.

A true **multinational corporation**, or MNC, is a business firm with extensive international operations in more than one foreign country. MNCs are more than just companies that "do business abroad," they are global concerns—exemplified by Ford, Royal-Dutch Shell, Sony and many others—whose missions and strategies are truly worldwide in scope. In addition, *multinational organizations* (MNOs) are ones with nonprofit missions and whose operations also span the globe. Examples are Amnesty International, the International Red Cross, the United Nations, and the World Wildlife Fund.

The truly global organization operates with a total world view and without allegiance to any one national "home." Futurist Alvin Toffler calls them *transnational organizations* that ". . . may do research in one country, manufacture components in another, assemble them in a third, sell the manufactured goods in a fourth, deposit surplus funds in a fifth, and so on." Although the pure transnational corporation may not yet exist, the strategic moves of giant multinationals certainly point them in this direction. And Toffler warns further that "the size, importance, and political power of this new player in the global game has skyrocketed."[36]

It is difficult to exaggerate the economic power and impact of the world's MNCs. Most of the largest ones have revenues in excess of $23 billion, and the 200 largest multinationals in the world have affiliates in 20 or more countries. Importantly, their activities can bring both benefits and controversies to host countries. This is noticeable in Mexico, where many *maquiladoras*, or foreign-owned plants, assemble imported parts and ship finished products to the United States. Labor is inexpensive for the foreign operators, and Mexico bene-

> A **multinational corporation** is a business with extensive international operations in more than one country.

fits from reduced unemployment and increased foreign exchange earnings. But some complain about the stress on housing and public services in Mexican border towns, inequities in the way Mexican workers are treated (wages, working conditions, production quotas) relative to their foreign counterparts, and the environmental impact of pollution from the industrial sites.[37]

**ETHICS AND
SOCIAL RESPONSIBILITY**

Information that Guatemalan workers earn 2 cents a pound while toiling in inhumane conditions to pick coffee beans that Starbucks sold for $8 a pound

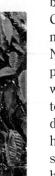

brought controversy to the successful chain. CEO Howard Schultz responded by setting a new standard for socially responsible business. New guidelines require overseas suppliers to pay wages that "address the basic needs of workers and their families," to not allow work to "interfere with mandated education" for children, and to help workers get "access to safe housing, clean water and health facilities and services." Starbucks' policy is praised by global human rights activists as a benchmark for importers of agricultural commodities.[38]

▼ MULTICULTURAL WORKFORCES

There are no easy answers for how to deal best with a multicultural workforce. Styles of leadership, motivation, decision making, planning, organizing, leading, and controlling vary from one country to the next.[39] The challenges of managing a construction project in Saudi Arabia with employees from Asia, the Middle East, Europe, and North America working side by side, will clearly differ from a domestic project. Likewise, a great deal of patience will be necessary to establish and successfully operate a joint venture in Kazakhstan, Nigeria, or Vietnam. In these and other international settings, political risks and bureaucratic difficulties further complicate the already difficult process of working across cultural boundaries.

The challenges of managing across cultures, however, is not limited to international operations alone. The term *domestic multiculturalism* describes cultural diversity within a given national population—a diversity that will be reflected in the workforces of local organizations.[40] Los Angeles, for example, is a popular home to many immigrant groups. Some 20 percent of the city's school children speak one of over 100 languages more fluently than they speak English. In Vancouver, British Columbia, only about 60 percent of the population speaks English as a native language; Chinese is the mother tongue of some 20 percent.

An **expatriate** works and lives in a foreign country for an extended time.

▼ EXPATRIATE WORK ASSIGNMENTS

People who work and live abroad for extended periods of time—**expatriates**—can be very expensive for the employer. An executive earning $100,000 per year in the United States may cost her company more than $300,000 in the first year—

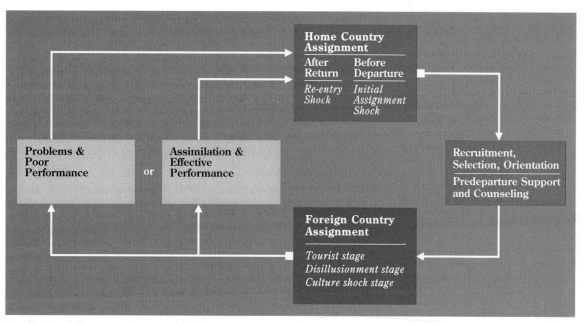

■ FIGURE 2.3

Stages in the expatriate international career cycle: adjustment problems in the home and foreign countries. [Source: Developed from Nancy J. Adler, *International Dimensions of Organizational Behavior*, 2nd ed. (Boston: Kent, 1991).

in terms of compensation, benefits, transfer, and other costs—if transferred to Great Britain. To get the most out of the investment, a progressive employer will maximize the potential of expatriate performance success by: carefully recruiting employees who have the right sensitivities and skills, providing good training and orientation to the foreign culture, actively supporting them while abroad, giving extra attention to the needs of family members, and paying careful attention to relocation when the employee and family return home.

Expatriates often face problems both when entering and working in a foreign culture, and when returning home. Figure 2.3 illustrates phases in the typical expatriate work assignment, beginning with the *initial assignment shock* experienced upon being informed of a foreign posting. The nature of the recruitment, selection, and orientation provided during this stage can have an important influence on the assignment's eventual success. Ideally, the employee, along with his or her spouse and family, is allowed to choose whether or not to accept the opportunity. Also ideally, proper predeparture support and counseling provide "realistic expectations" of what is to come.

There are three phases of adjustment to the new country.[41] First is the *tourist stage,* in which the expatriate enjoys discovering the new culture. Second is the *disillusionment stage,* in which his or her mood declines as difficulties become more evident. Typical problems include conversing well in the local language, obtaining personal products and food supplies of preference, and so on.

Third, the expatriate's mood often hits bottom in the stage of *culture shock*, where frustration and confusion result from the continuing challenge of living in the foreign environment. If culture shock is well handled the expatriate begins to feel better, function more effectively, and lead a reasonably normal life. If it isn't, work performance may suffer, even deteriorating to the point where a reassignment home may be necessary.

At the end of the expatriate assignment, perhaps after 3 or 4 years, the *reentry process* can be stressful also.[42] After an extended period away, the expatriate and his or her family have changed and the home country has changed as well. Instead of just being able to "fall back in," it takes time to get used to living at home again. In too many instances, furthermore, little thought may be given to assigning the returned expatriate a job that matches his or her current skills and abilities. While abroad, the expatriate has often functioned with a great degree of independence—something that may or may not be possible at home. Problems caused by such *reentry shock* can be minimized if the reentry is carefully planned. This includes maintaining adequate contact with the home office during the expatriate assignment as well as having all possible support for the move back. Employers should also identify any new skills and abilities, and assign returned expatriates to jobs commensurate with their abilities. As organizations utilize more and more expatriate assignments, their career planning and development systems must also operate on a global scale.

GLOBAL

When Noel Kreicker left the United States with her three small children for her husband's two-year business assignment in Colombia, she didn't expect to be back home within six months, but she was. Noel and her husband went to Colombia without any predeparture cross-cultural training and no logistical support after arrival. They were on their own; they had difficulty even buying a light bulb; and after a number of mishaps, the family decided to end the assignment and return home. Now Noel has her own company, International Orientation Resources, that specializes in assisting others as they prepare for international assignments. One of the many customized services that Noel's Chicago-based consulting firm offers is cross-cultural training for spouses and family members, as well as for the employees. Cross-cultural training programs include a variety of topics including conducting business in the destination country; daily living in the destination country; cultural etiquette, social customs and beliefs; history, economics and politics; and cultural transitions. Upon arrival in-country, IOR's Destination Assistance services are available to relocating families to help with locating housing, schooling research, community orientation, and such day-to-day necessities as shopping, banking, and other local registration requirements.[43]

A GLOBAL VIEW OF ORGANIZATIONAL LEARNING ◀

Organizational learning was defined in Chapter 1 as the process of acquiring the knowledge necessary to adapt successfully to a changing environment. Consistent with the themes of this chapter, the concept can be extended to **global organizational learning**—the ability to gather from the world at large the knowledge required for long-term organizational adaptation. Simply stated, people from different cultures and parts of the world have a lot to learn from one another about organizational behavior.

> **Global organizational learning** is the ability to gather from the world at large the knowledge required for long term organizational adaptation.

▼ ROLE OF STRATEGIC ALLIANCES

One indicator of the importance of a global approach to organizational learning is the fact that so many business firms increasingly find that they can't just "go it alone" anymore and succeed in the global economy. Things are just too complex, competitive, and costly. Firms are also finding that they can better meet some challenges by "teaming up" and cooperating with one another to meet certain objectives. *Strategic alliances,* in which two or more firms—often from different countries—join together on a temporary or continuing basis to accomplish a specific project, are becoming more common.

The partners in a strategic alliance should ideally both gain by learning from one other. In its partnership with General Motors at the California-based New United Motor Manufacturing Company, Inc. (NUMMI), Toyota has shown how important joint ventures can be in learning to operate in new markets. Not only has NUMMI done well as a business investment, but the Japanese company learned about American workers and markets and put the knowledge to good use when opening its own U.S. manufacturing facilities. Of course, GM also learned from Toyota some elements of the Japanese management approaches, including work team concepts eventually put to use in the firm's innovative Saturn facility.

▼ JAPANESE MANAGEMENT SYSTEMS

As the prior example suggests, Japanese management approaches have received considerable outside attention. The runaway popularity in the 1980s of William Ouchi's *Theory Z: How American Business Can Meet the Japanese Challenge* and Richard Tanner and Anthony Athos's *The Art of Japanese Management* evidenced the force with which western managers rushed to find out exactly what the Japanese were doing successfully.[44] The Japanese economy has had problems of its own since then, and the simplistic rush to copy its methods exactly and manage "the Japanese way" has been tempered. However, OB scholars still recognize many lessons to be learned from Japanese management, given proper research and cultural awareness.[45]

Japan's highly collectivist society contrasts markedly with the highly individualistic cultures of the United States and other western nations. Thus, it is only reasonable to expect differences in their management and organizational prac-

✳ SAMSUNG
*http://www.sam-
sung.com/*

The large Korean conglomerate or *chaebol*, Samsung, meets global competition in its own way. Consultant Kim II Suk says: "Because of the shortcomings and strong points of the Korean people and Korean culture, we cannot readily imitate Japan, Taiwan, or U.S. management styles. We need our own."[51]

tices.[46] Japanese firms have traditionally favored *lifetime employment* with strong employee–employer loyalty, seniority pay, and company unions.[47] Their operations have emphasized a *quality commitment,* the use of *teams* and *group decision making*, and career development based upon *slow promotions* and *cross-functional job assignments*.[48] But even though these general patterns can be identified, Japanese society is experiencing its own pressures for change. The emerging values and attitudes of younger Japanese workers contrast somewhat with those of the past.[49] Some observers note tendencies to be less loyal toward employers, to display greater concerns for self-interests, to focus more on monetary gain and tangible rewards, and to show more respect for equal work opportunities for women, who have suffered job discrimination in the past.

Still, the influence of learning from the Japanese approaches is evident in many of the workplace themes with which you will become familiar in this book. These include growing attention to the value of teams and work groups, consensus decision making, employee involvement, flatter structures, and strong corporate cultures. Organizations using these practices and related practices are sometimes identified by using Ouchi's term, *Theory Z management.*

▼ IMPLICATIONS FOR THE GLOBAL MANAGER

The special case of Japan is a good example of how important it is for managers in all countries and cultures to study and learn about the management and organizational practices of their counterparts in others. Importantly, however, any transfer of such practices must be done with due sensitivity to cultural differences. The Japanese themselves are learning this lesson as they operate overseas. For example, Japanese top managers at Magyar Suzuki in Hungary have experienced some difficulties operating in traditional Japanese ways. The Hungarians have complained about lack of extra pay for overtime, a smoking ban, and emphasis on quality workmanship.[50]

An appropriate goal in global organizational learning is to identify the "best practices" around the world. What is being done well in other settings may be of great value at home, whether that "home" is in North America, Asia, Europe, or anywhere else. And even though the world at large once looked mainly to the North Americans and Europeans for management insights, today we are more alert to the fact that potential "benchmarks" of excellence can be discovered anywhere.

The field of organizational behavior continues to mature in its international dimensions. As it does, we increasingly benefit from an expanding knowledge base that is enriched by cultural diversity. No one culture possesses all of the "right" answers to today's complex management and organizational problems. But, a sincere commitment to global organizational learning can bring fresh ideas to everyone's attention while still allowing for locally appropriate solutions to be implemented with cultural sensitivity.

CHAPTER 2 STUDY GUIDE

CHAPTER 2 STUDY GUIDE

What is the international context of organizational behavior?
- The global economy, with its complex worldwide networks of business competition, resource supplies, and product markets, is having a major impact on businesses, employers, and workforces around the world.
- Nations in Europe, North America, and Asia are forming regional trade agreements, such as the EU, NAFTA, and APEC, to gain economic strength in a highly competitive global economy.
- More and more organizations, large and small, do an increasing amount of business abroad; more and more local employers are "foreign" owned, in whole or in part.
- Wherever one lives and works, the domestic workforce is becoming multicultural and more diverse.
- All organizations need global managers with the special interests and talents needed to excel in international work and cross-cultural relationships.

SUMMARY

What is culture?
- Culture is the learned and shared ways of doing things in a society; it represents deeply ingrained influences on the way people from different societies think, behave, and solve problems.
- Popular dimensions of culture include observable differences in language, time orientation, use of space, and religion.
- Hofstede's five dimensions of national cultures include power distance, individualism–collectivism, uncertainty avoidance, masculinity–femininity, and long-term–short-term orientation.
- Trompenaars' framework for understanding cultural differences focuses on relationships among people, attitudes toward time, and attitudes toward the environment.
- Cross-cultural awareness requires a clear understanding of one's own culture; it requires the ability to overcome the limits of parochialism and ethnocentrism.

How does the international dimension affect people at work?
- Multinational corporations (MNCs) are global businesses that operate with a worldwide scope; they are powerful forces in the global economy.
- The challenges of dealing with multicultural workforces are significant for MNCs, for multinational organizations, and for any employer engaged in international business.
- Expatriate employees that work abroad for extended periods of time face special challenges, including possible adjustment problems abroad and reentry problems upon returning home.
- Increasingly, multiculturalism is a characteristic of the domestic workforce; everyone must be prepared to and willing to work well with people of different cultural backgrounds.

What is a global view on organizational learning?

- A global view on learning about OB seeks to understand the best practices from around the world, with due sensitivity to cultural differences.
- Many organizations are utilizing international strategic alliances to help them learn and stay abreast of best practices from the world's industries and organizations.
- Interest in Japanese management practices continues, with the traditional focus on long-term employment, emphasis on teams, quality commitment, careful career development, and participative decision making.
- The future will see global learning increasingly moving beyond the limits of North America, Europe, and Japan, to include the best practices found anywhere and everywhere in the world.

KEY TERMS

Culture (p. 26)	Individualism–collectivism (p. 28)	Monochronic culture (p. 27)
Expatriates (p. 32)	Long-term–short-term orientation (p. 28)	Multinational corporation (p. 31)
Global economy (p. 22)	Low-context culture (p. 26)	Polychronic culture (p. 26)
Global manager (p. 24)	Masculinity–femininity (p. 28)	Power distance (p. 28)
Global organizational learning (p. 35)		Uncertainty avoidance (p. 28)
High-context culture (p. 26)		

SELF-TEST 2

▼ MULTIPLE CHOICE

1. NAFTA, APEC, and the EU are examples of _____. (a) multinational corporations (b) agencies of the United Nations (c) regional economic groupings (d) government agencies regulating international trade
2. In _____ cultures, people tend to complete one activity at a time. (a) Asian (b) monochronic (c) polychronic (d) ethnocentric
3. Cultural values emphasizing respect for tradition, ordering of relationships, and protecting one's "face" are associated with _____. (a) religious differences (b) uncertainty avoidance (c) masculinity–femininity (d) Confucian dynamism
4. One would expect to find respect for authority and acceptance of status differences in high _____ cultures. (a) power distance (b) individualism (c) uncertainty avoidance (d) aggressiveness
5. The "Asian Dragons" are described on Hofstede's dimensions of national culture as generally high in _____. (a) uncertainty avoidance (b) short-term orientation (c) long-term orientation (d) individualism
6. _____ are foreign-owned plants that operate in Mexico, especially along the U.S. border, with special privileges. (a) *Estrellas* (b) *Escuelas* (c) *Maquiladoras* (d) *Cabezas*
7. In Trompenaars' framework for understanding cultural differences, _____ is used to describe different orientations toward nature. (a) inner directed versus outer directed (b) sequential versus polychronic (c) universal versus particular (d) neutral versus emotional
8. Management practices such as participative decision making and an emphasis on

teamwork are often characteristic of organizations in _____ cultures.
(a) monochronic (b) collectivist (c) paternalistic (d) uncertain

9. The joint venture is an example of how organizations from two different countries may cooperate in a _____ for mutual gain. (a) franchise (b) multinational organization (c) strategic alliance (d) *chaebol*

10. Which of the following is most characteristic of Japanese management practices? (a) consensus decisions (b) fast promotion (c) highly specialized career paths (d) all of these

▼ TRUE–FALSE

11. Implications of the global economy only apply to persons who will work in foreign countries and/or for multinational corporations. T F

12. The importance of foreign domestic investment in such economies as those of the United States, Canada, and the United Kingdom is decreasing. T F

13. Language is only important as a cultural variable when one is dealing with another person who speaks a different language. T F

14. A Canadian businessperson who expects foreign visitors to be able to conduct business negotiations in English is being very parochial about culture. T F

15. Respect based on performance is associated with an achievement oriented culture. T F

16. An American doing business in Hong Kong should be sensitive to the "silent language" of culture, such as that reflected in the use of space. T F

17. The reentry of expatriate employees returning from foreign assignments can be a source of problems for them and their employers. T F

18. Someone from a universalist culture is likely to be flexible and oriented toward relationships, rather than focused on rules. T F

19. Career advancement by promotion is typically faster in Japanese than in American businesses. T F

20. A global manager thinks with a world view and is tolerant of differences. T F

▼ SHORT RESPONSE

21. Why is the individualism–collectivism dimension of national culture important in OB?

22. How may differences in power distance values affect management practices across cultures?

23. What is a joint venture?

24. An organization operating with Theory Z management principles would do what?

▼ APPLICATIONS ESSAY

25. Stephen Bachand, the CEO of Canadian Tire, featured in the chapter opener, wants to keep his company "ahead of the pack" as foreign retailers try to penetrate the Canadian market. It used to be that the American firms such as Wal-Mart and Home Depot were the major threats; now he has learned that the Asian giant Yaohan and the well-known Sainsbury's from Britain are considering operations in Canada. Bachand has heard of your special consulting expertise in "global organizational learning." He is on the telephone now, and wants you to explain how the concept may help him keep his company a world-class competitor. With a large consulting contract at stake, what do you tell him about this concept?

DIVERSITY AND INDIVIDUAL DIFFERENCES

When the Bank of Montreal looked for ways to get an edge on its competitors, hiring employees who reflected the bank's customers became its number one priority. Johanne M. Totta, Vice President of Employee Programs and Workplace Equality, reports directly to the president of this 6000-branch international operation and plays a key role in implementing this ambitious priority. According to Totta, banks offer pretty much the same rate; it's the people who make the difference—the customer service.

Working closely with the board chair and the president, Totta established four task forces—one for women, one for people with disabilities, one for aboriginal (Native American) people, and one for visible minorities—to develop action plans for creating an equitable workplace and to take advantage of workplace diversity. Totta has been a key player in winning the Bank of Montreal numerous awards for its overall workplace equality programs and its efforts in advancing women.[1] (http://www.wsdinc.com/pgs www/w7234.shtml)

Throughout Canada, Europe, and the United States, the kinds of issues dealt with by Johanne Totta and the Bank of Montreal are assuming more and more importance in dealing with increasingly diverse workforces and becoming increasingly competitive. They involve an understanding of employees' individual demographic, competency, and personality differences and similarities, as well as insights into values and attitudes. This chapter will help provide you with this understanding and insight as well as some ways of managing workplace diversity and individual differences.

An understanding of individual differences and similarities is increasingly important in today's diverse organizations. As you read Chapter 3, keep in mind these key questions. ◀

- ◉ What is workforce diversity, and why is it important?
- ◉ What are demographic differences among individuals, and why are they important?
- ◉ What are aptitude and ability differences among individuals, and why are they important?
- ◉ What are personality determinants and differences among individuals, and why are they important?
- ◉ What are value and attitude differences among individuals, and why are they important?
- ◉ What does managing diversity and individual differences involve, and why is it important?

WORKFORCE DIVERSITY ◀

Much like the Bank of Montreal, more than 50 percent of Fortune 500 companies, including Colgate Palmolive, Corning, and Quaker Oats, are now providing incentives for executives to deal successfully with workforce di-

Workforce diversity is a workforce consisting of a broad mix of workers from different racial and ethnic backgrounds, of different ages and genders, and of different domestic and national cultures.

versity.[2] "Workforce diversity" refers to the presence of individual human characteristics that make people different from one another.[3] More specifically, we define **workforce diversity** in terms of key demographic differences among members of a given workforce. These differences include gender, race and ethnicity, age, and able-bodiedness.[4] Where once our society promoted a melting pot, it now emphasizes difference. The challenge is how to manage workforce diversity in a way that both respects individuals' unique perspectives and contributions and promotes a shared sense of organization vision and identity.

Workforce diversity is increasing in both the United States and Canada, as it is in much of the rest of the world. For example, in the United States, figures indicate that between 1990 and 2005, about 50 percent of the new entrants to the labor force will be women and such racial and ethnic groups as African Americans, Latinos and Asians. At the same time, those 55 and older are projected to make up nearly 15 percent of the labor force. All of this is in sharp contrast to the traditional, younger, mostly white American male, labor force. Canadian and U.K. trends for women are similar.[5]

As the workforce becomes increasingly diverse, the possibility of stereotyping and discrimination increases and managing diversity becomes more important. *Stereotyping* occurs when one thinks of an individual as assigned to a group or category—for instance, old person—and the characteristics commonly associated with the group or category are assigned to the individual in question—for instance, older people aren't creative. Demographic characteristics may serve as the basis of stereotypes that obscure individual differences and can prevent people from getting to know others as individuals and from accurately assessing their peformance potential. If you believe that older people are not creative, for example, you may mistakenly decide not to assign a very inventive 60-year-old person to an important task force.

Stereotyping and discriminating against certain people in the organization is not only a violation of United States, Canadian, and European Union (EU) laws, it is also counterproductive because the contribution of people who are discriminated against and ignored are not fully utilized. Like the Bank of Montreal, many firms in a variety of industries are increasingly recognizing that a diverse workforce that reflects societal differences helps bring them closer to their customers. Levi Straus is a prime example; 56 percent of its nontraditional workforce serves an increasingly diverse customer base.[6]

▼ MANAGING DIVERSITY VERSUS AFFIRMATIVE ACTION

Sometimes managing diversity is confused with affirmative action or other laws directed toward those with certain characteristics. Actually, the two concepts are quite different.[7] *Affirmative action* emphasizes achieving equality of opportunity in the work setting through the changing of organizational demographics—gender, age, racial and ethnic mixes, and the like. It is legally driven and requires written reports containing plans and statistical goals for specific groups of people. The reports are mandated by equal employment opportunity laws. Affirmative action is designed to benefit specific groups that have suffered from past wrongs. It primarily affects hiring and promotion decisions, opening doors for some but leading to perceived fears of reverse discrimination by others. Related laws, such as the Americans with Disabilities Act, have been passed to provide special treatment for the disabled or to discourage discrimination on the basis of sexual orientation. *Managing diversity*, in contrast, emphasizes appreciation of differences in creating a setting in which everyone feels valued and accepted. It is monitored by organizational surveys focusing on attitudes and perceptions. Managing diversity assumes that groups will retain their own characteristics and will shape the firm as well as be shaped by it, creating a common set of values. It is designed to affect employee perceptions and attitudes but is sometimes resisted because of fear of change and discomfort with differences. In Canada, for example, laws have been designed to encourage the management of diversity at the provincial level through Employment Equity Legislation.[8]

DIVERSITY

Mount Sinai Medical Center in New York City has pioneered several diversity strategies, says Dr. Gary Rosenberg, senior vice president. The hospital's employee orientation program trains staff members to be alert to how various cultures regard pain, patients' preferences to be alone or with family members, and food preferences, among other things. The staff members receive extensive training in how to draw out patients' medical, emotional, and other concerns. The hospital is also cooperating with a medical center in Kyoto, Japan, to see whether some of its approaches for treating elderly patients may work at Mount Sinai.[9]

DEMOGRAPHIC DIFFERENCES AMONG INDIVIDUALS

Demographic characteristics are the background characteristics that help shape what a person has become—one's gender, age, race and ethnicity, and able-bodiedness. They are sometimes called *biographic characteristics*. It's useful to think of these characteristics both in current terms, for example, a worker's current marital status, and historical terms, for example, where and how long a person has worked at various jobs.

Demographic characteristics are the heart and soul of workplace diversity. Those such as gender, age, racioethnicity, able-bodiedness, and even sexual preference are covered by a series of federal, state/provincial, and local laws outlawing workplace discrimination.[10] They also serve as the basis for stereotyping, as mentioned earlier. Finally, an approach known as *biodata* is sometimes used to establish a link between these characteristics and individual work performance

Demographic characteristics are background variables (e.g., age, gender) that help shape what a person becomes over time.

and human resource maintenance. Information is obtained on a wide range of characteristics, such as parents' socioeconomic background and the number of places an individual has lived while growing up. The biodata approach then compares demographic characteristics for high-performing and low-performing workers to provide a profile against which to compare new job applicants. To shed more light on and help dispel stereotypes concerning some of the key demographic characteristics, let's look at what the research data tell us.

▼ GENDER

The research on working women in general tells us that there are very few differences between men and women that affect job performance. Thus, there are no consistent differences in the problem-solving abilities, analytical skills, competitive drive, motivation, learning ability, or sociability of a man versus a woman.[11] However, women do tend to be more conforming and to have lower expectations of success than men do. Finally, women's absenteeism rates tend to be higher than are those of men. This finding may change, however, as we see men starting to play a more active role in raising children; absenteeism is also likely to be less frequent as telecommuting, flexible working hours, and the like become more prevalent.

Regardless of these general U.S. findings, and some Canadian data showing significant positive correlations between firm revenue and the percentage of women in the firm's workforce, evidence suggests that nearly 40 percent of respondents believe that increasing employment of women has led to a breakdown of the family and that women have obtained their current positions solely because they are women.[12] The following representative comment by a female employee reinforces this finding: "I feel most men are more qualified because they want to be the breadwinner in their homes and the women want to be at home."

Take-A-Note 3.1

TIPS IN DEALING WITH MALE AND FEMALE MANAGERS

- Do not assume that male and female managers differ in personal qualities.
- Make sure that policies, practices, and programs minimize creation of sex differences in managers' job experiences.
- Assume that managers of one sex are not superior to those of the other sex.
- Assume that there will be excellent, good, and poor managers within each sex.
- Assume that success requires the best use of talent, regardless of sex.

▼ AGE

The research findings concerning age are particularly important given the aging of the workforce. Those 50 years and older account for 85 percent of the projected labor force growth between 1990 and 2005.[13] A common stereotype concerns age and learning and flexibility. Many people associate the elderly with a sense of inertia; in reality, it depends on the individual. In fact, many elderly have shown themselves to be quite flexible.[14] Furthermore, age and performance generally have been found to be unrelated. That is, older people are no more likely than younger people to be unproductive. Whereas older workers have higher rates of unavoidable absences than do younger workers, their *avoidable* absences are less frequent. Older workers are also less likely to quit a job than are younger workers. Finally, the evidence indicates that job satisfaction sometimes increases with age and sometimes rises and then drops off with age; there is no definitive correlation.[15]

▼ ABLE-BODIEDNESS

A comprehensive survey of managers at all levels in small companies has reported that disabled workers do their jobs as well as do nondisabled employees. The study further indicates that the costs of accommodating disabled workers are generally not very high and are not an important barrier to hiring these workers.[16] Indeed, some firms are hiring both the physically and mentally disabled, as has Caprock Manufacturing.

▼ RACIAL AND ETHNIC GROUPS

Consistent with some current literature, we use the term *racial and ethnic groups* to reflect the broad spectrum of employees of differing ethnicities or races who make up an ever-increasing portion of the new workforce.[17] Besides white Americans, the four primary racial and ethnic groups receiving increasing attention are Native Americans, Asian Americans, African Americans, and Latino Americans. Once again, stereotypes exist for these as well as other racial and ethnic groups too numerous to mention, because each group tends to harbor stereotypes about the other. The research findings for each are not systematic enough to report, however.

▼ OTHER DEMOGRAPHIC CHARACTERISTICS

Some other general demographic characteristics that are considered are marital status, number of children, and experience.[18] In general, the research shows that married individuals tend to have fewer absences, lower turnover rates, and greater job satisfaction than do unmarried individuals. There is typically a positive relationship between number of children and absences and job satisfaction, whereas data for turnover are mixed.

Finally, a look at experience and performance shows that although many people expect experience to lead to increased performance, there is actually only a weak relationship between the two variables. More experienced workers tend to have low absence rates and relatively low turnover, however. In addition, turnover on a worker's previous job is strongly related to future turnover.

If carefully validated, the important demographic variables we have briefly examined can be used to assist in the selection process. Such validation is absolutely critical for demographics concerned with gender, age, racial and ethnic groups, or disability in terms of various governmental discrimination laws. Too often, demographics are used stereotypically, and individuals are not given a fair chance to demonstrate their true underlying capabilities in a work setting. Stereotypes can create special problems in today's increasingly diverse workplace.

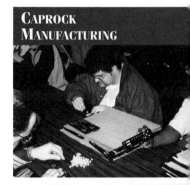

CAPROCK MANUFACTURING

Caprock Manufacturing, a plastics injection molding firm in Lubbock, Texas, has hired a number of physically and mentally disabled adults who have not only been productive but have led to improved attitudes, productivity, and understanding among its other workers.

APTITUDE AND ABILITY DIFFERENCES AMONG INDIVIDUALS

A second set of individual difference characteristics includes *aptitude* and *ability.* As we have seen, demographic characteristics are sometimes used erroneously as stereotypes in place of assessing a person's true aptitude or ability. For example, women may be stereotypically perceived as having better finger dexterity than men. Using this stereotype for hiring could lead to discrimination against men in jobs requiring high finger dexterity.

> **Aptitude** is the capability of learning something.

Aptitude represents a person's capability of learning something, whereas **ability** reflects a person's existing capacity to perform the various tasks needed for a given job and includes both relevant knowledge and skills.[19] In other words, aptitudes are potential abilities, whereas abilities are the knowledge and skills that an individual currently possesses.

> **Ability** is the capacity to perform the various tasks needed for a given job.

Aptitudes and abilities are important considerations for a manager when initially hiring or selecting candidates for a job. We are all acquainted with various tests used to measure mental aptitudes and abilities. Some of these provide an overall "IQ" score (e.g., the Stanford-Binet IQ Test). Others provide measures of more specific competencies that are required of people entering various educational programs or career fields. You have probably taken the ACT or SAT college entrance tests. Perhaps you plan to take a test for graduate study in law (LSAT), medicine (MCAT), or management (GMAT). All such tests are designed to facilitate the screening and selection of job applicants.

Of course, there is controversy over the validity of such tests and their trends over time, particularly as they apply to persons from the diverse backgrounds characteristic of today's workforce. For example, there is evidence that some racial and ethnic groups have average test scores as much as one standard deviation below those of white Americans on verbal, numerical, and related tests. Some argue that such scores do not truly measure the aptitudes or abilities of other racial and ethnic groups because the tests are based on the knowledge and experiences of middle-class white Americans to which other groups have not been exposed. A common way of dealing with this issue is to establish separate scoring norms within each racial or ethnic group—for example, African Americans and Latino Americans may each have a separate set of norms for candidate acceptance.[20] Such an approach is consistent with legal efforts by the courts to try to eliminate employment discrimination.

In addition to mental aptitudes and abilities, it is important to test for physical abilities for some jobs, such as firefighters and police. Muscular strength and cardiovascular endurance are two physical ability dimensions.[21]

QUALITY

Scholastic, a $630 million company, has become one of the world's leading publishers of children's books, classroom magazines, and instructional materials by emphasizing diversity strategies since the 1920s. Top management decided that one way to get input about what children from diverse backgrounds throughout the world wanted in educational materials was to hire women, minorities, and people who were bilingual and understood other cultures. This policy was unusual because, until the 1960s, the publishing industry was largely made up of white males. The firm has reinforced this diversity strategy with advice from experts concerning ways to capitalize on it. As a result Scholastic sells 160 million books a year worldwide, and 90 percent of U.S. classrooms use its materials.[22]

PERSONALITY

In addition to demographics, aptitude, and ability, a third important individual attribute is personality. The term **personality** represents the overall profile or combination of characteristics that capture the unique nature of a person as that person reacts and interacts with others. As an example, *Fortune* magazine has created a dubious award recognizing the "toughest CEOs in the United States"; they are characterized as extremely rigid personalities with extremely high expectations and unyielding natures that make them abusive and impossible to please.[23]

Personality combines a set of physical and mental characteristics that reflect how a person looks, thinks, acts, and feels. Sometimes attempts are made to measure personality with questionnaires or special tests. Frequently, personality can be implied from behavior alone, such as by the actions of the toughest bosses. Either way, personality is an important individual characteristic for managers to understand—an understanding of personality contributes to an understanding of organizational behavior in that we expect there to be a predictable interplay between an individual's personality and his or her tendency to behave in certain ways.

Personality is the overall profile or combination of traits that characterize the unique nature of a person.

▼ PERSONALITY DETERMINANTS AND DEVELOPMENT

Just what determines personality? Is personality inherited or genetically determined, or is it formed by experience? You may have heard someone say something like, "She acts like her mother." Likewise, someone may argue that "Bobby is the way he is because of the way he was raised." These two arguments illustrate the *nature/nurture controversy:* Is personality determined by heredity, that

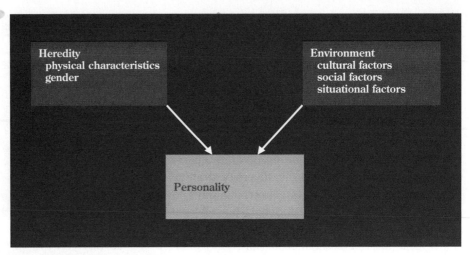

■ FIGURE 3.1

Heredity and environmental linkage with personality.

is, by genetic endowment, or by one's environment? As Figure 3.1 shows, these two forces actually operate in combination. *Heredity* consists of those factors that are determined at conception, including physical characteristics, gender, and personality factors. *Environment* consists of cultural, social, and situational factors.

There continues to be considerable debate concerning the impact of heredity on personality. Perhaps the most general conclusion we can draw is that heredity sets the limits on just how much personality characteristics can be developed; environment determines development within these limits. For instance, a person could be born with a tendency toward authoritarianism and that tendency could be reinforced in an authoritarian work environment. These limits appear to vary from one characteristic to the next. Across all the characteristics studied, however, the average proportion is about a 50–50 split between heredity and environment.[24]

As we show throughout this book, *cultural values* and norms play a substantial role in the development of an individual's personality and behaviors. Contrast the individualism of U.S. culture with the collectivism of Mexican culture, for example.[25] *Social factors* reflect such things as family life, religion, and the many kinds of formal and informal groups in which people participate throughout their lives—friendship groups, athletic groups, as well as formal work groups. Finally, *situational factors,* such as opportunity to assume increasingly challenging goals or to come back from failure, can influence personality.

Developmental Approaches   The developmental approaches of Chris Argyris and Daniel Levinson systematically examine the ways in which personality develops across time. A management expert concerned with conflicts between individuals and organizations, Argyris notes that people develop along a continuum of dimensions from immaturity to maturity.[26]

From Immaturity	To Maturity
Passivity	Activity
Dependence	Independence
Limited behavior	Diverse behavior
Shallow interests	Deep interests
Short time perspective	Long time perspective
Subordinate position	Superordinate position
Little self-awareness	Much self-awareness

Argyris believes that the nature of the mature adult personality can sometimes be inconsistent with work opportunities. That is, organizations and their managers may neglect the "adult" sides of people and instead use close supervision and control that is more typically needed by "infants" whose personalities are still immature. For example, a subordinate may raise a question about a task, and, instead of explaining, the boss simply says, "Don't worry about it, just do it the way I told you."

Others, such as Daniel Levinson, maintain that an individual's personality develops in a series of stages over time, as shown in Figure 3.2. For Levinson, there

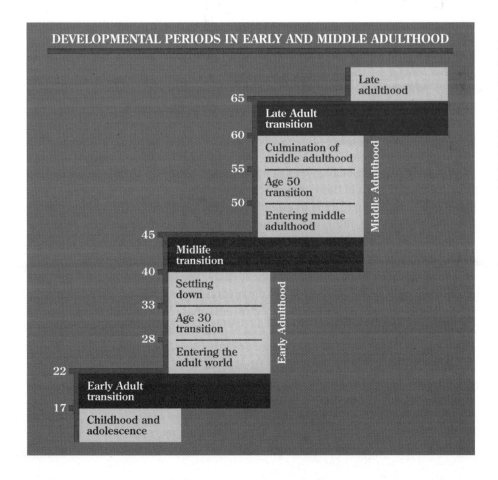

■ FIGURE 3.2
Developmental periods in early and middle adulthood. [Source: From *The Seasons of a Man's Life,* by Daniel J. Levinson, copyright © 1978 by Daniel J. Levinson. Reprinted by permission of Alfred A. Knopf, Inc.]

are four key transitions—age 30, midlife, age 50, and late adult—that have a crucial impact on a worker's job and career and on the employing organization.[27]

The point of both Argyris' and Levinson's work is that: (1) personalities develop in predictable ways over time, and (2) these developments require quite different managerial responses. Thus, an individual's needs and other personality
aspects of a person entering the organization for the first time can be expected to
change as he or she moves through Levinson's stages or moves toward more maturity, in Argyris' terms.

CLASSIFICATION FRAMEWORKS

Numerous lists of personality traits have been developed, many of which
have been used in OB research. We provide two frameworks that are useful
for grouping these traits—the first is the Big Five Framework; the second is
a framework based on J. C. Nunnally's work.

▼ BIG FIVE FRAMEWORK

Recent research has examined extensive lists of personality dimensions and distilled them into the "Big Five:"[28]

- *Extraversion*—Outgoing, sociable, assertive
- *Agreeableness*—Good-natured, trusting, cooperative
- *Conscientiousness*—Responsible, dependable, persistent
- *Emotional stability*—Unworried, secure, relaxed
- *Openness to experience*—Imaginative, curious, broad-minded

■ The "Big Five" person-
ality dimensions

Standardized personality tests determine how positively or negatively an individual scores on each of these dimensions. For instance, a person scoring high on
openness to experience tends to ask lots of questions and to think in new and unusual ways. You can think in terms of a person's individual personality profile
across the five dimensions. In terms of job performance, research has shown that
conscientiousness predicts job performance across five occupational groups of
professions—engineers, police, managers, sales, and skilled and semiskilled employees. Predictability of the other dimensions depends on the occupational
group. For instance, not surprisingly, extraversion predicts performance for sales
and managerial positions.

▼ NUNNALLY'S FRAMEWORK

Nunnally's framework (Figure 3.3) classifies several different kinds of personality
traits that are related to various OB aspects.[29]

Social Traits **Social traits** are surface-level traits that reflect the way a person
appears to others when interacting in various settings. Problem-solving style is

Social traits are surface-level traits that reflect the way one ap-
pears to others through
interactions.

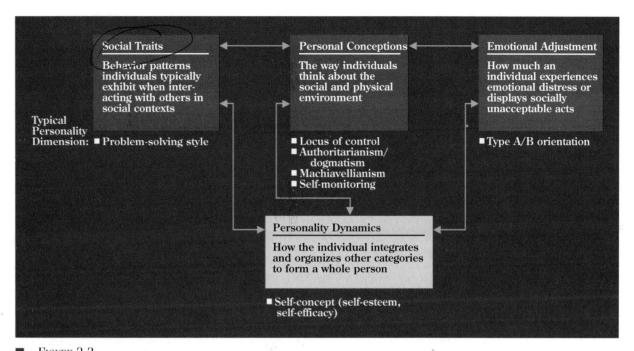

■ FIGURE 3.3

Personality classification framework. [Source: Based on a discussion by Nunnally, *Psychometric Theory* (New York: McGraw Hill, 1978), Ch. 14.]

one measure representing social traits;[30] it reflects the way a person goes about gathering and evaluating information in solving problems and making decisions.

Information gathering involves getting and organizing data for use. Styles of information gathering vary from sensation to intuitive. *Sensation-type individuals* prefer routine and order and emphasize well-defined details in gathering information; they would rather work with known facts than look for possibilities. By contrast, *intuitive-type individuals* prefer the "big picture." They like solving new problems, dislike routine, and would rather look for possibilities than work with facts.

The second component of problem solving, *evaluation,* involves making judgments about how to deal with information once it has been collected. Styles of information evaluation vary from an emphasis on feeling to an emphasis on thinking. *Feeling-type individuals* are oriented toward conformity and try to accommodate themselves to other people. They try to avoid problems that may result in disagreements. *Thinking-type individuals* use reason and intellect to deal with problems and downplay emotions.

When these two dimensions (information gathering and evaluation) are combined, four basic problem-solving styles result: sensation–feeling (SF), intuitive–feeling (IF), sensation–thinking (ST), and intuitive–thinking (IT), together with summary descriptions, as shown in Figure 3.4.

Research indicates that there is a fit between individuals' styles and the kinds of decisions they prefer. For example, STs (sensation-thinkers) prefer analytical

S

Sensation–Feeling	Sensation–Thinking
Interpersonal	Technical detail oriented
Specific human detail	Logical analysis of hard data
Friendly, sympathetic	Precise, orderly
Open communication	Careful about rules and procedures
Respond to people now	Dependable, responsible
Good at:	*Good at*:
Empathizing	Observing, ordering
Cooperating	Filing, recalling
Goal: To be helpful	*Goal*: Do it correctly
Illustrated by: Anita Rudick, CEO Body Shop International (International Cosmetics Organization)	*Illustrated by*: Enita Nordeck, President Unity Forest Products (a small and growing builder's supply firm)
Intuitive–Feeling	**Intuitive–Thinking**
Insightful, mystical	Speculative
Idealistic, personal	Emphasize understanding
Creative, original	Synthesize, interpret
Global ideas oriented to people	Logic-oriented ideas
Human potential	Objective, impersonal, idealistic
Good at:	*Good at*:
Imagining	Discovery, inquiry
New Combinations	Problem solving
Goal: To make things beautiful	*Goal*: To think things through
Illustrated by: Herb Kelleher, CEO Southwest Airlines (a fast-growing large, regional airline)	*Illustrated by*: Paul Allaire, CEO, Zerox Corporation (a huge multinational, recently innovatively reorganized)

F   T

I

■ FIGURE 3.4

Four problem-solving style summaries. [Source: Based on R. P. McIntyre and M. M. Capen, "A Cognitive Style Perspective on Ethical Questions," *Journal of Business Ethics* (1993), Vol. 12, p. 631; and D. Hellriegel, J. Slocum, and Richard Woodman, *Organizational Behavior,* 7th ed. (Minneapolis: West Publishing, 1995), Ch. 4.]

strategies—those that emphasize detail and method. IF's (intuitive-feelers) prefer intuitive strategies—those that emphasize an overall pattern and fit. Mixed styles (sensation-feelers or intuitive-thinkers), not surprisingly, select both analytic and intuitive strategies. Other findings also indicate that thinkers tend to have higher motivation than do feelers and that individuals who emphasize sensations tend to have higher job satisfaction than do intuitives. These and other findings suggest a number of basic differences among different problem-solving styles, emphasizing the importance of fitting such styles with a task's information processing and evaluation requirements.[31]

Measuring Problem-Solving Styles   Problem-solving styles are most frequently measured by the (typically 100-item) *Myers-Briggs Type Indicator,* which asks individuals how they usually act or feel in specific situations. Firms such as Apple, AT&T, and Exxon, as well as hospitals, educational institutions, and military organizations have used the Myers-Briggs for various aspects of management development.[32]

At the large aerospace conglomerate LTV, in management team meetings headed by an intuitive thinking manager, the manager would typically emphasize creative solutions rather than detailed facts. There were a number of sensation-thinkers involved, however, who felt very uncomfortable with the approach and missed meetings whenever possible. Ultimately, on the basis of these Myers-Briggs categorizations, a consultant intervened, and the manager began to emphasize the more factual aspects until the sensation-thinkers were satisfied. Then, the team moved into creative solutions. Both the team's effectiveness and its morale improved.[33]

Personal Conceptions As illustrated in Figure 3.3, *personal conceptions* represent the way individuals tend to think about their social and physical environment as well as their major beliefs and personal perspective concerning a range of issues.

Locus of Control The extent to which a person feels able to control his or her own life is concerned with a person's internal–external orientation and is measured by Rotter's **locus of control** instrument.[34] People have personal conceptions about whether events are controlled primarily by themselves, which indicates an internal orientation, or by outside forces, such as their social and physical environment, which indicates an external orientation. *Internals,* or persons with an internal locus of control, believe that they control their own fate or destiny. In contrast, *externals,* or persons with an external locus of control, believe that much of what happens to them is beyond their control and is determined by environmental forces.

> **Locus of control** is the internal–external orientation—the extent to which people feel able to affect their lives.

In general, externals are more extroverted in their interpersonal relationships and are more oriented toward the world around them. Internals tend to be more introverted and are more oriented toward their own feelings and ideas. Other differences between externals and internals are summarized in Figure 3.5.

Authoritarianism/Dogmatism Both "authoritarianism" and "dogmatism" deal with the rigidity of a person's beliefs. A person high in **authoritarianism** tends to adhere rigidly to conventional values and to obey recognized authority. This person is concerned with toughness and power and opposes the use of subjective feelings. An individual high in **dogmatism** sees the world as a threatening place. This person regards legitimate authority as absolute and accepts or rejects others according to how much they agree with accepted authority. Superiors possessing these latter traits tend to be rigid and closed. At the same time, dogmatic subordinates tend to want certainty imposed upon them.[35] From an ethical standpoint, we can expect highly authoritarian individuals to present a special problem because they are so susceptible to authority that they may behave unethically in their eagerness to comply.[36] For example, we might speculate that many of the Nazis

> **Authoritarianism** is a personality trait that focuses on the rigidity of a person's beliefs.

> **Dogmatism** is a personality trait that regards legitimate authority as absolute and accepts or rejects others based on their acceptance of authority.

FIGURE 3.5
Some ways in which internals differ from externals.

Information processing	Internals make more attempts to acquire information, are less satisfied with the amount of information they possess, and are better at utilizing information.
Job satisfaction	Internals are generally more satisfied, less alienated, less rootless, and there is a stronger job satisfaction/performance relationship for them.
Performance	Internals perform better on learning and problem-solving tasks, when performance leads to valued rewards.
Self-control, risk, and anxiety	Internals exhibit greater self-control, are more cautious, engage in less risky behavior, and are less anxious.
Motivation, expectancies, and results	Internals display greater work motivation, see a stronger relationship between what they do and what happens to them, expect that working hard leads to good performance, feel more control over their time.
Response to others	Internals are more independent, more reliant on their own judgment, and less susceptible to the influence of others; they are more likely to accept information on its merit.

who were involved in war crimes during World War II were high in authoritarianism or dogmatism; they believed so unquestioningly in authority that they followed their unethical orders without question.

Machiavellianism The third personal conceptions dimension shown in Figure 3.3 is Machiavellianism, which owes its origins to Niccolo Machiavelli. The very name of this sixteenth-century author evokes visions of a master of guile, deceit, and opportunism in interpersonal relations. Machiavelli earned his place in history by writing *The Prince,* a nobleman's guide to the acquisition and use of power.[37] The subject of Machiavelli's book is manipulation as the basic means of gaining and keeping control of others. From its pages emerges the personality profile of a **Machiavellian**—someone who views and manipulates others purely for personal gain.

Psychologists have developed a series of instruments called *Mach scales* to measure a person's Machiavellian orientation.[38] A *high-Mach personality* is someone with tendencies to behave in ways consistent with Machiavelli's basic principles. Such individuals approach situations logically and thoughtfully and are even capable of lying to achieve personal goals. They are rarely swayed by loyalty, friendships, past promises, or the opinions of others, and are skilled at influencing others.

Machiavellians are people who view and manipulate others purely for personal gain.

Research using the Mach scales has provided insight into the way high and low Machs may be expected to behave in various situations. A person with a "cool" and "detached" high-Mach personality can be expected to take control and try to exploit loosely structured environmental situations but will perform in a perfunctory, even detached, manner in highly structured situations. Low Machs tend to accept direction imposed by others in loosely structured situations; they work hard to do well in highly structured ones. For example, we might expect that, where the situation permitted, a high Mach would do or say whatever it took to get his or her way. In contrast, a low Mach would tend to be much more strongly guided by ethical considerations and would be less likely to lie or cheat or to get away with lying or cheating.

Self-Monitoring   A final personal conceptions dimension of special importance to managers is self-monitoring. **Self-monitoring** reflects a person's ability to adjust his or her behavior to external, situational (environmental) factors.[39]

High self-monitoring individuals are sensitive to external cues and tend to behave differently in different situations. Like high Machs, high self-monitors can present a very different appearance from their true self. In contrast, low self-monitors, like their low-Mach counterparts, aren't able to disguise their behaviors— "what you see is what you get." There is also evidence that high self-monitors are closely attuned to the behavior of others and conform more readily than do low self-monitors.[40] Thus, they appear flexible and may be especially good at responding to the kinds of situational contingencies emphasized throughout this book. For example, high self-monitors should be especially good at changing their leadership behavior to fit subordinates with high or low experience, tasks with high or low structure, and so on.

> **Self-monitoring** reflects a person's ability to adjust his or her behavior to external, situational factors.

Emotional Adjustment   Individuals also differ in their levels of emotional adjustment—that is, how much an individual experiences emotional distress or displays unacceptable acts. Often the person's health is affected. Although many such traits are cited in the literature, one frequently encountered is the Type A/Type B orientation.

Type A and Type B Orientation   To get a feel for this orientation, take the following quiz and then read on.[41] Circle the number that best characterizes you on each of the following pairs of characteristics.

Casual about appointments	1 2 3 4 5 6 7 8	Never late
Not competitive	1 2 3 4 5 6 7 8	Very competitive
Never feel rushed	1 2 3 4 5 6 7 8	Always feel rushed
Take one thing at a time	1 2 3 4 5 6 7 8	Try to do many things
Do things slowly	1 2 3 4 5 6 7 8	Do things fast
Express my feelings	1 2 3 4 5 6 7 8	Hold in my feelings
Many outside interests	1 2 3 4 5 6 7 8	Few outside interests

Total your points for the seven items in the quiz. Multiply this total by 3 to arrive at a final score. Use this total to locate your Type A/Type B orientation on the following list.

Final Points *A/B Orientation*
Below 90   B
90–99   B+
100–105   A–
106–119   A
120 or more A+

Individuals with a **Type A orientation** are characterized by impatience, desire for achievement, and perfectionism. In contrast, those with **Type B orientations** are characterized as more easygoing and less competitive in relation to daily events.[42]

Type A people tend to work fast and to be impatient, uncomfortable, irritable, and aggressive. Such tendencies indicate "obsessive" behavior, a fairly widespread—but not always helpful—trait among managers. Many managers are hard-driving, detail-oriented people who have high-performance standards and thrive on routine. But when such work obsessions are carried to the extreme, they may lead to greater concerns for the details than the results, resistance to change, overzealous control of subordinates, and various kinds of interpersonal difficulties, which may even include threats and physical violence. In contrast, Type B managers tend to be much more laid back and patient in their dealings with coworkers and subordinates.

Personality Dynamics Collectively, the ways in which an individual integrates and organizes the other categories and the traits they contain are referred to as *personality dynamics.* It is this category that makes personality more than just the sum of the separate traits. A key personality dynamic in your study of OB is the *self-concept.*

We can describe the **self-concept** as the view individuals have of themselves as physical, social, and spiritual or moral beings.[43] It is a way of recognizing oneself as a distinct human being. A person's self-concept is greatly influenced by his or her culture. For example, Americans tend to disclose much more about themselves than do the English; that is, Americans' self-concept is more assertive and talkative.[44]

Two related—and crucial—aspects of the self-concept are self-esteem and self-efficacy. *Self-esteem* is a belief about one's own worth based on an overall self evaluation.[45] People high in self-esteem see themselves as capable, worthwhile, and acceptable and tend to have few doubts about themselves. The opposite is true of a person low in self-esteem. Some OB research suggests that, whereas high self-esteem generally can boost performance and human resource maintenance, when under pressure, people with high self-esteem may become boastful and act egotistically. They also may be overconfident at times and fail to obtain important information.[46]

Type A orientation is characterized by impatience, desire for achievement, and perfectionism.

Type B orientation is characterized by an easygoing and less competitive nature.

Self-concept is the view individuals have of themselves as physical, social, and spiritual or moral beings.

56

Self-efficacy, sometimes called the "effectance motive," is a more specific version of self-esteem; it is an individual's belief about the likelihood of successfully completing a specific task. You could be high in self-esteem, yet have a feeling of low self-efficacy about performing a certain task, such as public speaking.

VALUES AND ATTITUDES

Joining demographic and personality characteristics as important individual difference characteristics are values and attitudes.

▼ VALUES

Values can be defined as broad preferences concerning appropriate courses of action or outcomes. As such, values reflect a person's sense of right and wrong or what "ought" to be.[47] "Equal rights for all" and "People should be treated with respect and dignity" are representative of values. Values tend to influence attitudes and behavior. For example, if you value equal rights for all and you go to work for an organization that treats its managers much better than it does its workers, you may form the attitude that the company is an unfair place to work, and, consequently, you may not produce well or perhaps leave the company. It's likely that if the company had had a more equalitarian policy, your attitude and behaviors would have been more positive.

> **Values** are global beliefs that guide actions and judgments across a variety of situations.

Sources and Types of Values   Parents, friends, teachers, and external reference groups can all influence individual values. Indeed, peoples' values develop as a product of the learning and experience they encounter in the cultural setting in which they live. As learning and experiences differ from one person to another, value differences result. Such differences are likely to be deep seated and difficult (though not impossible) to change; many have their roots in early childhood and the way a person has been raised.[48]

The noted psychologist Milton Rokeach has developed a well-known set of values classified into two broad categories.[49] **Terminal values** reflect a person's preferences concerning the "ends" to be achieved; they are the goals individuals would like to achieve during their lifetime. Rokeach identified 18 terminal values, as summarized in Figure 3.6.

> **Terminal values** are values that reflect a person's beliefs about ends to be achieved.

Instrumental values reflect the "means" for achieving desired ends. They represent how you might go about achieving your important end states, depending on the relative importance you attached to the instrumental values.

Illustrative research shows, not surprisingly, that both terminal and instrumental values differ by group (for example, executives, activist workers, and union members).[50] These preference differences can encourage conflict or agreement when different groups have to deal with each other.

> **Instrumental values** are values that reflect a person's beliefs about the means for achieving desired ends.

Terminal Values	Instrumental Values
A comfortable life (and prosperous)	Ambitious (hardworking, aspiring)
An exciting life (stimulating)	Broad-minded (open-minded)
A sense of accomplishment (lasting contribution)	Capable (competent, effective)
A world at peace (free of war and conflict)	Cheerful (lighthearted, joyful)
A world of beauty (beauty of nature and the arts)	Clean (neat, tidy)
Equality (brotherhood, equal opportunity)	Courageous (standing up for beliefs)
Family security (taking care of loved ones)	Forgiving (willing to pardon)
Freedom (independence, free choice)	Helpful (working for others' welfare)
Happiness (contentedness)	Honest (sincere, truthful)
Inner harmony (freedom from inner conflict)	Imaginative (creative, daring)
Mature love (sexual and spiritual intimacy)	Independent (self-sufficient, self reliant)
National security (attack protection)	Intellectual (intelligent, reflective)
Pleasure (leisurely, enjoyable life)	Logical (rational, consistent)
Salvation (saved, eternal life)	Loving (affectionate, tender)
Self-respect (self-esteem)	Obedient (dutiful, respectful)
Social recognition (admiration, respect)	Polite (courteous, well mannered)
True friendship (close companionship)	Responsible (reliable, dependable)
Wisdom (mature understanding of life)	Self-controlled (self-disciplined)

■   FIGURE 3.6

Rokeach value survey. [Source: Based on M. Rokeach, *The Nature of Human Values* (New York: Free Press, 1973).]

Another classification of human values was developed in the early 1930s by psychologist Gordon Allport and his associates. These values fall into six major types:[51]

■   Allport's six value categories

❶ *Theoretical*—Interest in the discovery of truth through reasoning and systematic thinking.

❷ *Economic*—Interest in usefulness and practicality, including the accumulation of wealth.

❸ *Aesthetic*—Interest in beauty, form, and artistic harmony.

❹ *Social*—Interest in people and love as a human relationship.

❺ *Political*—Interest in gaining power and influencing other people.

❻ *Religious*—Interest in unity and in understanding the cosmos as a whole.

Once again, groups differ in the way in which they rank order the importance of these values, as shown below.[52]

● *Ministers*—Religious, social, aesthetic, political, theoretical, economic.

● *Purchasing Executive*—Economic, theoretical, political, religious, aesthetic, social.

- *Industrial Scientists*—Theoretical, political, economic, aesthetic, religious, social

The previous value classifications have had a major impact on the values literature, but they were not specifically designed for people in a work setting. A more recent values schema has been developed by Meglino and associates and is aimed at people in the workplace:[53]

❶ *Achievement*—Getting things done and working hard to accomplish difficult things in life.

❷ *Helping and Concern for Others*—Being concerned with other people and helping others.

❸ *Honesty*—Telling the truth and doing what you feel is right.

❹ *Fairness*—Being impartial and doing what is fair for all concerned.

■ Meglino and associates value categories

These four values have been shown to be especially important in the workplace; thus, the framework should be particularly relevant for studying values in OB.

In particular, values can be influential through **value congruence,** which occurs when individuals express positive feelings upon encountering others who exhibit values similar to their own. When values differ, or are *incongruent,* conflicts over such things as goals and the means to achieve them may result. The Meglino et al. value schema was used to examine value congruence between leaders and followers. The researchers found greater follower satisfaction with the leader when there was such congruence in terms of achievement, helping, honesty, and fairness values.[54]

> **Value congruence** occurs when individuals express positive feelings upon encountering others who exhibit values similar to their own.

Patterns and Trends in Values   We should also be aware of applied research on values trends over time. Daniel Yankelovich, for example, is known for his informative public opinion polls.[55] Among North American workers, Yankelovich notes a movement away from valuing economic incentives, organizational loyalty, and work-related identity and toward valuing meaningful work, pursuit of leisure, and personal identity and self-fulfillment. Yankelovich believes that the modern manager must be able to recognize value differences and trends among people at work. For example, he reports finding higher productivity among younger workers who are employed in jobs that match their values and/or who are supervised by managers who share their values, reinforcing the concept of value congruence.

In a nationwide sample, managers and human resource professionals were asked to identify the work-related values they believed to be most important to individuals in the workforce, both now and in the near future.[56] The nine most popular values are: recognition for competence and accomplishments; respect and dignity; personal choice and freedom; involvement at work; pride in one's work; lifestyle quality; financial security; self-development; and health and wellness. These values are especially important for managers since they provide an indication of some key concerns of the new workforce. Even though each individual

KOREAN AIRLINES

The Hanjin conglomerate's Korean Airlines emphasizes the individual values of service orientation, creativity, and progressiveness that are consistent with the airline's emphasis on constantly moving forward to enhance its role in the transportation business.[57]

Attitudes are predispositions to respond in a positive or negative way to someone or something in one's environment.

worker places his or her own importance on these values, and even though the United States today has by far the most diverse workforce in its history, this overall characterization is a good place for managers to start when dealing with workers in the new workplace. It is important to note, however, that, although values are individual preferences, many tend to be shared within cultures and organizations.

▼ ATTITUDES

Attitudes are influenced by values, but they focus on specific people or objects, whereas values have a more general focus. "Employees should be allowed to participate" is a value; your positive or negative feeling about your job because of the participation it allows is an attitude. Formally defined, an **attitude** is a predisposition to respond in a positive or negative way to someone or something in one's environment. For example, when you say that you "like" or "dislike" someone or something, you are expressing an attitude. It's important to remember that an attitude, like a value, is a hypothetical construct; that is, one never sees, touches, or actually isolates an attitude. Rather, attitudes are *inferred* from the things people say, informally or in formal opinion polls or do—their behavior.

Cognitive components of an attitude are the beliefs, opinions, knowledge, or information a person possesses.

Figure 3.7 shows attitudes as accompanied by antecedents and results.[58] The beliefs and values antecedents in the figure form the **cognitive component** of an attitude: the beliefs, opinions, knowledge, or information a person possesses. **Beliefs** represent ideas about someone or something and the conclusions people draw about them; they convey a sense of "what is" to an individual. "My job lacks responsibility" is a belief shown in the figure. Note that the beliefs may or may not be accurate. "Responsibility is important" is a corresponding aspect of the cognitive component, which reflects an underlying value.

Beliefs represent ideas about someone or something and the conclusions people draw about them.

The **affective component** of an attitude is a specific feeling regarding the personal impact of the antecedents. This is the actual attitude itself, such as "I don't like my job." The **behavioral component** is an intention to behave in a certain way based on your specific feelings or attitudes. This intended behavior is a result of an attitude and is a predisposition to act in a specific way, such as "I'm going to quit my job."

Affective components of an attitude are the specific feelings regarding the personal impact of the antecedents.

Attitudes and Behavior   You should recognize that the link between attitudes and behavior is tentative. An attitude results in *intended* behavior; this intention may or may not be carried out in a given circumstance.

In general, the more specific attitudes and behaviors are, the stronger the relationship. For example, say you are a French-Canadian personal computer operator and you are asked about your satisfaction with your supervisor's treatment of French-Canadian PC operators. You also indicate the strength of your intent to look for another PC job in a similar kind of organization within the next 6 months. Here, both the attitude and the behavior are specifically stated (they refer to French-Canadian PC operators and identify a given kind of organization over a specific time period). Thus, we would expect to find a relatively strong relationship between these attitudes and how aggressively you actually start looking for another PC job.

Behavioral components of an attitude are the intentions to behave in a certain way based on a person's specific feelings or attitude.

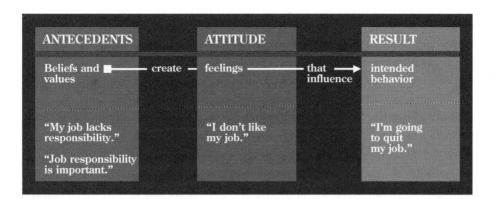

■ FIGURE 3.7
A work-related example of
the three components of
attitudes.

It is also important that there is a good deal of freedom available to carry out the intent. In the example just given, the freedom to follow through would be sharply restricted if the demand for PC operators dropped substantially.

Finally, the attitude and behavior linkage tends to be stronger when the person in question has had experience with the stated attitude. For example, assuming you are a business administration or management major, the relationship between your course attitude and/or your intent to drop the course and your later behavior of actually doing so would probably be stronger in your present OB course than in the first week of your enrollment in an advanced course in nuclear fission.[59]

Even though attitudes do not always predict behavior, the link between attitudes and potential or intended behavior is important for managers to understand. Think about your work experiences or conversations with other people about their work. It is not uncommon to hear concerns expressed about someone's "bad attitude." These concerns typically reflect displeasure with the behavioral consequences with which the poor attitude is associated. Unfavorable attitudes in the form of low job satisfaction can result in costly labor turnover, absenteeism, tardiness, and even impaired physical or mental health. One of the manager's responsibilities, therefore, is to recognize attitudes and to understand both their antecedents and their potential implications.

Attitudes and Cognitive Consistency Leon Festinger, a noted social psychologist, uses the term **cognitive dissonance** to describe a state of inconsistency between an individual's attitudes and his or her behavior.[60] Let's assume that you have the attitude that recycling is good for the economy but you don't recycle. Festinger predicts that such an inconsistency results in discomfort and a desire to reduce or eliminate it by (1) changing the underlying attitude, (2) changing future behavior, or (3) developing new ways of explaining or rationalizing the inconsistency.

Two factors that influence which of the above choices tend to be made are the degree of control a person thinks he or she has over the situation and the magnitude of the rewards involved. In terms of control, if your boss won't let you recycle office trash, you would be less likely to change your attitude than if you

> **Cognitive dissonance** is a state of perceived inconsistency between a person's expressed attitude and his or her actual behavior.

voluntarily chose not to recycle. You might instead choose the rationalization option. In terms of rewards, if they are high enough, rewards tend to reduce your feeling of inconsistency: If I'm rewarded even though I don't recycle, the lack of recycling must not be so bad after all.

MANAGING DIVERSITY AND INDIVIDUAL DIFFERENCES

The trick here is to reconcile the many conflicting pressures in managing the workforce of today and tomorrow and to enhance organizational competitiveness. Basically, we are talking about a match between the firm and specific jobs and the people recruited, hired, and trained. Once, not too long ago, this would have involved managing a homogeneous workforce of white males. Now, because of affirmative action; ethical considerations; local, national, and global competitive pressures; and a projected change in the nature of the workforce (a substantial decrease in traditional white males accompanied by an increasing number of females and nonwhites), it involves managing an increasingly diverse workforce. This is true not only in the United States but also in Canada and European Union countries, as well as in several countries in Asia.[61] Only the details differ.

So how do managers deal with all this? First, it is critical not to forget the organization–job–individual match. This involves determining the appropriate profile of individual difference characteristics needed to be successful in the organization and for given jobs. As previously discussed, these individual differences involve aptitude and ability characteristics, personality dimensions, and values and attitudes. In Chapter 6 we discuss *how* to match these individual difference characteristics with organizational and job requirements. We also show how to use selected demographic characteristics nonstereotypically as biodata for matching purposes.

Given the workforce realities noted earlier, the organization–job–individual matching should result not only in an organization–individual job fit but in an increasingly diverse workforce. To go beyond the fit and harness the potential competitive advantages of this diversity, firms are increasingly attempting to manage diversity. For example, General Motors has set up a broad-based diversity training program that includes the CEO and board of directors as well as all its 700,000 employees worldwide.[62] Such training is but one important aspect of managing diversity. A path-breaking study by Ann Morrison identified 52 practices, divided into the three areas of accountability, development, and recruitment. Without mentioning all 52 practices, let's briefly summarize the nature of these within each of the areas.

✳ NYNEX
http://www.nynex.com/

NYNEX, the 54,000-employee telephone company in New York, recently presented 10 awards to individuals and groups such as the Disability Support Organization and the Hispanic Support Organization in recognition of their efforts to manage diversity.[63]

▼ ACCOUNTABILITY PRACTICES

Accountability practices are related to a manager's responsibility to treat diverse workers fairly. They cover such practices as inclusion of diversity emphasis in

CHAPTER 3 STUDY GUIDE

management performance evaluations and promotion and management succession planning; work and family policies, attitude surveys; and policies against racism and sexism, including sexual harassment.

▼ DEVELOPMENT PRACTICES

Development practices prepare diverse workers for greater responsibility and advancement. In addition to diversity training, they involve such things as networks and support groups; job rotation; mentoring programs; entry development programs for high-potential new hires; and recognition events and awards.

▼ RECRUITMENT PRACTICES

Recruitment practices emphasize attracting job applicants at all levels who want to accept challenging work assignments and involve such activities as targeted recruitment of managers and nonmanagers, partnerships with educational institutions, internships, and publications that highlight diversity. For example, J. P. Morgan, the large financial firm, recently developed an in-house diversity internship program to identify undergraduate and graduate students to join the firm during summers.[64]

CHAPTER 3 STUDY GUIDE

SUMMARY

What is workforce diversity, and why is it important?
- Workforce diversity is the mix of gender, race and ethnicity, age, and able-bodiedness in the workforce.
- Workforces in the United States, Canada, and Europe are becoming more diverse, and valuing and managing such diversity is becoming increasingly more important to enhance organizational competitiveness and provide individual development.

What are demographic differences among individuals, and why are they important?
- Demographic differences are background characteristics that help shape what a person has become.
- Some are current (e.g., a person's current marital status); others are historical (e.g., how long a person has worked at various jobs).
- Gender, age, race and ethnicity, and ablebodiedness are particularly important demographic characteristics.
- They are important because they are covered by a series of federal, state/provincial, and local laws outlawing discrimination; they serve as the basis of stereotypes; and there are links between demographics and performance and human resource maintenance.

63

What are aptitude and ability differences among individuals, and why are they important?
- Aptitude is the capability of learning something.
- Ability is the existing capacity to do something.
- Aptitudes are potential abilities.
- Both mental and physical aptitudes and abilities are used in matching individuals to organizations and jobs.

What are personality determinants and differences among individuals, and why are they important?
- Personality captures the overall profile or combination of characteristics that represent the unique nature of an individual as that individual interacts with others.
- Personality is determined by both heredity and environment; across all personality characteristics, the mix of heredity and environment is about 50–50.
- The Big Five personality framework consists of extraversion, agreeableness, conscientiousness, emotional stability, and openness to experience.
- A personality framework based on J. C. Nunnally's work consists of social traits, personal conceptions, emotional adjustment, and personality dynamics; each category represents one or more personality dimensions.
- Personality characteristics are important because of their predictable interplay with an individual's behavior. Along with demographics and aptitude/ability differences, personality characteristics must be matched to organizations and jobs.

What are value and attitude differences among individuals, and why are they important?
- Values are broad preferences concerning courses of action or outcomes.
- Rokeach divides 18 values into terminal values (preferences concerning ends) and instrumental values (preferences concerning means.)
- Allport and his associates identify six value categories, ranging from theoretical to religious.
- Meglino and his associates classify values into achievement, helping and concern for others, honesty, and fairness.
- There have been societal changes in value patterns away from economic and organizational loyalty and toward meaningful work and self-fulfillment.
- Attitudes are a predisposition to respond positively or negatively to someone or something in one's environment; they are influenced by values but are more specific.
- Individuals desire consistency between their attitudes and their behaviors.
- Values and attitudes are important because they indicate predispositions toward behaviors.
- Along with demographics, aptitude/ability, and personality differences, values and attitudes need to be matched to organizations and jobs.

What does managing diversity and individual differences involve, and why is it important?
- Managing diversity and individual differences involves striving for a match between the firm, specific jobs, and the people recruited, hired, and developed, while recognizing an increasingly diverse workforce.

- Affirmative action; ethical considerations; local, national, and global competitive pressures; and a projected change in the nature of the workforce provide increasing workforce diversity.
- Once a match between organizational and job requirements and individual characteristics is obtained, it is necessary to manage the increasing diversity in the workforce.
- Firms now use a wide variety of practices in managing workforce diversity, which may be divided into accountability, development, and recruiting categories.

KEY TERMS

Ability (p. 46)
Affective component (p. 60)
Aptitude (p. 46)
Attitude (p. 60)
Authoritarianism (p. 53)
Beliefs (p. 60)
Behavioral component (p. 60)
Cognitive component (p. 60)

Cognitive dissonance (p. 61)
Demographic characteristics (p. 43)
Dogmatism (p. 53)
Instrumental values (p. 57)
Locus of control (p. 53)
Machiavellian (p. 54)
Personality (p. 47)
Self-concept (p. 56)

Self-monitoring (p. 55)
Social traits (p. 50)
Terminal values (p. 57)
Type A orientation (p. 56)
Type B orientation (p. 56)
Values (p. 57)
Value congruence (p. 59)
Workforce diversity (p. 42)

▼ MULTIPLE CHOICE

SELF-TEST 3

1. In the United States, Canada, the European Union, and much of the rest of the world, the workforce is __C__. (a) becoming more homogeneous (b) more highly motivated than before (c) becoming more diverse (d) less motivated than before
2. Stereotyping occurs when one thinks of an individual __b__. (a) as different from others in a given group (b) as possessing characteristics commonly associated with members of a given group (c) as like some members of a given group but different from others (d) as basically not very competent
3. Managing diversity and affirmative action are __C__ (a) similar terms for the same thing (b) both mandated by law (c) different but complementary (d) becoming less and less important
4. Demographic characteristics consist of __C__. (a) aptitude and ability (b) personality traits (c) background characteristics that help shape what a person has become (d) values and attitudes
5. Aptitudes and abilities are divided into __b__. (a) stereotypes (b) physical and mental (c) mental and personality (d) aggressive and passive
6. Personality characteristics tend to be determined by __C__. (a) environment (b) heredity (c) a mix of environment and heredity (d) a person's aptitudes and abilities.
7. The Big Five Framework consists of __d__. (a) five aptitudes and abilities (b) five demographic characteristics (c) extraversion, agreeableness, strength, emotional stability, and openness to experience (d) extraversion, agreeableness, conscientiousness, emotional stability, and openness to experience
8. Personality dynamics is represented by __a__. (a) self-esteem, self-efficacy (b) Type A/Type B orientation (c) self-monitoring (d) Machiavellianism

9. Values and attitudes are __C__. (a) similar to aptitudes and abilities (b) used interchangeably (c) related to each other (d) similar to demographic characteristics

10. Managing workforce diversity involves __a__. (a) matching organizational and job requirements with increasingly diverse individuals (b) giving preference to traditional white American males (c) giving preference to nontraditional, nonwhite male workers (d) making sure quotas of workers in various categories are emphasized

▼ TRUE–FALSE

11. The U.S. workforce is becoming less diverse. T **F**
12. Workforce diversity is another name for affirmative action. T **F**
13. Gender is one kind of demographic characteristic. **T** F
14. Aptitude is another name for ability. T **F**
15. Personality is determined by both environment and heredity. **T** F
16. Personality can develop across time. **T** F
17. The Big Five personality framework has been distilled from extensive lists of personality dimensions. **T** F
18. Attitudes often lead to values. T **F**
19. Both values and attitudes are predispositions to behave in certain ways. **T** F
20. An increasingly diverse workforce is exclusive to the United States. T **F**

▼ SHORT RESPONSE

21. What does managing diversity and individual differences mean in the workplace?
22. Why are diversity and individual differences important in the workplace?
23. In what ways are demographic characteristics important in the workplace?
24. Why are personality characteristics important in the workplace?

▼ APPLICATIONS ESSAY

25. Your boss is trying to figure out how to get the kinds of people she needs for her organization to do well, while at the same time dealing appropriately with an increasing number of nonwhite female and male workers. She has asked you to respond to this concern. Prepare a short report with specific suggestions for your boss.

4

PERCEPTION AND
ATTRIBUTION

As a young girl growing up on Ghana's coast, Beatrice Vormawah wasn't allowed to go near the water. She couldn't swim, and her mother was afraid she might drown. Beatrice obeyed, but today she is the only female ship's captain in Africa and one of only about a dozen, worldwide.[1] This is particularly remarkable in West Africa, where only about half of women are literate and less than a third go beyond primary school. Women who can't have children are considered "barren" and are outcasts. On the average, the women have six children each and live only into their mid-fifties.

Despite these odds, 22 years ago, Vormawah answered a newspaper ad for applicants to Ghana's Merchant Marine. She and two other women were accepted and graduated, and only four have done so since. A few months ago, Vor-mawah was promoted to captain, joining the ranks of 24 male captains. Surprisingly, Vormawah never encountered any discrimination or hostility, something she attributes to male assumptions that she would soon drop out. "They figured we'd stay on the job until we got married and had babies and then go back home." This lack of discrimination is even more remarkable given African beliefs that women on a ship would drive away the fish or anger the mermaids into starting up a squall.

Vormawah also differs sharply from other African women in that her husband handles most childcare duties for their three children, ages 8 to 14. She oversees a male crew of 42, and each of her round-trip voyages usually keeps her at sea for about 24 days at a time.[1] (http://www.cs.brown.edu/people/geb/ghana/government/html)

B eatrice Vormawah has been successful in her career, in spite of deviating

substantially from the general Ghanian perceptions of the role of women in their

society and their attributions about success at sea. Such gender perceptions and

attributions are part of the overall perceptual and attributional processes that are

critical components of OB and are the topics of this chapter.

Perceptions and attributions influence an individual's interpretation of his or
her environment. As you read Chapter 4, keep in mind these key questions.

- What is the perceptual process?
- What are common perceptual distortions?
- How can the perceptual process be managed?
- What is attribution theory?
- How can attribution be managed?

THE PERCEPTUAL PROCESS

L ook at Figure 4.1 and compare parts 1A and 1B, 2A and 2B, and 3AX, XD,
and XC. Are 1A and 1B the same or different lengths? Are 2A and 2B the
same or different lengths? What about 3AX, XD, and XC? If you are like most
people, the lines probably don't look the same length to you, when in fact they all
are.

Perception is the
process through which
people receive, orga-
nize, and interpret in-
formation from their en-
vironment.

This example illustrates the notion of **perception,** the process by which people select, organize, interpret, retrieve, and respond to information from the
world around them.[2] This information is gathered from the five senses of sight,
hearing, touch, taste, and smell. As the example above indicates, perception is
not necessarily the same as reality, nor are the perceptions or responses of any
two people necessarily the same when describing the same event.

Through perception, people process information inputs into responses involving feelings and action. Perception is a way of forming impressions about
oneself, other people, and daily life experiences. It also is a screen or filter

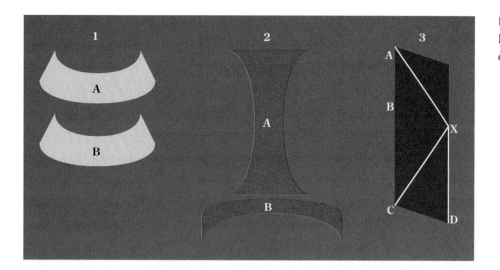

■ FIGURE 4.1
Line lengths in three different perceptual objects.

through which information passes before it has an effect on people. The quality or accuracy of a person's perceptions, therefore, has a major impact on his or her responses to a given situation.

Perceptions and responses can be long standing. For example, a spectacular catch—"the catch," a part of National Football League lore—made during the 1982 National Football Conference championship game, is perceived to have propelled Joe Montana, former San Francisco 49er quarterback, into the legendary status he enjoys today. The reverse effect is claimed to have occurred for Danny White; this Dallas Cowboy's quarterback fumbled in the final minute of the same game and never obtained the status of his predecessor, Roger Stauback, even though White took the Cowboys to the championship game 3 years in a row.[3]

Perceptual responses are also likely to vary between managers and subordinates. Consider Figure 4.2, which depicts contrasting perceptions of a performance appraisal between managers and subordinates. Rather substantial differences exist in the two sets of perceptions; the responses can be significant. In this case, managers who perceive that they already give adequate attention to past performance, career development, and supervisory help are unlikely to increase their emphasis on these points in future performance appraisal interviews. In contrast, their subordinates are likely to experience continued frustration since they perceive that these subjects are *not* being given sufficient attention.

▼ FACTORS INFLUENCING THE PERCEPTUAL PROCESS
A number of factors contribute to perceptual differences and the perceptual process among people at work. These are summarized in Figure 4.3 and include characteristics of the *perceiver,* the *perceived,* and the *situation.*

The Perceiver A person's past experiences, needs or motives, personality, and values and attitudes may all influence the perceptual process. A person with a strong achievement need tends to perceive a situation in terms of that need. If

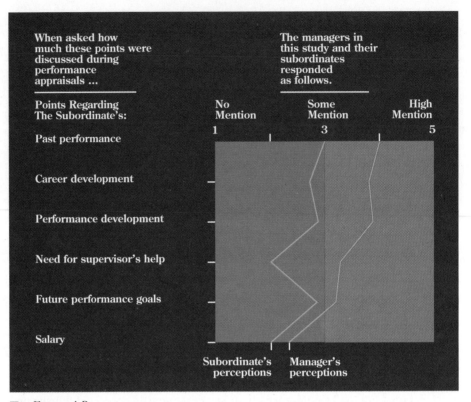

When asked how much these points were discussed during performance appraisals ...	The managers in this study and their subordinates responded as follows.		
Points Regarding The Subordinate's:	No Mention 1	Some Mention 3	High Mention 5
Past performance			
Career development			
Performance development			
Need for supervisor's help			
Future performance goals			
Salary			
	Subordinate's perceptions	Manager's perceptions	

■   FIGURE 4.2

Contrasting perceptions between managers and their subordinates: The case of the performance appraisal interview. [Source: Data reported in Edward E. Lawler III, Allan M. Mohrman, Jr., and Susan M. Resnick, "Performance Appraisal Revisited," *Organizational Dynamics,* Vol. 13 (Summer 1984), pp. 20–35.]

you see doing well in class as a way to help meet your achievement need, for example, you will tend to emphasize that aspect when considering various classes. By the same token, a person with a negative attitude toward unions may look for antagonisms even during routine visits by local union officials to the organization. These and other perceiver factors influence the various aspects of the perceptual process.

The Perceived   Characteristics of the perceived person, object, or event, such as contrast, intensity, figure–ground separation, size, motion, and repetition or novelty, are also important in the perceptual process. For example, one truck among six cars or one man among six women will be perceived differently than one of six trucks or one of six men—where there is less contrast. Intensity can vary in terms of brightness, color, depth, sound, and the like. A bright red sportscar stands out from a group of gray sedans; whispering or shouting stands out

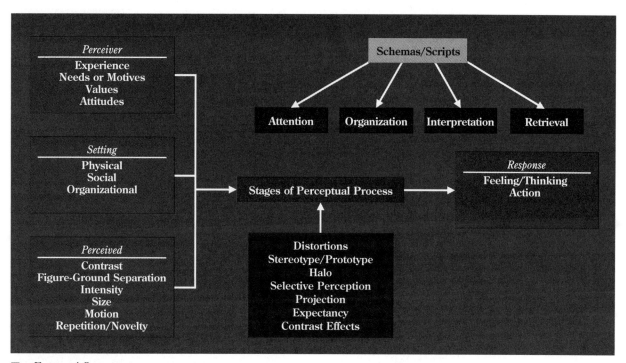

■ FIGURE 4.3

The perceptual process.

from ordinary conversation. The concept is known as figure–ground separation, and it depends on which image is perceived as the background, and which as the figure. To illustrate look at Figure 4.4. What do you see? Faces or a vase?

When it comes to size, very small or very large people tend to be perceived differently and more readily than average-sized people. Similarly, in terms of motion, moving objects are perceived differently from stationary objects. And, of course, advertisers hope that ad repetition or frequency will positively influence peoples' perception of a product. Television advertising blitzes for new models of automobiles or trucks are a case in point. Finally, the novelty of a situation affects its perception. A purple-haired teenager is perceived differently from a blond or a brunette, for example.

■ FIGURE 4.4

Figure–ground illustration.

The Setting The physical, social, and organizational context of the perceptual setting also can influence the perceptual process. Suppose you hear a coworker call his or her boss by a first name; you may perceive this situation quite differently if you observe it in an office hallway than you would at an evening social reception. And a conversation with the boss may be perceived differently when taking place in a casual reception area than when held behind closed doors in the boss's office.

▼ STAGES OF THE PERCEPTUAL PROCESS

So far we have discussed key factors influencing the perceptual process. Now we'll look at the stages involved in processing the information, that ultimately determines a person's perception and reaction, as shown in Figure 4.3. The information-processing stages are divided into information *attention* and *selection; organization* of information; information *interpretation,* and information *retrieval.*

Attention and Selection   Our senses are constantly bombarded with so much information that if we don't screen it, we quickly become incapacitated with information overload. *Selective screening* lets in only a tiny proportion of all of the information available. Some of the selectivity comes from controlled processing—consciously deciding what information to pay attention to and what to ignore. In this case, the perceivers are aware that they are processing information. Think about the last time you were at a noisy restaurant and screened out all the sounds but those of the person with whom you were talking.

In contrast to controlled processing, screening can also take place without the perceiver's conscious awareness. For example, you may drive a car without consciously thinking about the process of driving; you may be thinking about a problem you are having with your course work instead. In driving the car, you are affected by information from the world around you, such as traffic lights and other cars, but you don't pay conscious attention to that information. Such selectivity of attention and automatic information processing works well most of the time when you drive, but if a nonroutine event occurs, such as an animal darting into the road, you may have an accident unless you quickly shift to controlled processing.

Organization   Even though selective filtering takes place in the attention stage, it is still necessary to find ways to organize the information efficiently. Schemas help us do this. **Schemas** are cognitive frameworks that represent organized knowledge about a given concept or stimulus developed through experience.[4] A *self schema* contains information about a person's own appearance, behavior, and personality. For instance, a person with a decisiveness schema tends to perceive himself or herself in terms of that aspect in many circumstances, especially those calling for leadership.

Person schemas refer to the way individuals sort others into categories, such as types or groups, in terms of similar perceived features. The term "prototype," or "stereotype," is often used to represent these categories; it is an abstract set of features commonly associated with members of that category. Once the prototype is formed, it is stored in long-term memory and then retrieved when it is needed to compare how well a person matches the prototype's features. For instance, you may have a "good worker" prototype in mind, which includes hard work and punctuality; that prototype is used as a measure against which to compare a given worker. Stereotypes, as discussed in Chapter 3, may be thought of as prototypes based on such demographic characteristics as gender, age, able-bodiedness, and racial and ethnic groups. In the case of Beatrice Vormawah, we

Schemas are cognitive frameworks that represent organized knowledge about a given concept or stimulus developed through experience.

can assume that the African Merchant Marine had established a prototype of what a good Ghanian sea captain is like, and she fit that prototype well enough to be promoted.

The Moscow staff of HR Strategies, a human resource consulting firm, conducted a seminar for Russian human resource managers. During a cross-cultural awareness exercise, the participants— Russian, Tartar, Georgian, British, German, Swedish, and American—were asked to identify three positive and three negative traits about each of the nationalities represented. Americans, in general, were viewed by the others as arrogant, inflexible, and unwilling to listen. On the other hand, they were seen as always smiling. The purpose of the exercise? Once you have a feel for how people perceive you, you are in a position to determine what you can or should do differently.[5]

A *script schema* is defined as a knowledge framework that describes the appropriate sequence of events in a given situation.[6] For example, an experienced manager would use a script schema to call forth the appropriate steps involved in running a meeting. Finally, *person-in-situation schemas* combine schemas built around persons (self and person schemas) and events (script schemas).[7] Thus, a manager might organize his or her perceived information in a meeting around a decisiveness schema for both himself or herself and a key participant in the meeting. Here, a script schema would provide the steps and their sequence in the meeting; the manager would push through the steps decisively and would call on the selected participants, periodically throughout the meeting to respond decisively. Note that, although this approach might facilitate organization of important information, the perceptions of those attending might not be completely accurate because decisiveness of the person-in-situation schema did not allow the attendees enough time for open discussion.

As you can see in Figure 4.3, schemas are not only important in the organizing stage, they also affect other stages in the perception process. Furthermore, schemas rely heavily on automatic processing to free people up to use controlled processing as necessary. Finally, as we will show shortly, schemas are influenced in various ways by the characteristics and distortions shown in the figure.

Interpretation   Once your attention has been drawn to certain stimuli and you have grouped or organized this information, the next step is to uncover the reasons behind the actions. That is, even if your attention is called to the same information and you organize it the same way as your friend, you may interpret it differently or make different attributions about the reasons behind what you have perceived. For example, as a manager, you might attribute compliments from a friendly subordinate to his being an eager worker, whereas your friend would interpret the behavior as insincere flattery.

Retrieval   So far, we have discussed the stages of the perceptual process as if they all occurred at the same time. However, to do so ignores the important component of *memory*. Each of the previous stages forms a part of that memory and contributes to the stimuli or information stored there. The information stored in our memory must be retrieved if it is to be used. This leads us to the retrieval stage of the perceptual process summarized in Figure 4.3.

We have all experienced times when we can't retrieve information stored in our memory. More commonly, there is a decay in our memory, so that only some of the information is retrieved. Schemas play an important role here. Schemas make it difficult for people to remember things not included in them. For example, based on your prototype about the traits comprising a "high-performing employee," you may overestimate these traits and underestimate others when evaluating the performance of a subordinate whom you generally think of as good. Thus, you may overestimate that person's decisiveness if that were part of your high-performance prototype. Indeed, there is some evidence that people are as likely to recall nonexistent traits as they are to recall those that are really there. Furthermore, once formed, prototypes may be difficult to change and tend to last for a long time.[8]

▼ RESPONSE TO THE PERCEPTUAL PROCESS

Throughout this chapter, we have shown how the perceptual process influences numerous OB responses. Figure 4.3 classifies such responses into thoughts and feelings and actions. For example, if you witnessed coworkers kissing and if you perceived this act as sexual harassment, your thoughts and feelings would be quite different than if you perceived the kiss as a routine greeting. You might even take action by filing a sexual harassment charge. You also should be on the alert for the importance of perceptual responses covering thoughts, feelings, and actions as you cover the other OB topics in the book.

▼ COMMON PERCEPTUAL DISTORTIONS

Figure 4.3 shows some common kinds of distortions that can make the perceptual process inaccurate and affect the response. These are stereotypes or prototypes, halo effects, selective perception, projection, contrast effects, and expectancy.

Stereotypes or Prototypes   Earlier, we described stereotypes, or prototypes, as useful ways of categorizing information in order to deal with information overload. At the same time, stereotypes can cause inaccuracies in retrieving information, along with some further problems. In particular, stereotypes obscure individual differences; that is, they can prevent managers from getting to know people as individuals and from accurately assessing their needs, preferences, and abilities. Some common sources of negative stereotypes were discussed in Chapter 3, where we compared these stereotypes with research results and showed the errors that can occur when stereotypes are relied on for decision making. In spite of such errors, stereotypes continue to exist at the board of directors level in organizations. A recent survey from 133 Fortune 500 firms showed that female directors were favored for membership on only the relatively peripheral public affairs committee in these organizations, whereas males were favored for membership on the more important compensation, executive, and finance committees, despite the fact that females were equally or more qualified than their male counterparts in terms of experience.[9]

Here, we reiterate our previous message: Both managers and employees need to be sensitive to stereotypes and attempt to overcome them and recognize that an increasingly diverse workforce can be a truly competitive advantage.

Jeffrey Christian, CEO of the Cleveland-based search firm Christian and Timbers, argues that corporate America is *not* diversifying. He bases his argument on data from his firm showing that, of 6199 executives who responded to a questionnaire, 131 were African Americans, 183 were Asian American, 174 were Latino American, and 148 were Middle-Eastern/Indian Americans, but 5563 were white female Americans. Christian is concerned that only 14 percent of the executives are from diverse backgrounds; he is even more concerned that 90 percent of the diverse executives are white American women.[10]

Halo Effects A **halo effect** occurs when one attribute of a person or situation is used to develop an overall impression of the individual or situation. Like stereotypes, these distortions are particularly likely to occur in the organization stage of perception. Halo effects are common in our everyday lives. When meeting a new person, for example, a pleasant smile can lead to a positive first impression of an overall "warm" and "honest" person. The result of a halo effect is the same as that associated with a stereotype, however: Individual differences are obscured.

Halo effects are particularly important in the performance appraisal process since they can influence a manager's evaluations of subordinates' work performance. For example, people with good attendance records tend to be viewed as intelligent and responsible; those with poor attendance records are considered poor performers. Such conclusions may or may not be valid. It is the manager's job to try to get true impressions rather than allowing halo effects to result in biased and erroneous evaluations.

Selective Perception **Selective perception** is the tendency to single out those aspects of a situation, person, or object that are consistent with one's needs,

A **halo effect** occurs when one attribute of a person or situation is used to develop an overall impression of the person or situation.

Selective perception is the tendency to single out for attention those aspects of a situation or person that reinforce or emerge and are consistent with existing beliefs, values, and needs.

values, or attitudes; it has its strongest impact in the attention stage of the perceptual process. This perceptual distortion is identified in a classic research study involving executives in a manufacturing company.[11] When asked to identify the key problem in a comprehensive business policy case, each executive selected problems consistent with his or her functional area work assignments. For example, most marketing executives viewed the key problem area as sales, whereas production people tended to see it as a problem of production and organization. These differing viewpoints would certainly affect the way in which the executive would approach the problem; they might also create difficulties once these people tried to work together to improve things.

More recently, 121 middle- and upper-level managers attending an executive development program expressed broader views in conjunction with an emphasis on their own function. For example, a chief financial officer indicated an awareness of the importance of manufacturing, and an assistant marketing manager recognized the importance of accounting and finance along with their own functions.[12] Thus, this more current research demonstrated very little perceptual selectivity. The researchers were not able to say with certainty what accounted for the differing results, however.

These results suggest that selective perception is more important at some times than at others. Managers should be aware of this and test whether or not situations, events, or individuals are being selectively perceived. The easiest way to do this is to gather additional opinions from other people. When these opinions are contradictory with a manager's own, an effort should be made to check the original impression.

> **Projection** is the assignment of personal attributes to other individuals.

Projection   **Projection** is the assignment of one's personal attributes to other individuals; it is especially likely to occur in the interpretation stage of perception. A classic projection error is illustrated by the manager who assumes that the needs of his or her subordinates are the same as his or her own. Suppose, for example, that you enjoy responsibility and achievement in your work. Suppose, too, that you are the newly appointed manager of a group whose jobs seem dull and routine. You may move quickly to expand these jobs to help the workers achieve increased satisfaction from more challenging tasks because you want them to experience things that you, personally, value in work. But this may not be a good decision. If you project your needs on the subordinates, individual differences are lost. Instead of designing the subordinates' jobs to fit *their* needs best, you have designed their jobs to fit *your* needs. The problem is that the subordinates may be quite satisfied and productive doing jobs that seem dull and routine to you. Projection can be controlled through a high degree of self-awareness and *empathy*— the ability to view a situation as others see it.

> **Contrast effects** occur when an individual's characteristics are contrasted with those of others recently encountered who rank higher or lower on the same characteristics.

Contrast Effects   Earlier, when discussing the perceived, we mentioned how a red sportscar would stand out from others because of its contrast. Here, we show the perceptual distortion that can occur when, say, a person gives a talk following a strong speaker or is interviewed for a job following a series of mediocre applicants. We can expect a **contrast effect** to occur when an individual's characteris-

The chair and president of M.A.C. Cosmetics, a Canadian firm selling a line of professional cosmetics, have successfully projected their own perceptions about ethics onto M.A.C.'s marketplace. They feel strongly about social and charitable causes and shun print and television advertising to promote their products unless social and charitable causes are involved. The firm also champions numerous worthy causes. For example, all of the retail selling price of one of its lipstick lines is donated to AIDS home care support services, research and education. Also, M.A.C. supports alternatives to animal testing for cosmetics and gives free merchandise to customers for returning containers for recycling. The support of social causes is an integral part of the firm's identity.[13]

tics are contrasted with those of others recently encountered who rank higher or lower on the same characteristics. Clearly, both managers and employees need to be aware of the possible perceptual distortion the contrast effect may create in many work settings.

Expectancy   A final perceptual distortion that we consider is **expectancy**—the tendency to create or find in another situation or individual that which you expected to find in the first place. Expectancy is sometimes referred to as the "Pygmalion effect," named for a mythical Greek sculptor who created a statue of his ideal mate and then made her come to life.[14] His expectations came true! Through expectancy, you also may create in the work situation that which you expect to find.

Expectancy can have both positive and negative results for you as a manager. Suppose you assume that your subordinates prefer to satisfy most of their needs outside the work setting and want only minimal involvement with their jobs. Consequently, you are likely to provide simple, highly structured jobs designed to require little involvement. Can you predict the response of the subordinates to this situation? Their most likely response would be to show the lack of commitment that you assumed in the first place. Thus, your initial expectations are confirmed as a *self-fulfilling prophecy.*

There is a positive side to expectancy, however. Psychologists have found that rats introduced to their handlers as "maze bright" run mazes more quickly than do rats introduced to their handlers as "dumb," although there are no real differences between the group. Similarly, students identified to their teachers as

> **Expectancy** is the tendency to create or find in another situation or individual that which one has expected to find in the first place.

"intellectual bloomers" do better on achievement tests than do their counterparts who lack such a positive introduction. A particularly interesting example of the self-fulfilling prophesy is that of Israeli tank crews. The researcher told one set of tank commanders that test data indicated that some members of their assigned crews had exceptional abilities but others were only average. In reality, the crew members were assigned randomly, so the two test groups were equal in ability. Later, the commanders reported that the performance of the so-called exceptional crew members was better than that of the "average" members. The commanders had paid more attention to and praised the crew members for which they had the higher expectancies.[15] The expectancy effects in these cases argue strongly for managers to adopt positive and optimistic approaches to people at work.

MANAGING THE PERCEPTUAL PROCESS

A globally focused consumer products manufacturer with 50 facilities in 24 countries, the Gillette Company conducts an International Trainee Program that offers participants 18-month assignments in Boston, London or Singapore. Upon successful completion of the program, the trainees return to managerial positions in their home countries, thus broadening their schemas.[17]

To be successful, managers need to be alert to the perceptual process, the stages involved, and the impact the perceptual process can have on their own and others' responses. They must also be aware of the role of the perceiver, the setting, and the perceived in the perceptual process. Particularly important when focusing on the perceived is the concept of impression management—for both managers and others.

Impression management is the systematic attempt to behave in ways that create and maintain desired impressions of oneself in the eyes of others. First impressions are especially important and influence how people respond to one another. Impression management is influenced by such activities as associating with the "right people," doing favors to gain approval, flattering others to make oneself look better, taking credit for a favorable event, apologizing for a negative event while seeking a pardon, agreeing with the opinions of others, downplaying the severity of a negative event, and doing favors for others.[16] Successful managers learn how to use these activities to enhance their own images and are sensitive to their use by their subordinates and others in the organizations.

▼ PERCEPTUAL PROCESS AND DISTORTION MANAGEMENT

During the attention and selection stage, managers should be alert to balancing automatic and controlled information processing. Most of their responsibilities, such as performance assessment and clear communication, will call for controlled processing, which will take away from other job responsibilities. Along with more controlled processing, managers need to be concerned with increasing the frequency of observations and with getting representative information, rather than simply responding to the most recent information about a subordinate, for instance. Some organizations, such as long-distance trucking firms, provide computer-based monitoring of critical information to deal with the representativeness responsibility. Finally, managers should be seeking out disconfirming information to help provide a balance to their typical perception of information.

The various kinds of schemas and prototypes and stereotypes are particularly important at the information organizing stage. Managers should seek to broaden their schemas or even replace them with more accurate or complete ones.

At the interpretation stage, managers need to be especially attuned to the impact of attribution on information; we discuss this concept further in the section on managing the attributional process later in the chapter. At the retrieval stage, managers should be sensitive to the fallibility of memory. They should recognize the tendency to overrely on schemas, especially prototypes or stereotypes that may bias the nature of the information stored and retrieved.

Throughout the entire perception process, of course, managers should be sensitive to the information distortions caused by halo effects, selective perception, expectancy and contrast effects, in addition to the distortions of stereotypes and prototypes.

Take-A-Note 4.1

Creating Positive Self-Fulfilling Prophecies for Employees

- *Create a warmer interpersonal climate between your subordinates and you.*
- *Give more performance feedback to subordinates—make it as positive as possible, given their actual performance.*
- *Spend more time helping subordinates learn job skills.*
- *Provide more opportunities for subordinates to ask questions.*

Attribution Theory

Earlier in the chapter we mentioned attribution theory in the context of perceptual interpretation. **Attribution theory** aids in this interpretation by focusing on how people attempt to (1) understand the causes of a certain event, (2) assess responsibility for the outcomes of the event, and (3) evaluate the personal qualities of the people involved in the event.[18] In applying attribution theory, we are especially concerned with whether one's behavior has been internally or externally caused. Internal causes are believed to be under an individual's control—you believe Bill's performance is poor because he is lazy. External causes are seen as outside a person—you believe Sally's performance is poor because her machine is old.

Attribution theory is the attempt to understand the cause of an event, assess responsibility for outcomes of the event, and assess the personal qualities of the people involved.

According to attribution theory, there are three factors that influence this internal or external determination: *distinctiveness, consensus,* and *consistency.* Distinctiveness considers how consistent a person's behavior is across different situations. If Bill's performance is low, regardless of the machine on which he is working, we tend to give the poor performance an internal attribution; if the poor performance is unusual, we tend to assign an external cause to explain it.

Consensus takes into account how likely all those facing a similar situation are to respond in the same way. If all the people using machinery like Sally's have poor performance, we tend to give her performance an external attribution. If other employees do not perform poorly, we attribute internal causation to Sally's performance.

Consistency concerns whether an individual responds the same way across time. If Bill has a batch of low performance figures, we tend to give the poor performance an internal attribution. In contrast, if Bill's low performance is an isolated incident, we attribute it to an external cause.

In addition to these three influences, there are two errors that have an impact on internal versus external determination—the *fundamental attribution error* and the *self-serving bias*.[19] Figure 4.5 provides data from a group of health-care managers.[20] When supervisors were asked to identify, or *attribute,* causes of poor performance on the part of subordinates, they more often chose internal deficiencies of the individual—lack of ability and effort—than external deficiencies in the situation—lack of support. This demonstrates a **fundamental attribution error**—the tendency to underestimate the influence of situational factors and to overestimate the influence of personal factors in evaluating someone else's behavior. When asked to identify causes of their own poor performance, however, the supervisors overwhelmingly cited lack of support—an external, or situational, deficiency. This indicates a **self-serving bias**—the tendency to deny personal responsibility for performance problems but to accept personal responsibility for performance success.

To summarize, we tend to overemphasize other people's internal personal factors in their behavior and to underemphasize external factors in other people's behavior. In contrast, we tend to attribute our own success to our own internal factors and to attribute our failure to external factors.

The managerial implications of attribution theory can be traced back to the fact that perceptions influence responses. For example, a manager who feels that subordinates are *not* performing well and perceives the reason to be an internal lack of effort is likely to respond with attempts to "motivate" the subordinates to work harder; the possibility of changing external, situational factors to remove job constraints and to provide better organizational support may be largely ignored. This oversight could sacrifice major performance gains. It is also interest-

Fundamental attribution error is the tendency to underestimate the influence of situational factors and to overestimate the influence of personal factors in evaluating someone else's behavior.

Self-serving bias is the tendency to deny personal responsibility for performance problems but to accept personal responsibility for performance success.

Cause of Poor Performance by Their Subordinates	Most Frequent Attribution	Cause of Poor Performance by Themselves
7	Lack of *ability*	1
12	Lack of *effort*	1
5	Lack of *support*	23

■ FIGURE 4.5

Health-care managers' attributions of causes for poor performance.

ing to note that, because of the self-serving bias, when it came to evaluating their own behavior, the supervisors in the earlier study indicated that their performance would benefit from having better support. Thus, the supervisors' own abilities or willingness to work hard were not felt to be at issue.

Findings concerning the self-serving bias and fundamental attribution error are particularly interesting in cultures outside the United States.[21] In Korea, the self-serving bias was found to be negative, that is, Korean managers attribute work group failure to themselves—"I was not a capable leader"—rather than to external causes. In India, the fundamental attribution error overemphasizes external, rather than internal, causes for failure. Still another interesting cultural twist on the self-serving bias and fundamental attribution error is suggested in the opening example of the Ghanian sea captain. There, Africans attributed negative consequences—driving away fish and angering mermaids into creating squalls—to women but apparently not to men. Why these various differences occurred is not clear, but differing cultural values appear to play a role.

Finally, note that there is some evidence that U.S. females may be less likely to emphasize the self-serving bias than males.[22] This is not necessarily positive, however; ignoring the self-serving bias may hurt the women's self-esteem because they are less likely to explain away failure in terms of external causes while hesitating to take personal credit for successes.

MANAGING ATTRIBUTIONS ◀

The important thing is to be aware of the tendency in certain cultures, such as the United States, to overemphasize internal causes and underemphasize external causes. Such overemphasis may result in negative attributions toward employees. These negative attributions, in turn, can lead to disciplinary actions, negative performance evaluations, transfers to other departments, and over-reliance on training, rather than focusing on such external causes as lack of workplace support.[23]

Employees, too, take their cues from managerial misattributions and, through negative self-fulfilling prophesies, may reinforce managers' original misattributions. Employees and managers alike can be taught attributional realignment to help deal with such misattributions.[24]

Take-A-Note 4.2

KEYS IN MANAGING PERCEPTIONS AND ATTRIBUTIONS

- Be self-aware.
- Seek a wide range of differing information.
- Try to see a situation as others would.
- Be aware of different kinds of schemas.
- Be aware of perceptual distortions.
- Be aware of self and other impression management.
- Be aware of attribution theory implications.

CHAPTER 4 STUDY GUIDE

SUMMARY

What is the perceptual process?

- Individuals use the perceptual process to pay attention to and to select, organize, interpret, and retrieve information from the world around them.
- The perceptual process involves the perceiver, the setting, and the perceived.
- Responses to the perceptual process involve thinking and feeling and action classifications.

What are the common perceptual distortions?

Common perceptual distortions include

- stereotypes or prototypes.
- halo effects.
- selective perception.
- projection.
- contrast effects.
- expectancy.

How can the perceptual process be managed?

Managing the perceptual process involves

- impression management of self and others.
- managing the information attention and selection stages.
- managing the information organizing stage.
- managing the information interpretation stage.
- managing the information storage and retrieval stage.
- being sensitive to effects of the common perceptual distortions.

What is attribution theory?

Attribution theory involves

- emphasis on the interpretation stage of the perceptual process.
- consideration of whether individuals' behaviors result primarily from external causes or from causes internal to the individuals.
- consideration of three factors influencing an external or internal causal attribution: distinctiveness, consensus, and consistency.
- consideration of two errors influencing an external or internal causal attribution: fundamental attribution error and self-serving bias.

How can attributions be managed?

- Attributions can be managed by recognizing a typical overemphasis on internal causes of behavior and an underemphasis on external causes.
- An overemphasis on internal causes tends to lead to assignment of failure to employees and with accompanying, disciplinary actions, negative performance evaluations, and the like.

- An underemphasis on external causes tends to lead to lack of workplace support.
- Because of the self-fulfilling prophesy, employees tend to overemphasize internal causes of failure.
- Attributional realignment training can be used to change misattributions in the workplace.

KEY TERMS

Attribution theory (p. 79)   Halo effect (p. 75)   Schema (p. 72)
Contrast effects (p. 77)   Perception (p. 68)   Selective perception (p. 75)
Expectancy (p. 77)   Projection (p. 76)   Self-serving bias (p. 80)
Fundamental attribution
  error (p. 80)

SELF-TEST 4

▼ MULTIPLE CHOICE

1. Perception is the process by which people ____ information. (a) generate (b) retrieve (c) transmute (d) transmogrify
2. Which of the following is *not* a perceptual process stage? (a) Attention/selection. (b) Interpretation. (c) Follow through. (d) Retrieval.
3. Which of the following is *not* a perceptual distortion? (a) Stereotypes/prototypes. (b) Barnum effect. (c) Halo effect. (d) Contrast effect.
4. Perceptual distortions ____. (a) are quite rare (b) are quite common (c) affect only the interpretation stage (d) make the perceptual process more accurate
5. Impression management ____. (a) applies only to managers (b) applies only to subordinates (c) may involve agreeing with others' opinions and doing favors for others (d) may involve disobeying a superior to show how tough one is
6. Managing the perceptual process involves being concerned with ____. (a) information organizing and interpretation (b) information processing (c) narrowing schemas (d) seeking confirming information
7. Which of the following does *not* influence internal or external attribution of causation? (a) Distinctiveness. (b) Consensus. (c) Contrast. (d) Consistency.
8. In the self-serving bias, the influence of ____. (a) situational factors is overestimated (b) personal factors is overestimated (c) self-factors is overestimated (d) situational factors is underestimated
9. Overemphasizing internal causes can lead to ____. (a) additional workplace support (b) training to correct deficiencies (c) promotion of managers (d) positive self-fulfilling prophesies
10. Attribution ____. (a) is a trait managers are born or not born with (b) lends itself to training (c) is almost impossible to manage (d) is strongly related to participative management

▼ TRUE–FALSE

11. The perceptual process operates only in the perception of people.   T   F
12. The perceptual process involves four stages plus a response.   T   F
13. Stereotypes and prototypes are similar.   T   F
14. Expectancy is related to the self-fulfilling prophesy.   T   F
15. During the attention and selection stage, managers should concentrate primarily on automatic processing.   T   F

16. During the retrieval stage, there is a tendency to underemphasize schemas.   T   F
17. The fundamental attribution error seems to operate similarly throughout the world.   T   F
18. Distinctiveness influences internal or external causal determination.   T   F
19. There is a tendency in the United States to overemphasize internal causes of employee behavior.   T   F
20. Managerial misattributions can be influenced by training.   T   F

▼ SHORT RESPONSE

21. Draw and briefly discuss the text's model of the perceptual process.
22. Select two perceptual distortions, briefly define them, and show how they influence the perceptual process.
23. What is the relation of attribution theory to the perceptual process?
24. Briefly discuss the perceptual response categories and relate them to one OB topic area.

▼ APPLICATIONS ESSAY

25. Your boss has recently heard a little about attribution theory and has asked you to explain it to him in more detail, focusing on its possible usefulness in managing his department. How do you address his request?

5

MOTIVATION

It's different and it seems to work. Ben Sawatzky's lumber mill in Edmonton, Canada, operates on principles that will surely strike many as unusual, to say the least. A walk through the 160-person plant reveals a sauna and a gym with exercise machines. There are no supervisors. In teams, workers have specific production goals; once met, they get time off. The average work day is 6.75 hours. Workers are paid by the day, not the hour, and earn about double the industry average. They get 10-day paid vacations every year in Hawaii or Mexico. Says a lumber grader: "I get paid the same as the guy next to me. I have a few more responsibilities but everything is spread out among everybody in the crew." Ben Sawatzky says, in response: "By and large, I haven't run across any other company that has the loyalty of staff we have."

All this has earned Spruceland a reputation as a high-quality maker of specialized lumber products. The firm has won a Pinnacle award for outstanding entrepreneurship. Starting in 1983 with a personal investment of $1,128, a loan of $5,000, and 2 workers, Sawatzky built Spruceland into a company whose sales now total some $60 million. Japan is the company's largest market; the United States and Canada follow, respectively. The mission statement reads: "To be the supplier of first choice to our customers. To be the employer of first choice to our staff. To be the customer of first choice to our suppliers."[1]

Today's work environments are challenging, to say the least. Success for organizations and the people who make them run doesn't come easy. In this age of contrasts, the Spruceland story is refreshing. It opens the door for creativity in management, and it demonstrates the gains that may be made by employers who truly respect the needs of those who work for them. In our times, when the advent of new technologies, the pressures of global competition, and the quest for efficiency through downsizing and restructuring dominate attention, the loyalty of workers in many organizational settings is on the decline. Now, not later, the workplace must be designed and operated so that those who do the required work can achieve high-performance outcomes and experience a sense of personal satisfaction in the process.

Motivation is a key issue in any workplace, and a number of theories are helpful in understanding task performance and job satisfaction by people at work. As you read Chapter 5, keep in mind these study questions:

- What is motivation to work?
- What do the content theories suggest about individual needs?
- What do the process theories say about individual motivation?
- What is the relationship between motivation and job satisfaction?
- How can insights of the motivation theories be integrated?

WHAT IS MOTIVATION?

If asked to identify a major concern or problem at work, a manager is very likely to say "motivation—I need to do something that will encourage people to work harder." Formally defined, **motivation** refers to forces within an individual that account for the level, direction, and persistence of effort expended at work. *Level* refers to the amount of effort a person puts forth (e.g., a lot or a little); *direction* refers to what the person chooses when presented with a number of possible alternatives (e.g., whether to exert effort toward product quality or toward product quantity); and *persistence* refers to how long a person sticks with a given action (e.g., to try for product quantity and give up when it is found difficult to attain).

Motivation refers to forces within an individual that account for the level, direction, and persistence of effort expended at work.

▼ CONTENT AND PROCESS THEORIES

The theories of motivation can be conveniently divided into two broad categories.[2] First, **content theories** focus primarily on individual *needs*—the physiological or psychological deficiencies that we feel a compulsion to reduce or eliminate. These theories suggest that the manager's job is to create a work environment that responds positively to individual needs. They help to explain how poor performance, undesirable behaviors, low satisfaction, and the like, can be caused by "blocked" needs or needs that are not satisfied on the job. The motivational value of rewards can also be analyzed in terms of "activated" needs, to which a given reward either does or does not respond. Second, **process theories** focus on the thought or cognitive processes that take place within the minds of people and that act to influence their behavior. Whereas a content approach may identify job security as an important need for an individual, a process approach probes further to identify how this need leads the person to behave in particular ways relative to available rewards and work opportunities. Ultimately, we use the insights of both sets of theories to offer an integrated view of motivational dynamics that should be useful in any work setting.[3]

Content theories profile different needs that may motivate individual behavior.

Process theories seek to understand the thought processes that determine behavior.

▼ MOTIVATION ACROSS CULTURES

Before we examine the motivation theories in detail, an important caveat or word of warning is in order. These theories are subject to cultural limitations.[4] Although it can be said with confidence that worker motivation is a universal concern, the determinants of motivation and the best ways to deal with it are likely to vary considerably. As you learned in our discussion of cultures and the international dimensions of OB in Chapter 2, individual values and attitudes—both important aspects of motivation—have strong cultural ties. What proves "motivational" as a reward system in one culture, for example, may not work in another. Whereas Americans value individual rewards—a reflection of what Hofstede refers to as their high-individualism culture—the Japanese prefer group rewards, reflecting their high collectivism. We should be sensitive to these issues and avoid being parochial or ethnocentric by assuming that people in all cultures are motivated by the same things in the same ways.[5]

CONTENT THEORIES OF MOTIVATION

Four of the better known content theories have been proposed by Abraham Maslow, Clayton Alderfer, David McClelland, and Frederick Herzberg. Each of these scholars offers a slightly different view of the needs individuals may bring with them to work.

▼ HIERARCHY OF NEEDS THEORY

> Maslow's **hierarchy of needs theory** offers a pyramid of physiological, safety, social, esteem, and self-actualization needs.

Abraham Maslow's **hierarchy of needs theory**, as shown in Figure 5.1, identifies five distinct levels of individual needs: from self-actualization and esteem, at the top, to social, safety, and physiological at the bottom.[6] The notion of a needs hierarchy is important to Maslow, and he assumes that some needs are more important than others and must be satisfied before the other needs can serve as motivators. For example, the physiological needs must be satisfied before safety needs are activated, and safety needs must be satisfied before social needs are activated, and so on.

■ FIGURE 5.1
Higher order and lower order needs in Maslow's hierarchy of needs.

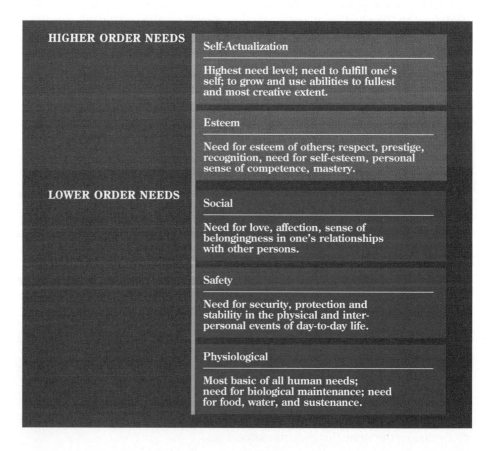

HIGHER ORDER NEEDS

Self-Actualization

Highest need level; need to fulfill one's self; to grow and use abilities to fullest and most creative extent.

Esteem

Need for esteem of others; respect, prestige, recognition, need for self-esteem, personal sense of competence, mastery.

LOWER ORDER NEEDS

Social

Need for love, affection, sense of belongingness in one's relationships with other persons.

Safety

Need for security, protection and stability in the physical and interpersonal events of day-to-day life.

Physiological

Most basic of all human needs; need for biological maintenance; need for food, water, and sustenance.

As indicated in Figure 5.1, Maslow identifies three **lower order needs.** First, the *physiological needs* are considered the most basic concerns. They consist of needs for food, water, and the like. Individuals try to satisfy these before turning to the next level of *safety needs,* which involve such things as security, protection, and stability. The *social needs* consist of a sense of belonging and a need for affiliation. Once the physiological and safety needs are satisfied, the need for relationships and belonging is activated. The kinds of work teams emphasized in total quality management and other high-performance systems are one means of satisfying these needs.

The **higher order needs** differ significantly from the lower order ones. The *esteem needs* are for both self-respect and for reputation or recognition in the eyes of others. They are the first to come into play once lower order needs are satisfied. Next come the *self-actualization needs,* the highest level in Maslow's hierarchy, consisting of the desire to achieve self-fulfillment through the creative and full use of one's talents.

> **Lower order needs** in Maslow's hierarchy are physiological, safety, and social.

> **Higher order needs** in Maslow's hierarchy are esteem and self-actualization.

Research and Global Implications   Research evidence fails to support the existence of a precise five-step hierarchy of needs as postulated by Maslow. The needs more likely operate in a flexible hierarchy. Some research suggests that there is a tendency for higher order needs to increase in importance over lower order needs as individuals move up the promotion ladder.[7] Other studies report that needs vary according to a person's career stage, the size of the organization, and even geographical location.[8] There is also no consistent evidence that the satisfaction of a need at one level decreases its importance and increases the importance of the next higher need.[9]

When the hierarchy of needs is examined across cultures, values such as those discussed in Chapter 2 clearly become important.[10] In those countries high in Hofstede's uncertainty avoidance, such as Japan or Greece, security tends to motivate more strongly than does self-actualization. Similarly, social needs tend to dominate in more collectivist countries, such as Mexico and Pakistan.[11]

The phrase *"no comprendo ingles"* has closed a lot of doors for Latino workers. Language barriers often limit job opportunities for Spanish-speaking individuals in the United States and Canada. After wrestling with difficulties faced by its Latino workers, California-based Weber Metals formed a partnership with the adult education division of the Paramount Unified School District. An innovative education program was begun to improve not only the employees' language skills, but also their opportunities for promotion and self-improvement. Weber gained in its ability to utilize their skills in total quality management programs.[12]

DIVERSITY

▼ ERG THEORY

Clayton Alderfer's **ERG theory** differs from Maslow's theory in three basic respects.[13] First, the theory collapses Maslow's five need categories into three: **existence needs**—the desire for physiological and material well-being; **relatedness needs**—the desire for satisfying interpersonal relationships; and **growth needs**—the desire for continued personal growth and development. Second, whereas Maslow's theory argues that individuals progress up the hierarchy as a result of the satisfaction of lower order needs, ERG theory includes a unique *frustration–regression* component. This suggests that an already satisfied lower level need can become activated when a higher level need cannot be satisfied. Thus, if a person is continually frustrated in his or her attempts to satisfy growth needs, relatedness needs can again surface as key motivators. Third, unlike Maslow's theory, ERG theory contends that more than one need may be activated at the same time.

Even though additional research is needed to shed more light on its validity, the supporting evidence on ERG theory is encouraging.[14] In particular, the allowance in the theory for regression back to lower level needs is a valuable contribution to our thinking. It may help to explain why in some settings, for example, the focus of workers' complaints is primarily on wages, benefits, and conditions of work—things relating to existence needs. Although these are certainly important, their concerns may be exaggerated because of the inability of the workers' jobs to otherwise satisfy relatedness and growth needs. ERG theory thus offers a more flexible approach to understanding human needs than does Maslow's strict hierarchy.

▼ ACQUIRED NEEDS THEORY

In the late 1940s, psychologist David I. McClelland and his coworkers began experimenting with the Thematic Apperception Test (TAT) as a way of measuring human needs.[15] The TAT is a projective technique that asks people to view pictures and write stories about what they see. In one case, McClelland showed three executives a photograph of a man sitting down and looking at family photos arranged on his work desk. One executive wrote of an engineer who was daydreaming about a family outing scheduled for the next day. Another described a designer who had picked up an idea for a new gadget from remarks made by his family. The third described an engineer who was intently working on a bridge-stress problem that he seemed sure to solve because of his confident look.[16]

McClelland identified three themes in such TAT stories, with each corresponding to an underlying need that he believes is important for understanding individual behavior. These needs are (1) **need for achievement** (*nAch*) —the desire to do something better or more efficiently, to solve problems, or to master complex tasks; (2) **need for affiliation** (*nAff*)—the desire to establish and maintain friendly and warm relations with others; and (3) **need for power** (*nPower*)—the desire to control others, to influence their behavior, or to be responsible for others.

Managerial Implications McClelland posits that these three needs are acquired over time, as a result of life experiences. He encourages managers to learn how to identify the presence of nAch, nAff, and nPower in themselves and in oth-

Alderfer's **ERG theory** identifies existence, relatedness, and growth needs.

Existence needs are desires for physiological and material well-being.

Relatedness needs are desires for satisfying interpersonal relationships.

Growth needs are desires for continued personal growth and development.

Need for achievement is the desire to do better, solve problems, or master complex tasks.

Need for affiliation is the desire for friendly and warm relations with others.

Need for power is the desire to control others and influence their behavior.

ers and to be able to create work environments that are responsive to the respective need profiles. The theory is particularly useful since each need can be linked with a set of work preferences. A high-need achiever will prefer individual responsibilities, challenging goals, and performance feedback. A high-need affiliator likes interpersonal relationships and opportunities for communication. The high need for power type seeks influence over others and likes attention and recognition.

If these needs are truly acquired, furthermore, it may be possible to acquaint people with the need profiles required to succeed in various types of jobs. Working with what he calls the "leadership motive pattern," McClelland has found that the combination of a moderate to high need for power and a lower need for affiliation is linked with senior executive success. High nPower creates the willingness to have influence or impact on others; lower nAff allows the manager to make difficult decisions without undue worry over being disliked.[17]

The power need is particularly interesting. The term "destructive achiever" has been used to describe executives who are high in nPower but who misuse that power. These people usually have the charisma and other characteristics needed to move up to high-level positions, but because they misuse their power they usually don't make it to the top. Why? They don't make it because they tend to get sabotaged by those they stepped on earlier. McClelland is careful to point out that nPower is most useful for managers when it is used to accomplish group and organization goals rather than selfishly motivated goals. This focus is sometimes termed "socialized power."

Research and Global Implications   Research lends considerable insight into nAch in particular and includes some especially interesting applications in developing nations. For example, McClelland trained businesspeople in Kakinda, India, to think, talk, and act like high achievers by having them write stories about achievement and participate in a business game that encouraged achievement. The businesspeople also met with successful entrepreneurs and learned how to set challenging goals for their own businesses. Over a 2-year period following these activities, the participants from the Kakinda study engaged in activities that created twice as many new jobs as those who hadn't received the training.[18]

Other work done outside the United States also suggests that societal culture can make a difference in the emphasis on nAch. Anglo-American countries such as the United Sates, Canada, and Great Britain tend to follow the high nAch pattern. But, this may lead to misunderstandings when dealing with other cultures where the influence of need for achievement is more subtle. When a major western chain built a new hotel in Tahiti, for example, a skilled totem carver was contacted to build a number of totems to provide atmosphere for the hotel. The carver quoted succeedingly higher prices for each totem. When queried about quantity discounts, the carver replied that the first totem was fun and that each additional one became less so.[19]

▼ TWO-FACTOR THEORY

Frederick Herzberg began research on his motivation theory by asking workers to report times they felt exceptionally good about their jobs and times they felt ex-

■ FIGURE 5.2
Sources of *dis*satisfaction and satisfaction in Herzberg's two-factor theory. [Source: Based on Frederick Herzberg, "One More Time: How Do You Motivate Employees?" *Harvard Business Review,* Vol. 46 (January/February, 1968), pp. 53–62.]

Hygiene factors in job context affect job *dis*satisfaction	Motivator factors in job context affect job satisfaction
Organizational policies	Achievement
Quality of supervision	Recognition
Working conditions	Work itself
Base wage or salary	Responsibility
Relationships with peers	Advancement
Relationships with subordinates	Growth
Status	
Security	

High   Job *Dis*satisfaction   0   Job Satisfaction   High

Herzberg's **two-factor theory** identifies job context as the source of job *dis*satisfaction and job content as the source of job satisfaction.

Hygiene factors in job context, the work setting, are sources of job *dis*satisfaction.

Motivator factors in job content, the tasks people actually do, are sources of job satisfaction.

ceptionally bad about them.[20] After analyzing nearly 4000 responses, as shown in Figure 5.2, Herzberg and his associates noted that the respondents identified somewhat different things in each case. From this they developed the **two-factor theory**, also known as the *motivator–hygiene theory,* which portrays different factors as primary causes of job satisfaction and job dissatisfaction.

According to the theory, **hygiene factors** are sources of job *dis*satisfaction. They are associated with the *job context* or work setting; that is, they relate more to the environment in which people work than to the nature of the work itself. Among the hygiene factors shown on the left in Figure 5.2, perhaps the most surprising is salary. Herzberg found that low salary makes people dissatisfied, but that paying them more does not necessarily satisfy or motivate them. Improved working conditions (e.g., special offices, air conditioning) act in the same way. This is because, in the two-factor theory, job satisfaction and job dissatisfaction are totally separate dimensions—improving a hygiene factor, such as working conditions, will not make people satisfied with their work; it will only prevent them from being *dis*satisfied.

To improve job satisfaction, the theory directs attention toward an entirely different set of factors—the **motivator factors** shown on the right in Figure 5.2. These factors are related to *job content,* what people actually do in their work. Adding these satisfiers or motivators to people's jobs is Herzberg's link to performance. These factors are such things as sense of achievement, recognition, and responsibility. According to Herzberg, when these opportunities are not available, low job satisfaction causes a lack of motivation and performance suffers.

Managerial Implications   The two-factor theory offers a particular discipline to managerial thinking about the use of rewards and incentives to improve motivation in the workplace. Specifically, managers sometimes allocate considerable time, attention, and other resources to issues that Herzberg would consider hygiene factors—ones that theoretically do not have a direct impact on job satisfaction and motivation, *per se*. Special office fixtures, piped-in music, fancy lounges, and high base salaries are some illustrations. The two-factor theory advises caution in focusing resources and attention solely on these hygiene factors to the exclusion of essential job content considerations. Here, also, Herzberg gets quite specific in terms of recommended applications. He suggests the technique of *job enrichment* as a way of building satisfiers into job content. This topic is given special attention in Chapter 8. For now, the notion is well summarized in this statement by Herzberg: "If you want people to do a good job, give them a good job to do."[21]

Research and Global Implications   OB scholars debate the merits of the two-factor theory.[22] Whereas Herzberg's continuing research and that of his followers support the theory, some researchers have used different methods and find that they are unable to confirm the theory. In particular, it is criticized as being method bound. This is a serious criticism, since the scientific approach requires that theories be verifiable when different research methods are used.

Herzberg's theory has met with other criticisms, such as: (1) the original sample of scientists and engineers probably is not representative of the working population; (2) the theory does not account for individual differences (e.g., pay is assumed to have a similar impact regardless of gender, age, and other important differences); and (3) the theory does not define the relationship between satisfaction and motivation.[23] Such criticisms may contribute to the mixed findings from research conducted in other cultures. For example, in New Zealand, supervision and interpersonal relationships were found to contribute significantly to satisfaction and not simply to reducing dissatisfaction. And certain hygiene factors were cited more frequently as satisfiers in Panama, Latin America, and a number of other countries than in the United States. In contrast, evidence from countries such as Finland tends to confirm U.S. results.[24] Of course, societal culture could be expected to influence these results, as it did for other approaches to motivation. Interestingly, consistent with societal culture differences, it has been argued that the individualistic masculine-oriented U.S. culture has tended to encourage the emphasis on job enrichment which emerges from the two-factor theory.[25]

PROCESS THEORIES ◀

The various content theories emphasize the "what" aspects of motivation; they tend to look for ways to improve motivation by dealing with activated or deprived needs. They do not delve formally into the thought processes through which people choose one action versus another in the workplace. For answers to these "why" and "how" questions, we must turn to the process motivation theories.

▼ EQUITY THEORY

Adams' **equity theory** posits that people will act to eliminate any felt inequity in the rewards received for their work in comparison with others.

Equity theory is based on the phenomenon of social comparison and is best applied to the workplace through the writing of J. Stacy Adams.[26] He argues that when people gauge the fairness of their work outcomes relative to others, any perceived inequity is a motivating state of mind. This occurs whenever someone believes that the rewards received for their work contributions compare unfavorably to the rewards other people appear to have received for theirs. When such perceived inequity exists, the theory states that people will be motivated to act in ways that remove the discomfort and restore a sense of felt equity. The equity comparison in a work situation can be described as:

$$\frac{\text{Personal rewards}}{\text{Personal contributions}} \quad \textit{<equity comparison>} \quad \frac{\text{Others' rewards}}{\text{Others' contributions}}$$

Felt negative inequity exists when an individual feels that he or she has received relatively less than others have in proportion to work inputs. *Felt positive inequity* exists when an individual feels that he or she has received relatively more than others have. When either exists, the individual will likely engage in one or more of the following behaviors to restore a sense of equity.

■ How to restore perceived equity

- Change work inputs (e.g., reduce performance efforts).
- Change the outcomes (rewards) received (e.g., ask for a raise).
- Leave the situation (e.g., quit).
- Change the comparison points (e.g., compare self to a different coworker).
- Psychologically distort the comparisons (e.g., rationalize that the inequity is only temporary and will be resolved in the future).
- Take actions to change the inputs or outputs of the comparison person (e.g., get a coworker to accept more work).

Managerial Implications   The equity comparison intervenes between the allocation of rewards and the ultimate impact on the recipients. What may seem fair and equitable to a group leader, for example, may be perceived as unfair and inequitable by a team member after comparisons are made with other teammates. Such feelings of inequity, furthermore, are determined solely by the individual's interpretation of the situation. It is not the reward giver's intentions that count, it is how the recipient perceives the reward that will determine actual motivational outcomes. The burden lies with the manager or team leader to take this into account and try to minimize the negative consequences of any equity comparisons.

Take-A-Note 5.1

STEPS FOR MANAGING THE EQUITY PROCESS

- *Recognize that equity comparisons are inevitable in the workplace.*
- *Anticipate felt negative inequities when rewards are given.*
- *Communicate clear evaluations of any rewards given.*
- *Communicate an appraisal of performance on which the reward is based.*
- *Communicate comparison points appropriate in the situation.*

As indicated in Figure 5.1, Maslow identifies three **lower order needs.** First, the *physiological needs* are considered the most basic concerns. They consist of needs for food, water, and the like. Individuals try to satisfy these before turning to the next level of *safety needs,* which involve such things as security, protection, and stability. The *social needs* consist of a sense of belonging and a need for affiliation. Once the physiological and safety needs are satisfied, the need for relationships and belonging is activated. The kinds of work teams emphasized in total quality management and other high-performance systems are one means of satisfying these needs.

The **higher order needs** differ significantly from the lower order ones. The *esteem needs* are for both self-respect and for reputation or recognition in the eyes of others. They are the first to come into play once lower order needs are satisfied. Next come the *self-actualization needs,* the highest level in Maslow's hierarchy, consisting of the desire to achieve self-fulfillment through the creative and full use of one's talents.

Lower order needs in Maslow's hierarchy are physiological, safety, and social.

Higher order needs in Maslow's hierarchy are esteem and self-actualization.

Research and Global Implications   Research evidence fails to support the existence of a precise five-step hierarchy of needs as postulated by Maslow. The needs more likely operate in a flexible hierarchy. Some research suggests that there is a tendency for higher order needs to increase in importance over lower order needs as individuals move up the promotion ladder.[7] Other studies report that needs vary according to a person's career stage, the size of the organization, and even geographical location.[8] There is also no consistent evidence that the satisfaction of a need at one level decreases its importance and increases the importance of the next higher need.[9]

When the hierarchy of needs is examined across cultures, values such as those discussed in Chapter 2 clearly become important.[10] In those countries high in Hofstede's uncertainty avoidance, such as Japan or Greece, security tends to motivate more strongly than does self-actualization. Similarly, social needs tend to dominate in more collectivist countries, such as Mexico and Pakistan.[11]

The phrase *"no comprendo ingles"* has closed a lot of doors for Latino workers. Language barriers often limit job opportunities for Spanish-speaking individuals in the United States and Canada. After wrestling with difficulties faced by its Latino workers, California-based Weber Metals formed a partnership with the adult education division of the Paramount Unified School District. An innovative education program was begun to improve not only the employees' language skills, but also their opportunities for promotion and self-improvement. Weber gained in its ability to utilize their skills in total quality management programs.[12]

DIVERSITY

> Alderfer's **ERG theory** identifies existence, relatedness, and growth needs.

> **Existence needs** are desires for physiological and material well-being.

> **Relatedness needs** are desires for satisfying interpersonal relationships.

> **Growth needs** are desires for continued personal growth and development.

> **Need for achievement** is the desire to do better, solve problems, or master complex tasks.

> **Need for affiliation** is the desire for friendly and warm relations with others.

> **Need for power** is the desire to control others and influence their behavior.

▼ **ERG THEORY**

Clayton Alderfer's **ERG theory** differs from Maslow's theory in three basic respects.[13] First, the theory collapses Maslow's five need categories into three: **existence needs**—the desire for physiological and material well-being; **relatedness needs**—the desire for satisfying interpersonal relationships; and **growth needs**—the desire for continued personal growth and development. Second, whereas Maslow's theory argues that individuals progress up the hierarchy as a result of the satisfaction of lower order needs, ERG theory includes a unique *frustration–regression* component. This suggests that an already satisfied lower level need can become activated when a higher level need cannot be satisfied. Thus, if a person is continually frustrated in his or her attempts to satisfy growth needs, relatedness needs can again surface as key motivators. Third, unlike Maslow's theory, ERG theory contends that more than one need may be activated at the same time.

Even though additional research is needed to shed more light on its validity, the supporting evidence on ERG theory is encouraging.[14] In particular, the allowance in the theory for regression back to lower level needs is a valuable contribution to our thinking. It may help to explain why in some settings, for example, the focus of workers' complaints is primarily on wages, benefits, and conditions of work—things relating to existence needs. Although these are certainly important, their concerns may be exaggerated because of the inability of the workers' jobs to otherwise satisfy relatedness and growth needs. ERG theory thus offers a more flexible approach to understanding human needs than does Maslow's strict hierarchy.

▼ **ACQUIRED NEEDS THEORY**

In the late 1940s, psychologist David I. McClelland and his coworkers began experimenting with the Thematic Apperception Test (TAT) as a way of measuring human needs.[15] The TAT is a projective technique that asks people to view pictures and write stories about what they see. In one case, McClelland showed three executives a photograph of a man sitting down and looking at family photos arranged on his work desk. One executive wrote of an engineer who was daydreaming about a family outing scheduled for the next day. Another described a designer who had picked up an idea for a new gadget from remarks made by his family. The third described an engineer who was intently working on a bridge-stress problem that he seemed sure to solve because of his confident look.[16]

McClelland identified three themes in such TAT stories, with each corresponding to an underlying need that he believes is important for understanding individual behavior. These needs are (1) **need for achievement** (*nAch*)—the desire to do something better or more efficiently, to solve problems, or to master complex tasks; (2) **need for affiliation** (*nAff*)—the desire to establish and maintain friendly and warm relations with others; and (3) **need for power** (*nPower*)—the desire to control others, to influence their behavior, or to be responsible for others.

Managerial Implications   McClelland posits that these three needs are acquired over time, as a result of life experiences. He encourages managers to learn how to identify the presence of nAch, nAff, and nPower in themselves and in oth-

Research and Global Implications   Research indicates that people who feel overpaid (perceived positive inequity) increase the quantity or quality of their work, whereas those who feel underpaid (perceived negative inequity) decrease the quantity or quality of their work.[27] The research is most conclusive in respect to felt negative inequity. It appears that people are less comfortable when they are underrewarded than when they are overrewarded. Such results, however, are particularly tied to individualistic cultures where self-interests tend to govern social comparisons. In more collectivist cultures, such as those of many Asian countries, the concern often runs more for equality than equity. This allows for solidarity with the group and helps to maintain harmony in social relationships.[28]

▼ EXPECTANCY THEORY

Victor Vroom's **expectancy theory** of work motivation seeks to answer this basic question: "What determines the willingness of an individual to exert personal effort to work at tasks that contribute to the performance of the work unit and the organization?"[29] The answer, according to expectancy theory, is found in the individual beliefs regarding effort–performance relationships and the desirabilities of various work outcomes that are associated with different performance levels. Simply put, the theory is based on the logic "People *will do* what they *can do* when they *want to*."[30] For example, if I want a promotion and see that high performance can lead to that promotion and believe that if I work hard I can achieve high performance, then I will be motivated to work hard.

Components of Expectancy Theory   Figure 5.3 presents the managerial foundations of expectancy theory. The three key components of the theory are:

❶ **Expectancy**—The probability assigned by an individual that work effort will be followed by a given level of achieved task performance. Expectancy would equal 0 if the person felt it were impossible to achieve the given per-

> Vroom's **expectancy theory** argues that work motivation is determined by individual beliefs regarding effort–performance relationships and work outcomes.

> **Expectancy** is the probability that work effort will be followed by performance accomplishment.

■ Key terms in expectancy theory

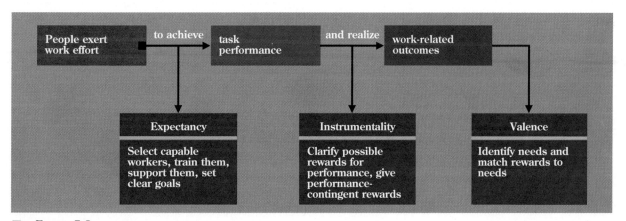

■ FIGURE 5.3
Key terms and managerial implications of Vroom's sxpectancy theory.

Instrumentality is the probability that performance will lead to various work outcomes.

Valence is the value to the individual of various work outcomes.

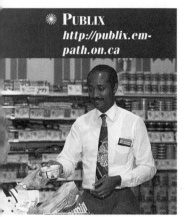

Publix, the nation's largest employee-owned supermarket, promotes from within. Most store managers begin their careers at the bottom, working their way up from entry-level positions. Publix offers employees a generous benefits and compensation package; store managers earn bonuses based on their stores' profits.

formance level; it would equal 1 if a person were 100 percent certain that the performance could be achieved.

❷ **Instrumentality**—The probability assigned by the individual that a given level of achieved task performance will lead to various work outcomes. Instrumentality also varies from 0 to 1.*

❸ **Valence**—The value attached by the individual to various work outcomes. Valences form a scale from –1 (very undesirable outcome) to +1 (very desirable outcome).

Vroom posits that motivation (M), expectancy (E), instrumentality (I), and valence (V) are related to one another by the equation: $M = E \times I \times V$. This *multiplier effect* means that the motivational appeal of a given work path is sharply reduced whenever any one or more of these factors approaches the value of zero. Conversely, for a given reward to have a high and positive motivational impact as a work outcome, the expectancy, instrumentality, and valence associated with the reward all must be high and positive.

Suppose that a manager is wondering whether or not the prospect of earning a merit raise will be motivational to someone. Expectancy theory predicts that motivation to work hard to earn the merit pay will be low if expectancy is low—if a person feels that he or she cannot achieve the necessary performance level. Motivation will be low if instrumentality is low—if the person is not confident a high level of task performance will result in a high merit pay raise. Motivation will also be low if valence is low—if the person places little value on a merit pay increase. And importantly, motivation will be low if any combination of these exists. Thus, the multiplier effect requires managers to act to maximize expectancy, instrumentality, *and* valence when seeking to create high levels of work motivation through the allocation of certain work rewards. A zero at any location on the right side of the expectancy equation will result in zero motivation.

Managerial Implications   Expectancy theory can accommodate multiple work outcomes in predicting motivation. In terms of the earlier case, the prospect of receiving a merit pay increase for high performance may not be the only thing that affects a person's decision to work hard. As shown in Figure 5.4, relationships with coworkers may also be important, and they may be undermined if the individual stands out from the group as a high performer. In that case, the motivational power of the possible pay increase can be cancelled out by any negative effects the high performance may have on the individual's relationships with coworkers. One of the advantages of expectancy theory is its ability to take into account such multiple outcomes when trying to determine the motivational value of various work rewards.

Expectancy logic argues that a manager must try to intervene actively in work situations to maximize work expectancies, instrumentalities, and valences that support organizational objectives. To influence expectancies, managers should select people with proper abilities, train them well, support them with

*Strictly speaking, Vroom's treatment of instrumentality would allow it to vary from –1 to +1. We use the probability definition here and the 0 to +1 range for pedagogical purposes; it is consistent with the instrumentality notion.

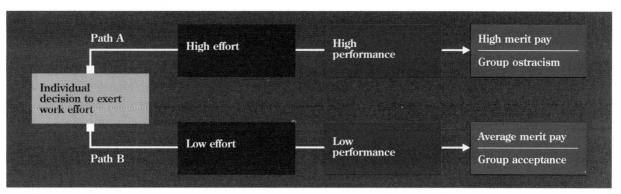

■ FIGURE 5.4

An expectancy theory view of a work situation.

needed resources, and identify clear performance goals. To influence instrumentality, managers should clarify performance–reward relationships and confirm these relationships when rewards are actually given for performance accomplishments. To influence valences, managers should identify the needs that are important to each individual and then try to adjust available rewards to match these needs.

Research and Global Implications   There is a great deal of research on expectancy theory, and good review articles are available.[31] Although the theory has received substantial support, specific details, such as the operation of the multiplier effect, remain subject to question. Researchers indicate, however, that their inability to generate more confirming data may be caused by problems of methodology and measurement rather than any inadequacy of the theory. Thus, while awaiting the results of more sophisticated research, experts seem to agree that expectancy theory is a useful source of insight into work motivation.

One of the more popular modifications of Vroom's original version of the theory distinguishes between work outcomes of two different types.[32] **Extrinsic rewards** are positively valued work outcomes that are given to the individual by some other person in the work setting. An example is pay. Workers typically do not pay themselves directly; some representative of the organization administers the reward. In contrast, **intrinsic rewards** are positively valued work outcomes that are received by the individual directly as a result of task performance. A feeling of achievement after accomplishing a particularly challenging task is an example.

Expectancy theory does not specify exactly which rewards will motivate particular groups of

> **Extrinsic rewards** are given to the individual by some other person in the work setting.

> **Intrinsic rewards** are received by the individual directly through task performance.

Take-A-Note 5.2

TIPS ON MANAGING THE VALENCE OF REWARDS

- Find out what each person wants most.
- Make a list of the available rewards.
- Discuss how well individual needs match available rewards.
- Make a list of what should be done to get desired rewards.
- Make a list of support needed to gain the desired rewards.
- Discuss possible negative outcomes and how best to avoid them.

workers. In this sense, it allows for the fact that the rewards and their link with performance are likely to be seen as quite different in various societal cultures. It helps to explain, for example, why a pay raise motivated one group of Mexican workers to work fewer hours (they wanted a certain amount of money in order to enjoy things other than work), and why the promotion to manager of a Japanese sales representative for a U.S. company adversely affected his performance (the promotion embarrassed him and distanced him from his colleagues).[33]

MOTIVATION AND JOB SATISFACTION

Job satisfaction is the degree to which individuals feel positively or negatively about their jobs.

Formally defined, **job satisfaction** is the degree to which individuals feel positively or negatively about their jobs. It is an attitude or emotional response to one's tasks as well as to the physical and social conditions of the workplace. At first glance, and from the perspective of Herzberg's two-factor theory, job satisfaction should be motivational in leading to positive employment relationships and high levels of individual job performance. But as we will discuss, the issues are more complicated than this conclusion suggests.

QUALITY

At Patagonia, a manufacturer of high-quality sports and outdoor equipment and clothing, the employees are a source of competitive advantage. And although the appeal of working for a sporting equipment company may get applicants in the door, Patagonia's passion for job satisfaction keeps them there. Employees are free to schedule their own work hours, other than core time between 9 a.m. and 3 p.m.; they have the option of 2- to 3-month leaves of absence without pay; and they are given a lot of job involvement—with responsible tasks and decision making input. Since the company is only about 1 mile from the beach, many employees go surfing during lunch for a couple of hours in the afternoon. But Patagoniacs, as they like to be called, work as hard as they play. Many of the employees who take off during the afternoon are back in the office in the evening working until 9:00.[34]

▼ COMPONENTS OF JOB SATISFACTION

Job satisfaction is just one among many important attitudes that influence human behavior in the workplace. It is closely related, for example, to "organizational commitment" and "job involvement." *Organizational commitment* refers to the degree to which a person strongly identifies with and feels a part of the organization. *Job involvement* refers to the willingness of a person to work hard and apply effort beyond normal job expectations. An individual who has high organizational commitment is considered very loyal; an individual who is highly involved in a job is considered very dedicated to it.

Given its importance, OB researchers are interested in accurately measuring job satisfaction and understanding its consequences for people at work. On a daily basis, managers must be able to infer the job satisfaction of others by careful observation and interpretation of what they say and do while going about their jobs. Sometimes, it is also useful to examine more formally the levels of job satisfaction among groups of workers. This is most frequently done through formal interviews or questionnaires. Increasingly, other methods are being used as well, including focus groups, and computer–based attitude surveys.[35]

Among the many available job satisfaction questionnaires that have been used over the years, two popular ones are the Minnesota Satisfaction Questionnaire (MSQ) and the Job Descriptive Index (JDI).[36] Both address things with which good managers should be concerned for the people reporting to them. For example, the MSQ measures satisfaction with working conditions, chances for advancement, freedom to use one's own judgment, praise for doing a good job, and feelings of accomplishment, among others. The five facets of job satisfaction measured by the JDI are:

❶ *The work itself*—responsibility, interest, and growth.
❷ *Quality of supervision*—technical help and social support.
❸ *Relationships with coworkers*—social harmony and respect.
❹ *Promotion opportunities*—chances for further advancement.
❺ *Pay*—adequacy of pay and perceived equity vis-à-vis others.

▼ JOB SATISFACTION AND EMPLOYMENT RELATIONSHIPS

The importance of job satisfaction can be viewed in the context of two decisions people make about their work. The first is the decision to belong, that is, to join and then stay a member of an organization. The second is the decision to perform, that is, to work hard in pursuit of high levels of task performance. Importantly, not everyone who belongs to an organization performs up to expectations.

The decision to belong concerns an individual's attendance and longevity at work. In this sense, job satisfaction influences **absenteeism**, or the failure of people to attend work. In general, workers who are satisfied with the job itself are more regular in attendance and are less likely to be absent for unexplained reasons than are dissatisfied workers. Job satisfaction can also affect **turnover**, or decisions by people to terminate their employment. Simply put, dissatisfied workers are more likely than satisfied workers to quit. When people fail to show up for work or quit their jobs, valuable human resources are wasted. The costs of turnover are especially high. They include the expenses of recruiting, selecting, and training replacements as well as productivity losses caused by any operational disruptions and low morale.

Still, neither absenteeism nor turnover should be viewed as entirely negative phenomena. *Functional absenteeism* has positive results for individuals and/or the organization. For example, people who are "burned out" or highly stressed in their work may benefit from a day or more of rest and relaxation. *Functional*

TUX & TAILS

Business strategy at Phoenix-based Tux and Tails is based on a simple truth: many consumers will pay premium prices for great service. Policies stress development and retention of quality employees. Training is backed by incentives that support continuous improvement.

■ Five facets of job satisfaction

Absenteeism is the failure of people to attend work.

Turnover results when people terminate their employment.

turnover also has positive results for individuals and/or the organization. For example, turnover can be an opportunity to bring replacements with creative ideas and new energy into the work unit. Functional turnover may also reduce conflict by removing a dissatisfied employee from the work setting and/or increase satisfaction by providing openings into which others may advance.[37]

Absenteeism and turnover sometimes develop because unrealistic expectations are created during the recruiting process. In contrast to traditional recruiting, which tries only to "sell" job candidates on the organization, realistic recruitment is the preferred approach. This method utilizes *realistic job previews,* which give prospective employees as much pertinent information—both good and bad—about the job as possible, without distortion.[38] This recruiting approach not only makes sense from a staffing perspective, it is also the only *ethical* thing to do.

▼ JOB SATISFACTION AND PERFORMANCE

"What is the relationship between job satisfaction and performance?" There is considerable debate on this issue, with three alternative points of view evident: (1) satisfaction causes performance, (2) performance causes satisfaction, and (3) rewards cause both performance and satisfaction.[39]

Argument: Satisfaction Causes Performance   If job satisfaction causes high levels of performance, the message to managers is quite simple: To increase people's work performance, make them happy. Research indicates that there is no simple and direct link between individual job satisfaction at one point in time and work performance at a later point in time, however. This conclusion is widely recognized among OB scholars, even though some evidence suggests that the relationship holds better for professional or higher level employees than for nonprofessionals or those at lower job levels. Job satisfaction alone is probably not a consistent predictor of individual work performance. But satisfaction may well be an important component of a larger set of variables that together can predict performance, and it may predict performance for certain people. Finally, regardless of whether or not job satisfaction causes work performance, it is certainly a part of human resource maintenance and, on the basis of this point alone, deserves attention.

Argument: Performance Causes Satisfaction   If high levels of performance cause job satisfaction, the message to managers is quite different. Rather than focusing first on people's job satisfaction, attention should be given to helping people achieve high-performance accomplishments; job satisfaction would be expected to follow. For example, a manager may carefully instruct a worker until the worker performs well. This high performance would make the worker feel good about his or her job and probably the supervisor as well.

Research indicates that an empirical relationship exists between individual performance measured at a certain time period and later job satisfaction. A basic model of this relationship, based on the work of Edward E. Lawler and Lyman Porter, maintains that performance accomplishment leads to rewards that, in turn, lead to satisfaction.[40] Rewards in this model are intervening variables; that is, they "link" performance with later satisfaction. In addition, a moderator variable— perceived equity of rewards—further affects the relationship. The moderator indicates that performance will lead to satisfaction *only if* rewards are perceived as equitable. If an individual feels that his or her performance is unfairly rewarded, the performance-causes-satisfaction effect will not hold.

Argument: Rewards Cause Both Satisfaction and Performance   This final argument in the job satisfaction–performance controversy is the most compelling. It suggests that a proper allocation of rewards can positively influence *both* performance *and* satisfaction. The key word in the previous sentence is "proper." Research indicates that people who receive high rewards report higher job satisfaction. But research also indicates that *performance-contingent rewards* influence a person's work performance. In this case, the size and value of the reward varies in proportion to the level of one's performance accomplishment. Large rewards are given for high performance; small or no rewards are given for low performance. And, whereas giving a low performer only small rewards initially may lead to dissatisfaction, the expectation is that the individual will make efforts to improve performance in order to obtain greater rewards in the future.

The point is that managers should consider satisfaction and performance as two separate but interrelated work results that are affected by the allocation of rewards. Whereas job satisfaction alone is not a good predictor of work performance, well-managed rewards can have a positive influence on both satisfaction and performance.

INTEGRATING THE MOTIVATION THEORIES

E ach of the theories presented in this chapter is potentially useful. Although the equity and expectancy theories have special strengths, current thinking argues forcefully for a combined approach that develops and tests contingency-type models that point out where and when various motivation theories work best. Thus, before leaving this discussion, we should pull the content and process theories together. An integrated model of individual performance and satisfaction is shown in Figure 5.5—a figure that has much in common with Vroom's expectancy theory and the Porter-Lawler framework just discussed.[41]

In the figure, job performance and satisfaction are separate, but potentially interdependent, work results. Performance is determined by individual attributes such as ability and experience, organizational support such as resources and technology, and work effort—the point at which an individual's level of motivation comes directly to bear. Individual motivation directly determines work effort, and the key to motivation is the ability to create a work setting that positively responds to individual needs and goals. Whether or not a work setting proves motivational for a given individual depends on the availability of rewards and their per-

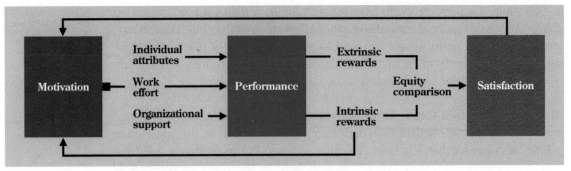

■   FIGURE 5.5

An integrated model of individual motivation to work.

ceived value. The content theories enter the model as the guide to understanding individual attributes and identifying the needs that give motivational value to the possible rewards. When the individual experiences intrinsic rewards for work performance, motivation will be directly and positively affected. Motivation can also occur when job satisfactions result from either extrinsic or intrinsic rewards that are felt to be equitably allocated. When felt negative inequity results, satisfaction will be low and motivation will be reduced.

CHAPTER 5 STUDY GUIDE

SUMMARY

What is motivation to work?

- Motivation is an internal force that accounts for the level, direction, and persistence of effort expended at work.
- Content theories, including the work of Maslow, Alderfer, McClelland, and Herzberg, focus on locating individual needs that influence behavior in the workplace.
- Process theories, such as equity and expectancy theory, examine the thought processes that affect decisions about alternative courses of action by people at work.

What do the content theories suggest about individual needs?

- Maslow's hierarchy of needs theory views human needs as activated in a five-step hierarchy ranging (from lowest) physiological, safety, social, esteem, and self-actualization (the highest).
- Alderfer's ERG theory collapses the five needs into three: existence, relatedness, and growth; more than one need can be activated at a time.
- McClelland's acquired needs theory focuses on the needs for achievement, affiliation, and power, and views needs as developed over time through experience and training.

- Herzberg's two-factor theory links job satisfaction to motivator factors, such as responsibility and challenge, associated with job content.
- Herzberg's two-factor theory links job *dis*satisfaction to hygiene factors, such as pay and working conditions, associated with job context.

What do the process theories say about individual motivation?
- Equity theory points out that social comparisons take place when people receive rewards, and that any felt inequity will motivate them to take actions to restore a sense of perceived equity.
- When felt inequity is negative, that is, when the individual feels unfairly treated, he or she may decide to work less hard in the future or to quit a job.
- Vroom's expectancy theory describes motivation as a function of an individual's beliefs concerning effort–performance relationships (expectancy), work–outcome relationships (instrumentality), and the desirability of various work outcomes (valence).
- Expectancy theory states that Motivation = Expectancy × Instrumentality × Valence, and suggests that managers should make each factor positive in order to ensure high levels of motivation.

What is the relationship between motivation and job satisfaction?
- Job satisfaction is a work attitude that reflects the degree to which people feel positively or negatively about a job and its various facets.
- Common aspects of job satisfaction relate to pay, working conditions, quality of supervision, coworkers, and the task itself.
- Job satisfaction is empirically related to employee turnover and absenteeism.
- The relationship between job satisfaction and performance is more controversial; current thinking focuses on how rewards influence both satisfaction and performance.

How can insights of the motivation theories be integrated?
- Expectancy theory, with the notion that people will exert effort to achieve performance if it is achievable and potentially rewarding, can be used to build an integrated model of motivation.
- The content theories help identify important needs and determine what a person values by way of rewards.
- The equity theory suggests that any rewards must be perceived as equitable in the social context of the workplace.
- Although motivation predicts work efforts, individual performance also depends on job-relevant abilities and organizational support.

KEY TERMS

Absenteeism (p. 99)	Expectancy theory (p. 95)	Hierarchy of needs theory (p. 88)
Content theories (p. 87)		
Equity theory (p. 94)	Extrinsic rewards (p. 97)	Hygiene factors (p. 92)
ERG theory (p. 90)	Growth needs (p. 90)	Instrumentality (p. 96)
Existence needs (p. 90)	Higher order needs (p. 89)	Intrinsic rewards (p. 97)
Expectancy (p. 95)		Job satisfaction (p. 98)

Lower order needs (p. 89)   Need for affiliation (p. 90)   Two-factor theory (p. 92)

Motivation (p. 87)   Need for power (p. 90)   Valence (p. 96)

Motivator factors (p. 92)   Process theories (p. 87)

Need for achievement   Relatedness needs (p. 90)
   (p. 90)   Turnover (p. 99)

SELF-TEST 5

▼ MULTIPLE CHOICE

1. A content theory of motivation is most likely to focus on _____. (a) cognitive processes (b) instrumentalities (c) equities (d) individual needs
2. The self-actualization need _____ in Maslow's hierarchy . (a) follows the social need (b) is a need for status or reputation in the eyes of others (c) reflects desires for creative use of one's talents (d) is a lower order need
3. A person high in need for achievement is most like to prefer _____ in their jobs. (a) group work (b) challenging goals (c) control over other people (d) little or no feedback
4. In Herzberg's two-factor theory, piped-in music, carpeting on the floor, and a comfortable office are examples of _____. (a) things relating to job dissatisfaction (b) things relating to job satisfaction (c) motivator factors (d) job content factors
5. In equity theory, the _____ is a key issue. (a) social comparison of rewards and efforts (b) equality of rewards (c) equality of efforts (d) absolute value of rewards
6. In expectancy theory, _____ is the probability that a given level of performance will lead to a particular work outcome. (a) expectancy (b) instrumentality (c) motivation (d) valence
7. One of the ways in which managers can influence the expectancy term in expectancy theory is by _____. (a) proper selection and training of workers (b) telling workers about performance–reward relationships (c) identifying individual needs (d) adjusting rewards to fit needs
8. Which statement about job satisfaction is most correct? (a) It causes performance. (b) It can affect turnover. (c) It cannot be measured. (d) It doesn't affect absenteeism.
9. In the integrated model of motivation, performance is determined by work effort, individual attributes, and _____. (a) fear of punishment (b) organizational support (c) organizational commitment (d) perceived equity of rewards
10. Because _____, the content and process theories of motivation must be cautiously applied in international management situations. (a) workers in most countries don't want to work hard (b) wages in some parts of the world are too high (c) cultural differences place limits on management theories (d) worker motivation is not a universal concern

▼ TRUE–FALSE

11. Motivation is defined as the forces leading to high performance in the workplace. T F
12. Because motivation is a universal concept, the theories apply equally well in all cultures. T F
13. There is no equivalent to Maslow's social need in Alderfer's ERG theory. T F

14. In McClelland's acquired needs theory, a high need for socialized power involves the desire to control others for the pursuit of group or organizational goals. T F
15. Creating better job content is a form of job enrichment in Herzberg's two-factor theory. T F
16. In equity theory, felt negative inequity is a motivating state but felt positive inequity is not. T F
17. An extrinsic reward is a positively valued work outcome received directly from task performance itself. T F
18. Job satisfaction is a work attitude. T F
19. A reward is performance contingent when its size and value vary in proportion to the achieved performance level. T F
20. The integrated model of motivation uses the process theories but not the content theories. T F

▼ SHORT RESPONSE

21. What is the "frustration–regression" component in Alderfer's ERG theory?
22. What is the difference between a motivator and a hygiene factor?
23. What is the "multiplier effect" in expectancy theory?
24. How can both absenteeism and turnover be functional for an organization?

▼ APPLICATIONS ESSAY

25. While attending a business luncheon, you overhear the following conversation at a nearby table. *Person A*: "I'll tell you this, if you make your workers happy they'll be productive." *Person B*: "I'm not so sure, if I make them happy maybe they'll be real good about coming to work but not very good about working really hard while they are there." Which person do you agree with and why?

6

PERFORMANCE MANAGEMENT AND REWARDS

Pic 'n Pay, a North Carolina–based shoe-retailing chain with nearly a thousand store managers, was having problems with employee turnover. To deal with this problem, top management decided to move the hiring decision from the store managers to a centralized electronic system. Interviews and hiring for all the stores are now done via headquarter's voice mail.

Applicants start by filling out an application in the store where they want to work. The store manager checks the application for obvious inconsistencies and has the candidate call an 800 number for a voice mail interview, which consists of a number of yes/no questions concerning personal habits, drug use, and honesty. Computers record the answers. Headquarter's interviewers review the candidate's information and develop questions for a followup live interview, whereby carefully trained interviewers interpret pauses, speech patterns, and the like.

Local managers can challenge headquarter's decisions but rarely do. Top management claims it has saved over $1 million as a result of reduced turnover and theft. It also plans to market its system to other high-turnover businesses.[1]

P ic 'n Pay illustrates the importance of how the key human resource manage-

ment function of employee selection can help with such OB concerns as

turnover and theft. This function is part of human resource planning for staffing

needs and fullfilling those needs. It also is part of the HR training and career de-

velopment, performance appraisal, and workforce reward functions that are the

topics of this chapter.

Human resource management functions and reward strategies are increasingly ◀
important in the new workplace. As you read Chapter 6, keep in mind the
following key questions.

- ◉ What is human resource strategic planning and staffing?
- ◉ What is training and career planning and development?
- ◉ What is performance appraisal?
- ◉ What are rewards?
- ◉ How does one manage pay as an extrinsic reward?
- ◉ How does one manage intrinsic rewards?

HUMAN RESOURCE STRATEGIC PLANNING AND STAFFING ◀

Human resource (HR) strategic planning is the process of providing capable and motivated people to carry out the organization's mission and strategy. A key part of this process is the *staffing function,* which involves the recruitment—generation of applicants; selection—hiring decisions for each applicant; and socialization—orienting new hires to the organization—of employees.[2] This function is a critical part of an organization's job requirements—the employee characteristics match emphasized so strongly in Chapter 3. Of course, once an HR staffing strategy is in place, managers must continue to assess current HR needs to make sure the organization continues to retain people to meet its strategic objectives.[3]

> **Human resource strategic planning** involves hiring capable, motivated people to carry out the organization's mission and strategy.

▼ JOB ANALYSIS

Staffing begins with an understanding of the positions or jobs for which individuals are needed in the organization. **Job analysis** provides this information; it is the process and procedures used to collect and classify information about tasks the organization needs to complete.[4] Job analysis assists in the understanding of job activities required in a work process and helps define jobs, their interrelationships, and the demographic aptitude and ability and personality characteristics needed to do these jobs. The results can be applied to job descriptions, job evaluation and classification, training and career development, performance appraisal, and other HR aspects.

> **Job analysis** is the procedure used to collect and classify information about tasks the organization needs to complete.

Information concerned with the job itself is laid out in the *job description.* The job description typically contains such information as job duties and responsibilities, equipment and materials used, working conditions and hazards, supervision, work schedules, standards of performance, and relationship to other jobs.[5]

The worker characteristics of job analysis to meet the job requirements specified in the job description are laid out in a *job specification.* A sample job specification might include such characteristics as education and experience, technical knowledge, physical aptitudes and abilities, interpersonal and communication skills, analytical aptitudes and abilities, and creative abilities.[6]

In addition to its other important contributions, job analysis is necessary to meet various legal requirements specifying that an organization's selection devices must be useful predictors of job performance.

▼ RECRUITMENT

Once job analysis provides the necessary job requirements and employee characteristics, qualified people need to be drawn in to apply for various positions. **Recruitment** is the process of attracting the best qualified individuals to apply for a given job.[7]

> **Recruitment** is the process of attracting the best qualified individuals to apply for a job.

Recruitment typically involves (1) advertisement of a position vacancy, (2) preliminary contact with potential job candidates, and (3) preliminary screening to obtain a pool of candidates. In the Pic 'n Pay example, we can assume that the firm has developed some kind of advertisement to bring in potential applicants to talk to store managers. Preliminary contact followed through the application process and discussions with the store manager. The store manager then did some initial preliminary screening by checking the application form; additional preliminary screening was conducted through the 800-number call-in.

Pic 'n Pay is an example of *external recruitment,* or attracting individuals from outside the organization. External recruitment involves such sources as general advertisements, often in newspapers, trade journals, or via external internet; word-of-mouth suggestions from current employees; use of employment agencies; and applicant walkins.

By contrast, *internal recruitment* is a process for attracting job applicants from those currently working for the firm. Posting vacant positions on bulletin boards, in internal memos, and over internal internets are frequently used means for internal recruitment.

Most firms tend to use a mix of external and internal recruitment. Some, such as the United States armed forces, rely heavily on external recruitment for entry-level positions and then fill higher level positions entirely from internal promotions. Both have advantages. Internal recruitment is encouraging to current employees, and external recruitment tends to bring in "new blood" and fresh ideas to the firm.

Realistic Job Previews   Traditionally, firms have attempted to "sell" their organization and jobs to build up the applicant pool. More recently, an approach called a *realistic job preview,* or RJP, is increasingly being used. In an RJP, applicants are provided with an objective description of the prospective organization and job. Such descriptions have been found to reduce turnover and to better prepare new hires to cope with their jobs.[8] A twist on this is the "few good men" theme used in Marine Corps recruiting—applicants are told that being a Marine is so tough that very few can be successful.

▼ SELECTION

Once an applicant pool has been recruited, the selection aspect of staffing comes into play. **Selection** involves the series of steps from initial applicant screening to finally hiring the new employee. The selection process involves the following steps: completing the application form, conducting an interview, completing any necessary tests, a background investigation, and a decision to hire or not.

> **Selection** is the series of steps from initial applicant screening to hiring.

Application Form Completion   Application form completion involves filling out a form prepared by the firm and calls for detailing various aspects of background and experience; sometimes resumés are used in lieu of or in addition to an application. Resumés include brief summaries of an applicant's background and qualifications. Most of you have probably completed an application form at one time or another and will prepare a resume before graduation, if you haven't already done so. Some application forms are built around the biodata notion mentioned in Chapter 3 and are much more comprehensive than typical application forms in terms of the amount of background information requested.

> ## Take-A-Note 6.1
> STEPS TO EMPHASIZE IN CONDUCTING HIRING INTERVIEWS
>
> - *Prepare yourself—check applicant's resumé and prepare agenda.*
> - *Initially put applicant at ease—use small talk.*
> - *Guard against stereotypes—emphasize applicant as individual.*
> - *Emphasize results-oriented questions—not only what applicant has done but results of these actions.*
> - *Allow for pauses to gather thoughts.*
> - *Bring interview to a natural close.*

Employment Interviews   Many of you have also probably experienced employment interviews at one time or another. Interviews are almost invariably used in the selection process, although they are prone to the kinds of perceptual distortions discussed in Chapter 4, as well as having other problems. Nevertheless, they are a mainstay of the selection process, perhaps because they can serve as public relations tools for the organization; at their best, interviews provide rough ideas concerning fit with the job and organization.[9]

Tests Tests may be administered either before or after the interview. They include cognitive aptitude or ability and personality tests and, increasingly, tests for drug use. Intelligence tests are the most common examples of cognitive tests. Other examples are clerical and mechanical tests. Personality tests evaluate the kinds of personality characteristics discussed in Chapter 3. For example, the California Personality Inventory measures such characteristics as dominance, sociability, and flexibility. Again, whatever kind of test is used must be validated against job requirements so that the organization is not guilty of discrimination.

Performance tests take many forms but often ask candidates to perform tasks identical to or at least closely related to what will be required on the job. For example, secretarial applicants are often required to take typing tests or to report results of such tests. Often a battery of tests is used to explore a range of job behaviors.

For managerial jobs in particular, but increasingly for other jobs as well, assessment centers are often used. *Assessment centers* are designed to provide a firm with a comprehensive view of a candidate by evaluating the candidate's performance across many situations. Such assessments typically involve one to four days of various tests, simulations, role plays, and interviews, all based on dimensions the person occupying the job will need to demonstrate. AT&T has used assessment centers for many years, with considerable effectiveness, spending as much as $1500 per employee in the process.[10] IBM and the FBI are also among the more than 2000 organizations that use assessment centers for managerial selection and promotion.[11]

Background Investigation Background investigation is also another step that can be used either early or late in the selection process. Typically, a background investigation involves reference checks. Generally, letters of reference tend to be positively biased and so are not highly related to job performance.[12] Further, unless the references, either written or provided over the phone, are very carefully worded, they can lead to lawsuits. References should only disclose information about the job duties the individual in question has been performing. Any personal descriptions should involve only information that can be objectively verified.

Decision to Hire Based on the previous steps, the organization may choose to make the hiring decision and present a formal job offer. This may be done by the potential employee's future boss or by a group of people. At this point, a physical examination may be required if shown to be relevant for job performance, and, for some jobs, negotiations concerning salary or other benefits may occur.

▼ SOCIALIZATION

Once hiring is completed, **socialization** is the final step in the staffing process. It involves orienting new employees to the firm and, specifically, to the work units in which they will be working. At this stage, the new employee is familiarized with the firm's policies and procedures and begins to get a feel for the organization's culture. Orientation can be conducted formally or informally or it may involve a combination of the two; in complex positions, orientation may take place

FRANK B. HALL & COMPANY

When Larry Buck's former boss at the Houston insurance firm of Frank B. Hall and Company described Buck as a "Jekyll and Hyde person" in responding to a telephone reference check, Buck sued and won close to $2 million for malicious slander and libel.[13]

Socialization involves orienting new employees to the firms and its work units.

over an extended period of time. Socialization can help with the job requirements–employee characteristics match by helping to fill in gaps.

TRAINING AND CAREER PLANNING AND DEVELOPMENT ◀

After an employee is selected, it is important that he or she undergo training and long-term career planning and development.

▼ TRAINING

Training is a set of activities that provides the opportunity to acquire and improve job-related skills.[14] Training occurs not only initially but anytime improved
skills are needed to meet changing job requirements.

Training can be on the job, off the job, or both. *On-the-job training* (OJT) involves job instruction while performing the job in the actual workplace. Internships, apprenticeships, and job rotation are common forms of OJT. *Internships* are
an opportunity for students to gain real-world experience. They are often offered
in the summer and may or may not be paid. *Apprenticeships* involve learning a
trade from an experienced worker. They are quite common in Europe and relatively uncommon in the United States. Related coaching or mentoring programs
for managerial and professional jobs are quite common in the United States, however. *Job rotation* provides a broad range of experience in different kinds of jobs
in a firm. It is often used to provide background for future managers and is sometimes used to try to alleviate worker boredom.

Off-the-job training commonly involves lectures, videos, and simulations. *Lectures* convey specific information and work well for problem-solving and technical
skills. *Videos* are particularly good for demonstrating various skills. *Simulations,*
such as experiential exercises, business games, and various computer-based exercises, are particularly useful for teaching interpersonal, leadership, strategic
management, and other complex skills.

A Canadian airline used a comprehensive combination of on- and off-the-job
training to deal with the impact of five mergers and to cope with an extremely dynamic environment. The training was done worldwide and was conducted in combination with American Airlines. Numerous Canadian/U.S. cultural differences
had to be worked through in the process.[15]

▼ CAREER PLANNING AND DEVELOPMENT

In addition to employee training for short-term jobs, both the employee and the
organization need to be concerned about longer term **career planning and development,** whereby individuals work with their managers and/or HR experts
on career issues.[16]

> **Training** provides the opportunity to acquire and improve job-related skills.

> **Career planning and development** involves working with managers and/or HR experts on career issues.

**ETHICS AND
SOCIAL RESPONSIBILITY**

Lucas Aerospace is taking steps to raise worker awareness of its strengthened ethics program. The program was launched first in the United States and later in the U.K. to deal with problems brought about by allegations of falsified tests on components supplied to the U.S. Government. Lucas Aerospace's 1,800 employees in the U.S. and 3,000 employees in the U.K. have received a booklet representing the company's new code of conduct, and more than 90 percent have been to ethics awareness presentations. At the end of each presentation, workers are asked to sign a tear-off slip to show that they understand the Lucas code of ethics. Employees are encouraged to report suspected breaches, either to their immediate supervisor or through an anonymous hot line without fear of retaliation or reprisal. Phil Griffiths, Lucas' U.K. corporate ethics officer, reports that there have been "surprisingly few" cynical reactions—it's as though workers believed that an ethical standard was already in place but that it had just now been written down.[17]

A basic, but useful, framework for formal career planning is offered in Figure 6.1. The five steps in the career planning framework begin with *personal assessment* and then progress through *analysis of opportunities, selection of career objectives,* and *implementation of strategies,* until the final point: *evaluation of results.* The process is recycled as necessary to allow for constructive revision of the career plan over time. Success in each of these steps entails a good deal of self-awareness and frank assessment. The message is clear: A successful career begins with sufficient insight to make good decisions about matching personal

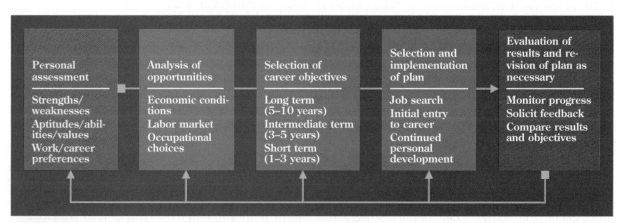

■ FIGURE 6.1

Five steps in formal career planning.

needs and capabilities with job opportunities over time. Importantly, the manager's responsibility concerning career planning is twofold: A good manager is successful at (1) planning and managing a personal career, and (2) assisting subordinates in assuming responsibility for their career planning and development.

Thoughts about careers take on a special relevance in the new workplace. We live and work in a time when the implications of constant change pressure us continually to review and reassess our career progress. In particular, businesses are becoming smaller in size and employing fewer people, and new, more flexible and adaptable forms are replacing the traditional organizational "pyramid." Accordingly, multifunctional understanding is increasingly important as organizations emphasize lateral coordination. Technical workers also are becoming increasingly important, whereas manufacturing operatives are becoming less important. In general, the nature of "work" is changing; future work will require continuous learning and will be less bound by the "9 to 5" traditions.

In this setting, the old notions of a career based within a single organization that takes responsibility for a person's career development are increasingly obsolete. In his book, *The Age of Unreason,* British scholar and consultant Charles Handy argues forcefully that each of us must take charge of our own careers and prepare for inevitable uncertainties and changes by building a "portfolio" of skills.[18] Importantly, this portfolio must be subject to continuous development; each new job assignment must be well selected and rigorously pursued as a learning opportunity. And, according to Handy, all of this is entirely a *personal* responsibility.

As director of institutional business (electronic equipment rental and integrated TV systems) for Hong Kong–based Thorn/EMI, Stephanie Ho came to the post with a broad mix of business experience and skills. While working with the Hong Kong Tourist Association, she completed an MBA part time at the Chinese University of Hong Kong. Stephanie then joined the advertising agency Ogilvy & Mather in what she calls a "strategic and opportunistic move." Another move brought her to Citicorp; she was then "headhunted" into Hong Kong Bank, where she moved into a variety of management posts. Upon hearing that the bank was entering the international card business, Stephanie asked to be assigned to the project. She visited every branch location, including Saudi Arabia, where she was the first female executive ever to visit from the bank. With 6 years of Hong Kong Bank experience behind her, Stephanie took a job with Rothman's as general manager of the tobacco firm's China operations. Within a year, she was headhunted again—this time by Thorn/EMI. Stephanie Ho's promising and still emerging executive career is now well supported by industry experience in tourism, advertising, banking, and tobacco. She also has functional experience in media, public relations, business development, and marketing.[19]

Initial Entry to a Career   The full implications of the new workplace become apparent at the point of initial entry to a career. Choosing a job and a work organization are difficult decisions; our jobs inevitably exert a lot of influence over our lives. Whenever a job change is considered, the best advice is to know yourself and to learn as much as possible about the new job and the organization. This helps to ensure the best person–job–organization match. By working hard to examine personal needs, goals, and capabilities and to gather relevant information, share viewpoints, and otherwise make the recruitment process as realistic as possible, you can help start a new job on the best possible note.

When considering a new job or when contemplating a possible job change, a "balance sheet" analysis of possible "gains" and "losses" can help you fully evaluate the opportunity. At least two questions should be asked and answered as part of such an analysis.[20] The first is, *What are my potential gains and losses?* Things to consider in answering this question include salary and fringe benefits, work hours and schedules, travel requirements, use and development of skills and competencies, and opportunities for challenging new job assignments. The second question is, *What are the potential gains and losses for significant others?* Things to consider in answering this question include income available to meet family responsibilities, time available to be with family and friends, implications of a geographical move on family and friends, and implications of work stress on nonwork life.

Adult Transitions and Career Stages   As people mature, they pass through an adult life cycle involving many different problems and prospects. It is helpful for you to recognize this cycle and to prepare to face its implications over the course of your career. It also is useful to recognize the effects of this cycle on other people with whom you work. Understanding their special problems and pressures can help you work with them better as a manager.

Adult Transitions   We introduced Daniel Levinson's ideas about personality development as a series of life stages in Chapter 3. Levison's basic point is that life unfolds with a number of *adult transitions* that have quite different implications for the work and personal aspects of one's life.[21] Three transitions relevant to our present interest in careers are early adulthood, midlife, and later adulthood. Each has its own personal and organizational implications.

The *young adulthood* stage marks a period of completing one's education, entering an occupation, and getting married. Parenthood follows, introducing new family and job responsibilities. This is a time of vitality, self-determination, and perhaps one or more job changes. The individual experiences an *adulthood and midlife transition* in his or her later thirties and early forties. At this time, the career is all important. Family complications stress this orientation, and personal crises can occur. Some frustration in the career also may occur and raise added questions of confidence, goals, and identity. For the first time, health and age become relevant concerns. In *later adulthood,* settling in begins, along with a knowledge of the "system" and a mellowing of goals. Concerns turn toward making a real impact at work, being a mentor to others, and balancing goals and reality.

This is a time of consolidating personal affairs and accepting career limitations. The next step is *retirement* and, perhaps, a new career.

Career Stages   As suggested in Figure 6.2, adult transitions and their special attributes can be linked to various **career stages** through which people move over the course of their lives. These are often referred to as the establishment, maintenance, and withdrawal career stages.[22]

Initial entry to a career is part of the *establishment stage.* Here, the individual begins on-the-job development of the skills and abilities essential to his or her career. It is also a point at which the socialization into the ways of an employing organization is first experienced and networks of peers and contacts are intially built. Increasingly, progressive employers are assigning their best managers or employees to serve as mentors—or "coaches"—to advise and counsel new employees, identify areas of strength and weakness, and help develop their management potential.

In the *advancement stage,* the individual seeks growth and increased responsibility through the continued development and utilization of these skills. Advancement may be pursued through internal career paths within a given organization or through external career paths that involve taking advantage of opportunities that require a change in employers. In either case, advancement is an exciting stage that must be balanced by a person's skills.

During the *maintenance stage,* individuals may experience continued growth of performance and accomplishments, or, by contrast, they may encounter career stability. Sometimes, a further change in employers is necessary to sustain advancement, but often the individual loses career flexibility. This may be a result of personal considerations, such as limited interest in learning new skills; organizational considerations, such as a basic lack of opportunity; and/or family consider-

> **Career stages** are different points of work responsibility and achievement through which people pass during the course of their work lives.

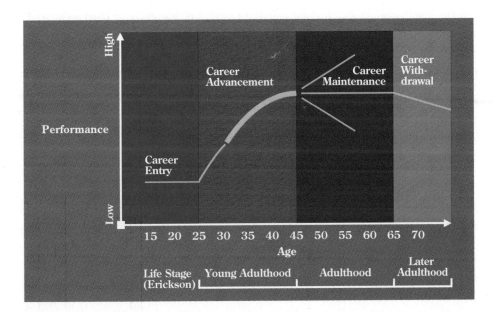

■ FIGURE 6.2
Career stages, individual performance, and the adult life cycle. [Source: From *Careers in Organizations,* by Douglas T. Hall. Copyright © 1976 by Scott, Foresman and Company. Reprinted by permission.]

A **career plateau** is a position from which someone is unlikely to move to advance to a higher level of responsibility.

ations that simply make it difficult either to change jobs or to take on added work responsibilities.

At this stage, many people encounter a **career plateau**—they find themselves in a position from which they are unlikely to move to advance to a higher level of responsibility. Career plateaus occur for one or more of the following reasons:[23] personal choice—the individual decides that he or she no longer wants to advance in responsibility; limited ability; or lack of opportunity. Managers must be prepared to deal with career plateaus, both personally and as their subordinates are affected. It can be difficult to maintain job satisfaction and a high-performance edge when caught in a career plateau that is a result of something other than individual choice. In such cases, it can be very easy to drift into low marginal performance levels. A manager's understanding of individual needs can help in developing appropriate responses on these occasions.

Finally, the *withdrawal stage* signifies the approach and acceptance of retirement. Depending on the individual, this can be either a very positive or a highly upsetting stage of one's career. More and more employers now provide training and support to help people make a positive transfer from the routines of regular employment to the flexibility of retirement.

PERFORMANCE APPRAISAL

Performance appraisal is a process of systematically evaluating performance and providing feedback on which performance adjustments can be made.

Still another key HR management function is performance appraisal, which helps both the manager and subordinate maintain the organization–job–employee characteristics match. Formally defined, **performance appraisal** is a process of systematically evaluating performance and providing feedback on which performance adjustments can be made.[25] If the desired level of performance exceeds actual levels, a performance variance requiring special attention exists. For example, if you have a sales quota of eight new cars per month—the desired performance—and you only sell two cars per month—your actual performance—there is a performance variance of six cars that requires the attention of the sales managers. The performance appraisal process should be based on the job analysis mentioned earlier. The job description, describing organizational job requirements, and the job specification, describing individual worker characteristics, provide the core.[24]

▼ PURPOSES OF PERFORMANCE APPRAISAL
Any performance appraisal system is central to an organization's human resource management activities. Performance appraisals are intended to:

■ Purposes of performance appraisal

❶ *Define the specific job criteria* against which performance will be measured.
❷ *Measure past job performance* accurately.

❸ *Justify the rewards* given to individuals and/or groups, thereby discriminating between high and low performance.

❹ *Define the development experiences* the ratee needs to enhance performance in the current job and to prepare for future responsibilities.

CHEVRON
http://www.chevron.com/

These four functions describe two general purposes served by good performance-appraisal systems: evaluation, and feedback and development. From an evaluative perspective, performance appraisal lets people know where they stand relative to objectives and standards. As such, the performance appraisal is an input to decisions that allocate rewards and otherwise administer the personnel functions of the organization. From a counseling perspective, performance appraisal facilitates implementing decisions relating to planning for and gaining commitment to the continued training and personal development of subordinates.

In downsizing its workforce by 6500 people, Chevron, the oil giant, redeployed nearly 1000 other employees into different jobs in different sections of the firm. For Vince Sgier, this *redeployment* meant a new lease on his 22-year career.[26]

Evaluative Decisions   Evaluative decisions are concerned with such issues as promotions, transfers, terminations, and salary increases. When these decisions are made on the basis of performance criteria, as opposed to some other basis, such as seniority, some sort of performance appraisal system is necessary. Performance appraisal information is also useful for making selection and placement decisions. In this case, performance results are matched against individual characteristics to determine which of these characteristics are most related to performance. For example, management checks various individual characteristics, such as education, mathematical ability, verbal ability, mechanical ability, and achievement motivation, to see how closely they are related to performance. Individuals who score well on those characteristics found to be closely tied to performance for a given job are considered for that position. In addition, if specific aspects of a ratee's performance are found to be inadequate, the performance appraisal process may lead to remedial training. Finally, appraisals form the basis of any performance-contingent reward system (i.e., any system that ties rewards, such as pay, to an individual's or groups's performance).

Feedback and Development Decisions   Performance appraisals also can be used to let ratees know where they stand in terms of the organization's expectations and performance objectives. Performance appraisal feedback should involve a detailed discussion of the ratee's job-related strengths and weaknesses. This feedback can then be used for developmental purposes. In terms of the expectancy motivation approach discussed in Chapter 5, feedback can help clarify the individual's sense of both instrumentality—it can help you better understand what kinds of rewards you will receive if you perform well—and expectancy—it lets you know what actions you need to take to reach that level of performance.

Performance appraisal feedback also can be used as a basis for individual coaching or training by the manager to help a subordinate overcome performance deficiencies. Surveys typically indicate that around two thirds of the sampled firms use performance appraisals for developmental purposes.

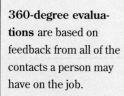

▼ WHO DOES THE PERFORMANCE APPRAISAL?

Performance appraisals traditionally have been conducted by an individual's immediate superior.[27] More and more, however, firms are moving to what are called **360-degree evaluations.**[28] These evaluations are based on feedback from the full circle of contacts that a person may have in performing his or her job. In addition to bosses, peers, subordinates, and the person him- or herself, these may also include customers and others with whom one deals outside the immediate work unit. The number of appraisals typically ranges from 5 to 10 per person under evaluation. Firms such as Alcoa and UPS now use 360-degree evaluations. They are made to order for the new, flatter, team-oriented organizations emphasizing total quality management, whereby input from many sources is crucial.

A distributor of pipe, valves, and fittings, and a 1990 winner of the coveted Baldrige National Quality Award, The Wallace Company combines self- and superior ratings in a very innovative way. The subordinate (called an "associate") rates himself or herself on the importance of a given job function to the associate's performance and on how well the associate thinks he or she is performing the function. The supervisor performs a similar evaluation of the associate. A computer program then highlights those areas on which there is the most disagreement. Only the associate gets the printout and may choose to discuss these areas with the supervisor. Both the timing and the specific content of such a meeting are at the discretion of the associate.

▼ DIMENSIONS AND STANDARDS OF PERFORMANCE APPRAISAL

In addition to performance outcomes, the behaviors or activities that *result* in these outcomes are frequently important to performance appraisal as well.

Output Measures A number of production and sales jobs provide ready measures of *work output.* For example, an assembler may have a goal of 30 completed industrial grease guns per hour. The number of grease guns is easily measurable, and it is possible for the organization to set standards concerning how many grease guns should be completed per hour. Here, the performance dimension of interest is a quantitative one: 30 completed grease guns per hour. However, the organization also may introduce a *quality* dimension. The individual may be evaluated not only in terms of the number of grease guns per hour but also by the number of units that pass a *quality control inspection* per hour. Now, both quantity and quality are important, and the individual cannot trade one for the other—assembling 40 guns per hour will not do if only 28 pass inspection, nor will having a larger proportion of guns pass inspection if only 25 guns are assembled per hour.

In addition, management may be interested in other performance dimensions, such as downtime of the equipment used for assembling. In this case, the assembler would be evaluated in terms of quantity and quality of assembly output and equipment downtime. In this way, management could not only ensure that a desirable product is being assembled at a desirable rate but that the employee is careful with the equipment as well.

360-degree evaluations are based on feedback from all of the contacts a person may have on the job.

Activity Measures In the preceding example, the output measures were straightforward, as was the measure of equipment downtime. Often, however, output measures may be a function of group efforts; or they may be extremely difficult to measure; or they may take so long to accomplish that they can't be readily determined for a given individual during a given time period. For example, it may be very difficult to determine the output of a research scientist attempting to advance new knowledge. In such a case, activity or behavioral measures may be called for, rather than output measures. The research scientist may be appraised in terms of his or her approach to problems, his or her interactions with other scientists, and the like.

Activity measures are typically obtained by some sort of observation and rating on the part of the evaluator. In contrast, output measures are often obtained directly from written records or documents, such as production records. Difficulty of obtaining output measures may be one reason for using activity measures. Activity measures are also typically more useful for employee feedback and development than are output measures alone. For example, a salesperson may sell 20 insurance policies a month when the quota is 25. However, activities such as number of sales calls per day or number of community volunteer events attended per week (where some potential clients are likely to be found) can provide more specific information than simply the percentage of monthly quota output measure. Where jobs lend themselves to systematic analysis, important activities can be inferred from the job analysis.

You also should be sensitive to the fact that sometimes output and activity measures convey different signals. In a classic example, the head basketball coach at the University of California received a congratulatory letter for beating UCLA by 22 points—an output measure. The athletic director had also scribbled a note in the margin: "Great game, keep up the good work." A few days later, the athletic director unexpectedly overheard the coach castigating his players in the locker room after a loss to Arizona State. Four days later, the coach was fired for verbal abuse—an activity measure.[29]

▼ PERFORMANCE APPRAISAL METHODS

A number of methods are commonly used in performance appraisal. We can divide these methods into two general categories: comparative methods and absolute methods.[30]

Comparative methods of performance appraisal seek to identify one's relative standing among those being rated; that is, comparative methods can establish that Bill is better than Mary, who is better than Leslie, who is better than Tom, on a performance dimension. Comparative methods can indicate that one person is better than another on a given dimension, but not *how much better*. These methods also fail to indicate whether the person receiving the better rating is "good enough" in an absolute sense. It may well be that Bill is merely the best of a bad lot. Three comparative performance appraisal methods are (1) ranking, (2) paired comparison, and (3) forced distribution.

In contrast, *absolute methods* of performance appraisal specify precise measurement standards. For example, tardiness might be evaluated on a scale ranging from "never tardy" to "always tardy." Four of the more common absolute rating procedures are (1) graphic rating scales, (2) critical incident diary, (3) behaviorally anchored ratings scales, and (4) management by objectives.

Ranking **Ranking** is the simplest of all the comparative techniques. It consists of merely rank ordering each individual from best to worst on each performance dimension being considered. For example, in evaluating work quality, I compare Smith, Jones, and Brown. I then rank Brown number 1, Smith number 2, and Jones number 3. The ranking method is relatively simple to use, although it can become burdensome when there are many people to consider.

> **Ranking** is a comparative technique of performance appraisal that involves rank ordering each individual from best to worst on each performance dimension.

Paired Comparison In a **paired comparison** method, each person is directly compared with every other person being rated. The frequency of endorsement across all pairs determines one's final ranking. Every possible paired comparison within a group of ratees is considered, as shown below (italics indicate the person rated better in each pair):

> **Paired comparison** is a comparative method of performance appraisal whereby each person is directly compared with every other person.

Bill	vs.	Mary	*Mary*	vs.	Leslie	*Leslie*	vs.	Tom
Bill	vs.	Leslie	*Mary*	vs.	Tom			
Bill	vs.	Tom						

Number of times Bill is better   = 3
Number of times Mary is better   = 2
Number of times Leslie is better = 1
Number of times Tom is better   = 0

The best performer in this example is Bill, followed by Mary, then Leslie, and, last of all, Tom. The paired comparison approach can be even more tedious than the ranking method when there are many people to compare.

> **Forced distribution** is a method of performance appraisal that uses a small number of performance categories, such as "very good," "good," "poor," and "very poor."

Forced Distribution In **forced distribution,** a small number of performance categories are used, such as "very good," "good," "adequate," "poor," and "very poor." Each rater is instructed to rate a specific proportion of employees in each of these categories. For example, 10 percent of employees must be rated very good; 20 percent must be rated good; etc. This method *forces* the rater to use all of the categories and to avoid rating everyone as outstanding, poor, average, or the like. It can be a problem if most of the people are truly superior performers or if most of the people perform about the same.

> **Graphic rating scales** list a variety of dimensions that are thought to be related to high-performance outcomes in a given job and that the individual is expected to exhibit.

Graphic Rating Scales **Graphic rating scales** list a variety of dimensions that are thought to be related to high-performance outcomes in a given job and that the individual is accordingly expected to exhibit, such as cooperation, initiative, and attendance. The scales allow the manager to assign the individual scores on each dimension. An example is shown in Figure 6.3. These ratings are sometimes given point values and combined into numerical ratings of performance.

The primary appeal of graphic rating scales is their ease of use. In addition, they are efficient in the use of time and other resources, and they can be applied

| Employee: *Jayne Burroughs* | | Supervisor: *Dr. Cutter* |
| Department: *Pathology* | | Date: *11-28-91* |

Work Quantity	Work Quality	Cooperation
1. Far below average ___	1. Far below average ___	1. Far below average ___
2. Below average ✓	2. Below average ___	2. Below average ✓
3. Average ___	3. Average ✓	3. Average ___
4. Above average ___	4. Above average ___	4. Above average ___
5. Far above average ___	5. Far above average ___	5. Far above average ___

| Employee: *John Watson* | | Supervisor: *Dr. Cutter* |
| Department: *Pathology* | | Date: *12-24-95* |

Work Quantity	Work Quality	Cooperation
1. Far below average ___	1. Far below average ___	1. Far below average ___
2. Below average ___	2. Below average ___	2. Below average ___
3. Average ✓	3. Average ___	3. Average ___
4. Above average ___	4. Above average ✓	4. Above average ___
5. Far above average ___	5. Far above average ___	5. Far above average ✓

■ FIGURE 6.3

Sixth-month performance reviews for Burroughs and Watson [Source: From Andrew D. Szilagi, Jr., and Marc J. Wallace, Jr., *Organizational Behavior and Performance* 3rd ed. (Glenview, IL: Scott, Foresman, 1983), pp. 393–394.]

to a wide range of jobs. Unfortunately, because of generality, they may not be linked to job analysis or to other specific aspects of a given job. This difficulty can be dealt with by ensuring that only relevant dimensions of work based on sound job analysis procedures are rated. However, there is a tradeoff: the more the scales are linked to job analyses, the less general they are when comparing people on different jobs.

Critical Incident Diary Supervisors may use **critical incident diaries** to record incidents of each subordinate's behavior that led to either unusual success or failure in a given performance aspect. These incidents are typically recorded in a diary-type log that is kept daily or weekly under predesignated dimensions. In a sales job, for example, following up sales calls and communicating necessary customer information might be two of the dimensions recorded in a critical incident diary. Descriptive paragraphs can then be used to summarize each salesperson's performance for each dimension as it is observed.

> A **critical incident diary** is a method of performance appraisal whereby supervisors record incidents of each subordinate's behavior that have led either to unusual success or failure in a given performance aspect.

121

This approach is excellent for employee development and feedback. Since the method consists of qualitative statements rather than quantitative information, however, it is difficult to use for evaluative decisions. To provide for such information, the critical incident technique is sometimes combined with one of the other methods.

Behaviorally Anchored Rating Scales   The **behaviorally anchored rating scales,** or BARS is a performance appraisal approach that has received increasing attention. The procedure for developing this type of scale starts with the careful collection of descriptions of observable job behaviors. These descriptions are typically provided by managers and personnel specialists and include both superior and inferior performance. Once a large sample of behavioral descriptions is collected, each behavior is evaluated to determine the extent to which it describes good versus bad performance. The final step is to develop a rating scale, in which the anchors are specific critical behaviors, each reflecting a different degree of performance effectiveness. An example of a BARS is shown in Figure 6.4 for a retail department manager.[31] Note the specificity of the behaviors and the scale values for each. Similar behaviorally anchored scales would be developed for other dimensions of the job.

As you can see, the BARS approach is detailed and complex. It requires lots of time and effort to develop. But the BARS also provides specific behaviors that are useful for counseling and feedback, combined with quantitative scales that are useful for evaluative comparative purposes. Initial results of the use of BARS suggested that they were less susceptible to common rating errors than were more traditional scales. More recent evidence suggests that the scales may not be as superior as originally thought, especially if an equivalent amount of developmental effort is put into other types of measures.[32] A somewhat simpler variation of behaviorally anchored scales is the *Behavioral Observation Scale* (BOS), which uses a five-point frequency scale (ranging from almost always to almost never) for each separate statement of behavior.[33]

Management by Objectives   Of all the appraisal methods available **management by objectives** (MBO) is linked most directly to means–ends chains and goal setting.[34] When an MBO system is used, subordinates work with their supervisor to establish specific task-related objectives that fall within their domains and serve as means to help accomplish the supervisor's higher level objectives. Each set of objectives is worked out between a supervisor and a subordinate for a given time period. The establishment of objectives is similar to a job analysis, except that it is directed toward a particular individual in his or her job rather than toward a particular job type alone. The increased discretion of the MBO approach means that each specific person is likely to have a custom-tailored set of work goals while still working within the action context of organizational means–ends chains.

MBO is the most individualized of all the appraisal systems and tends to work well for counseling if the objectives go beyond simply desired outputs and focus on important activities as well. In comparing one employee with another, a

Behaviorally anchored rating scales (BARS) are a performance appraisal approach that starts with the careful collection of descriptions of observable job behaviors, each of which is evaluated to determine the extent to which it describes good versus bad performance.

Management by objectives (MBO) is a process of joint goal setting between a supervisor and a subordinate.

Supervising Sales Personnel
Gives sales personnel a clear idea of their job duties and responsibilities; exercises tact and consideration in working with subordinates; handles work scheduling efficiently and equitably; supplements formal training with his or her own "coaching"; keeps informed of what the salespeople are doing on the job; and follows company policy in agreements with subordinates.

Effective 9   Could be expected to conduct full day's sales clinic with two new sales personnel and thereby develop them into top salespeople in the department.

        8   Could be expected to give his or her sales personnel confidence and strong sense of responsibility by delegating many important tasks.

        7   Could be expected never to fail to conduct weekly training meetings with his or her people at a scheduled hour and to convey to them exactly what is expected.

        6   Could be expected to exhibit courtesy and respect toward his or her sales personnel.

        5   Could be expected to remind sales personnel to wait on customers instead of conversing with one another.

        4   Could be expected to be rather critical of store standards in front of his or her own people, thereby risking their development of poor attitudes.

        3   Could be expected to tell an individual to come in anyway even though he or she called in to say he or she was ill.

        2   Could be expected to go back on a promise to an individual who he or she had told could transfer back into previous department if he or she did not like the new one.

Ineffective 1   Could be expected to make promises to an individual about his or her salary being based on department sales even when he or she knew such a practice was against company policy.

FIGURE 6.4
Example of a behaviorally anchored rating scale dimension.

key concern is the ease or difficulty of achieving the goals. If one person has an easier set of objectives to meet than another, then comparisons are unfair. Since MBO tends to rely less heavily on ratings than do other appraisal systems, rating errors are less likely to be a problem.

▼ MEASUREMENT ERRORS IN PERFORMANCE APPRAISAL

To be meaningful, an appraisal system must be both *reliable*—provide consistent results each time it is used—and *valid*—actually measure people on relevant job content. A number of measurement errors can threaten the reliability and/or validity of performance appraisals.[35]

Halo Errors A **halo error** results when one person rates another person on several different dimensions and gives a similar rating for each dimension. For example, a sales representative considered to be a "go-getter" and thus rated high on

> **Halo error** results when one person rates another person on several different dimensions and gives a similar rating for each one.

123

"dynamism" also would be rated high on dependability, tact, and whatever other performance dimensions were used. The rater fails to discriminate between the person's strong and weak points; a "halo" carries over from one dimension to the next. This effect can create a problem when each performance dimension is considered an important and relatively independent aspect of the job.

Leniency/Strictness Errors   Just as some professors are known as "easy A's," some managers tend to give relatively high ratings to virtually everyone under their supervision. This is known as a **leniency error.** Sometimes the opposite occurs; some raters tend to give everyone a low rating. This is called a **strictness error.** The problem in both instances is that there is very little discrimination between the good and poor performers. Leniency is especially likely to be a problem when peers assess one another, especially if they are asked to provide feedback to one another, because it is easier to discuss high ratings than low ones.

Central Tendency Errors   **Central tendency errors** occur when managers lump everyone together around the "average," or middle, category. This tendency gives the impression that there are no very good or very poor performers on the dimensions being rated. No true performance discrimination is made.

Recency Errors   A different kind of error, known as a **recency error,** occurs when a rater allows recent events to influence a performance rating over earlier events. Take, for example, the case of an employee who is usually on time but shows up 1 hour late for work the day before his or her performance rating. The employee is rated low on "promptness" because the one incident of tardiness overshadows his or her usual promptness.

Personal Bias Errors   Raters sometimes allow specific biases to enter into performance evaluations. When this happens, **personal bias errors** occur. For example, a rater may intentionally give higher ratings to white employees than to nonwhite employees. In this case, the performance appraisal reflects a racial bias. Bias toward members of other demographic categories, such as age, gender, and disability, also can occur, based on stereotypes the rater may have. Such bias appears to have been widespread in Monarch Paper Company, when a former vice president was demoted to a warehouse-maintenance job for not accepting an early retirement offer. A federal jury judged the firm guilty of age bias.[36] It is obvious from this example that raters must reflect carefully on their personal biases and guard against their interference with performance-based ratings of subordinates.

▼ IMPROVING PERFORMANCE APPRAISALS

As with most other issues in organizational behavior, there are tradeoffs that managers must recognize in setting up and implementing any performance appraisal system. In addition to the pros and cons already mentioned for each method, some specific issues to keep in mind to reduce errors and improve appraisals include:[37]

Leniency error is the tendency to give relatively high ratings to virtually everyone.

Strictness error occurs when a rater tends to give everyone a low rating.

Central tendency error occurs when managers lump everyone together around the average, or middle, category.

Recency error is a biased rating that develops by allowing the individual's most recent behavior to speak for his or her overall performance on a particular dimension.

Personal bias error occurs when a rater allows specific biases, such as racial, age, and gender, to enter into performance appraisals.

❶ Train raters so that they understand the evaluation process rationale and can recognize the various sources of measurement error.

❷ Make sure that raters observe ratees on an ongoing, regular basis and that they do not try to limit all their evaluations to the formally designated evaluation period, for instance, every 6 months or every year.

❸ Do not have the rater rate too many ratees. The ability to identify performance differences drops and fatigue sets in when the evaluation of large numbers of people is involved.

❹ Make sure that the performance dimensions and standards are stated clearly and that the standards are as noncontaminating and nondeficient as possible.

❺ Avoid terms such as "average" because different evaluators tend to react differently to the terms.

❻ Remember that appraisal systems cannot be used to discriminate against employees on the basis of age, gender, race, ethnicity, and so on. To help provide a legally defensible system in terms of governing legislation, the following recommendations are useful:[38]

- Appraisal must be based on an analysis of job requirements as reflected in performance standards.
- Appraisal is appropriate only where performance standards are clearly understood by employees.
- Clearly defined individual dimensions should be used rather than global measures.
- Dimensions should be behaviorally based and supported by observable evidence.
- If rating scales are used, avoid abstract trait names, such as "loyalty" unless they can be defined in terms of observable behaviors.
- Rating scale anchors should be brief and logically consistent.
- The system must be validated and psychometrically sound, as must the ratings given by individual evaluators.
- There must be an appeal mechanism in the event that the evaluator and the ratee disagree.

It is important to note that technological advances now provide various PC programs to facilitate the rating process. These allow for easier and more comprehensive scale construction, faster feedback, and the additional flexibility called for in today's new workplace.[39]

▼ GROUP EVALUATION

As indicated earlier, there is an increasing trend toward group or team performance evaluations. Such an evaluation is consistent with self-managed teams

■ Ways to improve performance appraisals

> *Take-A-Note 6.2*
>
> SUGGESTIONS FOR A GROUP PERFORMANCE EVALUATION SYSTEM[41]
>
> - Link the team's results to organizational goals.
> - Start with the team's customers and the team work process needed to satisfy those needs:
>   Customer requirements.
>   Delivery and quality.
>   Waste and cycle time.
> - Evaluate team and each individual member's performance.
> - Train the team to develop its own measures.

and an emphasis on TQM. Frequently, this emphasis is accompanied by a group-based compensation system such as discussed later in this chapter. Traditional individually oriented appraisal systems are no longer appropriate and need to be replaced with group ones.[40]

REWARDS

In addition to staffing, training, career planning and development, and performance appraisal, another key aspect of HR management is the design and implementation of reward systems. These reward systems emphasize a mix of extrinsic and intrinsic rewards. As we noted in Chapter 5, *extrinsic rewards* are positively valued work outcomes that are given to an individual or group by some other person or source in the work setting. In contrast, *intrinsic rewards* are positively valued work outcomes that are received by the individual directly as a result of task performance; they do not require the participation of another person or source. A feeling of achievement after accomplishing a particularly challenging task is an example of an intrinsic reward. In the remainder of this chapter, we emphasize the management of pay as an extrinsic reward. We touched on the management of intrinsic rewards in Chapter 5 on motivation and emphasize extrinsic rewards heavily in Chapter 7.

MANAGING PAY AS AN EXTRINSIC REWARD

Pay is an especially complex extrinsic reward. Pay can help organizations attract and retain highly capable workers, and it can help satisfy and motivate these workers to work hard to achieve high performance. But, if there is dissatisfaction with the salary, pay can also lead to strikes, grievances, absenteeism, turnover, and sometimes even poor physical and mental health.

Edward Lawler is a management expert whose work has contributed greatly to our understanding of pay as an extrinsic reward. His research generally concludes that, for pay to serve as a source of work motivation, high levels of job performance must be viewed as the path through which high pay can be achieved.[42] **Merit pay** is defined as a compensation system that bases an individual's salary or wage increase on a measure of the person's performance accomplishments during a specified time period. That is, merit pay is an attempt to make pay contingent upon performance.

Although research supports the logic and theoretical benefits of merit pay, it also indicates that the implementation of merit pay plans is not as universal or as easy as we might expect. In fact, surveys over the past 30 years have found that as

> **Merit pay** is a compensation system that bases an individual's salary or wage increase on a measure of the person's performance accomplishments during a specific time period.

many as 80 percent of respondents felt that they were not rewarded for a job well done.[43] An effective merit pay system is one approach to dealing with this problem.

To work well, a merit pay plan should be based on realistic and accurate measures of individual work performance and create a belief among employees that the way to achieve high pay is to perform at high levels. In addition, merit pay should clearly discriminate between high and low performers in the amount of pay reward received. Finally, managers should avoid confusing "merit" aspects of a pay increase with "cost-of-living" adjustments.

Creative Pay Practices   Merit pay plans are just one attempt to enhance the positive value of pay as a work reward. But some argue that merit pay plans are not consistent with the demands of today's organizations since they fail to recognize the high degree of task interdependence among employees, as illustrated particularly in TQM programs. Also, as we argued earlier, HR management strategies should be consistent with overall organization strategies. For example, the pay system of a firm with an emphasis on highly skilled individuals in short supply should emphasize employee retention, rather than performance.[44]

With these points in mind, let us examine a variety of creative pay practices. These practices are becoming more common in organizations with increasingly diverse workforces and increased emphasis on TQM or similar setups.[45] They include *skill-based pay, gain-sharing plans, lump-sum pay increases,* and *flexible benefit plans.*

Skill-Based Pay   **Skill-based pay** rewards people for acquiring and developing job-relevant skills. Pay systems of this sort pay people for the mix and depth of skills they possess, not for the particular job assignment they hold. In a typical manufacturing plant, for example, a worker may know how to perform several different jobs, each of which requires different skills. The worker would be paid for this "breadth" of capability, even though he or she would be working primarily in one job assignment. Of course, this person must be willing to use any of the compensated skills in other assignments and at any time in accordance with the company's needs.

Although only a small proportion of firms (about 5 percent) in the United States use skill-based pay, it is one of the fastest growing pay innovations.[47] Among the better known firms using skill-based pay is Polaroid.[48] Besides flexibility, some advantages of skill-based pay are employee cross-training—workers learn to do one another's job; fewer supervisors—workers can provide more of these functions themselves; and more individual control over compensation—workers know in advance what is required to receive a pay raise. One disadvantage is possible higher pay and training costs not offset by greater productivity. Another is that of deciding on appropriate monetary values for each skill.[49]

Gain-Sharing Plans   Cash bonuses, or extra pay for performance above standards or expectations, have been common practice in the compensation of managers and executives for a long time. Top managers in some industries earn an-

AMERICAN EXPRESS CANADA

American Express Canada's flexible, menu-based program, Express Yourself, allocates 150 "express dollars" to each of its 2000 employees to purchase extra benefit coverage. Leftover dollars may be used for additional vacation days or family-member life insurance.[46]

Skill-based pay is a pay system that rewards people for acquiring and developing job-relevant skills in number and variety relevant to the organization's needs.

nual bonuses of 50 percent or more of their base salaries. Attempts to extend such opportunities to all employees are growing in number and importance today. One popular plan is **gain-sharing,** which links pay and performance by giving workers the opportunity to share in productivity gains through enhanced earnings.

The Scanlon Plan is probably the oldest and best known gain-sharing plan. Others you may have heard about are the Lincoln Electric Plan, the Rucker Plan™, or IMPROSHARE™. Gain-sharing plans possess some similarities to profit-sharing plans, but they are not the same. Typically, profit-sharing plans grant individuals or work groups a specified portion of any economic profits earned by an organization as a whole. In contrast, gain-sharing plans involve a specific measurement of productivity combined with a calculation of a bonus designed to offer workers a mutual share of any increase in total organizational productivity. Usually, everyone responsible for the increase receives the bonus. Gain-sharing involves some kind of "hard productivity" measurement, whereas profit-sharing typically does not.[50]

The intended benefits of gain-sharing plans include increased worker motivation because of the pay-for-performance incentives, and a greater sense of personal responsibility for making performance contributions to the organization. Because they can be highly participative in nature, gain-sharing plans also may encourage cooperation and teamwork in the workplace. Although more remains to be learned about gain-sharing, the plans are receiving increasing attention from organizations.[51]

Lump-Sum Pay Increases Do you know what an annual pay raise of $1200 is worth when spread over 52 pay checks? It means exactly $23.08 per week! This figure is reduced even further when taxes and other deductions are made. Most of us don't have any choice in such matters. Our annual pay increases are distributed in proportionate amounts as part of weekly, biweekly, or monthly paychecks. And, as a result, they may lose considerable motivational impact in the process.

An interesting alternative is the **lump-sum increase** program, by which individuals can elect to receive an increase in one or more lump-sum payments. The full increase may be taken at the beginning of the year and used for some valued purpose, for example, a down payment on a car or a sizable deposit in a saving account. Or, a person may elect to take one half of the raise early and get the rest at the start of the winter holiday season. In either case, the individual should be more motivated because of the larger doses or because it is attached to something highly valued.

Another related but more controversial development in this area is the *lump-sum payment,* which differs from the *lump-sum increase.* The lump-sum payment is an attempt by employers to hold labor costs in line while still giving workers more money, if corporate earnings allow. It involves giving workers a one-time lump-sum payment, often based on a gain-sharing formula, instead of a yearly percentage wage or salary increase. In this way, a person's base pay remains fixed, whereas overall monetary compensation varies according to the bonus added to this figure by the annual lump-sum payment. American labor unions, in particular, are somewhat resistant to this approach since base pay does not increase and management determines the size of the bonus. However, survey information generally has shown that around two thirds of the respondents have favorable reactions and think that the plans have a positive effect on performance.[52]

Flexible Benefit Plans   An employee's total compensation package includes not only direct pay but also any fringe benefits that are paid by the organization. These fringe benefits often add an equivalent of 10 to 40 percent to a person's salary. It is argued that organizations need to allow for individual differences when developing such benefit programs. Otherwise, the motivational value of this indirect form of pay incentive is lost. One approach is to let individuals choose their total pay package by selecting benefits, up to a certain dollar amount, from a range of options made available by the organization. These **flexible benefit plans** allow workers to select benefits according to needs. A single worker, for example, may prefer quite a different combination of insurance and retirement contributions than would a married person.

> **Flexible benefits plans** are pay systems that allow workers to select benefits according to their individual needs.

INTRINSIC WORK REWARDS

As mentioned earlier, *intrinsic work rewards* are those rewards received by an individual directly as a result of task performance. You can think of these as rewards that people give to themselves in return for successful task completion. One example is the feeling of achievement that comes from completing a challenging project. Such feelings are individually determined and integral to the work itself. They are self-regulated in that a person is not dependent on an outsider, such as the manager, to provide them.

When we discussed extrinsic rewards in the previous section, we viewed the manager as responsible for allocating these rewards, such as pay, promotion, and verbal praise to employees. To serve in this capacity, a manager must be good at evaluating performance, maintaining an inventory of valued work rewards, and giving these rewards to employees contingent upon work performance. We have emphasized pay here, and we emphasize other kinds of extrinsic work rewards in Chapter 7. Managing intrinsic work rewards presents the additional challenge of designing a work setting so that employees can, in effect, reward themselves for a job well done. That is the topic of Chapter 8.

CHAPTER 6 STUDY GUIDE

SUMMARY

What are human resource planning and staffing?

- HR planning is the process of providing capable and motivated people to carry out the organization's mission and strategy.
- HR staffing involves job analysis, attracting individuals through recruitment, selecting those best qualified through screening and hiring, and socializing employees through initial orientation and followup over time.

What are training and career planning and development?

- Training is a set of activities that provides the opportunity to acquire and improve job-related skills.
- On-the-job training involves job instruction in the workplace and commonly utilizes internships, apprenticeships, and job rotation.
- Off-the-job training takes place off the job and commonly involves lectures, videos, and simulations.
- Career planning and development involves working with managers and HR experts on careers and involves the following: a five-stage planning framework; personal responsibilities for development of a portfolio of skills to keep one marketable at any time; a balance sheet approach to evaluating each career opportunity; recognition of the relationship between life stages and adult transitions from career entry through career withdrawal; and career plateaus, whereby individuals are unlikely to move to a higher level of responsibility.

What is performance appraisal?

- Performance appraisal involves systematically evaluating performance and providing feedback on which performance adjustments can be made.
- Performance appraisals serve the two general purposes of evaluation and feedback and development.
- Performance appraisals traditionally are done by an individual's immediate superior but are moving toward 360-degree evaluations involving the full circle of contacts a person may have in job performance.
- Performance appraisals use either or both output measures and activity measures.
- Performance appraisal methods involve comparative methods and absolute methods.
- There are at least five rater errors important in performance appraisal.
- There are six steps that can be used to reduce errors and improve performance appraisals.
- Group performance evaluation systems are being used increasingly.

What are rewards?

- Rewards are another key aspect of HR management and involve the design and implementation of positively valued work outcomes.

- Reward systems emphasize a mix of extrinsic and intrinsic rewards.

How does one manage pay as an extrinsic reward?
- Pay as an extrinsic reward involves merit pay and creative pay practices.
- Creative pay practices include skill-based pay, gain-sharing plans, lump-sum pay increases, and flexible benefit plans.

How does one manage intrinsic rewards?
- Managing intrinsic rewards involves the challenge of designing a work setting so employees can, in effect, reward themselves for a job well done.

KEY TERMS

Behaviorally anchored rating scales (BARS) (p. 122)
Career planning and development (p. 111)
Career plateau (p. 116)
Career stages (p. 115)
Central tendency error (p. 124)
Critical incident diary (p. 121)
Flexible benefits plans (p. 129)
Forced distribution (p. 120)

Gain sharing (p. 128)
Graphic rating scale (p. 120)
Halo error (p. 123)
Human resource strategic planning (p. 107)
Job analysis (p. 108)
Leniency error (p. 124)
Lump-sum pay increase (p. 128)
Management by objectives (MBO) (p. 122)
Merit pay (p. 126)
Paired comparison (p. 120)

Performance appraisal (p. 116)
Personal bias error (p. 124)
Ranking (p. 120)
Recency error (p. 124)
Recruitment (p. 108)
Selection (p. 109)
Skill-based pay (p. 127)
Socialization (p. 110)
Strictness error (p. 124)
Training (p. 111)
360-degree evaluations (p. 118)

SELF-TEST 6

▼ MULTIPLE CHOICE

1. HR staffing consists of all of the following *except* ____. (a) selection (b) socialization (c) recruitment (d) training
2. Job analysis is ____. (a) the same as job description (b) the same as job specification (c) involved with organizational tasks (d) the same as performance appraisal
3. Training ____. (a) is the same as socialization (b) is another name for career development (c) is a set of activities for improving job-related skills (d) precedes staffing
4. The notions of a career based within a single organization ____. (a) are truer than ever (b) are increasingly obsolete (c) were never really true (d) apply to some industries but not others
5. All of the following except *one* is a reason for a career plateau. (a) Personal choice. (b) Limited ability. (c) Lack of opportunity. (d) Too much stress.
6. Performance appraisal and job analysis are ____ (a) similar (b) unrelated (c) related such that the job analysis should be based on the performance appraisal (d) related such that the performance appraisal should be based on the job analysis.
7. Performance appraisals have the two general purposes of ____. (a) rewards and punishments (b) evaluating and development decisions (c) rewards and evaluative decisions (d) feedback and job analysis decisions

8. Two kinds of awards are ____. (a) extrinsic and intrinsic (b) internal and external (c) strong and weak (d) higher level and lower level
9. Merit pay ____. (a) rewards people for increased job-related skills (b) is a form of gain sharing (c) is similar to a lump-sum pay increase (d) enhances the positive value of pay as a work reward
10. In a flexible benefit plan ____. (a) workers select benefits according to needs (b) there are high benefits early in a job and lower ones later (c) there are low benefits early in a job and higher ones later (d) rewards can be split between salary and non-salary payouts.

▼ TRUE–FALSE

11. Staffing is narrower than recruitment.   T   F
12. Selection follows socialization.   T   F
13. Training can be on the job or off the job.   T   F
14. The career planning framework consists of five steps.   T   F
15. Adult transitions are linked to career stages.   T   F
16. Performance appraisals are best done by an immediate superior.   T   F
17. Performance appraisals can use output measures or activity measures.   T   F
18. Forced distribution is an absolute performance appraisal method.   T   F
19. Pay is an intrinsic reward.   T   F
20. Gain-sharing plans and profit-sharing plans are the same.   T   F

▼ SHORT RESPONSE

21. Discuss the relationship between an organization's mission and HR strategic planning.
22. Discuss how training and career development relate to the organization–job requirements–individual characteristics match.
23. Discuss the linkage between adult transitions and career stages.
24. Compare and contrast the evaluative and feedback and development aspects of performance appraisal.

▼ APPLICATIONS ESSAY

25. Assume you belong to a fraternity or sorority. Making any necessary assumptions, discuss, in some detail, how the human resource management concepts in this chapter could be applied at the national and local level of your fraternity.

7

LEARNING AND REINFORCEMENT

Wisconsin Power and Light Company's Jim Bindl has won one of the highly coveted annual Yoder-Heneman Creative Application Awards for turning an employee suggestion system into a successful reward system that employees both like and support.[1] The program is called "Employees Recognizing Employees." Employees at any level can reward colleagues immediately for brilliant ideas, outstanding cooperation, or hard work.

At the beginning of each year, each employee gets 10 certificates worth $20 each. Throughout the year, employees pass along these certificates to other workers, noting on the certificate why it is being given. The recipient can either redeem the certificate for cash at the end of the year or award it to another employee who, in turn, can cash it in or pass it on.

One Wisconsin Power and Light employee cashed in certificates totaling $840, and nearly 70 workers each received at least $400 in certificates. The pass-on feature was used 973 times for a total of close to $20,000.[1] (http://www.wpl.com/who/founda.html)

J im Bindl's plan shows the impact that reinforcement (especially that of colleagues) can have on the behavior of people in Wisconsin Power and, indeed, organizations in general. The certificate recipients have learned that if they engage in the kinds of behaviors desired they will receive positive reinforcement. Learning and reinforcement are important building blocks in organizational behavior, and we discuss these topics and the ways in which managers can use them in organizations. This chapter extends our discussion of pay as an extrinsic reward from Chapter 6 and considers other kinds of extrinsic rewards.

▶ Learning and reinforcement and the ways managers implement them in organizations are important building blocks in organizational behavior. As you read Chapter 7, keep in mind the following key questions.

- ◉ What is learning, and what are four general approaches to learning?
- ◉ What is reinforcement, its foundation, and its linkage to rewards?
- ◉ What is organizational behavior modification (OB Mod), and how are its four strategies implemented?
- ◉ What are some research and ethical issues involved in using reinforcement strategies?
- ◉ How are social learning theory and behavioral self-management related?

▶ # LEARNING

Learning is a relatively permanent change in behavior that occurs as a result of experience.

L earning, defined in Chapter 1 as a relatively permanent change in behavior resulting from experience, is an important part of rewards management. It is the process by which people acquire the competencies and beliefs that affect their behavior in organizations. Managers with an awareness of basic learning principles are well positioned to help others "learn" the behaviors necessary to achieve maximum positive outcomes from their work.

There are four general approaches to learning: classical conditioning, operant conditioning, cognitive learning, and social learning. Each of these approaches offers potentially valuable insights to managers and the field of OB.[2]

▼ CLASSICAL CONDITIONING

Classical conditioning is a form of learning through association. As shown in Figure 7.1, this type of learning involves the manipulation of a *stimulus* or *stimuli* to influence behavior. We'll define a **stimulus** as anything that incites action. Classical conditioning associates a previously neutral stimulus—one that has no effect on behavior—with another stimulus that does affect behavior. The former thus becomes a *conditioned stimulus,* which, upon its occurrence, also draws forth the now *conditioned response.* This process is illustrated by the well-known experiments conducted by Ivan Pavlov, the Russian psychologist who "taught" dogs to salivate—the conditioned response—at the sound of a bell—the conditioned stimulus—by ringing the bell when feeding the dogs. The sight of the food caused the dogs to salivate. Eventually, the dogs "learned," through the association of the bell with the presentation of meat, to salivate at the ringing of the bell alone. Involuntary or reflexive behaviors of humans are also susceptible to classical conditioning. Someone who is verbally reprimanded on several occasions after being "asked to step into the boss's office" may become conditioned to display apprehension and nervous reactions whenever asked to come into the office in the future.

Classical conditioning is quite common both inside and outside the workplace. But it often is hard to know just when it is taking place. For example, it may take both the manager and the employee a long time to figure out the stimulus and response connection shown in Figure 7.1. Nevertheless, the classical conditioning approach alerts good managers to such possibilities. They may then gain a better understanding of their subordinates. Further, the general stimulus response notion sets the stage for operant conditioning.

> **Classical conditioning** is a form of learning through association that involves the manipulation of stimuli to influence behavior.

> A **stimulus** is something that incites action.

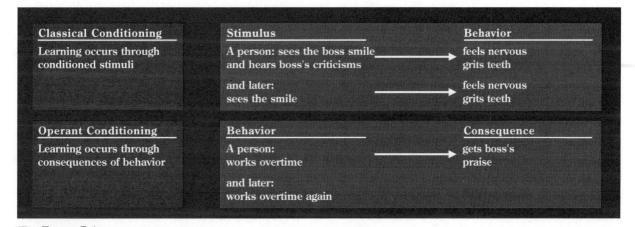

Classical Conditioning	Stimulus	Behavior
Learning occurs through conditioned stimuli	A person: sees the boss smile and hears boss's criticisms	feels nervous grits teeth
	and later: sees the smile	feels nervous grits teeth

Operant Conditioning	Behavior	Consequence
Learning occurs through consequences of behavior	A person: works overtime	gets boss's praise
	and later: works overtime again	

■ FIGURE 7.1

Differences between the classical and operant conditioning approaches to learning.

▼ OPERANT CONDITIONING

Operant conditioning is learning that is achieved when the *consequences* of a behavior lead to changes in the probability of its occurrence. Figure 7.1 clarifies how this operant, or *behaviorist,* approach contrasts with classical conditioning; the former approach views behavior as "operating" on its environment to produce consequences that affect its future occurrence.

The late noted psychologist B. F. Skinner popularized operant conditioning as a way of controlling behavior by manipulating its consequences.[3] The method consists of the three-component framework: *Antecedents → Behavior → Consequences,* sometimes called ABC contingencies or "if/then" relationships. Returning to Figure 7.1, the *antecedent (A)*—the condition leading up to or cueing behavior—may be an agreement between the boss and the employee to work overtime as needed. If the employee engages in the overtime *behavior (B)*—the *consequence (C)*—the results of the behavior—is the boss's praise.

Whereas classical conditioning works only on behaviors that are involuntary in nature, operant conditioning has a broader application to almost any human behavior. Thus, it has rather substantial applications in the workplace.

▼ COGNITIVE LEARNING

Cognitive learning is learning that is achieved by thinking about the perceived relationship between events and individual goals and expectations. The process motivation theories reviewed in Chapter 5 help illustrate how this learning perspective is applied to the work setting. These theories are concerned with explaining *how* and *why* people decide to do things by examining the ways in which people come to view various work activities as perceived opportunities to pursue desired rewards, to eliminate felt inequities, and the like. These cognitive explanations of learning differ markedly from the acognitive cognitive and behaviorist explanations of operant conditioning.

Take the example of an Omni hotel employee greeting a hotel customer with a pleasing smile and a friendly hello and receiving a compliment from his boss. Thereafter, the employee is observed to spend more time smiling at hotel customers. The question is, "why?" According to the cognitive learning explanation, the employee exhibits a friendly customer greeting, with the goal in mind of receiving compliments from his boss—something he highly values. The employee *reasons* that increased friendly greetings will please his boss and thus *decides* to seek out customers to greet. According to the operant conditioning explanation, the *antecedent* was a hotel orientation session emphasizing greeting customers in a friendly manner. The *behavior* of greeting a customer with a friendly hello was positively reinforced by the *consequence* of the boss's compliment. Having been positively reinforced, the behavior is repeated whenever the employee sees a customer in the future.

▼ SOCIAL LEARNING

Social learning is learning that is achieved through the reciprocal interactions among people, behavior, and environment. Social learning theory is expressed in the work of Albert Bandura and uses such reciprocal interactions to integrate op-

Operant conditioning is the process of controlling behavior by manipulating, or "operating" on, its consequences.

Cognitive learning is achieved by thinking about the perceived relationship between events and individual goals and expectations.

Social learning is achieved through the reciprocal interaction between people and their environments.

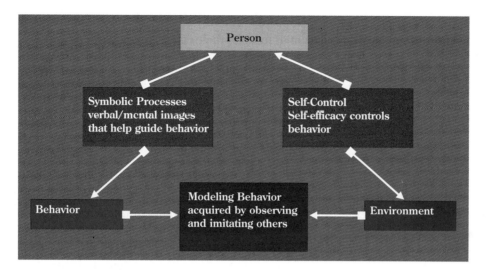

■ FIGURE 7.2
Social learning model.
[Source: Adapted from R.
Kreitner and F. Luthans, "A
Social Learning Approach
to Behavioral Management:
'Radical Behaviorists' Mel-
lowing Out," *Organiza-
tional Dynamics* (Autumn
1984), p. 55].

erant and cognitive learning approaches.[4] That is, environmental determinism and self-determinism are combined. Thus, behavior is seen not simply as a function of external antecedents and consequences, or solely of internal needs, satisfaction, or expectations (as discussed in Chapter 5), but as a combination of the two. Figure 7.2 illustrates and elaborates on this reciprocal interaction notion.

According to the figure, the individual uses modeling or vicarious learning to acquire behavior by observing and imitating others. The person then attempts to acquire these behaviors by modeling them through practice. The "models" may be the person's parents, friends, or even well-known celebrities. In the work situation, the model may be a manager or coworker who demonstrates desired behaviors. Mentors or senior workers who befriend younger and more inexperienced proteges can also be important models. Indeed, some have argued that a shortage of mentors for women in management is a major constraint to their progression up the career ladder.[5]

The symbolic processes depicted in Figure 7.2 are also important in social learning. Words and symbols used by managers and others in the workplace can help communicate values, beliefs, and goals and thus serve as guides to the individual's behavior. For example, a "thumbs up" or a symbol from the boss lets you know your behavior is appropriate. At the same time, the person's self-control is important in influencing his or her own behavior. *Self-efficacy*—the person's belief that he or she can perform adequately in a situation—is a very important part of such self-control. People with self-efficacy believe that they have the necessary ability for a given job; that they are capable of the effort required; and that no outside events will hinder them from obtaining their desired

---

Take-A-Note 7.1

KEY POINTS IN APPLYING SOCIAL LEARNING THEORY[6]

- Identify appropriate job behaviors.
- Help employees select an appropriate behavioral model.
- Work with employees to meet the requirements of the new behaviors.
- Structure the learning situation to enhance learning of the necessary behaviors.
- Provide appropriate rewards (consequences) for workers who perform the appropriate behaviors.
- Engage in appropriate managerial actions to maintain the newly learned behaviors.

performance level.[7] In contrast, people with low self-efficacy believe that no matter how hard they try, they cannot manage their environment well enough to be successful. For example, if you feel self-efficacious as a student, a low grade on one test is likely to encourage you to study harder, talk to the instructor, or do other things to enable you to do well the next time. In contrast, a person low in self-efficacy would probably drop the course or give up studying.

Of course, even people who are high in self-efficacy do not control their environment entirely. As a manager, you can have an impact on the environment and other factors listed in Figure 7.2, even though the impact is less than in the operant approach. This is especially the case in influencing a person's self-efficacy. A manager's expectations and peer support can go far in increasing a worker's self-efficacy and feelings of control. We examined this notion in Chapter 4, when we discussed the Pygmalion effect, or the self-fulfilling prophesy, whereby people tend to respond according to the expectations of others.

REINFORCEMENT

Reinforcement is the administration of a consequence as a result of behavior.

Reinforcement, or the administration of a consequence as a result of behavior, plays a key role in the learning process and is the means through which operant conditioning takes place. The foundation for this relationship is the **law of effect,** as stated by E. L. Thorndike.[8] Behavior that results in a pleasant outcome is likely to be repeated; behavior that results in an unpleasant outcome is not likely to be repeated. The implications of the law of effect are rather straightforward. Rewards are outcomes or environmental consequences that are considered by the reinforcement perspective to determine individual behavior. In Chapter 6, we discussed both intrinsic and extrinsic rewards. In terms of operant learning and reinforcement, our interest is in the latter.

The **law of effect** is the observation that behavior that results in a pleasing outcome is likely to be repeated; behavior that results in an unpleasant outcome is not likely to be repeated.

Recall that *extrinsic rewards* are positively valued work outcomes that are given to the individual by some other person. They are important external reinforcers or environmental consequences that can substantially influence people's work behaviors through the law of effect. Figure 7.3 presents a sample of extrinsic rewards that can be allocated by managers to their subordinates.[9] Some of these are *contrived,* or *planned,* rewards that have direct costs and budgetary implications; examples are pay increases and cash bonuses. A second category includes *natural* rewards that have no cost other than the manager's personal time and efforts; examples are verbal praise and recognition in the workplace.

Organizational behavior modification (OB Mod) is the systematic reinforcement of desirable work behavior and the nonreinforcement or punishment of unwanted work behavior.

We now use an approach called **organizational behavior modification,** or OB Mod, to bring together the application of operant conditioning, reinforcement, and extrinsic reward notions. You can think of OB Mod as the systematic reinforcement of desirable work behavior and the nonreinforcement or punishment of unwanted work behavior. OB Mod includes four basic reinforcement

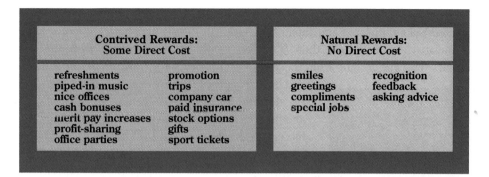

Contrived Rewards: Some Direct Cost		Natural Rewards: No Direct Cost	
refreshments	promotion	smiles	recognition
piped-in music	trips	greetings	feedback
nice offices	company car	compliments	asking advice
cash bonuses	paid insurance	special jobs	
merit pay increases	stock options		
profit-sharing	gifts		
office parties	sport tickets		

■ FIGURE 7.3
A sample of extrinsic rewards allocated by managers.

strategies: positive reinforcement, negative reinforcement (or avoidance), punishment, and extinction.[10]

▼ POSITIVE REINFORCEMENT

B. F. Skinner and his followers advocate **positive reinforcement**—the administration of positive consequences that tend to increase the likelihood of repeating the desirable behavior in similar settings. For example, a Texas Instruments manager nods to express approval to a subordinate after she makes a useful comment during a sales meeting. To use positive reinforcement well in the work setting, you must first be aware of the wide variety of things that have potential reward value. A number of these are listed in Figure 7.3.

To begin, we need to be aware that positive reinforcers and rewards are not necessarily the same. Recognition is both a reward and a positive reinforcer *only if* a person's performance later improves. Sometimes, however, apparent rewards turn out not to be positive reinforcers. For example, a supervisor at Boeing may praise a subordinate in front of other group members for finding errors in a report. But the group members may then give the worker the silent treatment. In response, the worker may stop looking for errors in the future. In this case, the supervisor's "reward" does not serve as a positive reinforcer.

To have maximum reinforcement value, a reward must be delivered only if the desired behavior is exhibited. That is, the reward must be *contingent* on the desired behavior, as in the contingent, if/then ABC model. This principle is known as the **law of contingent reinforcement.** In the previous Boeing example, the supervisor's praise was contingent on the subordinate's finding errors in the report, even though this praise did not turn out to be a positive reinforcer. Finally, the reward must be given as soon as possible after the desired behavior. This is known as the **law of immediate reinforcement.**[11] If the supervisor gave the praise as soon as the errors were found, that praise was consistent with this law.

Consider the Harris Company's example in terms of our earlier ABC analysis. If the associates do the kinds of things noted in performing their jobs, they will receive special recognition. The antecedents are the managers' communication of the program, the removal of obstacles, and the availability of opportunities for these kinds of activities. The behaviors are the performance of the activities.

Positive reinforcement is the administration of positive consequences that tend to increase the likelihood of repeating the behavior in similar settings.

The **law of contingent reinforcement** is the view that, for a reward to have maximum reinforcing value, it must be delivered only if the desired behavior is exhibited.

The **law of immediate reinforcement** states that the more immediate the delivery of a reward after the occurrence of a desirable behavior, the greater the reinforcing effect on behavior.

QUALITY

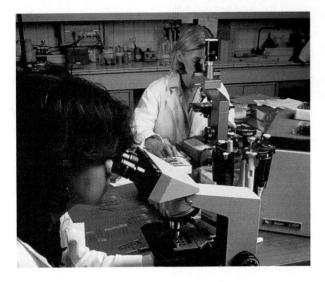

Harris is an independent contract research laboratory with locations in the United States, Europe, and Japan. The company's scientists and technology associates conduct more than 4 million tests a year for more than 6000 clients. The information from these experts improves the food, environment, and health of people throughout the world. Harris strongly believes that employees' feelings about their investment in time and energy for the organization go beyond what they are paid. Therefore, it provides special recognition for quality performance of its global experts through a yearly Scientific Achievement Day that includes awards for different facets of quality performance. Key criteria used in determining the awards range from positive scientific or technical recognition by clients to training and mentoring associates, publication of papers, and leadership in professional or technical organizations. Colleague committees determine the recipients of the awards.[12]

The consequences are the receipt of the awards at a special ceremony. Although it is hard to evaluate the program quantitatively, Harris feels very pleased with the results. In addition, the awards appear to be clearly linked to a range of desired behaviors, and, since the awards are determined by their own colleagues, they are likely to be especially valued by the recipients.

Shaping   In the above example, the behaviors were fairly general in nature. Sometimes, if the desired behavior is more specific in nature and is difficult to achieve, another form of positive reinforcement, called shaping, can be used. **Shaping** is the creation of a new behavior by the positive reinforcement of successive approximations to the desired behavior. For example, city workers in Bellevue, Washington, are awarded "points" with a monetary value on the cost of their health insurance. Currently, one point must be given up for each dollar of health benefits used, and the value of the points increases as the number of claims filed by all workers decreases. This is a straightforward positive reinforcement strategy.[13] But suppose the amount of money spent on insurance and the number of claims filed were still too high. The city might then set a goal that was harder to reach to contain its costs further. Rather than give rewards only for reaching the new goal, the city might continue with current rewards and then increase these rewards in increments until the new goal was reached. Once reached, the new level of rewards would continue to stabilize the behavior. In this way, behavior could be shaped gradually, rather than changed all at once.

Scheduling Positive Reinforcement   Positive reinforcement can be given according to either continuous or intermittent schedules. **Continuous reinforce-**

Shaping is the creation of a new behavior by the positive reinforcement of successive approximations to the desired behavior.

Continuous reinforcement is a reinforcement schedule that administers a reward each time a desired behavior occurs.

ment administers a reward each time a desired behavior occurs. **Intermittent reinforcement** rewards behavior only periodically. These alternatives are important since the two schedules may have very different impacts on behavior. In general, continuous reinforcement draws forth a desired behavior more quickly than does intermittent reinforcement. At the same time, continuous reinforcement is more costly in the consumption of rewards and is more easily extinguished when reinforcement is no longer present. In contrast, behavior acquired under intermittent reinforcement lasts longer upon the discontinuance of reinforcement than does behavior acquired under continuous reinforcement. In other words, it is more resistant to extinction.

Intermittent reinforcement, as shown in Figure 7.4 can be given according to fixed or variable schedules. The variable schedules typically result in more consistent patterns of desired behavior than do fixed reinforcement schedules. *Fixed interval schedules* provide rewards at the first appearance of a behavior after a given time has elapsed; *fixed ratio schedules* result in a reward each time a certain number of the behaviors has occurred. A *variable interval schedule* rewards behavior at random times, while a *variable ratio schedule* rewards behavior after a random number of occurrences.

Let's look at an example from Drankenfeld Colors, Washington, Pennsylvania, with 250 employees. The absenteeism rate of these employees was very low—under 1 percent; 44 percent of the employees had perfect attendance records in a recent year. The firm wanted to use positive reinforcement to showcase perfect attendance, even though attendance was already so positive. Consequently, it gave perfect attendance monetary awards of $50 at 6 and 12 months, with a $25 bonus for a full year of perfect attendance. Along with this incentive, the firm entered perfect attendees into a sweepstakes drawing at a special awards

> **Intermittent reinforcement** is a reinforcement schedule that rewards behavior only periodically.

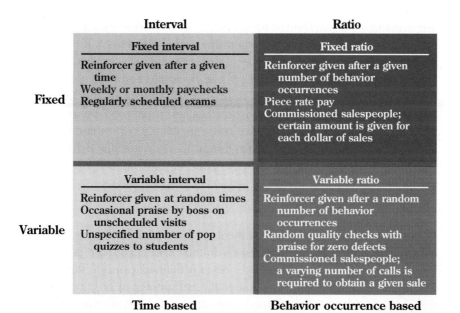

■ FIGURE 7.4
Four types of intermittent reinforcement schedules.

Take-A-Note 7.2

WORK GUIDELINES FOR ALLOCATING EXTRINSIC REWARDS

1. *Clearly identify the desired behaviors.*

2. *Maintain an inventory of rewards that have the potential to serve as positive reinforcers.*

3. *Recognize individual differences in the rewards that will have positive value for each person.*

4. *Let each person know exactly what must be done to receive a desirable reward. Set clear target antecedents and give performance feedback.*

5. *Allocate rewards contingently and immediately upon the appearance of the desired behaviors.*

6. *Allocate rewards wisely in terms of scheduling the delivery of positive reinforcement.*

banquet. The winner received an all-expense-paid trip for two to a resort. Perfect attendance increased from 44 percent to 62 percent in the program's first year.[14]

Let's consider what kind of reinforcement scheduling was used in this program. A strong argument can be made that a fixed ratio schedule was used, in conjunction with a variable ratio schedule. The first schedule gave an award for those attendance behaviors occurring within 6 months and 12 months or the specific number of work days' attendance occurring within these periods. Thus, for each of the periods in which a perfect number of attendance days occurred, a person received an award—a fixed ratio schedule one. The second schedule focuses on eligibility for the drawing and is a variable ratio because a random number of perfect attendance days must pass before a specific employee receives a trip. Maintaining perfect attendance to qualify for the drawing is similar to playing a slot machine. In this variable ratio system, players keep putting coins in the machines since they don't have any idea when they will hit the jackpot.[15] Lotteries similar to Drankenfeld's have been used by firms as different as new car dealerships and New York Life Insurance.[16] All these examples show the usefulness of using intermittent reinforcement schedules.

▼ NEGATIVE REINFORCEMENT (AVOIDANCE)

Negative reinforcement is the withdrawal of negative consequences which tends to increase the likelihood of repeating the behavior in a similar setting; it is also known as avoidance.

A second reinforcement strategy used in OB Mod is **negative reinforcement** or *avoidance*—the withdrawal of negative consequences, which tends to increase the likelihood of repeating the desirable behavior in similar settings. For example, a manager at McDonald's regularly nags a worker about his poor performance and then stops nagging when the worker does not fall behind one day. Note that there are two aspects here: *first,* the negative consequences, *then* the withdrawal of these consequences when desirable behavior occurs. The term "negative reinforcement" comes from this withdrawal of the negative consequences. This strategy is also sometimes called "avoidance" because its intent is for the person to avoid the negative consequence by performing the desired behavior. For instance, we stop at a red light to avoid a traffic ticket; or a worker who prefers the day shift is allowed to return to that shift if she performs well on the night shift.

▼ PUNISHMENT

Punishment is the administration of negative consequences that tend to reduce the likelihood of repeating the behavior in similar settings.

A third OB Mod strategy is punishment. Unlike positive reinforcement and negative reinforcement, punishment is not intended to encourage positive behavior but to *discourage* negative behavior. Formally defined, **punishment** is the administration of negative consequences or the withdrawal of positive consequences that tend to reduce the likelihood of repeating the behavior in similar settings.

The first type of punishment is illustrated by a Burger King manager who assigns a tardy worker to an unpleasant job, such as cleaning the restrooms. An example of withdrawing positive consequences is a Burger King manager who docks the employee's pay when she is tardy.

Some scholarly work illustrates the importance of punishment by showing that punishment administered for poor performance leads to *increased* performance without a significant effect on satisfaction. However, punishment seen by the workers as arbitrary and capricious leads to very low satisfaction as well as low performance.[17] Thus, punishment can be handled poorly, or it can be handled well. Of course, the manager's challenge is to know when to use this strategy and how to use it correctly.

Sometimes negative reinforcement and punishment are confused. A major difference lies in their effects on behavior. Negative reinforcement *increases* the likelihood of repeating the behavior, whereas punishment *decreases* that likelihood; negative reinforcement *removes* negative consequences following behavior—I stop yelling at you for being late when you start coming to work on time—whereas punishment *presents* negative consequences or the withdrawal of positive consequences following behavior—you are late to work for the third time in two weeks and I dock your pay.

Problems with the Punishment Strategy Resentment and sabotage may accompany a manager's use of punishment. A manager who frequently punishes subordinates may find that he or she has an unpleasant effect on the work unit even when not administering punishment. This manager has become so associated with punishment that his or her very presence in the work setting is an unpleasant experience for others. It is also wise to remember that although a behavior may be suppressed as a result of punishment, it may not be permanently abolished. For example, an employee may be reprimanded for taking unauthorized work breaks. The behavior may stop, but only when the manager is visible. As soon as the threat of punishment is removed from the situation, when the manager is no longer present, the employee may continue to take breaks.

Finally, punishment may be offset by positive reinforcement received from another source. A worker may be reinforced by peers at the same time that punishment is being received from the manager. Sometimes, the positive value of such peer support may be stong enough to cause the individual to put up with the punishment. Thus, the undesirable behavior continues. As many times as a student may be verbally reprimanded by an instructor for being late to class, for example, the "grins" offered by other students may well justify the continuation of the tardiness in the future.

Does all of this mean you should never punish? No. The important things to remember are to administer punishment selectively and then to do it right. Consider the following case.

A Case of Punishment Peter Ramirez is a forklift operator in a large supermarket warehouse.[19] This is the highest paid nonsupervisory job in the firm. It is considered a high-status job, and it took Peter 5 and a half years to earn the posi-

The Omni Royal Orleans Hotel places a heavy emphasis on its Omni Service Champion Program, recognizing desirable worker behaviors. A smiling greeting is one such desirable behavior, and the boss's praise is the consequence.[18]

Take-A-Note 7.3

GUIDELINES FOR USING PUNISHMENT

1. Tell the individual what is being done wrong.
2. Tell the individual what is right.
3. Punish in private.
4. Punish in accord with the laws of contingent and immediate reinforcement.
5. Make sure the punishment matches the behavior.

tion. Unfortunately, Peter is prone to "show off" by engaging in a variety of unsafe driving habits that violate federal safety codes. Pete's manager "chews him out" regularly, but the unsafe driving continues.

Pete's boss analyzed the situation from a reinforcement perspective. She sought to determine the environmental consequences associated with Pete's unsafe driving habits. As you may have predicted, she found that the undesirable behavior was typically followed by laughter and special attention from the other warehouse workers.

The next time Peter was observed driving unsafely, Pete's boss took him off the forklift truck, explained what he was doing wrong and what was desired, and reassigned him to general warehousing duties. When he was finally allowed back on the forklift, Peter drove more safely.

Alternatively, Pete's boss could have combined punishment with positive reinforcement. For example, she could praise Pete's performance when he drove safely. Then Peter would know exactly what was wrong and the unpleasant consequences associated with that behavior and what was right and the pleasant consequences associated with that behavior.[20]

▼ EXTINCTION

Extinction is the withdrawal of the reinforcing consequences for a given behavior.

The final OB Mod reinforcement strategy is **extinction**—the withdrawal of the reinforcing consequences for a given behavior. For example, Jack is often late for work, and his coworkers cover for him (positive reinforcement). The manager instructs Jack's coworkers to stop covering for him, withdrawing the reinforcing consequences. The manager has deliberately used extinction to get rid of an undesirable behavior. This strategy decreases the frequency of or weakens the behavior. The behavior is not "unlearned"; it simply is not exhibited. Since the behavior is no longer reinforced, it will reappear if reinforced again. Whereas positive reinforcement seeks to establish and maintain desirable work behavior, the goal of extinction is to weaken and eliminate undesirable behavior.

A Case of Extinction A manager at Motorola is worried.[21] One of her bright young assistants is developing a problem behavior that could eventually erode his credibility. At the weekly staff meeting, Jason has started acting more like a comedian than an aspiring executive. He interjects one-liners and increasingly makes wisecracks during discussions. As a result, the meetings are often disrupted. The manager is becoming annoyed and is especially concerned because Jason's behavior has gotten worse during the last month. If you were the manager, how would you use reinforcement theory to analyze this situation?

The manager in this case decided not to reprimand Jason. Rather, she tried to analyze his behavior in terms of the environmental consequences it produced for him. She reasoned that his behavior must be receiving some sort of positive reinforcement. At the next two meetings, she closely observed Jason's disruptive behavior and its results. She noticed that two other staff members usually acknowledged Jason's remarks by smiling and nodding approval. In fact, the manager noticed that Jason immediately looked to these coworkers each time after making one of his disruptive comments.

In terms of reinforcement theory, the manager has found that Jason is being positively reinforced by these two people for a behavior that is organizationally undesirable. Given this diagnosis, the manager decided on a strategy of extinction. She privately mentioned to Jason's two colleagues that their smiles reinforced Jason's disruptive behavior and asked if they would stop. They did so. In future meetings, the frequency of Jason's disruptive behavior decreased dramatically.

Extinction can be especially powerful when combined with positive reinforcement. In this case, extinction caused Jason to stop making disruptive comments. However, the manager was still concerned that Jason maintain and even increase his useful contributions. Whenever Jason made such a valuable comment, therefore, he was provided with immediate acknowledgment and approval. These extrinsic rewards had a positive reinforcing effect on desirable behavior. Thus, the combined strategy of extinction and positive reinforcement is a most useful tool for managers.

▼ A SUMMARY OF OB MOD STRATEGIES

Figure 7.5 summarizes the use of each of the OB Mod strategies using the ABC framework. They are all designed to direct work behavior toward practices desired by management. Both positive and negative reinforcement are used to strengthen the desirable behavior of improving work quality when it occurs. Punishment is used to weaken the undesirable behavior of high error rate and consists of either administering negative consequences or withdrawing positive consequences. Likewise, extinction is used deliberately to weaken the undesirable high error rate behavior when it occurs. Note also, however, that extinction is used inadvertently to weaken the desirable low error rate behavior. Finally, don't forget that these strategies may be used in combination as well as independently.

REINFORCEMENT PERSPECTIVES:
RESEARCH AND ETHICAL ISSUES

The effective use of reinforcement strategies can assist in the management of human behavior at work. Testimony to this effect is found in the application of these strategies in many large firms, such as General Electric and B. F. Goodrich, and even in small ones, such as Mid-America Building Maintenance.[22] A janitorial services firm in Wichita, Kansas, Mid-America Building Maintenance, provides an incentive program to employees who work 90 consecutive work days

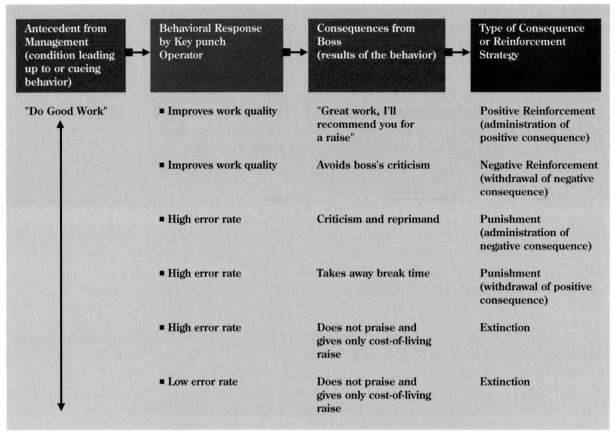

Antecedent from Management (condition leading up to or cueing behavior)	Behavioral Response by Key punch Operator	Consequences from Boss (results of the behavior)	Type of Consequence or Reinforcement Strategy
"Do Good Work"	■ Improves work quality	"Great work, I'll recommend you for a raise"	Positive Reinforcement (administration of positive consequence)
	■ Improves work quality	Avoids boss's criticism	Negative Reinforcement (withdrawal of negative consequence)
	■ High error rate	Criticism and reprimand	Punishment (administration of negative consequence)
	■ High error rate	Takes away break time	Punishment (withdrawal of positive consequence)
	■ High error rate	Does not praise and gives only cost-of-living raise	Extinction
	■ Low error rate	Does not praise and gives only cost-of-living raise	Extinction

■ FIGURE 7.5

Applying the ABC framework in a work setting.

without an absence. Reinforcement strategies are also supported by the growing number of consulting firms that specialize in reinforcement techniques.

GLOBAL

The Performance Advisory Service (PAS) of the World Bank, a financial institution concentrating on international development, was recently involved with reinforcement strategies in dealing with a performance problem. The problem was that managers' administrative assistants chronically procrastinated in answering phones and disseminating time-sensitive information. When this procrastination occurred, the managers nagged the assistants, and when that did not work, simply performed the tasks themselves—thus reinforcing low performance. The five-person PAS team recommended that the managers should specifically describe the current work-performance issues and behaviors that were unacceptable, delineate the assistants' job responsibilities and performance expectations, and specify the reinforcement and consequences that would be taken for performance and nonperformance. The managers followed through, and their nagging problem disappeared.[23]

We must also recognize that managerial use of these approaches is not without criticism, however. For example, some reports on the "success" of specific programs are single cases that have been analyzed without the benefit of scientific research designs. It is hard to conclude definitively whether the observed results were *caused* by reinforcement dynamics. In fact, one critic argues that the improved performance may well have occurred only because of the goal setting involved; that is, because specific performance goals were clarified, and workers were individually held accountable for their accomplishment.[24]

Another criticism rests with the potential value dilemmas associated with the use of applied operant conditioning techniques to influence human behavior at work. For example, there is expressed concern that the systematic use of reinforcement strategies leads to a demeaning and dehumanizing view of people that stunts human growth and development.[25] Another criticism is that managers abuse the power of their position and knowledge by exerting external control over individual behavior.

Advocates of the reinforcement approach attack the problem head on: They agree that behavior modification involves the control of behavior, but they also argue that behavior control is an irrevocable part of every manager's job. The real question is how to ensure that this manipulation is done in a positive and constructive fashion. William Scott and Philipp Podsakoff, two advocates of reinforcement, argue that managers can avoid exploitation in organizational behavior modification only by a careful examination of the controlling features of their own behavior and of the short- and long-range results of their practices. Managers need to promote self-control and to avoid weakening subordinates by ignoring worker self-interest, since leaders are only as effective as the subordinates they lead.[26]

Others have argued that the ethics of social influence processes, such as organizational behavior modification, may be judged by how much these processes promote freedom of choice. Such choice can be increased by recognizing individuals' preferences in the design of the reinforcement contingencies and by designing self-reinforcement systems whereby people regulate their own behavior. These self-management systems and their ethics have been treated by Fred Luthans and Robert Kreitner and are discussed further later. It follows that managers should be sensitive to possible exploitation by carefully examining their own behavior and practices, by involving subordinates in the design of the system, and by encouraging self-reinforcement systems whenever feasible.[27]

In spite of criticisms such as these, we expect continuing research primarily to refine our knowledge of the reinforcement strategies rather than dramatically change existing insights. Further research is likely to tell us, as managers, how better to use the various reinforcement strategies. Such use should be tempered with a strong managerial emphasis on employee involvement wherever possible and by explicit efforts to avoid exploitation. In other words, reinforcement should always be pursued from strong ethical foundations.

3M encourages behavioral self-management actions among its employees wherever possible. People are encouraged to "work outside the boxes" to facilitate new product innovations.[28]

SOCIAL LEARNING THEORY AND
BEHAVIORAL SELF-MANAGEMENT

Some scholars have applied social learning theory in the workplace to encourage employees to help manage or lead themselves. Figure 7.6 shows self-management strategies recommended by one set of authors. Notice how these strategies build on social learning theory to emphasize both behavioral and

SELF-MANAGEMENT STRATEGIES	
BEHAVIORAL FOCUSED STRATEGIES	
Behavior	**Strategy**
Self-Set Goals	Setting goals for your own work efforts.
Management of Cues	Arranging and altering cues in the work environment to facilitate your desired personal behaviors.
Rehearsal	Physical or mental practice of work activities before you actually perform them.
Self-Observation	Observing and gathering information about your own specific behaviors that you have targeted for change.
Self-Reward	Providing yourself with personally valued rewards for completing desirable behaviors.
Self-Punishment	Administering punishments to yourself for behaving in undesirable ways (this strategy is generally *not* very effective).
COGNITIVE FOCUSED STRATEGIES	
Building Natural Rewards into Tasks	Self-redesign of where and how you do your work to increase the level of natural rewards in your job. Natural rewards that are part of, rather than separate from, the work (i.e., the work, like a hobby, becomes the reward) result from activities that cause you to feel: • a sense of competence • a sense of self-control • a sense of purpose
Focusing Thinking on Natural Rewards	Purposely focusing your thinking on the naturally rewarding features of your work.
Establishing Constructive Thought Patterns	Establishing constructive and effective habits or patterns in your thinking (e.g., a tendency to search for opportunities rather than obstacles embedded in challenges) by managing your: • beliefs and assumptions • mental imagery • internal self-talk

■   FIGURE 7.6

Self-management strategies.

cognitive focuses. Their use is designed to enhance self-efficacy and the worker's feeling of self-control.

Consistent with our thrust in this part of the book, this chapter has emphasized workers as individuals. However, many of the self-management strategies can be extended to self-managed teams as well, which are discussed later in the book.

CHAPTER 7 STUDY GUIDE

SUMMARY

What is learning, and what are four general approaches to learning?
- Learning is a relatively permanent change in behavior resulting from experience and is the process by which people acquire the competencies and beliefs that affect their behavior in organizations.
- The four general approaches to learning are classical conditioning, operant conditioning, cognitive learning, and social learning.

What are reinforcement, its foundation, and its linkage to rewards?
- Reinforcement is the means through which operant conditioning takes place and is the administration of a consequence as a result of behavior.
- Reinforcement's foundation is the law of effect, which states that behavior will be repeated or extinguished depending on whether the consequences are positive or negative.
- Reinforcement is related to extrinsic rewards in that these rewards serve as environmental consequences influencing behaviors through the law of effect.

What is organizational behavior modification (OB Mod), and how are its four strategies implemented?
- OB Mod is the systematic reinforcement of desirable work behavior and the nonreinforcement or punishment of unwanted work behavior.
- Positive reinforcement is one OB Mod strategy and is the administration of positive consequences that tend to increase the likelihood of a person's repeating a behavior in similar settings.
- Positive reinforcement should be contingent and immediate, and it can be scheduled continuously or intermittently, depending on resources and desired outcomes.
- Negative reinforcement (avoidance) is used to encourage desirable behavior through the withdrawal of negative consequences for previously undesirable behavior.
- Punishment is the administration of negative consequences or the withdrawal of positive consequences, which tends to reduce the likelihood of repeating an undesirable behavior in similar settings.
- Extinction is the withdrawal of reinforcing consequences for a given behavior.

What are some research and ethical issues involved in using reinforcement strategies?
- A number of success stories have been reported concerning various OB Mod strategies, but some argue that other variables may account for the success. Nevertheless, we believe the support is strong enough to utilize the theories but we should be alert to new findings.
- Some have argued that using reinforcement strategies may be unethical because they manipulate workers and lead to managerial abuse of power.
- OB Mod advocates respond that all managerial strategies are manipulative in some sense and that managers must be sensitive to the potential abuse of power.
- To minimize manipulation, employees can be encouraged to provide input into the design of the system and to use behavioral self-management whenever feasible.

How are social learning theory and behavioral self-management related?
- Social learning theory advocates learning through the reciprocal interactions among people, behavior, and environment.
- Social learning theory combines operant and cognitive learning approaches.
- Behavioral self-management builds on social learning theory to emphasize both behavioral and cognitive thrusts.
- Behavioral self-management has a special emphasis on enhancing a person's self-efficacy and feeling of self-control.
- Behavioral self-management is useful in treating workers both as individuals and as parts of self-managed teams.

KEY TERMS

Classical conditioning (p. 135)
Cognitive learning (p. 136)
Continuous reinforcement (p. 140)
Extinction (p. 144)
Intermittent reinforcement (p. 141)
Law of contingent reinforcement (p. 139)

Law of effect (p. 138)
Law of immediate reinforcement (p. 139)
Learning (p. 134)
Negative reinforcement (p. 142)
Organizational behavior modification (OB Mod) (p. 138)

Operant conditioning (p. 136)
Positive reinforcement (p. 139)
Punishment (p. 142)
Reinforcement (p. 138)
Shaping (p. 140)
Social learning (p. 136)
Stimulus (p. 135)

SELF-TEST 7

▼ MULTIPLE CHOICE

1. Learning is ____. (a) a temporary change in behavior resulting from experience (b) a change in attitude but not behavior (c) a relatively permanent change in behavior resulting from experience (d) best demonstrated through physical conditioning
2. Social learning ____. (a) is achieved through reciprocal interactions among people, behavior, and environment (b) is achieved by thinking about the perceived relationship between events and individual goals and expectations (c) avoids using symbolic processes (d) avoids using modeling of behavior
3. Reinforcement ____. (a) is based mostly on contrived rewards (b) emphasizes cog-

nitions (c) often uses shaping (d) has its greatest impact when a continuous schedule is used.

4. Negative reinforcement ____. (a) is similar to punishment (b) seeks to discourage undesirable behavior (c) seeks to encourage desirable behavior (d) is also known as escapism

5. Reinforcement emphasizes ____. (a) intrinsic rewards (b) extrinsic rewards (c) the law of diminishing returns (d) social learning

6. OB Mod reinforcement strategies ____. (a) have much carefully controlled research support (b) have been criticized because the observed results may confuse causality (c) are not used much in large firms (d) are mostly useful in large firms

7. OB Mod emphasizes ____. (a) the systematic reinforcement of desirable work behavior (b) noncontingent rewards (c) noncontingent punishment (d) extinction in preference to positive reinforcement

8. Reinforcement strategies ____. (a) violate ethical guidelines (b) involve the control of behavior (c) work best when they restrict freedom of choice (d) have largely been replaced by computer technology

9. Social learning theory ____. (a) is useful for employee self-management (b) is not used much anymore (c) has largely replaced OB Mod (d) is used almost exclusively in groups

10. Self-management strategies ____. (a) are almost entirely cognitive (b) are almost entirely behavioral (c) combine cognitive and behavioral emphases (d) are almost entirely group focused

▼ TRUE–FALSE

11. Cognitive learning is a form of OB Mod.   T   F
12. Classical conditioning is another name for operant conditioning.   T   F
13. The foundation for reinforcement is based on intrinsic rewards.   T   F
14. Reinforcement is the administration of a consequence as the result of behavior.   T   F
15. OB Mod uses ABC analysis.   T   F
16. OB Mod especially emphasizes the concepts of punishment and extinction.   T   F
17. OB Mod has a lot of carefully controlled research support.   T   F
18. OB Mod is unethical to use.   T   F
19. Social learning theory is another name for OB Mod.   T   F
20. Behavioral self-management has a special emphasis on self-efficacy.   T   F

▼ SHORT RESPONSE

21. Briefly compare and contrast classical conditioning and operant conditioning.
22. Briefly discuss how reinforcement is linked to extrinsic rewards.
23. Briefly compare and contrast negative reinforcement and punishment.
24. Briefly discuss behavioral self-management in the context of social learning theory.

▼ APPLICATIONS ESSAY

25. You have worked hard and qualified yourself to teach OB. For a class of 90 students, discuss how you will use an OB Mod approach to encourage attendance and preparation for each class.

JOB DESIGN,
GOAL SETTING, AND
WORK ARRANGEMENTS

Proudly, John Hazen White refers to Taco, Inc., his Cranston, Rhode Island, pump and valve manufacturing plant as "the prettiest little factory you'd ever want to see." The family-owned business employs some 450 employees, including a fair proportion of recent Latino, African, and Southeast Asian immigrants. But what strikes the visitor immediately is the company's Learning Center. The company spends $700 or more annually per employee on education. Courses offered through the center range from traditional business-related topics, such as ISO 9000 auditing and customer service, to general education courses, such as conversational Spanish, computing, and algebra. But there's more. The company tries to link the education and training to its workers' lives as evidenced by other courses such as "citizenship," business ethics, art, and music. Hazen White is quick to point out that the investments in his employees pay a good return to the company: "It comes back in the form of attitude. People feel they're playing in the game, not being kicked around in it." When faced with a recession and necessary layoffs, White was honest and direct. "We assured the employees that layoff was it," he says, ". . . the layoff was survival, not displacement." Then he turned to the employees for ideas on "how to fix the place." With the goal of competitiveness and cost efficiency, work flows and processes were redesigned with their inputs; new skills were developed with the assistance of the Learning Center; equipment was updated with the understanding that people would not be automated out of jobs. The result to date has been a 20 percent productivity increase. (http://www.taco-hvac.com/html/tacovii.html)[1]

152

The same *Fortune* magazine article that tells the story of Taco, Inc., reminds its readers that "The kind of schooling Taco offers is rare."[2] Unfortunately, too many people are still working today without substantial opportunities for personal growth, creative contribution, and job satisfaction. As a student once told us, for many people: "Even the best day at work can never be as good as the worst day of golf." This chapter on job design, goal setting, and work schedules takes a more positive view, suggesting that jobs can and should be designed for both high-performance outcomes and satisfaction. When a job is properly defined, when the tasks are clear, when the goals are challenging but attainable, and when the schedules of work respect individual needs, both outcomes are possible. Simply put, good jobs facilitate performance, quality, and continuous improvement while allowing also for job satisfaction.

Chapter 8 introduces the essentials of job design, goal setting, and work scheduling as important motivational strategies. As you read the chapter, keep in mind these key questions.

- What are the basic job-design approaches?
- What is the job characteristics model?
- How does technology influence job design?
- How can goal setting improve job outcomes?
- What alternative work arrangements are used today?

APPROACHES TO JOB DESIGN

> **Job design** is the process of defining job tasks and the work arrangements to accomplish them.

Job design is the planning and specification of job tasks and the work arrangements through which they are to be accomplished. Figure 8.1 shows how alternative job design approaches differ in the way required tasks are defined and in the amount of intrinsic motivation provided for the worker. Obviously, the "best" job design is always one that meets organizational requirements for high performance, offers a good fit with individual skills and needs, and provides opportunities for job satisfaction.

▼ SCIENTIFIC MANAGEMENT

The history of scholarly interest in job design can be traced in part to Frederick Taylor's work with "scientific management" in the early 1900s.[3] Taylor and his contemporaries sought to increase the efficiency of people at work. Their approach was to study a job carefully, break it into its smallest components, establish exact time and motion requirements for each task to be done, and then train workers to do these tasks the same ways over and over again. These early efforts were forerunners of current industrial engineering approaches to job design that emphasize efficiency. Such approaches attempt to determine the best processes, methods, work-flow layouts, output standards, and person–machine interfaces for various jobs.

> **Job simplification** standardizes tasks and employs people in very routine jobs.

Today the term **job simplification** is used to describe the approach of standardizing work procedures and employing people in very clearly defined and highly specialized tasks. The machine-paced automobile assembly line is a classic example of this job-design strategy. The potential advantages of this approach in-

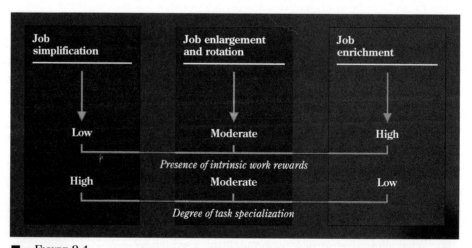

■ FIGURE 8.1

A continuum of job design strategies.

clude increased operating efficiency by deskilling work to emphasize low-cost labor, minimum job-training requirements, and repetitive tasks. However, the potential disadvantages include loss of efficiency because of poor work quality, high rates of absenteeism and turnover, and the need to pay higher wages to get people to do unattractive jobs.

▼ JOB ENLARGEMENT AND JOB ROTATION

One of the basic issues in job design relates to the number or variety of different tasks performed. In job simplification the variety is limited. Although this makes the tasks easier to master, the repetitiveness can reduce motivation. Thus, a second set of job-design approaches adds breadth to the variety of tasks performed. **Job enlargement** increases task variety by combining into one job two or more tasks that were previously assigned to separate workers. Sometimes called *horizontal loading,* this approach increases job "breadth" by having the worker perform more tasks of the same level of responsibility. **Job rotation**, another horizontal loading approach, increases task variety by periodically shifting workers among jobs involving different tasks. Again, the responsibility level of the tasks stays the same. The rotation can be arranged according to almost any time schedule, such as hourly, daily, or weekly schedules.

Many contemporary businesses use job enlargement and job rotation. However, the results have sometimes been disappointing since the nature of the tasks performed largely remains unchanged. An important benefit of job rotation, though, is training. It allows workers to become more familiar with different tasks and increases the flexibility with which they can be moved from one job to another.

> **Job enlargement** increases job breadth and task variety by adding new tasks of similar difficulty to a job.

> **Job rotation** increases job breadth and task variety by shifting workers among jobs involving tasks of similar difficulty.

▼ JOB ENRICHMENT

According to Frederick Herzberg, whose two-factor theory is discussed in Chapter 5, high levels of motivation should not be expected from jobs designed according to the rules of simplification, enlargement, or rotation.[4] "Why" asks Herzberg, "should a worker become motivated when one or more 'meaningless' tasks are added to previously existing ones or when work assignments are rotated among equally 'meaningless' tasks?" Instead of pursuing one of these job design strategies, therefore, Herzberg recommends "job enrichment."

Job enrichment is the practice of building motivating factors—such as responsibility, achievement, recognition—into job content. This job-design strategy differs from the previous ones in that it expands job content by adding some of the planning and evaluating duties normally reserved for managers. These changes increase the "depth" of a job, something Herzberg calls *vertical loading.* According to Herzberg, the added responsibility of enriched jobs will respond positively to people's higher order needs and therefore increase their motivation to work.

> **Job enrichment** increases job depth by giving workers more responsibility for planning and evaluating duties.

Despite the inherent appeal of Herzberg's job enrichment concept, some basic questions deserve to be asked and answered before we go further. *Is job enrichment expensive?* Job enrichment can be very costly, particularly when it re-

Take-A-Note 8.1

JOB ENRICHMENT PRINCIPLES

· *Allow workers to plan.*

· *Allow workers to control.*

· *Maximize job freedom.*

· *Increase task difficulty.*

· *Help workers become task experts.*

· *Provide performance feedback.*

· *Increase performance accountability.*

· *Provide complete units of work.*

quires major changes in work flows, facilities, and/or equipment. *Will workers demand higher pay?* Herzberg argues that if employees are being paid a truly competitive wage or salary, then the intrinsic rewards of performing enriched tasks will be adequate compensation. Other researchers are more skeptical, advising that pay must be carefully considered.[5] *What do the unions say?* One union official sounded this note of caution: ". . . better wages, shorter hours, vested pensions, a right to have a say in their working conditions, the right to be promoted on the basis of seniority . . . That's the kind of job enrichment that unions believe in."[6]

JOB CHARACTERISTICS THEORY

O B scholars are reluctant to apply job enrichment as a universal solution to all job performance and satisfaction problems. A diagnostic approach developed by Richard Hackman and Greg Oldham offers a broader and contingency-based framework for job design.[7]

The current version of this **job characteristics theory** is shown in Figure 8.2. Five core job characteristics are identified as particularly important to job designs; a job that is high in these core characteristics is said to be enriched. The core job characteristics are:

■ Core job characteristics

❶ *Skill variety:* The degree to which a job includes a variety of different activities and involves the use of a number of different skills and talents of the employee.

❷ *Task identity:* The degree to which the job requires completion of a "whole" and identifiable piece of work, one that involves doing a job from beginning to end with a visible outcome.

❸ *Task significance:* The degree to which the job is important and involves a meaningful contribution to the organization or society in general.

❹ *Autonomy:* The degree to which the job gives the employee substantial freedom, independence, and discretion in scheduling the work and determining the procedures used in carrying it out.

❺ *Job Feedback:* The degree to which carrying out the work activities provides direct and clear information to the employee regarding how well the job has been done.

Job characteristics theory identifies five core job characteristics of special importance to job design—skill variety, task identity, task significance, autonomy, and feedback.

To apply their model, Hackman and Oldham recommend that a job first be measured carefully in terms of its status on each of the core characteristics. In or-

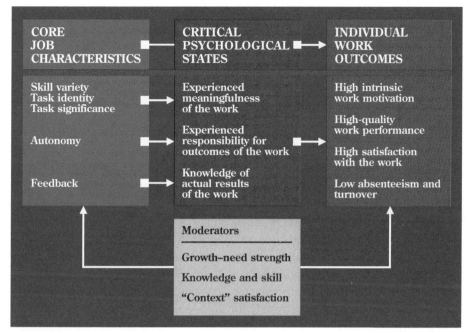

■ FIGURE 8.2
Job design implications of job characteristics theory. [Adapted from J. Richard Hackman and Greg R. Oldham, "Development of the Job Diagnostic Survey," *Journal of Applied Psychology,* Vol. 60 (1975), p. 161. Used by permission.]

der to enrich it, changes can then be made to improve upon each characteristic. Doing so, they point out, brings the advantage of positively influencing three critical psychological states that increase intrinsic work motivation: (1) experienced meaningfulness in the work; (2) experienced responsibility for the outcomes of the work; and (3) knowledge of actual results of the work activities.

▼ INDIVIDUAL DIFFERENCE MODERATORS

Importantly, job characteristics theory recognizes that the five core job characteristics do not affect all people in the same way. Simply put, not everyone's job should be enriched, and not all job-design changes should improve upon the core characteristics. The goal, instead, is to arrive at the best match of core characteristics and individual needs. In general, people whose capabilities match the requirements of an enriched job are likely to experience positive feelings and to perform well; people who are inadequate or who feel inadequate in this regard are likely to have difficulties.

Figure 8.2 highlights three individual difference moderators that can influence individual preferences in job design. First, *growth-need strength* is the degree to which a person desires the opportunity for self-direction, learning, and personal accomplishment at work. It is similar to Maslow's esteem and self-actualization and Alderfer's growth needs. The theory predicts that people with strong growth needs will respond positively to enriched jobs, whereas people low in

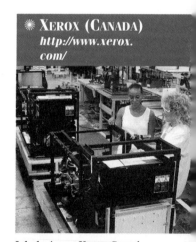

※ XEROX (CANADA)
http://www.xerox.com/

Job design at Xerox Canada is customer focused. A new business excellence process links every person's job to work objectives that support and serve customer needs. Each employee receives special training in process improvements, problem solving, group communication, and benchmarking.[8]

157

growth-need strength will find enriched jobs a source of anxiety. Second, people with the *knowledge and skill* needed for performance on an enriched job are predicted to feel good about the enrichment. Once again, we see how important a sense of competency or self-efficacy can be to people at work. Third, *context satisfaction* is the extent to which an employee is satisfied with the kind of contextual factors emphasized by Herzberg. For example, those satisfied with salary levels, supervision, and working conditions are more likely to support job enrichment than are their dissatisfied colleagues.

▼ RESEARCH RESULTS

Considerable research has been done on the job characteristics approach in a variety of work settings, including banks, dentists' offices, corrections departments, telephone companies, and in such organizations as the federal government, IBM, and Texas Instruments. Experts generally agree that the job diagnostic approach is quite useful, but it is not a universal panacea.[9] On the average, job characteristics affect performance, but not nearly as much as they do satisfaction. The research also emphasizes the importance of growth-need strength. Job characteristics tie to performance more strongly for high–growth need employees than for low–growth need employees. The relationship is about as strong as with satisfaction. It is also clear that job enrichment can fail when job requirements are increased beyond the level of individual capabilities and/or interests. Finally, it is important to note that employee perceptions of job characteristics are different from objective measures and from those of independent observers. Positive results typically are strongest when an overall performance measure is used rather than a separate measure of quality or quantity. In summary, jobs high in core characteristics (especially as perceived by employees) tend to increase both satisfaction and performance, particularly among high–growth need employees.

▼ SOCIAL INFORMATION PROCESSING

Gerald Salancik and Jeffrey Pfeffer reviewed the literature serving as a base for the job diagnostic approach to job design.[10] They questioned whether jobs have stable and objective characteristics to which individuals respond predictably and consistently. As an alternative to the job characteristics model, their **social information–processing theory** argues that individual needs, task perceptions, and reactions are a result of socially constructed realities. Thus, social information in the workplace influences a worker's perception of the job and his or her responses to it. It is very much like a student's perception of a class. For example, suppose several of your friends tell you that the instructor for a certain course is bad, the course content is boring, and the class requires too much work. You may then think that the critical characteristics of the class are the instructor, the content, and the workload, and that they are all bad. All of this may substantially influence your class perception and responses, regardless of the actual characteristics of the course.

Research on the social information–processing approach provides mixed results. Essentially, the results indicate that although social information processing does influence task perceptions and attitudes, the kinds of job characteristics de-

> The **social information–processing approach** believes that individual needs and task perceptions result from socially constructed realities.

scribed earlier are also important. The social information–processing research suggests that perceptions of job characteristics are likely to be a function of both objective characteristics and social information in the workplace. Thus, their stability and predictability, in the eye of the job holder, is determined by both objective and subjective factors.

▼ MANAGERIAL AND GLOBAL IMPLICATIONS

Once again, we can utilize a question and answer framework to summarize some final points and implications worth remembering about job enrichment. First, *should everyone's job be enriched?* The answer is "No." The logic of individual differences suggests that not everyone will want an enriched job. Individuals most likely to have positive reactions to job enrichment are those who need achievement, who hold middle-class working values, and/or who are seeking higher order growth-need satisfaction at work. Job enrichment also appears to be most advantageous when dissatisfiers are not present in job context and when workers have the abilities needed to do the enriched job. Furthermore, costs, technological constraints, and work group or union opposition may make it difficult to enrich some jobs.[12]

Second, *can job enrichment apply to groups?* The answer is "Yes." The application of job design strategies at the group level is growing in many types of settings. In the next book part we discuss creative work group designs, including cross-functional work teams and self-managing teams.

Finally, *what is the impact of culture on job enrichment?* The answer is "Substantial." Research has been conducted on perceptions of the nature of work in Belgium, Israel, Japan, The Netherlands, the United States, and Germany. Unique aspects of what constitute work were found in each country.[13] Work was most strongly seen as something expected by society in Belgium and Japan; it was seen as least so by the Germans. Work was seen as something done for money in all countries but Belgium. In most cases, however, work was seen as having an economic component and a societal contribution component. These results, as well as differences in such national culture dimensions as power distance and individualism, reinforce arguments that job enrichment needs to recognize cultural as well as individual difference considerations.

❋ **UPS**
http://www.ups.com

United Parcel Service (UPS) is well known for its operating efficiency and engineered job designs, including prescribed routes for drivers and clear delivery time guidelines. A new approach that empowers drivers to modify routes is improving customer satisfaction and productivity.[11]

TECHNOLOGY AND JOB DESIGN

The concept of **sociotechnical systems** is used in organizational behavior to indicate the importance of integrating people and technology to create high-performance organizational systems.[14] As computers and high technology make their way more and more into the modern workplace, this concept remains an important point of reference in successfully incorporating technological advancements into job designs. [15]

Sociotechnical systems integrate people and technology into high performance work settings.

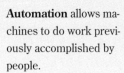

Automation allows machines to do work previously accomplished by people.

Flexible manufacturing uses adaptive technology and integrated job designs as ways to shift production among alternative products.

VOLKSWAGEN WOLFSBURG, GERMANY

Volkswagen's Wolfsburg, Germany, car plant is the world's largest and most highly automated. Robots do 80 percent of welding work and can be programmed to perform different tasks. Computers control the assembly line, adjusting production to fit schedules for different models and options.[16]

▼ ROBOTICS

Earlier in the chapter, we mentioned that highly simplified jobs often cause problems because they offer little in terms of intrinsic motivation for the worker. In such cases, the tasks have been defined so narrowly that they lack challenge and lead to boredom when the worker repeats them over and over again. Given the high technology available now, one way to deal with this is complete **automation**—allowing a machine to do the work previously accomplished through human effort. This approach increasingly involves the use of robots, which are becoming ever more versatile and reliable.

▼ FLEXIBLE MANUFACTURING

Flexible manufacturing cells utilize adaptive computer-based technologies and integrated job designs to shift work among alternative products. This approach is increasingly common, for example, with machined metal products, such as cylinder heads and gear boxes.[17] Here, a cellular manufacturing system contains a number of automated production machines that cut, shape, drill, and fasten together various metal components. Each machine is connected to the others by convertible conveyor grids that allow quick change from manufacturing one product to another—perhaps from air conditioner compressors to engine crankshafts. Some machines are turned on, others are turned off, and different conveyors are activated to connect the machines being used. Using this kind of approach, more than 100 different products can be made without substantial changes to the cell.[18] Workers in these cells perform very few routine assembly-line tasks. What they do is make sure the operations are handled correctly and deal with the changeover from one product configuration to another. Thus, each worker needs to develop expertise across the wide range of functions necessary to keep production flowing smoothly. It follows that the highly automated cells offer the potential for enriched core job characteristics.

▼ ELECTRONIC OFFICES

Electronic office technology was the key when U.S. Healthcare, a large, private practice–based health maintenance organization (HMO), became interested in improving the quality of its health-care services. The company installed large electronic bulletin boards that monitored progress toward a range of performance goals. It also installed an electronic mail (E-mail) system, put in robots to deliver the paper mail, and installed a computerized answering machine. Essentially, the company tried to automate as many tasks as possible to free people for more challenging work.[19] Similarly, Mutual Benefit Life completely reorganized the way it serviced insurance application forms—once handled by as many as 19 people across five departments. Mutual created a new case manager position responsible for processing applications from their inception until policies were issued. Accompanying this radical change in job design were powerful PC-based workstations designed to assist decision making and connected to a variety of automated subsystems on a mainframe.[20]

Continuing developments in electronic offices offer job enrichment possibilities for those workers who are equipped to handle the technology. But, they can be stressful and difficult for those who do not have the necessary education or skills. One survey showed that even in highly developed countries, such as those in Europe, 54 percent of workers possessed inadequate skills to operate a computer; the proportion was about one third in the United States.[21] People are also beginning to experience physical ailments, such as carpal tunnel syndrome, as a result of working at computer terminals and the like for long periods of time. Clearly, the high technologies of the new workplace must be carefully integrated with the human factor.

▼ WORK-FLOW AND PROCESS REENGINEERING

One of the latest approaches for improving job designs and performance is based on the concept of **process reengineering**—the analysis, streamlining, and reconfiguration of actions and tasks required to reach a work goal.[22] The process design approach systematically breaks processes down into their specific components and subtasks, analyzes each for relevance and simplicity, and then does everything possible to reconfigure the process to eliminate wasted time, effort, and resources. A classic example might be the various steps required to gain approval for a purchase order to buy a new computer. The process reengineering approach looks at every step in the process, from the search for items and vendors, to the obtaining of bids, to the completion of necessary forms, to the securing of required "signatures" and approvals, to the actual placing of the order, and so on to the point at which the new computer actually arrives, is checked in, is placed into an equipment inventory, and then is finally delivered to the workplace. In all this, one simple question drives the reengineering approach: What is necessary and what can be elminated?

> **Process reengineering** analyzes, streamlines, and reconfigures actions and tasks to achieve work goals.

Novell Corporation, a leading software vendor for groups and networking environments, isn't letting the great potential of work-flow and business process

reengineering pass unnoticed. The company offers GroupWise Workflow as a graphical tool for managing the decision processes involved in such reengineering approaches. The software focuses user attention first on roles—who does what in the process—and then on processes—when and how they do it and at what stage in the cycle. The firm believes that the software encourages people to work together in the reengineering process and supports the notion of worker enpowerment in the search for continuous organizational improvement.[23]

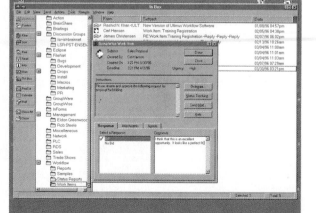

GOAL SETTING

G oals are important aspects of any job design. Without proper goals, employees may suffer a direction problem. Some years ago, for example, a Minnesota Vikings' defensive end gathered up an opponent's fumble. Then, with obvious effort and delight, he ran the ball into the *wrong* end zone. Clearly, the athlete did not lack motivation. Unfortunately, though, he failed to channel his energies toward the right goal. Similar problems are found in many work settings. They can be eliminated, or at least reduced, by the proper setting and clarification of task goals.

▼ GOAL-SETTING THEORY

Goal setting is the process of developing and setting motivational performance objectives.

Goal setting is the process of developing, negotiating, and formalizing the targets or objectives that a person is responsible for accomplishing.[24] Over a number of years, Edwin Locke and his associates have developed a comprehensive framework linking goals to performance as shown in Figure 8.3. The model uses elements of expectancy theory from Chapter 5 to help clarify the implications of

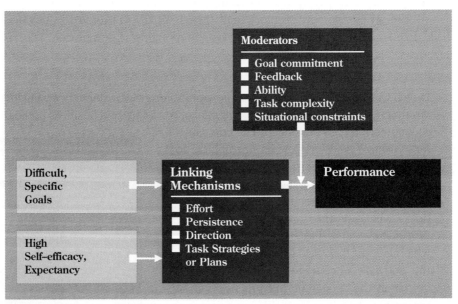

■   FIGURE 8.3

Essentials of the Locke and Latham goal-setting framework. [Based on Edwin A. Locke and Gary P. Latham "Work Motivation and Satisfaction: Light at the End of the Tunnel," *Psychological Science,* Vol. 1, No. 4 (July 1990), p. 244.]

goal setting for performance while taking into account certain moderating conditions, such as ability and task complexity.

▼ MANAGERIAL AND GLOBAL IMPLICATIONS

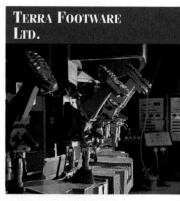

TERRA FOOTWARE LTD.

Research using and extending these predictions is now quite extensive. Indeed, there is more research for goal setting than for any other theory related to work motivation.[25] Nearly 400 studies have been conducted in several countries, including Australia, England, Germany, Japan, and the United States.[26] The basic precepts of goal-setting theory remain a most important source of advice for managing human behavior in the work setting.

Managerially speaking, the implications of the Locke and Latham model and related goal-setting research can be summarized as follows.[27] First, *difficult goals are more likely to lead to higher performance than are less difficult ones.* However, if the goals are seen as *too* difficult or impossible, the relationship with performance no longer holds. For example, you are likely to sell more if you have a goal of six refrigerators a month than if you have a goal of three. However, if your goal is 60 refrigerators a month, you may see that as impossible, and your performance very likely will be lower than with a goal of six.

Second, *specific goals are more likely to lead to higher performance than are no goals or vague or very general ones.* All too often people work with very general goals such as the encouragement to "do your best." Research clearly indicates that more specific goals, such as selling six computers a day, are much more motivational than a simple "do your best" goal.

Third, *task feedback, or knowledge of results, is likely to motivate people toward higher performance by encouraging the setting of higher performance goals.* Feedback lets people know where they stand and whether they are on course or off course in their efforts. For example, think about how eager you are to find out how well you did on an examination.

Fourth, *goals are most likely to lead to higher performance when people have the abilities and the feelings of self-efficacy required to accomplish them.* The individual must actually be able to accomplish the goals and feel confident in those abilities. For example, you may actually be able to do what's required to sell six computers a day and feel confident that you can. However, if your goal is 16 computers a day, you may have neither the ability nor the confidence to accomplish it.

Fifth, *goals are most likely to motivate people toward higher performance when they are accepted and there is commitment to them.* Participating in the goal-setting process helps build such acceptance and commitment. It helps create "ownership" of the goals. However, Locke and Latham report that goals assigned by someone else can be equally effective. The assigners are likely to be authority figures, and that can have an impact. Also, the assignment implies that the subordinate can actually reach the goal. Moreover, assigned goals often are a challenge. Finally, assigned goals help define the standards people use to attain self-satisfaction with their performance. According to Locke and Latham, assigned goals lead to poor performance only when they are curtly or inadequately explained.

Sophisticated CAD/CAM technology has reduced the time for prototype development from weeks to hours for Terra Footwear Ltd. With satellite linkages and well-trained workers, a boot designed in Terra's Ontario facility can be manufactured in its Newfoundland plant on the very same day.[28]

As Chief Learning Officer at General Electric, former business school professor Stephen Kerr advocates stretch goals. He says that "if done right, a
stretch target, which basically is an extremely
ambitious goal, gets your people to perform in
ways they never imagined possible." But he also
cautions that stretch goals must be carefully
managed. They cannot be too easy or impossible
to reach; they shouldn't punish high performers
who are already working at peak levels; they require proper support from management, including training and tools; and, importantly, stretch
goals much be accompanied by a commitment to
not punish failure.[29]

▼ GOAL SETTING AND MBO

When we speak of goal setting and its potential to influence individual performance at work, the concept of *management by objectives,* or MBO, immediately
comes to mind. The essence of MBO is a process of *joint* goal setting between a
supervisor and a subordinate.[30] It involves managers working with their subordinates to establish performance goals and plans that are consistent with higher
level work unit and organizational objectives. When this process is followed
throughout an organization, MBO helps clarify the hierarchy of objectives as a series of well-defined means–end chains.

Figure 8.4 shows a comprehensive view of MBO. The concept is consistent
with the notion of goal setting and its associated principles discussed above. Notice how joint supervisor–subordinate discussions are designed to extend participation from the point of initial goal establishment to the point of evaluating results in terms of goal attainment. In addition to these goal-setting steps, a
successful MBO system calls for careful implementation. This means that the

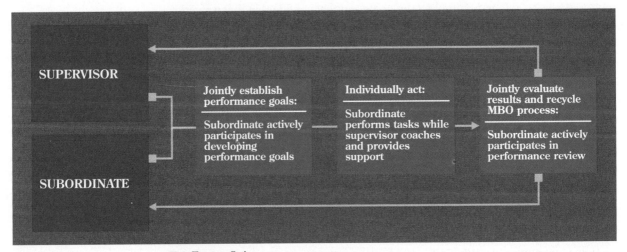

■ FIGURE 8.4
How the management by objectives process works.

previous steps are translated into the kinds of strategies or plans mentioned earlier that will lead to goal accomplishment. Subordinates must have freedom to carry out the required tasks; managers may have to do considerable coaching and counseling.

Although there is a fair amount of research based on case studies of MBO success, not much has been rigorously controlled, and what there is reports mixed results.[31] In general, and as an application of goal-setting theory, MBO has much to offer, but it is by no means easy to start and keep going. MBO also may need to be implemented organization-wide if it is to work well. Many firms have started and dropped the approach because of difficulties experienced early on. As with other applied OB programs, managers should be aware of MBO's potential costs as well as its benefits. Some specific problems to recognize include: too much emphasis on goal-oriented rewards and punishments, too much paperwork documenting goals and accomplishments, too much emphasis on top-down goals, too much emphasis on goals that are easily stated in objective terms, and too much emphasis on individual instead of group goals.

ALTERNATIVE WORK ARRANGEMENTS

Alternative ways of scheduling time at work are increasingly common. These arrangements essentially reshape the traditional 40-hour a week, 9 to 5 schedules where work is done on the premises. Virtually all such plans are designed to influence employee satisfaction and to help employees balance demands of their work and nonwork lives.[32] They are becoming more and more important in fast-changing societies where demands for more "family friendly" employers grow ever more apparent.[33] Members of our increasingly diverse workforces are increasingly concerned with fitting work responsibilities with individual needs. For example, dual-career families with children, part-time students, older workers (retired or near retirement age), single parents, and others are all candidates for alternative work arrangements. In addition, new schedules can offer more flexibility for employers as business expands or contracts.

▼ COMPRESSED WORK WEEK

A **compressed work week** is any scheduling of work that allows a full-time job to be completed in fewer than the standard 5 days. The most common form of compressed work week is the "4—40," or 40 hours of work accomplished in four 10-hour days. There are many possible benefits to this work schedule. Added time off is a major feature for the worker. The individual often benefits from increased leisure time, more 3-day weekends, free weekdays to pursue personal business, and lower commuting costs. The organization can benefit, too, in terms of reduced energy consumption during 3-day shutdowns, lower employee absenteeism, improved recruiting of new employees, and the extra time available for building and equipment maintenance.

> A **compressed work week** allows a full-time job to be completed in less than five full workdays.

The disadvantages of the compressed work week may include increased fatigue from the extended workday and family adjustment problems for the individual, as well as increased work scheduling problems and possible customer complaints because of breaks in work coverage. In addition, occasional union opposition and laws that require some organizations to pay overtime for work that exceeds 8 hours of individual labor in any 1 day are possible constraints.

Research results are mixed on the compressed work week.[34] This schedule sometimes has a positive effect on productivity, absenteeism, and the like, but this is most likely to occur when the compressed work week is first implemented. One study found that reaction to the compressed work week was most favorable for employees who had participated in the decision to compress the work week, who had their jobs enriched as a result of the new schedule, and who had strong higher order needs. The enrichment occurred because fewer employees were on duty at any one time and because job duties were changed and enriched to accommodate this reduction, since the organization was kept open the same number of days as before.

▼ FLEXIBLE WORKING HOURS

> **Flexible working hours** give employees some daily choice in scheduling arrival and departure times from work.

Flexible working hours, or *flextime,* is defined as "any work schedule that gives employees daily choice in the timing between work and nonwork activities."[35] A survey showed that of 259 companies, 42 percent used some form of flexible working time. More than 9 million workers are estimated to be on a flexible working schedule.[36] An example is one that requires employees to work 4 hours of "core" time. They are then free to choose their remaining 4 hours of work from among flexible time blocks. On the international scene an even more dramatic version of flextime is under consideration. In Austria and Germany, several firms have considered the possibility of a "flexyear." Here, workers would decide on the number of hours they want to work in the coming year and allocate them as they see fit. Their pay would be equalized each month, but their hours of work could vary.[37]

Flextime increases individual autonomy in work scheduling. Early risers may choose to come in early and leave at 4:00 p.m.; late sleepers may choose to start at 10:00 a.m. and leave at 6:00 p.m. In between these two extremes are opportunities to attend to such personal affairs as dental appointments, home emergencies, visiting the bank, and so on. Proponents of this scheduling strategy argue that the discretion it allows workers in scheduling their own hours of work encourages them to develop positive attitudes and to increase commitment to the organization. Research tends to support this position. An Aetna manager, commenting on the firm's flexible working hours program, says: "We're not doing flexible work scheduling to be nice, but because it makes business sense.[38]

Take-A-Note 8.2

BENEFITING FROM FLEXTIME

For organizations:	For workers:
Lower absenteeism	Less commuting time
Less tardiness	More leisure time
Less turnover	More job satisfaction
More commitment	Greater responsibility
Higher performance	Easier personal scheduling

▼ JOB SHARING

In **job sharing**, one full-time job is assigned to two or more persons, who then divide the work according to agreed-upon hours. Often, each person works half a day, but job sharing can also be done on weekly or monthly sharing arrangements. Although it is still practiced by only a relatively small percentage of employers, human-resource experts believe that job sharing is a valuable alternative work arrangement.[39]

> **Job sharing** allows one full-time job to be divided among two or more persons.

Organizations can benefit from job sharing when they are able to attract talented people who would otherwise be unable to work. An example is the qualified teacher who also is a parent. This person may feel unable to be away from the home a full day but is able to work half a day. Through job sharing, two such persons can be employed to teach one class. Some job sharers report less burnout and claim that they feel recharged each time they report for work. Finding the right people is very important since they must work well with each other. When middle managers Sue Mannix and Charlotte Shutzman worked together at Bell Atlantic, for example, they faithfully covered each other's absences and oversights at work. Shutzman worked Mondays, Tuesdays, and Wednesday mornings; Mannix worked the rest of the work week.[40]

Job sharing should not be confused with *work sharing,* a more controversial subject. Work sharing occurs when workers agree to cut back on the number of hours worked in order to protect against layoffs. It might be agreed for workers to voluntarily reduce 20 percent of hours worked and pay received rather than to have 20 percent of the workforce cut by the employer during difficult economic times. This practice is prohibited in some settings by legal restrictions. In Canada, for example, requests from Bell Canada to implement such programs have been turned down in the past.[41]

▼ PART-TIME WORK

Part-time work has become a work arrangement of increasing prominence and controversy. There are two kinds of part-time work: **temporary part-time work** (an employee is classified as "temporary" and works less than the standard 40-hour work week) and **permanent part-time work** (a worker is considered "permanent" but works fewer hours than the standard work week). Note that employees involved in job sharing typically fit this latter category.

> **Temporary part-time work** is when someone temporarily works fewer than the standard 40 hours in 1 week.

Temporary part-timers are usually easy to release and hire as needs dictate. Accordingly, many organizations use part-time work to hold down labor costs and to help smooth out peaks and valleys in the business cycle. Employers also may use part-time work to better manage what may be called "retention quality." These are highly skilled individuals committed to their careers who want to continue to develop professionally but who can only work part time. Part-time nurses, among others, fall in this category.[42]

> **Permanent part-time work** is when someone permanently works fewer than the standard 40 hours in 1 week.

The part-time work schedule can be a benefit to people who also hold full-time jobs or who want something less than a full work week for a variety of personal reasons. For someone who is holding two jobs, including at least one part time, the added burdens can be stressful and may affect performance in either one or both work settings. Furthermore, part-timers often fail to qualify for fringe benefits, such as health care, life insurance, and pensions, and they may be paid less then their full-time counterparts. Nevertheless, part-time work schedules are of growing practical importance because of the organizational advantages listed previously.

▼ TELECOMMUTING

Telecommuting is work at home or in remote location that uses computer and other electronic communication linkages with the corporate office.

High technology is influencing another alternative work arrangement that is increasingly prominent in many employment sectors of our society—from higher education to government, and from manufacturing to services. **Telecommuting** describes work done at home or in a remote location via use of a computer and/or facsimile machine linked to a central office or some other employment location. Sometimes this arrangement is called *flexiplace*. At IBM, Canada, "flexiplace" means working from a home office and coming to IBM offices for meetings.[43] At other firms it means being on the road with a "virtual office" or being physically located at a customer's site while linked electronically with the home office. In these and other cases, telecommuting emphasizes place rather than scheduling, although working at home does allow flexible working hours. Estimates are that some $8\frac{1}{2}$ million workers are telecommuting in the United States, and the numbers are growing daily.[44]

QUALITY

Many members of American Express Travel Related Services Company's 240-person core sales staff telecommute to work daily. Groupware, modems, cellular telephones, and a home or mobile office are ways of life. Managers send daily messages; sales representatives are only occasionally in the corporate office. But they are always in the information "loop" and job performance hasn't suffered. If asked, in fact, most would probably find many reasons that telecommuting is far better than being tied to standard hours and a home office berth.[45]

For the individual, telecommuting offers the potential advantages of flexibility, the comforts of home, and choice of locations consistent with one's lifestyle. In terms of advantages to the organization, a Denver employment agency owner reports that he cut central office overhead from 16 consultants to 4. He gave the other 12 consultants office furniture, and they work from their homes.[46] In contrast, firms have tried telecommuting and dropped it. Managerial considerations in dealing with remote employees seem to be a prime reason. Other reasons are a sense of isolation from coworkers, decreased identification with the work team, and technical difficulties with computer linkages.

CHAPTER 8 STUDY GUIDE

SUMMARY

What are the basic job-design approaches?

- Job design is the creation of tasks and work settings for specific jobs.
- Job design by scientific management or job simplification standardizes work and employs people in very clearly defined and specialized tasks.
- Job enlargement increases task variety by combining two or more tasks previously assigned to separate workers.
- Job rotation increases task variety by periodically rotating workers among jobs involving different tasks.
- Job enrichment builds bigger and more responsible jobs by adding planning and evaluating duties.

What is the job characteristics theory?

- Job characteristics theory offers a diagnostic approach to job enrichment based on the analysis of five core job characteristics: skill variety, task identity, task significance, autonomy, and feedback.
- The theory does not assume that everyone wants an enriched job; it indicates that job enrichment will be more successful for persons with high growth needs, requisite job skills, and context satisfaction.
- The social information–processing theory points out that information from coworkers and others in the workplace influences a worker's perceptions and responses to a job.
- Not everyone's job should be enriched; job enrichment can be done for groups as well as individuals; cultural factors may influence job enrichment success.

How does technology influence job design?

- Well-planned sociotechnical systems integrate people and technology for high performance.
- Robotics and complete automation are increasingly used to replace people to perform jobs that are highly simplified and repetitive.
- Workers in flexible manufacturing cells utilize the latest technology to produce high-quality products with short cycle times.
- The nature of office work is being changed by computer workstation technologies, networks, and various forms of electronic communication.
- Work-flow and business process reengineering analyzes all steps in work sequences to streamline activities and tasks, save costs, and improve performance.

How can goal setting improve job outcomes?

- Goal setting is the process of developing, negotiating, and formalizing performance targets or objectives.
- Research supports predictions that the most motivational goals are challenging and specific, allow for feedback on results, and create commitment and acceptance.

- The motivational impact of goals may be affected by individual difference moderators such as ability and self-efficacy.
- Management by objectives is a process of joint goal setting between a supervisor and worker.
- The management by objectives process is a good action framework for applying goal-setting theory on an organization-wide basis.

What alternative work arrangements are used today?
- Today's complex society is giving rise to a number of alternative work arrangements designed to balance the personal demands on workers with job responsibilities and opportunities.
- The compressed work week allows a full-time work week to be completed in under 5 days, typically offering four 10-hour days of work and 3 days free.
- Flexible working hours allow employees some daily choice in timing between work and nonwork activities.
- Job sharing occurs when two or more people divide one full-time job according to agreements among themselves and the employer.
- Part-time work requires less than a 40-hour work week, and can be done on a schedule classifying the worker as temporary or permanent.
- Telecommuting involves work at home or at a remote location while communicating to the home office as needed via computer and related technologies.

KEY TERMS

Automation (p. 160)

Compressed work week (p. 165)

Flexible manufacturing (p. 160)

Flexible working hours (p. 166)

Goal setting (p. 162)

Job characteristics theory (p. 156)

Job design (p. 154)

Job enlargement (p. 155)

Job enrichment (p. 155)

Job rotation (p. 155)

Job sharing (p. 167)

Job simplification (p. 154)

Permanent part-time work (p. 167)

Process reengineering (p. 161)

Social Information processing (p. 158)

Sociotechnical systems (p. 159)

Telecommuting (p. 168)

Temporary part-time work (p. 167)

SELF-TEST 8

▼ MULTIPLE CHOICE
1. Job simplification is closely associated with _____ as originally developed by Frederick Taylor. (a) vertical loading (b) horizontal loading (c) scientific management (d) self-efficacy
2. Job _____ increases job _____ by combining into one job several tasks of similar difficulty. (a) rotation; depth (b) enlargement; depth (c) rotation; breadth (d) enlargement; breadth
3. In job characteristics theory, _____ indicates the degree to which an individual is able to make decisions affecting his or her work. (a) task variety (b) task identity (c) task significance (d) autonomy

4. The basic logic of sociotechnical systems is that: (a) people must be integrated with technology. (b) technology is more important than people. (c) people are more important than technology. (d) technology alienates people.

5. Which goals tend to be more motivating? (a) challenging goals (b) easy goals (c) general goals (d) low-feedback goals

6. The MBO process emphasizes _____ as a way of building worker commitment to goal accomplishment. (a) authority (b) joint goal setting (c) infrequent feedback (d) general goals

7. _____ is one of the concerns sometimes raised about organization-wide MBO programs. (a) Too much paperwork (b) Too little paperwork (c) Too little emphasis on top-down goals (d) Too much emphasis on group instead of individual goals

8. The "4—40" is a type of _____ work arrangement. (a) compressed work week (b) flextime (c) job sharing (d) permanent part-time

9. The flexible working hours schedule allows workers to choose _____. (a) days of week to work (b) total hours to work in week (c) location of work (d) starting and ending times for work days

10. Today's society is creating a demand for more jobs that by design _____. (a) are easy to perform (b) minimize the need for employee skills (c) are family friendly (d) have low performance goals

▼ TRUE–FALSE

11. In some cases, job enrichment may be difficult to implement because of the expenses involved and/or union opposition. T F

12. The characteristic of task significance indicates the degree to which a job is meaningful to the organization or society. T F

13. According to job characteristics theory, everyone's job should be enriched. T F

14. The social information–processing approach stresses the importance of objective job characteristics to motivation and performance. T F

15. Job enrichment is a management practice that is not universally applicable in all cultural settings. T F

16. One sure way to motivate through goal setting is to tell people to simply "do your best." T F

17. Goals are most likely to lead to higher performance for people high in feelings of self-efficacy. T F

18. Flextime is unique in that it offers advantages to the individual worker with no disadvantages for the employer. T F

19. Trends seem to indicate that telecommuting has considerable appeal to members of the emerging and diverse workforce. T F

20. The presence of more part-time work is a uniformly positive trend from a societal perspective. T F

▼ SHORT RESPONSE

21. How does "vertical loading" create job enrichment?

22. What role does growth-need strength play in job characteristics theory?

23. How can a manager increase employee commitment to stated task goals?

24. What is the difference between temporary part-time and permanent part-time work?

▼ APPLICATIONS ESSAY

25. When Jean-Paul Latrec opened his first "Outfitter's Plus" store, he wanted to create a motivational work environment for his sales associates. He decided to implement MBO as a core management strategy. Over time he became well known in Quebec City for his success. If you were to visit his store to study Jean-Paul's MBO approach, what would you expect to find him doing to make the program work so well?

9

THE NATURE OF GROUPS

Stanford University Professor Harold J. Leavitt has been writing about human behavior at work for many years. Author of the popular book *Managerial Psychology,* Leavitt is well known as an advocate for the power and usefulness of groups in organizations. His classic article "Suppose We Took Groups Seriously" is a widely cited appeal for groups to be given more attention—an appeal that has largely been heard, given recent developments with teams and teamwork in the modern organization. His recent article on "hot groups" carries the theme even further. Along with his colleague Jean Lipman-Blumen, Leavitt now speaks about special groups of high-achieving members who are excited and turned on to highly challenging tasks. The characteristics of hot groups are described as "vital, absorbing, full of debate, laugh-

ter, and very hard work" regardless of whether they are called committees, task forces, or teams. The original team that created Apple's Macintosh computer is cited as a prime example. Working in a separate building flying the "Jolly Roger," the team members combined youthful enthusiasm with great expertise and commitment to an exciting task. The result was a benchmark computer produced in record time. Hot groups are best at creativity and innovation in short time frames. They thrive in conditions of crisis and competition. They require special treatment and support. And, they can generate special returns for the organization and for their members. "For many people," say Leavitt and Lipman-Blumen, "membership in such a group is a peak experience." (http://www-mech.ust.hk/faculty/pcheng.html)[1]

Without any doubt, the new workplace values change and adaptation. Pressures abound for organizations to experiment continually with new ways of operating in the quest for higher productivity, total quality and service, customer satisfaction, and better quality of working life. And among the many trends and developments, none is more important than attempts to tap the full potential of groups more creatively as critical organizational resources. Groups of various forms and types are increasingly prominent as organizations seek the advantages of smaller size, flatter structures, and more flexible operations. To meet competitive demands in challenging environments, the best organizations mobilize groups in many capacities and help them reach their full potential as high-performance systems.

Groups can be important sources of performance, creativity, and enthusiasm. This chapter introduces you to the basic attributes of groups as they are found in organizations. As you read Chapter 9, keep in mind these study questions:

- How do groups help organizations?
- What are the stages of group development?
- What are the foundations of group effectiveness?
- What are group dynamics?
- How do groups make decisions?

GROUPS IN ORGANIZATIONS

Formally defined, a **group** is a collection of two or more people who work with one another regularly to achieve one or more common goals. In a true group, members are mutually dependent on one another to achieve common goals, and they interact with one another regularly to pursue those goals over a sustained period of time.[2] Importantly, groups are good for both organizations and their members. Groups help accomplish important tasks, and they help maintain a high-quality workforce. The noted scholar Harold J. Leavitt points out the following benefits of the organizational use of groups.[3]

Groups involve two or more people working together regularly to achieve common goals.

- Groups are good for people.
- Groups can improve creativity.
- Groups sometimes make better decisions.
- Groups can increase commitments to decisions.
- Groups have control over their members.
- Groups help offset effects of large organization size.

■ Advantages of groups

▼ GROUPS AND TASK PERFORMANCE

Groups can help organizations accomplish important tasks. In particular, groups offer the potential for **synergy**—the creation of a whole that is greater than the sum of its parts. When synergy occurs, groups accomplish more than the total of their members' individual capabilities. Group synergy is necessary for organizations to become competitive and achieve long-term prosperity in today's dynamic times.[4]

Synergy is the creation of a whole greater than the sum of its parts.

When asked how Chrysler is able to turn out fleet after fleet of best selling cars, CEO Robert Eaton answers in one word—"empowerment." He's referring to a team-oriented approach to new model development. Workers from engineering, manufacturing, design, finance, marketing, and other areas come together in cross-functional teams. They work together to meet vehicle design, performance, and cost goals sketched out by a top management group. Given that contract, says Eaton, team members "then go away and do it, and they don't get back to us unless they have a major problem."[5]

QUALITY

Research shows that groups often have three performance advantages over individuals acting alone.[6] First, when the presence of an "expert" is uncertain, groups seem to make better judgments than does the average individual alone. Second, when problem solving can be handled by a division of labor and the sharing of information, groups are typically more successful than individuals. And third, because of their tendencies to make more risky decisions, groups can be more creative and innovative than individuals.

At the same time, however, we know that groups can also have problems. The very word "group" raises both positive and negative reactions in the minds of most people. Although it is said that "Two heads are better than one," we are also warned that "Too many cooks spoil the broth." The issue here is how well group members work together to accomplish a task. This includes a concern for **social**

Social loafing occurs when people work less hard in groups than they would individually.

loafing, also known as the "Ringelmann effect."[7] Ringlemann, a German psychologist, pinpointed this by asking people to pull as hard as they could on a rope, first alone and then in a group. He found that average productivity dropped as more people joined the rope-pulling task. Thus, the Ringlemann effect acknowledges that people may tend not to work as hard in groups as they would individually, for two reasons: (1) their contribution is less noticeable and (2) they prefer to see others carry the workload. One reason for studying groups in OB is to learn how to minimize social loafing and maximize performance outcomes.

▼ GROUPS AND INDIVIDUAL NEEDS

Groups can have a substantial impact on their members' attitudes and behaviors in the workplace. Ideally, this influence is beneficial to the organization and the individuals, helping to improve both task performance and job satisfaction. For example, groups are places where many people really learn how to do their jobs and share job skills and knowledge. The learning environment and pool of experience within a group can be used to solve difficult and unique problems, something especially helpful to newcomers who often need help in their jobs. In a good group, members offer one another support and performance feedback. This helps them acquire and improve job competencies, and may even make up for deficiencies in organizational training systems.

Group members also communicate expectations to one another that may encourage or discourage high levels of work effort. For example, a new employee soon learns from coworkers who the "bad" supervisors are and who can and cannot be "trusted." These influences may even extend to how the individual should feel about his or her job and the organization. Again, managers would like all influences within groups to be as positive and supportive of organizational goals as possible.

Perhaps the most apparent function of groups is their ability to satisfy the needs of their members. Groups offer opportunities for social interactions and interpersonal relations. Groups can provide individual security in the form of direct work assistance and technical advice, and they can offer emotional support in times of special crisis or pressure. Groups also give their members a sense of identification and offer opportunities for ego involvement by allowing them to assist in group activities.

▼ FORMAL AND INFORMAL GROUPS

Formal groups are officially designated for a specific organizational purpose.

Progressive managers in the new workplace are finding ways to utilize groups in ways that benefit group members and organizations. This requires an awareness of different types of groups and their potential applications. A **formal group** is officially designated to serve a specific organizational purpose. An example is the work unit headed by a manager and consisting of one or more direct reports. Such a group has been created by the organization to perform a specific task, typically involving the use of resources to create a product such as a report, decision, service, or commodity.[8] The head of a formal group is responsible for the group's performance accomplishments, but it is the members who largely do the required work.

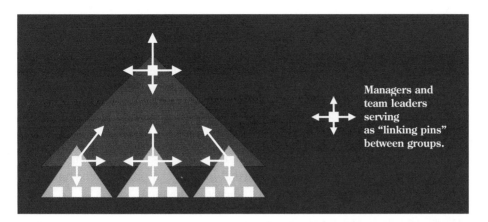

As shown in Figure 9.1, one way to view organizations is as interlocking networks of work groups.[9] In this network structure managers play "linking-pin" roles by serving as superiors in one work group and as subordinates in another at the next higher level. Whereas the manager of a branch bank is "in charge" of the branch, for example, she is also one of several branch managers who report to the bank president at the next higher level.

Formal groups may be permanent or temporary in nature. *Permanent work groups,* or command groups, often appear on organization charts as departments (e.g., market research department), divisions (e.g., consumer-products division), or teams (e.g., product-assembly team), among others. Such groups can vary in size from very small departments or teams of just a few people to large divisions employing a hundred or more people. In all cases, permanent work groups are officially created to perform a specific function on an ongoing basis. They continue to exist until a decision is made to change or reconfigure the organization for some reason.

In contrast, *temporary work groups,* or task groups, are created for a specific purpose—to solve a specific problem or to perform a defined task—and typically disband once that purpose has been accomplished.[10] Examples are the many temporary committees and task forces that are important components of any organization. Indeed, today's organizations tend to make more use of *cross-functional task forces* for special problem-solving efforts. The president of a company, for example, might convene a task force to examine the possibility of implementing flexible work hours for nonmanagerial employees. Usually, such temporary groups appoint chairpersons or heads who are held accountable for results, much as is the manager of a work unit. Another common form is the *project team* that is formed, often cross-functionally, to complete a specific task with a well-defined end point. Examples include installing a new E-mail system and introducing a new product modification.[11]

Informal groups emerge without being officially designated by the organization. They form spontaneously and are based on personal relationships or special interests, not because of specific organizational endorsement. Importantly, they are commonly found within most formal groups. *Friendship groups* consist of per-

ROVER GROUP

"Teamwork in engineering" was the motto when Rover Group of Great Britain set out to develop a new car engine. Supported by special training and careful selection of members, cross-functional project groups and teams brought commitment and insight to a high-quality final product.[12]

> **Informal groups** are unofficial and emerge to serve special interests.

sons with natural affinities for one another; they may tend to work together, sit together, take breaks together, and even do things together outside of the workplace. *Interest groups* consist of persons who share common interests; these may be job-related interests, such as an intense desire to learn more about computers, or nonwork interests, such as community service, sports, or religion.

Informal groups often help people get their jobs done. They offer a network of interpersonal relationships with the potential to "speed up" the work flow or "gain favors" in ways that formal lines of authority fail to provide. They also help individuals satisfy needs that are thwarted or otherwise left unmet in a formal group. In these and related ways, informal groups can provide their members with social satisfactions, security, and a sense of belonging.

STAGES OF GROUP DEVELOPMENT

Groups typically pass through different stages in their life cycles and, depending on the stage it is at, a group may have different challenges and management needs. The five stages of group development are: (1) forming, (2) storming, (3) norming, (4) performing, and (5) adjourning.[13]

▼ FORMING STAGE

In the *forming stage* of group development, a primary concern is the initial entry of members to a group. At this point, individuals ask a number of questions as they begin to identify with other group members and with the group itself. Their concerns may include: "What can the group offer me?" "What will I be asked to contribute?" "Can my needs be met at the same time I contribute to the group?" People are interested in discovering what is considered acceptable behavior, in determining the real task of the group, and in defining group rules. All this is likely to be more complicated in the workplace than in other settings. Members of a new task force, for example, may have been in the organization for a substantial period of time. Such factors as multiple group memberships and identifications, prior experience with group members in other contexts, and impressions of organization philosophies, goals, and policies may affect how these members initially behave in the newly formed task force.

▼ STORMING STAGE

The *storming stage* of group development is a period of high emotionality and tension among the group members. Hostility and infighting may occur during this stage, and the group typically experiences many changes. Membership expectations tend to be clarified and further elaborated. Attention begins to shift toward obstacles standing in the way of group goals. Individuals begin to understand one another's interpersonal styles, and efforts are made to find ways to accomplish group goals while also satisfying individual needs. Outside demands, including premature expectations for performance results, may create pressures at this time. Depending on the group's size and membership composition, coalitions or cliques may form. Conflict may develop over leadership and authority, as individuals compete to impose their preferences on the group and to achieve their desired status position.

▼ NORMING STAGE

The *norming stage* of group development, sometimes referred to as the *initial integration stage,* is the point at which the group really begins to come together as a coordinated unit. At this point, the interpersonal probes and jockeying behaviors of the storming phase give way to a precarious balancing of forces. In their pleasure at the new sense of harmony, group members will most likely strive to maintain this balance; minority viewpoints and tendencies to deviate from or to question group directions will be discouraged. Initial integration provides group members with a preliminary sense of closeness; consequently, members will want to protect the group from disintegration. Indeed, holding the group together may become more important to some than successfully working on the group's tasks. Thus, this stage may be misperceived by some group members as one of ultimate maturity. In fact, the sense of premature accomplishment needs to be carefully managed as a "stepping stone" to a higher level of group development and not an end in itself.

▼ PERFORMING STAGE

The *performing stage* of group development, sometimes referred to as the *total integration stage,* sees the emergence of a mature, organized, and well-functioning group. The integration begun in the previous stage is completed during this period. The group is now able to deal with complex tasks and to handle membership disagreements in creative ways. Group structure is stable, and members are motivated by group goals and are generally satisfied. The primary challenges of this stage relate largely to continued work on relationships and performance, but with a strong commitment to continuing improvement and self-renewal. Group members should be able to adapt successfully as opportunities and demands change over time. A group that has achieved the level of total integration typically scores high on the criteria of group maturity shown in Figure 9.2.

▼ ADJOURNING STAGE

A well-integrated group is able to disband, if required, when its work is accomplished. The *adjourning stage* of group development is especially important for the many temporary groups that are increasingly common in the new workplace, including task forces, committees, and the like. Members of these groups must be able to convene quickly, do their jobs on a tight schedule, and then adjourn— often to reconvene later if needed. The willingness of members to disband when the job is done and to work well together in future responsibilities, group or otherwise, is an important long-run test of group success.

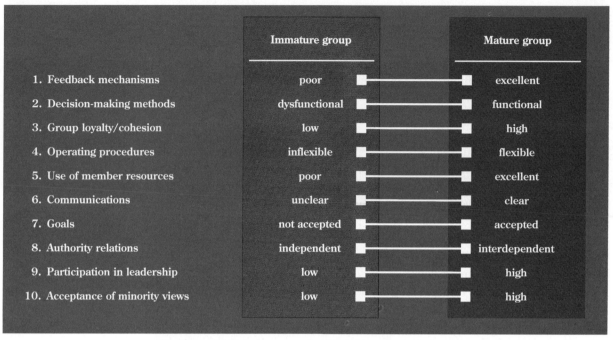

	Immature group			Mature group
1. Feedback mechanisms	poor			excellent
2. Decision-making methods	dysfunctional			functional
3. Group loyalty/cohesion	low			high
4. Operating procedures	inflexible			flexible
5. Use of member resources	poor			excellent
6. Communications	unclear			clear
7. Goals	not accepted			accepted
8. Authority relations	independent			interdependent
9. Participation in leadership	low			high
10. Acceptance of minority views	low			high

■ FIGURE 9.2

Ten criteria for measuring the "maturity" of a group. [Source: Developed from Edgar H. Schein, *Process Consultation,* Vol. 1. Copyright © 1988. Addison-Wesley Publishing Company, Inc., Chapter 6.]

FOUNDATIONS OF GROUP EFFECTIVENESS

The success of organizations depends in large part on how their internal networks of formal and informal groups perform. Like individuals, groups must "do well" for the organization to prosper over the long run. But just what does this mean?

Effective groups achieve high levels of both task performance and human resource maintenance.

An **effective group** is one that achieves high levels of both task performance and human resource maintenance over time. In respect to *task performance,* an effective group achieves its performance goals—in the standard sense of timely and high-quality work results. For a permanent work group, such as a manufacturing team, this may mean meeting daily work targets; for a temporary group, such as a new policy task force, this may involve submitting a draft of a new organizational policy to the company president. In respect to *human resource maintenance,* an effective group is one whose members are sufficiently satisfied with their tasks, accomplishments, and interpersonal relationships to work well together on an ongoing basis. For a permanent work group, this means that the members work well together workday after workday; for a temporary work group, it means that the members work well together for the duration of the assignment.

The systems model in Figure 9.3 shows how, like organizations, groups interact with their environments to transform resource inputs into product outputs.[14]

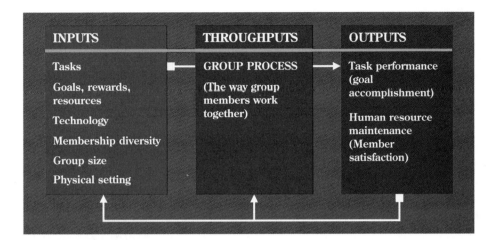

■ FIGURE 9.3
The work group as an open system transforming resource inputs into product outputs.

The inputs are the initial "givens" in a group situation; they are the foundations for all group action. In general, it can be said that the stronger the input foundations, the better the chances for long-term group effectiveness.

▼ TASKS

Different tasks place various demands on a group. *Technical demands* include: How unique is the task to be accomplished? How difficult is the task? How dispersed is the information needed to accomplish the task? Compared to simple tasks, complex tasks are technically more demanding. They require unique solutions and they require more information processing to make this performance possible. *Social demands* relate to ego involvement and agreements on issues of ends and means. Compared to simple tasks, complex ones are more socially demanding. Although very ego involving, they also make it more difficult to reach agreement on either the ends or the means for accomplishing them.

It is usually harder to achieve group effectiveness when the task is highly complex.[15] To master complexity, group members must apply and distribute their efforts broadly; they must also cooperate more to achieve desired results. When successful, however, group members usually experience high levels of satisfaction from accomplishing complex tasks.

▼ GOALS, REWARDS, AND RESOURCES

Appropriate goals, well-designed reward systems, and essential resources are all necessary for group members to work hard together in support of long-term performance accomplishments. As in the case of individuals, a group's performance can suffer when goals are unclear, insufficiently challenging, or arbitrarily imposed from the outside. Groups can also suffer if goals and rewards are focused too much on individual outcomes. Organizational resources important to the work group include such things as adequate budgets, the right facilities, good work methods and procedures, and the best technologies. A good work setting supports a group or team by providing the resources needed to utilize the members' talents fully and achieve high-performance results.

A task force formed to ex-amine problems with GTE's Mobilnet business had un-expected results. Members liked the job so much that most decided to stay on af-ter the assignment was fin-ished. They formed a nine-person mobile SWAT team to help local operations de-bug the system.[16]

Status congruence in-volves consistency be-tween a person's status within and outside of a group.

▼ TECHNOLOGY

Technology is the means through which work gets accomplished, and having the right technology is an important group asset. The nature of the technology can also influence the way group members interact with one another while working on tasks. It is one thing to be part of a group that crafts products to specific cus-tomer requests; it is quite another to be part of a group whose members staff one section of a machine-paced assembly line. The former technology allows for more interaction among group members. It will probably create a closer knit group that has a stronger sense of identity than the one formed around one small segment of an assembly line.

▼ MEMBERSHIP DIVERSITY

The attributes and diversity of individual group members can also affect both the way the group operates and what it accomplishes. A *heterogeneous group* whose members differ greatly in basic characteristics—age, gender, race, ethnicity, ex-perience, and the like—has a wide pool of human resources that it can bring to bear on complex problems. But the members may have some difficulty working together because of their differences. Research, for example, suggests that di-verse groups may encounter short-term difficulties as they learn to work to-gether. Once they do learn this, however, the groups have high-performance po-tential.[17] Members in a *homogeneous group,* by contrast, may work easily and well together. But, they may also have performance limitations if their collective skills and experiences are not a good match for complex tasks.

Having the right *skills and competencies* available for group problem solving is obviously critical to performance success. Although talents alone cannot guar-antee desired results, they establish an important baseline of potential perfor-mance accomplishments. When the input competencies are insufficient in any way, a group will operate with performance limits that are difficult to overcome.

The mix of personalities is also important in a group or team. The *FIRO-B theory* helps explain how people orient themselves toward one another based on their needs to express and receive feelings of inclusion, control, and affection.[18] The theory points out that groups whose members are "compatible" on these needs are more likely to be effective than are groups whose members are more "incompatible" on them. Symptoms of harmful incompatibilities include the pres-ence of withdrawn members, open hostilities, struggles over control, and domina-tion of the group by a few members. William Schutz, whose FIRO-B Scale mea-sures needs for inclusion, control, and affection, states the management implications this way: "If at the outset we can choose a group of people who can work together harmoniously, we shall go far toward avoiding situations where a group's efforts are wasted in interpersonal conflicts."[19]

Another diversity issue relates to a person's *status,* or relative rank, prestige, or standing in a group. This standing can be based on any number of factors, in-cluding someone's age, work seniority, occupation, education, work accomplish-ments, or status in other groups. **Status congruence** occurs when members are placed in positions within the group that are equivalent with the status of their po-sitions outside of the group. In high–power distance cultures, such as Hong Kong and Malaysia, the chair of a committee is expected to be the highest ranking or senior member of the group. The maintenance of such status congruity allows the group members to feel comfortable and for the group to proceed more harmoniously with its work. Status *in*congruity, however, may cause problems in groups. This may arise if the senior member is not appointed to head the committee. Likewise, it may occur when a young college graduate is appointed to chair a project group composed of older and more experienced workers.

▼ GROUP SIZE

The size of a group, as measured by the number of members, can make a difference in its effectiveness. As a group becomes larger, more people are available to divide up the work and accomplish needed tasks. This can boost performance and member satisfaction, up to a point. As a group continues to grow larger, however, communication and coordination problems often set in. Satisfaction may dip, and turnover, absenteeism, and social loafing may increase. Even logistical matters, such as finding time and locations for meetings, become more difficult with larger groups, negatively affecting performance.[20]

In problem-solving groups of *fewer than five members,* there are less people to share responsibilities. This typically results in more personal discussions and more participation by all members. In problem-solving groups of *more than seven members,* there tend to be fewer opportunities for participation, and members may be more inhibited in offering ideas. There is also the possibility of domination by aggressive members and tendencies for the larger group to split into coalitions or subgroups.[21] Thus, a good size for problem-solving groups is between five and seven members.

Groups with an *even number of members* seem more prone to sustained disagreement and conflict while working on tasks. The even number makes it harder for a dominant coalition to form or for one position to get a majority if a vote is taken. It seems easier for groups with an *odd number of members* to form coalitions and to take majority votes to resolve disagreements. Where speed is required, this form of conflict management behavior is useful, and odd-numbered groups may be preferred. But where careful deliberations are required, and the emphasis is more on consensus, such as in jury duty or very complex problem solving, even-numbered groups may be more effective; unless the members deadlock.[22]

GROUP DYNAMICS

Group effectiveness, as shown in Figure 9.3, always depends in part on how well members work together to utilize resource inputs to produce task outputs. This is an issue of **group dynamics**—the forces operating in groups which affect task performance and human resource maintenance. If the group is an open system that transforms resource inputs into product outputs, group dynamics are the "processes" through which this transformation is accomplished.

> **Group dynamics** are the forces operating in groups that affect the ways members work together.

SAN FRANCISCO'S
FAIRMONT HOTEL

The service goals of San
Francisco's Fairmont Hotel
are enhanced by front-desk
clerks who are empowered
to respond as they see fit to
a variety of customer re-
quests. One clerk says:
"We pretend like it's our
hotel, and we can take care
of problems ourselves."[24]

Intergroup dynamics
are relationships be-
tween groups cooperat-
ing and competing with
one another.

▼ REQUIRED AND EMERGENT BEHAVIORS

In George Homans' classic model of group dynamics *required behaviors* are what the organization formally requests from group members as a basis for continued affiliation and support.[23] They may include such work-related behaviors as punctuality, customer respect, and assistance to coworkers. *Emergent behaviors* are what group members do in addition to, or in place of, what is formally asked of them by the organization. They exist purely as matters of individual or group choice. Often, they are things people do that go beyond formal job requirements and help get the job done. An example might be E-mailing an absent member to make sure he or she is informed about what happened during a group meeting. Indeed, the presence of supportive emergent behaviors is essential if any group or organization is to perform effectively. Rarely can the required behaviors be specified so perfectly that they meet all the demands that arise in a work situation. This is especially true in dynamic and uncertain environments, where conditions change over time.

▼ ACTIVITIES, INTERACTIONS, AND SENTIMENTS

Activities are the verbal and nonverbal actions in which group members engage. They are the things people do in groups and include task-oriented behaviors as well as more social or interpersonal ones. Both required and emergent activities will be found in any group, and both must be understood in order to best utilize groups as organizational resources. The concept of empowerment, often discussed in this book, reflects a willingness to place less reliance on formal requirements and more on emergent and discretionary activities.

Interactions are communications and interpersonal contacts that occur between and among group members. The essence of any interaction is the sending and receiving of information through oral, written, and nonverbal communication (facial gestures, hand signals, body posture). Although groups may require certain interactions, many are emergent.

Sentiments are the feelings, attitudes, beliefs, or values held by group members. Sentiments may be brought into the group from the outside by individuals or they may be learned as a result of becoming a group member. They are especially subject to emergent forces. Although it may be easy to require positive attitudes toward work, such as a respect for authority or belief in company rules and procedures, it is more difficult to achieve these results in actual practice. Furthermore, when the goals of the emergent system support those of the required system, group process is likely to facilitate rather than impede group effectiveness. If the sentiments turn negative, however, such as when a dispute arises with management, the lack of willingness to engage in such behaviors can adversely affect performance.

▼ INTERGROUP COMPETITION AND COOPERATION

The term **intergroup dynamics** refers to the dynamics that operate between two or more groups. Any organization ideally operates as a cooperative system in which the various groups are willing and able to help one another as needed. In the real world, however, there are many ways and reasons for competition and intergroup problems to develop. Although there may be times when a bit of competition can help groups maintain their creative edge, too much competition can work to the detriment of the larger system. When intergroup rivalries and antagonisms detract from the ability of the groups to cooperate with one another, the organization will lose the desired synergy.

Groups in competition may experience changes to their internal group dynamics. This may be seen as an increase in in-group loyalty, a greater concern for the group task, more acceptance of a single group leader, and tendencies to structure and better organize group activities. Between competing groups, changes also take place. The competition may divert energies away from the performance of important tasks as members focus more on dealing with the other groups. Also common is the emergence of "grudges," animosities, or biased and selective viewpoints of one group toward another. In all likelihood, each group views the other as some sort of an "enemy," associates it with negative stereotypes, and underestimates its strengths.

Hostilities tend to escalate between competing groups as intergroup communication decreases.[25] When this happens within an organization such as between manufacturing and sales units, the poor working relationships can have very negative performance consequences. On the other hand, there can be a positive side to competition—if it is properly managed. When groups compete with others, they may work harder, become more focused on key tasks, develop more internal cohesion and satisfaction, or achieve a higher level of creativity in problem solving. Japanese companies, for example, often use competitive themes to motivate their organization-wide workforces. At Sony, the slogan "BMW" stands for "Beat Matsushita Whatsoever."[26]

One way to handle the dynamics of intergroup competition, is to deal with them after the competition occurs.[27] This may be accomplished by working with competing groups to identify a common enemy, appeal to a common goal, hold direct negotiations, and train members to work more cooperatively. Another approach is to take action before it occurs, that is, to prevent its occurrence in the first place. Recommended ways for preventing destructive intergroup competition include avoiding win–lose reward systems, focusing rewards on contributions to the total organization, rewarding groups for helping one another, increasing interactions and even rotating members among different groups, and preventing groups from withdrawing and becoming isolated from one another.

DECISION MAKING IN GROUPS ◀

A key activity for any group is decision making. Obviously, the decisions made can have an important impact on group effectiveness. The fundamentals of *decision making*—the process of choosing among alternative courses of action—are discussed in detail in Chapter 16. Our present interest is with the

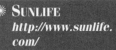

Sun Life of Canada created a task force to develop and implement an AIDS education program for employees in the workplace. A team representing the Human Resources, Law, Medical, and Public Relations departments from the company's home office pooled their views and recommended that outside (The Aids Action Committee) experts be used in a company-wide AIDS educational program.[29]

Consensus is a group decision that has the expressed support of most members.

alternative ways in which groups make decisions as their members communicate and work together on various tasks.

▼ HOW GROUPS MAKE DECISIONS

Edgar Schein, a noted scholar and consultant, has worked extensively with groups to analyze and improve their decision-making processes. He observes that groups may make decisions through any of the following six methods: lack of response, authority rule, minority rule, majority rule, consensus, or unanimity.[28]

In *decision by lack of response,* one idea after another is suggested without any discussion taking place. When the group finally accepts an idea, all others have been bypassed and discarded by simple lack of response rather than by critical evaluation. In *decision by authority rule,* the chairperson, manager, or some other authority figure makes a decision for the group. This can be done with or without discussion and is very time efficient. Whether the decision is a good one or a bad one, however, depends on whether or not the authority figure has the necessary information and on how well this approach is accepted by other group members. In *decision by minority,* two or three people are able to dominate or "railroad" the group into making a decision to which they agree. This is often done by providing a suggestion and then forcing quick agreement by challenging the group with such statements as "Does anyone object? . . . Let's go ahead then."

One of the most common ways groups make decisions, especially when early signs of disagreement set in, is *decision by majority rule.* Here, formal voting may take place, or members may be polled to find the majority viewpoint. This method parallels the democratic political system and is often used without awareness of its potential problems. The very process of voting can create coalitions; that is, some people will be "winners" and others will be "losers" when the final vote is tallied. Those in the minority—the "losers"—may feel left out or discarded without having had a fair say. As a result, they may be less enthusiastic about implementing the decision of the "majority," and lingering resentments may impair group effectiveness in the future.

Another alternative is *decision by consensus.* Formally defined, **consensus** is a state of affairs whereby discussion leads to one alternative being favored by most members and the other members agreeing to support it. When a consensus is reached, even those who may have opposed the chosen course of action know that they have been listened to and have had a fair chance to influence the decision outcome. Consensus, therefore, does not require unanimity. What it does require is the opportunity for any dissenting members to feel they have been able to speak . . . and that they have been listened to.[30]

A *decision by unanimity* may be the ideal state of affairs. Here, all group members agree totally on the course of action to be taken. This is a "logically perfect" group decision method that is extremely difficult to attain in actual practice. One of the reasons that groups sometimes turn to authority decisions, majority voting, or even minority decisions is the difficulty of managing the group process to achieve consensus or unanimity.[31]

▼ ASSETS AND LIABILITIES OF GROUP DECISION MAKING

The best groups don't limit themselves to just one decision-making method. Instead, they change methods to best fit the problems at hand. Indeed, an important group leadership skill is helping a group choose the "right" decision method—that which provides for a timely and quality decision and one to which the members are highly committed. The *potential advantages of group decision making* are: (1) *information*—more knowledge and expertise is applied to solve the problem; (2) *alternatives*—a greater number of alternatives are examined, avoiding tunnel vision; (3) *understanding and acceptance*—the final decision is better understood—and accepted—by all group members; and, (4) *commitment*—there is more commitment among all group members to make the final decision work.[32]

There is more to group decision making than these potential benefits alone, however. We all know that groups can experience problems making decisions. *Potential disadvantages of group decision making* include: (1) *social pressure to conform*—individuals may feel compelled to go along with the apparent wishes of the group; (2) *minority domination*—the group's decision may be forced or "railroaded" by one individual or a small coalition; and (3) *time demands*—with more people involved in the dialogue and discussion, group decisions usually take longer to make than individual decisions.

> ### *Take-A-Note 9.1*
> #### GUIDELINES FOR GROUP CONSENSUS
>
> 1. *Don't argue blindly; consider others' reactions to your points.*
> 2. *Don't change your mind just to reach quick agreement.*
> 3. *Avoid conflict reduction by voting, coin tossing, bargaining.*
> 4. *Try to involve everyone in the decision process.*
> 5. *Allow disagreements to surface so that information and opinions can be deliberated.*
> 6. *Don't focus on winning versus losing; seek alternatives acceptable to all.*
> 7. *Discuss assumptions, listen carefully, encourage participation by everyone.*

▼ GROUPTHINK

An important potential disadvantage of group decision making, identified by social psychologist Irving Janis, is **groupthink**—the tendency of members in highly cohesive groups to lose their critical evaluative capabilities.[33] Janis believes that, because highly cohesive groups demand conformity, there is a tendency for their members to become unwilling to criticize one another's ideas and suggestions. Desires to hold the group together and to avoid unpleasant disagreements lead to an overemphasis on agreement and an underemphasis on critical discussion. The possible result is a poor decision. Group leaders and members, therefore, must be on guard to spot the symptoms of groupthink and take any necessary action to prevent its occurrence.[34]

> **Groupthink** is the tendency of cohesive group members to lose their critical evaluative capabilities.

▼ TECHNIQUES FOR IMPROVING GROUP DECISION MAKING

As you can see, the process of making decisions in any group is a complex and even delicate process. To take full advantage of the group as a decision-making resource, care must be taken to manage group dynamics to balance individual contributions and group operations.[35]

Take-A-Note 9.2

HOW TO AVOID GROUPTHINK

· Assign the role of critical evaluator to each group member.
· Have the leader avoid seeming partial to one course of action.
  Create subgroups to work on the same problem.
· Have group members discuss issues with outsiders and report back.
· Invite outside experts to observe and react to group processes.
· Assign someone to be a "devil's advocate" at each meeting.
· Write alternative scenarios for the intentions of competing groups.
· Hold "second-chance" meetings after consensus is apparently achieved.

Brainstorming involves generating ideas through "freewheeling" and without criticism.

The **nominal group technique** involves structured rules for generating and prioritizing ideas.

Over the years, social scientists have studied ways of maximizing the assets of group decision making while minimizing its liabilities. A particular concern is with the process losses that often occur in free-flowing meetings, such as a committee deliberation or a staff meeting to address a specific problem. These are settings in which the risk of social pressures to conform, domination, time pressures, and even highly emotional debates may detract from the purpose at hand. They are also settings in which special group decision techniques may be used to increase participation and ensure that the creative potential of the group is tapped to the fullest.[36] As discussed in Chapter 10, each of the following techniques lends itself to the increasingly popular electronic or virtual group meeting formats.

Brainstorming In **brainstorming**, group members actively generate as many ideas and alternatives as possible, and they do so relatively quickly and without inhibitions. Four rules typically govern the brainstorming process. First, *all criticism is ruled out*. No one is allowed to judge or evaluate any ideas until the idea-generation process has been completed. Second, *"freewheeling" is welcomed*. The emphasis is on creativity and imagination; the wilder or more radical the ideas, the better. Third, *quantity is wanted*. The emphasis is also on the number of ideas; the greater the number, the more likely that a superior idea will appear. Fourth, *"piggy-backing" is good*. Everyone is encouraged to suggest how others' ideas can be turned into new ideas or how two or more ideas can be joined into still another new idea.

Because brainstorming bans evaluation during the idea generation process, it tends to reduce participants' fears of criticism or failure. Typical results include enthusiasm, involvement, and a free flow of ideas. Researchers consider brainstorming superior to open-group discussions when the goals are creative thinking and the generation of alternative solutions to identified problems.

Nominal Group Technique In any group, there will be times when the opinions of members differ so much that antagonistic arguments will develop. It is hard to make decisions under such circumstances. There are other times when the group is so large that open discussion is awkward. Again, it can be hard to make decisions under such circumstances. In such cases, a form of structured group decision making called the **nominal group technique** may be helpful.[37]

This technique puts people in small groups of six to seven members and asks everyone to respond individually and in writing to a "nominal question" (e.g., "What should be done to improve the effectiveness of this work team?"). Everyone is encouraged to list as many alternatives or ideas as they can come up with.

Next, participants read aloud their responses to the nominal question in round-robin fashion. The recorder writes each response on large newsprint as it is offered; no criticism is allowed. The recorder asks for any questions that may clarify items on the newsprint. This is again done in round-robin fashion and no evaluation is allowed. The goal is simply to make sure that everyone present fully understands each response.

A structured voting procedure is then used to prioritize responses to the nominal question. Participants are given 3 x 5 cards and are asked to rank the five or seven responses they consider most valuable. The balloting is tallied to create a rank ordering of each response on the master list. These final steps are repeated as desired to refine the list further in order to identify the most preferred response or responses to the original nominal question.

Overall, the structured nature of the nominal group and the voting procedure allows ideas to be evaluated without risking the inhibitions, hostilities, and distortions that may occur in an open meeting. This makes the nominal group technique very useful in otherwise difficult or unwieldy group decision situations.

Delphi Technique   A third group decision approach, the **Delphi technique**, was developed by the Rand Corporation for use in situations where group members are unable to meet face to face. In this procedure, a series of questionnaires are distributed to a panel of decision makers, who submit initial responses to a decision coordinator. The coordinator summarizes the solutions and sends the summary back to the panel members, along with a followup questionnaire. Panel members again send in their responses, and the process is repeated until a consensus is reached and a clear decision emerges.

Teams of copywriters and art directors at Leo Burnett Advertising Agency brainstorm ideas. Their efforts have created award-winning and heart-tugging ad campaigns for such companies as McDonald's, Kellogg's, Hallmark, and Maytag.

The **Delphi technique** involves generating decision making alternatives through a series of survey questionnaires.

CHAPTER 9 STUDY GUIDE

SUMMARY

How do groups help organizations?
- A group is a collection of people who interact with one another regularly to attain common goals.
- Groups can help organizations by helping their members to improve task performance and experience more satisfaction from their work.
- One way to view organizations is as interlocking networks of groups, whose managers serve as leaders in one group and subordinates in another.
- Synergy occurs when groups are able to accomplish more than their members could by acting individually.
- Formal groups are designated by the organization to serve an official purpose; examples are work units, task forces, committees, and the like.
- Informal groups are unofficial and emerge spontaneously because of special interests; they may work for or against organizational needs.

What are the stages of group development?

- Groups pass through various stages in their life cycles, and each stage poses somewhat distinct management problems.
- In the forming stage, groups have problems managing individual entry.
- In the storming stage, groups have problems managing expectations and status.
- In the norming or initial integration stage, groups have problems managing member relations and task efforts.
- In the performing or total integration stage, groups have problems managing continuous improvement and self-renewal.
- In the adjourning stage, groups have problems managing task completion and the process of disbanding.

What are the foundations of group effectiveness?

- An effective group is one that achieves both high levels of task accomplishment and good human resource maintenance; it is able to perform successfully over the long term.
- As open systems, groups must interact successfully with their environments to obtain resources that are transformed into product outputs.
- Group input factors establish the core foundations for effectiveness.
- Important group input factors include goals, rewards, resources, technology, the task, membership characteristics, and group size, among other possibilities.

What are group dynamics?

- Group dynamics are the way members work together to utilize inputs; they are another foundation of group effectiveness.
- Group dynamics are based on the interactions, activities, and sentiments of group members.
- Group dynamics are based on the required and emergent ways in which members work together.
- Intergroup dynamics are the forces that operate between two or more groups.
- Although groups in organizations ideally cooperate with one another, they often become involved in dysfunctional conflicts and competition.
- The disadvantages of intergroup competition can be reduced through management strategies to direct, train, and reinforce groups to pursue cooperative instead of purely competitive actions.

How do groups make decisions?

- Groups can make decisions by lack of response, authority rule, minority rule, majority rule, consensus, and unanimity.
- The potential assets to more group-oriented decision making include having more information available and generating more understanding and commitment.
- The potential liabilities to more group-oriented decision making include social pressures to conform and greater time requirements.
- "Groupthink" is the tendency of some groups to lose critical evaluative capabilities.
- Techniques for improving creativity in group decision making include brainstorming, the nominal group technique, and the Delphi method.

Brainstorming (p. 188)

Consensus (p. 186)

Delphi technique (p. 189)

Effective group (p. 180)

Formal group (p. 176)

Group (p. 175)

Group dynamics (p. 183)

Groupthink (p. 187)

Informal group (p. 177)

Intergroup dynamics
(p. 184)

Nominal group technique
(p. 188)

Social loafing (p. 176)

Status congruence (p. 182)

Synergy (p. 175)

KEY TERMS

▼ MULTIPLE CHOICE

SELF-TEST 9

1. The Ringelmann effect is another term for _____ in groups. (a) creativity (b) social loafing (c) dominating members (d) conformity

2. It is during the _____ stage of group development that members begin to really come together as a coordinated unit. (a) storming (b) norming (c) performing (d) total integration

3. An effective group is defined as one that achieves high levels of both _____ and _____. (a) performance, human resource maintenance (b) productivity, efficiency (c) coordination, performance (d) synergy, satisfaction

4. Task characteristics, reward systems, and group size are all _____ that make a difference in group effectiveness. (a) group processes (b) group dynamics (c) group inputs (d) human resource maintenance factors

5. The best size for a problem-solving group is usually _____ members. (a) no more than 3 or 4 (b) 5 to 7 (c) 8 to 10 (d) around 12 to 13

6. When two groups are in competition with one another, within each group _____ may be expected. (a) more in-group loyalty (b) less reliance on the leader (c) less task focus (d) more conflict

7. The tendency of groups to lose their critical evaluative capabilities during decision making is a phenomenon called _____. (a) groupthink (b) the Ringlemann effect (c) decision congruence (d) group consensus

8. When a decision requires a high degree of commitment for its implementation, a/an _____ decision is generally preferred. (a) authority (b) majority vote (c) group consensus (d) groupthink

9. Written responses to a question, structured round-robin sharing of responses, and a written record of responses listed on newsprint are all part of the _____ technique for improving group creativity. (a) brainstorming (b) Delphi (c) step ladder (d) nominal group

10. When organizations are viewed as interlocking networks of groups, the managers of these groups serve in _____ roles. (a) task (b) maintenance (c) linking pin (d) devil's advocate

▼ TRUE–FALSE

11. The creation of a whole that is greater than the sum of its parts defines synergy. T F

12. Informal groups tend to hurt organizations and should not be tolerated by managers. T F

13. Generally speaking, members of homogeneous groups are expected to work easily and well with one another. T F

14. Poor attitudes toward work are examples of sentiments that may exist in group dynamics. T F

15. Decision by majority voting is the only group decision method without any disadvantages. T F
16. The potential liabilities or disadvantages of group decision making include social pressures to conform. T F
17. When group members are not getting along well together, the brainstorming technique is a good approach for improving creativity in decision making. T F
18. Devil's advocate roles and second-chance meetings are good ways for members to avoid the dangers of nominal grouping. T F
19. Increasing interactions among members is one way of dealing with dysfunctional intergroup relationships. T F
20. Overall, there is little doubt that group decision making is always superior to individual decision making. T F

▼ SHORT RESPONSE

21. How can groups be good for organizations?
22. What types of formal groups are found in organizations today?
23. What is the difference between required and emergent behaviors in group dynamics?
24. How can intergroup competition be bad for organizations?

▼ APPLICATIONS ESSAY

25. Alejandro Puron recently encountered a dilemma in working with his quality circle (QC) team. One of the team members claims that the QC must always be unanimous in its recommendations. "Otherwise," she says, "we will not have a true consensus." Alejandro, the current QC leader, disagrees. He believes that unanimity is desirable but not always necessary to achieve consensus. You are a management consultant specializing in group utilization in organizations. Alejandro calls you for advice. What would you tell him and why?

10

TEAMWORK AND
WORKGROUP DESIGN

The San Diego Zoo has been steadily reorganizing to show its animals in natural environments. In this new arrangement, animals and plants from a particular region are housed together in cageless enclosures designed to resemble natural settings. The elephants are splitting up, and the crocodiles and alligators are headed their separate ways, as each is moved to an appropriate bioclimatic zone. And with the switch to bioclimatic zones the zoo itself has started shedding its old organizational skin and replacing it with a fresh approach that uses on-site, cross-trained, self-managing teams. Each bioclimatic zone has its own team, typically consisting of 7 to 10 employees from the old departments, who now work together to accomplish one goal: to run their bioclimatic zone successfully. A typical team is likely to be made up of mammal specialists, bird experts, horticulturists, and maintenance and construction workers. Team members share responsibility for the entire zone. Their jobs blend and merge, making it difficult sometimes to tell who does what. This shared responsibility means that each team member is responsible for seeing that the work of the team gets done. Gone is the "it's-not-my-job" syndrome that plagued the zoo in the past. Now, if something needs to be done, it is not just the responsibility of a specific department, it is the job of the entire team. This restructuring has created a challenge for the zoo's department managers. They have had to learn to let go of the managerial practices they've employed and develop new skills that are better matched to the new team concept.[1]

"**W**ho needs a boss?" reads the headline of a *Fortune* magazine article. "Not the employees who work in self-managed teams," answers the first paragraph.[2] Indeed, many managers consider teams and teamwork as the keys to productivity and quality of working life improvements in the new workplace. But putting these concepts to work is a major challenge for people used to more traditional ways of working. As more and more jobs are turned over to teams, special problems relating to group and intergroup dynamics may occur. It is not enough for visionary managers to implement creative work group designs. They must also be prepared to do what is needed to help the group members properly develop and maintain themselves as high-performance teams.

Teamwork is one benchmark of a successful organization. This chapter introduces the essentials of teamwork and work group design for high-performance systems. As you read Chapter 10, keep in mind these questions:

- What are the essentials of high-performance teams?
- How do team processes affect performance?
- What are employee involvement groups?
- Why are self-managing teams important today?
- What are new developments with virtual teams?

HIGH-PERFORMANCE TEAMS

Teams work together to achieve a purpose for which they are all accountable.

When we think of the word "teams," a variety of popular sporting teams usually comes to mind. Work groups also are **teams** to the extent that they meet this definition: a team is a small group of people with complementary skills, who work together to achieve a common purpose for which they hold themselves collectively accountable.[3]

▼ THE NATURE OF TEAMWORK

In the workplace, there are three common types of teams.[4] First, there are *teams that recommend things*. Established to study specific problems and recommend solutions to them, these teams typically work with a target completion date and disband once their purpose has been fulfilled. They are temporary groups including task forces, ad hoc committees, project teams, and the like. Members of these teams must be able to learn quickly how to work well together, accomplish the assigned task, and make good action recommendations for followup work by other people.

Second, there are *teams that make or do things*. These are functional groups that perform ongoing tasks, such as marketing or manufacturing, and are considered permanent; that is, they operate without scheduled dates for disbanding. Members of these teams must have long-term working relationships as well as good operating systems and the external support needed to achieve effectiveness over a sustained period of time.

Third, there are *teams that run things*. These *management teams* consist of people with the formal responsibilitity of leading other groups. For example, top management teams consist of an organization's most senior executives. Key issues for such teams include identifying overall organizational purposes, goals, and values and helping others fulfill them. It is increasingly common today to find such teams formally designated in the top management structures of organizations.[5]

The ability to build effective teams is increasingly considered an essential managerial capability; the ability to contribute successfully to team performance is increasingly considered an essential capability of any worker. All teams need members who are motivated to actively work with others to accomplish important tasks—whether those tasks involve recommending things, making or doing things, or running things. The members of true teams feel "collectively accountable" for what they accomplish through "teamwork." Formally stated, **teamwork** occurs when team members work together in such a way that their respective skills are all well utilized to achieve a common purpose. A commitment to teamwork is found in the willingness of every member to "listen and respond constructively to views expressed by others, give others the benefit of the doubt, provide support, and recognize the interests and achievements of others."[7]

▼ CHARACTERISTICS OF HIGH-PERFORMANCE TEAMS

Creating high-performance teams is a challenging task in any setting.[8] The essential values and characteristics of high-performance teams may be described in this way. First, *high-performance teams have strong core values* that help guide their attitudes and behaviors in directions consistent with the team's purpose. Such values act as an internal control system for a group or team, and can substitute for much of the outside direction that might otherwise be provided by a supervisor. Second, *high-performance teams turn a general sense of purpose into specific performance objectives*. Whereas a shared sense of purpose gives general direction to a team, it is commitment to specific performance results—such as reducing the time of getting the product to market by half—that makes this pur-

ALCOA

The top management team at Alcoa is taking full advantage of a new high-tech corporate headquarters. CEO Paul H. O'Neill and the other senior executives work in open cubicles around a central "communications center" where they hold frequent impromptu meetings.[6]

Teamwork occurs when group members work together in ways that utilize their skills well to accomplish a purpose.

pose truly meaningful. Specific objectives provide a focus for solving problems and resolving conflicts, and they set standards for measuring results and obtaining performance feedback. They also help group members understand the need for "collective" versus purely individual efforts. Third, *members of high-performance teams have the right mix of skills.* These include technical skills, problem-solving and decision-making skills, and interpersonal skills. Finally, *high-performance teams possess creativity.* In the new workplace, teams must use their creativity to assist organizations in continuous improvement of operations—including productivity and customer service—and in continuous development of new products, services, and markets.

▼ THE TEAM-BUILDING PROCESS

Teamwork, and high performance in particular, doesn't always happen naturally in a group; it is something that team members and leaders must work hard to achieve. In the sports world, for example, coaches and managers focus on teamwork when building new teams at the start of each season. As you are aware, even experienced teams often run into problems as a season progresses. Members slack off or become disgruntled; some retire, and others are traded to other teams. Even world-champion teams have losing streaks, and the most talented players can lose motivation at times, quibble among themselves, and end up in slumps. When these things happen, the owners, managers, and players are apt to examine their problems and take corrective action to rebuild the team and restore the teamwork that is needed to achieve high-performance results.

> ### *Take a Note 10.1*
> HOW TO BUILD A HIGH-PERFORMING TEAM
>
> - *Communicate high-performance standards.*
> - *Set the tone in the first team meeting.*
> - *Create a sense of urgency.*
> - *Make sure members have the right skills.*
> - *Establish clear rules for team behavior.*
> - *As a leader, model expected behaviors.*
> - *Find ways to create early "successes."*
> - *Continually introduce new facts and information.*
> - *Make sure members spend a lot of time together.*
> - *Give positive feedback and reward high performance.*

Team building is a collaborative way to gather and analyze data to improve teamwork.

Work groups and teams have similar difficulties. When newly formed, they must master challenges in the early stages of group development. Even when they are mature most work teams encounter problems of insufficient teamwork at different points in time. When difficulties occur, or as a means of preventing them from occurring, "team-building" activities can help. Formally defined, **team building** is a sequence of planned activities designed to gather and analyze data on the functioning of a group and to initiate changes designed to improve teamwork and increase group effectiveness.[9]

The steps and continuous improvement theme highlighted in Figure 10.1 are typical of most team building activities. The process begins when someone notices that a problem exists or may develop. Group members then work together to gather data relating to the problem, analyze these data, plan for improvements, and implement the action plans. Importantly, the entire team-building process is highly collaborative. Everyone is expected to participate actively as group operations are evaluated and decisions are made on what needs to be done to improve the team's functioning in the future. This process can and should become an on-

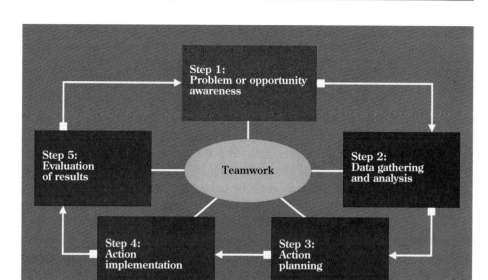

going part of any team's work agenda. It is an approach to continuous improvement that can be very beneficial to long-term team effectiveness.

▼ HOW TEAM BUILDING WORKS

Team-building is participative and data based. Whether the data are gathered by questionnaire, interview, nominal group meeting, or other creative methods, the goal is to get good answers to such questions as "How well are we doing in terms of task accomplishment?" and "How satisfied are we as individual members with the group and the way it operates?" There are a variety of ways for such questions to be asked and answered in a collaborative and motivating manner.

Formal Retreat Approach   In the *formal retreat approach,* team-building takes place during an off-site "retreat." During this retreat, which may last from 2 to 7 or more days, group members work intensively on a variety of assessment and planning tasks. They are often initiated by a review of data gathered through survey, interviews, or structured interactions such as the nominal group technique. Formal retreats are typically held with the assistance of a consultant, who is either hired from the outside or made available from in-house staff. Team-building retreats are quite common and offer opportunities for intense and concentrated efforts to examine group accomplishments and operations.

Continuous Improvement Approach   Not all team building is done in a formal retreat format or with the assistance of consultants. In a *continuous improvement approach,* the manager, team leader, and/or group members themselves take responsibility for regularly engaging in the team-building process. This method can be as simple as periodic meetings that implement the team-building steps; it can also include self-managed formal retreats. In all cases, the team members commit to monitoring group development and accomplishments continuously and making the day-to-day changes needed to ensure group effectiveness. Such continuous improvement of teamwork is essential to the total quality and total service management themes so important to organizations today.

Outdoor Experience Approach   In addition, the *outdoor experience approach* is an increasingly popular team-building aactivity that may be done on its own or in combination with other approaches. The outdoor experience places group members in a variety of physically-challenging situations that must be mastered through teamwork, not individual work. By having to work together in the face of difficult obstacles, team members are supposed to experience increased self-confidence, more respect for others' capabilities, and a greater commitment to teamwork. A popular sponsor of team building through outdoor experience is the Outward Bound Leadership School, but many others exist. For a group that has never done team building before, outdoor experience can be an exciting way to begin; for groups familiar with team-building, it can be a way of further enriching the experience.

GLOBAL

The Françoise-Mast Outdoor Management Program, a Malaysian–Australian joint venture, utilizes a variety of outdoor sites in Malaysia to help companies build high-performance teams. Participants in a typical program engage in a variety of activities—from rock climbing to obstacle courses—with the assistance of experienced group facilitators. Team members learn the importance of communicating with one another and realize the need to support one another to accomplish a task, and they learn that several brains are often better than one. Françoise-Mast emphasizes developing each member of a team to achieve his or her full potential.[10]

BUILDING TEAM PROCESSES

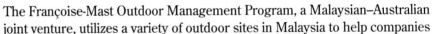

L ike many changes in the new workplace, the increased emphasis on teams and teamwork is a major challenge for people used to more traditional ways of working. As more and more jobs are turned over to groups, special problems relating to team processes may arise. Team leaders and members alike must be prepared to deal positively with such problems as disagreements on goals and responsibilities, delays and disputes when making decisions, and the inevitable friction and interpersonal conflicts. Given the nature of group dynamics, team building in a sense is never done. Something is always happening that creates the need for further efforts to help improve teamwork and group effectiveness.

▼ INDIVIDUAL ENTRY PROBLEMS

Special difficulties are likely to occur when members first get together in a new group or work team, or when new members join an existing one. Problems often arise as new members try to understand what is expected of them while dealing with anxiety and discomfort in a new social setting. New members, for example, may worry about: *Participation*—"Will I be allowed to participate?" *Goals*—"Do I share the same goals as others?" *Control*—"Will I be able to influence what takes place?" *Relationships*—"How close do people get?" *Processes*—"Are conflicts likely to be upsetting?"

Edgar Schein, a noted scholar and group consultant, points out that people may try to cope with individual entry problems in self-serving ways that may hinder group operations.[11] He identifies three behavior profiles that are common in such situations.

The Tough Battler   The first entry problem is *the tough battler*. This is a group member who is frustrated by his or her lack of identity in the new group situation. The tough battler may act aggressively and resist the ideas offered by others. He or she may also reject the authority of others. Tough battlers are seeking to establish their identities within the team. They want answers to the question, "Who am I in this group?" Until the individual resolves this issue, either alone or with the assistance of others, the group may suffer.

The Friendly Helper   A second entry problem appears as *the friendly helper*. This is a group member who is experiencing the uncertainties of intimacy and control. Out of insecurity, this person may show extraordinary support for others, behave in a dependent way, and seek alliances in subgroups or cliques. This behavior may detract from the potential contribution of personal skills to group needs. The friendly helper needs to know whether he or she will be liked by the other group members and whether he or she will be able to exert any control over their behavior.

The Objective Thinker   The third entry problem profiled by Schein is *the objective thinker*. This group member is anxious and concerned about whether or not personal needs and goals will be satisfied through teamwork. People join groups for various reasons. When a group member seems unduly passive, very reflective, and even single minded, the reasons may be traced to uncertainty over the "fit" between individual goals and group directions. The objective thinker, in such cases, is trying to determine whether group goals include opportunities to satisfy personal needs. Until this matter is settled, it may be difficult to tap the full potential of this member as a group resource.

▼ DISTRIBUTED LEADERSHIP

Research in social psychology suggests that the achievement of sustained high performance by groups requires that two important needs be met—"task needs" and "maintenance needs."[12] Although anyone formally appointed as group leader should help fulfill these needs, the responsibility is also shared by all group members. This sharing of responsibility for meeting group task and maintenance needs is sometimes called **distributed leadership** in group dynamics.[13]

Distributed leadership is the sharing of responsibility for meeting group task and maintenance needs.

Group Task Activities   **Task activities** are the various things members do that directly contribute to the performance of important group tasks. If task activities are not adequate, the group will have difficulty accomplishing its objectives. In an effective group, by contrast, members contribute important task activities as needed and as building blocks for performance success. Among the essential task activities are:[14]

Task activities directly contribute to the performance of important group tasks.

■ Task activities that help groups

- *Initiating*—offering new ideas or ways of defining problems; suggesting solutions to group difficulties.
- *Seeking information*—attempting to clarify suggestions in terms of factual accuracy; asking for ideas of others.
- *Giving information*—offering authoritative and relevant information and facts.
- *Clarifying*—clarifying relations among various suggestions or ideas; attempting to coordinate member activities.
- *Summarizing*—assessing group functioning; raising questions about the logic and practicality of member suggestions.

Group Maintenance Activities   Whereas task activities directly advance the performance agenda of a group, **maintenance activities** support the social and interpersonal relationships among its members. They help the group stay intact and healthy as an ongoing social system. When maintenance is poor, members become dissatisfied with one another and their group membership. This sets the stage for conflicts that can drain energies otherwise needed for task performance. In an effective group, by contrast, maintenance activities help build and sustain relationships needed for group members to work and stay together over time. Examples of important group maintenance activities include:

Maintenance activities support the emotional life of the group as an ongoing social system.

■ Maintenance activities that help groups

- *Encouraging*—praising, accepting, or agreeing with other members' ideas; indicating solidarity and warmth.
- *Harmonizing*—mediating squabbles within the group; reconciling differences; seeking opportunities for compromise.
- *Setting standards*—expressing standards for the group to achieve or use in evaluating group process.
- *Following*—going along with the group; agreeing to try out the ideas of others.
- *Gatekeeping*—encouraging participation of group members; trying to keep some members from dominating.

Disruptive Behaviors in a Group   All group members share the additional responsibility of avoiding *disruptive behaviors*—ones that harm the group process. Full participation in distributed leadership means avoiding the following behaviors . . . and helping others do the same:

- Being overly aggressive toward other members.
- Withdrawing and refusing to cooperate with others.
- Horsing around when there is work to be done.
- Using the group as a forum for self-confession.
- Talking too much about irrelevant matters.
- Trying to compete for attention and recognition.

■ Disruptive behaviors that harm groups

▼ ROLES AND ROLE DYNAMICS

In groups, members—new and old alike—need to know what others expect of them and what they can expect from others. It is common to use the term **role** to describe the set of expectations associated with a job or position on a team. The people who hold these expectations are considered members of the *role set*; the person who is supposed to fulfill them is the *role incumbent*. Members of a task force, for example, would be part of the role set for the person serving as its chair; the person to whom the chair reports would also be part of his or her role set. Problems in groups and work teams are sometimes caused by difficulties in defining and managing roles.

A **role** is a set of expectations for a team member or person in a job.

Role Ambiguity   **Role ambiguity** occurs when the role incumbent is uncertain about his or her role. That is, the expectations of one or more members of the role set are unclear and therefore difficult to satisfy. To do their jobs well, people need to know what is expected of them. In new group or team situations, role ambiguities may create problems as members find that their work efforts are wasted or unappreciated by others. Even on mature groups and teams, the failure of members to share expectations and listen to one another may at times create a similar lack of understanding. Role ambiguity can be stressful for the individual, resulting in lowered self-confidence and decreased job satisfaction. It may also cause difficulties in relationships with members of the role set.

Role ambiguity occurs when someone is uncertain about what is expected of him or her.

Role Overload and Underload   Another common difficulty is *role overload,* which occurs when too much is expected of the role incumbent at any given time. By the same token, *role underload* can also create difficulties when a person is asked to do too little and subsequently feels underutilized in a role. Both role overload and underload can increase job stress and may lead to performance and satisfaction problems. One of the things that must be achieved in any group is a clear set of realistic expectations regarding the contributions of each member.

Role Conflict   **Role conflict** occurs when the role incumbent is unable to meet the expectations of one or more members of the role set. The individual understands what needs to be done, but for some reason cannot comply with them. The resulting tension can reduce job satisfaction and affect both work performance

Role conflict occurs when someone is unable to respond to role expectations that conflict with one another.

and relationships with other group members. Among the most common forms of role conflict are the following:

■ Forms of role conflict

- *Intrasender role conflict*—occurs when the same person sends conflicting expectations (e.g. a purchasing agent is asked by the boss to buy materials unavailable through normal channels; the boss also says company procedures should not be violated).
- *Intersender role conflict*—occurs when different people send conflicting expectations (e.g. a manager's boss expects her to be very direct and to exercise close control over subordinates; the subordinates want more freedom in their work).
- *Person–role conflict*—occurs when one's values and needs conflict with role expectations (e.g., pressure is put on a senior executive to agree secretly to fix prices with competing firms; this violates the personal ethics of the executive).
- *Interrole conflict*—occurs when the expectations of two or more roles held by the same individual become incompatible (e.g. a task force head must choose between weekend work to meet a deadline and attending family gatherings).

Role Negotiation   *Role negotiation* is a process through which individuals negotiate to clarify the role expectations each holds for the other. Often used as part of team-building, role negotiations can be very effective in clarifying roles and improving work relationships. Sample results from an actual role negotiation are shown in Figure 10.2. Note the presence of "give and take" in the final written agreements between negotiators. The agreement is reached after each person first lists what is expected of the other and then both share their lists and discuss them with the goals of role clarification and agreement.[15]

QUALITY

Dr. Dennis Freidan, owner and president of the Memphis Center for Cosmetic Dentistry, has learned that, for a practice to prosper, it must be well managed. "There must be a commitment on everyone's part to function as a team," Freiden says. His team staff begins each day by meeting as a group to discuss the day's goals, decide who will do what that day, and share any personal information that may affect their work performance. This way everyone knows how to pitch in to help that person and to make sure that all responsibilities are met. The group also meets before going home to talk about the day's successes and frustrations.[16]

▼ GROUP NORMS

Group **norms** are ideas or beliefs about the behaviors that group members are expected to display. They are often referred to as "rules" or "standards" of behav-

ROLE NEGOTIATIONS

Issue Diagnosis Form

Messages from   Jim

       to   Diane

If you were to do the following, it would help me to increase my performance:

- Be more receptive to improvement suggestions
- Give help on new software
- Work harder to get bigger budget
- Stop asking for so many detailed progress reports
- Keep providing full information in our weekly meetings
- Keep being available when I need to talk with you

■ FIGURE 10.2
A sample role negotiations agreement.

ior that apply to group members.[17] Norms help clarify the expectations associated with a person's membership in a group. They allow members to structure their own behavior and to predict what others will do; they help members gain a common sense of direction; and, they reinforce a desired group or organizational culture. When someone violates a group norm, other members typically respond in ways that are aimed at enforcing the norm. These responses may include direct criticisms, reprimands, expulsion, social ostracism, and the like.

> **Norms** are rules or standards for the behavior of group members.

Managers, task force heads, committee chairs, and team leaders must all try to help their groups adopt positive norms that support organizational goals.[18] A key norm in any setting is the *performance norm* which conveys expectations about how hard group members should work. Other norms are important too. In order for a task force or a committee to operate effectively, for example, norms regarding attendance at meetings, punctuality, preparedness, criticism, and social behaviors are needed. Groups also commonly have norms on how to deal with supervisors, colleagues, and customers, as well as those establishing guidelines for honesty and ethical behaviors. The following list shows how various norms may have both positive and negative implications for groups and organizations.[19]

- *Organizational and personal pride norms*—"It's a tradition around here for people to stand up for the company when others criticize it unfairly" (positive); "In our company, they are always trying to take advantage of us" (negative).
- *High-achievement norms*—"On our team, people always try to work hard" (positive); "There's no point in trying harder on our team, nobody else does" (negative).
- *Support and helpfulness norms*—"People on this committee are good listeners and actively seek out the ideas and opinions of others" (positive); "On this committee it's dog-eat-dog and save your own skin" (negative).

■ Types of group norms

Take a Note 10.2

SEVEN STEPS TO POSITIVE NORMS

1. Act as a positive role model.
2. Hold meetings to agree on goals.
3. Select members who can and will perform.
4. Provide support and training for members.
5. Reinforce and reward desired behaviors.
6. Hold meetings for feedback and performance review.
7. Hold meetings to plan for improvements.

Cohesiveness is the degree to which members are attracted to a group and motivated to remain a part of it.

- *Improvement and change norms*—"In our department people are always looking for better ways of doing things" (positive); "Around here, people hang on to the old ways even after they have outlived their usefulness" (negative).

▼ GROUP COHESIVENESS

Group **cohesiveness** is the degree to which members are attracted to and motivated to remain part of a group.[20] Cohesiveness tends to be high in groups or teams whose members are homogeneous in age, attitudes, needs, and backgrounds. It is also high in groups of small size, where members respect one another's competencies, agree on common goals, and work on interdependent tasks. Cohesiveness tends to increase when groups are physically isolated from others, and when they experience performance success or crisis.

Persons in a highly cohesive group value their membership and strive to maintain positive relationships with other group members. In this sense, cohesive groups and teams are good for their members. In contrast to less cohesive groups, members of highly cohesive ones tend to be more energetic when working on group activities, less likely to be absent, and more likely to be happy about performance success and sad about failures. Cohesive groups generally have low turnover and satisfy a broad range of individual needs, often providing a source of loyalty, security, and esteem for their members.

Conformity to Norms Even though cohesive groups are good for their members, they may or may not be good for the organization. Figure 10.3 demonstrates the performance implications for a basic *rule of conformity in group dynamics:* the more cohesive the group, the greater the conformity of members to group norms. When the performance norms are positive in a highly cohesive work group or team, the resulting conformity to the norms should have a positive effect on task performance as well as member satisfaction. This is a "best case" situation for everyone. When the performance norms are negative in a highly cohesive group, however, the same power of conformity can have undesirable results. As shown in the figure, this creates a "worst case" situation for the organization. Although team members are highly motivated to support group norms, the organization suffers from poor performance results. In between these two extremes are mixed-case situations in which a lack of cohesion fails to rally strong conformity to the norm. With its strength reduced, the outcome of the norm is somewhat unpredictable and will most likely fall on the moderate or low side.

Influencing Group Cohesiveness Team leaders and managers must be aware of steps that can be taken to build group cohesiveness, such as in a team that has positive norms but suffers from low cohesiveness. They must also be

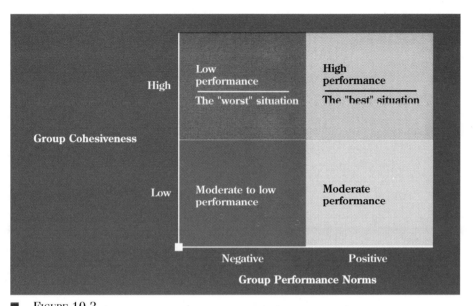

■ FIGURE 10.3
How cohesiveness and conformity to norms affect group performance.

ready to deal with situations when cohesiveness needs to be lowered, at least temporarily because of the effects of negative and hard-to-change performance norms. As shown in Figure 10.4, group cohesiveness can be increased or decreased by making changes in group goals, membership composition, interactions, size, rewards, competition, location, and duration.

How To Decrease Cohesion	TARGETS	How To Increase Cohesion
Create disagreement	Goals	Get agreement
Increase heterogeneity	Membership	Increase homogeneity
Restrict within group	Interactions	Enhance within group
Make group bigger	Size	Make group smaller
Focus within group	Competition	Focus on other groups
Reward individual results	Rewards	Reward group results
Open up to other groups	Location	Isolate from other groups
Disband the group	Duration	Keep group together

■ FIGURE 10.4
Ways to increase and decrease group cohesiveness.

TEAMWORK AND EMPLOYEE INVOLVEMENT GROUPS

Managers in the new workplace are adopting many innovative ways of better using teams and groups to improve organizational performance. The watchwords of these new approaches to teamwork are *empowerment, participation,* and *involvement.*

DIVERSITY

When it was time to reengineer its order-to-delivery process to eliminate an uncompetitive and costly 26-day cycle time, Hewlett-Packard turned to a team. With two experienced managers in the lead, some 35 members from HP and two outside companies went to work. In nine months they slashed the time to eight days, improved service, and cut costs. How did they do it? Team leader Julie Anderson says: "We took things away: no supervisors, no hierarchy, no titles, no job descriptions . . . the idea was to create a sense of personal ownership." Says a team member: ". . . no individual is going to have the best idea, that's not the way it works—the best ideas come from the collective intelligence of the team."[21]

▼ WHAT IS AN EMPLOYEE INVOLVEMENT GROUP?

> Members of **employee involvement groups** meet regularly to examine work-related problems and opportunities.

Among the creative ways to use teams in organizations is the **employee involvement group.** This term applies to a wide variety of groups whose members meet regularly to collectively examine important workplace issues. The goals of an employee involvement group often relate to the implementation of *total quality and total service concepts* and the quest for *continuous improvement* in all operations. Typically consisting of 5 to 10 members, these groups discuss ways to enhance quality, better satisfy customers, raise productivity, and improve the quality of work life.

Employee involvement groups allow workers to have more influence over matters affecting them and their work. They also help to mobilize the advantages of group decision making. These include bringing the full extent of worker knowhow to bear on problems and gaining the commitment needed to fully implement solutions. For employee involvement to succeed, however, managers must be sincere in their willingness to allow participation and empowerment. The opportunities for the group members to have an influence on what happens must be real.

▼ QUALITY CIRCLES AND EMPLOYEE INVOLVEMENT

> Members of a **quality circle** meet regularly to find ways for continuous improvement of quality operations.

A **quality circle**, or QC for short, is a small group of persons who meet periodically (e.g., an hour or so, once a week) to discuss and develop solutions for problems relating to quality, productivity, or cost.[22] This special type of employee involvement group is very common in the new workplace.

Originally developed in Japan to promote employee involvement, encourage innovation, and improve efficiency, QCs are now very popular in organizations around the world. But, as useful as they are, quality circles cannot be looked upon as panaceas for all of an organization's ills. To be successful, members of QCs should receive special training in group dynamics, information gathering, and problem analysis techniques. Leaders of quality circles should also be trained in participation and team building. Any solutions to problems should be jointly pursued with the support of both QC members and organizational management. And, efforts must be made to keep a quality circle program from becoming just another management "gimmick." In order for QCs to work best, they require a clear emphasis on quality in the organization's goals, a culture that supports participation and empowerment, management willingness to trust and share important information, and a "team spirit" in the QC group.

SELF-MANAGING TEAMS ◀

A new type of work group design is increasingly popular today. Known as **self-managing teams**, these are small groups that are empowered to make the decisions needed to essentially manage themselves on a day-to-day basis.[23] Although there are different variations of this theme, members of a true self-managing work team make decisions on scheduling work, allocating tasks, training in job skills, evaluating performance, selecting new team members, and controlling quality of work. Importantly, members of a self-managing team are collectively held accountable for the team's overall performance results.

Self-managing teams are empowered to make decisions about planning, doing, and evaluating their daily work.

▼ HOW SELF-MANAGING TEAMS WORK

Self-managing teams—also called *self-directed teams* or *empowered teams*—are permanent and formal elements in the organizational structure. They replace the traditional work group headed by a supervisor. What differentiates self-managing teams from the more traditional alternatives, is the decision making authority just described. Indeed, the very concept of the self-managing team is that its members take on duties otherwise performed by a manager or first-line supervisor—such things as planning and work scheduling, performance evaluation, and quality control.

Members of self-managing teams are given substantial discretion in determining work pace and in distributing tasks. This is made possible, in part, by **multiskilling**, whereby team members are trained in performing more than one job on the team. In self-managing teams, each person is typically expected to be able to perform many different jobs—even all of the team's jobs—as needed. The more "skills" someone masters, the higher the base pay. Importantly, team members themselves are the ones who conduct the job training and certify one another as having mastered the required skills.

Multiskilling occurs when team members are trained in skills to perform different jobs.

QUALITY

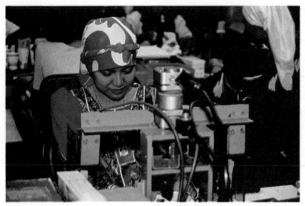

If you visit the Texas Instruments plant in Malaysia you will find more than 2000 workers and no traditional supervisors. The plant uses self-managing teams that make decisions on quality and production issues, schedule work and work breaks, and keep track of work hours on the "honor system." When teams were first introduced, people were anxious. Management styles had to be changed, and rigid job descriptions were eliminated. But the changes increased productivity, improved product quality, and reduced staff absenteeism. Says a TI senior executive: "Teams bring about better sharing of ideas and learning. Better decisions are made and implementation of ideas takes less time."[24]

A self-managing team should probably include between 5 and 15 members. The teams must be large enough to provide a good mix of skills and resources, but they must also be small enough to function efficiently. Team members must meet as often as necessary to get the job done. If the team gets too big, the large size makes "self-management" just as difficult to accomplish as traditional external supervision. It is also helpful for someone to serve in the "team leader" role. At the Texas Instruments Malaysia plant, for example, this person is called a facilitator. Although the choice of title isn't important, it is important that someone be always prepared to represent the team with higher management and other groups, and to formally convene the team as day-to-day events may require. It is probably best if this person is not permanently assigned to the leader role. Ideally, all team members are trained for and able to fill this leadership role when asked.

USAA

At USAA, QCs add to a total service commitment. "The logic is that the people who would do the work know the most about it and are the best qualified to improve it," says a former coordinator. "With that support and the enthusiasm of our employees, there's no limit to what we can accomplish."[25]

▼ OPERATIONAL IMPLICATIONS OF SELF-MANAGING TEAMS

When self-managing teams are added to an organization, a number of benefits are expected. They include productivity and quality improvements, production flexibility and faster response to technological change, reduced absenteeism and turnover, and improved work attitudes and quality of work life. Although these potential benefits are quite substantial, they are not guaranteed and they may be accompanied by additional consequences.

Implementing self-managing teams brings about structural changes in job classifications and management levels. Simply put, with a "self-managing" team you don't need the traditional first-line supervisor anymore. The possible extent of this change is shown in Figure 10.5, where the first level of supervisory management has been eliminated and replaced by self-managing teams. Note also that many traditional tasks of the supervisor are reallocated to the team. Although this may not have major consequences when the self-managing teams are designed into a new or start-up setting, the situation is quite different when they are being introduced into an ongoing one. For persons used to more traditional work arrangements, learning to work in such teams for the first time can be chal-

FIGURE 10.5

Organizational and management implications of self-managing teams. [Source: John R. Scher-merhorn, Jr., *Management,* 5th ed. (New York: John Wiley & Sons, 1996), p. 274. Used by permission.]

lenging; for managers learning to deal with self-managing teams rather than individual workers, the change-over can be challenging; for the former supervisors who have been displaced by the self-managing team, the implications are even more personal and threatening.

Given this, a question must be asked: "Should all work groups operate as self-managing teams?" The best answer is "No." Self-managing teams are probably not right for all organizations, work situations, and people. They are of great potential, but they also require a proper setting and support. At a minimum, the essence of any self-managing team—participation and empowerment—must be consistent with the values and culture of the organization. If not, the use of self-managing teams may create more problems than it resolves. Implementing self-managing teams also requires major changes in the structure of the organization and in the ways in which managers have traditionally approached their jobs. Unless the people involved are willing to make personal adjustments and unless the organization is able to provide them with the necessary training, self-managing teams will have a difficult time living up to expectations.

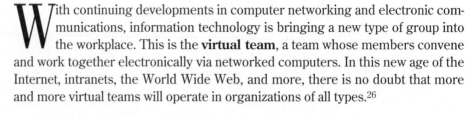

VIRTUAL TEAMS

A **virtual team** convenes and operates with members linked together electronically via networked computers.

With continuing developments in computer networking and electronic communications, information technology is bringing a new type of group into the workplace. This is the **virtual team**, a team whose members convene and work together electronically via networked computers. In this new age of the Internet, intranets, the World Wide Web, and more, there is no doubt that more and more virtual teams will operate in organizations of all types.[26]

▼ ELECTRONIC MEETINGS

Until recently, "group" decision making was confined to those circumstances in which members could be physically face to face. The advent of group decision support systems and sophisticated computer programs known as *groupware* has changed all that. Groupware allows for computer-mediated meetings and decision making in a variety of situations, ranging from a common electronic meeting or decision rooms to global area networks. The growing use of *electronic brainstorming* is one example of the trend toward virtual meetings. Assisted by special software, participants use personal computers to enter ideas at will, either through simultaneous interaction or over a period of time. The software compiles and disseminates the ideas in return. This electronic version of traditional brainstorming seems to offer several advantages. They include the benefits of anonymity, greater number of ideas generated, efficiency of recording and storing for later use, and ability to handle large groups with geographically dispersed members.[27]

Marriott uses an electronic group meeting room employing VisionQuest software. Group members work via computer mediation to share information, process ideas, and solve problems. Time saving and vastly expanded idea pools are among the cited advantages.[28]

▼ VIRTUAL TEAM DYNAMICS

Members of virtual teams typically do the same things as members of face-to-face teams. They share information, make decisions, and complete tasks. Hopefully, they also experience the satisfactions of performance accomplishment. With the computer as the "go-between" for virtual team members, however, group dynamics can emerge with a slightly different form than found in face-to-face settings.[29]

Although technology can help to overcome great distance in making communication possible among a group of people, it may also create teams whose members do not share much, if any, direct "personal" contact. Whereas this may have an advantage of focusing interaction and decision making on facts and objective information rather than emotional considerations, it also may increase risks as decisions are made in a limited social context. Virtual teams may suffer from less social rapport and less direct interaction among members. Finally, the cost of supporting technology and training to bring virtual teams on-line can be high.[30]

Virtual teams are an everyday phenomenon at Texas Instruments, where physical distance doesn't stop people from working together. On any given
day you can find computer designers working together from all over the world—linked via computers—to pool ideas and create new products. Talented engineers in Bangalore, India, may work with other group members in Japan and Texas to develop a new chip. When the design is finished it is sent via computer to Texas for fabrication and then goes back to Bangalore for any required "debugging." Says a TI group vice president, "Problems that used to take three years now take a year."[31]

CHAPTER 10 STUDY GUIDE

What are the essentials of high-performance teams?

SUMMARY

- A team is a small group of people working together to achieve a common purpose for which they hold themselves collectively accountable.
- Teamwork occurs when members of a team work together so that their skills are well utilized to accomplish common goals.
- High-performance teams have core values, clear performance objectives, the right mix of skills, and creativity.
- Team building is a data-based approach to analyzing group performance and taking steps to improve it in the future.
- Team building is participative and engages all group members in collaborative problem solving and action.

How do team processes affect performance?

- Individual entry problems are common when new teams are formed and when new members join existing teams.
- Task leadership involves initiating and summarizing, making direct contributions to the group's task agenda; maintenance leadership involves gatekeeping and encouraging, helping to support the social fabric of the group over time.
- Role difficulties occur when expectations for group members are unclear, overwhelming, underwhelming, or conflicting.
- Norms, rules or standards for what is considered appropriate behavior by group members, can have a significant impact on group processes and outcomes.
- Members of highly cohesive groups value their membership and are very loyal to the group, they also tend to conform to group norms.

- When performance norms are positive, cohesiveness and conformity work to the benefit of the organization; when performance norms are negative, cohesiveness and conformity to norms work against the organization's interests.

What are employee involvement groups?
- An employee involvement group is any group whose members meet regularly to address important work-related problems and concerns.
- Members of a quality circle, a popular type of employee involvement group, meet regularly to deal with issues of quality improvement in work processes.
- "Participation" is the true key to employee involvement.

Why are self-managing teams important today?
- Self-managing teams are small work groups that operate with empowerment and essentially manage themselves on a day-to-day basis.
- Members of self-managing teams collectively take responsibility for making many of the "supervisory" decisions common in traditional work groups.
- Members of self-managing teams typically plan, complete, and evaluate their own work; train and evaluate one another in job tasks; and share tasks and responsibilities.
- Self-managing teams can contribute to improved productivity for organizations and improved quality of working life for their members.
- Self-managing teams have structural and management implications for organizations since they largely eliminate the first-line supervisors.

What are new developments with virtual teams?
- A virtual team is one whose members convene and work together via networked computers.
- A wide variety of group decision support software is available for virtual teams, allowing them to operate in electronic decision rooms and wide area networks.
- The electronic rather than face-to-face interaction on virtual teams can have an impact on group dynamics.
- Potential advantages of virtual teams include a greater focus on objective facts and information; potential disadvantages relate to the loss of face-to-face social interaction among the members.

KEY TERMS

Cohesiveness (p. 204)	Multiskilling (p. 207)	Self-managing team
Distributed leadership	Norm (p. 203)	(p. 207)
(p. 200)	Quality circle (p. 206)	Task activities (p. 200)
Employee involvement	Role (p. 201)	Team (p. 194)
group (p. 206)	Role ambiguity (p. 201)	Teamwork (p. 195)
Maintenance activities	Role conflict (p. 201)	Team building (p. 196)
(p. 200)		Virtual team (p. 210)

▼ **MULTIPLE CHOICE**
1. High-performance teams _____. (a) operate with general performance goals (b) are task oriented but lack creativity (c) have the right mix of membership skills (d) don't need strong core values

2. The team-building process can best be described as _____. (a) participative (b) data based (c) action oriented (d) all of these

3. When a new group member is anxious about questions such as, "Will I be able to influence what takes place?" the underlying issue is one of _____. (a) relationships (b) goals (c) processes (d) control

4. A person facing an ethical dilemma involving differences between personal values and employer expectations is experiencing _____ conflict. (a) person–role (b) intrasender role (c) intersender role (d) interrole

5. The statement "*On our team, people always try to do their best*" is an example of a _____ norm. (a) support and helpfulness (b) high-achievement (c) organizational pride (d) organizational improvement

6. Highly cohesive groups tend to _____. (a) be bad for organizations (b) be good for their members (c) have more social loafing among members (d) have greater membership turnover

7. To increase group cohesiveness, one would _____. (a) make the group bigger (b) increase membership diversity (c) isolate the group from others (d) relax performance pressures

8. Self-managing teams _____. (a) reduce the number of different job tasks members need to master (b) largely eliminate the need for a traditional supervisor (c) rely heavily on outside training to maintain job skills (d) add another management layer to overhead costs

9. Which statement about self-managing teams is correct? (a) They can improve performance but not satisfaction. (b) They should have limited decision making authority. (c) They should operate without any team leaders. (d) They should let members plan work schedules.

10. A group member who does a good job at summarizing discussion, offering new ideas, and clarifying points made by others is contributing _____ activities to the group process. (a) required (b) disruptive (c) task (d) maintenance

▼ TRUE–FALSE

11. Collective accountability for results is essential for a true team.   T F
12. Team building should only be done in a formal retreat with the help of an outside consultant.   T F
13. Group members work best with role ambiguity and unclear expectations.   T F
14. Role overload is bad; role underload is good.   T F
15. The only norm that is really important to group success is the performance norm. T F
16. A quality circle is an example of an employee involvement group.   T F
17. Quality circles are unique in that they work well in all situations.   T F
18. Through multiskilling, members of self-managing teams are capable of switching job tasks.   T F
19. Self-managing teams seem to work well in all work settings.   T F
20. A lack of social interaction may cause problems for people working together as a virtual team.   T F

▼ SHORT RESPONSE

21. What is the team-building process?
22. How can a team leader help build positive group norms?

23. How do cohesiveness and conformity to norms influence group performance?

24. What are members of self-managing teams typically expected to do?

▼ APPLICATIONS ESSAY

25. While "surfing the Internet" one day you encounter this note posted in your RPG discussion group. *Help. I have just been assigned to head a new product design team at my company. The division manager has high expectations for the team and me, but I have been a technical design engineer for 4 years since graduating from university. I have never "managed" anyone, let alone led a team. The manager keeps talking about her confidence that I will create a "high-performance team." Does anyone out there have any tips to help me master this challenge? Help. /s/Galahad.* As a good citizen of the net you decide to answer. What message will you send out?

11

Basic Attributes of Organizations

At First Community Financial, CEO Jim Adamany faced a conventional but vexing problem. First Community Financial is a modest-sized small business lender specializing in loans backed by the assets of small firms and factoring (loans based on invoices a firm has sent to clients who have yet to pay). Analyzing the credit worthiness for conventional loans and factoring calls for different skills are typically organized in separate departments. Small business clients rarely understand the use of loans or factoring, and they often don't see how a firm such as First Community can help them grow even though the financial firm charges somewhat higher rates on its higher risk loans and factoring.

Jim's solution was simple and elegant. He organized the firm into three major groups: (1) marketing organized around client groups with a single business development officer for each client, (2) a finance division for loans in which employees analyze client credit worthiness and recommend approval for loans, and (3) a factoring division in which employees evaluate the account receivables of a client. Of course, the structure means that marketing will want to make loans and factoring agreements even to clients with very questionable credit ratings, whereas the finance and factoring managers only want to approve the highest quality loans. To minimize this problem Jim relies extensively on personal methods of coordination across the three groups. Employees from all three groups work together with Jim to develop an acceptable tradeoff between risk and sales for each potential client. There are no easy answers, but Jim knows that his experienced staff realizes that solving this problem is a key to success. (First Community Financial)[1]

I n Chapter 1, we defined an organization as a collection of people working to-

gether in a division of labor to achieve a common purpose. In this chapter we will

expand this definition to provide you with a working knowledge of organizational

goals and the division of labor and the supporting structures organizations use to

become successful.

The traditional basics of organizing and the ways in which firms are modifying traditions to compete in the 1990s are important topics in organizational behavior. As you read Chapter 11, keep in mind these study questions:

- ◉ What types of contributions do organizations make and what types of goals do they adopt?

- ◉ What is the formal structure of the organization and what is meant by the term "division of labor"?

- ◉ How is vertical specialization used to allocate formal authority within the organization?

- ◉ How does the firm control the actions of its members?

- ◉ What different patterns of horizontal specialization can be used in the organization?

- ◉ Which personal and impersonal coordination techniques should the organization use?

CONTRIBUTIONS AND GOALS OF ORGANIZATIONS

W ithout organizations our modern societies would cease to function. Economies would collapse, governments would evaporate, religion would fade, and education would all but come to a halt. We would need to revert to older forms of social organization based on royalty, clans, and tribes. Our world is one of organizations from the time we are born. They are so pervasive and so commonplace that it is sometimes easy to forget that organizations may be viewed as entities with specific goals.[2]

Jim Adamany of First Community Financial knows these basics and recognizes that there are many different ways to improve his corporation. He is aware that the goals he emphasizes are often multifaceted and often conflict with one another. These goals are common to individuals within the organization only to the extent that managers, such as Jim Adamany and other members are aware of how an individual's interests can be partially served by the organization. In this section, we examine how the organization intends to serve society. We then examine the types of goals organizations adopt in their attempts to survive.

▼ SOCIETAL CONTRIBUTIONS OF ORGANIZATIONS

Organizations do not operate in a social vacuum but reflect the needs and desires of the societies in which they operate. **Societal goals** reflect the intended contributions of an organization to the broader society.[3] Organizations normally serve a specific societal function or an enduring need of the society.[4] Astute top-level managers build on the professed societal contribution of the organization by relating specific organizational tasks and activities to higher purposes.[5] **Mission statements**—written statements of organizational purpose—may include these corporate ideas of service to the society. Weaving a mission statement together with an emphasis on implementation to provide direction and motivation is an executive order of the first magnitude.

> **Societal goals** are goals reflecting the intended contributions of an organization to the broader society.

> **Mission statements** are written statements of organizational purpose.

QUALITY

Bread Loaf Construction Company, in Middlebury, Vermont, is proud of its mission statement.[6] And well it should be, because it was a successful attempt by cofounders Mac McLaughlin and John Leehman to take a little more control of their destiny. The Bread Loaf mission statement reads:

We are Bread Loaf, a team of building professionals dedicated to and empowered by the strength of our people.

We seek challenges to create innovative solutions which make statements demonstrating our commitment to excellence.

We shall continually focus on profitability, employee wellness, community involvement, and a sensitive balance between personal and professional fulfillment.

The statement was not developed just by the cofounders but involved a cross section of salaried and hourly employees, who queried their counterparts to spot current problems and scout long-term potentials in the highly cyclical construction industry. To implement this mission, all agreed to participate in cross-sectional ad hoc teams to make the mission a reality. The teams were charged with spotting new opportunities for Bread Loaf. Of course, to ensure continuity, the cofounders also developed a "vision threading" team with rotating membership to keep the mission and implementation in sync.

217

Such a sense of mission in a political party may be to generate and allocate power for the betterment of all citizens. Universities attempt to develop and disseminate knowledge. Churches instill values and protect the spiritual wellbeing of all. Courts integrate the interests and activities of citizens. Finally, business firms provide economic sustenance and material wellbeing to society.

Societal contributions form a basis that allows organizations to make claims over resources, individuals, markets, and products. Organizations that can effectively translate the character of their societal contribution for their members have an advantage—they have an additional set of motivational tools that are based on a shared sense of noble purpose.

▼ PRIMARY BENEFICIARIES

Whereas some organizations may provide benefits to the society as a whole, most target their efforts toward a particular group.[7] In the United States, for example, it is generally expected that the *primary beneficiary* of business firms is the stockholder. Political organizations are formed to serve the common good, and culturally based organizations, such as churches, may emphasize contributions to their members. In contrast to the internal focus of churches, social-service organizations, such as hospitals, are expected to emphasize service to their clients and customers.

Although each organization may have a primary beneficiary, its mission statement may also recognize the interests of many other parties. Thus, business mission statements often include service to customers, the organization's obligations to employees, and its intention to support the community.

The view of organizational goals in many traditional Japanese firms is quite different. Instead of making stockholders the primary beneficiaries, Japanese senior executives place long-time workers at the center of the firm. This approach ensures that those individuals with the proper expertise and greatest stake in maintaining the company form the core of the organization. This approach is also consistent with the belief among Japanese managers that their role is to develop and expand the business to provide employment security and economic growth for the country. Stockholders are not given the priority of long-term employees. Instead, they are seen as important suppliers of money, just as component suppliers provide a manufacturer with vital raw materials.

▼ OUTPUT GOALS

Many larger organizations have found it useful to state very carefully which business they are in.[8] This statement can form the basis for long-term planning and may help prevent huge organizations from diverting too many resources to peripheral areas. For some corporations, answering this question may yield a more detailed statement concerning their products and services. These product and service goals provide an important basis for judging the quality of an organization's major contributions to society.

Output goals define the type of business an organization is in and provide some substance to the more general aspects of mission statements. In the 1990s firms are clarifying and narrowing their output goals.

Data General will attempt to "take silicon, put it into world-class machines"; and the company is "not going to stray very far from our engineering roots."[9]

Output goals are the goals that define the type of business an organization is in.

▼ SYSTEMS GOALS AND ORGANIZATIONAL SURVIVAL

Fewer than 10 percent of the businesses founded in a typical year can be expected to survive to their twentieth birthday.[10] The survival rate for public organizations is not much better. Even in organizations for which survival is not an immediate problem, managers seek specific types of conditions within their firms that minimize the risk of demise and promote survival. These conditions are positively stated as systems goals.

Systems goals are concerned with the conditions within the organization that are expected to increase the organization's survival potential. The list of systems goals is almost endless, since each manager and researcher links today's conditions to tomorrow's existence in a different way. For many organizations, however, the list includes growth, productivity, stability, harmony, flexibility, prestige, and, of course, human resource maintenance. In some businesses, analysts consider market share and current profitability important systems goals. Other recent studies suggest that innovation and quality are also considered important.[11] In a very practical sense, systems goals represent short-term organizational characteristics that higher level managers wish to promote. Systems goals must often be balanced against one another. For instance, a productivity and efficiency drive, if taken too far, may reduce the flexibility of an organization.

Different parts of the organization may be asked to pursue different types of systems goals. For example, higher level managers may expect to see their production operations strive for efficiency while pressing for innovation from their R&D lab and promoting stability in their financial affairs.

The relative importance of different systems goals can vary substantially across various types of organizations. Although we may expect the University of British Columbia or the University of New South Wales to emphasize prestige and innovation, few expect such businesses as Siemans or AT&T to emphasize prestige over growth and profitability.

> **Systems goals** are goals concerned with conditions within the organization that are expected to increase its survival potential.

At Motorola, executives are asked to carry a card on them at all times showing the central focus of the corporation on customers and its commitment to key beliefs, goals, and initiatives. On the front, in bold letters, it says, "OUR FUNDAMENTAL OBJECTIVE (Everyone's Overriding Responsibility), TOTAL CUSTOMER SATISFACTION." On the back, it lists key beliefs on how executives will act. The two listed are constant respect for people and uncompromising integrity. To match these beliefs it provides the following goals: increased global market share and best in class (people, marketing, technology, product, manufacturing, service). It then provides some key mechanisms Motorola will use in the jargon of the firm: Six Sigma Quality, Total Cycle Time Reduction, Product and Manufacturing Leadership, Profit Improvement, and Participative Management Within and Cooperation Between Organizations.

QUALITY

KEY BELIEFS—*how we will always act*
* Constant Respect for People
* Uncompromising Integrity

KEY GOALS—*what we must accomplish*
* Best in Class
  —*People*
  —*Marketing*
  —*Technology*
  —*Product: Software, Hardware and Systems*
  —*Manufacturing*
  —*Service*
* Increased Global Market Share
* Superior Financial Results

KEY INITIATIVES—*how we will do it*
* Six Sigma Quality
* Total Cycle Time Reduction
* Product, Manufacturing and Environmental Leadership
* Profit Improvement
* Empowerment for all, in a Participative, Cooperative and Creative Workplace

Rev. 8-92

OUR FUNDAMENTAL OBJECTIVE
(Everyone's Overriding Responsibility)

Total Customer Satisfaction

 **MOTOROLA**

Systems goals are so important to firms because they provide a road map to assist in linking together various units of an organization to assure its survival. Well-defined systems goals are practical and easy to understand; they focus the manager's attention on what needs to be done. Furthermore, accurately stated systems goals offer managers flexibility in devising ways to meet important targets. They can be used to balance the demands, constraints, and opportunities facing the firm. They can form a basis for dividing the work of the firm into manageable pieces. In short, a firm's systems goals provide a basis for developing a formal structure.

FORMAL STRUCTURES AND THE DIVISION OF LABOR

To help accomplish their goals, managers develop an intended *formal structure* that shows the general, planned configuration of positions, job duties, and the lines of authority among different parts of the enterprise. Traditionally, the formal structure of the firm has also been called the "division of labor." Some still use this term to separate issues concerning the formal structure of the firm from related questions, such as those concerning the division of markets, the choice of businesses, and/or the selection of a technology. The formal structure is important because it provides the foundations for managerial action. It outlines the job to be done, the person(s) (in terms of position) who are to perform specific activities, and the ways in which the total task of the organization is to be accomplished. In other words, it is the skeleton of the organization.

Organization charts
are diagrams that depict the formal structures of organizations.

Organization charts are diagrams that depict the formal structures of organizations. A typical chart shows the various positions, the position holders, and the lines of authority that link them to one another. Figure 11.1 is a partial organization chart for a large university. The total chart allows university employees to locate their positions in the structure and to identify the lines of authority linking them with others in the organization. For instance, in this figure, the treasurer reports to the vice president of administration, who, in turn, reports to the president of the university.

VERTICAL SPECIALIZATION

Vertical specialization
is a hierarchical division of labor that distributes formal authority.

In larger organizations, there is a clear separation of authority and duties by hierarchical rank. This separation represents **vertical specialization,** a hierarchical division of labor that distributes formal authority and establishes where and how critical decisions are to be made. This division creates a hierarchy of authority—an arrangement of work positions in order of increasing authority.

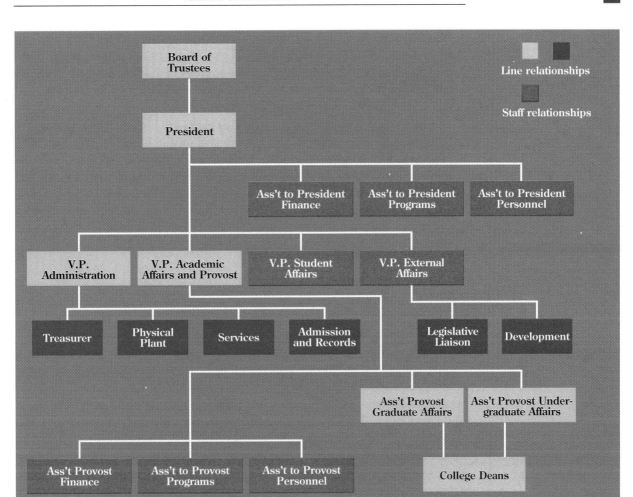

■ Figure 11.1

A partial organization chart for a state university.

In the United States, the distribution of formal authority is evident in the responsibilities typical of managers. Top managers or senior executives plan the overall strategy of the organization and plot its long-term future.[12] They also act as final judges for internal disputes and serve to certify promotions, reorganizations, and the like. Middle managers guide the daily operations of the organization, help formulate policy, and translate top-management decisions into more specific guidelines for action. Lower level managers supervise the actions of subordinates to ensure implementation of the strategies authorized by top management and compliance with the related policies established by middle management.

Managers in Japan often have different responsibilities than do managers in the typical U.S. firm. Japanese top managers do not develop and decide the overall strategy of the firm. Instead, they manage a process involving middle managers. The process involves extensive dialogue about actions the firm needs to take. Lower level managers are also expected to act as advocates for the ideas and suggestions of their subordinates. The strategy of the firm emerges from dialogue and discussion, and implementation proceeds according to the ideas and suggestions of lower managers and nonmanagers.

In many European firms, the senior managers are highly trained in the core of their business. For example, it is not unusual for the head of a manufacturing firm to have a Ph.D. in engineering. Thus, many European executives become more centrally involved in plotting the technical future of their firm. In contrast, few U.S. or Japanese executives have the necessary technical background to tackle this responsibility. Despite the differences in managerial responsibilities across Japan, Europe, and North America, all organizations have vertical specialization.

▼ CHAIN OF COMMAND AND THE SPAN OF CONTROL

Executives, managers, and supervisors are hierarchically connected through the *chain of command.* Individuals are expected to follow their supervisors' decisions in the areas of responsibility outlined in the organization chart. Traditional management theory suggests that each individual should have one boss and each unit one leader. Under the circumstances, there is a "unity of command." Unity of command is considered necessary to avoid confusion, to assign accountability to specific individuals, and to provide clear channels of communication up and down the organization. Under traditional management, with unity of command, the number of individuals a manager can supervise directly is obviously limited. The number of individuals reporting to a supervisor is called the **span of control.** Narrower spans of control are expected when tasks are complex, when subordinates are inexperienced or poorly trained, and/or when tasks call for team effort. Unfortunately, narrow spans of control yield many organizational levels. The excessive number of levels is not only expensive, it also makes the organization unresponsive to necessary change. Communications in such firms often become less effective because they are successively screened and modified so that subtle but important changes get ignored. Furthermore, with many levels, managers are removed from the action and become isolated. Only when facing an identifiable, obvious, and direct threat might the firm with many levels be able to react quickly.

In the 1990s, firms have begun to experiment with new patterns of vertical specialization. They are dramatically cutting the number of levels of management, and they are expanding the span of control. In many cases, organizations are modifying the traditional notion of unity of command. At Nucor, for instance, senior managers pioneered the development of "minimills" for making steel and developed what they call "lean" management. At the same time, management has expanded the span of control with extensive employee education and training. The senior managers now promote team development to help replace direct supervision by a single manager. The result: Nucor has four levels of management from the bottom to the top.

> **Span of control** refers to the number of individuals reporting to a supervisor.

▼ LINE AND STAFF UNITS

A very useful way to examine the vertical division of labor is to separate line and staff units. **Line units** and personnel conduct the major business of the organization. The production and marketing functions are two examples. In contrast, **staff units** and personnel assist the line units by providing specialized expertise and services, such as accounting and public relations. For example, the vice president of administration in a university (Figure 11.1) heads a staff unit, as does the vice president of student affairs. All academic departments are line units since they constitute the basic production function of the university.

A useful distinction to be made for both line and staff units concerns the amount and types of contacts each maintains with outsiders to the organization. Some units are mainly internal in orientation; others are more external in focus. In general, *internal line units* (e.g., production) focus on transforming raw materials and information into products and services, whereas *external line units* (e.g., marketing) focus on maintaining linkages to suppliers, distributors, and customers. *Internal staff units* (e.g., accounting) assist the line units in performing their function. Normally they specialize in specific technical and/or financial areas. *External staff units* (e.g., public relations) also assist the line units, but the focus of their actions is on linking the firm to its environment and buffering internal operations.

What To Do With the Staff   On the surface, it appears that firms need to handle all potentially useful staff functions. Someone needs to keep the books, hire and train the personnel, deal with the press, and conduct the research and development.

Figure 11.2 shows how the placement of staff alters the appearance of the firm. Staff units can be assigned predominantly to senior, middle, or lower level managers. When staff is assigned predominantly to senior management, the capability of senior management to develop alternatives and make decisions is expanded. When staff is at the top, senior executives can directly develop information and alternatives and check on the implementation of their decisions. Here, the degree of vertical specialization in the firm is comparatively lower because senior managers plan, decide, and control via their centralized staff. In this case, lower level managers and employees often report that formal authority is concentrated at the top. To increase responsiveness some firms, such as Owens-Illinois have shifted staff from top management to middle management. When staff are removed to the middle of the organization, middle managers see more delegation. They now have the specialized help necessary to expand their role.

In the 1990s, firms are also beginning to ask whether certain staff should be a permanent part of the organization at all. Some are outsourcing many of their staff functions. Manufacturing firms are spinning off much of their accounting, personnel, and public relations activities to small, specialized firms. These manufacturing firms are developing joint research and development agreements with suppliers, distributors, and even potential competitors to concentrate on their core operations. They are finding that with highly trained managers and employ-

> **Line units** are work groups that conduct the major business of the organization.

> **Staff units** are groups that assist the line units by performing specialized services to the organization.

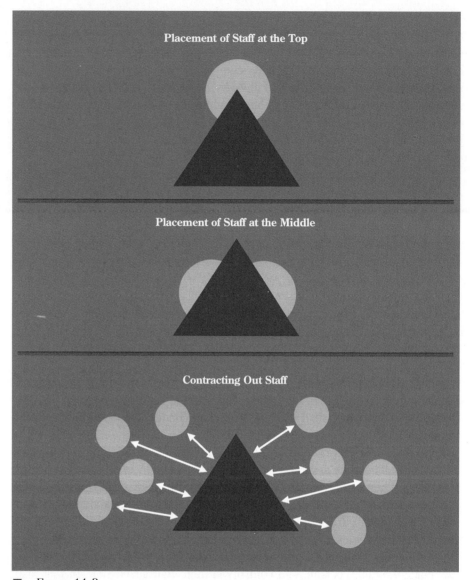

■ FIGURE 11.2

How placement of staff changes the look of an organization.

ees, middle and lower level managers can contract out for the necessary staff services.[13]

Outsourcing by large firms has been a boon for smaller corporations. For instance, José Taylor is the owner–manager of a software development firm under a long-term contract with a giant Japanese computer corporation. Taylor's operation is just one part of the Japanese firm's research and development arm in its reach into the U.S. market. Software Tayloring is assigned to develop programs that convert Japanese software into programs compatible with U.S. machines, and vice versa.

Figure 11.2 shows the use of staff via "contracting out."In large part, the elimination of staff units can happen only when the firm uses another important tool in vertical specialization: managerial techniques.

▼ MANAGERIAL TECHNIQUES

One of the foremost trends in modern industry involves streamlining operations and reducing staff in order to lower costs and raise productivity.[14] One way to facilitate these actions is to provide line managers and employees with managerial techniques designed to expand on their analytical and decision-making capabilities, thereby eliminating the need for staff "experts." Good examples are the ever-increasing role of the computer and associated decision support software in all areas of management.

In one sense, managerial techniques, such as computer-based expert systems, are substitutes for both line and staff managers and staff units.[15] Managerial techniques may be used to detect problems and opportunities, to select among alternative courses of action, and to monitor the progress of implementation. For instance, those studying financial management recognize the importance of financial planning models (in detecting problems), financial decision aids, such as capital budgeting models and discounted cash-flow analyses (for selecting among alternatives), and budgets (to monitor progress and ensure that managers stay within financial limits). With computer programs each of these is now accessible to all levels of management and is no longer restricted to financial staff.

Although a great variety of managerial techniques have been available to managers for decades, only with the widespread use of computers have the costs of these techniques been reduced. It is no longer necessary for middle managers to file reports on the accomplishments of others. Via computer, employees can file such reports themselves or have them filed as a natural byproduct of their work. Employees can use their own reports to better plan and improve their own work without waiting for management to intervene.

Managerial techniques are employed to expand the volume and scope of operations a manager can administer.[16] They can allow the manager to handle more sophisticated operations. *Decision support systems* (DSS) combine advances in computer hardware and software with the development of extensive information bases to aid line managers in decision making. More and more "expert systems" are also being created. These sophisticated computer programs can be used to duplicate the judgments of experts in areas calling for considerable skill, experience, intuition, and judgment.

Most organizations use a combination of line and staff units, alliances with specialized providers, plus managerial techniques to specialize the division of labor vertically (e.g., to distribute formal authority). The most appropriate pattern of vertical specialization depends on the environment of the organization, its size, its technology, and its goals. Generally, as organizations grow, vertical specialization increases. We will return to this theme in the next chapter. For now, let us turn our attention to those issues relating to control of the organization.

CONTROL

> **Control** is the set of mechanisms used to keep actions and outputs within predetermined limits.

Control is the set of mechanisms used to keep action and/or outputs within predetermined limits. Control deals with setting standards, measuring results versus standards, and instituting corrective action. Although controls are needed in all organizations, just a few controls may go a long way. Astute managers need to be aware of the danger of too much control in the organization.

▼ OUTPUT CONTROLS

Earlier in this chapter, we suggested that systems goals could be used as a road map to tie together the various units of the organization toward achieving a practical objective. Developing targets or standards, measuring results against these targets, and taking corrective action are all steps involved in developing output controls. **Output controls** focus on desired targets and allow managers to use their own methods for reaching defined targets.

> **Output controls** are controls that focus on desired targets and allow managers to use their own methods for reaching defined targets.

Most modern organizations use output controls as a part of an overall method of managing by exception. At Heinz, for example, Senior Vice President David Sculley explains, "We manage by exception generally. There's a goal post that is clear for every member of the company—yearly and quarterly. . . . When we see a problem developing we jump on it." Output controls are popular because they promote flexibility and creativity as well as facilitate dialogue concerning corrective action.

Reliance on outcome controls separates *what* is to be accomplished from *how* it is to be accomplished. Thus, the discussion of goals is separated from the dialogue concerning methods. This separation can facilitate the movement of power down the organization, as senior managers are reassured that individuals at all levels will be working toward the goals senior management believes are important, even as lower level managers innovate and introduce new ways to accomplish these goals.

▼ PROCESS CONTROLS

Few organizations run on outcome controls alone. Once a solution to a problem is found and successfully implemented, managers do not want the problem to recur, so they institute process controls. **Process controls** attempt to specify the manner in which tasks are accomplished. There are many types of process controls, but three groups have received considerable attention: (1) policies, rules, and procedures; (2) formalization and standardization; and (3) quality management controls.

> **Process controls** are controls that attempt to specify the manner in which tasks are to be accomplished.

Policies, Rules, and Procedures   Most organizations implement a variety of policies, rules, and procedures to help specify how goals are to be accomplished. Procedures indicate the best method for performing a task, show which aspects of a task are the most important, or outline how an individual is to be rewarded.

Usually, we think of a *policy* as a guideline for action that outlines important objectives and broadly indicates how an activity is to be performed. A policy allows for individual discretion and minor adjustments without direct clearance by a higher level manager. For example, most U.S. firms have a stated policy toward diversity that not only enunciates the firm's goals for increasing the diversity of its work force but also specifies the general procedures to be used in hiring.

Rules and procedures are more specific, rigid, and impersonal than policies. They typically describe in detail how a task or a series of tasks is to be performed. They are designed to apply to all individuals, under specified conditions. For example, most car dealers have detailed instruction manuals for repairing a new car under warranty, and they must follow very strict procedures to obtain reimbursement from the manufacturer for warranty work.

Rules, procedures, and policies are often employed as substitutes for direct managerial supervision. Under the guidance of written rules and procedures, the organization can specifically direct the activities of many individuals. It can ensure virtually identical treatment across even distant work locations. For example, a McDonald's hamburger and fries taste much the same whether they are purchased in Hong Kong, Indianapolis, London, or Toronto simply because the ingredients and the cooking methods follow written rules and procedures.

Rules, procedures, and policies also allow organizations to practice management by exception. Managers need not concentrate on the routine activities or decisions. They can spend their time on more important, unusual, or unique conditions that may have a more direct impact on performance and/or satisfaction.

> ## Take-a-Note 11-1
> ### SIGNS OF TOO MUCH CONTROL
>
> 1. Too much emphasis on one measured goal to the exclusion of all others.
> 2. Too much emphasis on the quick fix and an unwillingness to look for underlying causes of problems or new opportunities.
> 3. A tradition of across-the-board cuts rather than reductions linked to demands, constraints, and opportunities.
> 4. Too many vague and unrealistic expectations that breed defeat.
> 5. Raising quotas without rewarding employees, particularly after implementing employee suggestions for change.

Formalization and Standardization   **Formalization** refers to the written documentation of rules, procedures, and policies to guide behavior and decision making. Beyond substituting for direct management supervision, formalization is often used to simplify jobs. Written instructions allow individuals with less training to perform comparatively sophisticated tasks. Written procedures may also be available to ensure that a proper sequence of tasks is executed, even if this sequence is performed only occasionally.

> **Formalization** is the written documentation of work rules, policies, and procedures.

Most organizations have developed additional methods for dealing with recurring problems or situations. **Standardization** is the degree to which the range of allowable actions in a job or series of jobs is limited. It involves the creation of guidelines so that similar work activities are repeatedly performed in a similar fashion. Such standardized methods may come from years of experience in dealing with typical situations, or they may come from outside training. For instance, managers may be trained to handle crises by setting priorities and dealing

> **Standardization** is the degree to which the range of actions in a job or series of jobs is limited.

with them at all costs. Obviously, such situations call for judgment and cannot be handled by written rules—no written rules can anticipate every possible crisis.

Total Quality Management   The process controls discussed so far—policies, rules, procedures, formalization, and standardization—represent the lessons of experience within an organization. That is, managers institute these process controls based on past experience. Another way to institute process controls is to establish a total quality management process within the firm.

The late W. Edwards Deming is the modern-day founder of what is now referred to as the *total quality management movement*. When Deming's ideas were not generally accepted in the United States, he found an audience in Japan. Thus, to some managers, Deming's ideas appear in the form of the best Japanese business practices.

The heart of Deming's approach is to institute a process approach to continual improvement based on statistical analyses of the firm's operations. Around this core idea, Deming built a series of 14 points for managers to implement.[17] They are:

■ Deming's 14 points

1. Create a consistency of purpose in the company to
   a. innovate.
   b. put resources into research and education.
   c. put resources into maintaining equipment and new production aids.
2. Learn a new philosophy of quality to improve every system.
3. Require statistical evidence of process control and eliminate financial controls on production.
4. Require statistical evidence of control in purchasing parts; this will mean dealing with fewer suppliers.
5. Use statistical methods to isolate the sources of trouble.
6. Institute modern on-the-job training.
7. Improve supervision to develop inspired leaders.
8. Drive out fear and instill learning.
9. Break down barriers between departments.
10. Eliminate numerical goals and slogans.
11. Constantly revamp work methods.
12. Institute massive training programs for employees in statistical methods.
13. Retrain people in new skills.
14. Create a structure that will push, everyday, on the above 13 points.

Note that all levels of management are to be involved in the quality program. Managers are to improve supervision, train employees, retrain employees in new skills, and create a structure that pushes the quality program. Where the properties of the firm's outcomes are well defined, as in most manufacturing operations, Deming's system and emphasis on quality appears to work well. Where the products of the firm and the methods of production are more subjective, successful application of statistical methods is more difficult. Regardless, the emphasis on training, learning, and consistency of purpose appear to be important lessons that all organizations need to be reminded of constantly.

Reimer Express employs some 1000 Canadians and is one of the nation's largest trucking companies.[18] In this highly competitive business, quality of

service often is as important as cost in keeping valued customers. Traditionally, Reimer Express would match new employees with experienced ones so that new employees would pick up the proper focus on customer quality. The results were uneven, so management instituted a training program based on total quality management to reinforce precisely what was needed to compete effectively.

▼ ALLOCATING FORMAL AUTHORITY: CENTRALIZATION AND DECENTRALIZATION

Different firms use very different mixes of vertical specialization, output controls, process controls, and managerial techniques to allocate the authority or discretion to act. For employees the key to understanding the mix is knowing how they, as individuals, respond to the degree of discretion or freedom to act they are given.

The farther up the hierarchy of authority the discretion to spend money, to hire people, and to make similar decisions is moved, the greater the degree of **centralization.** The more such decisions are delegated, or moved down the hierarchy of authority, the greater the degree of **decentralization.** Generally speaking, greater decentralization provides higher subordinate satisfaction and a quicker response to problems. Decentralization also assists in the on-the-job training of subordinates for higher level positions. Decentralization is now a popular approach in many industries. For instance, Union Carbide is pushing responsibility down the chain of command, as are General Motors, Ford, and Chrysler.[19] In each case, the senior managers hope to improve both performance quality and organizational responsiveness.

Closely related to decentralization is the notion of *participation.* Many people want to be involved in making decisions that affect their work. Participation results when a manager delegates some authority for such decision making to subordinates. Employees may want a say both in what the unit objectives should be and in how they may be achieved.[20] Especially in recent years, and in light of the challenge from the Japanese forms of participation, even conservative firms are experimenting with new ways to decentralize parts of their operations. Throughout this book, we have provided numerous examples of employee empowerment. The foundation of empowerment on the part of the organization is the development of decentralization matched with extensive participation and supported by few managerial levels and few bureaucratically based controls (such as rules and procedures). In recent years, many firms, such as Intel Corporation, Eli Lilly, Apple Computer, Boeing, Dow Chemical, and Hoffman-LaRoche, have experimented by moving decisions down the chain of command and increasing participation. These firms found that just cutting the number of organizational levels

Centralization is the degree to which the authority to make decisions is restricted to higher levels of management.

Decentralization is the degree to which the authority to make decisions is given to lower levels in an organization's hierarchy.

229

was insufficient; they also needed to alter their controls toward quality, to stress constant improvement, and to change other basic features of the organization, such as the division of work among units or the firm's horizontal specialization.

HORIZONTAL SPECIALIZATION

Vertical specialization and control are only half the picture. Managers must also divide the total task into separate duties and group similar people and resources together.[21] **Horizontal specialization** is a division of labor that establishes specific work units or groups within an organization; it is often referred to as the process of departmentation. There are a variety of pure forms of departmentation.

> **Horizontal specialization** is a division of labor through the formation of work units or groups within an organization.

▼ DEPARTMENTATION BY FUNCTION

Grouping individuals by skill, knowledge, and action yields a pattern of *functional departmentation*. Figure 11.3 shows the organization chart for a nuclear power plant, in which each department has a technical specialty considered necessary for safe and efficient operation of the plant. In business, marketing, finance, production, and personnel are important functions. In many small firms, this functional pattern dominates. For instance, Apple Computer used this pattern early in its development. Figure 11.3 also summarizes the advantages of the functional pattern. With all these advantages, it is not surprising that the functional form is extremely popular. It is used in most organizations, particularly toward the bottom of the hierarchy. Of course, functional specialization also has some disadvantages, which are also summarized in Figure 11.3. Organizations that rely heavily on functional specialization may expect the following tendencies to emerge over time: an emphasis on quality from a technical standpoint, rigidity to change, and difficulty in coordinating the actions of different functional areas.

▼ DEPARTMENTATION BY DIVISION

Divisional departmentation groups individuals and resources by products, services, clients, and/or legal entities. Figure 11.4 shows a divisional pattern of organization grouped around products, regions, and customers for three divisions of a conglomerate. This pattern is often used to meet diverse external threats and opportunities. As shown in Figure 11.4 the major advantages of the divisional pattern are its flexibility in meeting external demands, spotting external changes, integration of specialized individuals deep within the organization, and focusing on the delivery of specific products to specific customers. Of course, it also has disadvantages, such as duplication of effort by function, the tendency for divisional goals to be placed above corporate interests, and conflict among divisions. It is also not the structure most desired for training individuals in technical areas and firms relying upon this pattern may fall behind competitors with a functional pattern.

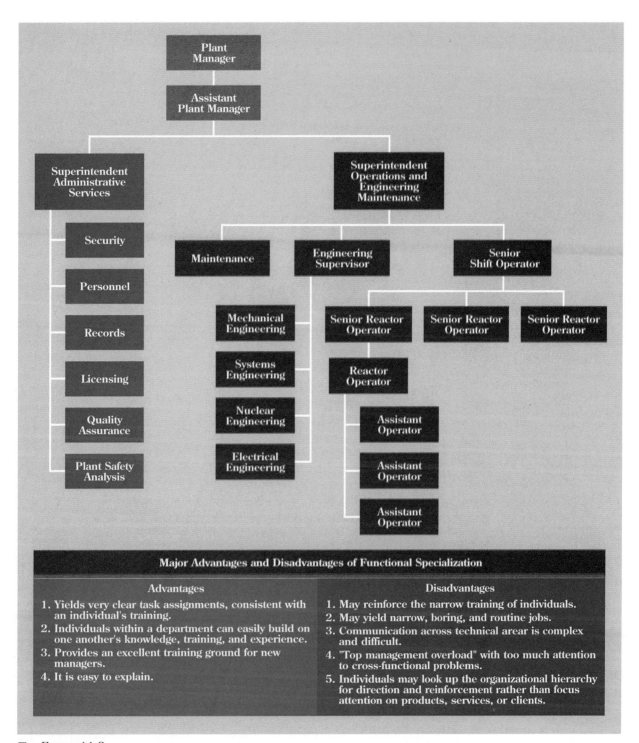

FIGURE 11.3

A functional pattern of departmentation for a nuclear power plant.

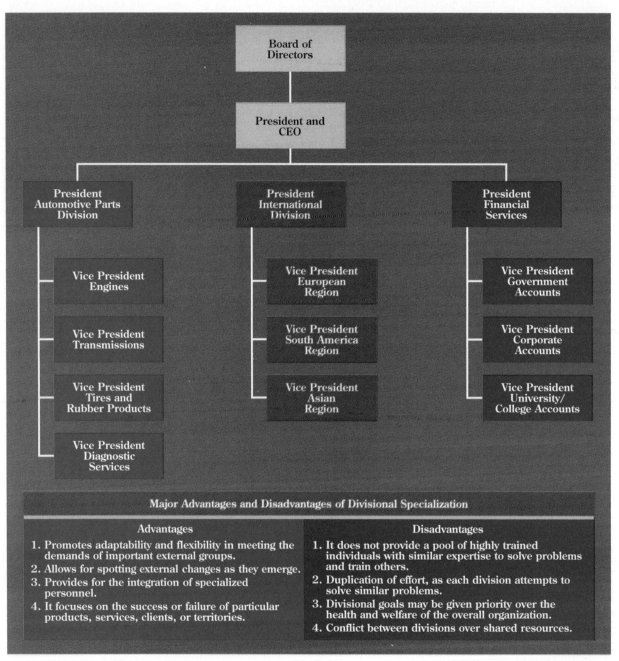

A divisional pattern of departmentation for a conglomerate.

232

Many larger, geographically dispersed organizations that sell to national and international markets may rely upon *departmentation by geography.* The savings in time, effort, and travel can be substantial, and each territory can adjust to regional differences. Organizations that rely on a few major customers may organize their people and resources by client. Here, the idea is to focus attention on the needs of the individual customer. To the extent that customer needs are unique, departmentation by customer can also reduce confusion and increase synergy. Organizations expanding internationally may also form divisions to meet the demands of complex host country ownership requirements. For example, NEC, Sony, Nissan, and many other Japanese corporations have developed U.S. divisional subsidiaries to service their customers in the U.S. market. Some huge Europe-based corporations such as Philips and Nestlé have also adopted a divisional structure in their expansion to the United States. Similarly, most of the internationalized United States based firms, such as IBM, GE, and Dupont, have incorporated the divisional structure as part of their internalization programs.

▼ DEPARTMENTATION BY MATRIX

From the aerospace industry, a third unique form of departmentation has developed; it is now called **matrix departmentation.**[22] In aerospace efforts, projects are technically very complex, and they involve hundreds of subcontractors located throughout the world. Precise integration and control is needed across many sophisticated functional specialties and corporations. This is often more than a functional or divisional structure can provide. Thus, *matrix departmentation* uses both the functional and divisional forms simultaneously. Figure 11.5 shows the basic matrix arrangement for an aerospace program. Note the functional departments on one side, and the project efforts on the other. Workers and supervisors in the middle of the matrix have two bosses—one functional and one project.

> **Matrix departmentation** is a combination of functional and divisional patterns wherein an individual is assigned to more than one type of unit.

 In a recent reorganization of its worldwide engineering operations, Ford Motor Company moved from a functional structure, with engineering departments for engines and transmissions, to a global matrix across its North American and European operations. Now engineers report to two bosses—their old functional boss and a new supervisor in one of five so-called platform groups. One of the platform groups for small cars is Europe based, with engineers in both North America and Western Europe reporting to supervisors in Germany. Alex Trotman, CEO of Ford, hopes the new matrix arrangement will not only speed product development but help make Ford more responsive to its global customers. One of the first new cars scheduled to come from this new structure will be the updated Escort. Although designed primarily by European engineers, it will be manufactured in Europe and North America and sold throughout the world.

GLOBAL

233

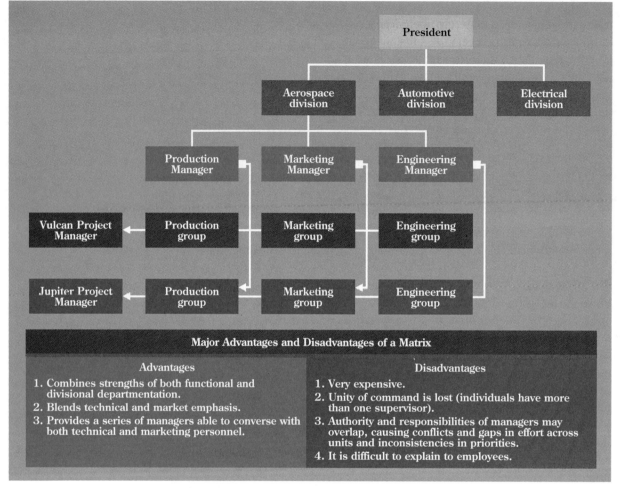

Major Advantages and Disadvantages of a Matrix

Advantages	Disadvantages
1. Combines strengths of both functional and divisional departmentation.	1. Very expensive.
2. Blends technical and market emphasis.	2. Unity of command is lost (individuals have more than one supervisor).
3. Provides a series of managers able to converse with both technical and marketing personnel.	3. Authority and responsibilities of managers may overlap, causing conflicts and gaps in effort across units and inconsistencies in priorities.
	4. It is difficult to explain to employees.

■ FIGURE 11.5

A matrix pattern of departmentation in an aerospace division.

The major advantages and disadvantages of the matrix form of departmentation are also summarized in Figure 11.5. The key disadvantage of the matrix method is the loss of unity of command. Individuals can be unsure as to what their jobs are, whom they report to for specific activities, and how various managers are to administer the effort. It can also be a very expensive method since it relies on individual managers to coordinate efforts deep within the firm. In Figure 11.5, note that the number of managers in a matrix structure almost doubles compared to either a functional or a divisional structure. Despite these limitations, however, the matrix structure provides a balance between functional and divisional concerns. Many problems can be resolved at the working level, where the balance among technical, cost, customer, and organizational concerns can be dealt with.

Many organizations also use elements of the matrix structure without officially using the term "matrix." For example, special project teams, coordinating committees, and task forces can be the beginnings of a matrix. Yet, these temporary structures can be used within a predominantly functional or divisional form and without upsetting the unity of command or hiring additional managers.

▼ MIXED FORMS OF DEPARTMENTATION

Which form of departmentation should be used? As the matrix concept suggests, it is possible to departmentalize by two different methods at the same time. Actually, organizations often use a mixture of departmentation forms. In fact, it is often desirable to divide the effort (group people and resources) by two methods at the same time in order to balance the advantages and disadvantages of each.

COORDINATION

Coordination is the set of mechanisms that an organization uses to link the actions of its units into a consistent pattern.[23] Much of the coordination within a unit is handled by its manager. Smaller organizations may rely on their management hierarchy to provide the necessary consistency and integration. As the organization grows, however, managers become overloaded. The organization then needs to develop more efficient and effective ways of linking work units to one another.

> **Coordination** is the set of mechanisms used in an organization to link the actions of its subunits into a consistent pattern.

▼ PERSONAL METHODS OF COORDINATION

Personal methods of coordination produce synergy by promoting dialogue, discussion, innovation, creativity, and learning, both within and across organizational units. Personal methods allow the organization to address the particular needs of distinct units and individuals simultaneously.

There are a wide variety of personal methods of coordination. Perhaps the most popular is direct contact between and among organizational members. In recent years, a number of new technologies have improved the potential for developing and maintaining effective contact networks. For example, many executives use E-mail and direct computer links to supplement direct personal communication.

Direct personal contact is also associated with the ever-present "grapevine." Although the grapevine is notoriously inaccurate in its role as the corporate rumor mill, it is often both accurate enough and quick enough that managers cannot ignore it. Instead, managers need to work with and supplement the rumor mill with accurate information.

Managers are also often assigned to numerous committees to improve coordination across departments. Even though committees are generally expensive and have a very poor reputation, they can become an effective personal mecha-

Take-A-Note 11.2

ADJUSTING COORDINATION EFFORTS

The astute manager should recognize that some individuals and/or units:

1. *Have their own views of how best to move toward organizational goals.*

2. *Emphasize immediate problems and quick solutions; others stress underlying problems and longer-term solutions.*

3. *Have their own unique vocabulary and standard way of communicating.*

4. *Have pronounced preferences for formality or informality.*

nism for mutual adjustment across unit heads. Committees can be effective in communicating complex qualitative information and in helping managers whose units must work together to adjust schedules, workloads, and work assignments to increase productivity.

As more organizations develop flatter structures with greater delegation, they are finding that *task forces* can be quite useful. Whereas committees tend to be long lasting, task forces are typically formed with a more limited agenda. Individuals from different parts of the organization are assembled into a task force to identify and solve problems that cut across different departments.

There is no magic involved in selecting the appropriate mix of personal coordination methods and tailoring them to the individual skills, abilities, and experience of subordinates. Managers need to know the individuals involved, their preferences, and the accepted approaches in different organizational units. Different personal methods can be tailored to match different individuals.

Of course, personal methods are only one important part of coordination. The manager may also establish a series of impersonal mechanisms.

▼ IMPERSONAL METHODS OF COORDINATION

Impersonal methods of control produce synergy by stressing consistency and standardization so that individual pieces fit together. Impersonal coordination methods are often refinements and extensions of process controls with an emphasis on formalization and standardization. Most larger organizations have written policies and procedures, such as schedules, budgets, and plans, that are designed to mesh the operations of several units into a whole by providing predictability and consistency.

The most highly developed form of impersonal coordination comes with the adoption of a matrix form of departmentation. As noted earlier, this form of departmentation is expressly designed to coordinate the efforts of diverse functional units. Although a few organizations rely exclusively upon a matrix structure, many firms are using cross-functional task forces. These task forces are replacing specialized staff units that once mainly dealt with ensuring coordination.

The final example of impersonal coordination mechanisms is undergoing radical change in many modern organizations. Originally, *management information systems* were developed and designed so that senior managers could coordinate and control the operations of diverse subordinate units. These systems were intended to be computerized substitutes for schedules, budgets, and the like. In some firms, the management information system still operates as a combined process control and impersonal coordination mechanism. In the hands of astute managers, the management information system becomes an electronic network, linking individuals throughout the organization. Using decentralized communication systems, supplemented with the phone, fax machine, and E-mail, a once centrally controlled system becomes a supplement to personal coordination.

In the 1990s, firms are finding that personal coordination mechanisms supplemented with modern communications networks are providing for more effective coordination to meet the ever-changing needs of a highly competitive marketplace. Whereas firms recognize that impersonal methods appear cheaper, they are also aware that those methods are less flexible and cannot support the mutual adjustment necessary in today's businesses.

CHAPTER 11 STUDY GUIDE ◀

What types of contributions do organizations make and what types of goals to they adopt?

SUMMARY

- Organizations make specific contributions to society.
- Firms often concentrate on primary beneficiaries and specify output goals (specific products and services).
- A societal contribution focused on a primary beneficiary may be represented in the firm's mission statement.
- Corporations have systems goals to show the conditions managers believe will yield survival and success.

What is the formal structure of the organization and what is meant by the term "division of labor"?

- The formal structure defines the intended configuration of positions, job duties, and lines of authority among different parts of the enterprise.
- The formal structure is also known as the firm's division of labor.

How is vertical specialization used to allocate formal authority within the organization?

- Vertical specialization is the hierarchical division of labor that specifies where formal authority is located.
- Typically, a chain of command exists to link lower level workers with senior managers.
- The distinction between line and staff units also indicates how authority is distributed with line units conducting the major business of the firm and staff providing support.
- Managerial techniques, such as decision support and expert computer systems, are used to expand the analytical reach and decision-making capacity of managers to minimize staff.

How does the firm control the actions of its members?

- Control is the set of mechanisms the organization uses to keep action and/or outputs within predetermined levels.
- Output controls focus on desired targets and allow managers to use their own methods for reaching the desired target.
- Process controls specify the manner in which tasks are to be accomplished through (1) policies, rules, and procedures; (2) formalization and standardization; and (3) total quality management processes.
- Firms in the 1990s are learning that decentralization often provides substantial benefits

What different patterns of horizontal specialization can be used in the organization?

- Horizontal specialization is the division of labor that results in various work units and departments in the organization.
- Three main types or patterns of departmentation are observed: functional, divisional, and matrix. Each pattern has a mix of advantages and disadvantages.
- Organizations may successfully use any type, or a mixture, as long as the strengths of the structure match the needs of the organization.

Which personal and impersonal coordination techniques should the organization use?

- Coordination is the set of mechanisms an organization uses to link the actions of separate units into a consistent pattern.
- Personal methods of coordination produce synergy by promoting dialogue, discussion, innovation, creativity, and learning.
- Impersonal methods of control produce synergy by stressing consistency and standardization so that individual pieces fit together.
- In the 1990s computer networks and E-mail are blurring the distinction between personal and impersonal mechanisms such as the centralized staff units that have traditionally been used in large corporations.

KEY TERMS

Centralization (p. 229)
Control (p. 226)
Coordination (p. 235)
Decentralization (p. 229)
Formalization (p. 227)
Horizontal specialization (p. 230)
Line units (p. 223)
Matrix departmentation (p. 233)
Mission statements (p. 217)
Organization charts (p. 220)
Output controls (p. 226)
Output goals (p. 218)
Process controls (p. 226)
Societal goals (p. 217)
Span of control (p. 222)
Staff units (p. 223)
Standardization (p. 227)
Systems goals (p. 219)
Vertical specialization (p. 220)

SELF-TEST 11

▼ MULTIPLE-CHOICE QUESTIONS

1. In order to increase survival potential, organizations create____. (a) mission statements (b) process controls (c) matrix specializations (d) systems goals (e) line and staff units

2. The formal structures of organizations may be shown in a(n) ____. (a) environmental diagram (b) organization chart (c) horizontal diagram (d) matrix depiction (e) labor assignment chart

3. A major distinction between line and staff units concerns the ____. (a) amount of resources each is allowed to utilize (b) linkage of their jobs to the goals of the firm (c) amount of education and/or training they possess (d) amount of responsibility they have (e) amount of prestige they have

4. The division of labor by grouping people and material resources deals with ____. (a) specialization (b) coordination (c) divisionalization (d) vertical specialization (e) goal setting.

5. Control involves all but ____. (a) measuring results (b) establishing goals (c) taking corrective action (d) comparing results with goals (e) selecting personnel

6. Grouping individuals and resources in the organization around products, services, clients, territories, and/or legal entities is an example of ____ horizontal specialization. (a) divisional (b) functional (c) matrix (d) mixed form (e) outsourced specialization

7. Grouping resources into departments by skill, knowledge, and action is the ____ pattern. (a) functional (b) divisional (c) vertical (d) means-end chains (e) matrix

8. A matrix structure ____. (a) reinforces unity of command (b) is inexpensive (c) is easy to explain to employees (d) shows overlap of authority and responsibilities of managers (e) yields a minimum of organizational politics

9. Formalization ____. (a) groups individuals and resources by product, service, client, territory, or legal entity (b) groups individuals and resources by skill, knowledge, and action (c) groups individuals and resources by the goals of an organization (d) provides written documentation of work rules, policies, and procedures (e) yields the combination of knowledge and technology that creates a product or serves output for an organization

10. ____ is the concern for proper communication enabling the units to understand one another's activities. (a) Control (b) Coordination (c) Specialization (d) Departmentation (e) Division of labor

▼ TRUE–FALSE

11. Mission statements are written statements of organizational purpose. T F

12. A specific group, such as a political campaign, is an example of a primary beneficiary. T F

13. The configuration of positions, job duties, and lines of authority among the component parts of an organization is called its structure. T F

14. The hierarchy of authority is the process of breaking work into small components that serve the organization's purpose. T F

15. Specialization and coordination are two core issues in the concept of organizational structure. T F

16. The span of control distributes formal authority and establishes where and how critical decisions are to be made. T F

17. Grouping people together by skill, knowledge, and action yields a divisional pattern of departmentation. T F

18. Line units and personnel in an organization provide specialized expertise and services to staff units and personnel. T F

19. One of the advantages of a matrix structure is that it helps provide a blending of technical and market emphases in organizations operating in exceedingly complex environments.   T F
20. As opposed to committees, task forces are typically formed with a limited agenda to identify and solve problems that cut across different departments.   T F

▼ SHORT RESPONSE

21. Compare and contrast the major types of goals for an organization.
22. Describe vertical specialization and contrast it to a flat hierarchy of authority. What are the advantages and disadvantages of each?
23. What are the major advantages and disadvantages of functional specialization?
24. What are the major advantages and disadvantages of divisional specialization?

▼ APPLICATIONS ESSAY

25. Describe some of the side effects of organizational controls in a large mechanistically structured organization, such as the United States Postal Service.

12

ORGANIZATIONAL DESIGN AND LEARNING

In the early 1980s, Lee Iacocca took over failing Chrysler as CEO and, through strong centralized leadership and dramatic cost cutting and downsizing, saved the company. Of the company's top 33 executives, 32 immediately left the firm as Lee centralized decision making in the office of the CEO.

By the mid 1980s, however, the company started to repeat some of its history by overextending itself. It diversified yet again into aerospace, and it attempted the ill-fated development of a new luxury sports coupe in partnership with Maserati. Even with all of the cost cutting, and partially as a result of centralizing so many decisions in Iacocca's office, Chrysler was top heavy. There were too many levels of management, and the firm had to sell too many cars to break even.

Chrysler management reacted by developing a better way to make cars, based on careful study of Honda's success. In one sense, the company returned to its own history of engineering excellence and use of outside suppliers in the design of a new model. Chrysler radically decentralized car development. Instead of modifying the design himself at its final stages, Iacocca relied on the judgment of a design team made up of stylists, engineers, manufacturing representatives, and a host of outside suppliers, all working in a new design center. The first trial of this system produced a new model called the Viper in less than half the usual time.

In 1992, Iacocca retired and was succeeded by Robert J. Eaton, who continued to nurture the development teams and set up new programs to ensure quality. Chrysler was quickly becoming a more participative, decentralized, and nimble maker of automobiles. (http://www-europe.sgi.com/Headlines/1995/sep/lutz.html)[1]

241

In order to meet a number of competitive challenges in the 1990s, organizations are beginning to redefine themselves and the way they are structured. We all recognize that a Chrysler auto assembly plant and the musical group Nirvana are quite different. Auto assembly plants are organized to emphasize routine, efficient production. In contrast, the musical group is loose, experimental, and organized for artistic expression, even though the logistics of travel, the movement of the equipment, and the sale of the tickets are highly organized. In this chapter, we discuss how managers adjust the basic elements of organizational structure to fit the scale of the operation, the job to be done, the demands of outsiders, and the ways in which senior management intends to compete.

Today, although many firms appear to be announcing revolutionary structures, most are implementing small variations around well-tested and well-known designs. As you read Chapter 12, keep in mind these study questions.

- What is organizational design, and how do the designs of small and large firms differ?
- Does the technology of the firm influence its organizational design?
- What is the relationship between environmental conditions and organizational design?
- What is strategy, and how are firms combining generic strategies and their own unique competencies?
- What is organizational learning?
- How are organizational learning cycles helpful in understanding organizational behavior?

ORGANIZATIONAL DESIGN AND FIRM SIZE ◀

Organizational design is the process of choosing and implementing a structural configuration.[2] The choice of an appropriate organizational design is contingent upon several factors, including the size of the firm, its technology, its environment, and the strategy it selects for growth and survival.

Large organizations cannot be just bigger versions of their smaller counterparts. Whereas there are many reasons for this, we concentrate here on three important differences size makes in the design of the organization.

As the number of individuals in a firm increases arithmetically, the number of possible interconnections among them increases geometrically. In other words, direct interpersonal contact among all members in a large organization is impossible to maintain. Thus, impersonal coordination techniques must be substituted for direct personal contact. Policies, rules, and procedures are used as substitutes for direct supervision both to save money and to ensure consistency.

One of the competitive strengths of larger organizations can be their efficiency. There are potential economies of scale when an organization can produce products and services efficiently through repetition. Specialization of labor, equipment, and departments is one way of capturing the potential economies of scale. Increasing specialization calls for increased control and coordination to ensure that action is directed toward common goals and linked together in a meaningful way.

Larger organizations are often more complex than are smaller ones in terms of their products, production processes, geographical locations, and the like. This additional complexity calls for a more sophisticated organizational design. Yet even very large organizations also rely upon simple design elements.

> **Organizational design** is the process of choosing and implementing a structural configuration for an organization.

▼ THE SIMPLE DESIGN FOR SMALLER UNITS AND FIRMS

The **simple design** is a configuration involving one or two ways of specializing individuals and units. That is, vertical specialization and control typically emphasize levels of supervision without elaborate formal mechanisms (e.g., rule books, policy manuals), and the majority of the control is based with the manager. One or two ways of organizing departments are used, and coordination mechanisms are often personal. The organization visually resembles a "pyramid" with few staff individuals or units.

The simple design is appropriate for many small firms, such as family businesses, retail stores, and small manufacturing firms.[3] The strengths of the simple design are simplicity, flexibility, and responsiveness to the desires of a central manager—in many cases, the owner. Since a simple design relies heavily on the manager's personal leadership, however, this configuration is only as effective as is the senior manager.

> A **simple design** is a configuration involving one or two ways of specializing individuals and units.

QUALITY

B&A Travel is a comparatively small travel agency run by Helen Druse. Reporting to Helen are two staff members—Jane Bloom for accounting and finance, and Ken Wiener for training and market development. The operations

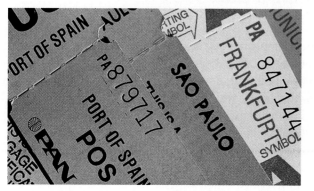

arm is headed by Joan Wiland, who supervises 10 lead travel agents. Whereas each of the lead travel agents specializes in a geographical area, all but Sue Connely and Bart Merve take client requests for all types of trips. Sue is in charge of three major business accounts, and Bart heads a tour group. Each of the 10 lead agents heads a group of 5 to 7 associates. Coordination is achieved through weekly meetings and a lot of personal contact by Helen and Joan. Control is enhanced by the computerized reservation system they all use. Helen makes sure each agent has a monthly sales target, and she routinely chats with important clients about their level of service. She realizes that developing participation from even the newest associate is an important tool in maintaining a "fun" atmosphere.

Bureaucracy is an ideal form of organization, the characteristics of which were defined by the German sociologist Max Weber.

▼ THE BUREAUCRACY

As the organization grows, additional layers of management and more specialized departments are added. The nature of the organization changes as layers of management increase, as the division of labor and coordination mechanisms become more elaborate, and as formal controls are established.[4] Reliance on a single senior manager is downplayed, and "levels" of management exercise varying degrees of authority.

The famous German sociologist Max Weber suggested that large organizations would thrive if they relied on legal authority, logic, and order.[5] Weber argued that organizations should become **bureaucracies** by relying on a division of labor, hierarchical control, promotion by merit with career opportunities for employees, and administration by rule. He argued that bureaucracies were superior to the simple design to the extent that they fitted ideal descriptions. Although not found in reality, these "ideal types" highlighted important aspects of organizations. What we have called the simple design, for example, Weber called a "charismatic" ideal type organization because its success depends so much on the talents of one individual. For efficiency, Weber preferred the bureaucracy to the simple structure. He hoped that it could also be fairer to employees and provide more freedom for individual expression. Although far from perfect, the bureaucracy, or some variation of this ideal form, was predicted by Weber to dominate modern society.

Take-A-Note 12.1
THE NATURAL DYSFUNCTIONAL TENDENCIES OF A BUREAUCRACY

1. Overspecialization and neglect to mitigate the resulting conflicts of interest resulting from specialization.
2. Overuse of the formal hierarchy and emphasis on adherence to official channels rather than problem solving.
3. Reification of senior mangers as superior performers on all tasks and as rulers of a political system rather than as individuals who should help others reach goals.
4. Overemphasis on insignificant conformity that limits individual growth.
5. Treatment of rules as ends in and of themselves rather than as poor mechanisms for control and coordination.

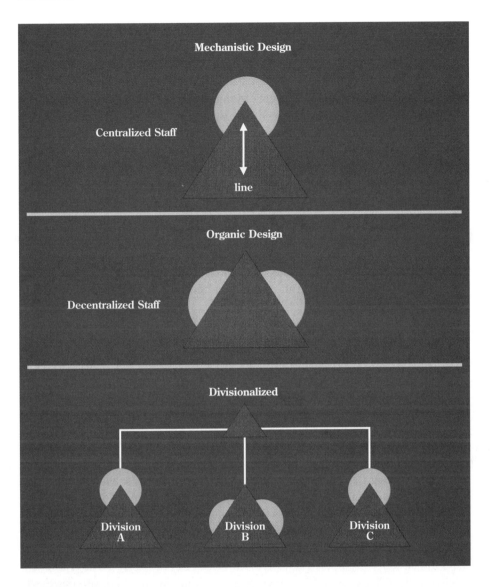

■ FIGURE 12.1
Different basic organizational design options.

Whereas all but a few large organizations are bureaucracies, there are subtle but important differences in the way each organization is designed. A sound design builds on the firm's strengths and minimizes its weaknesses. No one design is preferred. The organizational design adopted by a particular firm needs to "fit" a whole series of internal and external realities. Before these contingencies are discussed, however, it is important to present some basics of organizational design. Figure 12.1 illustrates three popular basic designs: the mechanistic, the organic, and the divisionalized approaches.

Mechanistic Designs   The **mechanistic design** is a highly bureaucratic organization that emphasizes vertical specialization and control. Organizations of this type stress rules, policies, and procedures; specify techniques for decision making; and emphasize developing well-documented control systems backed by a strong middle management and supported by a centralized staff. Henry

A **mechanistic design** is a highly bureaucratic organization that emphasizes vertical specialization and control, an extensive use of managerial techniques, impersonal coordination and control, and a heavy reliance on rules, policies, and procedures.

Mintzberg uses the term *machine bureaucracy* to describe an organization that is entirely structured in this manner.[6]

The mechanistic design results in a management emphasis on routine for efficiency. It is quite popular in basic industries with large-scale operations, such as banks, insurance companies, and government offices. When the organization is too rigid and centralized, however, the design may backfire. Employees do not like rigid designs and key employees may leave. Mechanistic designs can hinder an organization's capacity to adjust to external changes or new technologies.

> **Organic design** is an organizational structure that emphasizes horizontal specialization, an extensive use of personal coordination, and loose rules, policies, and procedures.

Organic Designs   The **organic design** is much less vertically oriented than is the mechanistic design; it emphasizes horizontal specialization. Procedures are minimal, and those that do exist are not as formalized. The organization relies on the judgments of experts and personal means of coordination. When controls are used, they tend to back up professional socialization, training, and individual reinforcement. Staff units tend to be placed toward the middle of the organization. Because this is a popular design in professional firms Mintzberg calls it a *professional bureaucracy*.[7]

Your university is probably a professional bureaucracy that looks like a broad, flat pyramid with a large bulge in the center for the professional staff. It is important to note that power in this ideal type rests with knowledge. Further, the elaborate staff typically helps the line managers and often has very little formal power. Yet, control is enhanced by the standardization of professional skills and the adoption of professional routines, standards, and procedures. Other examples include hospitals, consulting firms, libraries, and social service agencies.

The organic design stresses communication across the organization and focuses attention on customers and/or technology. Although not as efficient as the mechanistic design, the organic design is better for problem solving and for serving individual customer needs. Since lateral relations and coordination are emphasized, centralized direction by senior management is less intense. Thus, this design is good at detecting external changes and adjusting to new technologies, but at the sacrifice of responding to central management direction.[8]

> **Divisionalized design** is an organizational structure that establishes a separate structure for each business or division.

Divisionalized Designs   Many very large firms find that neither the mechanistic nor the organic design is suitable for all their operations. Adopting a machine bureaucracy would overload senior management and yield too many levels of management.[9] Yet, adopting an organic design would mean losing control and becoming too inefficient. Some industries find that although their businesses are related, some call for an organic structure, whereas others call for a mechanistic one. In the **divisionalized design,** the firm establishes a separate structure for each business or division. The classic divisional organization was created by Alfred Sloan for General Motors, when he divided GM's operations into divisions for designing and producing Chevys, Oldsmobiles, Pontiacs, Buicks, and Cadillacs.[10] Each division was treated as a separate business; each business competed against all the others.

In the divisionalized organization, coordination across businesses is provided by a comparatively small centralized staff that provides support, such as financial services and legal expertise. Senior line management provides direction and control over the presumably "autonomous" divisions. In very large organizations, this approach can free top management to establish strategy and concentrate on large, long-term problems. Divisional heads run their own businesses and compete for resources, yet each enjoys the support (financial, personnel, legal, etc.) of the larger parent.

Although this form is expensive, since redundant staff and support units must be developed for each division, it allows the firm greater flexibility to respond to different markets and customers. Yet, tension between divisional management and senior management is quite often apparent. It is very difficult for corporate executives and corporate staff to allow the divisions to operate as independent businesses. Over time, senior staff may grow in size and force "assistance" on the divisions. Since they compete for common resources, coordination across divisions is often also quite difficult.

▼ THE CONGLOMERATE

In the 1960s, a few organizations began to grow by buying unrelated businesses. On the surface, these firms looked like divisionalized firms, but the various businesses of the divisions were so unrelated that a new term had to be invented. Firms that own several different unrelated businesses are called **conglomerates**.[11] For instance, General Electric is a conglomerate that has divisions in quite unrelated businesses and industries, ranging from producing light bulbs, to designing and servicing nuclear reactors, to building jet engines, to operating the National Broadcasting Company.

> **Conglomerates** are firms that own several different, unrelated businesses.

With the wave of mergers and acquisitions in the 1980s and 1990s, several corporations became conglomerates, as raiders bought and sold various busi-

GLOBAL

In the late 1980s, Japan's Sony Corporation decided it needed to expand its role in the marketplace by adding enterprises related to its core consumer electronics business. Sony, along with producing electronics goods, attempted to create media sources as well—what some analysts took to calling a "synergistic" approach to business. By controlling parts of the media establishment and combining it with consumer electronics, Sony hoped to develop an unbeatable advantage. Sony acquired Columbia Pictures for $5 billion and then poured hundreds of millions of dollars into studio improvements and renovations. But the electronics and movie businesses just did not fit together. Even with this significant investment, however, Sony realized that it would take time to make Columbia profitable and the hopes of synergy faded. "Over the long run," says Peter Dekom, an entertainment lawyer, "Sony's asset [Columbia] will appreciate and eat up their mistakes. The key is to hang on long enough to capitalize on that appreciation."[12]

247

nesses. Here, structure and organizational design, other than with respect to cost cutting, were not important; financial manipulation was the key to short-term success. For example, RJR-Nabisco was created through a series of financial maneuvers that brought together a food company and a tobacco firm. Several international firms also hope to develop synergistic global businesses, often with mixed success, because they have found that running one type of business in one industry is not the same as managing a conglomerate.

Many state and federal entities are also, by necessity, conglomerates. For instance, a state governor is the chief executive officer of those units concerned with higher education, welfare, prisons, highway construction and maintenance, police, and the like.

TECHNOLOGY AND ORGANIZATIONAL DESIGN

While the design of an organization needs to reflect its size, it must also be adjusted to fit technological requirements.[13] That is, successful organizations are said to arrange their internal structures to meet the dictates of their dominant "technologies" or work flows.[14]

Technology is the combination of resources, knowledge, and techniques that creates a product or service output for an organization. The term is used in various ways in the OB literature, so it will help you to become acquainted with two of the more common classification schemes used by theorists and managers to describe the technologies of organizations.

> **Technology** is the combination of resources, knowledge, and techniques that creates a product or service output for an organization.

▼ THOMPSON'S VIEW OF TECHNOLOGY

James D. Thompson classifies technologies as intensive, mediating, or long linked. Under *intensive technology,* there is uncertainty as to how to produce desired outcomes.[15] A group of specialists must be brought together to use a variety of techniques to solve problems. Examples are found in a hospital emergency room or a research and development laboratory.

Mediating technology links parties that want to become interdependent. For example, banks link creditors and depositors and store money and information to facilitate such exchanges. Whereas all depositors and creditors are interdependent, the reliance is pooled through the bank. *Long-linked technology* is also called mass production or industrial technology. In this case, since the way to produce the desired outcomes is known, the task is broken down into a number of sequential and interdependent steps. A classic example is the automobile assembly line.

▼ WOODWARD'S VIEW OF TECHNOLOGY

Joan Woodward also divides technology into three categories: small-batch, mass production, and continuous-process manufacturing.[16] In units of *small-batch production,* a variety of custom products are tailor made to fit customer specifications, such as tailor-made suits. The machinery and equipment used are generally not very elaborate, but considerable craftsmanship is often needed. In *mass production,* the organization produces one or a few products with an assembly-line type of system. The work of one group is highly dependent on another; the equipment is typically sophisticated; and the workers are given very detailed instructions. Automobiles and refrigerators are produced in this way. Organizations using *continuous-process technology* produce a few products with considerable automation. Classic examples are automated chemical plants and oil refineries.

From her studies, Woodward concluded that the combination of structure and technology was critical to the success of the organizations. When technology and organizational design were properly matched, a firm was more successful. Specifically, successful small-batch and continuous-process plants had flexible structures with small work groups at the bottom; more rigidly structured plants were less successful. In contrast, successful mass production operations were rigidly structured and had large work groups at the bottom. This technological imperative has since been supported by various investigations. Yet, today we recognize that technology is just one factor involved in the success of an organization.[17]

▼ WHERE TECHNOLOGY DOMINATES: THE ADHOCRACY

The influence of technological considerations is most clearly seen in small organizations and in specific departments within large ones. In some instances, managers and employees simply do not know the appropriate way to service a client or to produce a particular product. This is the extreme of Thompson's intensive type of technology, and it may be found in some small-batch processes where a team of individuals must develop a unique product for a particular client.

Mintzberg suggests that at these technological extremes, the "adhocracy" may be an appropriate structure.[18] An **adhocracy** is characterized by few rules, policies, and procedures; substantial decentralization; shared decision making among members; extreme horizontal specialization (as each member of the unit may be a distinct specialist); few levels of management; and virtually no formal controls.

The adhocracy is particularly useful when an aspect of the firm's technology presents two sticky problems: (1) the tasks facing the firm vary considerably and provide many exceptions, as in a hospital, or (2) problems are difficult to define and resolve.[19]

The adhocracy places a premium on professionalism and coordination in problem solving. This structure is particularly suited to helping professionals solve technical problems. As such, adhocracies are often used as a supplement to other designs to offset their dysfunctional effects.[20] Firms use temporary task forces, form special committees, and even contract consulting firms to provide the creative problem identification and problem solving that the adhocracy promotes. For instance, Lotus Development Corporation creates new autonomous departments to encourage talented employees to develop new software programs. Allied Chemical and 3M also set up quasi-autonomous groups to work through new ideas.

> **Adhocracy** is an organizational structure that emphasizes shared, decentralized decision making; extreme horizontal specialization; few levels of management; the virtual absence of formal controls; and few rules, policies, and procedures.

ENVIRONMENT AND ORGANIZATIONAL DESIGN

An effective organizational design reflects powerful external forces as well as size and technological factors. Organizations, as open systems, need to receive various inputs from the environment and to sell various outputs to their environment. Therefore, it is important to understand what the environment is and what elements are likely to be important.[21]

The *general environment* is the set of cultural, economic, legal–political, and educational conditions found in the areas in which the organization operates. The owners, suppliers, distributors, government agencies, and competitors with which an organization must interact to grow and survive constitute its *specific environment*. A firm typically has much more choice over the composition of its specific environment than of its general environment. It can develop policies and strategies to alter the mix of owners, suppliers, distributors, and competitors with which it interacts.

Although it is often convenient to separate the general and specific environmental influences on the firm, designers need to recognize the combined impact of both. Choosing some businesses, for instance, means entering global competition with advanced technologies.

GLOBAL

When Procter and Gamble entered the European market, its organization centered around country locations.[22] Today, however, its organization is centered around regional locations. It always focused on product lines, such as laundry detergent or soap. This not only facilitates more coordinated and integrated marketing, it also helps management focus on the profitability of a category rather than on that of an individual brand. This also makes it easier for P&G to stay close to its customers, enabling staff to keep track of cultural trends and market opportunities. Procter and Gamble's organization also enables it to purchase ingredients and packages in volumes scaled to match individual markets. Production scheduling on a Europe-wide basis maximizes the use of manufacturing facilities, minimizes warehousing, and ensures a consistent product quality. The benefits are reflected by the bottom line: The European market is now responsible for about one third of P&G's total sales.

▼ ENVIRONMENTAL COMPLEXITY

A basic concern that must be addressed in analyzing the environment of the organization is its complexity. A more complex environment provides an organization with more opportunities and more problems. **Environmental complexity** is an estimate of the magnitude of the problems and opportunities in the organization's environment, as evidenced by three main factors: the degree of richness, the degree of interdependence, and the degree of uncertainty stemming from both the general and the specific environment.[23]

Environmental com-plexity is the magnitude of the problems and opportunities in the organization's environment as evidenced by the degree of richness, interdependence, and uncertainty.

Environmental Richness   Overall, the environment is richer when the economy is growing, when individuals are improving their education, and when others the organization relies upon are prospering. For businesses, a richer environment means that economic conditions are improving, customers are spending more money, and suppliers (such as banks) are willing to invest in the future of the organization. In a rich environment, more organizations survive, even if they have poorly functioning organizational designs. A richer environment is also filled with more opportunities and dynamism––the potential for change. The organizational design must make the company able to recognize these opportunities and capitalize on them.

The opposite of richness is decline. For business firms, a general recession is a good example of a leaner environment. Whereas corporate reactions vary, it is instructive to examine three typical responses to decline. In Japan, core manufacturing firms do not lay off core workers. Instead, they cut the hours of females, move some individuals to long-term suppliers, and initiate training for the remaining workers to prepare for a recovery.

In the United States, firms have traditionally reacted to decline by first issuing layoffs to nonsupervisory workers and then moving up the organizational ladder as the environment becomes leaner. In the 1990s, however, large firms have started to alter their organizational designs by cutting staff units and the number of organizational levels in response to more sustained periods of decline. This downsizing is traumatic but can be minimized.

Many European firms find it very difficult to cut full-time employees legally when the economy deteriorates. In many cases, firms have turned to national governments for help in sustained periods of decline. Much like United States–based firms, changes in organizational design are viewed as a last but increasingly necessary resort.

> ## Take-A-Note 12.2
> ### AVOIDING MORE PROBLEMS WITH DOWNSIZING
>
> When downsizing, firms should keep in mind that they must:
> 1. Accurately identify the causes of the decline.
> 2. Avoid grandiose attempts to reverse the past history.
> 3. Avoid the tendency to increase centralization and rigidity and to reduce participation.
> 4. Target cuts and retrain employees wherever possible.
> 5. Keep employees informed to alleviate fear.
> 6. Systematically work to rebuild morale and emphasize more participation.

Environmental Interdependence   The link between external interdependence and organizational design is often subtle and indirect. The organization may co-opt powerful outsiders by including them. For instance, many large corporations have financial representatives from banks and insurance companies on their boards of directors. The organization may also adjust its overall design strategy to absorb or buffer the demands of a more powerful external element. Per-

251

haps the most common adjustment is the development of a centralized staff department to handle an important external group. For instance, few large U.S. corporations are without some type of governmental relations group at the top. Where service to a few large customers is considered critical, the organization's departmentation is likely to switch from a functional form to a divisionalized one.

Uncertainty and Volatility Environmental uncertainty and unpredictable volatility can be particularly damaging to large bureaucracies. In times of change, investments quickly become outmoded, and internal operations no longer work as expected. The obvious organizational design response to uncertainty and volatility is to opt for a more organic form. At the extremes, movement toward an adhocracy may be important. However, these pressures may run counter to those that come from large size and technology. It may be too hard or too time consuming for some organizations to make the design adjustments in these cases. Thus, the organization may continue to struggle while adjusting its design just a little bit at a time.

Small, unsuccessful attempts at marginal adjustments to the design can often be followed by abrupt and massive changes. Such was the case with Sears. In the 1970s, Sears was the largest U.S. retailer, with its combined emphasis on catalog sales and stand-alone retail stores. Throughout the 1980s, Sears kept its unusual mix of products in both its catalog and, to a somewhat lesser extent, its retail stores. Although its success seemed assured in hard goods (e.g., tools and washing machines) Sears was constantly adjusting in terms of from whom and how it bought soft goods (e.g., women's clothing). At one time, all purchases were centralized; then they were decentralized; and then there was a shared arrangement, whereby some clothes sold in the catalog were purchased centrally, whereas others not sold in the catalog were purchased on a regional basis. Finally, in 1993, Sears recognized that these small adjustments were not enough. Sears was losing money on its general catalog and was now the number three retailer, behind Wal-Mart and K-mart. Sears announced a massive reorganization that included the closing of over 100 small stand-alone stores, the demise of the general catalog, and the termination of over 50,000 employees.

▼ USING ALLIANCES WHERE ENVIRONMENTAL FACTORS DOMINATE

In high-tech areas, such as robotics, semiconductors, advanced materials (ceramics and carbon fibers), and advanced information systems, a single company often does not have all the knowledge necessary to bring new products to the market. Often, the firms with the knowledge are not even in the same country. In this case, the organizational design must go beyond the boundaries of the organization into **interfirm alliances**—announced cooperative agreements or joint ventures between two independent firms. Often, these agreements involve corporations that are headquartered in different nations.[24]

Alliances are quite common in such high-technology industries, because they seek not only to develop technology but to make sure that their solutions become standardized across regions of the world. In some cases, the fight for a dominant design pits one nation against another. For instance, Zenith joined

Interfirm alliances are announced cooperative agreements or joint ventures between two independent firms.

forces with AT&T to develop one high-definition television (HDTV) system, and Toshiba, Sony, and some 30 other Japanese firms formed a strategic network to develop their own system. The winner in the United States will likely get the lion's share of the estimated $20 billion HDTV market in North America.

Firms may also develop alliances to explore potentials for future collaboration. One of the largest and potentially most influential strategic alliances is the cooperation between West Germany's Daimler-Benz and Japan's Mitsubishi. The two companies agreed to share technology and to develop joint ventures, market-based cooperations, or high-tech consortia, as the need arises.[25]

In more developed industries, interfirm alliances are also quite popular, but they are often known by other names. In Europe, for example, they are called *informal combines* or *cartels:* Competitors work cooperatively to share the market to decrease uncertainty and improve favorability for all. Except in rare cases, these arrangements are often illegal in the United States.

In Japan, alliances among well-established firms in many industries are quite common. The network of relationships is called a *keiretsu*. There are two common forms. The first is a *bank-centered keiretsu,* where firms are linked to one another directly via cross ownership and through historical ties to one bank. The Mitsubishi group is a good example. The second type has been called a *vertical keiretsu*. Here, a key manufacturer is at the hub of a network of supplier firms. The manufacturer typically has both long-term supply contracts with members as well as cross-ownership ties. These arrangements help isolate Japanese firms from stockholders and provide a mechanism for sharing and developing technology. Toyota is an example of a firm at the center of a vertical keiretsu.

The United States is beginning to see the evolution of the network organization as well. Here, the central firm specializes in a core activity, such as design and assembly. The firm works with a comparatively small number of participating suppliers on a long-term basis for both component development and manufacturing efficiency. Nike and Chrysler are leaders in the development of these relationships. At Chrysler, engineers from key suppliers are integrated into design

QUALITY

When Phil Knight, CEO of Nike, entered the athletic shoe business, he envisioned owning a company that produced inexpensive, high-quality running shoes for serious athletes. Knight's true love, however, was the research and development of shoes.[26] In its early years, the company did not have the resources to purchase a factory or employ large numbers of workers. Since labor was cheap in the Far East, Knight negotiated deals with a number of Asian suppliers to sell him set numbers of shoes. As a result, the cost of producing a pair of Nikes was far less than that of the company's primary competition, Adidas, which made its shoes in labor-expensive Germany. By focusing on its competencies and outsourcing production, Nike is now one of the largest and most successful firms in the shoe business.

253

teams. Their firms help both design and build key components. More extreme variations of this network design are also emerging to meet apparently conflicting environmental, size, and technological demands simultaneously. Firms are spinning off staff functions to reduce their overall size and concentrate their internal design on technological dictates.

STRATEGY AND ORGANIZATIONAL DESIGN

> **Organizational strategy** is the process of positioning the organization in the competitive environment and implementing actions to compete successfully.

For many firms, size, technology, and environment call for slightly different organizational designs. For these companies, organizational design scholars recommend that the design follow the strategy of the firm. **Organizational strategy** is the process of positioning the organization in its competitive environment and implementing actions to compete successfully.[27] The study of linking strategy, organizational design, and firm performance has a long tradition in organizational analysis. In the 1960s, Alfred Chandler studied the evolution of major U.S. firms and concluded that structure follows from the strategy established predominantly by senior management. More recent work suggests that a winning strategy is more likely when the firm recognizes both the importance of a singular direction and the unique skills and abilities within the firm. Forming a strategy is an interactive process. Senior managers select those systems goals they believe should define corporate success, form these goals into a vision, select a target position within the general and specific environments, and develop a design to accomplish the vision.

▼ GENERIC STRATEGIES

Senior managers often use so-called generic strategies to help guide their choices. Generic strategies are specific combinations of goals, technology, and environmental characteristics expected to yield success. Four types of generic strategies are common to many businesses:[28]

■ Four types of generic strategies

1. Focused differentiation.
2. Focused cost leadership.
3. Differentiation.
4. Cost leadership.

These four strategic types are shown in Figure 12.2 and are based on some simplified assumptions. The first assumption is that management must decide on the scope of its operations. If the firm is large and selects a broad range of customers and markets, it has *breadth*. If the choice is narrow, the firm has *focus*. The second assumption is that management selects technology to produce either comparatively inexpensive, standardized products or more expensive, tailor-made products and services. If the firm competes by providing lower cost, stan-

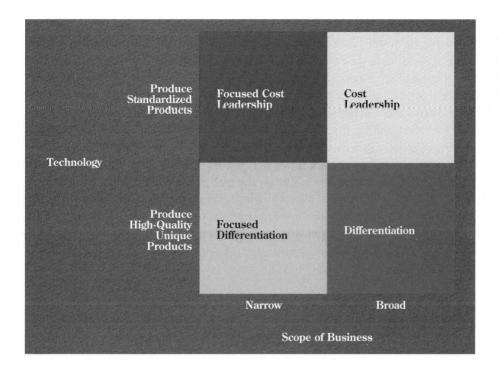

■ FIGURE 12.2
Types of generic strategies as affected by the organization's scope of business and technology.

dardized products, it relies on the economies of scale for cost leadership. If it produces higher quality, unique products (even if only in the minds of customers), it differentiates itself.

▼ COMPETENCY-BASED STRATEGIES

Although the list of generic strategies provides a quick overall guide for many senior managers, it is obvious that a firm needs to have the skills and abilities to capitalize on the intended generic strategy; just saying you want your firm to be a technical leader and instituting an adhocracy does not get the job done. Over time, the firm may develop specific administrative and technical competencies. As middle and lower level managers institute minor modifications and adjustments to solve specific problems and capitalize on specific opportunities, they and their firms may learn new skills. These skills may be recognized by senior management and give them the opportunity to adjust, modify, and build upon a generic strategy to develop a so-called competency strategy.

A key to success for most organizations is an appropriate modification of the generic strategy so that the organization builds upon and refines its unique experience and competencies. In the process of building upon its capabilities, the firm may actually shift generic strategies and/or combine elements of two generic strategies. The history of Chrysler is a good example.

In the 1990s, generic strategies are providing the jumping-off point for many corporations, because they must rely on the creativity, innovation, and skills of all their employees. IBM was once known as a successful second-to-market imitator with broad-scale differentiation in mainframe computers. It was not the technical leader, but it developed the standard for others, provided excellent service, and

※ **KODAK CANADA**
*http://www.
solutions-4u.
com/barter/
49063a73.htm/*

After a significant restructuring under Gord Wilson, Kodak Canada is entering into alliances to improve its technical competence in electronic imaging. These moves go beyond personal empowerment or employee participation in implementing the reorganization. Employees and middle managers are building a unique strategy based on their skills and abilities.[29]

offered a wide array of mainframe products and services. In the 1990s, IBM, or "Big Blue," is on the move. It has turned to flexible manufacturing for its personal computers to increase efficiency, accompanied by fewer levels of management and substantially greater participation. It is also reaching out to become the hub in a network of high-tech computer firms to service the expanding network computer market. IBM is fighting a history of very traditional management as it seeks to cut levels of management, reduce staff, stress innovation, and infuse a sound generic strategy with unique competencies.

Senior executives at such firms as Ford, AT&T, and Dow are now recognizing that an effective strategy builds on the competence of employees. Technical skills combined with astute management in an organizational design that reinforces employee contributions are fundamental to organizational success in the 1990s and beyond. This emphasis on individuals has also brought attention to the important topic of organizational learning. Executives now recognize that their firms must learn or die.

ORGANIZATIONAL LEARNING

Organizational learning is the process of knowledge acquisition, information distribution, information distribution, information interpretation, and organizational retention.

Organizational learning is the process of knowledge acquisition, information distribution, information interpretation, and organizational retention in adapting successfully to changing circumstances.[30] In simpler terms, organizational learning involves the adjustment of the organization's actions based on its experience and that of others. The challenge is doing to learn and learning to do.

▼ KNOWLEDGE ACQUISITION

All firms learn by obtaining information in a variety of ways and at different rates during their histories. Perhaps the most important information is obtained from sources outside the firm at the time of its founding. During the firm's initial years, its managers copy, or mimic, what they believe are the successful practices of others.[31] As they mature, however, firms can also acquire knowledge through experience and systematic search.

Mimicry is the copying of the successful practices of others.

Mimicry Mimicry is important to the new firm because (1) it provides workable, if not ideal, solutions to many problems; (2) it reduces the number of decisions that need to be analyzed separately, allowing managers to concentrate on more critical issues; and (3) it establishes legitimacy or acceptance by employees, suppliers, and customers and narrows the choices calling for detailed explanation.

One of the key factors involved in examining mimicry is the extent to which managers attempt to isolate cause-effect relationships. Simply copying others without attempting to understand the issues involved often leads to failure. The literature is filled with examples of firms that have tried to implement quality circles, empowerment, and decentralization simply because they have been used successfully by others. Too many firms have abandoned these techniques because managers failed to understand why and under what conditions they worked for other firms. When mimicking others, managers need to adjust for the unique circumstances of their corporation.

3M
http://www.ansi.org/iisp/95-0063.html/

An experiment to develop a new glue at 3M appeared to be a failure. It had very little adhesion. Years later, however, researchers applied the glue to paper, and the Post-It Note was born.

Experience   Of course, a primary way of acquiring knowledge is through experience. All organizations and managers can learn in this manner. Besides learning by doing, managers can also systematically embark upon structured programs to capture the lessons to be learned from failure and success. For instance, a well-designed research and development program allows managers to learn as much through failure as through success.

Learning by doing in an intelligent way is at the heart of many Japanese corporations, with their emphasis on statistical quality control, quality circles, and other such practices. Many firms have discovered that numerous small improvements can cumulatively add up to a major improvement in both quality and efficiency. The major problem with emphasizing learning by doing is the inability to forecast precisely what will change and how it will change. Managers need to believe that improvements can be made, listen to suggestions, and actually implement the changes. It is so much more difficult to do than to say, however.

Vicarious Learning   Vicarious learning involves capturing the lessons of others' experiences. Some firms have learned that the process of searching for new information may not always be structured or planned in conjunction with an identified problem or opportunity. Managers may embark upon learning in less systematic ways, including scanning, grafting, and contracting out.

Scanning involves looking outside the firm and bringing back useful solutions. At times, these solutions may be applied to recognized problems. More often, these solutions float around management until they are needed to solve a problem.[32] Astute managers can contribute to organizational learning by scanning external sources, such as competitors, suppliers, industry consultants, customers, and leading firms. For instance, by reverse engineering the competitor's products (developing the engineering drawings and specifications from the existing product), an organization can quickly match all standard product features; by systematically exploring the proposed developments from suppliers, a firm may become a lead user and be among the first to capitalize on the developments of suppliers.

Scanning is looking outside the firm and bringing back useful solutions to problems.

Grafting is the process of acquiring individuals, units, and/or firms to bring in useful knowledge. Almost all firms seek to hire experienced individuals from other firms simply because experienced individuals may bring with them a whole new series of solutions. For instance, at Dayton-Hudson senior management hired a new vice president for one of their department stores from a leading competitor, Nordstroms. They wanted to know the winning ways of this industry leader.

Of course, the critical problem in grafting is much the same as in scanning: Just obtaining the knowledge is not enough; it must be translated into action. A key

Grafting is the process of acquiring individuals, units, and/or firms to bring in useful knowledge to the organization.

problem with grafting one unit onto an existing organization is discussed in Chapter 13, on organizational culture. That is, there may be a clash of cultures, and instead of getting new solutions, both units may experience substantial conflict.

Contracting out is the reverse of grafting and involves asking outsiders to perform a particular function. Whereas all organizations contract out, the key question for managers is often what to keep. Generally, firms that out source peripheral or staff functions can benefit from the expertise of others. If operations critical to the competitive success of the firm are contracted out, however, the firm may lose its long-term competitive advantage. For instance, in the 1970s, RCA was the U.S. leader in making televisions. But with the advent of the transistor, Japanese firms became the technical leaders. Thinking it was too expensive to gain the needed knowledge, RCA contracted out much of its production and subsequently lost its competitive edge. Now, only the brand name remains RCA. The firm no longer makes televisions.

▼ INFORMATION DISTRIBUTION

Once information is obtained, managers must establish mechanisms to distribute relevant information to the individuals who may need it. One of the primary challenges in larger firms is to locate quickly who has the appropriate information and who needs specific types of information. A partial solution is the development of computer and electronic networks that connect related organizational units. The use of electronic networks allows managers to disperse information outside the normal hierarchical channels specified in the organization's design. For instance, to promote teamwork among geographically disbursed employees, Ben and Jerry's has invested over $140,000 in videoconferencing systems. The dedicated TV hookups allow teams of 10 to 15 employees from different locations to work as a team on common total quality management issues.[33] Although data collection is helpful, just providing the data is not enough; the information must be interpreted.

▼ INFORMATION INTERPRETATION

Data are not information. Information within organizations is a collective understanding of the firm's goals and of how the data relate to one of the firm's stated or unstated objectives within the current setting. Unfortunately, the process of developing multiple interpretations is often thwarted by a number of common problems.[34]

Self-Serving Interpretations   A manager's ability to interpret events, conditions, and history to his or her own advantage is almost universal. Managers and employees alike often see what they have seen in the past or see what they want to see. Rarely do they see what is or can be.

Managerial Scripts   A *managerial script* is a series of well-known routines for problem identification and alternative generation and analysis common to managers within a firm.[35] Different organizations have different scripts, often based on what has worked in the past. In a way, the script is a ritual that reflects what the "memory banks" of the corporation hold. Managers become bound by what they have seen. The danger is that they may not be open to what actually is occurring.

The script may be elaborate enough to provide an apparently well-tested series of solutions based on the firm's experience. Larger, older firms are rarely structured for learning; rather, they are structured for efficiency. That is, the organizational design emphasizes repetition, volume processing, and routine. In order to learn, the organization needs to be able to switch routines, to obtain information quickly, to provide various interpretations of events, and to tap into external archives.[36]

Few managers question a successful script. Consequently, they start solving today's problems with yesterday's solutions. Managers have been trained, both in the classroom and on the job, to initiate corrective action within the historically shared view of the world; that is, managers often initiate small, incremental improvements based on existing solutions instead of creating new approaches to identify the underlying problems.

Common Myths An **organizational myth** is a commonly held cause-effect relationship or assertion that cannot be empirically supported. Even though myths cannot be substantiated, both managers and workers may base their interpretations of problems and opportunities on the potentially faulty views. Three common myths often block the development of multiple interpretations.

The first common myth is the presumption that *there is a single organizational truth.* This myth is often expressed as, "Although others may be biased, I am able to define problems and develop solutions objectively." We are all subject to bias in varying degrees and in varying ways. The more complex the issue, the stronger the likelihood that there will be many different supportable interpretations.

A second common myth is the *presumption of competence.* Managers at all levels are subject to believing that their part of the firm is okay and just needs minor improvements in implementation. As we have documented throughout this book, such is rarely the case. We are in the middle of a managerial revolution, in which all managers need to reassess their general approach to managing organizational behavior.

A third common myth is the *denial of tradeoffs.* Most managers believe that their group, unit, or firm can avoid making undesirable tradeoffs and simultaneously please nearly every constituency. Whereas the denial of tradeoff is common, it can be a very dangerous myth in some firms. For instance, when complex, dangerous technologies are involved, safe operations may come at some sacrifice to efficiency. Yet, some firms claim that "an efficient operation is a safe one" and aggressively move to improve efficiency. While managers are stressing efficiency, they may fail to work on improving safety. The result may be a serious accident.[37]

> An **organizational myth** is a commonly held cause–effect relationship or assertion that cannot be empirically supported.

▼ ORGANIZATIONAL RETENTION

Organizations contain a variety of mechanisms that can be used to retain useful information.[38] Six important mechanisms are: individuals, culture, transformation procedures, formal structures, ecology, and external archives.

Of course, individuals are the most important storehouses of information for organizations. Organizations that retain a large and comparatively stable group of experienced individuals are expected to have a higher capacity to acquire, retain, and retrieve information. Collectively, the organizational culture is an important repository of the shared experiences of corporate members. The culture often maintains the organizational memory via rich, vivid, and meaningful stories that outlive those who actually experienced the event.

Documents, rule books, written procedures, and even standard but unwritten methods of operation are all mechanisms used to store accumulated information. In cases where operations are extremely complex but rarely needed, written sources of information are often invaluable. Pacific Gas and Electric, for example, maintains an extensive library for its Diablo Canyon nuclear power plant. In the library, one can find the complete engineering drawings for the whole plant plus all the changes made since the plant opened, as well as a step-by-step plan for almost every possible accident scenario.

The organizational structure and the positions in an organization are less obvious but equally important mechanisms for storing information. When an aircraft lands on the deck of a U.S. Navy aircraft carrier, there are typically dozens of individuals on the deck, apparently watching the aircraft land. Actually, each person on the deck is there for a specific purpose. Each can often trace his or her position to a specific accident that would not have occurred had some individual originally been assigned that position.

Physical structures (or "ecology," in the language of learning theorists) are potentially important but often neglected mechanisms used to store information. For example, a traditional way of ordering parts and subcomponents in a factory is known as the "two-bin" system. One bin is always kept in reserve. Once an individual opens the reserve bin, he or she automatically orders replacements. In this way, the plant never runs out of components.

Finally, external archives can be tapped to provide valuable information on most larger organizations. Former employees, stock market analysts, suppliers, distributors, and the media can be important sources of valuable information. These external archives are important because they may provide a view of events quite different from that held in the organization.

ORGANIZATIONAL LEARNING CYCLES

Throughout the 1990s, a common headline running in the business press seems to have been: "Major Corporation Downsizes." Whether the corporation was AT&T, General Motors, or IBM, the message appeared to be the same: major United States-based corporations were in trouble. They were finally adjusting to a new competitive reality, on the backs of their workers and managers.

Although there are many causes of downsizing, many of these firms have simply been unable to learn in a systematic manner and to make the needed incremental changes and decisions along the way. Instead, they engage in massive attempts to redirect themselves when it is apparent to all that change is overdue. Some recent work on learning cycles helps explain why many organizations apparently fail to learn, while others appear to improve rapidly.[39]

▼ DEFICIT CYCLES

A **deficit cycle** is a pattern of deteriorating performance that is followed by even further deterioration. Firms that are continually downsizing, such as AT&T, are examples of firms in a deficit cycle. The same problems keep reoccurring, and the firm fails to develop adequate mechanisms for learning. The firm often has problems in one or more phases of the learning process. The past inability to adjust yields more problems and fewer resources available to solve the next wave of problems, and the firm continues to deteriorate.

Major factors associated with deficit cycles are still being uncovered. However, three are obvious from current research.[40] One is *organizational inertia*. It is very difficult to change organizations, and the larger the organization the more inertia it often has. A second is *hubris*. Too few senior executives are willing to challenge their own actions or those of their firms because they see a history of success. They fail to recognize that yesterday's successful innovations are today's outmoded practices. A third is the issue of *detachment*. Executives often believe they can manage far-flung, diverse operations by analysis of reports and financial records. They lose touch and fail to make the needed unique and special adaptations required of all firms. One consultant has made millions advising executives to focus on improvement and practice management by walking around the office to avoid detachment.

> A **deficit cycle** is a pattern of deteriorating performance that is followed by even further deterioration.

▼ BENEFIT CYCLES

Although common, inertia, hubris, and detachment are not automatically the fate of all corporations. As we have repeatedly demonstrated, managers are trying to reinvent their firms each and every day. They hope to initiate a **benefit cycle**—a pattern of successful adjustment followed by further improvements. Microsoft is an example of a firm experiencing a benefit cycle. In this cycle, the same problems do not keep reoccurring as the firm develops adequate mechanisms for learning. The firm has a few major difficulties with the learning process, and managers continually attempt to improve knowledge acquisition, information distribution, information interpretation, and organizational memory.

> A **benefit cycle** is a pattern of successful adjustment followed by further improvements.

Just as a prior inability to adjust yields more problems and fewer resources for solving the next wave of problems, organizations that successfully adapt can ride the benefit cycle. Inertia can work for managers if they do not become overconfident and if they can stay directly involved with the key operations of the firm.

CHAPTER 12 STUDY GUIDE

SUMMARY

What is organizational design, and how do the organizational designs of small and large firms differ?

- Organizational design is the process of choosing and implementing a structural configuration for an organization.
- Smaller firms often adopt a simple structure, whereas larger firms often adopt a bureaucratic form.
- The bureaucracy is an ideal form based on legal authority, logic, and order.

Does the technology of the firm influence its organizational design?

- Technology and organizational design are interrelated.
- In highly intensive and small-batch technologies, organizational designs may tend toward the adhocracy, a very decentralized form of operation.

What is the relationship between environmental conditions and organizational design?

- Environmental and organizational design are interrelated.
- In analyzing environments, both the general (background conditions) and specific (key actors and organizations) environments are important.
- The more complex the environment, the greater the demands on the organization, and firms should respond with more complex designs, such as the use of interfirm alliances.

What is strategy, and how are firms combining generic strategies and their own unique competencies?

- Strategy and organizational design are interrelated. The organizational design must support the strategy if it is to prove successful.
- Four generic strategies pursued by businesses are differentiation, focused differentiation, cost leadership, and focused cost leadership.
- Effective managers are able to build upon competency based strategies to modify and extend the generic strategies.

What is organizational learning?

- Organizational learning is the process of knowledge acquisition, information distribution, information interpretation, and organizational memory used to adapt successfully to changing circumstances.

How are organizational learning cycles helpful in understanding organizational behavior?

- Organizational learning cycles help us understand how some organizations continually decline while others appear to be rising stars.

KEY TERMS

Adhocracy (p. 249)

Benefit cycle (p. 261)

Bureaucracy (p. 244)

Conglomerate (p. 247)

Deficit cycle (p. 261)

Divisionalized design
(p. 246)

Environmental complexity
(p. 251)

Grafting (p. 257)

Interfirm alliances (p. 252)

Mechanistic design (p. 245)

Mimicry (p. 256)

Organic design (p. 246)

Organizational design
(p. 243)

Organizational learning
(p. 256)

Organizational myth
(p. 259)

Organizational strategy
(p. 254)

Scanning (p. 257)

Simple design (p. 243)

Technology (p. 248)

SELF-TEST 12

▼ MULTIPLE CHOICE

1. The design of the organization needs to be adjusted to all but ___. (a) the environment of the firm (b) the strategy of the firm (c) the size of the firm (d) the technology of the firm (e) the personnel to be hired by the firm

2. Which is *not* a characteristic of bureaucracy. (a) members have administrative careers and work on a fixed salary. (b) there is little hierarchy of authority. (c) labor is specialized. (d) Members are subject to rules and controls. (e) Members are selected and promoted on the basis of technical competency.

3. ___ characterizes an organic organization. (a) Centralized authority (b) Ambiguous division of authority (c) Many rules and procedures (d) Intensive vertical specialization (e) Formal methods of coordination and control

4. When an organization's goals are oriented toward efficiency, the __ organizational design is most appropriate. (a) conglomerate (b) free form (c) organic (d) mechanistic (e) adhocracy

5. Which of the following is an inaccurate statement about an adhocracy? (a) Division of labor is ambiguous. (b) There are many rules and policies. (c) Use of managerial techniques is minimal. (d) It handles routine problems efficiently (e) It is quite common.

6. One key difference between the divisional and conglomerate designs is the ___. (a) degree of synergy among businesses (b) size of the organizations (c) environment in which the designs are successful (d) sophistication of the technology (e) role of management.

7. The set of cultural, economic, legal–political, and educational conditions in the areas in which a firm operates is called the ___. (a) task environment (b) specific environment (c) industry of the firm (d) environmental complexity (e) general environment

8. The process of acquiring knowledge, organizational retention, and distributing and interpreting information is called ___. (a) vicarious learning (b) experience (c) organizational learning (d) an organizational myth (e) a self-serving interpretation

9. Three methods of vicarious learning are ___. (a) scanning, grafting, and contracting out (b) grafting, contracting out, and mimicry (c) maladaptive specialization, scanning, and grafting (d) scanning, grafting, and mimicry (e) experience, mimicry, and scanning

10. Three important factors that block information interpretation are ___. (a) detachment, scanning, and common myths (b) self-serving interpretations, detachment, and common myths (c) managerial scripts, maladaptive specialization, and common myths (d) contracting out, common myths, and detachment (e) common myths, managerial scripts, and self-serving interpretations

▼ TRUE–FALSE

11. The general environment of organizations includes other organizations with which an organization must interact in order to obtain inputs and dispose of outputs.
    T F

12. Organizations with well-defined and stable technologies have more opportunity to substitute managerial techniques for managerial judgment than do firms relying on more variable technologies.   T F

13. Organic organizations tend to favor vertical specialization and control.   T F

14. In a mechanistic organization, staff is typically decentralized.   T F

15. A divisionalized design consolidates all divisions within an organization under a single, unitary design.   T F

16. The conglomerate is an example of a mechanistic organization design.   T F

17. An adhocracy is an extreme example of a mechanistic organization.   T F

18. Mimicry is the copying of successful practices of others.   T F

19. The key to effective organizational learning is manipulation.   T F

20. A deficit cycle is a pattern of deteriorating performance that is followed by further deterioration.   T F

▼ SHORT RESPONSE

21. Max Weber developed what he called the ideal bureaucracy. What are the characteristics associated with Weber's ideal bureaucracy?

22. Mechanistic and organic designs are very different. Compare and contrast these two designs.

23. Describe the effect technology has on an organization from both Thompson's point of view and Woodward's point of view.

24. What are the three primary determinants of environmental complexity?

▼ APPLICATIONS ESSAY

25. Why would Ford Motors want to shift to a matrix design organization for the design and development of cars and trucks but not do so in their manufacturing and assembly operations?

13

ORGANIZATIONAL CULTURE

Be they in California, Florida, Japan, or France, all new Disney employees are told the story of Walt Disney. He was said to have emphasized the idea that everyone is a child at heart and that every individual in the Disney theme parks is a performer. This emphasis is commonly attributed to his founding philosophy. Actually, Walt Disney was a perfectionist. A harder boss would be difficult to find, and several times Disney bet the entire firm on the success of one picture. The emphasis on "everyone is a performer" did not come from a philosophy but from hard-won experience. In fact, the initial opening of Disneyland in California was not a success until the firm eliminated much of the staff whose experience was limited to county fairs. They were replaced by an inexperienced crew of young employees trained by Disney.

In France, Euro Disney is still seeking an answer to the question of how to match European culture and Disney's created culture. It is a challenge of managing a corporate culture to fit both its history and its current situation. (http://www.ensicaen.ismra.frl~aubry/disney/perso/ee.html)

265

As we approach the beginning of a new century, a transformation is occurring in many organizations—from the giant auto manufacturers to the small software design firms. At all levels of operations, people are striving for productivity. Quality, innovation, and value are replacing the drive toward short-term efficiency. Managers are recognizing the need to build viable organizations that stand for something. They are rediscovering the critical importance of human resources. The old methods of command and control are being replaced by new methods of participation and involvement. Managers are becoming facilitators, helpers, guides, and coaches. In our terminology, they are changing their organization's "culture." One chief OB mechanism used to change the culture is organizational development (OD).

The not-so-hidden advantage of some leading firms is their corporate cultures. As you read Chapter 13, keep in mind these questions:

- What is the concept of organizational culture?
- What are the observable aspects of corporate culture?
- Can common assumptions link individuals together?
- Can the corporate culture be "managed," or are "nurtured" and "guided" more appropriate terms?
- How can organization development be used to manage corporate culture?
- What are some organization development interventions?

THE CONCEPT OF ORGANIZATIONAL CULTURE

Organizational culture is the system of shared actions, values, and beliefs that develops within an organization and guides the behavior of its members.[1] In the business setting, this system is often referred to as the *corporate culture*. Just as no two individual personalities are the same, no two organizational cultures are perfectly identical. Most significantly, management scholars and consultants increasingly believe that cultural differences can have a major impact on the performance of organizations and the quality of work life experienced by their members.

▼ THE FUNCTIONS AND COMPONENTS OF ORGANIZATIONAL CULTURE

Through their collective experience, members of an organization solve two extremely important survival issues.[2] The first is the question of external adaptation: What precisely needs to be accomplished and how can it be done? The second is the question of internal integration: How do members resolve the daily problems associated with living and working together?

External Adaptation *External adaptation* involves reaching goals and dealing with outsiders. Issues concerned are the tasks to be accomplished, the methods used to achieve the goals, and methods of coping with success and failure.

Through their shared experiences, members may develop common views that help guide their day-to-day activities. Organizational members need to know the real mission of the organization, not just the pronouncements to key constituencies, such as stockholders. Members will naturally develop an understanding of how they contribute to the mission via interaction. This view may emphasize the importance of human resources, or it may emphasize the role of employees as cogs in a machine, or it may emphasize a cost to be reduced.

Closely related to the organization's mission and view of its contribution are the questions of responsibility, goals, and methods. For instance, at 3M, employees believe that it is their responsibility to innovate and contribute creatively. They see these responsibilities reflected in achieving the goal of developing new and improved products and processes.

Each collection of individuals in an organization also tends to (1) separate more important from less important external forces; (2) develop ways to measure their accomplishments; and (3) create explanations for why goals are not always met. Chrysler's managers, for example, have moved away from judging their progress against specific targets to estimating the degree to which they are moving a development process forward. Instead of blaming a poor economy or upper level managers for the firm's failure to reach a goal, Chrysler managers have set hard goals that are difficult to reach and have redoubled their efforts to improve participation and commitment.

Organizational or **corporate culture** is the system of shared actions, values, and beliefs that develops within an organization and guides the behavior of its members.

External adaptation involves reaching goals and dealing with outsiders. Issues concerned are the tasks to be accomplished, the methods used to achieve the goals, and methods of coping with success and failure.

DEC
http://proto.
convergent.com/
unixcd/digital/
cohesion-sees/
team-see-pcms/
ts-/pg.txt/

Digital Equipment Corporation's culture emerged
from the entrepreneurial
approach of its founder Ken
Olsen, whose way of seeing
the world has guided gen-
erations of DEC managers:
Focus on opportunities not
problems; solve customer
problems and create new
opportunities. Wherever you
go in DEC, in the United
States or in other countries,
personnel share common
assumptions about how the
business should be run.[3]

The final issues in external adaptation deal with two important, but often neglected, aspects of coping with external reality. First, individuals need to develop
acceptable ways of telling outsiders just how good they really are. At 3M, for example, employees talk about the quality of their products and the many new useful products they have brought to the market. Second, individuals must collectively know when to admit defeat. At 3M, the answer is easy for new projects: At
the beginning of the development process, members establish "drop" points at
which to quit the development effort and redirect it.

In sum, external adaptation involves answering important instrumental or
goal-related questions concerning coping with reality: What is the real mission?
How do we contribute? What are our goals? How do we reach our goals? What external forces are important? How do we measure results? What do we do if specific targets are not met? How do we tell others how good we are? When do we
quit?

Internal Integration   The corporate culture also provides answers to the problems of internal integration. *Internal integration* deals with the creation of a collective identity and with finding ways of matching methods of working and living
together.

The process of internal integration often begins by the establishment of a
unique identity; that is, each collection of individuals and each subculture within
the organization develops some type of unique definition of itself. Through dialogue and interaction, members begin to characterize their world. They may see
it as malleable or fixed, filled with opportunity or threatening. Real progress toward innovation can begin when group members collectively believe that they
can change important parts of the world around them and that what appears to be
a threat is actually an opportunity for change.[4]

Three important aspects of working together are (1) deciding who is a member and who is not; (2) developing an informal understanding of acceptable and
unacceptable behavior; and (3) separating friends from enemies. Effective total
quality management holds that subgroups in the organization need to view their
immediate supervisors as members of the group, who are expected to represent
them to friendly higher managers.

To work together effectively, individuals need to decide collectively how to allocate power, status, and authority. They need to establish a shared understanding of who will get rewards and sanctions for specific types of actions. Too often,
managers fail to recognize these important aspects of internal integration. For example, a manager may fail to explain the basis for a promotion and to show why
this reward, the status associated with it, and the power given to the newly promoted individual are consistent with commonly shared beliefs.

Collections of individuals need to work out acceptable ways to communicate
and to develop guidelines for acceptable friendships. Although these aspects of
internal integration may appear esoteric, they are vital. To function effectively as
a team, individuals must recognize that some members will be closer than others;
friendships are inevitable. However, the basis for friendships can be inappropriately restricted. At the U.S. Department of Interior, for example, recent budget

cuts may have had a beneficial effect. At one time, the political appointees could be found eating together in their own executive dining room. Now, all employees eat at the Interior Department lunchroom, and even the political appointees are making new friends with the career civil servants.

In sum, internal integration involves answers to important questions associated with living together. What is our unique identity? How do we view the world? Who is a member? How do we allocate power, status, and authority? How do we communicate? What is the basis for friendship? Answering these questions is important to organizational members because the organization is more than a place to work; it is a place where individuals spend much of their adult life.[5]

Take-A-Note 13.1
PICKING A FIRM BY ITS CULTURE

One study suggests that there are four dominant types of corporate cultures:

1. Academies—individuals are carefully moved through training programs for career development.
2. Fortresses—individuals are asked to engage in a turn-around and a fight for corporate survival.
3. Clubs—seniority, loyalty, status, commitment, and "fitting in" are most important.
4. Baseball teams—talent and performance are considered critical.

▼ SUBCULTURES AND COUNTERCULTURES

It is often important to recognize distinct groups within a culture. **Subcultures** are groups of individuals with a unique pattern of values and philosophy that is not inconsistent with the organization's dominant values and philosophy.[6] Interestingly, strong subcultures are often found in high-performance task forces, teams, and special project groups in organizations. The culture emerges to bind individuals working intensely together to accomplish a specific task.

In contrast, **countercultures** have a pattern of values and a philosophy that reject the surrounding culture.[7] The antiapartheid counterculture in South Africa and the Solidarity movement in Poland in the 1980s are two vivid examples of countercultures on a national scale. In the first week of President Clinton's term in 1993, the press was filled with arguments regarding whether or not homosexuals should be allowed to state their sexual preference and still serve in the military. Some argued it was time to be more inclusive, and others were shocked and morally outraged at the idea. Each side of the controversy claimed the other was a minority counterculture.

Within an organization, mergers and acquisitions may produce countercultures. Employers and managers of an acquired firm may hold values and assumptions that are quite inconsistent with those of the acquiring firm. This is known as the "clash of corporate cultures."[8] In the 1980s, Coca Cola bought Columbia Pictures and began integrating Columbia operations into the Coca Cola family. The soft-drink company found out too late that the picture business was quite different from selling beverages, however. It sold Columbia, with its unique corporate culture, to Sony rather than fight a protracted clash of cultures.[9]

Subcultures are unique patterns of values and philosophies within a group that are consistent with the dominant culture of the larger organization or social system.

Countercultures are the patterns of values and philosophies that outwardly reject those of the larger organization or social system.

Importing Subcultures Every large organization imports potentially important subcultural groupings when it hires employees from the larger society. In North America, for instance, subcultures and countercultures may naturally form based on ethnic, racial, gender, generational, or locational similarities. In Japanese organizations, subcultures often form based on the date of graduation from a university, gender, or geographic location. In European firms, ethnicity and language play an important part in developing subcultures, as does gender. In many less developed nations, language, education, religion, or family social status are often grounds for forming societally popular subcultures and countercultures.

The difficulty with importing groupings from the larger societies lies in the relevance these subgroups have to the organization as a whole. At the one extreme, senior managers can merely accept these divisions and work within the confines of the larger culture. There are three primary difficulties with this approach. First, subordinated groups, such as members of a specific religion or ethnic group, are likely to form into a counterculture and to work more to change their status than to better the firm. Second, the firm may find it extremely difficult to cope with broader cultural changes. For instance, in the United States the expected treatment of women, ethnic minorities, and the disabled has changed dramatically over the last 20 years. Firms that merely accept old customs and prejudices have experienced a greater loss of key personnel and increased communication difficulties, as well as greater interpersonal conflict, than have their more progressive counterparts. Third, firms that accept and build upon natural divisions from the larger culture may find it extremely difficult to develop sound international operations. For example, many Japanese firms have had substantial difficulty adjusting to the equal treatment of women in their U.S. operations.

Promoting Cultural Diversity   Managers can work to eradicate all naturally occurring subcultures and countercultures. In the 1990s, firms are groping to develop what Taylor Cox calls the "multicultural organization." The *multicultural organization* is a firm that values diversity but systematically works to block the transfer of societally based subcultures into the fabric of the organization.[10] Because Cox focuses on some problems unique to the United States, his prescription for change may not apply to organizations located in other countries with much more homogeneous populations.

Cox suggests a five-step program for developing the multicultural organization. First, the organization should develop pluralism with the objective of multibased socialization. To accomplish this objective, members of different naturally occurring groups need to school one another to increase knowledge and information and to eliminate stereotyping. Second, the firm should fully integrate its structure so that there is no direct relationship between a naturally occurring group and any particular job, for instance, that there are no distinct male or female jobs. Third, the firm must integrate the informal networks by eliminating barriers and increasing participation; that is, it must break down existing societally based informal groups. Fourth, the organization should break the linkage between naturally occurring group identity and the identity of the firm. In other words, the firm should not be just for the young, old, men, women, and so on. Fifth, the organization must actively work to eliminate interpersonal conflict based on either the group identity or the natural backlash of the largest societally based grouping.

Of course, the key problems with fully implementing Cox's program are separating the firm from the larger culture in which it must operate and eliminating some societally based groupings that are relevant for achieving the firm's goals. For instance, the U.S. military is barred from fully implementing Cox's recommendations simply because it is not currently legal to put women into combat roles. The issue of generational groupings provides another example. Implementing Cox's recommendations would call for 20 year olds to be represented proportionally in the senior management ranks; most corporations want and need the judgment honed by experience.

▼ LEVELS OF CULTURAL ANALYSIS

Figure 13.1 depicts three important levels of cultural analysis in organizations: observable culture, shared values, and common assumptions.[11] These may be envisioned as layers. The deeper one gets, the more difficult it is to discover the culture.

The first level concerns *observable culture,* or "the way we do things around here." These are the methods the group has developed and teaches to new members. The observable culture includes the unique stories, ceremonies, and corporate rituals that make up the history of a successful work group.

The second level of analysis recognizes that *shared values* can play a critical part in linking people together and can provide a powerful motivational mechanism for members of the culture. Many consultants suggest that organizations should develop a "dominant and coherent set of shared values."[12] The term "shared" in cultural analysis implies that the group is a whole. Every member may not agree with the shared values, but they have all been exposed to them and have often been told they are important. At Hewlett-Packard, for example, "quality" is part of everyone's vocabulary. The firm was founded with a belief that everyone could make a creative contribution to developing quality products.

At the deepest level of cultural analysis are *common assumptions,* or the taken-for-granted truths that collections of corporate members share as a result of their joint experience. It is often extremely difficult to isolate these patterns, but doing so helps explain why culture invades every aspect of organizational life.

✳ **MARY KAY COSMETICS**
http://www.wwbcity.com/maryk.htm/

Rituals and ceremonies are an important aspect of Mary Kay's motivational strategy, including rousing all-day peptalks, where top performers enthusiastically share their success stories, and where awards —Mary Kay's famous pink luxury cars—are given to the highest achievers.

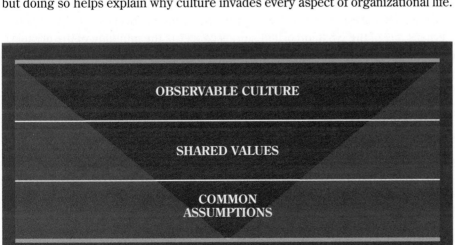

OBSERVABLE CULTURE

SHARED VALUES

COMMON ASSUMPTIONS

■ FIGURE 13.1
Levels of cultural analysis.

QUALITY

Common assumptions may surface in an organizational crisis. At Mills College the board of trustees voted to admit men to the all-women school to avert bankruptcy. They claimed that changing to coeducation was an economic necessity. The board retreated, however, when students, alumnae, and administrators demonstrated the educational importance and unique contributions of an all-women's liberal arts college. These often separate constituencies united to develop a new plan to save the tradition and philosophy that they all believed to be fundamental to Mills.

OBSERVABLE ASPECTS OF ORGANIZATIONAL CULTURE

Important parts of an organization's culture emerge from the collective experience of its members. These emergent aspects of the culture help make it unique and may well provide a competitive advantage for the organization. Some of these aspects may be directly observed in day-to-day practices. Others may have to be discovered—for example, by asking members to tell stories of important incidents in the history of the organization. We often learn about the unique aspects of the organizational culture through descriptions of very specific events.[13] By observing employee actions, listening to stories, and asking members to interpret what is going on, one can begin to understand the organization's culture.

▼ STORIES, RITES, RITUALS, AND SYMBOLS

Organizations are rich with stories of winners, losers, successes, and failures. Perhaps one of the most important stories concerns the founding of the organization. The *founding story* often contains the lessons learned from the heroic efforts of an embattled entrepreneur, whose vision may still guide the firm. The story of the founding may be so embellished that it becomes a **saga**—a heroic account of accomplishments.[14] Sagas are important because they are used to tell new members the real mission of the organization, how the organization operates, and how individuals can fit into the company. Rarely is the founding story totally accurate, and it often glosses over some of the more negative aspects of the founders.

If you have job experience, you may well have heard stories concerning the following questions: How will the boss react to a mistake? Can someone move from the bottom to the top of the company? What will get me fired? These are common story topics in many organizations.[15] Often, the stories provide valuable hidden information about who is more equal than others, whether jobs are se-

Sagas are embellished heroic accounts of the story of the founding of an organization.

cure, and how things are really controlled. In essence, the stories begin to suggest how organizational members view the world and live together.

Some of the most obvious aspects of organizational culture are rites and rituals. **Rites** are standardized and recurring activities that are used at special times to influence the behaviors and understanding of organizational members; **rituals** are systems of rites. It is common, for example, for Japanese workers and managers to start their work days together with group exercises and singing of the "company song." Separately, the exercises and song are rites. Together, they form part of a ritual. In other settings, such as the Mary Kay Cosmetics company, scheduled ceremonies reminiscent of the Miss America pageant (a ritual) are used regularly to spotlight positive work achievements and reinforce high-performance expectations with awards, including gold and diamond pins and fur stoles.

Rituals and rites may be unique to particular groups within the organization. Subcultures often arise from the type of technology deployed by the unit, the specific function being performed, and the specific collection of specialists in the unit. The boundaries of the subculture may well be maintained by a unique language. Often, the language of a subculture, and its rituals and rites, emerge from the group as a form of jargon. In some cases, the special language starts to move outside the firm and begins to enter the larger society. For instance an ad for a Hewlett-Packard hand-held computer reads "All the features you need are built right in. MS-DOS, Lotus 1-2-3 . . . and a 512 K RAM version of the HP 95LX." Not everyone finds this a user-friendly ad.[16]

Another observable aspect of corporate culture is the symbols found in organizations. A **cultural symbol** is any object, act, or event that serves to transmit cultural meaning. Good examples are the corporate uniforms worn by UPS and Federal Express delivery personnel. Although many such symbols are quite visible, their importance and meaning may not be.

> **Rites** are standardized and recurring activities used at special times to influence the behaviors and understanding of organizational members.

> **Rituals** are systems of rites.

> A **cultural symbol** is any object, act, or event that serves to transmit cultural meaning.

▼ CULTURAL RULES AND ROLES

Organizational culture often specifies when various types of actions are appropriate and where individual members stand in the social system. These cultural rules and roles are part of the normative controls of the organization and emerge from its daily routines.[17] For instance, the timing, presentation, and methods of communicating authoritative directives are often quite specific to each organization. In one firm, meetings may be forums for dialogue and discussion, where managers set agendas and then let others offer new ideas, critically examine alternatives, and fully participate. In another firm, the "rules" may be quite different: The manager goes into the meeting with fixed expectations. Any new ideas, critical examinations, and the like are expected to be worked out in private before the meeting takes place. The meeting is a forum for letting others know what is being done and for passing out orders on what to do in the future.

▼ THE EVOLUTION OF SHARED MEANINGS FROM OBSERVABLE CULTURE

What you see as an outside observer may or may not be what organizational members see. You may see NASA personnel on television filling the tanks of a booster rocket for the space shuttle. If you could ask the workers directly what they are doing, you might be surprised by the answer. They are not just filling booster tanks; they are assisting with an important part of exploring space. Through interaction with one another, and as reinforced by the rest of the organization, the workers have infused a larger shared meaning—or sense of broader purpose—into their tasks. In this sense, organizational culture is a "shared set of meanings and perceptions that are created and learned by organizational members in the course of interactions."[18] This set of shared meanings may be accompanied by shared values.

VALUES AND ORGANIZATIONAL CULTURE

To describe more fully the culture of an organization it is necessary to go deeper than the observable aspects. To many researchers and managers, shared common values lie at the very heart of organization culture. Shared values help turn routine activities into valuable, important actions, tie the corporation to the important values of society, and may provide a very distinctive source of competitive advantage.

In organizations, what works for one person is often taught to new members as the correct way to think and feel. Important values are then attributed to these solutions to everyday problems. By linking values and actions, the organization taps into some of the strongest and deepest realms of the individual. The tasks a person performs are given not only meaning but value; what one does is not only workable but correct, right, and important.

Some successful organizations share some common cultural characteristics.[19] Organizations with "strong cultures" possess a broadly and deeply shared value system. Unique, shared values can provide a strong corporate identity, enhance collective commitment, provide a stable social system, and reduce the need for formal and bureaucratic controls. A strong culture can be a double-edged sword, however. A strong culture and value system can reinforce a singular view of the organization and its environment. If dramatic changes are needed, it may be very difficult to change the organization. General Motors may have a "strong" culture, for example, but the firm faces enormous difficulty in its attempts to adapt its ways to a dynamic and highly competitive environment.

Take-A-Note 13.2

ELEMENTS OF STRONG CORPORATE CULTURES

- A widely shared real understanding of what the firm stands for, often embodied in slogans.
- A concern for individuals over rules, policies, procedures, and adherence to job duties.
- A recognition of heroes whose actions illustrate the shared philosophy and concerns of the company.
- A belief in ritual and ceremony as important to members and to building a common identity.
- A well-understood sense of the informal rules and expectations so that employees and managers understand what is expected of them.
- A belief that what employees and managers do is important and that it is important to share information and ideas.

COMMON ASSUMPTIONS AND ORGANIZATIONAL CULTURE

COMMON ASSUMPTIONS AND ORGANIZATIONAL CULTURE

In many corporate cultures, one finds a series of common understandings known to most everyone in the corporation: "We are different." "We are better at . . . ." "We have unrecognized talents." Senior managers often share common assumptions, such as, "We are good stewards." "We are competent managers." "We are practical innovators." In many firms, broadly shared common assumptions by senior management go even further. The firm may have a well-developed management philosophy.

▼ MANAGEMENT PHILOSOPHY

A **management philosophy** links key goal-related issues with key collaboration issues and comes up with a series of general ways by which the firm will manage its affairs. A well-developed management philosophy is important because (1) it establishes generally understood boundaries on all members of the firm; (2) it provides a consistent way of approaching new and novel situations; and (3) it helps hold individuals together by assuring them of a known path toward success. Wal-Mart has a clearly identified management philosophy linking growth and profitability with customer service and individual employee commitment. Each manager runs "a store within a store," supported by more senior management and corporate buyers. This concept both liberates individuals to try new initiatives and bounds their efforts within managerial constraints and purchasing realities. Profit sharing and the individual recognition given by the traveling CEO help bind individuals together. The philosophy is expressed in some old-fashioned values, such as customer service, frugality, hard work, and service toward employees.

> **Management philosophy** is a philosophy that links key goal-related issues with key collaboration issues to come up with general ways by which the firm will manage its affairs.

Elements of the management philosophy may be formally documented in a corporate plan, a statement of business philosophy, or a series of goals. Yet, it is the unstated but well-understood fundamentals these written documents signify that actually form the heart of a well-developed management philosophy.

▼ ORGANIZATIONAL MYTHS

In many firms, the management philosophy is supported by a series of organizational myths. **Organizational myths** are unproven and often unstated beliefs that are accepted uncritically. In a study of safety in nuclear power plants, senior managers were asked whether they felt there was a tradeoff between safeness and efficiency. The response was clear: A safe plant is an efficient plant. Yet, most of these executives had seen data showing that measures of safeness and efficiency were quite independent. To admit there was a tradeoff raised the issue of making choices between efficiency and safety. All wanted to believe that to do one was to promote the other.[20]

> **Organization myth** is an unproven and often unstated belief that is accepted uncritically.

Whereas some may scoff at these organizational myths and want to see rational, hard-nosed analysis replace mythology, each firm needs a series of managerial myths.[21] Myths allow executives to redefine impossible problems into more manageable components. Myths can facilitate experimentation and creativity, and they allow managers to govern. For instance, senior executives are not just decision makers or rational allocators of resources. All organization members hope these individuals will also be fair, just, and compassionate.

▼ NATIONAL ROOTS OF COMMON ASSUMPTIONS

It is often possible to trace widely held common assumptions to the larger culture of the corporation's host society.[22] The difference between Sony's corporate emphasis on group achievements and Zenith's emphasis on individual engineering excellence, for example, can be traced to the Japanese emphasis on collective action verses the U.S. emphasis on individualism.

National culture values may also become embedded in the expectations of important organizational constituencies and in generally accepted solutions to problems. When moving across national cultures, managers need to be sensitive to national cultural differences so that their actions do not violate common assumptions in the underlying national culture. In Japan and Western Europe, for example, executives are expected to work cooperatively with government officials on an informal basis. Informal business–government relations that are perfectly acceptable in these countries are considered influence pedaling in the United States. Whereas some South American executives expect to pay directly for some government services, in the United States such payments are considered bribes.

Inappropriate actions that violate common assumptions drawn from national culture can have an important impact on performance and may alienate organizational members, even if managers have the best intentions. To improve morale at General Electric's new French subsidiary, Chi. Generale de Radiologie, American mangers invited all the European managers to a "get acquainted" meeting near Paris. The Americans gave out colorful T-shirts with the GE slogan "Go for One," a typical maneuver in many American training programs. The French resented the T-shirts. One outspoken individual said, "It was like Hitler was back, forcing us to wear uniforms. It was humiliating."

✴ **IBM JAPAN**
*http://launcher.
g-search.or.jp/jeida/
www/datashow/e/
c013-e.htm/*

Newly hired Japanese workers at IBM Japan were shocked when an American executive indicated that the goal of the firm was to maximize stockholder wealth. In Japan, stockholders are a less important corporate stakeholder than are core employees.

MANAGING ORGANIZATIONAL CULTURE

The culture should be considered as critical as structure and strategy in establishing the organizational foundations of high performance. Good managers are able to reinforce and support an existing strong culture; good managers are also able to help build resilient cultures in situations where they are absent.

For instance CEO Mike Walsh of Union Pacific has brought a new and fresh approach to the firm with what *Fortune* magazine called an "introverted corporate culture." Cultural changes under Walsh's leadership include the empowerment of managers at all levels, who have responded, "We were so elated the company was willing to give new authority that we wanted it to work."

Two broad strategies for managing the corporate culture have received considerable attention in the OB literature. One strategy calls for managers to help modify observable culture, shared values, and common assumptions directly. A second strategy involves the use of organizational development techniques to modify specific elements of the culture.

▼ BUILDING, REINFORCING, AND CHANGING CULTURE DIRECTLY

Managers can modify the visible aspects of culture, such as the language, stories, rites, rituals, and sagas. They can change the lessons to be drawn from common stories and even encourage individuals to see the reality they see. Because of their positions, senior managers can interpret situations in new ways and can adjust the meanings attached to important corporate events. They can create new rites and rituals. This takes time and enormous energy, but the long-run benefits can also be great.

Top managers, especially, can set the tone for a culture and for cultural change. Managers at Aetna Life and Casualty Insurance built on its humanistic traditions to provide basic skills to highly motivated but underqualified individuals. Frances Hesselbein of the Girl Scouts stressed a clear mission of helping girls reach their highest potential—in today's world, not yesterday's. Even in the highly cost-competitive steel industry, Chairperson F. Kenneth Iverson of Nucor built on basic entrepreneurial values in U.S. society to reduce the number of management levels by half. And, at Procter and Gamble, Richard Nicolosi evoked the shared values for greater participation in decision making dramatically to improve creativity and innovation.

Each of these examples illustrates how managers can help foster a culture that provides answers to important questions concerning external adaptation and internal integration. Recent work on the linkages among corporate culture and financial performance reaffirm the importance of an emphasis on helping employees to adjust to the environment. It also suggests that this emphasis alone is not sufficient. Neither is an emphasis solely on stockholders or customers associated with long-term economic performance. Instead, managers must work to emphasize all three issues simultaneously. Of course, this emphasis on customers, stockholders, and employees comes at a cost of emphasizing management. Large offices, multimillion-dollar salaries, golden parachutes (protections for executives if the firm is bought by others), as well as the executive plane, dining room, and country club are out.

Sometimes, however, managers attempt to revitalize an organization by dictating major changes rather than by building on shared values. Although things may change a bit on the surface, a deeper look often shows whole departments resisting change and many key people who do not want to learn new ways. Such

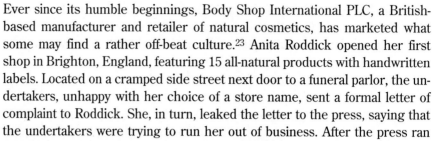

**ETHICS AND
SOCIAL RESPONSIBILITY**

Ever since its humble beginnings, Body Shop International PLC, a British-based manufacturer and retailer of natural cosmetics, has marketed what some may find a rather off-beat culture.[23] Anita Roddick opened her first shop in Brighton, England, featuring 15 all-natural products with handwritten labels. Located on a cramped side street next door to a funeral parlor, the undertakers, unhappy with her choice of a store name, sent a formal letter of complaint to Roddick. She, in turn, leaked the letter to the press, saying that the undertakers were trying to run her out of business. After the press ran

the story, Roddick's business boomed, and within a year Roddick began franchising. Today, there are franchises in over 40 countries. The product line has grown from the original 15 to hundreds of products. Every Body Shop retail store echoes Roddick's unique sentiments. Campaigns highlighting issues ranging from endangered rain forests to amnesty for those imprisoned for political reasons are waged throughout each store in the forms of posters, window displays, leaflets, and shopping bags. Mailers and brochures help educate customers on the products and causes that Body Shop promotes, and employees are expected to advocate the issue of the day through their clothing and customer education.

responses may indicate that the responsible managers are insensitive to the effects of their proposed changes on shared values. They fail to ask whether the changes are contrary to important values that have emerged from participants within the firm, a challenge to historically important corporate-wide assumptions, and inconsistent with important common assumptions derived from the national culture, outside the firm.

Whereas reshaping shared values is an executive challenge of the first order, few executives are able to reshape common assumptions or "the taken for granted truths" in a firm without drastic, radical action. Roger Smith of General Motors realized this challenge and established a new division to produce the Saturn. At Harley Davidson, a new senior management team had to replace virtually all of the company's middle managers to establish a new, unique, and competitive culture. All too often, however, executives are unable to realize that they too can be captured by the broadly held common assumptions within their firms. Just as executives in Eastern European firms must reexamine the philosophical foundation of their firms as their countries adopt market economies, so must managers in the United States and other Western nations, as they anticipate the exciting challenges of a new century.

USING ORGANIZATION DEVELOPMENT TO MANAGE CORPORATE CULTURE

To keep the culture fresh and competitive, the challenge today is to engage in a process of continuous self-assessment and planned change in order to stay abreast of problems and opportunities in a complex and demanding environment. **Organization development** (OD) is a comprehensive approach to planned change that is designed to improve the overall effectiveness of organizations. Formally defined, OD is the application of behavioral science knowledge in a long-range effort to improve an organization's ability to cope with change in its external environment and to increase its internal problem-solving capabilities.[24]

Organization development is used to improve performance in organizations of all types, sizes, and settings. It includes a set of tools with which any manager who is concerned about achieving and maintaining high levels of productivity will want to be familiar. Because of its comprehensive nature and scientific foundations, OD is frequently implemented with the aid of an external consultant or internal professional staff member. But its basic concepts can and should be used routinely by all managers.

> **Organization development (OD)** is the application of behavioral science knowledge in a long-range effort to improve an organization's ability to cope with change in its external environment and increase its problem-solving capabilities.

▼ GOALS AND PRINCIPLES UNDERLYING OD

OD is not a panacea or surefire cure for all that ails an organization and/or its members. However, OD does offer a systematic approach to planned change in organizations that addresses two main goals: process goals and outcome goals. *Process goals* include achieving improvements in such things as communication, interaction, and decision making among an organization's members. These goals focus on how well people work together and stress improving internal integration. *Outcome goals* include achieving improvements in task performance by improving external adaptation capabilities. In OD, these goals focus on what is actually accomplished through individual and group efforts.

In pursuit of these goals, OD is intended to help organizations and their members by (1) creating an open problem-solving climate throughout an organization, (2) supplementing formal authority with that of knowledge and competence, (3) moving decision making to points where relevant information is available, (4) building trust and maximizing collaboration among individuals and groups, (5) increasing the sense of organizational "ownership" among members, and (6) allowing people to exercise self-direction and self-control at work.[25]

Organization development is designed to improve the contributions of individual members in achieving the organizational goals, and it seeks to do so in ways that respect the organization's members as mature adults who need and deserve high-quality experiences in their working lives. The foundations for achieving change in this manner are a number of well-established behavioral science principles introduced throughout this book.[26] It is important to review these to show what interventions can be made at all levels of the organization.

At the individual level, OD is guided by principles that reflect an underlying respect for people and their capabilities. It assumes that individual needs for growth and development are most likely to be satisfied in a supportive and challenging work environment. And it assumes that most people are capable of taking responsibility for their own actions and of making positive contributions to organizational performance.

At the group level, OD is guided by principles that reflect a belief that groups can be good for both people and organizations. It assumes that groups help their members satisfy important individual needs and can also be helpful in supporting organizational objectives. And it assumes that effective groups can be created by people working in collaboration to meet individual and organizational needs.

At the organizational level, OD is guided by principles that show a respect for the complexity of an organization as a system of interdependent parts. It assumes

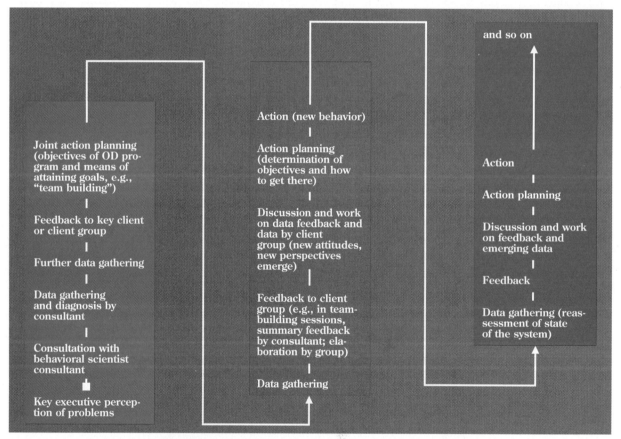

■   FIGURE 13.2

An action-research model for organization development. [Source: Copyright 1969 by the Regents of the University of California. Reprinted from the *California Management Review,* Vol. XII, No. 2, p. 26, Figure 1, by permission of the Regents.]

that changes in one part of the organization will affect other parts as well. It also assumes that the culture of the organization will affect the nature and expression of individual feelings and attitudes. And it assumes that organizational structures and jobs can be designed to meet the needs of individuals and groups as well as of the organization.

▼ THE PROCESS OF ORGANIZATION DEVELOPMENT

A general model of OD and its relationship to the planned change process is shown in Figure 13.2. Organization development begins with *diagnosis*—a stage of gathering and analyzing data to assess a situation and set appropriate change objectives to help pinpoint appropriate action directions. After diagnosis, OD enters the stage of *active intervention.* Here, change objectives are pursued through a variety of specific activities. The last stage of organization development is one of *reinforcement.* At this point, changes are monitored, reinforced, and evaluated. Refreezing of change is supposed to occur at this time, and the foundations for future replication of similar diagnosis–intervention–reinforcement cycles should be set.

QUALITY

Bob Westwater, president of Atlantic-Tracy, a power transmission house located in Somerville, Massachusetts, with branches throughout New England, began thinking about quality control after attending a professional meeting.[27] One of the lectures focused on quality control and the competitive advantage it provides businesses. Westwater returned from the meeting ready to find a creative approach to improving quality at Atlantic-Tracy. Rather than contract outside consultants, the company went to its own employees. It created an eight-page questionnaire asking all employees to find quality improvements they could make in their own areas, and it began an employee suggestion program. The information Atlantic-Tracy received from its employees included homespun insights about ways to improve service and concrete suggestions that could be readily implemented. One of the first of more than 400 suggestions was to declare the company an "Error-Free Zone." The suggestion took hold and is still used today as an MBO that inspires Atlantic-Tracy's search for quality.

Organization development seeks to achieve change in such a way that the organization's members become more active and confident in taking similar steps to maintain longer run organization effectiveness. A large part of any OD program's success in this regard rests with the strength of its action-research foundations.

Action Research and Organization Development   The model of OD just described emphasizes data-based reflection and action planning. OD practitioners

> **Action research** is the process of systematically collecting data on an organization, feeding it back for action planning, and evaluating results by collecting and reflecting on more data.

refer to **action research** as the process of systematically collecting data on an organization, feeding it back to the members for action planning, and evaluating results by collecting and reflecting on more data after the planned actions have been taken. This is a data-based and collaborative approach to problem solving and organizational assessment. When used in the OD process, action research helps identify action directions that may enhance an organization's effectiveness.

In a typical action-research sequence depicted in Figure 13.2 the sequence is initiated when someone senses a performance gap and decides to analyze the situation systematically for the problems and opportunities it represents. The process continues through the following steps: data gathering, data feedback, data analysis, and action planning. It continues to the point at which action is taken and results are evaluated. The evaluation or reassessment stage may or may not generate another performance gap. If it does, the action-research cycle begins anew.

Data gathering is a major element in the action-research process. There are many different ways of gathering data for this purpose. They include questionnaires, interviews, observation, and use of secondary sources. Each method has its advantages and disadvantages; a manager or OD practitioner must be careful to choose those methods that best suit the situation at hand.

■ FIGURE 13.3
Diagnostic foundations of organization development: concerns for individual, group, and organizational effectiveness.

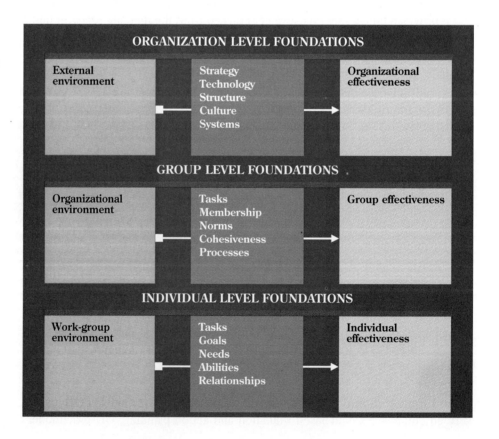

Interviews and written questionnaires are very common ways of gathering action research data for OD. These means of data collection are, in themselves, organization development activities. In addition, formal written surveys of employee attitudes and needs are growing in popularity. Many of those available have been tested for reliability and validity. Some even have "norms" against which one organization can compare its results with those from a broader sample of organizations. However, no data-gathering method can stand on its own as an OD activity unless it is properly integrated within an OD process that covers all three stages: diagnosis, intervention, and reinforcement.

Figure 13.3 identifies one set of frameworks that can assist OD practitioners in accomplishing the required diagnoses. These foundations apply the open systems framework and OB concepts with which you are already familiar from earlier parts of this book. At the organizational level, the figure indicates that effectiveness must be understood with respect to forces in the external environment and major organizational aspects, such as strategy, technology, structure, culture, and management systems. At the group level, effectiveness is viewed in a context of forces in the internal environment of the organization and major group aspects, such as tasks, membership, norms, cohesiveness, and group processes. At the individual level, effectiveness is considered in relationship to the internal environment of the work group and individual aspects, such as tasks, goals, needs, and interpersonal relationships.

ORGANIZATION DEVELOPMENT INTERVENTIONS ◀

The basic responsibility of the OD practitioner is to engage members of the client system in activities designed to accomplish the required diagnoses and to develop and implement plans for constructive change. Action research, data collection, and the diagnostic foundations should come together through the OD practitioner's choice and use of **OD interventions.** These are activities that are initiated by the consultant or manager to facilitate planned change and to assist the client system in developing its own problem-solving capabilities. As with the diagnostic frameworks just presented, the major OD interventions can be categorized with respect to their major impact at the organizational, group, and individual levels of action.[28]

> **Organization development interventions** are activities initiated to support planned change and improve work effectiveness.

▼ ORGANIZATION-WIDE INTERVENTIONS

An effective organization is one that achieves its major performance objectives while maintaining a high quality of work life for its members. OD interventions designed for system-wide application include the following.

Survey feedback is a popular intervention that begins with the collection of data via questionnaire responses from organization members, or a representative

> **Survey feedback** begins with the collection of data via questionnaires from organization members or a representative sample of them.

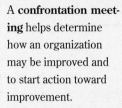

A **confrontation meeting** helps determine how an organization may be improved and to start action toward improvement.

sample of such responses. The data are then presented, or "fed back," to the members. They subsequently engage in a collaborative process to interpret the data and to develop action plans in response.

Confrontation meetings are designed to help determine quickly how an organization may be improved and to take initial actions to improve the situation.[29] The intervention involves a 1-day meeting conducted by an OD facilitator for a representative sample of organizational members, including top management. In a structured format, the consultant asks participants to make individual lists of what they feel can be done to improve things. Then, through a series of small-group work sessions and sharing of results, these ideas are refined into a tentative set of actions that top management then endorses for immediate implementation.

Structural redesign involves realigning the structure of the organization or major subsystem in order to improve performance.

Structural redesign involves realigning the structure of the organization or major subsystems to improve performance. This includes examining the best fit between structure, technology, and environment. In today's highly dynamic environments, and in light of the increasing involvement of organizations in international operations, it is easy for a structure to grow out of date. Thus, structural redesign is an important OD intervention that can be used to help maintain the best fit between organizational structures and situational demands.

Collateral organization involves a representative set of members in periodic small-group, problem-solving sessions.

Collateral organization is designed to make creative problem solving possible by pulling a representative set of members out of the formal organization structure to engage in periodic small-group problem-solving sessions.[30] These collateral, or "parallel," structures are temporary in nature and exist only to supplement the activities of the formal structure.

▼ GROUP AND INTERGROUP INTERVENTIONS

OD interventions at the group level are designed to improve group effectiveness. The major interventions at this level are team building, process consultation, and intergroup team building.

Team building is designed to gather and analyze data on the functioning of a group and implement changes to increase its operating effectiveness.

Team building essentially involves a manager or consultant engaging the members of a group in a series of activities designed to help them examine how the group functions and how it may function better. Like survey feedback at the organizational level, team building involves some form of data collection and feedback. The key elements, however, are a collaborative assessment of the data by all members of the group and the achievement of consensus regarding what may be done to improve group effectiveness. Team building is often done at "retreats" or off-site meetings, where group members spend 2 to 3 days working intensely together on this reflection–analysis–planning process.

Process consultation helps a group improve on such things as norms, cohesiveness, decision-making methods, communication, conflict, and task and maintenance activities.

Process consultation involves structured activities that are facilitated by the OD practitioner and is designed to improve group functioning. Process consultation has a more specific focus than does team building, however; its attention is directed toward the key "processes" through which members of a group work with one another. The process consultant is concerned with helping a group function better on such things as norms, cohesiveness, decision-making methods, communication, conflict, and task and maintenance activities.

Intergroup team building is a special form of team building. It is designed to help two or more groups improve their working relationships with one another and, it is hoped, to experience improved group effectiveness as a result. Here, the OD practitioner engages the groups or their representatives in activities that increase awareness of how each group perceives the other and is perceived by the other in return. Given this understanding, collaborative problem solving can take place to improve coordination between the groups and to encourage more mutual support of one another as important components in the total organization.

> **Intergroup team building** helps groups improve their working relationships with one another and experience improved group effectiveness.

▼ INDIVIDUAL INTERVENTIONS

Task performance and job satisfaction are important concerns with respect to improving individual effectiveness in the workplace. OD interventions at this level of attention range from those that address very personal issues to those that deal more with specific job and career considerations. Individual-level OD interventions include the following.

Sensitivity training is designed to increase the self-awareness of individuals and their "sensitivity" toward others. It typically involves a number of persons—usually strangers—working together with a professional trainer in a small group, called a *T-group* (training group). In this setting, T-group participants are encouraged to share feelings and concerns and to listen to those expressed by others. Since the opportunity exists for people to get very personal—both in exposing their emotions and in responding to others—this is a controversial type of intervention. It must be exercised only under the guidance of a highly skilled group facilitator.

> **Sensitivity training** increases the self-awareness of individuals and their sensitivity toward other people.

Role negotiation is a means for clarifying what individuals expect to give and receive of one another in their working relationship. Because roles and personnel change over time, role negotiation can be an important means for maintaining task understandings among individuals in an organization. This kind of understanding is quite easily accomplished by helping people who work together clarify what they need from one another to do their jobs well.

> **Role negotiation** is a process through which individuals clarify expectations about what each should be giving and receiving as group members.

Job redesign is the process of adjusting task demands to achieve and maintain this fit. A good example is the Hackman and Oldham[31] diagnostic approach to job enrichment, which involves (1) analyzing the core characteristics of a job or group of jobs, (2) analyzing the needs and capabilities of workers in those jobs, and (3) taking action to adjust the core job characteristics either to enrich or to simplify the jobs to best match individual preferences.

> **Job redesign** creates long-term congruence between individual goals and organizational career opportunities.

Career planning takes the form of structured opportunities for individuals to work with their managers and/or staff experts from the personnel or human resources department on career issues. They may map career goals, assess personal development needs, and actively plan possible short-term and long-term career moves. Increasingly, career planning is becoming a major part of the support provided by highly progressive organizations for their members.

> **Career planning** creates long-term congruence between individual goals and organizational career opportunities.

▶

CHAPTER 13 STUDY GUIDE

SUMMARY

What is the concept of corporate culture?
- Organizational or corporate culture is the system of shared actions, values, and beliefs that develops within an organization and guides the behavior of its members.
- Corporate culture can assist in responding to both external adaptation and internal integration issues.
- Organizations can also experience the strains of dealing with subcultures among various work units and subsystems, as well as possible countercultures that can become the source of potentially harmful conflicts.
- Organizational cultures may be analyzed in terms of observable actions, shared values, and common assumptions (the taken-for-granted truths).

What are the observable aspects of corporate culture?
- Observable aspects of culture include the stories, rites, rituals, and symbols that are shared by organization members.
- Cultural rules and roles specify when various types of actions are appropriate and where individual members stand in the social system .
- Shared meanings and understandings help everyone know how to act and expect others to act in various circumstances.

Can common assumptions link individuals together?
- Common assumptions are the taken-for-granted truths that are shared by collections of corporate members.
- Some organizations express these truths in a management philosophy that links key goal-related issues with key collaboration issues into a series of general ways in which the firm will manage its affairs.
- The management philosophy is supported by a series of corporate myths.

Can the corporate culture be "managed," or are "nurtured" and "guided" more appropriate terms?
- Executives may manage many aspects of the observable culture directly.
- Nurturing shared values among the membership is a major challenge for many executives.
- Adjusting actions to common understandings may limit the decision scope of even the CEO.

How can organization development be used to manage corporate culture?
- All managers may use organization development (OD) techniques in their attempts to manage, nurture, and guide cultural change.
- OD is a special application of knowledge gained from behavioral science to create a comprehensive effort to improve organizational effectiveness.
- OD has both outcome goals, with respect to improved task accomplishments, and

process goals, with respect to improvements in the way organization members work together.

What are some organization development interventions?

- With a strong commitment to collaborative efforts and human values, OD utilizes basic behavioral science principles in respect to individuals, groups, and organizations.
- Organization-wide interventions include survey feedback, confrontation meetings, structural redesign, and collateral organization.
- Group and intergroup interventions include team building, process consultation and intergroup team building.
- Individual interventions include sensitivity training, role negotiation, job redesign, and career planning.

KEY TERMS

Action research (p.282)
Career planning (p. 285)
Collateral organization (p.284)
Confrontation meeting (p. 284)
Corporate culture (p. 267)
Counterculture (p. 269)
Cultural symbol (p. 273)
External adaptation (p. 267)
Intergroup team building (p. 285)

Job redesign (p. 285)
Management philosophy (p. 275)
Organizational culture (p. 267)
Organizational myth (p. 275)
Organization development (OD) (p. 279)
Organization development intervention (p. 283)

Process consultation (p. 284)
Rite (p. 273)
Ritual (p. 273)
Role negotiation (p. 285)
Saga (p. 272)
Sensitivity training (p. 285)
Structural redesign (p. 284)
Subcultures (p. 269)
Survey feedback (p. 283)
Team building (p. 284)

SELF-TEST 13

▼ MULTIPLE CHOICE

1. Culture concerns all of the following except ____. (a) the collective concepts shared by members of a firm (b) acquired capabilities (c) the personality of the leader (d) the beliefs of members (e) members' view of their collective personality

2. The three levels of cultural analysis highlighted in the text concern ____. (a) observable culture, shared values, and common assumptions (b) stories, rites, and rituals (c) symbols, myths, and stories (d) manifest culture, latent culture, and observable artifacts (e) cultural symbols, myths, and sagas

3. ____both value diversity and systematically work to block the transfer of societally based subcultures into the fabric of the organization. (a) Organizational cultures (b) Ethical climates (c) Multicultural organizations (d) Shared values (e) Subcultures

4. Internal integration concerns ____. (a) the process of deciding the collective identity and how members will live together (b) the totality of the daily life of members as they see and describe it (c) expressed unproven beliefs that are accepted uncritically and used to justify current actions (d) groups of individuals with a pattern of values that rejects those of the larger society (e) the process of coping with outside forces

5. When Japanese workers start each day with the company song this is an example of a(n) ____ . (a) symbol (b) myth (c) underlying assumption (d) ritual (e) saga

6. ____ is a sense of broader purpose that workers infuse into their tasks as a result of interaction with one another. (a) A rite (b) A cultural symbol (c) A foundation myth (d) A shared meaning (e) An internal integration

7. The story of a corporate turnaround attributed to the efforts of a visionary manager is an example of a(n) ____ . (a) saga (b) foundation myth (c) internal integration (d) latent cultural artifact (e) common assumption

8. OD is designed primarily to improve ____ . (a) the overall effectiveness of an organization (b) intergroup relations (c) synergy (d) the planned change process (e) group dynamics

9. The three stages in the OD process are ____. (a) data collection, intervention, and evaluation (b) diagnosis, intervention, and reinforcement (c) intervention, application, and innovation (d) diagnosis, intervention, and evaluation (e) planning, implementing, and evaluating

10. OD is planned change plus ____. (a) evaluation (b) intervention (c) ability for self-renewal (d) any future changes that may occur (e) reinforcement

▼ TRUE–FALSE

11. The system of shared beliefs and values that develops within an organization is called organizational culture.   T F

12. The belief that senior managers can manage all levels of the corporate culture is a myth.   T F

13. External adaptation concerns such issues as the real mission of the firm, its goals, and how goals are reached.   T F

14. Who gets rewards and punishments is part of external adaptation.   T F

15. Rites and rituals often emerge from a subculture.   T F

16. A ritual is a standardized activity used to manage anxiety.   T F

17. Any object, art, or event that serves to transmit cultural meaning is called a rite. T F

18. The organization-wide OD interventions are: survey feedback, confrontation meeting, structural redesign, management by objectives, and collateral organization. T F

19. The confrontation meeting is an OD intervention used to handle conflicts.   T F

20. MBO is an organization-wide OD intervention.   T F

▼ SHORT RESPONSE

21. Describe the five steps Taylor Cox suggests need to be developed to help generate a multicultural organization or pluralistic company culture.

22. List the three aspects that help individuals and groups work together effectively and illustrate them through practical examples.

23. Give an example of how cultural rules and roles affect the atmosphere in a college classroom. Provide specific examples from your own perspective.

24. What are the major elements of a strong corporate culture?

▼ APPLICATIONS ESSAY

25. Discuss the process of OD and provide an overview of its diagnostic foundations in a small business.

14

POWER AND POLITICS

Microsoft founder and billionaire Bill Gates has been continuously able to build the sales and profitability of his company through practical empowerment.[1] Microsoft's DOS operating system was used in 95 percent of the personal computers built in the 1980s. In the 1990s, its new Windows 95 is a smash hit. With new innovative products, Microsoft's growth seems unstoppable. Gates has been able to empower his researchers and product managers by arranging them in small task-oriented groups. Microsoft's leadership has found that by eliminating bureaucracy, new products can make it from conception to production much more quickly. As a result, Microsoft is now able to develop its products significantly faster than can its competitors. According to Gates, "Big groups of programmers often create bad software more slowly than small ones who make good software." A key to the small-group process is found in the open lines of communication from the top of the organization to the bottom. Access to information and new ideas is important to the success of any high-tech firm, and Gates works hard to keep all parts of his organization well linked by allowing a free flow of information between departments. (http://www. microsoft.de/psql2.htm)

Individuals rarely join a corporation simply to work for the firm's stated goals. They join for their own reasons to meet their own goals. As individuals vie for their own interests in a hierarchical setting, analyses of power and politics are a key to understanding the behavior of individuals within organizations. As discussed throughout this chapter, power and politics have two sides. On the one hand, power and politics represent the seamy side of management, since organizations are not democracies composed of individuals with equal influence. On the other hand, power and politics are important organizational tools that managers must use to get the job done. In effective organizations, power is delicately developed, nurtured, and managed by astute individuals. Politics is always infused into the organization, yet it is possible to isolate many instances where individual and organizational interests are compatible. The astute manager knows how to find these opportunities.[2]

Analysis of power and politics is crucial to understanding the roles of individuals in organizations. As you read this chapter, keep in mind these study questions.

◉ What is power within the context of the organization, and why do managers have power?

◉ What are the relationships among power, formal authority, and obedience? How does the manager get the power needed to get the job done?

◉ What is empowerment and how can management empower others?

◉ Are organizational politics inevitable, and must the manager live in a political world?

◉ How does organizational politics differ for the individual supervisor, the middle manager, and the chief executive officer?

POWER

In OB, **power** is defined as the ability to get someone to do something you want done or the ability to make things happen in the way you want them to. The essence of power is control over the behavior of others.[3] One of the interesting things about power is that it has no verb form. You do not "power" something. You can, however, **influence** something. Power is the force you use to make things happen in an intended way, whereas influence is what you have when you exercise power and is expressed by others' behavioral response to your exercise of power. Managers derive power from both organizational and individual sources. These sources are called *position power* and *personal power,* respectively.[4]

> **Power** is the ability to get someone else to do something you want done or the ability to make things happen or get things done the way you want.

▼ POSITION POWER

Three bases of power are available to a manager solely as a result of his or her position in the organization: reward, coercive, and legitimate power.

Reward power is the extent to which a manager can use extrinsic and intrinsic rewards to control other people. Examples of such rewards include money, promotions, compliments, or enriched jobs. Although all managers have some access to rewards, success in accessing and utilizing rewards to achieve influence varies according to the skills of the manager.

Power can also be founded on punishment instead of reward. For example, a manager may threaten to withhold a pay raise, to transfer, demote, or even recommend the firing of a subordinate who does not act as desired. Such **coercive power** is the extent to which a manager can deny desired rewards or administer punishments to control other people. The availability of coercive power also varies from one organization and manager to another. The presence of unions and organizational policies on employee treatment can weaken this power base considerably.

> **Influence** is a behavioral response to the exercise of power.

> **Reward power** is the extent to which a manager can use extrinsic and intrinsic rewards to control other people.

The third base of "position" power is **legitimate power,** or *formal authority.* It stems from the extent to which a manager can use subordinates' internalized values or beliefs that the "boss" has a "right of command" to control their behavior. For example, the boss may have the formal authority to approve or deny such employee requests as job transfers, equipment purchases, personal time off, or overtime work. Legitimate power represents a special kind of power a manager has because subordinates believe it is legitimate for a person occupying the managerial position to have the right to command. If this legitimacy is lost, authority will not be accepted by subordinates.

> **Coercive power** is the extent to which a manager can deny desired rewards or administer punishment to control other people.

▼ PERSONAL POWER

Personal power resides in the individual and is independent of the position the individual holds. Personal power is important in many well-managed firms. Two bases of personal power are expertise and reference.

> **Legitimate power** or formal authority is the extent to which a manager can use the "right of command" to control other people.

291

Expert power is the ability to control another person's behavior through the possession of knowledge, experience, or judgment that the other person does not have but needs. A subordinate obeys a supervisor possessing expert power because the boss is felt to know more about what is to be done or how it is to be done than does the subordinate.

> **Expert power** is the ability to control another's behavior because of the possession of knowledge, experience, or judgment that the other person does not have but needs.

Expert power is relative, not absolute. Between superiors and subordinates, access to or control over information is an important element in this particular power base. The supervisor may also have more access to key organizational decision makers. Of course an individual's ability to contact key persons informally can offset some of the expert power sources of the supervisor. Access may include special participation in the definition of a problem or issue, alteration in the flow of information to decision makers, and/or lobbying for use of special criteria in decision making. Thus, whereas expert power is personal, it is relational and it is embedded within the organizational context. As the organizational context changes, personal sources of power may become more important.

Referent power is the ability to control another's behavior because the person wants to identify with the power source. In this case, a subordinate obeys the boss because he or she wants to behave, perceive, or believe as the boss does. This may occur, for example, because the subordinate likes the boss personally and therefore tries to do things the way the boss wants them done, or because the subordinate perceives that advancement depends upon doing things the boss's way. In a sense, the subordinate behaves in order to avoid doing anything that would interfere with the pleasing boss subordinate relationship.

> **Referent power** is the ability to control another's behavior because of the individual's wanting to identify with the power source.

▼ POWER, FORMAL AUTHORITY, AND OBEDIENCE

As we have shown, power is the potential to control the behavior of others, and formal authority is the potential to exert such control through the legitimacy of a managerial position. Yet, we also know that people who seem to have power don't always get their way. Why do some people obey directives, and others do not? More specifically, why should subordinates respond to a manager's authority, or "right to command," in the first place? Furthermore, given that subordinates are willing to obey, what determines the limits of obedience?

▼ THE MILGRAM EXPERIMENTS

These last questions may be answerable from Stanley Milgram's seminal research on obedience.[5] Milgram designed an experiment to determine the extent to which people obey the commands of an authority figure, even if they believe that they are endangering the life of another person. Subjects, ranging in age from 20 to 50 and representing a diverse set of occupations (engineers, salespeople, school teachers, laborers, and others), were paid a nominal fee for participation in the project.

The subjects were falsely told that the purpose of the study was to determine the effects of punishment on learning. The subjects were to be the "teachers." The "learner" was a confederate of Milgram's, who was strapped to a chair in an adjoining room with an electrode attached to his wrist. The "experimenter," another confederate of Milgram's, was dressed in a gray laboratory coat. Appearing impassive and somewhat stern, the experimenter instructed the teacher to read a series of word pairs to the learner and then to reread the first word along with four other terms. The learner was supposed to indicate which of the four terms was in the original pair by pressing a switch that caused a light to flash on a response panel in front of the teacher.

The teacher was instructed to administer a shock to the learner each time a wrong answer was given. This shock was to be increased one level of intensity each time the learner made a mistake. The teacher controlled switches that ostensibly administered shocks ranging from 15 to 450 volts. In reality, there was no electric current in the apparatus, but the learners purposely "erred" often and responded to each level of "shock" in progressively distressing ways.

If a "teacher" (subject) proved unwilling to administer a shock, the experimenter used the following sequential prods to get him or her to perform as requested: (1) "Please continue" or "Please go on"; (2) "The experiment requires that you continue"; (3) "It is absolutely essential that you continue"; and (4) "You have no choice, you must go on." Only when the "teacher" refused to go on after the fourth prod would the experiment be stopped. When would you expect the "teachers" to refuse to go on?

Milgram asked some of his students and colleagues the same question. Most felt that few, if any, of the subjects would go beyond the "very strong shock" level. Actually, 26 subjects (65 percent) continued to the end of the experiment and shocked the "learners" to the maximum.

None stopped before 300 volts, the point at which the learner pounded on the wall. The remaining 14 subjects refused to obey the experimenter at various intermediate points.

Most people are surprised by these results, as was Milgram. The question is why other people would have a tendency to accept or comply with authoritative commands under such extreme conditions. Milgram conducted further experiments to try to answer this question. The subjects' tendencies toward compliance were somewhat reduced (1) when experimentation took place in a rundown office (rather than a university lab), (2) when the victim was closer, (3) when the experimenter was farther away, and (4) when the subject could observe other subjects. However, the level of compliance was still much higher than most of us would expect.

Obedience and the Acceptance of Authority   As the Milgram experiments suggest, there are strong tendencies among individuals to follow the instructions of the boss. Direct defiance within organizational settings is quite rare. If the tendency to follow instructions is great and defiance is rare, then why do so many organizations appear to drift into apparent chaos?

The answer to this question can be found in work by the famous management writer Chester Barnard.[7] Essentially, Barnard's argument focused on the "consent of the governed" rather than on the rights derived from ownership. He argued that subordinates accepted or followed a directive from the boss only under special circumstances.

LABATT'S

Gerry Burke, Labatt's General Manager in Newfoundland, finds that his role has changed from just directing subordinates to being a coach and mentor. Now he must develop his personal bases of power, not just his formal authority.[6]

Take-A-Note 14.1

HOW TO ISSUE A DIRECTIVE

1. Always assume that the subordinate has a choice of following or ignoring the "request."

2. Make sure the individual understands what is to be done, how it is to be accomplished, and when the task is due.

3. Make sure the individual believes he or she can perform the task. Do not assume he or she can; ask.

4. Explain why the request is related to firm goals and why it is important to the firm.

5. Present the request in a manner that is consistent with the individual's interests.

All four of these circumstances must be met: (1) the subordinate can and must understand the directive; (2) the subordinate must feel mentally and physically capable of carrying out the directive; (3) the subordinate must believe that the directive is not inconsistent with the purpose of the organization; and (4) the subordinate must believe that the directive is not inconsistent with his or her personal interests.

These four conditions are very carefully stated. For instance, to accept and follow an order, the subordinate does not need to understand how the proposed action will help the organization. He or she only needs to believe that the requested action is not inconsistent with the purpose of the firm. The astute manager will not take these guidelines for granted. In giving directives, the astute manager recognizes that the acceptance of the request is not assured.

If the directive is routine, it is not surprising that the subordinate may merely comply without enthusiasm. Of course, the manager needs to understand what subordinates consider acceptable or unacceptable actions.

Obedience and the Zone of Indifference   Most people seek a balance between what they put into an organization (contributions) and what they get from an organization in return (inducements). Within the boundaries of the psychological contract, therefore, employees will agree to do many things in and for the organization because they think they should. In exchange for certain inducements, subordinates recognize the authority of the organization and its managers to direct their behavior in certain ways. Based on his acceptance view of authority, Chester Barnard calls this area in which directions are obeyed the *"zone of indifference."*[8]

A zone of indifference is the range of authoritative requests to which a subordinate is willing to respond without subjecting the directives to critical evaluation or judgment. Directives falling within the zone are obeyed. Requests or orders falling outside the zone of indifference are not considered legitimate under terms of the psychological contract. Such "extraordinary" directives may or may not be obeyed. This link between the zone of indifference and the psychological contract is shown in Figure 14.1.

The zone of indifference is not fixed. There may be times when a boss would like a subordinate to do things falling outside the zone. This requires efforts on the manager's part to enlarge the zone to accommodate additional behaviors. In these attempts, a manager most likely will have to use more incentives than pure position power. In some instances, no power base may be capable of accomplishing the desired result. Consider your own zone of indifference and tendency to obey. When will you say "No" to your boss? When should you be *willing* to say

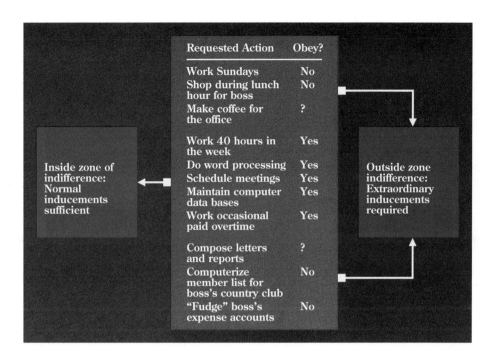

■ FIGURE 14.1
Hypothetical psychological contract for a secretary.

"No"? At times, the situation may involve ethical dilemmas, where you may be asked to do things that are illegal, unethical, or both.

Research on ethical managerial behavior shows that supervisors are singled out by their subordinates as sources of pressure to do such things as support incorrect viewpoints, sign false documents, overlook the supervisor's wrongdoing, and do business with the supervisor's friends.[9] Most of us will occasionally face such ethical dilemmas during our careers. For now, we must simply remember that saying "No" or "refusing to keep quiet" can be difficult and potentially costly.

▼ ACQUIRING AND USING POWER AND INFLUENCE

A considerable portion of any manager's time is directed toward what is called "power-oriented" behavior, that is, behavior directed primarily at developing or using relationships in which other people are to some degree willing to defer to one's wishes.[10] Figure 14.2 shows three basic dimensions of power and influence with which a manager will become involved in this regard: downward, upward, and lateral. Also shown in the figure are some preliminary ideas for achieving success along each of these dimensions.

The effective manager is one who succeeds in building and maintaining high levels of both position and personal power over time. Only then is sufficient power of the right types available when the manager needs to exercise influence on downward, lateral, and upward dimensions.

Building Position Power Position power can be enhanced when managers are able to demonstrate to others that their work units are highly relevant to or-

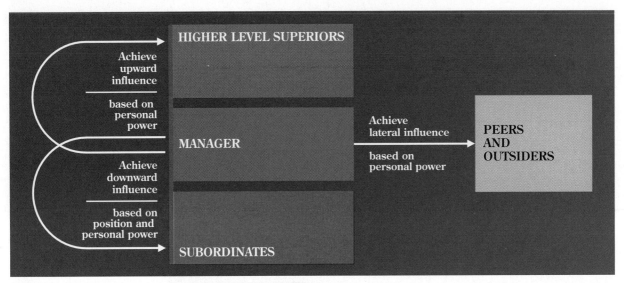

■ FIGURE 14.2

Three dimensions of managerial power and influence.

Power flows from consistent high performance. Sara Lee top executive John Bryan observes that performance leads to an ability to "take on" superiors and more easily "resist" staff people. A high performer, he says, "becomes a star, and over time comes to seem indispensable."

ganizational goals and are able to respond to urgent organizational needs.[11] To increase centrality and criticality in the organization, managers may seek to acquire a more central role in the work flow by having information filtered through them, making at least part of their job responsibilities unique, expanding their network of communication contacts, and occupying an office convenient to main traffic flows.

Managers may also attempt to increase the relevance of their tasks to the organization. There are many ways to do this, including (1) becoming an internal coordinator or external representative, (2) providing unique services and information to other units, (3) becoming a trainer or mentor for new members, and (4) becoming involved in decisions central to the organization's top-priority goals. To expand their position, managers may also delegate routine activities, expand the task variety and novelty for subordinates, initiate new ideas, and get involved in new projects.

There are also ways managers attempt to build influence that may or may not have a positive effect on the organization. Managers may attempt to define tasks so that they are difficult to evaluate, such as by creating an ambiguous job description or developing a unique language for their work. Of course, most managers also attempt to increase the visibility of their job performance by (1) expanding the number of contacts they have with senior people, (2) making oral presentations of written work, (3) participating in problem-solving task forces, (4) sending out notices of accomplishment, and (5) generally seeking additional opportunities to increase personal name recognition.

Building Personal Power   Personal power arises from the personal characteristics of the manager rather than from the location and other characteristics of his or her position in the organization's hierarchy of authority. Two primary bases of personal power rest in expertise and reference.

Three personal characteristics are singled out for their special potential to enhance personal power in an organization.[12] The most obvious is *building expertise.* Additional expertise may be gained by advanced training and education, participation in professional associations, and involvement in the early stages of projects. Related to personal expertise is special access to data and/or people.

A manager's reference power is increased by characteristics that *enhance his or her "likability" and create personal attraction in relationships* with other people. These include pleasant personality characteristics, agreeable behavior patterns, and attractive personal appearance. The demonstration of sincere hard work on behalf of task performance can also increase personal power by enhancing both expertise and reference. A person who is perceived to try hard may be expected to know more about the job and thus be sought out for advice. A person who tries hard is also likely to be respected for the attempt and may even become depended on by others to maintain that effort.

▼ TURNING POWER INTO RELATIONAL INFLUENCE

Actually using position and personal power well to achieve the desired influence over other people is a challenge for most managers. Practically speaking, there are many useful ways of exercising relational influence. The most common strategies involve the following:[13]

- *Reason* Using facts and data to support a logical argument.
- *Friendliness* Using flattery, goodwill, and favorable impressions.
- *Coalition* Using relationships with other people for support.
- *Bargaining* Using the exchange of benefits as a basis for negotiation.
- *Assertiveness* Using a direct and forceful personal approach.
- *Higher authority* Gaining higher level support for one's requests.
- *Sanctions* Using organizationally derived rewards and punishments.

■ Strategies for exercising influence

Research on these strategies suggests that reason is the most popular strategy overall.[14] In addition, friendliness, assertiveness, bargaining, and higher authority are used more frequently to influence subordinates than to influence supervisors. This pattern of influence attempts is consistent with our earlier contention that downward influence generally includes mobilization of both position and personal power sources, whereas upward influence is more likely to draw on personal power.

There is not much research available on the specific subject of upward influence in organizations. This is unfortunate, since truly effective managers are able to influence their bosses as well as their subordinates. One study reports that reason, or the logical presentation of ideas, is viewed by both supervisors and subordinates as the most frequently used strategy of upward influence.[15] When queried on reasons for success and failure, however, both similarities and differences are found in the viewpoints of the two groups. The perceived causes of success in upward influence are similar for both supervisors and subordinates and involve the favorable content of the influence attempt, a favorable manner of its presentation, and the competence of the subordinate.[16] The two groups disagree on the causes of failure, however. Subordinates attribute failure in upward influence to the closemindedness of the supervisor, unfavorable content of the influence attempt, and unfavorable interpersonal relationships with the supervisor. In contrast, supervisors attribute failure to unfavorable content of the attempt, the unfavorable manner in which it was presented, and lack of competence of the subordinate.

EMPOWERMENT

Empowerment is allowing individuals or groups to make decisions that affect them or their work.

Empowerment is the process by which managers help others to acquire and use the power needed to make decisions affecting themselves and their work. More than ever before, managers in progressive organizations are expected to be good at—and highly comfortable with—empowering the people with whom they work. Rather than considering power to be something to be held only at higher levels in the traditional "pyramid" of organizations, this view considers power to be something that can be shared by everyone working in flatter and more collegial structures.

The concept of empowerment is part of the sweeping change being witnessed in today's industry. Corporate staff is being cut back; layers of management are being cut back; the number of employees is being cut back. What is left is a leaner and trimmer organization staffed by fewer managers who must share more power as they go about daily tasks. As suggested by Corning's Chairperson John R. Houghton, it may well be that "the age of the hierarchy is over."[17] Indeed, empowerment is a key foundation of the increasingly popular self-managing work teams and other creative worker involvement groups.

▼ THE POWER KEYS TO EMPOWERMENT

One of the bases for empowerment is a radically different view of power itself. So far, our discussion has focused on power that is exerted over other individuals. In this traditional view, power is relational in terms of individuals. In contrast, the concept of empowerment emphasizes the ability to make things happen. Power is still relational, but in terms of problems and opportunities, not individuals. Cutting through all the corporate rhetoric on empowerment is quite difficult, since the term has become quite fashionable in management circles. Each individual empowerment attempt needs to be examined in light of how power in the organization will be changed.

Changing Position Power   When an organization attempts to move power down the hierarchy, it must also alter the existing pattern of position power. Changing this pattern raises some important questions. Can "empowered" individuals give rewards and sanctions based on task accomplishment? Has their new right to act been legitimized with formal authority? All too often, attempts at empowerment disrupt well-established patterns of position power and threaten middle and lower level managers. As one supervisor said, "All this empowerment stuff sounds great for top management. They don't have to run around trying to get the necessary clearances to implement the suggestions from my group. They never gave me the authority to make the changes, only the new job of asking for permission."

Expanding the Zone of Indifference   When embarking on an empowerment program, management needs to recognize the current zone of indifference and systematically move to expand it. All too often, management assumes that its directive for empowerment will be followed; management may fail to show precisely how empowerment will benefit the individuals involved, however. Management at Montgomery Ward, for example, told salesclerks that they were "empowered" to accept merchandise returns. At the same time, management cut full-time staff, hired more part-time salespeople at minimum wage, and refused to consider offering full benefits to part-time workers. Although management wanted salesclerks to do more work, they cut their staff's zone of indifference by reducing the level of inducements. Now, in many Montgomery Ward stores, all merchandise returns are processed in one central location under the direct supervision of the store manager.

Power as an Expanding Pie   Along with empowerment, employees need to be trained to expand their power and their new influence potential. This is the most difficult task for managers and a difficult challenge for employees, for it often changes the dynamic between supervisors and subordinates. The key is to change the concept of power within the organization from a view that stresses power over others to one that emphasizes the use of power to get things done. Under the new definition of power, all employees can be more powerful.

A clearer definition of roles and responsibilities may help managers empower others. For instance, senior managers may choose to concentrate on long-term, large-scale adjustments to a variety of challenging and strategic forces in the external environment. If top management tends to concentrate on the long term and downplay quarterly mileposts, others throughout the organization must be ready and willing to make critical operating decisions to maintain current profitability. By providing opportunities for creative problem solving coupled with the discretion to act, real empowerment actually increases the total power available in an organization. In other words, the top levels don't have to give up power in order for the lower levels to gain it. Note that senior managers must give up the illusion of control—the false belief that they can actually direct the actions of employees five or six levels of management below them.

The same basic arguments hold true in any manager–subordinate relationship. Empowerment means

---

Take-A-Note 14.2

GUIDELINES FOR IMPLEMENTING EMPOWERMENT

1. *Delegation of authority to lower levels should be clear and unambiguous.*

2. *Planning must be integrated and participative at all levels.*

3. *Managers at all levels, but especially the top, should exercise strong communication skills.*

that all managers need to emphasize different ways of exercising influence. Appeals to higher authority and sanctions need to be replaced by appeals to reason. Friendliness must replace coercion, and bargaining must replace orders for compliance. Given the all too familiar history of an emphasis on coercion and compliance within firms, special support may be needed for individuals so that they become comfortable in developing their own power over events and activities.

ORGANIZATIONAL POLITICS

Any study of power and influence inevitably leads to the subject of "politics." This word may conjure up thoughts of illicit deals, favors, and special personal relationships. Perhaps this image of shrewd, often dishonest, practices of obtaining one's way is reinforced by Machiavelli's classic fifteenth-century work *The Prince,* which outlines how to obtain and hold power via political action. It is important, however, to adopt a perspective that allows politics in organizations to function in a much broader capacity.[18]

▼ THE TWO TRADITIONS OF ORGANIZATIONAL POLITICS

There are two quite different traditions in the analysis of **organizational politics.** One tradition builds on Machiavelli's philosophy and *defines politics in terms of self-interest and the use of nonsanctioned means.* In this tradition, organizational politics may be formally defined as the management of influence to obtain ends not sanctioned by the organization or to obtain sanctioned ends through nonsanctioned influence means.[19] Managers are often considered political when they seek their own goals, use means not currently authorized by the organization, or use means that push legal limits. It is also important to recognize that where there is uncertainty or ambiguity, it is often extremely difficult to tell whether a manager is being political in this self-serving sense.[20] For instance, was Michael Milkin a great innovator when he used "junk bonds" to fund corporate takeovers and created a "market" for corporate control of major U.S. firms? Or was he just another common criminal out for the money any way he could make it? Clearly, Milkin violated insider trading rules (using information from inside a firm that is not known by others to make money on changes in the stock price) established by the U.S. Securities and Exchange Commission (SEC). Consequently, he was sentenced to 10 years in prison. Did Drexel, Burnham and Lambert, the investment banking firm Milkin worked for, know he was conducting illegal activities, or did it just turn its back while he was making everyone a fortune? Or, as often happens in the world of corporate politics, could all these statements be partially true?

The second tradition *treats politics as a necessary function resulting from differences in the self-interests of individuals.* Here, organizational politics is viewed as the art of creative compromise among competing interests. In a heterogeneous

> **Organizational politics** is the management of influence to obtain ends not sanctioned by the organization or to obtain sanctioned ends through nonsanctioned means of influence.

society, individuals will disagree on whose self-interests are most valuable and whose concerns should therefore be bounded by collective interests. Politics arise because individuals need to develop compromises, avoid confrontation, and live together. The same holds true in organizations, where individuals join, work, and stay together because their self-interests are served. Further, it is important to remember that the goals of the organization and the acceptable means are established by organizationally powerful individuals in negotiation with others. Thus, organizational politics is also the use of power to develop socially acceptable ends and means that balance individual and collective interests.

In the late 1980s, Caterpillar's CEO, Donald V. Fites, saw his new labor contract produce substantial benefits for both workers and management.[21] The 1986 labor agreement with 17,000 veteran United Auto Workers (UAW) shifted power from management to floor personnel. To complement this ambitious new contract, Fites invested over $2 billion in plant modernization. This program worked extremely well for Caterpillar's management and its hourly workers. But in 1991 everything began to change again, because management wanted to lower costs and increase their own bonuses by cutting union benefits and changing work rules. The strike started in November of 1991 and was ended in the spring of 1992, when Cat management threatened to permanently replace strikers. When Cat management took a hard line, UAW members came back but, in key plants, started a work slowdown. A second strike ensued in June 1994 and was never settled. Cat management allowed former UAW members to return to work without a contract in December of 1995 because it posted record profits and executive bonuses. For now, power sharing is a thing of the past at CAT because it is relying upon being lean and mean.

QUALITY

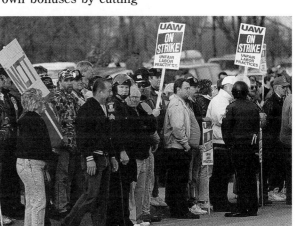

▼ THE DOUBLE-EDGED SWORD OF ORGANIZATIONAL POLITICS

The two different traditions of organizational politics are reflected in the ways in which executives describe their effects on managers and their organizations. In one survey, some 53 percent of those interviewed indicated that organizational politics enhanced the achievement of organizational goals and survival.[22] Yet, some 44 percent suggested that it distracted individuals from organizational goals. In this same survey, 60 percent of respondents suggested that organizational politics was good for career advancement; 39 percent reported that it led to a loss of power, position, and credibility.

Organizational politics is not automatically good or bad. It can serve a number of important functions, including overcoming personnel inadequacies, coping with change, and substituting for formal authority.

Even in the best managed firms, mismatches arise among managers who are learning, burned out, lacking in needed training and skills, overqualified, or lacking the resources needed to accomplish their assigned duties. Organizational politics provides a mechanism for circumventing these inadequacies and getting the job done. Organizational politics can facilitate adaptation to changes in the environment and technology of an organization. Organizational politics can help identify such problems and move ambitious, problem-solving managers into the breach. It is quicker than restructuring. It allows the firm to meet unanticipated problems with people and resources quickly, before small headaches become major problems. Finally, when a person's formal authority breaks down or fails to apply to a particular situation, political actions can be used to prevent a loss of influence. Managers may use political behavior to maintain operations and to achieve task continuity in circumstances where the failure of formal authority may otherwise cause problems.

▼ ORGANIZATIONAL POLITICS AND SELF-PROTECTION

Whereas organizational politics may be helpful to the organization as a whole, it is probably more commonly known and better understood in terms of self-protection.[23] Whether management likes it or not, all employees recognize that in any organization they must watch out for themselves first. In too many organizations, if the employee doesn't protect himself or herself, no one will.

There are three common strategies individuals employ to protect themselves. They can (1) avoid action and risk taking, (2) redirect accountability and responsibility, or (3) defend their turf.

Avoidance *Avoidance* is quite common in controversial areas where the employee must risk being wrong or where actions may yield a sanction. Perhaps the most common reaction is to "work to the rules." That is, employees are protected when they strictly adhere to all of the rules, policies, and procedures or do not allow deviations or exceptions. Perhaps one of the most frustrating but effective techniques is to "play dumb." We all do this at some time or another. When was the last time you said, "Officer, I didn't know the speed limit was 35. I couldn't have been going 52!"

Although working to the rules and playing dumb are common techniques, experienced employees often practice somewhat more subtle techniques of self-protection. These include depersonalization and stalling. Depersonalization involves treating individuals, such as customers, clients, or subordinates, as numbers, things, or objects. Senior managers don't fire long-term employees; the organization is merely "downsized" or "delayered." Routine stalling involves slowing down the pace of work to expand the task so that the individuals look as if they are working hard. With creative stalling, the employees may spend the time supporting the organization's ideology, position, or program and delaying implementation.

Redirecting Responsibility Politically sensitive individuals will always protect themselves from accepting blame for the negative consequences of their actions.

Again, there are a variety of well-worn techniques for *redirecting responsibility.* "Passing the buck" is a common method employees and managers use. The trick here is to define the task in such a way that it becomes someone else's formal responsibility. The ingenious ways individuals can redefine an issue to avoid action and transfer responsibility are often amazing.

Both employees and managers may avoid responsibility by *buffing,* or *rigorous documentation.* Here, individuals only take action when all the paperwork is in place and it is clear that they are merely following procedure. Closely related to rigorous documentation is the "blind memo," which explains an objection to an action implemented by the individual. Here, the required action is taken, but the blind memo is prepared should the action come into question. Politicians are particularly good at this technique. They will meet with a lobbyist and then send a memo to the files confirming the meeting. Any relationship between what was discussed in the meeting and the memo is accidental.

As the last example suggests, a convenient method some managers use to avoid responsibility is merely to rewrite history. If a program is successful, the manager claims to have been an early supporter. If a program fails, the manager was the one who expressed serious reservations in the first place. Whereas a memo in the files is often nice to have to show one's early support or objections, some executives don't bother with such niceties. They merely start a meeting by recapping what has happened in such a way that makes them look good.

For the really devious, there are three other techniques for redirecting responsibility. One technique is to blame the problem on someone or some group that has difficulty defending themselves. Fired employees, outsiders, opponents, and minorities are often targets of such scapegoating. Closely related to scapegoating is blaming the problem on uncontrollable events. The really astute manager goes far beyond the old "the-dog-ate-my-homework" routine. A perennial favorite is, "Given the unexpected severe decline in the overall economy, firm profitability was only somewhat below reasonable expectations." Meaning, the firm lost a bundle.

Of course, should these techniques fail, there is always another possibility: Facing apparent defeat, the manager can escalate commitment to a losing cause of action. That is, when all appears lost, assert your confidence in the original action, blame the problems on not spending enough money to implement the plan fully, and embark on actions that call for increased effort. The hope is that you will be promoted or retired by the time the negative consequences are actually recognized.

Defending Turf   Defending turf is a time-honored tradition in most large organizations. As noted earlier in the chapter, managers seeking to improve their power attempt to expand the jobs their groups perform. Defending turf also results from the coalitional nature of organizations. That is, the organization may be seen as a collection of competing interests that are held by various departments and groups. As each group attempts to expand its influence, it starts to encroach on the activities of other groups. Turf protection can be seen more easily in the following analysis of political action and the manager.

POLITICAL ACTION AND THE MANAGER

Managers may gain a better understanding of political behavior by placing themselves in the positions of other persons involved in critical decisions or events. Each action and decision can be seen as having benefits for and costs to all parties concerned. Where the costs exceed the benefits, the manager may act to protect his or her position.

Figure 14.3 shows a sample payoff table for two managers, Lee and Leslie, in a problem situation involving a decision as to whether or not to allocate resources to a special project. If both managers authorize the resources, the project gets completed on time, and their company keeps a valuable client. Unfortunately, if they do this, both Lee and Leslie overspend their budgets. Taken on its own, a budget overrun would be bad for the managers' performance records. Assume that the overruns are acceptable only if the client is kept. Thus, if both managers act, both they and the company win, as depicted in the upper left block of the figure. Obviously, this is the most desirable outcome for all parties concerned.

Assume that Leslie acts, but Lee does not. In this case, the company loses the client, Leslie overspends the budget in a futile effort, but Lee ends up within budget. While the company and Leslie lose, Lee wins. This scenario is illustrated in the lower left block of the figure. The upper right block shows the reverse situation, where Lee acts but Leslie does not. In this case, Leslie wins, while the company and Lee lose. Finally, if both Lee and Leslie fail to act, they each stay within the budget and therefore gain, but the company loses the client.

The company clearly wants both Lee and Leslie to act. But will they? Would you take the risk of overspending the budget, knowing that your colleague may refuse? The question of trust is critical here, but building trust among comanagers and other workers takes time and can be difficult. The involvement of higher level managers may be needed to set the stage better. Yet, in many organizations both Lee and Leslie would fail to act because the "climate" or "culture" too often encourages people to maximize their self-interest at minimal risks.

▼ POLITICAL ACTION AND SUBUNIT POWER

Political action links managers more formally to one another as representatives of their work units. Five of the more typical lateral, intergroup relations in which you may engage as a manager are work flow, service, advisory, auditing, and approval.[24] *Work-flow linkages* involve contacts with units that precede or follow in a sequential production chain. *Service ties* involve contacts with units established to help with problems. For instance, an assembly-line manager may develop a service link by asking the maintenance manager to fix an important piece of equipment on a priority basis. In contrast, *advisory connections* involve formal staff units having special expertise, such as a manager seeking the advice of the personnel department on evaluating subordinates. *Auditing linkages* involve units having the right to evaluate the actions of others after action has been taken,

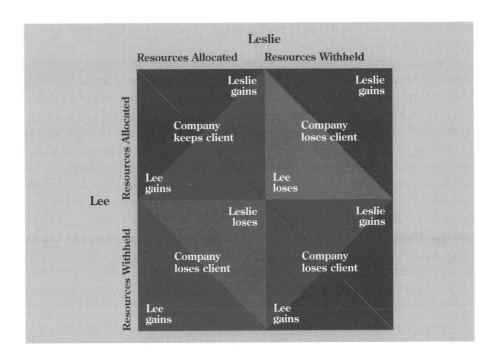

■ FIGURE 14.3
Political payoff matrix for
the allocation of resources
on a sample project.

whereas *approval linkages* involve units whose approval must be obtained before action may be taken.

To be effective in political action, managers should understand the politics of subunit relations. Line units are typically more powerful than are staff groups, and units toward the top of the hierarchy are often more powerful than are those toward the bottom. In general, units gain power as more of their relations with others are of the approval and auditing types. Work-flow relations are more powerful than are advisory associations, and both are more powerful than are service relations.

▼ POLITICAL ACTION IN THE CHIEF EXECUTIVE SUITE

From descriptions of the 1890s' robber barons such as Jay Gould to the actions of Microsoft's Bill Gates, Americans have been fascinated with the politics of the chief executive suite. An analytical view of executive suite dynamics may lift some of the mystery behind the political veil at the top levels in organizations.

Resource Dependencies   Executive behavior can sometimes be explained in terms of *resource dependencies*—the firm's need for resources that are controlled by others.[25] Essentially, the resource dependence of an organization increases as (1) needed resources become more scarce, (2) outsiders have more control over needed resources, and (3) there are fewer substitutes for a particular type of resource controlled by a limited number of outsiders. Thus, one political role of chief executives is to develop workable compromises among the competing resource dependencies facing the organization—compromises that enhance the executive's power. To create such compromises, executives need to diagnose the relative power of outsiders and to craft strategies that respond differently to various external resource suppliers.

For larger organizations, many strategies may center on altering the firm's degree of resource dependence. Through mergers and acquisitions, a firm may bring key resources within its control. By changing the "rules of the game," a firm may also find protection from particularly powerful outsiders. For instance, markets may be protected by trade barriers, or labor unions may be put in check by "right to work" laws. Yet, there are limits on the ability of even our largest and most powerful organizations to control all important external contingencies. International competition has narrowed the range of options for chief executives; they can no longer ignore the rest of the world. Some may need to redefine fundamentally how they expect to conduct business. For instance, once U.S. firms could go it alone without the assistance of foreign corporations. Now, chief executives are increasingly leading them in the direction of more joint ventures and strategic alliances with foreign partners from around the globe. Such "combinations" provide access to scarce resources and technologies among partners, as well as new markets and shared production costs.

GLOBAL

Corning is involved in more than 40 joint ventures with United States and foreign firms—many from Europe and Japan. CEO James R. Houghton believes that interfirm alliances are an idea whose time has come. He says Corning's competitors these days "aren't merely companies but combinations of companies, or entire nations and even combinations of nations. No one's strong enough to go it alone, to bend all others to its will."

On the seamier side there is a new wrinkle in the discussion of resource dependencies for the 1990s—excessive CEO pay for short-term corporate gains. Traditionally U.S. CEOs made about 30 times the pay of the average worker. This was similar to CEO pay scales in Europe and Japan.[26] By 1995 many U.S. CEOs were making 3000 times the average pay of workers. How did they get so rich? CEOs may tie themselves to the short-term interests of powerful stockholders. Their pay may be directly linked to short-term stock price increases, even though CEOs are most often expected to focus on the long-term health of the firm. When a CEO downsizes, embarks upon a merger campaign, or cuts such benefits as worker health care, short-term profits may jump dramatically. While the long-term health of the firm may be put in jeopardy, few U.S. CEOs seem able to resist the temptation. It is little wonder that there is renewed interest in how U.S. firms are governed.

> **Organizational governance** is the pattern of authority, influence, and acceptable managerial behavior established at the top of the organization.

Organizational Governance **Organizational governance** refers to the pattern of authority, influence, and acceptable managerial behavior established at the top of the organization. This system establishes what is important, how issues will be defined, who should and should not be involved in key choices, and the boundaries for acceptable implementation. In an era of corporate downsizing resulting from technological changes and international competition, some firms, such as Pitney Bowes, exemplify how it may be done in a way that does not damage the long-term prospects for the firm.

QUALITY

In 1989, Pitney Bowes was faced with the unpleasant task of downsizing. To find the best solution, Pitney Bowes went to its employees. At a company meeting, the need to reduce the workforce by 1500 people worldwide was announced. Rather than terminate employees, workers were encouraged to volunteer to leave. Those choosing to leave were given 75 percent to their annual pay or 2 weeks pay for every year of service, whichever was greater. Part of the leaving package also included an option to return to the company after 3 years, although employees would not be granted their former seniority. More than 1000 employees accepted the offer; no terminations were made at the time. A displaced-persons program was also established. People whose jobs disappeared were assigned to a pool, and managers considered these people before recruiting from outside the company.

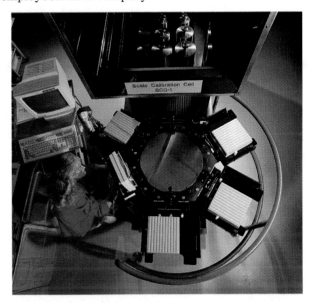

Students of organizational governance suggest that a "dominant coalition" comprised of powerful organizational actors is a key to understanding a firm's governance.[27] Although one expects many top officers within the organization to be members of this coalition, the dominant coalition occasionally includes outsiders with access to key resources. Thus, analysis of organizational governance builds on the resource dependence perspective by highlighting the effective control of key resources by members of a dominant coalition.

This view of the executive suite recognizes that the daily practice of organizational governance is the development and resolution of issues. Via the governance system, the dominant coalition attempts to define reality. By accepting or rejecting proposals from subordinates, by directing questions toward the interests of powerful outsiders, and by selecting individuals who appear to espouse particular values and qualities, the pattern of governance is slowly established within the organization. Furthermore, this pattern rests, at least in part, on very political foundations.

Whereas organizational governance was an internal and rather private matter in the past, it is now becoming more public and openly controversial in many instances. This was evidenced to some extent in the many well-publicized hostile takeovers of the 1980s. Whereas some argue that senior managers don't represent shareholder interests well enough, others are concerned that they give too little attention to broader constituencies.

It has been estimated that the Fortune 500 corporations have cut some 8 million positions over the last 15 years of downsizing.[28] In 1995 the estimate was almost 526,000 jobs. Once, managers and employes of these firms felt confident that the management philosophy of their firm included their interests; in the 1990s only a few seem to believe this anymore.

Public concerns about U.S. corporations, especially those organizations with high-risk technologies such as chemical processing, medical technology, and integrated oil refineries, appears on the rise. For instance, Dow-Corning's survival is questionable because it has been accused of selling breast implants that cause immune systems problems. Dow-Corning cites the lack of scientific evidence linking their product with such problems, but jury after jury seems willing to award damages to women who have had Dow-Corning implants and immune system problems. Juries are holding Dow-Corning management accountable.

Imbalanced organizational governance by some U.S. corporations may limit their ability to manage global operations effectively. Although U.S. senior managers may blame such externalities as unfavorable trade laws for their inability to compete in Japan, their critics suggest that it's just a lack of global operating savvy that limits the corporations these managers are supposed to be leading. Organizational governance is too tied to the short-term interests of stockholders and the pay of the CEO.

On a more positive note, there are bright spots suggesting that the governance of some U.S. firms, such as South Shore Bank, is extending well beyond the limited interests of the owners and into communities.

ETHICS AND SOCIAL RESPONSIBILITY

South Shore Bank was the first for-profit community development bank to open in the United States.[29] Started in 1973 on the South Shore of Chicago,

the bank started by making small business loans and individual mortgages in the neighborhood. Throughout the 1970s and 1980s, as other banks invested in the suburbs, foreign loans, and corporate takeovers, South Shore concentrated on developing its local area by supporting entrepreneurs and local citizens. By 1990, even the other Chicago banks had started to invest in the South Shore area. Today, the firm is expanding into the Austin area on Chicago's near west side.

Cavanagh, Moberg, and Velasquez argue that organizational governance should have an ethical base.[30] They suggest that from the CEO to the lowest employee, a person's behavior must satisfy the following criteria to be considered ethical. First, the behavior must result in optimization of satisfactions of people both inside and outside the organization to produce the greatest good for the greatest number of people. Second, the behavior must respect the rights of all affected parties, including the human rights of free consent, free speech, freedom of conscience, privacy, and due process. Third, the behavior must respect the rules of justice by treating people equitably and fairly, as opposed to arbitrarily.

There may be times when a behavior is unable to fulfill these criteria but can still be considered ethical in the given situation. This special case must satisfy the criterion of overwhelming factors, in which the special nature of the situation results in (1) conflicts among criteria (e.g., a behavior results in some good and some bad being done), (2) conflicts within criteria (e.g., a behavior uses questionable means to achieve a positive end), and/or (3) incapacity to employ the criteria (e.g., a person's behavior is based on inaccurate or incomplete information).

Choosing to be ethical often involves considerable personal sacrifice and, at all corporate levels, involves avoiding common rationalizations. CEOs and employees alike may justify unethical actions by suggesting that (1) the behavior is not really illegal and so could be moral; (2) the action appears to be in the firm's best interests; (3) the action is unlikely ever to be detected; and (4) it appears that the action demonstrates loyalty to the boss, the firm, or short-term stockholder interests. Whereas these rationalizations may appear compelling at the moment of action, each deserves close scrutiny if the organizational governance system of the firm is to avoid falling into being dominated by the seamier side of organizational politics.

CHAPTER 14 STUDY GUIDE

SUMMARY

What is power within the context of the organization, and why do managers have power?
- Power is the ability to get someone else to do what you want him or her to do.
- Power vested in managerial positions derives from three sources: rewards, punishments, and legitimacy (formal authority).

What are the relationships among power, formal authority, and obedience?
- Power, authority, and obedience are interrelated.
- Formal authority is based on the manager's position in the hierarchy of authority, whereas personal power is based on one's expertise and referent capabilities.
- People may have a tendency to obey directives coming from people who appear powerful and authoritative.
- The zone of indifference defines the boundaries within which people in organizations let others influence their behavior.
- Ultimately, power and authority work only if the individual "accepts" them.

What is empowerment and how can management empower others?
- Managers can pursue various ways of acquiring both position and personal power.

- They can also become skilled at using various tactics, such as reason, friendliness, ingratiation, and bargaining, to influence superiors, peers, and subordinates.

What is empowerment and how can management empower others?
- Empowerment is the process through which managers help others acquire and use the power needed to make decisions that affect themselves and their work.
- Empowerment emphasizes power as the ability to get things done rather than the ability to get others to do what you want.
- Clear delegation of authority, integrated planning, and the involvement of senior management are all important to implementing empowerment.

Are organizational politics inevitable, and must the manager live in a political world?
- Organizational politics are inevitable.
- Politics involves the use of power to obtain ends not officially sanctioned and the use of power to find ways of balancing individual and collective interests in otherwise difficult circumstances.

How does organizational politics differ for the individual supervisor, the middle manager, and the chief executive officer?
- For the manager, politics often occurs in decision situations where the interests of another manager or individual must be reconciled with one's own.
- For managers, politics also involves subunits that jockey for power and advantageous positions vis-à-vis one another.
- For chief executives, politics come into play as resource dependencies with external environmental elements must be strategically managed.
- Organizational governance is the pattern of authority, influence, and acceptable managerial behavior established at the top of the organization.
- CEOs and managers can develop an ethical organizational governance system that is free from rationalizations.

KEY TERMS

Coercive power (p. 291)	Legitimate power (p. 291)	Power (p. 291)
Empowerment (p. 298)	Organizational governance	Referent power (p. 292)
Expert power (p. 292)	(p. 306)	Reward power (p. 291)
Influence (p. 291)	Organizational politics	
	(p. 300)	

SELF-TEST 14

▼ MULTIPLE CHOICE

1. The three bases of position power are ___. (a) reward, expertise, and coercive power (b) legitimate, experience, and judgment power (c) knowledge, experience, and judgment power (d) reward, coercive, and knowledge power (e) reward, coercive, and legitimate power

2. A student following the rules of his or her instructor is explained by ___power. (a) expert (b) legitimate (c) reward (d) coercive (e) charismatic

3. A worker who behaves in a certain manner to ensure an effective boss subordinate relationship shows ___ power. (a) expert (b) reward (c) coercive (d) approval (e) referent

4. ___ are the three guidelines for enhancing personal power. (a) Coercion, effort, and influence (b) Referent power, knowledge/information, and effort (c) Personal attractiveness, expert power, and coercion (d) Knowledge/information, effort, and reward power (e) Personal attractiveness, knowledge/information, and effort

5. The range of authoritative requests to which a subordinate is willing to respond without subjecting the directives to critical evaluation or judgment is called the ___. (a) psychological contract (b) zone of indifference (c) Milgram experiments (d) functional level of organizational politics (e) power vector

6. The three basic power relationships to ensure success are ___. (a) upward, downward, and lateral (b) upward, downward, and oblique (c) downward, lateral, and oblique (d) downward, lateral, and external (e) internal, external, and oblique

7. In which dimension of power and influence would a manager find the use of both position power and personal power most advantageous? (a) upward (b) lateral (c) downward (d) work flow (e) advisory

8. Reasons, coalition, bargaining, and assertiveness are strategies for ___. (a) enhancing personal power (b) enhancing position power (c) exercising referent power (d) exercising influence (e) enhancing coercive power

9. Negotiating the interpretation of a union contract is an example of ___. (a) organizational politics (b) lateral relations (c) an approval relationship (d) an auditing linkage (e) unethical behavior

10. One guideline for implementing a successful empowerment strategy is that ___. (a) delegation of authority should be left ambiguous and open to individual interpretation (b) managers should refrain from communicating effectively to subordinates (c) planning should be separated according to the level of empowerment (d) it can be assumed that any empowering directives from management will be automatically followed (e) the authority delegated to lower levels should be clear and precise

▼ TRUE–FALSE

11. Coercion is a behavioral response to the exercise of power.   T   F

12. Reference is an example of power derived from personal, as opposed to organizational, sources.   T   F

13. Position power includes the ability to control another's behavior through possession of knowledge.   T   F

14. Legitimate power and formal authority are one and the same.   T   F

15. Reward power is the extent to which a manager can use extrinsic and intrinsic rewards to control other people.   T   F

16. The acceptance theory of authority indicates that subordinates will always accept the orders of their superiors in organizations.   T   F

17. The Milgram experiments demonstrate that persons are generally unwilling to obey the commands of authoritative persons.   T   F

18. The process by which managers help others acquire and use the power needed to make decisions is called organizational politics.   T   F

19. A resource dependence perspective suggests that one of the key roles played by top management is to develop and allocate power.   T   F

20. Increasing knowledge and attractiveness are ways to increase position power.   T   F

▼ SHORT RESPONSE

21. Explain how the various bases of position and personal power do or do not apply to the classroom relationship between instructor and student. What sources of power do students have over their instructors?

22. Identify and explain at least three guidelines for the acquisition of (a) position power and (b) personal power by managers.

23. Identify and explain at least four strategies of managerial influence. Give examples of how each strategy may or may not work when exercising influence (a) downward and (b) upward in organizations.

24. Define "organizational politics" and give an example of how it operates in both functional and dysfunctional ways.

▼ APPLICATIONS ESSAY

25. How does the "strategic contingencies" notion apply to political action and subunit relations in a large firm such as Canadian Tire?

15

LEADERSHIP

Dick Grove spent much of the 1980s using his computer mostly to display his Post-it Notes.[1] Today, he is CEO of the public relations firm Primetime Publicity and Media Consulting Corporation, and he is at the cutting edge of technology. Grove has his high-tech tools at arms length at all times, whether he is blasting across the country on his Harley-Davidson or working at his farm in the nation's midsection. He packs his Macintosh Duo 210 laptop, AT&T cellular phone, and ORA Data Link connector in his saddlebags and hits the road. Recently, in the Grand Tetons, Grove parked his Harley under the stars, set up his portable office, and began editing an important contract that had just been beamed to his fax/modem.

Dick Grove leads his virtual corporation with the same emphasis on flexibility. His nine media representatives can work when and where they please. They are based in home offices all across the country and communicate with their clients, Grove, and one another through daily Internet and progress reports. The digital traffic is routed through a main server located at the firm's headquarters on the Pacific Coast.

Three years ago, Grove determined to create a virtual corporation and supplied each employee with a Macintosh computer, a modem, and access to the Internet. He claims that the $50 thousand investment paid for itself almost immediately, and he now projects next year's revenues at $2 million. He spends much of his time on his farm and on the road, including trips abroad, and claims that he attracts the best employees because he offers them so much freedom.

Dick Grove captures for many the essence of leadership: the vision to seize

the day and make a difference. Although most people probably agree that leader-

ship makes a difference, some argue that it isn't important. For them, leaders are

so bound by constraints that they just don't have much impact. Some also see

leadership as so mystical that they can't define it but know it when they see it. In

this chapter, we address all these views and more in examining how leadership

fits in the organization.

Leadership is a special form of influence, as noted in Chapter 14 on Power and
Politics. As you read Chapter 15, keep in mind these key questions.

◉ What is leadership, and how does it differ from management?

◉ What are trait theories of leadership?

◉ What are behavioral theories of leadership?

◉ What are situational contingency theories of leadership?

◉ How does attribution theory relate to the new leadership?

◉ What is multiple-level leadership, and how does leadership apply to high
performance work teams?

LEADERSHIP AND MANAGEMENT

In the chapters in Part 1, we talked about managers and management functions, roles, activities, and skills. The question to ask now is how are leaders
and leadership linked to all this?

Currently, there is heated controversy concerning whether or not leaders are
different from managers or management is different from leadership and, if so,
how. One way of differentiating is to argue that the role of *management* is to pro-

mote stability or to enable the organization to run smoothly, whereas the role of *leadership* is to promote adaptive or useful changes.[2] A person in a managerial position could be involved with both management and leadership activities, or he or she could emphasize one activity at the expense of the other. Both are needed, however, and if the manager doesn't assume responsibility for both, he or she needs to make sure that the neglected activity is handled by someone else.

Leadership also is compared and contrasted with the kinds of influence and power discussed in Chapter 14. For our purpose, we will treat **leadership** as a special case of influence that gets an individual or group to do what the leader or manager wants done. Leadership appears in two forms: (1) *formal leadership,* which is exerted by persons appointed to or elected to positions of formal authority in organizations; and (2) *informal leadership,* which is exerted by persons who become influential because they have special skills that meet the needs and resources of others. Both types are important in organizations, although most of our emphasis in this chapter is on formal leadership.

> **Leadership** is a special case of interpersonal influence that gets an individual or group to do what the leader wants done.

The leadership literature is vast—more than 10,000 studies—and consists of numerous approaches.[3] We have organized the theories into two categories: traditional leadership and new leadership.[4] As you will see, both are important for a leader. The traditional perspectives go back many years, and they vary in the emphasis they place on the role of leadership.

TRAIT THEORIES

Trait approaches assume that, in one way or another, selected personal traits have a major impact on leadership outputs; that is, according to these theories, leadership is central, and other variables are relatively less important.

The *great man–trait theory* is the earliest approach used to study leadership and dates back to as early as the turn of the century. The early studies attempted to identify those traits that differentiated the "great person" in history from the masses (e.g., How did Catherine the Great differ from her subjects?).[5] This approach led to a research emphasis that tried to separate leaders from nonleaders or more effective leaders from less effective leaders. The argument was that certain traits such as height, integrity, intelligence, and the like, are related to success and that, once identified, these traits could be used to select leaders.

For various reasons, including inadequate theorizing and measurement of many traits and failure to recognize possible differences in organizations and situations, the studies were not successful enough to provide a general trait theory.[6] But they laid the groundwork for consideration of certain traits, in combination with other leadership aspects, such as behaviors, that form the basis for some of the more current theories.

BEHAVIORAL THEORIES

Like the trait approach, the behavioral theories approach assumes that leadership is central to performance and human resource maintenance. In this case, however, instead of dealing with underlying traits, behaviors or actions are considered. Two classic research programs, at the University of Michigan and Ohio State University, provide useful insights into leadership behaviors.

▼ MICHIGAN STUDIES

In the late 1940s, researchers at the University of Michigan introduced a program of research on leadership behavior. The researchers were concerned with identifying the leadership pattern that results in effective performance. From interviews of high- and low-performing groups in different organizations, the researchers derived two basic forms of leader behaviors: employee centered and production centered. *Employee-centered supervisors* are those who place strong emphasis on the welfare of their subordinates. In contrast, *production-centered supervisors* tend to place a stronger emphasis on getting the work done. In general, employee-centered supervisors were found to have more productive work groups than did the production-centered supervisors.[7]

These behaviors may be viewed on a continuum, with employee-centered supervisors at one end and production-centered supervisors at the other. Sometimes, the more general terms "human relations oriented" and "task oriented" are used to describe these alternative leader behaviors.

▼ OHIO STATE STUDIES

An important leadership research program was started at Ohio State University at about the same time as the Michigan studies. A questionnaire was administered in both industrial and military settings to measure subordinates' perceptions of their superiors' leadership behavior. The researchers identified two dimensions similar to those found in the Michigan studies: *consideration* and *initiating structure*.[8] A highly considerate leader is sensitive to people's feelings and, much like the employee-centered leader, tries to make things pleasant for his or her followers. In contrast, a leader high in initiating structure is more concerned with spelling out task requirements and clarifying other aspects of the work agenda; he or she might be seen as similar to a production-centered supervisor. These dimensions are related to what people sometimes refer to as socioemotional and task leadership, respectively.

At first, it seemed to the Ohio State researchers that a leader high on consideration, or socioemotional warmth, would have more highly satisfied and/or better performing subordinates. Later results indicated that leaders should be high on *both* consideration and initiating structure behaviors, however. This dual emphasis is reflected in the leadership grid approach.

▼ THE LEADERSHIP GRID

Developed by Robert Blake and Jane Mouton, the Leadership Grid perspective measures a manager's *concern for people* and *concern for production*.[9] The results are plotted on a nine-position grid that places concern for people on the vertical axis and concern for production on the horizontal axis, as shown in Figure 15.1. As the figure shows, a person with a 9,1 score is a "country club manager"—9 on concern for people, 1 on concern for production. Some other positions are 1,1— impoverished management style—and 1,9—task management style. A 5,5 style, in the middle of the grid, is a middle-of-the-road management style. The ideal position is a 9,9 "team manager," high on both dimensions.

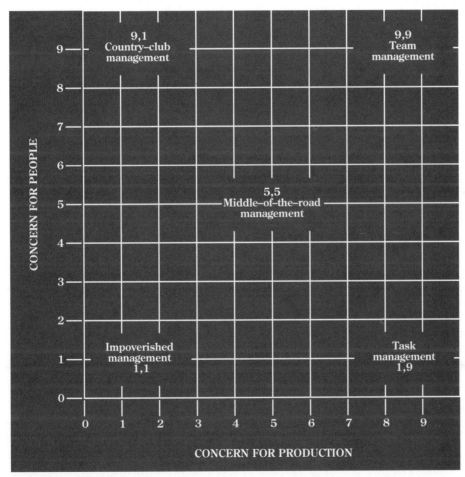

■ FIGURE 15.1

The leadership grid. [Source: From The Leadership Grid® Figure from *Leadership Dilemmas—Grid Solutions,* by Robert R. Blake and Anne Adams McCanse (formerly the Managerial Grid Figure by Robert R. Blake and Jane S. Mouton) (Houston: Gulf Publishing Company), p. 29. Copyright © 1991, by Scientific Methods, Inc. Reproduced by permission of the owners.]

▼ GRAEN'S LEADER–MEMBER EXCHANGE THEORY

In contrast to the approaches just described, leader–member exchange theory (LMX) emphasizes the behaviors of both leaders and individual followers in determining whether followers will be part of the leader's "in group" or "out group."[10] In-group followers tend to function as assistants, lieutenants, or advisers and to have higher quality personalized exchanges with the leader than do out-group followers. The latter tend to emphasize more formalized job requirements, and a relatively low level of mutual influence exists between leaders and out-group followers.

The more personalized in-group exchanges typically involve a leader's emphasis on assignments to interesting tasks, delegation of important responsibilities, information sharing, and participation in the leader's decisions, as well as special benefits, such as personal support and approval, favorable work schedules, and the like.

Research suggests that high-quality LMX is associated with increased follower satisfaction and productivity, decreased turnover, increased salaries, and faster promotion rates.[11] These findings are encouraging, and the approach continues to receive increasing emphasis in the literature. One unanswered but especially important question for the new workplace remains, however: What happens if there is too much disparity in the treatment of in-group and out-group members? Will out-group members become resentful and sabotage team efforts?[12] In addition, more needs to be learned about how the in-group/out-group exchange starts in the first place.

▼ EVALUATION AND APPLICATION OF TRAIT AND BEHAVIORAL APPROACHES

Underlying the Michigan, Ohio State, and leadership grid theories is an emphasis on people- versus task-oriented behaviors; the LMX theory also emphasizes these behaviors in a slightly different form than the others. A timely question is: How well do these dimensions transfer internationally?

Recent work in the United States, Britain, Hong Kong, and Japan shows that although the behaviors seem to be generally important in all these countries, they must be carried out in different ways in alternative cultures. For instance, British leaders are seen as considerate if they show subordinates how to use equipment, whereas in Japan the highly considerate leader helps subordinates with personal problems.[13] Similarly, the underlying notion of LMX theory, which maintains that leader behaviors toward in-group members are different from those toward out-group members, has been shown to operate in Japan.[14]

Finally, in some organizations or units other kinds of traits or behaviors have a major impact on leadership outputs. In these cases, the leader traits or behaviors can be treated as leader-individual characteristics, much the way individual characteristics were dealt with in Chapter 3. For example, it may be found that extroversion and dominance are particularly important traits. Further, certain leader behaviors may be important, and training programs borrowing from the ideas of the leadership grid and related approaches may be used.

SITUATIONAL CONTINGENCY THEORIES

Often, leader traits and/or behaviors act in conjunction with *situational contingencies*—other important aspects of the leadership situation—to determine outcomes. The major contributions to this second traditional leadership perspective include the work of Fred Fiedler, Robert House, Paul Hersey and Kenneth Blanchard, and Steven Kerr and John Jermier.

▼ FIEDLER'S LEADERSHIP CONTINGENCY THEORY

Fred Fiedler's work essentially began the situational contingency era in the mid-1960s.[15] His theory holds that group effectiveness depends on an appropriate match between a leader's style and the demands of the situation. Specifically, Fiedler considers **situational control**—the extent to which a leader can determine what his or her group is going to do as well as the outcomes of the group's actions and decisions.

Fiedler uses an instrument called the **least preferred coworker (LPC) scale** to measure a person's leadership style. Respondents are asked to describe the person with whom they have been able to work least well—their least preferred coworker, or LPC—using a series of adjectives such as the two listed below:

Unfriendly
| 1 | 2 | 3 | 4 | 5 | 6 | 7 | 8 |
Friendly

Pleasant
| 1 | 2 | 3 | 4 | 5 | 6 | 7 | 8 |
Unpleasant

Fiedler argues that high-LPC leaders (those describing their LPC very positively) have a relationship-motivated style, while low-LPC leaders have a task-motivated style. He considers this task or relationship motivation to be a trait that leads to either directive or nondirective behavior, depending on whether the leader has high, moderate, or low situational control, as described above. In other words, a task-motivated leader tends to be nondirective in high-control situations and directive in moderate- and low-control situations. A relationship-motivated leader tends to be the opposite.

Figure 15.2 shows the task-oriented leader as having greater group effectiveness under high and low situational control, whereas the relationship-oriented leader has a more effective group under a moderate control situation. The figure also shows that Fiedler measures high, moderate, and low control with the following three variables arranged in the situtional combinations indicated:

- *Leader–member relations* (good/poor)—Membership support for the leader.
- *Task structure* (high/low)—Spelling out the leader's task goals, procedures, and guidelines in the group.

> **Situational control** is the extent to which leaders can determine what their group is going to do and what the outcomes of their actions and decisions are going to be.

> The **least preferred coworker (LPC) scale** is a measure of a person's leadership style based on a description of the person with whom respondents have been able to work least well.

> ■ Fiedler's three situational control variables

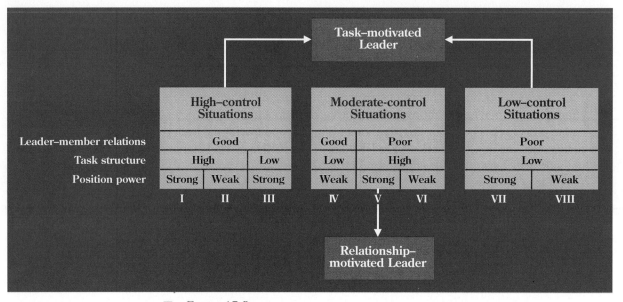

	High–control Situations			Moderate-control Situations			Low-control Situations	
Leader–member relations	Good			Good	Poor		Poor	
Task structure	High		Low	Low	High		Low	
Position power	Strong	Weak	Strong	Weak	Strong	Weak	Strong	Weak
	I	II	III	IV	V	VI	VII	VIII

Task–motivated Leader

Relationship–motivated Leader

■ FIGURE 15.2

Predictions from Fiedler's contingency theory of leadership.

● *Position power* (strong/weak)—The leader's task expertise and reward or punishment authority.

Consider an experienced and well-trained supervisor of a group manufacturing a part for a car engine. The leader is highly supported by his group members and can grant raises and make hiring and firing decisions. This supervisor has very high situational control and is operating in situation I in Figure 15.2. Those leaders operating in situations II and III would have high situational control, although lower than our production supervisor. For these high-control situations, a task-oriented leader behaving directively would have the most effective group.

Now, consider the chair of a student council committee of volunteers (the chair's position power is weak) who are unhappy about this person being the chair and who have the low-structured task of organizing a Parents' Day program to improve university–parent relations. This low-control situation VIII calls for a task-motivated leader who needs to behave directively to keep the group together and focus on the ambiguous task; in fact, the situation demands it.

Finally, consider a well-liked academic department chair with tenured faculty. This is a cell IV moderate-control situation with good leader–member relations, low task structure, and weak position power, calling for a relationship-motivated leader. The leader should emphasize nondirective and considerate relationships with the faculty.

Fiedler's Cognitive Resource Theory Fiedler recently moved beyond his contingency theory by developing the *cognitive resource theory.*[16] Cognitive resources are abilities or competencies. According to this approach, whether a leader should use directive or nondirective behavior depends on the following situational contingencies: (1) the leader's or subordinate group members' ability or competency, (2) stress, (3) experience, and (4) group support of the leader. Basically, cognitive resource theory is most useful because it directs us to leader or subordinate group-member ability, an aspect not typically considered in other leadership approaches.

The theory views directiveness as most helpful for performance when the leader is competent, relaxed, and supported. In this case, the group is ready, and directiveness is the clearest means of communication. When the leader feels stressed, he or she is diverted. In this case, experience is more important than is ability. If support is low, then the group is less receptive, and the leader has less impact. Group-member ability becomes most important when the leader is nondirective and receives strong support from group members. If support is weak, then task difficulty or other factors have more impact than do either the leader or the subordinates.

Evaluation and Application   The roots of Fiedler's contingency approach date back to the 1960s and have elicited both positive and negative reactions. The biggest controversy concerns exactly what Fiedler's LPC instrument measures. Some question Fiedler's behavioral interpretation, whereby the specific behaviors of high- and low-LPC leaders change, depending on the amount of situational control. Furthermore, the approach makes the most accurate predictions in situations I and VIII and IV and V; results are less consistent in the other situations.[17] Tests of cognitive resource theory have shown mixed results.[18]

In terms of application, Fiedler has developed *leader match training,* which has been used by Sears Roebuck and other organizations. Leaders are trained to diagnose the situation to match their high and low LPC scores with situational control, as measured by leader–member relations, task structure, and leader position power, following the general ideas shown in Figure 15.2. In those cases where there is no match, the training shows how each of these situational control variables can be changed to obtain a match. Alternatively, another way of getting a match is through leader selection or placement based on LPC scores.[19] For example, a high-LPC leader would be selected for a position with high situational control, as in our earlier example of the manufacturing supervisor. As in the case of Fiedler's contingency theory, a number of studies have been designed to test leader match. Although they are not uniformly supportive, more than a dozen such tests have found increases in group effectiveness following the training.[20]

We conclude that although there still are unanswered questions concerning Fiedler's contingency theory, especially concerning the meaning of LPC, the theory and the leader match program have relatively strong support.[21] The approach and training program are also especially useful in encouraging situational contingency thinking.

▼ HOUSE'S PATH–GOAL THEORY OF LEADERSHIP
Another well-known approach to situational contingencies is one developed by Robert House based on the earlier work of others.[22] This theory has its roots in

the expectancy model of motivation discussed in Chapter 5. The term "path–goal" is used because of its emphasis on how a leader influences subordinates' perceptions of both work goals and personal goals and the links, or paths, found between these two sets of goals.

The theory assumes that a leader's key function is to adjust his or her behaviors to complement situational contingencies, such as those found in the work setting. House argues that when the leader is able to compensate for things lacking in the setting, subordinates are likely to be satisfied with the leader. For example, the leader could help remove job ambiguity or show how good performance could lead to more pay. Performance should improve as the paths by which (1) effort leads to performance—expectancy—and (2) performance leads to valued rewards—instrumentality—become clarified.

The details of House's approach are summarized in Figure 15.3. The figure shows four types of leader behavior—directive, supportive, achievement oriented, and participative—and two categories of situational contingency variables—subordinate attributes and work-setting attributes. The leader behaviors are adjusted to complement the situational contingency variables in order to influence subordinate satisfaction, acceptance of the leader, and motivation for task performance.

Directive leadership has to do with spelling out the what and how of subordinates' tasks and is much like the initiating structure mentioned earlier. *Supportive leadership* focuses on subordinate needs and well-being and promoting a friendly work climate; it is similar to consideration. *Achievement-oriented leadership* emphasizes setting challenging goals, stressing excellence in performance, and showing confidence in the group members' ability to achieve high standards of performance. *Participative leadership* focuses on consulting with subordinates and seeking and taking their suggestions into account before making decisions.

■ FIGURE 15.3
Summary of major path–goal relationships in House's leadership approach. [Source: Adapted from Richard N. Osborn, James G. Hunt, and Lawrence R. Jauch, *Organizational Theory: An Integrated Approach* (New York: John Wiley & Sons, 1980), p. 464.]

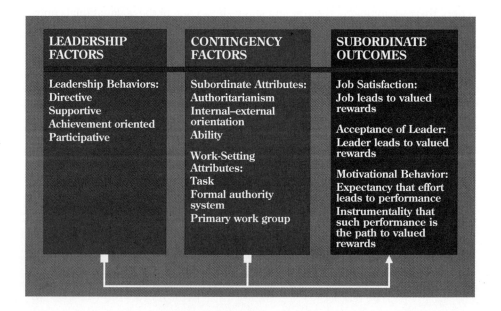

LEADERSHIP FACTORS

Leadership Behaviors:
Directive
Supportive
Achievement oriented
Participative

CONTINGENCY FACTORS

Subordinate Attributes:
Authoritarianism
Internal–external orientation
Ability

Work-Setting Attributes:
Task
Formal authority system
Primary work group

SUBORDINATE OUTCOMES

Job Satisfaction:
Job leads to valued rewards

Acceptance of Leader:
Leader leads to valued rewards

Motivational Behavior:
Expectancy that effort leads to performance
Instrumentality that such performance is the path to valued rewards

Important subordinate characteristics are *authoritarianism* (close minded-ness, rigidity), *internal–external orientation* (e.g., locus of control), and *ability*. The key work-setting factors are the *nature of the subordinates' tasks* (task structure), the *formal authority system,* and the *primary work group*.

Predictions from the Theory   Directive leadership is predicted to have a positive impact on subordinates when the task is ambiguous; it is predicted to have just the opposite effect for clear tasks. In addition, the theory predicts that when ambiguous tasks are being performed by highly authoritarian and close-minded subordinates, even more directive leadership is called for.

Supportive leadership is predicted to increase the satisfaction of subordinates who work on highly repetitive tasks or on tasks considered to be unpleasant, stressful, or frustrating; the leader's supportive behavior helps compensate for these adverse conditions. For example, many would consider traditional assembly-line auto worker jobs to be highly repetitive, perhaps even unpleasant and frustrating. A supportive supervisor could help make these jobs more pleasant.

Achievement-oriented leadership is predicted to encourage subordinates to strive for higher performance standards and to have more confidence in their ability to meet challenging goals. For subordinates in ambiguous, nonrepetitive jobs, achievement-oriented leadership should increase their expectancies that effort leads to desired performance.

Participative leadership is predicted to promote satisfaction on nonrepetitive tasks that allow for the ego involvement of subordinates. For example, on a challenging research project, participation allows employees to feel good about dealing with the challenge of the project on their own. On repetitive tasks, open-minded or nonauthoritarian subordinates will also be satisfied with a participative leader. On a task where employees screw nuts on bolts hour after hour, for example, those who are nonauthoritarian will appreciate having a leader who allows them to get involved in some ways to help break the monotony.

Evaluation and Application   House's path–goal approach has now been with us for more than 20 years. Early work provided some support for the theory in general and for the particular predictions discussed earlier.[23] However, current assessments by well-known scholars have pointed out that many aspects have not been tested adequately and there is very little recent research concerning the theory.[24] House, himself, recently revised and extended path–goal theory into the "Theory of Work Unit Leadership." It's beyond our scope to discuss details of this new theory while using path–goal notions here. However, as a base, the new theory expands the list of leader behaviors beyond those in path–goal theory, including aspects of both traditional and new leadership.[25] It remains to be seen how much research it will generate.

In terms of application, there is enough support for original path–goal theory to suggest a couple of possibilities. First, training could be used to change leadership behavior to fit the situational contingencies. Second, the leader could be taught to diagnose the situation and to learn how to try to change the contingencies, as in leader match.

▼ HERSEY AND BLANCHARD'S SITUATIONAL LEADERSHIP THEORY

Like other situational contingency approaches, the situational leadership theory developed by Paul Hersey and Kenneth Blanchard posits that there is no single best way to lead.[26] Hersey and Blanchard focus on the situational contingency of maturity, or "readiness," of followers, in particular. *Readiness* is the extent to which people have the ability and willingness to accomplish a specific task. Hersey and Blanchard argue that "situational" leadership requires adjusting the leader's emphasis on task behaviors, for instance, giving guidance and direction, and relationship behaviors, for instance, providing socioemotional support, according to the readiness of followers to perform their tasks.

Figure 15.4 shows the essence of this model of situational leadership. The figure identifies four leadership styles: delegating, participating, selling, and telling. Each emphasizes a different combination of task and relationship behaviors by the leader. As you can see, the figure also suggests the following situational matches as the best choice of leadership style for followers at each of four readiness levels.

■ Situational leadership styles

A "telling" style is best for low follower readiness. The direction provided by this style defines roles for people who are unable and unwilling to take responsibility themselves; it eliminates any insecurity about the task that must be done.

A "selling" style is best for low to moderate follower readiness. This style offers both task direction and support for people who are unable but willing to take task responsibility; it involves combining a directive approach with explanation and reinforcement in order to maintain enthusiasm.

A "participating" style is best for moderate to high follower readiness. Able but unwilling followers require supportive behavior in order to increase their motivation; by allowing followers to share in decision making, this style helps enhance the desire to perform a task.

A "delegating" style is best for high readiness. This style provides little in terms of direction and support for the task at hand; it allows able and willing followers to take responsibility for what needs to be done.

This situational leadership approach requires the leader to develop the capability to diagnose the demands of situations and then to choose and implement the appropriate leadership response. The theory gives specific attention to followers and their feelings about the task at hand. It also suggests that an effective leader reassess situations over time, giving special attention to emerging changes in the level of readiness of the people involved in the work.

Evaluation and Application In spite of its history—the theory has been around more than 20 years and has been incorporated into training programs by a large number of firms—the situational leadership approach has only recently begun to receive systematic research attention. That research attention provides very little support.[27]

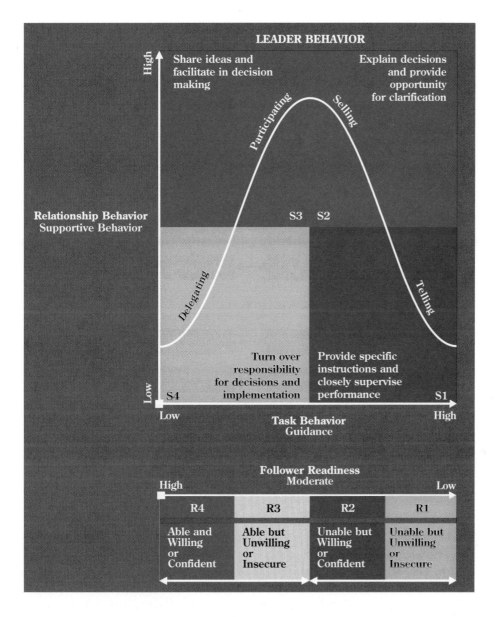

Hersey and Blanchard model of situational leadership. [Source: From Paul Hersey and Kenneth H. Blanchard, *Management of Organizational Behavior* (Prentice-Hall, Englewood Cliffs, N.J., 1988), p. 171. Used by permission.]

The approach does include a very elaborate training program that has been developed to train leaders to diagnose and emphasize appropriate behaviors. Internationally, this program is particularly popular in Europe, where an organization headquartered in Amsterdam provides situational leadership training for leaders in many countries.

▼ SUBSTITUTES FOR LEADERSHIP

In contrast to the previous traditional leadership approaches, the substitutes for leadership theory argue that sometimes hierarchical leadership makes essentially no difference. John Jermier and others contend that there are certain individual, job, and organizational variables that can either serve as substitutes for

■ FIGURE 15.5

Some example leadership
substitutes and neutralizers. [Source: Based on
Steven Kerr and John Jer-
mier, "Substitutes for Leadership: Their Meaning and
Measurement," *Organiza-
tional Behavior and Human
Performance,* Vol. 22
(1978), p. 387; and Fred
Luthans, *Organizational Behavior,* 6th ed. (New York;
McGraw-Hill, 1992), Ch.
10.]

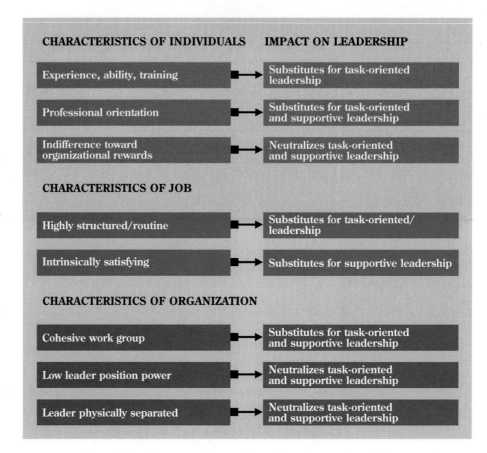

CHARACTERISTICS OF INDIVIDUALS   **IMPACT ON LEADERSHIP**

Experience, ability, training	→	Substitutes for task-oriented leadership
Professional orientation	→	Substitutes for task-oriented and supportive leadership
Indifference toward organizational rewards	→	Neutralizes task-oriented and supportive leadership

CHARACTERISTICS OF JOB

| Highly structured/routine | → | Substitutes for task-oriented/ leadership |
| Intrinsically satisfying | → | Substitutes for supportive leadership |

CHARACTERISTICS OF ORGANIZATION

Cohesive work group	→	Substitutes for task-oriented and supportive leadership
Low leader position power	→	Neutralizes task-oriented and supportive leadership
Leader physically separated	→	Neutralizes task-oriented and supportive leadership

leadership or can neutralize a leader's impact on subordinates.[28] Some examples
of these variables are shown in Figure 15.5.

Substitutes for leadership make a leader's influence both unnecessary and redundant in that they replace a leader's influence. For example, in Figure 15.5, it
will be unnecessary and perhaps not even possible for a leader to provide the
kind of task-oriented direction already available from a very experienced, talented, and well-trained subordinate's background.

In contrast, neutralizers prevent a leader from behaving in a certain way or
nullify the effects of a leader's actions. If a leader has low position or formal authority or is physically separated, for example, his or her leadership may be nullified even though task structuring and supportiveness may still be needed.

Evaluation and Application   There has been some work comparing Mexican
and United States workers, as well as workers in Japan, that suggests both similarities and differences between various substitutes in the countries examined.
More generally, a recent review of 17 studies in the United States as well as other
countries found mixed results for the substitutes theory. Among other things, the
authors argued that the kinds of characteristics and leader behaviors should be
broadened and that the approach appeared to be especially important for high-
performance work teams.[29] Concerning the latter, for example, in place of a hier-

archical leader specifying standards and ways of achieving goals (task-oriented behaviors), the team might set its own standards and substitute those for the leader's.

ATTRIBUTION THEORY AND THE NEW LEADERSHIP ◀

The traditional leadership theories discussed above have all been based on the assumption that leadership and its substantive effects can be identified and measured pretty easily. This is not always the case. Attribution theory addresses this very point—that of individuals trying to understand causes, to assess responsibilities, and to evaluate personal qualities, as all of these are involved with certain events. Attribution theory is particularly important in our understanding of leadership.

For openers, think about a work group or student group that you see as performing really well. Now assume that you are asked to describe the leader on one of the leadership scales discussed earlier in the chapter. If you are like many others, the group's high performance probably encouraged you to describe the leader favorably; in other words, you attributed good things to the leader based on the group's performance. Similarly, leaders themselves make attributions about subordinate performance and react differently depending on those attributions. For example, if leaders attribute an employee's poor performance to lack of effort they may issue a reprimand, whereas if they attribute the poor performance to an external factor, such as work overload, they will probably try to fix the problem. There is currently a great deal of evidence supporting these attributional views of subordinates and leaders.[30]

There is also evidence that people have in their minds a picture of what makes a "good leader" or ways in which "real leaders" would act in a given situation. This view sometimes is called a *leadership prototype,* whereby people have an image in their minds of what a model leader should look like.[31] These implicit theories or prototypes are usually made up of a mix of specific and more general characteristics. For example, a prototype of a bank president would differ in many ways from that of a high-ranking military officer. However, there would probably also be some core characteristics reflecting leaders in our society in general—for example, integrity and self-efficacy. Given the importance of national culture, even these core characteristics are likely to be partly a function of preferences based on differences in cultural values.[32]

The following are some predicted overall preferences for an effective leader prototype as a function of different national culture value clusterings:

- A high degree of directiveness, structuring, even manipulation—preferred in high–power distance cultures, such as those in Arabic, Far Eastern, and Latin clusterings.

HARMON AUTO PARTS

At Harmon Auto Parts, Paul Reeves, a production supervisor, taught workers to take over his job by helping them increase their experience and ability. Each worker spent half days with Reeves and eventually was able to help him perform his duties. These employees now function effectively as a self-managed work team.

■ Cultural leadership preferences

327

- A strong emphasis on participation—preferred in low–power distance societies, such as Norway, Finland, Denmark, and Sweden.
- A strong emphasis on group facilitation—preferred in collectivist societies, such as those in the Near Eastern countries, e.g., Turkey and West Pakistan; and the Far Eastern countries, e.g., Thailand and Singapore.

For example, a prototype in high–power distance Arabic, Far Eastern, and Latin country clusters probably will emphasize a high degree of structuring and even manipulative characteristics. In contrast is the strong group facilitation prototype that is likely to be preferred in collectivist societies such as those in the Near Eastern countries (e.g., Turkey and West Pakistan) and the Far Eastern countries (e.g., Thailand, Singapore).

The closer the behavior of a person in a leadership position is to the implicit theories of his or her followers, the more favorable the leader's relations and key outcomes tend to be.[33] Both of the attributional treatments above emphasize leadership as something largely symbolic or residing in the eye of the beholder. This general notion has also carried over to a related set of research directions. Ironically, the first of these argues that leadership makes little or no real difference in organizational effectiveness. The second tends to attribute greatly exaggerated importance to leadership and ultimately leads us into charisma and other aspects of the new leadership.

▼ LEADERSHIP MAKES NO REAL DIFFERENCE

Jeffrey Pfeffer has looked at what happens when leaders are changed at the top of the organization. Pfeffer is among those contending that even CEOs of large corporations have little leadership impact on profits and effectiveness compared to environmental and industry forces. The recent profit losses of defense contractors in response to cutbacks in the federal defense budget show the impact these forces can have on organizations.

Further, these leaders are typically accountable to so many groups of people for the resources they use that their leadership impact is greatly constrained. Pfeffer argues that in light of such forces and constraints, much of the impact a top leader does have is symbolic; leaders and others develop explanations to legitimize the actions they take.[34]

▼ LEADERSHIP HAS EXAGGERATED IMPORTANCE

This exaggeration or attribution occurs particularly when performance is either extremely high or extremely low or when the situation is such that many people could have been responsible for the performance. James Meindl and his colleagues call this phenomenon the "romance of leadership," whereby people attribute romantic, almost magical, qualities to leadership.[35] A common example is the firing of a baseball manager or football coach whose team doesn't perform well. Neither the owner nor anyone else is really sure why the team didn't do well. But the owner can't fire all the players, so a new team manager is brought in to symbolize "new leadership" that is sure to turn the team around (or so the owner claims).

▼ SUMMARY AND TRANSITION TO THE NEW LEADERSHIP

The focus on leadership attributions and symbolic aspects moves us away from traditional leadership and into the new leadership. The *new leadership* is comprised of approaches emphasizing charismatic, transformational, and visionary aspects that are considered especially important in changing and transforming individuals and organizations.[36]

▼ CHARISMATIC APPROACHES

Robert House and his associates have done a lot of recent work based on extensions of an earlier charismatic theory House developed, not to be confused with House's path–goal theory or its extension, discussed earlier in the chapter.[37] Especially interesting is the fact that House's theory uses both trait and behavior combinations.

House's **charismatic leaders** are those who, by force of their personal abilities, are capable of having a profound and extraordinary effect on followers. Essentially, these leaders are high in need for power and have high feelings of self-efficacy and conviction in the moral rightness of their beliefs. That is, the need for power motivates these people to want to be leaders. This need is then reinforced by their conviction of the moral rightness of their beliefs. The feeling of self-efficacy, in turn, makes these people feel that they are capable of being leaders. These traits then influence such charismatic behaviors as role modeling, image building, articulating goals (focusing on simple and dramatic goals), emphasizing high expectations, showing confidence, and arousing follower motives.

Some of the more interesting and important work based on aspects of House's charismatic theory involves a study of U.S. presidents.[38] The research showed that behavioral charisma was indeed substantially related to presidential performance and that the kind of personality traits in House's theory, along with response to crisis, among other things, predicted behavioral charisma for the sample of presidents.

House and his colleagues also summarize several other studies that support various aspects of the theory. Some of the more interesting related work has shown that negative, or "dark-side," charismatic leaders emphasize personalized power—focus on themselves—while positive, or "bright-side," charismatics emphasize socialized power that tends to empower their followers. This helps explain differences between such dark-side leaders as Adolph Hitler, David Koresh, and Reverend Jim Jones and a bright-side Martin Luther King, Jr.[39]

Jay Conger has developed a four-stage charismatic leadership theory based on his work with Rabindra Kanungo.[40] In the first stage, the leader develops a vision of idealized change that moves beyond the status quo. For example, President Kennedy had a vision of putting a man on the moon by the end of the 1960s. In the second stage, the leader communicates the vision and motivates the followers to go beyond the status quo. In stage three, the leader builds trust by exhibiting qualities such as expertise, success, risk taking, and unconventional actions. Martin Luther King, Jr. displayed several of these qualities. In the final stage, the leader demonstrates ways to achieve the vision by means of empowerment, behavior modeling for followers, and so forth. Conger and Kanungo have

> **Charismatic leaders** are those who, by force of their personal abilities, are capable of having a profound and extraordinary effect on followers.

■ FIGURE 15.6

Descriptions of characteristics of distant and close-up charismatics. [Source: Based on Boas Shamir, "Social Distance and Charisma: Theoretical Notes and an Exploratory Study," *The Leadership Quarterly,* Vol. 6(1995), pp. 19–48.]

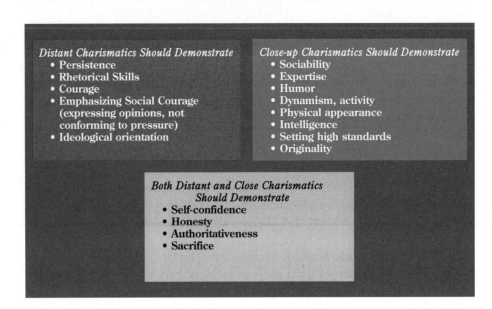

argued that if leaders use behaviors such as vision and articulation, environmental sensitivity, and unconventional behavior, rather than maintaining the status quo, followers will attribute charismatic leadership to them. Such leaders are also seen as behaving quite differently from those labeled "noncharismatic."[41]

Finally, an especially important question about charismatic leadership is whether it is described the same way for close-up or at-a-distance leaders. Boas Shamir recently examined this issue in Israel.[42] He found that descriptions of distant charismatics, for instance former Israeli prime minister Golda Meir, and close-up charismatics, for instance a specific teacher, were generally more different than they were similar. Figure 15.6 shows high points of his findings. It seems clear that leaders with whom followers have close contact and those with whom they seldom, if ever, have direct contact are both described as charismatic but possess quite different traits and behaviors.

▼ TRANSFORMATIONAL AND TRANSACTIONAL APPROACHES

Building on notions originated by James MacGregor Burns, as well as ideas from House's work, Bernard Bass has developed an approach that focuses on both transformational and transactional leadership.[43]

Transactional leadership involves daily exchanges between leaders and subordinates and is necessary for achieving routine performance that is agreed upon between leaders and subordinates. These exchanges involve four dimensions. *Contingent rewards* provide various kinds of rewards in exchange for mutually agreed upon goal accomplishment—your boss pays you a $500 bonus if you complete an acceptable article by a certain date. *Active management by exception* involves watching for deviations from rules and standards and taking corrective action—your boss notices that you have an increasing number of defects in your work and helps you adjust your machine to correct them. *Passive management by exception* involves in-

In **transactional leadership** the leader exerts influence during daily leader-subordinate exchanges without much emotion.

tervening only if standards are not met—your boss comes to see you after noticing your high percentage of rejects in the weekly production report. *Laissez-faire* involves abdicating responsibilities and avoiding decisions—your boss is seldom around and does not follow through on decisions that need action.

Transformational leadership goes beyond this routine accomplishment, however. For Bass, **transformational leadership** occurs when leaders broaden and elevate the interests of their followers, when they generate awareness and acceptance of the purposes and mission of the group, and when they stir their followers to look beyond their own self-interests for the good of others.

Transformational leadership has four dimensions: charisma, inspiration, intellectual stimulation, and individualized consideration. *Charisma* provides vision and a sense of mission and instills pride, along with follower respect and trust; for example, Steve Jobs, former head of Apple Computer, showed charisma by emphasizing the importance of creating the Macintosh as a radical new computer. *Inspiration* communicates high expectations, uses symbols to focus efforts, and expresses important purposes in simple ways; for example, in the movie *Patton,* George C. Scott stood on a stage in front of his troops with a wall-sized American flag in the background and pearl-handled revolvers in holsters at his side. *Intellectual stimulation* promotes intelligence, rationality, and careful problem solving; for example, your boss encourages you to look at a very difficult problem in a new way. *Individualized consideration* provides personal attention, treats each employee individually, and coaches and advises; for example, your boss drops by and makes remarks reinforcing your worth as a person.

Bass concludes that transformational leadership is likely to be strongest at the top-management level, where there is the greatest opportunity for proposing and communicating a vision. It is by no means *restricted* to the top level, however; it is found throughout the organization. Furthermore, transformational leadership operates *in combination with* transactional leadership. Transactional leadership is similar to most of the traditional leadership approaches mentioned earlier, and leaders need both transformational and transactional leadership in order to be successful, just as they need both leadership and management.

> In **transformational leadership** the followers' goals are broadened and elevated and confidence is gained to go beyond expectations.

 Jan Carlzon, CEO of Scandinavian Airline Systems (SAS), visualizes SAS as being one of the handful of international airlines successfully operating in the 1990s. Carlzon stresses originality, a strong focus on employees and passengers, and the ability to adopt a long-term perspective. He has communicated this vision in many ways, not the least of which is a cartoon book showing how employees contribute to achieving the vision and how they can profit from it.[44]

GLOBAL

Evaluation and Application   A recent book by Bryman summarizes a large number of studies using Bass's approach, ranging from six studies on the extra effort of followers, to 16 studies on performance or effectiveness, to nearly a dozen covering various aspects of satisfaction. Still other studies cover such outcomes as burnout and stress and the predisposition to act as innovation champions. The strongest relationships tend to be associated with charisma or inspirational leadership, although, in most cases, the other dimensions are also important. These findings are consistent with those reported elsewhere.[45] They are indeed impressive and broaden leadership outcomes beyond those cited in traditional leadership studies.

▼ THE NEW LEADERSHIP REVISITED

In addition to contrasting the core themes of traditional and new leadership, it is important to examine a number of issues concerning the role of new leadership in the workplace.

First, *can people be trained in new leadership?* Research in this area argues that training in new leadership *is* possible. Bass and his colleagues have put a lot of work into such training efforts. For example, they have created one workshop that lasts from 3 to 5 days, with later followup. Initially, leaders are given feedback on their scores on Bass's measures. The leaders then devise improvement programs to strengthen their weaknesses and work with the trainers in a variety of ways to develop their leadership skills. Bass and Avolio report findings that demonstrate beneficial effects from this training. They also report team training and programs tailored to individual firms' needs.[46] Similarly, Conger and Kanungo propose training to develop the kinds of behaviors summarized in their model.[47]

A couple of approaches with a special emphasis on vision emphasize training. Kouzas and Posner report results of a week-long training program they helped design at AT&T. The program involved training of leaders on five dimensions oriented around developing, communicating, and reinforcing a shared vision. According to Kouzas and Posner, leaders showed an average 15 percent increase in these visionary behaviors 10 months after participating in the program.[48] Similarly, Sashkin has developed a leadership approach that emphasizes various aspects of vision and organizational culture change. Sashkin discusses a number of ways to go about training leaders to be more visionary and to enhance the culture change.[49] All of the new leadership training programs involve a heavy hands-on workshop emphasis so that leaders do more than just read about vision.

Second, it is important to note that *new leadership is not always good.* As we pointed out earlier, dark-side charismatics, such as Adolph Hitler, can have very negative effects on the population of followers. Similarly, *new leadership is not always needed.* Sometimes emphasis on a vision diverts energy from more important day-to-day activities. It is also important to note that *new leadership by itself is not sufficient.* New leadership needs to be used in conjunction with traditional leadership. Finally, new leadership is not important only at the top. Although generally considered most important at the top levels, a number of experts argue that new leadership applies at all organizational levels.

Take-A-Note 15.1

FIVE CHARISMATIC SKILLS

- *Sensitivity to most appropriate contexts for charisma— Emphasis on critical evaluation and problem detection*
- *Visioning—Emphasis on creative thinking to learn and think about profound change*
- *Communication—Working with oral and written linguistic aspects*
- *Impression management—Emphasis on modeling, appearance, body language, and verbal skills*
- *Empowering—Emphasis on communicating high-performance expectations, improving participation in decision making, loosening up bureaucratic constraints, setting meaningful goals, and establishing appropriate reward systems*

MULTIPLE-LEVEL LEADERSHIP AND LEADERSHIP OF HIGH-PERFORMANCE TEAMS

T he new leadership suggests a special emphasis on top-level leadership with a visionary emphasis. This focus is broadened by first looking at *multiple-level leadership,* an approach that considers differences in leadership from the top to the bottom of the organization.[50] We then examine the *group-oriented leadership* involved in high-performance teams.

▼ MULTIPLE-LEVEL LEADERSHIP

The multiple-level perspective argues that there are three different organizational domains, each comprising no more than two managerial levels: (1) the production domain, at the bottom levels of the organization; (2) the *organization domain,* at the middle levels; and (3) the *systems domain,* at the top. Each domain and level gets more complex than those beneath it in terms of its leadership and managerial requirements. But even the largest and most complicated organizations can be designed to require no more than seven levels, from the lowest level—the employees—to the highest level—the manager.

One way of expressing the increasing complexity is in terms of how long it takes to see the results of the key decisions required at a given level. These range from 3 months or so, at the lowest managerial level, to 20 years or more, at the top.

Since the requirements become increasingly complex, it is expected that managers at each succeeding level must have increasing cognitive and behavioral complexity to deal with the increasing hierarchical complexity. One way of measuring the manager's cognitive complexity is in terms of how far into the future he or she can develop a vision. Notice that this measure is a trait, similar in some ways to intelligence but different in others. Accompanying such vision should be increasing sophistication across a wide range of traditional and new leader behaviors. Thus, successful higher level leaders are expected to both think and act more complexly as they move up the organization.

This approach is relatively new and is notable for emphasizing the impact of the leadership of those at the top as it cascades deep within the organization and for its emphasis on both leadership "in organizations" in the bottom two domains and leadership "of organizations" in the top domain. Recent work has applied the multiple-level leadership approach to help explain the sharp decline in General Motor's market share and performance during CEO Roger Smith's decade-long tenure (1981–1990). Smith's lack of success with his 21st century, ultra-high-tech vision for GM was interpreted primarily in terms of his and others' lack of behavioral complexity.[51]

▼ LEADING HIGH-PERFORMANCE TEAMS

Earlier in this chapter, we argued that substitutes for hierarchical leadership coming from the work team are likely to become more and more important in high-performance teams. Here, we look at leadership of these teams from a different angle: What are the kinds of leadership needed for team coordinators? Figure 15.7 offers a sample of behaviors from 21 of those reported by Manz and Sims.[52]

The key is not so much the behavior descriptions themselves as the *team focus* of the behaviors. The behaviors are clearly oriented toward the coordinators influencing the team members to lead or manage themselves. Like team substitutes for hierarchical leadership, such behaviors are becoming increasingly important in high-performance work teams. Notice that even though they are empowering, these behaviors do not appear to be very charismatic; they should work best when reinforced by new leadership from bright-side leaders higher up in the organization.

QUALITY

Employees in General Electric's plant in Bromont, Quebec, where compressor vanes for jet engines are built, are involved in high-performance work

teams. Every effort is made to downplay hierarchical relationships, including elimination of such traditional job titles as "foreman." Some of the leadership issues handled by the team members are decision making, dispute resolution, and getting each individual team member to take on increased responsibilities. Organizing work around these teams has made it possible to increase productivity by over 300 percent since the early 1980s.[53]

VARIABLE NAME	VARIABLE DESCRIPTION
Encourages self-reinforcement	Leader encourages work group to be self-reinforcing of high group performance.
Encourages self-criticism	Leader encourages work group to be self-critical of low group performance.
Encourages self-observation/evaluation	Leader encourages work group to monitor, be aware of, and evaluate level of performance.
Encourages rehearsal	Leader encourages work group to go over an activity and "think it through" before actually performing the activity.
Facilitates equipment supplies	Leader facilitates obtaining equipment and supplies for the work group.
Communicates between groups	Leader communicates group views to and from other groups.
Truthfulness	Leader communicates in a way that is truthful and believable to group members.

■ FIGURE 15.7

Sample leader behaviors for high-performance work teams.

CHAPTER 15 STUDY GUIDE

SUMMARY

What is leadership, and how does it differ from management?

- Leadership is a special case of interpersonal influence that gets an individual or group to do what the leader wants done.
- Leadership and management differ in that management is designed to promote stability or to make the organization run smoothly, whereas the role of leadership is to promote adaptive change.

What are trait theories of leadership?

- Trait, or great man, approaches argue that leader traits have a major impact on outcomes.
- The traits are considered relatively innate and hard to change.
- Traits are often used in conjunction with leader behaviors in situational contingency or even "new leadership" approaches, both summarized below.
- They are especially suitable for leader selection.

What are behavioral theories of leadership?

- Similar to trait approaches, behavioral theories argue that leader behaviors have a major impact on outcomes.
- The Michigan, the Ohio State, and Graen's Leader–Member Exchange approaches are well-known behavioral theories.
- Behavioral theories are especially suitable for leadership training.

What are situational contingency theories of leadership?

- Leader situational contingency approaches argue that leadership, in combination with various situational contingency variables, can have a major impact on outcomes.
- Fiedler's contingency theory, House's path–goal theory, and Hersey and Blanchard's situational leadership theory are major situational contingency approaches.
- Sometimes, as in the case of the substitutes for leadership approach, the role of the situational contingencies replaces that of leadership so that leadership has little or no impact in itself.

How does attribution theory relate to the new leadership?

- Attribution theory overlaps traditional trait, behavioral, and situational contingency approaches by emphasizing the importance of the symbolic aspects of leadership.
- Such symbolic aspects are a key part of the new leadership: charismatic, visionary, transformational, and related perspectives, according to which followers tend to attribute extraordinary leadership abilities to a leader when they observe certain behaviors.
- These attributions then help transform followers to achieve goals that transcend their own self-interests and help transform the organization.

- Among the better known new leadership perspectives are Bass's transformational theory and House's and Conger and Kanungo's charismatic approaches.
- Transformational approaches are broader than charismatic ones and sometimes include charisma as one of their dimensions.
- The new leadership, in general, is important because it goes beyond traditional leadership in facilitating change in the increasingly fast-moving workplace.

What is multiple-level leadership, and how does leadership apply to high-performance work teams?

- Multiple-level leadership emphasizes differences in leadership requirements from the top to the bottom of the organization.
- This leadership is divided into domains and levels with assumed increasingly complex leadership requirements at each higher level and domain.
- Leaders are expected to demonstrate more cognitive and behavioral complexity to deal with the more complex requirements.
- Leadership in high-performing teams changes the leadership role by making it a facilitative one to encourage team members to lead themselves.
- Behaviors of team coordinators are assumed to work best when reinforced by leaders who provide empowerment and stress various aspects of the new leadership.

KEY TERMS

Charismatic leaders
   (p. 329)
Leadership (p. 315)
Least preferred coworker
   (LPC) scale (p. 319)

Situational control (p. 319)
Transactional leadership
   (p. 330)
Transformational leadership (p. 331)

SELF-TEST 15

▼ MULTIPLE CHOICE

1. "Leadership is central, and other variables are less important," best describes ____ theories. (a) trait and behavioral (b) attribution (c) situational contingency (d) substitutes for leadership
2. Leader trait and behavioral approaches assume that traits and behaviors are ____. (a) equally important with other variables (b) more important than other variables (c) caused by other variables (d) symbolic of leadership
3. In comparing leadership and management, ____. (a) leadership promotes stability, management promotes change (b) leadership promotes change, management promotes stability (c) leaders are born but managers are developed (d) the two are pretty much the same
4. The earliest theory of leadership stated that individuals become leaders by ____. (a) the behavior of those they lead (b) the traits they possess (c) the particular situation in which they find themselves (d) being very tall
5. In Fiedler's contingency theory, the three situational control variables are leader–member relations, task structure, and ____. (a) command power (b) position power (c) discretionary power (d) complexity
6. Which leadership theory argues that a leader's key function is to act in ways that complement the work setting? (a) trait (b) behavioral (c) path–goal (d) multiple influence

7. A leadership prototype ____. (a) is useful primarily for selection and training (b) uses LPC as an important component (c) depicts the image of a model leader (d) emphasizes leadership skills

8. Conger and Kanungo's model emphasizes all of the following *except* ____. (a) active management by exception (b) development of a vision of an idealized change (c) trust building (d) communication of vision or motivation

9. In multiple-level leadership ____. (a) leadership becomes simpler as one moves higher in the organization (b) each domain and level gets more complex than those beneath (c) teams are used at the top and individual efforts at the bottom (d) leaders need to be more cognitively complex and less behaviorally complex at each higher level and domain

10. Leadership of high-performance teams ____. (a) emphasizes charisma (b) emphasizes team-member empowerment (c) emphasizes leader traits (d) has been replaced by technology

▼ TRUE–FALSE

11. The earliest studies of leadership tended to focus on leader behaviors.   T   F
12. Leadership and management usually are considered the same.   T   F
13. The University of Michigan studies concluded that employee-centered leaders tended to have more productive work groups.   T   F
14. Hersey and Blanchard's situational leadership theory focuses on the maturity or readiness of the followers.   T   F
15. Neutralizers prevent a leader from behaving in a certain way or nullify the effects of a leader's actions.   T   F
16. In the romance of leadership, it is argued that leaders have little impact on profits and effectiveness.   T   F
17. Transformational leadership acts in combination with transactional leadership.   T   F
18. Charismatic and transformational leadership are part of the "new leadership."   T   F
19. Multiple-level leadership is replacing the new leadership.   T   F
20. Leadership of high-performing teams emphasizes charisma in the team.   T   F

▼ SHORT RESPONSE

21. Define leadership and contrast it with management.
22. Discuss the role of leader trait and behavior approaches in leadership.
23. Discuss the role of situational contingency approaches in leadership.
24. Compare and contrast traditional leadership and the new leadership.

▼ APPLICATION ESSAY

25. You have just been called in as a consultant to analyze the role of leadership in the virtual corporation in the chapter opener and suggest ways to develop it further. Making any necessary assumptions, discuss how you would handle this assignment.

16

COMMUNICATION

At his Laguna Hills, California, repair shop Mechanical Mann, owner Duane Delp says: "It's the little things that hurt a business." How do you deal successfully with the little things? Delp puts it this way: "I'll sit and work with the technician as he works and we bounce ideas off one another." Rather than try to handle everything himself, Delp isn't afraid to ask for help from those who know best—the ones doing the work. "I do a lot of management by wandering around," he says. New employees are asked to carry notepads and write down things that concern them or things that they believe might be changed. Getting good suggestions depends on a sense of trust and willingness to listen and respond. Delp has changed lighting in work bays, parking lot designations, equipment locations, and washroom facilities. Management consultant Thomas Timmons says: "If you judge ideas too quickly," he says, "people will stop giving ideas." He encourages business owners to ask their employees two questions: "What three ideas do you have for increasing income, and what three ideas do you have for decreasing costs?" Then he encourages them to act. Duane Delp knows from experience that you can't implement every idea that is suggested, but he tries to acknowledge all of them and follow up. Everyone deserves to know that his or her ideas have at least been heard.[1]

Everyone knows that "communication" is vital to an organization. But not everyone is able to create the type of information-rich environment that has just been described at Mechanical Mann. This achievement requires an extraordinary commitment to open up communication linkages and opportunities among people in organizations, and between them and their customers.[2] It also requires a culture of trust that encourages a free flow of ideas and suggestions. The payoffs are found in both organizational performance and worker satisfaction. Duane Delp's experience in his small California business is a good example of how important communication skills and systems can be as foundations for success in a competitive environment.

Chapter 16 examines the process of communication, with special attention to both interpersonal and organizational challenges. As you read this chapter, keep in mind these questions:

- What is the communication process?
- What makes effective communication?
- What barriers interfere with effective communication?
- What is organizational communication?

THE COMMUNICATION PROCESS

Communication is a word like "organization." Everyone ostensibly knows what it means until asked to state its formal definition. It is useful to think of **communication** as a process of sending and receiving messages with attached meanings.[3] Communication in a wide variety of forms is essential to organizations, but new technologies have brought a dramatic increase in attention to the role of electronic communication in particular.

Communication is the process of sending and receiving symbols with attached meanings.

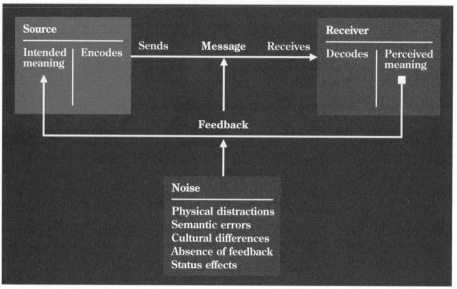

■   FIGURE 16.1

The communication process and possible sources of "noise."

> **Noise** is anything that interferes with the effectiveness of communication.

The key elements in the communication process are illustrated in Figure 16.1. They include a *source,* who *encodes* an *intended meaning* into a *message,* and a *receiver,* who *decodes* the message into a *perceived meaning.* The receiver may or may not give feedback to the source. Although this process may appear to be very elementary, it is not quite as simple as it looks. **Noise** is the term used to describe any disturbance within the communication process that disrupts it and interferes with the transference of messages.

▼ THE INTENDED COMMUNICATION

The information source is a person or group trying to communicate with someone else. The reasons for the source to communicate include changing the attitudes, knowledge, or behavior of the receiver. A team leader, for example, may want to communicate with a division manager to explain why the team needs more time or resources to finish an assigned project.

The next step in communication is *encoding*—the process of translating an idea or thought into meaningful symbols. The resulting message may consist of verbal, written, and/or nonverbal symbols (such as gestures), or some combination of them. This message is then transmitted through various possible **channels**, or delivery mediums. The possible channels include face-to-face meetings, electronic mail, written letters or memorandums, among others. Importantly, the choice of channel can have an important impact on the communication process. Some people are better at using certain channels over others, and some messages are better handled by specific channels. In the earlier case of the team

> **Channels** are the pathways through which messages are communicated.

leader communicating with the division manager, for example, it may make a difference whether the message is sent face to face, in a written memo, or by e-mail.

▼ THE RECEIVED COMMUNICATION

The communication process is not completed just because a message is sent. The receiver is the individual or group of individuals to whom a message is directed. In order for meaning to be assigned to any received message its contents must be interpreted through *decoding*. This process of translation is complicated by many factors, including the knowledge and experience of the receiver and his or her relationship with the sender. A message may also be interpreted with the added influence of other points of view, such as those offered by friends, coworkers, or organizational superiors. Ultimately, the decoding may result in the receiver interpreting a message in a way that is different from that originally intended by the source.

▼ FEEDBACK

Most receivers are well aware of the potential gap between the intended message of the source and the perceived meaning assigned to it by the recipient. One way in which these gaps are identified is through **feedback**, the process through which the receiver communicates with the sender by returning back another message. The exchange of information through feedback can be very helpful in improving the communication process, and the popular advice to always "keep the feedback channels open" is good to remember.

> **Feedback** is the process of communicating how one feels about something another person has done or said.

In practice, the giving of "feedback" is often associated with one person communicating an evaluation of what another person has said or done. There is an art to giving this special type of feedback so that it is accepted and used constructively by the receiver. The first requirement in giving feedback is to recognize when it is intended truly to benefit the receiver and when it is purely an attempt to satisfy a personal need of the sender. A manager who berates a secretary for errors in a computer data base, for example, may actually be mad about personally failing to give clear instructions in the first place.

Giving criticism is certainly one of the most difficult of all communication situations faced by managers. What is intended to be polite and constructive can easily end up being unpleasant and even hostile. This risk is particularly evident in the performance appraisal process discussed in Chapter 6. A manager or group leader must be able to do more than just complete an appraisal form and document another person's performance for the record. To serve the person's developmental needs, feedback regarding the results of the appraisal—both the praises and the criticism—must be well communicated.[4]

Take-A-Note 16.1

HOW TO GIVE CONSTRUCTIVE FEEDBACK

- Give directly and in a spirit of mutual trust.
- Be specific rather than general; use good clear examples.
- Give at a time when the receiver is most ready to accept it.
- Be accurate; check with others to ensure validity.
- Focus on things the receiver can do something about.
- Limit it to what the receiver can handle at the time.

341

EFFECTIVE COMMUNICATION

Effective communication results when the intended meaning and perceived meaning are virtually the same.

Effective communication occurs when the intended meaning of the source and the perceived meaning of the receiver are virtually the same.[5] Although this should be the goal in any communication, it is not always achieved. Even now, we worry whether or not you are interpreting these written words exactly as we intend. Our confidence would be higher if we were face to face in class together and you could ask clarifying questions. Opportunities to offer feedback and ask questions are important ways of increasing the effectiveness of communication.

Efficient communication is low cost in its use of resources.

Efficient communication occurs at minimum cost in terms of resources expended. Time, for example, is an important resource to all of us and it often plays a role in how we communicate with others. Picture your instructor taking the time to communicate individually with each student in your class about the course subject matter. It would be virtually impossible to do so. And, even if it were possible, it would be very costly in terms of time. People at work often choose not to visit one another personally to communicate messages. Instead, they rely on the efficiency of written memos, posted bulletins, group meetings, e-mail, voice-mail, or video conferences.

As efficient as these latter forms of communication may be, however, they are not always effective. A change in policy posted by efficient e-mail may save time for the sender, but it may not achieve the desired results in terms of the receivers' interpretations and responses. Similarly, an effective communication may not be efficient. For a business manager to visit each employee and explain a new change in procedures may guarantee that everyone truly understands the change, but it may also be prohibitively expensive in terms of the required time expenditure.

QUALITY

Springfield ReManufacturing Corporation is a benchmark for others trying to improve their internal communication systems. On any given day, one may find a group of outsiders wandering around this Missouri-based company to

learn about "open book management." Touted by CEO Jack Stack as a key for any business, this involves training employees to understand financial data and then regularly sharing it with them. Given the numbers and their implications, Stack finds people work better and with greater satisfaction. Of course, Stack makes sure the rewards match the performance, once passing out 400 leather bags to plant workers who logged 1.5 million person hours without a costly accident.[6]

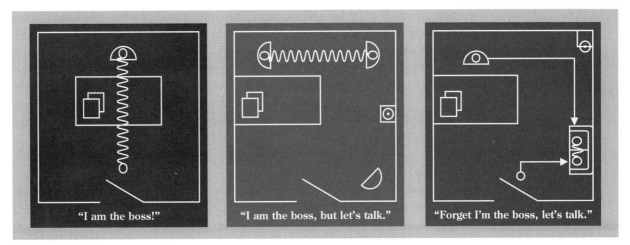

"I am the boss!"   "I am the boss, but let's talk."   "Forget I'm the boss, let's talk."

■ FIGURE 16.2

Furniture placement and nonverbal communication in the office.

▼ NONVERBAL COMMUNICATION

Nonverbal communication takes place through facial expressions, body position, eye contact, and other physical gestures rather than as written or oral expression. *Kinesics,* or the study of gestures and body postures, has achieved a rightful place in communication theory and research.[7] The nonverbal side to communication can often hold the key to what someone is really thinking or meaning. It can also affect the impressions we make on others. Interviewers, for example, tend to respond more favorably to job candidates whose nonverbal cues, such as eye contact and erect posture, are positive than to those displaying negative nonverbal cues, such as looking down or slouching. The art of impression management in these and other situations requires careful attention to one's nonverbal as well as verbal communication skills.

Nonverbal communication can also take place through the physical arrangement of space, such as that found in various office layouts. *Proxemics,* the study of the way space is utilized, is important to communication.[8] Figure 16.2 shows three different office arrangements and the messages they may communicate to visitors. Check the diagrams against the furniture arrangement in your office or that of your instructor or a person with whom you are familiar. What are you/they saying to visitors by the choice of furniture placement?[9]

> **Nonverbal communication** occurs by facial expressions, body motions, eye contact, and other physical gestures.

▼ ACTIVE LISTENING

The ability to listen well is a distinct asset to anyone whose job involves a large proportion of time spent "communicating" with other people. After all, there are always two sides to the communication process: (1) sending a message, or "telling," and (2) receiving a message, or "listening." There is legitimate concern that too many people may emphasize the former and neglect the latter, however, especially in their working relationships.[10] Everyone in the new workplace should develop good skills in **active listening**—the ability to help the source of a mes-

> **Active listening** by encouraging and paraphrasing helps people say what they really mean.

sage say what he or she really means. The concept comes from the work of counselors and therapists, who are trained to help people express themselves and talk about things that are important to them.[11]

Take a moment to more thoroughly consider the guidelines for active listening. One of the conversations below involves active listening on the part of the branch manager; the other does not. Read both of these examples—ideally speaking the words out loud, and think through how you would feel as the group leader in the case.

Example 1

Group leader: Hey, Al, I don't get this production order. We can't handle this run today. What do they think we are?

Branch manager: But that's the order. So get it out as soon as you can. We're under terrific pressure this week.

Group Leader: Don't they know we're behind schedule already because of that press breakdown?

Branch manager: Look, Kelly, I don't decide what goes on upstairs. I just have to see that the work gets out, and that's what I'm gonna do.

Group leader: The group isn't gonna like this.

Branch manager: That's something you'll have to work out with them, not me.

Example 2

Group leader: Hey, Ross, I don't get this production order. We can't handle this run today. What do they think we are?

Branch manager: Sounds like you're pretty sore about it, Kelly.

Group leader: I sure am. We were just about getting back to schedule after that press breakdown. Now this comes along.

Branch manager: As if you didn't have enough work to do, huh?

Group leader: Yeah, I don't know how I'm gonna tell the group about this.

Branch manager: Hate to face 'em with it now, is that it?

Group leader: I really do. They're under a real strain today. Seems like everything we do around here is rush, rush, rush.

Branch manager: I guess you feel like it's unfair to load anything more on them.

Group leader: Well, yeah, I know there must be plenty of pressure on everybody up the line, but—well, if that's the way it is . . . guess I'd better get the word to 'em.

The branch manager in Example 2 possesses active listening skills. He responded to the group leader's communication in a way that increased the flow of information. The manager ended up receiving important information about the work situation and should be able to use this information for constructive re-

---

Take-A-Note 16.2

GUIDELINES FOR ACTIVE LISTENING

1. *Listen for content—try to hear exactly what is being said.*

2. *Listen for feelings—try to identify how the source feels about things.*

3. *Respond to feelings—let the source know that his or her feelings are recognized.*

4. *Note all cues—be sensitive to both verbal and nonverbal expressions.*

5. *Reflect back—repeat in your own words what you think you are hearing.*

sults. The group leader also felt better after having been able to really say what she thought, and after being heard!

▼ COMMUNICATION CHANNELS

As noted earlier, a communication channel is the medium through which messages are sent and received, e.g., face-to-face or through e-mail. Research in the area of *channel richness,* the capacity of a channel to convey information effectively, lends insight into how various channel alternatives may be used depending on the type of message to be conveyed.[12] In general, the richest channels are face to face. Next are telephone, e-mail, written memos and letters. The leanest channels are posted notices and bulletins. When messages get more complex and open ended, richer channels are necessary to achieve effective communication; leaner channels work well for more routine and straightforward messages, such as announcing the location of a previously scheduled meeting.

Another issue relates to the use of formal versus informal channels of communication. **Formal channels** follow the chain of command established by an organization's hierarchy of authority. For example, an organization chart indicates the proper routing for official messages passing from one level or part of the hierarchy to another. Because formal channels are recognized as authoritative, it is typical for communication of policies, procedures, and other official announcements to adhere to them.

Although necessary and important, the use of formal channels constitutes only one part of a person's communication responsibilities in the workplace. In Chapter 1, we identified interpersonal "networking" as an essential activity for effective managers.[13] In the present context, such networks represent the use of the formal channels just described plus a wide variety of **informal channels** that do not adhere to the organization's hierarchy of authority. These informal channels coexist with the formal channels but frequently diverge from them by skipping levels in the hierarchy and/or cutting across vertical chains of command. The importance of informal channels for communication in organizations is highlighted in the book *In Search of Excellence.* Its authors, Thomas J. Peters and Robert H. Waterman, Jr., report that "excellent companies are a vast network of informal, open communications. The patterns and intensity cultivate the right people's getting into contact with each other."[14] Peters and Waterman offer the examples of Levi Strauss, where management calls its open-door policy the "fifth freedom," and Corning Glass, where management installed escalators instead of elevators in a new engineering building to increase opportunities for face-to-face contact.

One familiar informal channel is the **grapevine**—the network of friendships and acquaintances through which rumors and other unofficial information are passed from person to person. Grapevines have the advantage of being able to transmit information quickly and efficiently. Every experienced worker realizes that a message well placed in a grapevine can often travel faster and with greater impact than can the same message passed through formal channels. Grapevines also help fulfill the needs of people involved in them. Being part of a grapevine can provide a sense of security from "being in the know" when important things

Formal communication channels follow the official chain of command.

Informal communication channels do not follow the chain of command.

A **grapevine** transfers information through networks of friendships and acquaintances.

are going on. It also provides social satisfaction as information is exchanged interpersonally. The primary disadvantage of grapevines occurs when they transmit incorrect or untimely information. Rumors can be very dysfunctional, both to people and to organizations. Astute managers get to know the grapevines operating in their work settings and try to use them to good advantage. After all, one of the best ways to avoid incorrect rumors is to make sure that key persons in a grapevine get the right information to begin with.

COMMUNICATION BARRIERS

To improve communications, it is important to understand the six sources of noise common to most interpersonal exchanges: physical distractions, semantic problems, cultural differences, mixed messages, absence of feedback, and status effects. Each of these sources of noise should be recognized and controlled to create more effective communication. They are shown in Figure 16.1 as potential threats to the communication process.

▼ PHYSICAL DISTRACTIONS

Any number of physical distractions can interfere with the effectiveness of a communication attempt. Some of these distractions are evident in the following conversation between an employee, George, and his manager.[15]

> Okay, George, let's hear your problem (phone rings, boss picks it up, promises to deliver the report, "just as soon as I can get it done"). Uh, now, where were we—oh, you're having a problem with your secretary. She's (the manager's secretary brings in some papers that need immediate signatures; he scribbles his name where she indicates; secretary leaves) . . . you say she's depressed a lot lately, wants to leave . . . ? I tell you what, George, why don't you (phone rings again, lunch partner drops by) . . . uh, take a stab at handling it yourself. I've got to go now.

Besides what may have been poor intentions in the first place, George's manager allowed physical distractions to create information overload. He was letting too many requests for information processing occur at once. As a result, the communication with George suffered. The mistake of processing too much information at once can be eliminated by setting priorities and planning. If George has something to say, his manager should set aside adequate time for the meeting. In addition, interruptions such as telephone calls, secretarial requests, and drop-in visitors should be prevented. At a minimum, George's manager could start by closing the door to the office and instructing his secretary not to disturb them.

▼ SEMANTIC PROBLEMS

Semantic barriers to communication occur in the form of encoding and decoding errors and mixed messages. Simply put, they involve a poor choice and/or use of words. We generally do not realize how easily semantic errors occur. In fact, they abound. The following illustrations of the "bafflegab" that once tried to pass as actual "executive communication" are a case in point.[16]

A. "We solicit any recommendations that you wish to make, and you may be assured that any such recommendations will be given our careful consideration."

B. "Consumer elements are continuing to stress the fundamental necessity of a stabilization of the price structure at a lower level than exists at the present time."

One has to wonder why the prior messages weren't more simply stated: (A) "Send us your recommendations. They will be carefully considered," and (B) "Consumers want lower prices."

Another semantic problem occurs as **mixed messages**, the situation where a person's words communicate one thing while actions or "body language" communicate another. It is important to spot mixed messages since the nonverbals can often add important insight into what is really being said in face-to-face communication.[17] For instance, someone may voice a cautious "Yes" during a business meeting at the same time that her facial expression shows stress and she begins to lean back in her chair. The body language in this case may suggest the existence of important reservations even though the words indicate agreement. Such sensitivity may be particularly important when communicating across cultures. In some Asian cultures people are hesitant to respond negatively to ideas or requests of foreign visitors. Although they may reluctantly agree with a visitor's point, the aware observer may well spot discomfort in the nonverbal signals. In response, she or he may politely withdraw the request or shift to a more agreeable subject of discussion.

> **Mixed messages** occur when words say one thing while nonverbal cues communicate another.

▼ CULTURAL DIFFERENCES

Clearly, people must always exercise caution when involved in cross-cultural communication. This includes communication between persons of different geographical or ethnic groupings within one country, as well as between persons of different national cultures. A common problem is *ethnocentrism*—the tendency to consider one's culture and its values superior to others. Very often, such tendencies are accompanied by an unwillingness to try to understand alternative points of view and to take the values they represent seriously. This can be highly disadvantageous when trying to conduct business and maintain effective working relationships with people of diverse backgrounds.

The difficulties with cross-cultural communication are perhaps most obvious when it comes to language differences among people. A convenient illustration is the case of advertising messages that work well in one country but encounter difficulty when translated into the language of another. Consider these international business mistakes. Two often-cited examples from the advertising world are the Coca-Cola Company, whose ad "Coke Adds Life" was confusing to some Asians who translated the message to mean "Coke Brings You Back From the Dead," and General Motors, whose "Nova" model name translated literally into Spanish as "Chevrolet no go."

The same issues hold in respect to nonverbal communication. Gestures, in particular, may be used quite differently in the various cultures of the world. Consider these examples of how practices common to Anglo cultures may run into difficulty elsewhere: whereas crossed legs in the United Kingdom are quite acceptable, they are rude in Saudia Arabia if the sole of the foot is directed toward someone; pointing at someone to get the person's attention may be acceptable in Canada, but in Asia it would be considered inappropriate; a joined thumb and index finger (making an "o") means "okay" in the United States, but it carries an obscene intent in Latin America.[18]

▼ ABSENCE OF FEEDBACK

One-way communication is sender to receiver, as in the case of a written memo or a voice-mail message. There is no direct and immediate feedback from the recipient. Two-way communication, by contrast, is sender to receiver and back to sender. It is characterized by the normal interactive conversations in our daily experiences. Research indicates that two-way communication is more accurate and effective than is one-way communication, even though it is also more costly and time consuming. Because of their efficiency, however, one-way forms of communication—memos, letters, e-mail, voice-mail, and the like—are frequently used in work settings. Because they do not allow immediate feedback one-way messages can be comfortable to the sender but very frustrating for the receiver, who may be left unsure of just what the sender means or wants done.

▼ STATUS EFFECTS

Status differentials in organizations create special communication barriers between persons of higher and lower ranks. On the one hand, given the authority of their positions, managers may be inclined to do a lot of "telling" but not much "listening." On the other hand, communication is frequently biased when flowing upward in organizational hierarchies.[19] Subordinates may *filter* information; that is, they tell their superiors only what they think the boss wants to hear. Whether the reason is a fear of retribution for bringing bad news, an unwillingness to identify personal mistakes, or just a general desire to please, the result is the same: The higher level decision maker may end up taking the wrong actions because of biased and inaccurate information supplied from below.

To avoid such problems, managers and group leaders must develop trust in their working relationships with subordinates and team members, and take advantage of all opportunities for face-to-face communications. *Management by wandering around*, or MBWA for short, is now popularly acclaimed as one way to achieve this.[20] It simply means getting out of the office and talking to people regularly as they do their jobs. Managers who spend time walking around can greatly reduce the perceived "distance" between themselves and their subordinates. MBWA can also reduce tendencies toward selective perception by reducing the gap between what individuals want to hear and see and what is actually occurring. It further helps to create an atmosphere of open and free-flowing communication between the ranks. As a result, more and better information is available for decision making, and the relevance of decisions to the needs of operating workers increases. Of course, the "wandering around" must be a genuine attempt to communicate. It should not be perceived as just another way to monitor the workplace.

ORGANIZATIONAL COMMUNICATION

Communication among members of an organization as well as between them and external customers, suppliers, distributors, alliance partners, and a host of outsiders provides vital information for the enterprise. Formally defined, **organizational communication** is the specific process through which information moves and is exchanged throughout an organization.[21] Information flows through both formal and informal structures, and it flows downward, upward, and laterally. Today, more than ever before, computer technology plays a major role in how information is shared and utilized in organizations.

> **Organizational communication** is the process by which information is exchanged in the organizational setting.

GLOBAL

The Intranet is proving its worth for Eli Lilly & Co. Consultant John Swartzendruber hooked up 3000 desktop computers in 24 countries and plans eventually to link two thirds of Lilly's worldwide staff. The company's Intranet uses a series of Web pages to make information from all parts of the company available to its users. At a meeting in Indiana, use of the Intranet can identify regulatory procedures for clearing a new drug in other countries. Previously this information would have had to be gathered through e-mail, telephone calls, and the like. Amazingly, the company's initial investment to set up the Intranet was only $80,000.[22]

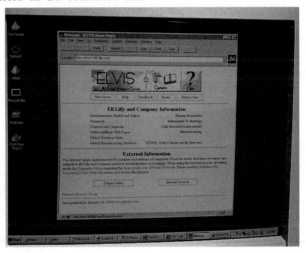

▼ INFORMATION FLOWS

As shown in Figure 16.3, *downward communication* follows the chain of command top to bottom. One of its major functions is to inform. Lower level personnel need to know what higher levels are doing and to be regularly reminded of key policies, strategies, objectives, and technical developments. Of special importance is feedback and information on performance results. Sharing such information helps minimize the spread of rumors and inaccuracies regarding higher level intentions. It also helps create a sense of security and involvement among receivers, who feel they know the whole story. Truly effective leaders use downward communication in a comprehensive sense. They use it to empower people,

■ FIGURE 16.3
Directions for information
flows in organizations.
[Source: John R. Schermerhorn, Jr., *Management,* 5th
ed. (New York: John Wiley
& Sons, 1996), p. 377. Used
by permission.]

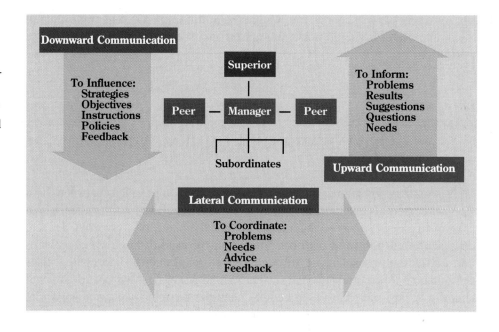

※ CULTURAL
EXCHANGE
ENTERTAINMENT
CORP./CULTURAL
TOYS®

It's fun working at Culture
Exchange Entertainment
Corp./Cultural Toys® and
CEO Jacob R. Miles III intends to keep it that way.
Miles's firm develops children's entertainment properties and products, multicultural toys, books and
electronic learning aids. He
also listens to retailers, creating packaging, features,
and pricing to meet their
customers' needs.[25]

to recognize and reinforce task accomplishments, and to encourage high-performance aspirations.

Research in Canada and the United States indicates that the supervisor is the
most preferred source of higher level information for employees.[23] Unfortunately,
a lack of adequate downward communication is often cited as a management failure. On the issue of corporate downsizing, for example, one sample showed 64
percent of employees not believing what management said, 61 percent feeling un-
informed about company plans, and 54 percent complaining that decisions were
not well explained.[24]

The flow of messages from lower to higher levels in an organization's hierarchy of authority is *upward communication.* As shown in Figure 16.3, it serves several purposes. Upward communication keeps higher levels informed about what
lower level workers are doing, what their problems are, what suggestions they
have for improvements, and how they feel about the organization and their jobs.
But, as you should recall, status effects can potentially interfere with the effectiveness of upward communication.

The importance of *lateral communication* in the new workplace has been a
recurrent theme in this book. Organizational success in a dynamic environment
depends on high-quality decision making and problem solving at all points of responsibility. Today's customer sensitive organizations need timely and accurate
feedback and product information. To serve customer needs they must get the
right information—and get it fast enough—into the hands of workers. Inside the
organization, furthermore, people must be willing and able to communicate
across departmental or functional boundaries and to listen to one another's needs
as "internal customers." Lateral communication, as shown in Figure 16.3, serves
the important purposes of informing, supporting, and coordinating activities
across internal organizational boundaries.

An organization's informal structures and grapevines can be very helpful in improving lateral communications. But increasingly, more formal channels in the form of cross-departmental committees, teams, or task forces and the matrix organization are important as well. New organization designs are emphasizing lateral communication as a basic requirement of everyday operations. Among the developments in this respect is growing attention to *organizational ecology*—the study of how building design may influence communication and productivity. When investing in new facilities or the rearrangement of existing ones, managers are now giving more attention to how a good facility design may enhance performance through better lateral communications.

▼ COMMUNICATION NETWORKS

Figure 16.4 depicts three interaction patterns and communication networks that are common ways information moves within organizations.[26] Some work arrangements involve *interacting groups* whose members work closely together on tasks, and in which close coordination of activities takes place. This interaction pattern results in a **decentralized communication network**—one in which all group members communicate directly with one another. Sometimes these are also referred to as *all-channel* or *star communication networks.*[27]

Other work arrangements involve *coacting groups* whose members work on tasks independently, while linked through some form of central coordination. The required work is divided up and then largely completed by individuals working alone. Each individual's activities are coordinated and results pooled by a cen-

Decentralized communication networks link all group members directly with one another.

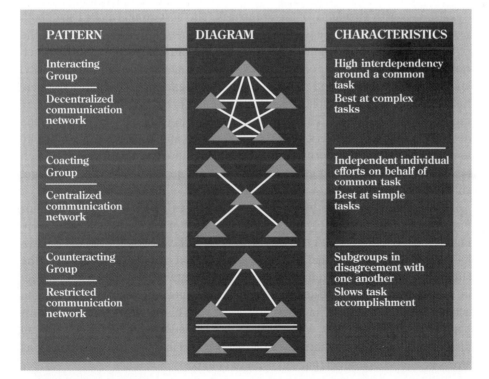

■ FIGURE 16.4
Interaction patterns and communication networks in groups.

351

tral control point. Coacting groups tend to work best when tasks are easily routinized or subdivided. In a coacting group, most communication flows back and forth between individual members and the control point. This creates a **centralized communication network,** with the central person serving as the "hub." As shown in the figure, this structure is sometimes referred to as a *wheel* or *chain communication network.*

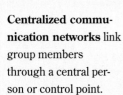

Centralized communication networks link group members through a central person or control point.

Counteracting groups exist when subgroups disagree on some aspect of workplace operations. The subgroups may experience issue-specific disagreements, such as a temporary debate over the best means to achieve a goal, or the disagreements may be of longer-term duration, such as labor–management disputes. In either case the resulting interaction pattern involves a **restricted communication network**, in which polarized subgroups contest one another's positions and maintain sometimes antagonistic relations. As would be expected, communication between the groups is often limited and biased. Problems of destructive competition in intergroup dynamics are likely under such circumstances.

Restricted communication networks link subgroups that disagree with one another's positions.

Having the right interaction pattern and communication network can make a big difference in the way groups function and the results they achieve. In general, members tend to be most satisfied when they are involved in interacting groups using decentralized communication networks. The "all-channel" nature of communication gives everyone opportunities to be involved. Information is well distributed among the members, and with this comes the satisfaction of active participation. In coacting groups using centralized communication networks, it is usually the central or "hub" person who experiences this satisfaction. After all, he or she alone is most involved in all aspects of group information processing.

The performance results achieved by the different communication networks can also vary with the nature of the group task. The best groups make use of both types of communication networks, but they use them in the right ways, at the right times, and for the right tasks. In general, centralized communication networks seem to work better on simple tasks. These tasks require little creativity, information processing, and problem solving and lend themselves to more centralized control. Thus, simple tasks tend to be performed faster and more accurately by coacting groups. The reverse is true for more complex tasks. Here, the decentralized networks work better since they are able to support the more intense interactions and information processing required to perform under such task conditions. Interacting groups tend to be the top performers when tasks get complicated.

When communication within a group becomes restricted and subgroups form, task accomplishment typically suffers, at least in the short run. If the coacting group is able to restore good group processes, it can benefit from the creativity and critical evaluation that typically accompanies conflict. Often, however, the subgroups drift further and further apart, until negative intergroup dynamics set in. Emotions, antagonisms, and other biases may intervene to make it difficult to achieve desired group outcomes in this situation. This is sometimes found in labor–management relations, where strikes and extended contract bargaining can disrupt normal work routines. New directions in labor–management relations stress greater cooperation that can work to both party's benefits.

The new Honda Civic is a product of lateral communications. The company merged two teams that started working in two different countries, Japan and the United States, to collaborate on the final design. The teams developed ways to cut costs by working with suppliers and talking to manufacturing workers. One American paint shop employee suggested a way to improve bumper design, but Japanese engineers resisted. She persisted, offering different alternatives in response to their questions. A compromise resulted in savings of $1.2 million. Says one of the Japanese team members: "We weren't accustomed to hearing from the factory so early on."[28]

▼ COMMUNICATION TECHNOLOGIES

One of the greatest changes in organizations and in everyday life in recent years has been the great explosion in new communication technologies. In today's workplace we have moved from the world of the telephone, mail, photocopying, and face-to-face meetings into one of voice mail, e-mail, facsimile transmission, computer-mediated conferencing, and use of the Internet and Intranets. The ability to participate effectively in the electronic office and communications environment is now well established as an essential career skill.[29]

The impact of the new technologies has been discussed elsewhere in this book with respect to job design and the growth of telecommuting, organizational design and the growth of network organizations, and teamwork and the availability of software for electronic meetings and decision making. The principal advantages of the new communication technologies are that (1) they distribute information much faster than before; (2) they make more information available than ever before; (3) they allow broader and more immediate access to this information; and (4) they encourage participation in the sharing and use of information.

Along with these advantages, however, the potential disadvantages of electronic communications must also be recognized. To begin, they are largely impersonal; people interact with machines, not with one another. Electronics also remove nonverbal communications from the situation—aspects that may otherwise add important context to a situation. The electronic medium can also influence the emotional aspects of communication. Some argue, for example, that it is far easier to be blunt, overly critical, and insensitive when conveying messages electronically rather than face-to-face. The term "flaming" is sometimes used to describe rudeness in electronic communication. In this sense, the use of computer mediation may make people less inhibited and more impatient in what they say.[30]

Another risk of the new communication technologies is information overload. In some cases, too much information may find its way into the communication networks and e-mail systems and basically overload the systems—organizational and individual. Individual users may have difficulty sorting the useful from the trivial, and may become impatient while doing so. The development of information protocols is occurring in more organizations as information managers try to ensure that the new technologies are used to best advantage and that misuse is minimized.

In all this, one point remains undeniable: New communication technologies will continue to keep changing the nature of work and the nature of office work in particular. The once conventional office—with its telephones, mail rooms, clerical support, and file space—is giving way to new forms such as telecommuting and the use of electronic networks. Workers in the future will benefit as new technologies allow them to spend more time out of the traditional office, more time working with customers, and more time working on terms that best fit individual needs.[31] They should also benefit as further research adds to our understanding of how to best integrate technology with the human dimensions of the workplace.

▼ CURRENT ISSUES AND CONTROVERSIES

An issue of emerging interest in organizational communication and management involves the *different communication styles of men and women*. More and more people are asking the question, "Are women better communicators than men?" A study by the consulting firm Lawrence A. Pfaff and Associates suggests they may well be.[32] The survey shows that supervisors rank women managers higher than men managers on communication, approachability, evaluations, and empowering others; they are ranked higher on these same items by their subordinates.

One explanation for this pattern is that early socialization and training better prepare women for the soft skills involved in communication and makes them more sensitive in interpersonal relationships. Men, by contrast, may be more socialized toward aggression, competitiveness, and individualism.[33] The flip side of this issue, however, relates to what happens in *communication between men and women*. To the extent that different styles are possible, gender dynamics become a potential communication barrier. It is suggested that men may tend to use communications to advance status, whereas women tend to use communications to improve connections. One result is that the genders may get frustrated with one another as these styles and intentions come into conflict.[34] In considering such possibilities, however, it is important to avoid gender stereotyping and focus instead on the point of ultimate importance—how communication in organizations can be made most effective.[35]

Among the controversies in organizational communication is the issue of *privacy*. A state law in Illinois now makes it legal for bosses to listen in on employees' telephone calls. But, the law leaves the boundaries of appropriateness unclear. One area where the practice is common is airlines reservations. Here, a union leader describes its potential impact on telephone reservations agents as: "It's the George Orwell type of thing."[36] The privacy issue is likely to increase in importance and controversy as communication technologies continue to make it easier for employers to monitor the performance and communications of their workers.

Another area of controversy lies with the *political correctness* of communications in the workplace. The vocabulary of work is changing and people are ever more on guard not to let their choice of words offend another individual or group. We now hear references to "people of color," "physically challenged," and "seniors"; not too long ago the references may have been different, and they may be different again in the future. Organizations are taking more notice of this issue and offering more training to their members. Especially in these times of growing workforce diversity and employer desires to fully tap the potential of these workforces, efforts are being made to eliminate any possible sources of intolerance and insensitivity. Some 2000 AT&T workers, for example, annually attend a workshop entitled "Homophobia in the Workplace."[37]

CHAPTER 16 STUDY GUIDE ◀

SUMMARY

What is the communication process?
- Communication is the process of sending and receiving messages with attached meanings.
- The communication process involves encoding an intended meaning into a message, sending the message through a channel, and receiving and decoding the message into perceived meaning.
- Noise is anything that interferes with the communication process.
- Feedback is a return message from the original recipient back to the sender.
- To be constructive, feedback must be direct, specific, and given at an appropriate time.

What makes effective communication?
- Communication is effective when both sender and receiver interpret a message in the same way.
- Communication is efficient when messages are transferred at a low cost.
- Nonverbal communication occurs through facial expressions, body position, eye contact, and other physical gestures.
- Active listening encourages a free and complete flow of communication from the sender to the receiver; it is nonjudgmental and encouraging.
- Communication in organizations uses a variety of formal and informal channels; the richness of the channel, or its capacity to convey information, must be adequate for the message.

What barriers interfere with effective communication?
- The possible barriers to communication include such things as physical distractions, semantic problems, and cultural differences, among others.
- Mixed messages that give confused or conflicting verbal and nonverbal cues may interfere with communications.

- The absence of feedback can make it difficult to know whether or not an intended message has been accurately received.
- Status effects in organizations may result in restricted and filtered information exchanges between subordinates and their superiors.

What is organizational communication?

- Organizational communication is the specific process through which information moves and is exchanged within an organization.
- Organizations depend on complex flows of information, upward, downward, and laterally, to operate effectively.
- Groups in organizations work with different interaction patterns and use different communication networks.
- Interacting groups with decentralized networks tend to perform well on complex tasks; coacting groups with centralized networks may do well at simple tasks.
- Restricted communication networks are common in counteracting groups involving subgroup disagreements.
- New electronic communication technologies that are changing the workplace have both advantages and potential disadvantages.
- Current issues and controversies in organizational communication include gender differences in communication styles, and concerns for both privacy and political correctness in workplace communications.

KEY TERMS

Active listening (p. 343)

Centralized communication network (p. 352)

Channels (p. 340)

Communication (p. 339)

Decentralized communication network (p. 351)

Effective communication (p. 342)

Efficient communication (p. 342)

Feedback (p. 341)

Formal communication channels (p. 345)

Grapevine (p. 345)

Informal communication channels (p. 345)

Mixed messages (p. 347)

Noise (p. 340)

Nonverbal communication (p. 343)

Organizational communication (p. 349)

Restricted communication networks (p. 352)

SELF-TEST 16

▼ MULTIPLE CHOICE

1. When criticism is given to someone, this feedback should be _____. (a) general and nonspecific (b) given whenever the sender feels the need (c) tied to things the recipient can really do something about (d) given all at once to get everything over with

2. In _____ communication the cost is low, whereas in _____ communication the intended message is fully received. (a) effective, electronic (b) efficient, electronic (c) electronic, face-to-face (d) efficient, effective

3. Which channel is more appropriate for sending a complex and open-ended message? (a) Face-to-face. (b) Written memorandum. (c) E-mail. (d) Telephone call.

4. When someone's words convey one meaning and their body posture conveys some-

thing else, a(n) _____ is occurring. (a) ethnocentric message (b) mixed message (c) semantic problem (d) status effect

5. Management by wandering around is a technique that can help to overcome the limitations of _____ in the communication process. (a) status effects (b) semantics (c) physical distractions (d) proxemics

6. A coacting group is most likely to use a(n) _____ communication network. (a) interacting (b) decentralized (c) centralized (d) restricted

7. A complex problem is best dealt with by a group using a(n) _____ communication network. (a) all-channel (b) wheel (c) chain (d) linear

8. Although new communication technologies have the advantage of handling large amounts of information, they may also make organizational communication _____. (a) less accessible (b) less participative (c) more impersonal (d) more personal

9. The physical arrangement of office furniture and its impact on communication is a concern of _____. (a) kinesics (b) proxemics (c) semantics (d) channel richness

10. In _____ communication the sender is likely to be most comfortable, whereas in _____ communication the receiver is likely to feel more informed. (a) one-way, two-way (b) top-down, bottom-up (c) bottom-up, top-down (d) two-way, one-way

▼ TRUE–FALSE

11. Encoding translates an intended message into perceived meaning in the communication process.   T F

12. Proxemics is the study of mixed messages in organizations.   T F

13. A rule of active listening is to avoid reflecting back or paraphrasing what the other person has said.   T F

14. Grapevines can have a positive impact on communication in organizations.   T F

15. Research reported in the chapter indicates that poor downward communication is often cited as a management failure.   T F

16. New trends in organizational design place increased emphasis on lateral communications in organizations.   T F

17. Developments in organizational ecology are facilitating informal communication.   T F

18. Members in a coacting group tend to interact frequently and share information directly with one another.   T F

19. A tendency toward "flaming" to express intense anger is a possible drawback of electronic communication.   T F

20. Concerns about the political correctness of communications seem less important in the modern workplace.   T F

▼ SHORT RESPONSE

21. Why is channel richness a useful concept for managers?

22. What place do informal communication channels have in organizations today?

23. Why are communications between lower and higher organizational levels sometimes filtered?

24. Is there a gender difference in communication styles?

▼   APPLICATIONS ESSAY

25.   "People in this organization don't talk to one another anymore. Everything is e-mail, e-mail, e-mail. If you are mad at someone, you can just say it and then hide behind your computer." With these words, Wesley expressed his frustrations with Delta General's operations. Xiaomei echoed his concerns, responding, "I agree, but surely the managing director should be able to improve organizational communication without losing the advantages of e-mail." As a consultant overhearing this conversation, what would you suggest the managing director might do in response to Xiaomei's challenge?

17

DECISION MAKING

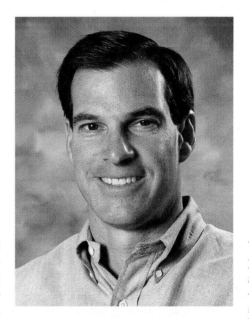

The local supermarket's produce counter probably has it; sales run over $450 million per year for Steve Taylor's Fresh International Corp. What's the product? Its Fresh Express's salad-in-a-bag. It offers everything from a standard garden salad to a fancy Mexican salad with all the accoutrements—fresh, and ready to eat, all in a plastic bag.

Getting salads to stay fresh in a bag, however, hasn't been an easy process. It took perseverance and creativity. The idea originated with Steve Taylor's father, who was trying to find a way to reduce the risks associated with his family's commodity lettuce business. He had the gut feeling that serving-size salads packaged in plastic bags would sell, but the problem was that lettuce and green vegetables turned brown in a bag. They just wouldn't stay fresh long enough. But Taylor didn't give in; he kept pushing to find a way to make his idea work. The eventual breakthrough came with the development, and patenting, of a new plastic bag. As it turns out, the principal cause of decay in lettuce is the overabsorption of oxygen and a self-induced fast rate of decomposition. Taylor's scientists eventually created a bag that allowed more carbon dioxide to escape and less oxygen to enter; they also injected the bag with nitrogen. The result is a green salad that can stay fresh for weeks . . . inside a bag.[1]

Organizations depend for their success on day-to-day decisions made by their members. The quality of these decisions influences both the long-term performance of an organization and its day-to-day "character" . . . in the eyes of employees, customers, and society at large. Today's challenging environments, furthermore, demand ever more rigor and creativity in the decision-making process. New products, such as the salad-in-a-bag, and new manufacturing and service processes all come from ideas. Organizations must provide for decision making that encourages the free flow of new ideas and supports the efforts of people who want to make their ideas work. And just as with organizations themselves, the success of our individual careers depends on the quality of the decisions we make regarding our jobs and employment situations.

Chapter 17 examines the many aspects of decision making in organizations, with special attention to decision making in the modern workplace. As you read the chapter, keep in mind these key questions.

- How are decisions made in organizations?
- How do intuition, judgment, and creativity affect decision making?
- How can the decision-making process be managed?
- What current issues affect organizational decision making?

DECISION-MAKING APPROACHES

Decision making is choosing a course of action to deal with a problem.

Formally defined, **decision making** is the process of choosing a course of action for dealing with a problem or opportunity.[2] The five basic steps involved in systematic decision making are:

❶ Recognize and define the problem or opportunity.
❷ Identify and analyze alternative courses of action.
❸ Choose a preferred course of action.
❹ Implement the preferred course of action.
❺ Evaluate the results and follow up as necessary.

■ Five steps in decision making

▼ DECISION ENVIRONMENTS

Problem-solving decisions in organizations are typically made under three different conditions or environments: certainty, risk, and uncertainty.[3] **Certain environments** exist when information is sufficient to predict the results of each alternative in advance of implementation. When a person invests money in a savings account, for example, absolute certainty exists about the interest that will be earned on that money in a given period of time. Certainty is an ideal condition for managerial problem solving and decision making. The challenge is simply to locate the alternative offering the best or ideal solution. Unfortunately, certainty is the exception instead of the rule in organizational decision environments.

Risk environments exist when decision makers lack complete certainty regarding the outcomes of various courses of action, but have some awareness of the probabilities associated with their occurrence. A *probability,* in turn, is the degree of likelihood of an event's occurrence. Probabilities can be assigned through objective statistical procedures or through personal intuition. On the one hand, statistical estimates of quality rejects in production runs can be made; on the other hand, a senior production manager can make similar estimates based on past experience. Risk is a common decision environment in today's organizations.

Uncertain environments exist when managers lack information to the point where they are unable to even assign probabilities to various alternatives and their possible outcomes. This is the most difficult of the three decision environments. Uncertainty forces decision makers to rely heavily on individual and group creativity to succeed in problem solving. It requires unique, novel, and often totally innovative alternatives to existing patterns of behavior. Responses to uncertainty are often heavily influenced by intuition, educated guesses, and hunches.

▼ TYPES OF DECISIONS

The many routine and nonroutine problems in the modern workplace call for different types of decisions to be made. *Routine problems* arise on a regular basis and can be addressed through standard responses, called **programmed decisions**. These decisions simply implement solutions that have already been determined by past experience as appropriate for the problem at hand. Examples of programmed decisions are reordering inventory automatically when stock falls below a predetermined level and issuing a written reprimand to someone who violates a certain personnel procedure.

Nonroutine problems are unique and new, having not been encountered before. Because standard responses are not available, these circumstances call for creative problem solving. These **nonprogrammed decisions** are specifically

Certain environments provide full information on the expected results for decision-making alternatives.

Risk environments provide probabilities regarding expected results for decision-making alternatives.

Uncertain environments provide no information to predict expected results for decision-making alternatives.

Programmed decisions are determined by past experience as appropriate for a problem at hand.

Nonprogrammed decisions are created to deal uniquely with a problem at hand.

crafted or tailored to the situation at hand. Higher level managers generally spend a greater proportion of their decision-making time dealing with nonroutine problems. An example is a senior marketing manager faced with the problem of responding to the introduction of a new product by a foreign competitor. Although past experience may help deal with this competitive threat, the immediate decision requires a creative solution based on the unique characteristics of the present market situation.

▼ DECISION-MAKING MODELS

The field of organizational behavior recognizes and contrasts the two alternative approaches to decision making shown in Figure 17.1—classical and behavioral.[4] **Classical decision theory** views the manager as acting in a world of complete certainty. The manager faces a clearly defined problem, knows all possible action alternatives and their consequences, and then chooses the alternative that offers the best, or "optimum," solution to the problem. Clearly, this *optimizing* style is an ideal way to make decisions. This classical approach is normative and prescriptive, and is often used as a model for how managers ideally should make decisions.

Behavioral scientists are cautious regarding the applicability of classical decision theory to many decision situations. They recognize that the human mind is a wonderful creation, capable of infinite achievements. But they also recognize that human beings have *cognitive limitations* that restrict their information-processing capabilities.[5] Information deficiencies and overload compromise the ability of decision makers to achieve complete certainty and otherwise operate according to the classical model. Human decision makers also operate with *bounded rationality*, as they interpret and make sense of things within the context of the situation within which they are operating.[6] Acting "within the box" of a simplified view of a more complex reality, so to speak, makes it difficult to realize the ideal of classical decision making. As a result, the classical model does not give a full and accurate description of how most decisions are made in organizations.[7]

> **Classical decision theory** views decision makers as acting in a world of complete certainty.

■ FIGURE 17.1
Decision making viewed from the classical and behavioral perspectives.

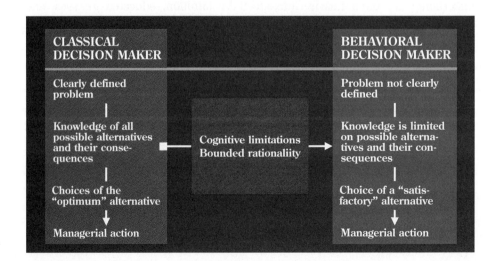

CLASSICAL
DECISION MAKER

Clearly defined
problem

Knowledge of all
possible alternatives
and their conse-
quences

Choices of the
"optimum" alternative

Managerial action

Cognitive limitations
Bounded rationaliity

BEHAVIORAL
DECISION MAKER

Problem not clearly
defined

Knowledge is limited
on possible alterna-
tives and their con-
sequences

Choice of a "satis-
factory" alternative

Managerial action

Behavioral decision theory accepts the notion of bounded rationality and suggests that people act only in terms of what they perceive about a given situation. Because these perceptions are frequently imperfect, most organizational decision making does not take place in a world of complete certainty. Rather, the behavioral decision maker is viewed as acting most often under uncertain conditions and with limited information. Organizational decision makers face problems that are often ambiguous, and they have only a partial knowledge about the available action alternatives and their consequences. This leads to a phenomenon described by Herbert Simon as **satisficing**—decision makers choose the first alternative that appears to give an acceptable or satisfactory resolution of the problem. Simon states: "Most human decision making, whether individual or organizational, is concerned with the discovery and selection of satisfactory alternatives; only in exceptional cases is it concerned with the discovery and selection of optimal decisions."[8]

> **Behavioral decision theory** views decision makers as acting only in terms of what they perceive about a given situation.

> **Satisficing** in decision making chooses the first satisfactory decision alternative.

Intuition, Judgment, and Creativity ◀

The key difference between a manager's ability to make an optimum decision in the classical style and the tendency to make a satisfying decision in the behavioral style is the availability of information. The organizational realities of bounded rationality and cognitive limitations affect the way people define problems, identify action alternatives, and choose preferred courses of action. By necessity, most decision making in organizations involves more than the linear and step-by-step rational choice models often suggest. Decisions must be made under risk and uncertainty, decisions must be made to solve nonroutine problems, and decisions must be made under the pressures of time and information limitations. These decisions always bear the unique imprint of the individuals who make them.

▼ Intuition in Decision Making

A key element in decision making under risk and uncertainty is **intuition**, defined as the ability to know or recognize quickly and readily the possibilities of a given situation.[9] Intuition adds elements of personality and spontaneity to decision making; as a result, it offers potential for creativity and innovation.

A debate among scholars regarding how managers really plan helps to clarify the role and importance of intuition in the decision-making process. On one side of the issue are those who believe that planning can be taught and accomplished in a systematic step-by-step fashion. On the other side are those who believe that the very nature of managerial work makes this hard to achieve in actual practice. The ideas of Henry Mintzberg, whose research on managerial behavior is introduced in Chapter 1, are illustrative here. Mintzberg argues as follows.[10] Managers favor verbal communication. Thus, they are more likely to gather data and

> **Intuition** is the ability to know or recognize quickly the possibilities of a situation.

Take-A-Note 17.1

WAYS TO IMPROVE INTUITION

Relaxation Techniques
- Drop the problem for a while.
- Spend some quiet time by yourself.
- Try to clear your mind.

Mental Exercises
- Use images to guide your thinking.
- Let ideas run freely without a specific goal.
- Accept ambiguity and lack of total control.

Analytical Techniques
- Talk with people of different viewpoints.
- Tackle problems at times of maximum personal alertness.
- Take creative pauses before making final decisions.

to make decisions in a relational or interactive way than in a systematic step-by-step fashion. Managers often deal with impressions. Thus, they are more likely to synthesize than to analyze data as they search for the "big picture" in order to make decisions. Managers work fast, do a variety of things, and are frequently interrupted. Thus, they do not have a lot of quiet time alone to think, plan, or make decisions systematically.

With this background, we can answer the question, "Is systematic decision making useful?" with a clear "Yes." Managers and other decision makers should think systematically and take full advantage of rational choice models that offer step-by-step guidance. But, the answer to the additional question, "Is intuitive decision making useful?" is also a clear "Yes." Decision makers and managers do work in environments such as the one described by Mintzberg. This reality should be accepted and decision makers should hone and be confident in using their intuitive skills. They should combine analytical and intuitive approaches to create new and novel solutions to complex problems.[11]

▼ JUDGMENTAL HEURISTICS

Judgment, or the use of one's intellect, is important in all aspects of decision making. When we question the ethics of a decision, for example, we are questioning the "judgment" of the person making it. Research shows that people are prone to mistakes and biases that often interfere with the quality of any decisions made.[12] These can be traced to the use of *heuristics*—simplifying strategies or "rules of thumb" used to make decisions. Heuristics serve a useful purpose in making it easier to deal with uncertainty and limited information in problem situations. But they can also lead to systematic errors that affect the quality, and perhaps the ethical implications, of any decisions made. It is helpful to understand the common judgmental heuristics of availability, representativeness, and anchoring and adjustment.[13]

The **availability heuristic** bases a decision on recent events relating to the situation at hand.

The **availability heuristic** involves assessing a current event based on past occurrences that are easily available in one's memory. An example is the product development specialist who bases a decision not to launch a new product on her recent failure with another product offering. In this case, the existence of a past product failure has negatively, and perhaps inappropriately, biased the decision maker's judgment of how to best handle the new product.

The **representative heuristic** bases a decision on similarities between the situation at hand and stereotypes of similar occurrences.

The **representativeness heuristic** involves assessing the likelihood of an event's occurring based on its similarity to one's stereotypes of similar occurrences. An example is the team leader who selects a new member not because of any special qualities of the person, but only because the individual comes from a department known to have produced high performers in the past. In this case, it is the individual's current place of employment—and not his or her job qualifications—that are the basis for the selection decision.

The **anchoring and adjustment heuristic** involves assessing an event by taking an initial value from historical precedent or an outside source, and then incrementally adjusting this value to make a current assessment. An example is the executive who makes salary increase recommendations for key personnel by simply adjusting their current base salaries by a percentage amount. In this case, the existing base salary becomes an "anchor" that drives subsequent salary increases. In some situations this anchor may be inappropriate, such as the case of an individual whose market value has become substantially higher than the base salary plus increment can reflect.

In addition to using the common judgmental heuristics, decision makers are also prone to more general biases in decision making. One bias is the **confirmation trap**, whereby the decision maker seeks confirmation for what is already thought to be true and neglects opportunities to acknowledge or find disconfirming information. A form of selective perception, this involves seeking only those cues in a situation that support a pre-existing opinion. A second bias is the **hindsight trap**, whereby the decision maker overestimates the degree to which he or she really could have predicted an event that has already taken place. One of the risks of hindsight, is that it may foster feelings of inadequacy or insecurity in dealing with future decision situations.

▼ CREATIVITY FACTORS

Creativity in decision making involves the development of unique and novel responses to problems and opportunities of the moment. In a dynamic environment full of nonroutine problems, creativity in crafting decisions often determines how well people and organizations do in response to complex challenges.[14]

In Part 3 of this book we examined the group as an important resource for improving creativity in decision making. Indeed, making good use of such traditional techniques as brainstorming, nominal groups, and the Delphi method can greatly expand the creative potential of people and organizations. The addition of new computer-based group meeting and decision-making techniques extends this great potential even further.

Creative thinking can be thought of as unfolding in a series of five stages. First is *preparation*.[15] Here people engage in the active learning and day-to-day sensing required to deal successfully with complex environments. The second stage is one of *concentration*, whereby actual problems are defined and framed so that alternatives can be considered for dealing with them. The third stage is one of *incubation*. Here, people look at the problems in diverse ways that allow for the consideration of unusual alternatives, avoiding tendencies toward purely linear and systematic problem solving. The fourth stage is *illumination*. Here, people respond to flashes of insight and recognize when all pieces to the puzzle suddenly fit into place. The fifth and final stage is *verification*, which proceeds with logical analysis to confirm that good problem-solving decisions have really been made.[16]

All of these stages of creativity need support and encouragement in the organizational environment. However, creative thinking in decision making can be

---

The **anchoring and adjustment heuristic** bases a decision on incremental adjustments to an initial value determined by historical precedent or some reference point.

The **confirmation trap** is the tendency to seek confirmation for what is already thought to be true and to not search for disconfirming information.

The **hindsight trap** is a tendency to overestimate the degree to which an event that has already taken place could have been predicted.

Creativity generates unique and novel responses to problems.

limited by a number of factors. Judgmental heuristics like those just reviewed can limit the search for alternatives. When attractive options are left unconsidered, creativity can be limited. Cultural and environmental blocks can also limit creativity. This occurs when people are discouraged from considering alternatives viewed as inappropriate by cultural standards or inconsistent with prevailing norms.

GLOBAL

The idea for well-known Nike traces to a college term paper written by Phil Knight, a former track star. His concept was to import high-quality running

shoes and run a company with a unique culture and values and an athlete-like high-performance thrust. He went on to do it. Knight decided early on to link Nike's manufacturing to low-cost Asian producers and sell products with the endorsement of "name-brand" athletes. He once built an entire new product line around basketball star Michael Jordan. But now his competitors, such as Reebok, have adopted this strategy. Knight doesn't want to be just like them and wonders how far the sports hero strategy can go in the future.[17]

MANAGING THE DECISION-MAKING PROCESS

People working at all levels, in all areas, and in all types and sizes of organizations aren't supposed just to make decisions; they are supposed to make *good* decisions. Sometimes, this means being willing to override previous commitments and to discontinue a course of action that is just not working out the way it should. Frequently, it means developing creative solutions to novel problems. Always, it means making the right decisions in the right way at the right time.

▼ PROBLEM CHOICE

Most people are too busy and have too many valuable things to do with their time to respond personally by making decisions on every problem or opportunity that comes their way. The effective manager and team leader knows when to delegate decisions to others, how to set priorities, and when to abstain from acting altogether. When faced with the dilemma of whether or not to deal with a specific problem, asking and answering the following questions can sometimes help.[18]

Is the problem easy to deal with? Small and less significant problems should not get as much time and attention as should bigger ones. Even if a mistake is made, the cost of decision error on small problems is also small. *Might the problem resolve itself?* Putting problems in rank order leaves the less significant for last. Surprisingly, many of these less important problems resolve themselves or are solved by others before you get to them. One less problem to solve leaves decision-making time and energy for other uses. *Is this my decision to make?* Many problems can be handled by other persons. They should be delegated to people best prepared to deal with them; ideally, they should be delegated to people whose work they most affect. Finally, *is this a solvable problem within the context of the organization?* The astute decision maker recognizes the difference between problems that realistically can be solved and those that are simply not solvable for all practical purposes.

▼ PARTICIPATION AND INVOLVEMENT

A mistake commonly made by many new managers and team leaders is presuming that they must solve every problem by making every decision themselves. In practice, good organizational decisions get made by individuals acting alone, by individuals consulting with others, and by groups of people working together.

When **individual decisions** are made, the manager or team leader uses information that he or she possesses and decides what to do without involving others. Also called an *authority decision,* this decision method often reflects the prerogatives of a person's position of formal authority in the organization. In **consultative decisions**, by contrast, inputs on the problem are solicited from other persons. Based on this information and its interpretation, the decision maker arrives at a final choice. In other cases, true **group decisions** can be made by both consulting with others and allowing them to help make the final choice. Although sometimes difficult and time consuming, the group decision is the most participative of the three methods.

Victor Vroom, Philip Yetton, and Arthur Jago have developed a framework for helping managers choose which of the prior decision-making methods is most appropriate for various problem situations.[19] The central proposition in their model is that the decision-making method used should always be appropriate to the problem being solved. The challenge is to know when and how to implement each of the possible methods as the situation demands. They further clarify individual, consultative, and group decision options as follows.

❶ AI (*first variant on the authority decision*): The manager solves the problem or makes the decision alone, using information available at that time.

❷ AII (*second variant on the authority decision*): The manager obtains the necessary information from subordinate(s) or other group members and then decides on the problem solution. The manager may or may not tell subordinates what the problem is before obtaining the information from them. The subordinates provide the necessary information but do not generate or evaluate alternatives.

❸ CI (*first variant on the consultative decision*): The manager shares the problem with relevant subordinates or other group members individually, getting their ideas and suggestions without bringing them together as a group. The manager then makes a decision that may or may not reflect the subordinates' input.

> **Individual decisions** are made by one individual in behalf of a group.

> **Consultative decisions** are made by one individual after seeking input from or consulting with members of a group.

> **Group decisions** are made by all members of the group.

■ Decision-making methods

❹ CII (*second variant on the consultative decision*): The manager shares the problem with subordinates or other group members, collectively obtaining their ideas and suggestions. The manager then makes a decision that may or may not reflect the subordinates' input.

❺ G (*the group or consensus decision*): The manager shares the problem with the subordinates as a total group and engages the group in consensus seeking to arrive at a final decision.

In the most recent version of this decision-making framework, Vroom and Jago use the flowchart in Figure 17.2 to help managers analyze problem situations and choose the most appropriate decision-making methods. Key issues involve the quality requirements of a decision, the availability and location of the relevant information, the commitments needed to fully implement the decision, and the amount of time available. While this model appears complex and cumbersome, its underlying logic offers a useful decision-making discipline. Try it by working through Figure 17.2 for an organizational problem with which you are familiar. The analysis forces you to recognize how time, quality requirements, information availability, and subordinate acceptance issues can affect decision outcomes. It also reminds you that all of the decision methods are important and useful. The key to effectively managing participation in decision making is first knowing when to use each decision method, and then knowing how to implement each of them well.

QUALITY

President Chris Carey of Datatec Industries does his best to unlock the power of employee involvement and group participation. As part of a long-run quality improvement campaign he sponsors values of honesty, openness, empowerment, and acceptance of failure. The New Jersey maker of in-store computer systems has even extended employee participation to the point of doing "reverse reviews"—using a special survey, employees at all levels rate management and the company on such things as communication of goals, attention to ideas, support, and general fairness. Results are distributed company-wide and action plans are developed for areas of change.[20]

> **Escalating commitment** is the tendency to continue a previously chosen course of action even when feedback suggests that it is failing.

▼ ESCALATING COMMITMENTS

Social psychologists recognize a common tendency that can hinder decision making and block creativity. Called **escalating commitment**, this is the tendency to continue with a previously chosen course of action even though it is not working.[21] Escalating commitment is reflected in the popular adage, "If at first you don't succeed, try, try, again." Current OB thinking supports an alternative view, one expressed in these words attributed to the late W. C. Fields: "If at first you don't succeed, try, try, again. Then quit."

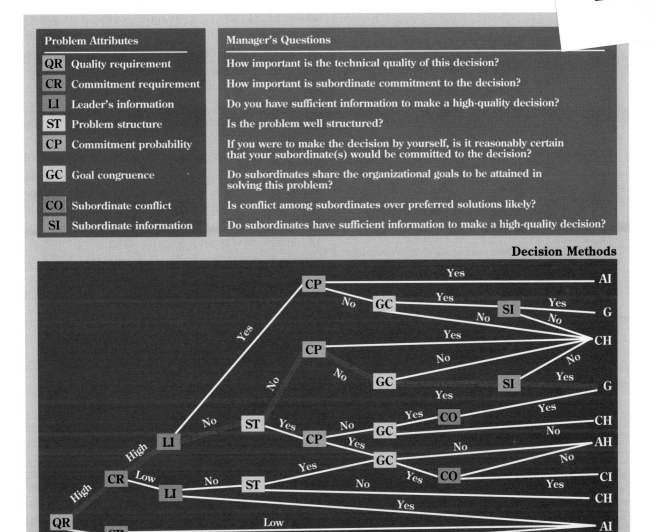

Problem Attributes		Manager's Questions
QR	Quality requirement	How important is the technical quality of this decision?
CR	Commitment requirement	How important is subordinate commitment to the decision?
LI	Leader's information	Do you have sufficient information to make a high-quality decision?
ST	Problem structure	Is the problem well structured?
CP	Commitment probability	If you were to make the decision by yourself, is it reasonably certain that your subordinate(s) would be committed to the decision?
GC	Goal congruence	Do subordinates share the organizational goals to be attained in solving this problem?
CO	Subordinate conflict	Is conflict among subordinates over preferred solutions likely?
SI	Subordinate information	Do subordinates have sufficient information to make a high-quality decision?

Decision Methods

State the Problem

■ FIGURE 17.2

Selecting alternative decision-making methods: The Vroom and Jago decision process flow chart. [Source: Reprinted from Victor H. Vroom and Arthur G. Jago, *The New Leadership* (Englewood Cliffs, NJ: Prentice-Hall, 1988), p. 184. Used by permission of the authors.]

Good decision makers know when to call it quits. They are willing to reverse previous decisions and stop investing time and other resources in unsuccessful courses of action. The self-discipline required to admit mistakes and change direction, however, is sometimes difficult to achieve. The tendency to escalate commitments often outweighs the willingness to disengage from them. Decision

369

Take-A-Note 17.2

AVOIDING THE ESCALATION TRAP

1. Set limits on your commitment ahead of time and then stick to them.
2. Don't let what others are doing serve as a model for what you should be doing.
3. Stop periodically to assess why you are continuing with a course of action.
4. Stop periodically to assess what it will cost to continue with a course of action.
5. Stay vigilant for creeping commitments that continue existing courses of action.

makers may rationalize negative feedback as simply a temporary condition, protect their egos by not admitting that the original decision was a mistake, and/or characterize any negative results as a "learning experience" that can be overcome with added future effort.[22]

Escalating commitments are a form of decision entrapment that leads people to do things that are not justified based on the facts of a situation. We should be proactive in spotting "failures" and more open to reversing decisions or dropping plans that do not appear to be working.[23] But again, this is easier said than done. After continued commitment of millions of dollars to Ontario Hydro's Darlington nuclear power project, for example, a former CEO had this to say about such huge projects: "Once you commit to them, there's very little you can do to reverse that commitment."[24]

CURRENT ISSUES IN ORGANIZATIONAL DECISION MAKING

In today's environments the problems facing organizational decision makers seem to get harder and more complex. We face difficult stresses and strains as the quest for ever-higher productivity challenges the needs, talents, and opportunities of people working in positions of all levels of responsibility. Prominent among the current issues relating to decision making in the modern workplace are those dealing with ethics, culture, technology, and careers.

▼ ETHICAL DECISION MAKING

The subject of ethical behavior in the workplace cannot be overemphasized, and it is worth reviewing once again the framework for ethical decision making first introduced in Chapter 1. An *ethical dilemma* was defined as a situation in which a person must decide whether or not to do something that, although personally or organizationally beneficial, may be considered unethical and perhaps illegal. Often, ethical dilemmas are associated with risk and uncertainty, and with nonroutine problem situations. Just how decisions are handled under these circumstances, ones that will inevitably appear during your career, may well be the ultimate test of your personal ethical framework. Consider this short case.[25]

You are a new financial analyst for a small project engineering firm. Your job is to analyze competitive proposals for the electrical portion of a construction project supervised by your firm. Three proposals have been received so far, and one is clearly the best. Your boss's assistant puts a copy of this proposal in an envelope and tells you to hand carry it to a "friend" of the boss's who runs an electrical contracting business. "He always gets a chance to look at the other bids before submitting one himself," the assistant says. Your boss is out of town for the next 2 days. What should you do?

A Take-A-Note in Chapter 1 introduced a useful decision-making checklist for resolving ethical dilemmas, such as the one just described. Before any decision is made the checklist tests the preliminary decision with stiff questions.[26] First, it would have you ask: "Is my action legal? Is it right? Is it beneficial?" Second, it would have you ask: "How would I feel if my family found out about this? How would I feel if my decision were printed in the local newspaper?" Only after these questions are asked and satisfactorily answered, does the model suggest you should take action.

Remember, too, that people in organizations all too frequently use after-the-fact rationalizations to "excuse" or "explain away" *un*ethical behavior. Common rationalizations to be guarded against include (1) pretending the decision is not really unethical or illegal, (2) excusing the intended behavior by saying it's really in the organization's or your own best interests, (3) assuming the decision is acceptable because no one else would ever find out about it, and (4) expecting your superiors to support and protect the decision if anything should go wrong.[27]

▼ CULTURE AND DECISION MAKING

The forces of globalization and workforce diversity have brought increased attention to how culture may influence decision making. Fons Trompenaars defines *culture* specifically as "the way in which a group of people solves problems."[29] Given this, it is only reasonable to expect that as cultures vary so too will decision-making tendencies and processes.

Time spent living and working abroad is increasingly valued in the world of business. Dick Ferry of Korn/Ferry International says: "A foreign posting somtime in your career is now almost required for senior-level jobs."[30]

The cultural dimensions of power distance and individualism-collectivism have special implications for decision making. Workers from high power distance cultures may expect their supervisors to make the decisions and may be less inclined than individualists to expect or wish to be involved in decision making processes. Signs of good managers in cultures emphasizing and respecting status differences may include a willingness to act as an expert in problem solving and to be decisive; a manager who seems uncomfortable making decisions without group involvement and consensus may be less favorably viewed.

Values relating to individualism–collectivism also affect cultural tendencies toward participation in decision making. Trompenaars describes decision making in collectivist cultures as time consuming, with every effort being made to gain consensus. The results are slower decisions but smooth implementation. Decision making in individualist cultures, by contrast is oriented more toward being decisive, saving time, and the use of voting to resolve disagreements. The results

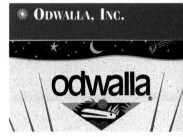

Greg Steptenpohl didn't want to just start a business, he wanted one that ". . . didn't wreak havoc on the environment." The result was Odwalla Inc., a regional fresh juice company based in the Pacific northwest. Its no-preservative and not-pasteurized fruit and vegetable juices are proving popular.[28]

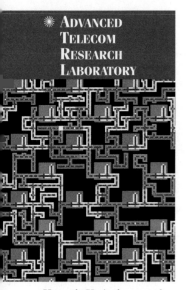

ADVANCED TELECOM RESEARCH LABORATORY

Hugo de Varis dreams of the day when a computer possesses brainpower equal to that of all humans that have ever lived. At Advanced Telecom Research Laboratory in Japan, he is part of a brain-builder team creating computer chips that act like the human brain and central nervous system.[36]

Artificial intelligence, or AI, studies how computers can be made to think like the human brain.

are often implementation problems and delays.[31] In collectivist Japan, for example, many companies use the *ringi* system—a group decision approach whereby workers indicate written approval of proposals prior to their acceptance and implementation.[32] In more individualist France, it is common for decisions made at higher corporate levels to be passed down the hierarchy for implementation.

Culture may even play a role in determining whether or not a decision is necessary at all—in other words, whether or not the situation should be changed. North Americans tend to perceive situations as problems to be solved and want to do something about them. Other cultures, such as Thai and Indonesian, are more prone to accept situations as they are.[33] To make plans, a decision maker must be able to visualize the future, believe that the future can be influenced, and believe that it is desirable to influence the future. Cultural differences in attitudes toward time will influence planning decisions. The stereotypical "American dream" and rush toward the future, for example, may contrast markedly with French tendencies to respect and treasure the past.[34] The degree and detail of planning, as well as the time frame of decisions and plans may be affected by such cultural differences in time orientation.

▼ TECHNOLOGY AND DECISION MAKING

There is no doubt that today's organizations are becoming ever more sophisticated in applying computer technologies to facilitate decision making in new structures and under new conditions. Developments in the field of **artificial intelligence**, the study of how computers can be programmed to think like the human brain, are many and growing.[35] Nobel Laureate and decision scientist Herbert Simon is convinced that computers will someday be more intelligent than humans. Already, the applications of "AI" to organizational decision making are significant. We have access to decision-making support from *expert systems* that reason like a human expert and follow "either–or" rules to make deductions, *fuzzy logic* that reasons beyond either–or choices in more imprecise territory, and *neural networks* that reason inductively by simulating the brain's parallel processing capabilities. Uses for such systems may be found everywhere from banks—where they may help screen loan applications, to hospitals—where they check laboratory results and check possible drug interactions, to the factory floor—where they schedule machines and people for maximum production efficiencies, to a wide and growing variety of other settings.

Computer support for group decision making, including developments with the Internet and with Intranets, breaks the decision-making meeting out of the confines of face-to-face interactions. With the software now available, problems can be defined and decisions can be made by people working in geographically dispersed locations. Emerging research confirms that group decision software can be especially useful for generating ideas, such as in electronic brainstorming, and improving time efficiency of decisions.[37] People working under electronically mediated conditions tend to stay focused on tasks and avoid the interpersonal conflicts and other problems common in face-to-face deliberations. On the negative side, decisions made by "electronic groups" carry some risks of being impersonal and perhaps less compelling in terms of commitments to implementation and follow-through. There is evidence, furthermore, that the use of computer technology for decision making is better accepted by today's college students than by persons who are already advanced in their organizational careers.[38]

▼ CAREER DECISIONS IN THE NEW WORKPLACE

Thoughts and decisions about careers take on a special relevance in the new workplace. We live and work in a time when the realities of turmoil and constant change in organizations and job markets require continuous reviews of our career progress and objectives. In addition to issues of ethics, culture, and technology, for example, workplace trends giving credence to this point include:[39]

- Businesses are becoming smaller in size; they are doing more outsourcing and employing fewer full-time workers.
- New, more flexible and adaptable organizational forms are replacing the traditional pyramid structures.
- Multifunctional understanding is increasingly important as organizations emphasize lateral coordination.
- Workers with both technical knowledge and team skills are becoming increasingly sought after.
- The nature of "work" is in flux as jobs change fast, require continuous learning, and are less bound by the "9 to 5" traditions.

■ Key workplace trends

In this complicated setting, the old notion of a career based within a single organization that takes responsibility for one's career development is increasingly obsolete; new thinking about self-managed and multifaceted careers is needed. In his book *The Age of Unreason,* British scholar and consultant Charles Handy argues forcefully for everyone to take personal charge of their careers and prepare for inevitable uncertainties and changes by maintaining an up-to-date "portfolio" of skills and competencies.[40] This portfolio should always be marketable and attractive to many possible employers. As Handy says: "executives will begin to think of their careers as a sequence of jobs that may or may not be in the same organization."[41] Importantly, this portfolio must be subject to continuous development; each new job assignment must be well selected and rigorously pursued as a learning opportunity. And, according to Handy, all of this is entirely a personal responsibility. He states: "the new executive must look out for himself or herself ... the future is not guaranteed ... education in those circumstances becomes an investment, wide experience is an asset provided that it is wide and not shallow."[42] In short, personal career decisions must meet the test of the marketplace ... both today and everyday in the future.

CHAPTER 17 STUDY GUIDE

SUMMARY

How are decisions made in organizations?

- Decision making is a process of identifying problems and opportunities and choosing among alternative courses of action for dealing successfully with them.
- Organizational decisions are often made in risky and uncertain environments, where situations are ambiguous and information is limited.
- Routine and repetitive problems can be dealt with through programmed decisions; nonroutine or novel problems require nonprogrammed decisions that are crafted to fit the situation at hand.
- According to classical decision theory, optimum decisions are made after carefully analyzing all possible alternatives and their known consequences.
- According to behavioral decision theory, most organizational decisions are made with limited information and by satisficing—choosing the first acceptable or satisfactory solutions to problems.

How do intuition, judgment, and creativity affect decision making?

- Intuition is the ability to recognize quickly the action possibilities for resolving a problem situation.
- Both systematic decision making and intuitive decision making are important in today's complex work environments.
- The use of judgmental heuristics, or simplifying rules of thumb, is common in decision making, but can lead to biased results.
- Common heuristics include availability—decisions based on recent events; representativeness—decisions based on similar events; and anchoring and adjustment—decisions based on historical precedents.
- Creativity in finding unique and novel solutions to problems can be enhanced through both individual and group problem-solving strategies.

How can the decision-making process best be managed?

- Good managers know that not every problem requires an immediate decision; they also know how and when to delegate decision-making responsibilities.
- A common mistake is for a manager or team leader to make all decisions alone; instead, a full range of individual, consultative, and group decision-making methods should be utilized.
- The Vroom-Yetton/Jago model offers a way of matching problems with appropriate decision methods, based on quality requirements, information availability, and time constraints.
- Tendencies toward escalating commitment, continuing previously chosen courses of action even when they are not working, should be recognized in work settings.

What current issues affect organizational decision making?

- Ethics are important; everyone should have a framework for confronting ethical dilemmas and making decisions that meet high ethical standards.
- Culture counts; differences in such dimensions as power distance and individualism–collectivism can influence how decisions get made and by whom in various settings.
- Technological developments are continuing to change the nature of organizational decision making, both in respect to ever-more sophisticated decision support systems and to new interactive software used by electronic groups.
- Career decisions are challenging and complex; they must ultimately be made with personal responsibility and supported by portfolios of skills and competencies consistent with the changing demands of the new workplace.

KEY TERMS

Anchoring and adjustment
  heuristic (p. 365)
Artificial intelligence
  (p. 372)
Availability heuristic
  (p. 364)
Behavioral decision theory
  (p. 363)
Certain environments
  (p. 361)
Classical decision theory
  (p. 362)

Confirmation trap (p. 365)
Consultative decisions
  (p. 367)
Creativity (p. 365)
Decision making (p. 360)
Escalating commitment
  (p. 368)
Group decisions (p. 367)
Hindsight trap (p. 365)
Individual decisions
  (p. 367)
Intuition (p. 363)

Nonprogrammed decisions
  (p. 361)
Programmed decisions
  (p. 361)
Representative heuristic
  (p. 364)
Risk environment (p. 361)
Satisficing (p. 363)
Uncertain environment
  (p. 361)

SELF-TEST 17

▼ MULTIPLE CHOICE

1. After a preferred course of action has been implemented, the next step in the decision-making process is to _____. (a) recycle the process (b) look for additional problems or opportunities (c) evaluate results (d) document the reasons for the decision

2. In which environment does the decision maker deal with probabilities regarding possible courses of action and their consequences? (a) certain (b) risk (c) speculative (d) uncertain

3. A manager who must deal with limited information and uncertainty is most likely to make decisions based on _____. (a) optimizing (b) classical decision theory (c) behavioral decision theory (d) escalation

4. A team leader who makes a decision not to launch a new product because the last new product launch failed, is falling prey to the _____ heuristic. (a) anchoring (b) availability (c) adjustment (d) representativeness

5. The five steps in the creativity process are preparation, _____, illumination, _____, and verification. (a) extension, evaluation (b) reduction, concentration (c) adaptation, extension (d) concentration, incubation

6. In Vroom's model of decision making, the choice among individual and group decision methods is based on criteria that include quality requirements, availability of

information, and _____. (a) need for implementation commitments (b) size of organization (c) number of people involved (d) position power of leader

7. The saying "If at first you don't succeed, try and try again" is most associated with a decision making tendency called _____. (a) groupthink (b) the confirmation trap (c) escalating commitment (d) the hindsight trap

8. Preferences for leader or authority-based decision making are most consistent with _____ cultures. (a) individualistic (b) high power distance (c) neutral (d) universalist

9. Although the decisions may take longer because of a search for consensus, implementation may be quicker in _____ cultures. (a) collectivist (b) low power distance (c) emotional (d) particularist

10. Among the developments with artificial intelligence, _____ attempt to have computers reason inductively in solving problems. (a) neural networks (b) expert systems (c) fuzzy logics (d) electronic brainstorms

▼ TRUE–FALSE

11. Most managerial decisions take place in certain environments.   T F
12. Nonprogrammed decisions fit best with routine and repetitive problems.   T F
13. Systematic decision making is always preferred to intuitive decision making.   T F
14. Managers do not have to solve every problem that comes their way.   T F
15. Escalating commitments is a way of improving implementation of group decisons. T F
16. A good way to resolve an ethical dilemma is to have greater confidence that the organization will stand by you even though the actions being taken are of a questionable nature.   T F
17. The *ringi* system is a Japanese approach to making participative decisions.   T F
18. Group consensus is always preferred to the authority decision.   T F
19. Impersonality in relationships is one possible disadvantage of electronic group decision making.   T F
20. In the final analysis, the turbulence in today's work environments makes any type of career planning useless. T F

▼ SHORT RESPONSE

21. What are heuristics and how can they affect individual decision making?
22. What are the main differences among individual, consultative, and group decisions?
23. What is escalating commitment and why is it important to recognize in decision making?
24. What questions might a manager or team leader ask to help determine which problems to deal with and with what priorities?

▼ APPLICATIONS ESSAY

25. You have been asked to represent your college at a career assembly for local high school seniors. Specifically, you have been requested to share with them some insights on career planning and development based on Charles Handy's concept of the "portfolio person." What will you tell this audience?

18

CONFLICT AND NEGOTIATION

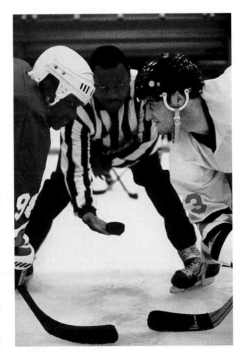

When you think of hockey do you think of conflict or do you think about successful negotiations? League president John Ziegler, and National Hockey League Players Association (NHLPA) president Bob Goodenow have had a lot of experience with both. Disagreements led to a strike 2 weeks before the 1992 playoffs were to begin. This was when the owners made a large portion of their profits, whereas the players made little financially from the playoff games. After a 10-day players' walkout, Goodenow and Ziegler shook hands on a compromise deal, saving the NHL's seventy-fifth anniversary season. A joint player–management committee was inaugurated to examine the problems and promises of the hockey business.

But this helped only temporarily. A strike erupted again in the 1994–1995 season, resulting in a shortened schedule. Now both Goodenow and Ziegler are working to develop an approach to help hockey expand while increasing player salaries and team revenues. (http:// www .tribnet.com/~tnt/news/39013.htm)

T here is no doubt that the daily work of managers is intensely based on interpersonal relationships and the exchange of information; this is the way networks are developed and maintained and action agendas are enacted.[1] But interpersonal relationships also open the door for potential differences and disagreements to creep into the workplace, causing difficulties that affect not only what people may accomplish in their work but also their satisfaction. A manager who understands the fundamentals of conflict and negotiation is better prepared to deal successfully with these situations, inevitable as they are.

This chapter introduces you to conflict and negotiation as two processes of organizational behavior that can have a substantial impact on the performance and satisfaction of people at work. As you read Chapter 18, keep in mind these study questions.

- What is conflict?
- How can conflict be managed by indirect and direct approaches?
- What is negotiation?
- What are the different strategies to negotiation?

CONFLICT

Conflict occurs when parties disagree over substantive issues or when emotional antagonisms create friction between them.

C onflict occurs whenever disagreements exist in a social situation over issues of substance or whenever emotional antagonisms create frictions between individuals or groups.[2] Managers are known to spend up to 20 percent of their time dealing with conflict, including conflicts in which the manager is directly involved as one of the principal actors.[3] In other situations, the manager may act as a mediator, or third party, whose job it is to resolve conflicts between other people. In all cases, the manager must be a skilled participant in the dynamics of interpersonal conflict. He or she must also be able to recognize situations that have the potential for conflict and deal with these situations to best serve the needs of both the organization and the people involved.

▼ SUBSTANTIVE AND EMOTIONAL CONFLICTS

Substantive conflict is a fundamental disagreement over ends or goals to be pursued and the means for their accomplishment.[4] A disagreement with one's boss over a plan of action to be followed, such as the marketing strategy for a new product, is an example of substantive conflict. When people work together day in and day out, it is only normal that different viewpoints on a variety of substantive workplace issues will arise. It is common for people to disagree at times over such things as group and organizational goals, the allocation of resources, the distribution of rewards, policies and procedures, and task assignments. Dealing successfully with such conflicts is an everyday challenge for most managers.

> **Substantive conflict** involves fundamental disagreement over ends or goals to be pursued and the means for their accomplishment.

Emotional conflict involves interpersonal difficulties that arise over feelings of anger, mistrust, dislike, fear, resentment, and the like.[5] It is commonly known as a "clash of personalities." Emotional conflicts can drain the energies of people and distract them from other important work priorities. They can emerge from a wide variety of settings and are common among coworkers as well as in superior subordinate relationships. Superior subordinate emotional conflict is perhaps the most upsetting organizational conflict for any person to experience. Unfortunately, competitive pressures in today's business environment and the resulting emphasis on downsizing and restructuring have created more situations in which the decisions of a "tough" boss can create emotional conflict.

> **Emotional conflict** involves interpersonal difficulties that arise over feelings of anger, mistrust, dislike, fear, resentment, and the like.

▼ LEVELS OF CONFLICT

When it comes to dealing personally with conflicts in the workplace, the relevant question becomes: "How well prepared are you to encounter and deal successfully in your experiences with conflicts of various types?" In particular, people at work may encounter such conflicts at the intrapersonal level (conflict within the individual), the interpersonal level (individual-to-individual conflict), the intergroup level, or the interorganizational level.

Intrapersonal Conflict   Among the significant conflicts that affect behavior in organizations are those that involve the individual alone. These **intrapersonal conflicts** often involve actual or perceived pressures from incompatible goals or expectations of the following types: *Approach–approach conflict* occurs when a person must choose between two positive and equally attractive alternatives. An example is having to choose between a valued promotion in the organization or a desirable new job with another firm. *Avoidance–avoidance conflict* occurs when a person must choose between two negative and equally unattractive alternatives. An example is being asked either to accept a job transfer to another town in an undesirable location or to have one's employment with an organization terminated. *Approach–avoidance conflict* occurs when a person must decide to do something that has both positive and negative consequences. An example is being offered a higher paying job, but one whose responsibilities entail unwanted demands on one's time.

> **Intrapersonal conflict** occurs within the individual because of actual or perceived pressures from incompatible goals or expectations.

Interpersonal Conflict   **Interpersonal conflict** occurs between two or more individuals who are in opposition to one another; the conflict may be substantive or emotional in nature, or both. Two persons debating aggressively over each other's views on the merits of hiring a job applicant is an example of a substantive interpersonal conflict. Two persons continually in disagreement over each other's choice of work attire is an example of an emotional interpersonal conflict.

> **Interpersonal conflict** occurs between two or more individuals in opposition to each other.

Intergroup Conflict   Another level of conflict in organizations occurs among groups. Such **intergroup conflict** can also have substantive and/or emotional underpinnings. Intergroup conflict is quite common in organizations, and it can make the coordination and integration of task activities very difficult.[6] Many firms, such as Canadian Tire; Electroglass, a semiconductor component supplier in California; and Northern States Power, are instituting peer group conflict resolution programs to deal with interpersonal conflicts.

> **Intergroup conflict** occurs among groups in an organization.

Interorganizational Conflict   **Interorganizational conflict** is most commonly thought of in terms of the competition and rivalry that characterizes firms operating in the same markets. A good example is the continuing battle between U.S. businesses and their Japanese rivals, with the Americans charging the Japanese with unfair trade practices. But interorganizational conflict is really a much broader issue than that represented by market competition alone. Consider, for example, disagreements between unions and the organizations employing their members; between government regulatory agencies and the organizations subject to their surveillance; and, more generally, between organizations and those who supply them with raw materials.

> **Interorganizational conflict** occurs between organizations.

GLOBAL   CAMI, a joint venture between Suzuki Motor Company of Japan and GM of Canada, relies heavily upon sustained conflict resolution and negotiations to run its Ingersoll, Ontario plant. With unionized workers and a Japanese approach to managing, the potential for conflict is ever present. Yet both the union and management want to support the extensive use of teams and involvement that can yield higher quality and productivity. Rather than form an

 elaborate bureaucratic system, union and management have decided to use teams and involvement on the shop floor to prevent small disputes from escalating. All stewards and shop foremen are trained in conflict resolution and encouraged to maintain direct face-to-face communication to help resolve problems. As a result CAMI's Ingersoll plant is rated one of the best for efficiency and quality.[7]

▼ CONSTRUCTIVE AND DESTRUCTIVE CONFLICTS

Conflict in organizations can be upsetting both to the individuals directly involved and to others who may observe it or are affected by its occurrence. It can be quite uncomfortable, for example, to work in an environment in which two coworkers are continually hostile toward each other. In OB, however, two sides to conflict are recognized—the constructive side and the destructive side. They are depicted in Figure 18.1.

Constructive conflict results in positive benefits to individuals, the group, or the organization. It offers the people involved a chance to identify otherwise neglected problems and opportunities; creativity and performance can improve as a result. Indeed, an effective manager is able to stimulate constructive conflict in situations in which satisfaction with the status quo inhibits needed change and development.

For instance, suppliers and manufacturers in the United States have experienced constant conflict over price, quality, and service, whereas the Japanese have worked together creatively to turn this potentially destructive relationship into constructive conflict. Recently, U.S. firms are attempting much the same. As Chrysler's vice president for purchasing, Thomas T. Stallkamp, says, "When you start to see your suppliers as experts, then they become valuable partners instead of a switchable commodity." Under Stallkamp's leadership, Chrysler has eliminated competitive bidding to gain supplier contracts. Instead, Chrysler provides suppliers with detailed specifications and then asks them to meet the specifications and cut costs. In return, Chrysler agrees to share the savings with the suppliers and to give long-term purchase contracts. Part of Chrysler's overall TQM approach, this cooperative approach to supplier relationships, is called SCORE: Supplier Cost Reduction Effort. It has been credited with over 4600 cost-saving ideas and actual savings of some $235 million.[8]

Destructive conflict works to the individual's, group's, or organization's disadvantage. It occurs, for example, when two employees are unable to work together because of interpersonal hostilities (a destructive emotional conflict) or when the members of a committee fail to act because they cannot agree on group goals (a destructive substantive conflict). Destructive conflicts of these types can

> **Constructive conflict** results in positive benefits to the group.

> **Destructive conflict** works to the group's or organization's disadvantage.

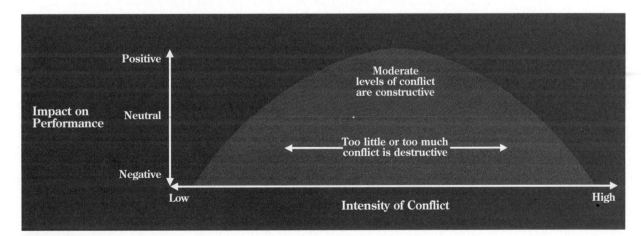

■ FIGURE 18.1
The two faces of conflict: constructive conflict and destructive conflict.

decrease work productivity and job satisfaction and contribute to absenteeism and job turnover. Managers must be alert to destructive conflicts and be quick to take action to prevent or eliminate them or at least minimize their resulting disadvantages.

MANAGING CONFLICT

Conflict in organizations is inevitable. But the process of managing conflict to achieve constructive rather than destructive results is clearly essential to organizational success. This process of conflict management can be pursued in a variety of ways. An important goal always should be to achieve or set the stage for true **conflict resolution**—that is, a situation in which the underlying reasons for a given destructive conflict are eliminated. The process begins with a careful diagnosis of the specific conflict situation.

Conflict resolution occurs when the reasons for a conflict are eliminated.

▼ SPECIFIC CONFLICT SITUATIONS FACED BY MANAGERS

The very nature of the manager's position in an organization guarantees that managing conflict will be a part of his or her work experience. A manager's ability to deal with specific situations may, in large part, determine whether the outcome is constructive or destructive.

The process of managing conflict begins with the manager recognizing each of the following conflict situations.[9] *Vertical conflict* occurs between hierarchical levels. It commonly involves supervisor–subordinate disagreements over resources, goals, deadlines, or performance results. *Horizontal conflict* occurs between persons or groups at the same hierarchical level. These disputes commonly involve goal incompatibilities, or resource scarcities, or purely interpersonal factors. A common variation of horizontal conflict is *line–staff conflict*. Conflict that occurs between line and staff representatives commonly involves disagreements over who has authority and control over certain matters such as personnel selection and termination practices. Note that these specific conflict situations are built into the organization. They may be compounded by role conflict. *Role conflict* occurs when the communication of task expectations proves inadequate or upsetting. It commonly involves uncertainties of expectations, overloads or underloads in expectations, or incompatibilities among expectations.

The built-in conflict situations may turn from latent disputes into open disagreements when units and individuals are required to cooperate to meet challenging goals.[10] In general, interdependencies among individuals and units can breed conflicts. *When work-flow interdependence is high*—that is, when a person or group must rely on task contributions from one or more others to achieve its goals—conflicts often occur. You will notice this, for example, in a fast-food restaurant, when the people serving the food have to wait too long for it to be delivered from the cooks.

The potential for destructive conflict also escalates when individuals or groups operate with a lack of adequate task direction or clarity of goals. For individuals, ambiguity can be stressful. At the group or department level, similar effects in terms of *domain ambiguities* can occur. These ambiguities involve misunderstandings over such things as customer jurisdiction or scope of authority. Conflict is likely when individuals and/or groups are placed in situations where it is difficult for them to understand just who is responsible for what. Ambiguity combined with work-flow interdependence can dramatically increase the chances of destructive conflict.

Actual or perceived *resource scarcity* can yield destructive competition as well. When resources are scarce, working relationships are likely to suffer. This is especially true in organizations experiencing downsizing or financial difficulties. As cutbacks occur, various individuals or groups try to position themselves to gain or retain maximum shares of the shrinking resource pool. They are also likely to try to resist resource redistribution, or to employ countermeasures to defend their resources from redistribution to others, even if such attempts reduce goal attainment.

Finally, *power* or *value asymmetries* in work relationships can make it more difficult for individuals to deal with high work-flow interdependencies, ambiguity, and resource scarcity. Power or value asymmetries exist when interdependent people or groups differ substantially from one another in status and influence or in values. Conflict resulting from asymmetry is prone to occur, for example, when a low-power person needs the help of a high-power person, who does not respond; when people who hold dramatically different values are forced to work together on task; or when a high-status person is required to interact with and perhaps be dependent on someone of lower status. The latter case occurs when a manager is forced to deal with another manager only through his or her secretary.

▼ STAGES OF CONFLICT

Most conflicts develop in stages, as shown in Figure 18.2. Managers should recognize that unresolved prior conflicts help set the stage for future conflicts of the same or related sort. Rather than try to deny the existence of conflict or settle on a temporary resolution, it is always best to deal with important destructive conflicts so that they are completely resolved. These stages include antecedent conditions, perceived and felt conflict, manifest conflict, conflict resolution or suppression, and conflict aftermath.[11]

The conditions that create conflict, as discussed above, are examples of conflict antecedents. *Conflict antecedents* establish the conditions from which conflicts are likely to develop. When the antecedent conditions actually become the basis for substantive or emotional differences between people and/or groups, the stage of *perceived conflict* exists. Of course, this perception may be held by only one of the conflicting parties.

It is important to distinguish between perceived conflict and the stage of *felt conflict*. When conflict is felt, it is experienced as tension that motivates the person to take action to reduce feelings of discomfort. For conflict to be resolved, all parties should both perceive it and feel the need to do something about it.

■   FIGURE 18.2
The stages of conflict.

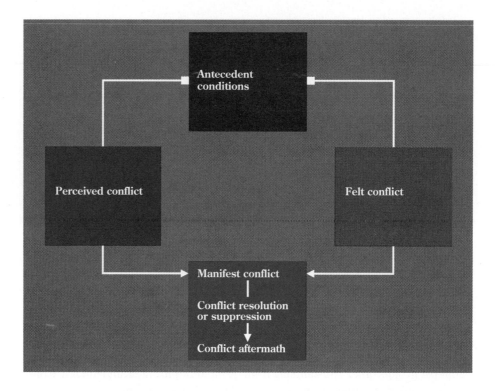

When conflict is openly expressed in behavior it is said to be manifest. A state of *manifest conflict* may be resolved by removing or correcting its antecedents. It can also be suppressed. With suppression, no change in antecedent conditions occurs; the manifest conflict behaviors are controlled. For example, one or both parties may choose to ignore the conflict in their dealings with one another. *Suppression* is a superficial and often temporary form of conflict resolution. Indeed, we have already noted that unresolved conflicts—and a suppressed conflict falls into this category—may continue to fester and cause future conflicts over similar issues. It may be the best a manager can do, however, until antecedent conditions can be changed.

Unresolved substantive conflicts can result in sustained emotional discomfort and escalate into dysfunctional emotional conflict between individuals. In contrast, truly resolved conflicts may establish conditions that reduce the potential for future conflicts and/or make it easier to deal with them. Thus, any manager should be sensitive to the influence of conflict aftermath on future conflict episodes.

▼ INDIRECT CONFLICT MANAGEMENT APPROACHES

Managers should first consider the use of *indirect conflict management approaches*. They include reducing interdependence, appeals to common goals, hierarchical referral, organizational redesign, and alterations in the use of mythology and scripts.

Reducing Interdependence When work-flow interdependencies exist, conflicts often arise. Managers have a number of options available to reduce conflicts by adjusting the level of interdependency among units or individuals.[12] One simple option is to reduce the required contact between conflict parties. In some cases, the tasks of the units can be adjusted to reduce the number of required points of coordination. The conflicting units can then be separated from one another, and each can be provided separate access to valued resources. Although such *decoupling* may reduce conflict, it may also result in duplication and a poor allocation of valued resources. Often the question is whether the conflict costs more than do the inefficiencies of resource allocation.

Buffering is another approach that can be used when the inputs of one group are the outputs of another group. The classic buffering technique is to build an inventory, or buffer, between the two groups so that any output slowdown or excess is absorbed by the inventory and does not directly pressure the target group. Although it reduces conflict, this technique is increasingly out of favor because it increases inventory costs. This consequence is contrary to the elements of "just-in-time" delivery that is now valued in operations management.

Conflict management can be facilitated by assigning people to serve as formal *linking pins* between groups that are prone to conflict.[13] Persons in linking-pin roles, such as project liaison, are expected to understand the operations, members, needs, and norms of their host group. Linking pins are supposed to use this knowledge to help their group work better with other groups to accomplish mutual tasks. Although expensive, this technique is often used when different specialized groups, such as engineering and sales, must closely coordinate their efforts on complex and long-term projects.

Appeal to Common Goals When ambiguity is a driving factor, an *appeal to common goals* can focus the attention of potentially conflicting parties on one mutually desirable conclusion. By elevating the potential dispute to a common framework wherein the parties recognize their mutual interdependence in achieving common goals, petty disputes can be put in perspective. However, this can be difficult to achieve when prior performance is poor and individuals or groups disagree over how to improve performance. In this negative situation, the manager needs to remember the attributional tendency of individuals to blame poor performance on others and/or external conditions. In this case, conflict resolution begins by making sure that the parties take personal responsibility for improving the situation.

Hierarchical Referral *Hierarchical referral* makes use of the chain of command for conflict resolution. Here, problems are simply referred up the hierarchy for more senior managers to reconcile. The managers involved are typically those to whom the conflicting parties mutually report. They are managers who ultimately have the formal authority to resolve such disputes by changing key antecedent conditions.

Whereas hierarchical referral can be definitive in a given case, it also has limitations. If conflict is severe and recurring, the continual use of hierarchical referral may not result in true conflict resolution. Managers removed from day-to-day affairs may have difficulty accurately diagnosing the antecedents of conflict. Busy managers may tend to consider most conflicts as results of poor interpersonal relations. Such is the case particularly when long-standing substantive conflict is accompanied by emotional conflict. More senior managers may want to see outward signs of harmony. They may act quickly to replace a person with a perceived "personality" problem.[14] In so doing, they may actually fail to diagnose the real causes of a conflict, and conflict resolution may be superficial. Subordinates may also learn that it is best not to refer any conflict upward. Thus, conflicts may be kept from view until they finally erupt into major problems.

Organizational Redesign   A sustained pattern of destructive conflict among individuals and departments may be a sign of a poor organizational design that no longer fits the demands, constraints, and opportunities from the environment, the technology, or the size of the organization. One signal of an inappropriate design is the extensive use of liaison groups.[15] A liaison group, team, or department coordinates the activities of certain units to prevent destructive clashes between them. Members of the department may be given formal authority to resolve disputes on everything from technical matters to resource claims to work assignments. Although liaison groups can reduce conflict, they are quite expensive and only should be used in anticipation of new organizational designs.

Scripts and Myths   In some situations, conflict is superficially managed by *scripts,* or behavioral routines that become a part of the organization's culture.[16] The scripts become rituals that allow the conflicting parties to vent their frustrations and to recognize that they are mutually dependent on one another via the larger corporation. An example is a monthly meeting of "department heads," held presumably for purposes of coordination and problem solving but that actually become just a polite forum for superficial agreement.[17] Managers in such cases know their scripts and accept the difficulty of truly resolving any major conflicts. By sticking with the script—expressing only low-key disagreement and then quickly acting as if everything has been resolved, for instance—the managers publicly act as if problems are being addressed. Astutely managed firms recognize the danger that emerging conflicts involving employees may be swept under the rug. Consequently, they routinely conduct employee surveys and use the results to improve employee relations. Unfortunately, the major issues are usually avoided.

Conflict may also be hidden by *myths* that deny the necessity to make trade-offs. For example, in complex, dangerous technologies, safe operations may come at some sacrifice to efficiency. Some organizations hide this fact by proclaiming that "an efficient operation is a safe one." Analyses of operating statistics on safety and efficiency suggest otherwise. Such myths may become "social facts." People may begin to act them out. For example, managers may begin to stress efficiency and say that they are also improving safety. This attitude could result in a serious accident.

▼ DIRECT CONFLICT MANAGEMENT TECHNIQUES

Consultants and academics generally agree that true conflict resolution can occur only when the underlying substantive and emotional reasons for the conflict are identified, resulting in a solution that allows both conflicting parties to "win."[18] Let's examine this issue of "Who wins?" from the perspective of each conflicting party.

Lose–Lose Conflict *Lose–lose conflict* occurs when nobody really gets what he or she wants. No one achieves his or her true desires, and the underlying reasons for the conflict remain unaffected. In this case, future conflict of a similar nature is likely to occur.

Lose–lose conflicts often result from conflict management by avoidance, smoothing, and/or compromise. **Avoidance** is an extreme form of nonattention, wherein everyone involved pretends that the conflict does not really exist and hopes that it will simply go away. **Accommodation,** or **smoothing,** involves playing down differences among the conflicting parties and highlighting similarities and areas of agreement. Whereas smoothing may promote peaceful coexistence through a recognition of common interests in the goal, it ignores the real essence of a given conflict and often yields higher levels of frustration and resentment. **Compromise** in conflict management occurs when each party gives up something of value to the other. As a result, neither party gains its full desires, and the antecedent conditions for future conflicts are established. Although a conflict may appear to be settled for a while through compromise, it may well reappear at some future time.

Win–Lose Conflict In *win–lose conflict*, one party achieves its desires at the expense and to the exclusion of the other party's desires. This may result from outright competition. In **competition** a victory is achieved through force, superior skill, or domination. It may also occur as a result of **authoritative command,** whereby a formal authority simply dictates a solution and specifies what is gained and what is lost by whom. When the authority is a party to the conflict, it is easy to predict who will be the winner and who the loser.

Win–lose strategies fail to address the root causes of the conflict and tend to suppress the desires of at least one of the conflicting parties. As a result, future conflicts over the same issues are likely to occur.

Win–Win Conflict *Win–win conflict* is achieved by collaboration to address the real issues and the use of problem solving to reconcile differences. **Collaboration** involves a recognition by all conflicting parties that something is wrong and needs attention. **Problem solving** stresses gathering and evaluating information in solving disputes and making choices. When success is achieved through problem solving, true conflict resolution has occurred. Win–win conditions eliminate the reasons for continuing or resurrecting the conflict since nothing has been avoided or suppressed. All relevant issues are raised and openly discussed. The ultimate test for a win–win solution is whether or not the conflicting parties see that the so-

Avoidance involves pretending a conflict does not really exist.

Accommodation or **smoothing** involves playing down differences and finding areas of agreement.

Compromise occurs when each party gives up something of value to the other.

Competition seeks victory by force, superior skill, or domination.

Authoritative command uses formal authority to end conflict.

Collaboration involves recognition that something is wrong and needs attention through problem solving.

Problem solving uses information to resolve disputes.

lution (1) achieves each other's goals, (2) is acceptable to both parties, and (3) establishes a process whereby all parties involved see a responsibility to be open and honest about facts and feelings.[19]

Sustained conflict resolution calls upon the parties to develop a responsible attitude toward conflict resolution. They need to develop a desire to satisfy each other's concerns in a conflict situation, as well as their own. The paradox is that individuals who are both very cooperative and assertive are more likely to be involved in win–win solutions. Uncooperative and unassertive individuals are likely to engage in avoidance, whereas those who value cooperation but are not assertive often favor accommodation to withdraw from conflict. Assertive individuals who place little emphasis on cooperation are more likely to opt for competition. Of course, most of us are somewhat assertive and somewhat cooperative and most of us opt for compromise. Yet, in most organizational settings, higher self-assertion and a higher emphasis on cooperation can yield collaboration and problem solving.[20] In the ever-shifting competitive field of the 1990s, firms are finding that a first step to win–win solutions is to focus internally to see where conflicts are actually arising.

> ## Take-A-Note 18.1
> ### WHEN TO USE CONFLICT MANAGEMENT STYLES
>
> - *Collaboration and problem solving is preferred to gain true conflict resolution if time and cost permits and the parties are willing to be both assertive and collaborative.*
> - *Avoidance may be used when an issue is trivial or more important issues are pressing, or when people need to cool down temporarily and regain perspective.*
> - *Authoritative command may be used when quick and decisive action is vital or when unpopular actions must be taken.*
> - *Accommodation may be used when conflict issues are more important to others than to oneself or when a person wants to build "credits" for use in later issues.*
> - *Compromise may be used for temporary settlements to complex issues or to arrive at expedient solutions when time is limited.*

QUALITY

As a U.S. Department of Energy lab, Los Alamos National Laboratory (LANL) of Los Alamos, New Mexico, is part of the billion dollar network of applied research organizations that built the A-bomb.[21] Since the end of the cold war, LANL has had to expand its horizons beyond national defense. As expected in changing times, incidents of manifest conflict have increased. Managers recently analyzed 500 employee relations cases to determine the major areas of employee and management concerns. The results were surprising: 45 percent of the 500 cases involved conflicts related to the relationships between coworkers. The results were used to develop a new conflict-resolution program for the whole lab.

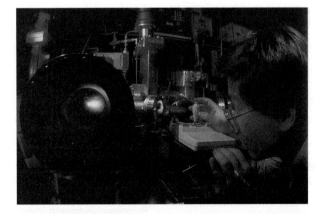

Although collaboration and problem solving are generally favored, you should be aware of some limitations based upon the nature of the conflict, the parties involved, and the overall organizational setting. One limitation is the time and energy needed to engage in win–win conflict resolution. The source of the conflict, the degree of conflict, or the degree of interdependence may not be suffi-

◀

cient to warrant the time and expense to use collaboration and problem solving. It is also important to realize that both parties to the conflict need to be both assertive and cooperative to develop a win–win joint solution.

Collaboration and problem solving may not be feasible if the dominant culture of the firm does not place a value on cooperation. In fact, efforts to use collaboration and problem solving may backfire and the openness and honesty that are required may be seen as a sign of weakness. In such a setting, attempts to use collaboration may merely serve to escalate the level of conflict and evoke competition from other parties.[22]

NEGOTIATION

◀

Picture yourself trying to make a decision in the following situation: You have ordered a new state-of-the-art computer for your department. Another department has ordered a different brand of computer. Your boss indicates that only one brand will be ordered.

This is just a sample of a negotiation situation that involves managers and other people in the workplace. **Negotiation** is the process of making joint decisions when the parties involved have different preferences. It can be considered a way of getting what you want from others in the process of making decisions.[23] Negotiation is especially significant in today's work settings, where more people are being offered opportunities to be involved in decisions affecting them and their work. As more people get involved, disagreements are likely to arise over such diverse matters as wage rates, task objectives, performance evaluations, job assignments, work schedules, work locations, and special privileges. Since organizations are becoming increasingly participative, a manager's familiarity with basic negotiation concepts and processes is increasingly important for dealing with such day-to-day affairs. As a manager, you will be asked to play the role of a negotiator.[24] To begin with, it is important to discuss what is meant by a "successful negotiation."

> **Negotiation** is the process of making joint decisions when the parties involved have different preferences.

▼ SUCCESSFUL NEGOTIATIONS

In our discussion of conflict resolution we suggested that collaboration and problem solving could yield a win–win solution that would help prevent future conflict. When it comes to negotiation, the evaluation of success is a little different. In negotiation there are substantive and relational goals. *Substance goals* are concerned with outcomes relative to the "content" issues at hand. The dollar amount of a wage agreement in a collective bargaining situation is one example. *Relationship goals* are concerned with outcomes relating to how well people involved in the negotiation and any constituencies they may represent are able to work with one another once the process is concluded. An example is the ability of union members and management representatives to work together effectively after a contract dispute has been settled.

To maintain working relationships, managers, like anyone involved in negotiation, should strive for high ethical standards. This may be particularly difficult since self-interests are paramount. The motivation to behave ethically in negotiations is put to the test by the desire of each party to "get more" than the other from the negotiation coupled with a belief that there are insufficient resources to satisfy all parties. The parties need to search for outcomes defined as "fair" beyond their own narrow, short-term perspective.[25]

After the heat of negotiations dies down, the parties involved often try to rationalize or explain away questionable ethics as unavoidable, harmless, or justified. Such after-the-fact rationalizations may be offset by long-run negative consequences, such as not being able to achieve one's wishes again the next time. At the very least, the unethical party may be the target of "revenge" tactics by those who were disadvantaged. Furthermore, once some people have behaved unethically in one situation, they may become entrapped by such behavior and be expected to display it again in the future.[26]

Unfortunately, many negotiations result in a sacrifice of relationships, as parties become preoccupied with substance goals and self-interests. In contrast, *effective negotiation* occurs when substance issues are resolved and working relationships are maintained or even improved.

The parties involved in negotiation may find themselves at an impasse when there are no overlapping interests and the parties fail to find common points of agreement. But agreement in negotiation can mean different things—and the agreement may be either "for the better" or "for the worse" for either or both parties involved. Effective negotiation results in overlapping interests and joint decisions that are "for the better" of all parties. The trick is knowing how to get there.

Take-A-Note 18.2

CRITERIA OF AN EFFECTIVE NEGOTIATION

- *Quality — The negotiation results offer a "quality" agreement that is wise and truly satisfactory to all sides.*
- *Harmony — The negotiation is "harmonious" and fosters rather than inhibits good interpersonal relations.*
- *Efficiency — The negotiation is "efficient" and no more time consuming or costly than absolutely necessary.*

▼ ORGANIZATIONAL SETTINGS FOR NEGOTIATION

It is useful to recognize that the situations in which managers become involved in negotiations are varied. Figure 18.3 shows that managers should be prepared to participate in at least four major action settings for negotiations: (1) in *two-party negotiation* the manager negotiates directly with one other person; (2) in *group negotiation* the manager is part of a team or group whose members are negotiating to arrive at a common decision; (3) in *intergroup negotiation* the manager is part of a group that is negotiating with another group to arrive at a decision regarding a problem or situation affecting both; and (4) in *constituency negotiation* the manager is involved in negotiation with other persons, and each individual party represents a broad constituency. A common example of constituency negotiation is a team representing management negotiating with a team representing labor to arrive at a collective bargaining agreement.

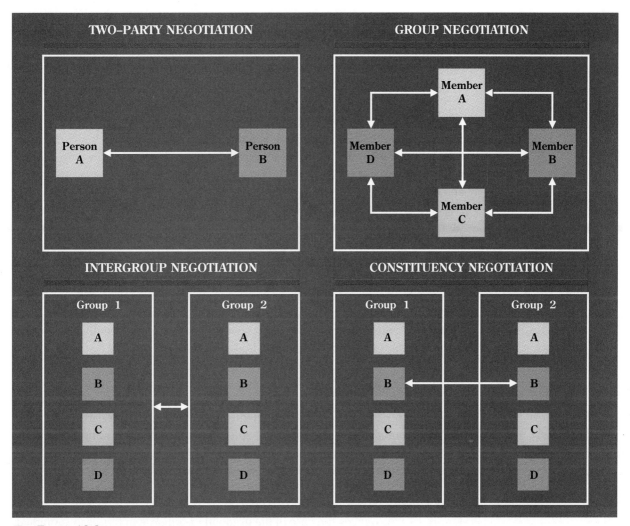

■ FIGURE 18.3

Four types of negotiation situations faced by managers.

DISTRIBUTIVE AND INTEGRATIVE NEGOTIATION STRATEGIES

Managers and other workers frequently negotiate with one another over access to scarce organizational resources. These resources may be money, time, people, facilities, equipment, and so on. In all such cases, the general approach to or strategy for the negotiation can have a major influence on its outcomes. It is useful to discuss two alternative strategies: distributive negotiation and integrative negotiation.[27]

Distributive negotia-
tion focuses on "posi-
tions" staked out or de-
clared by the parties
involved who are each
trying to claim certain
portions of the available
"pie."

Integrative negotia-
tion focuses on the
merits of the issues,
and the parties involved
try to enlarge the avail-
able "pie" rather than
stake claims to certain
portions of it.

In **distributive negotiation,** the focus is on "positions" that are staked out or declared by conflicting parties. Each party is trying to "claim" certain portions of the available "pie." In **integrative negotiation,** sometimes called *principled negotiation,* the focus is on the "merits" of the issues. Everyone involved tries to enlarge the available "pie" rather than stake claims to certain portions of it.

▼ HARD AND SOFT DISTRIBUTIVE BARGAINING

In distributive bargaining approaches, the participants would each ask the question, "Who is going to get this resource?" This question, and the way in which it frames subsequent behavior, will have a major impact on the negotiation process and outcomes.

A case of distributive negotiation usually unfolds in one of two directions, neither of which yields optimal results. *"Hard" distributive negotiation* takes place when each party holds out to get its own way. This leads to competition, whereby each party seeks dominance over the other and tries to maximize self-interests. *"Soft" distributive negotiation* takes place when one party is willing to make concessions to the other to get things over with. In this case, one party tries to find ways to meet the other's desires. A soft approach leads to *accommodation*—one party gives in to the other—or to *compromise*—each party gives up something of value in order to reach agreement.

The hard approach may lead to a win–lose outcome, whereby one party dominates and gains, or to an impasse. The soft approach may lead to *accommodation*—again, only one party may be satisfied. But even in this case there is likely to be at least some latent dissatisfaction on the part of the party who accommodates. Even when the soft approach results in *compromise* (e.g., splitting the difference between the initial positions equally), dissatisfaction may exist since each party is still deprived of what it originally wanted.

▼ CLASSIC TWO-PARTY NEGOTIATION

Figure 18.4 introduces the case of the graduating senior.[28] In this case, a graduating senior is negotiating a job offer with a corporate recruiter. The example illustrates the basic elements of classic two-party negotiation in many contexts.

To begin, look at the situation from the graduate's perspective. She has told the recruiter that she would like a salary of $45,000; this is her initial offer. But she also has in mind a minimum reservation point of $35,000—the lowest salary that she will accept for this job. Thus, she communicates a salary request of $45,000 but is willing to accept one as low as $35,000. Now, the situation is somewhat reversed from the recruiter's perspective. His initial offer to the graduate is $30,000, and his maximum reservation point is $40,000; this is the most he is prepared to pay.

The **bargaining zone** is defined as the range between one party's minimum reservation point and the other party's maximum reservation point. In Figure 18.4, the bargaining zone is $40,000–$45,000; it is a positive bargaining zone since the reservation points of the two parties overlap. Whenever a positive bargaining zone exists, bargaining has room to unfold. Had the graduate's minimum reservation point been greater than the recruiter's maximum reservation point (for ex-

The **bargaining zone**
is the zone between one
party's minimum reser-
vation point and the
other party's maximum
reservation point in a
negotiating situation.

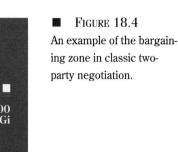

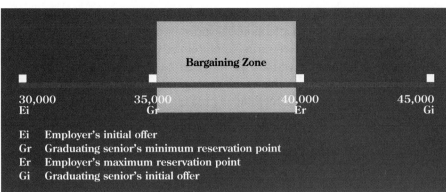

Bargaining Zone

| 30,000 | 35,000 | 40,000 | 45,000 |
| Ei | Gr | Er | Gi |

Ei   Employer's initial offer
Gr   Graduating senior's minimum reservation point
Er   Employer's maximum reservation point
Gi   Graduating senior's initial offer

ample, $42,000), no room would have existed for bargaining. Classic two-party bargaining always involves the delicate tasks of first discovering the respective reservation points (one's own and the other's) and then working toward an agreement that lies somewhere within the resulting bargaining zone and is acceptable to each party.

▼ USING INTEGRATIVE NEGOTIATION

In the integrative approach to negotiation participants would ask, "How can the resource best be utilized?" Notice that this is a very different question from the one described for distributive negotiation. It is much less confrontational, and it allows for a broader range of alternatives.

 Xerox Corporation has long been touted as a role model in the area of good labor relations.[29] Because of successful negotiating with the Amalgamated Clothing & Textile Workers Union (ACTWU), jobs have been saved, plants have remained open, costs have been reduced, and the company has been

able to maintain its position as the largest copier company in the world. Yet, Paul Allaire, chairman of Xerox, felt that there was room for improvement. So he brought Joseph W. Laymon on board as Xerox's director of corporate industrial relations. Laymon worked with the union to develop and implement a training program on conflict resolution. The result was smoother negotiations conducted in weeks rather than months. Part of the success of the talks may be found in one of Laymon's key principles: "You have to have an open book and treat the union and your workers as a partner."

The integrative approach to negotiation has much more of a "win–win" orientation than does the distributive approach; it seeks ways of satisfying the needs and interests of all parties. At one extreme, this may involve selective avoidance,

393

wherein both parties simply realize that there are more important things on which to focus their time and attention. The time, energy, and effort needed to negotiate may not be worth the rewards. Compromise can also play a role in the integrative approach, but it must have an enduring basis. This is most likely to occur when the compromise involves each party giving up something of perceived lesser personal value to gain something of greater value. For instance, in the classic two-party bargaining case over salary, both the graduate and the recruiter could go beyond the initial numbers to include the starting date of the job. Since it will be a year before the candidate's first vacation, she may be willing to take a little less money if she can start a few weeks later.

Finally, integrative negotiation may involve true *collaboration*. In this case, the negotiating parties engage in problem solving to arrive at a mutual agreement that truly maximizes benefit to each.

▼ GAINING INTEGRATIVE AGREEMENTS

Underlying the concept of "principled" negotiation is negotiation based on the "merits" of the situation. The foundations for gaining truly integrative agreements cover three main areas: attitudes, behaviors, and information.[30]

To begin, there are three *attitudinal foundations of integrative agreements*. First, each party must approach the negotiation with a *willingness to trust* the other party. Now you should see why ethics and maintaining relationships are emphasized in judging negotiations. Second, each party must be *willing to share information* with the other party. Without shared information, it is highly unlikely that effective problem solving can occur. Third, each party must be *willing to ask concrete questions* of the other party.

During a negotiation, all behavior is important both for its actual impact and for the impressions it leaves behind. Accordingly, the following *behavioral foundations of integrative agreements* must be carefully considered and included in any negotiator's repertoire of skills and capabilities:

■ Behavioral foundations of integrative agreements

- The ability to separate the people from the problem to avoid allowing emotional considerations to affect the negotiation.
- The ability to focus on interests rather than positions.
- The ability to avoid making premature judgments and to keep the acts of alternative creation separate from evaluation.
- The ability to judge possible agreements on an objective set of criteria or standards.

BATNA is the best alternative to a negotiated agreement, or each party's position on what he or she must do if an agreement can't be reached.

The information foundations of integrative agreements are substantial; they involve each party becoming familiar with the **BATNA,** or "best alternative to a negotiated agreement." That is, each party must know what he or she will do if an agreement can't be reached. This requires that both negotiating parties identify and understand their personal interests in the situation. They must know what is really important to them in the case at hand, and they must come to understand the relative importance of the other party's interests. As difficult as it may seem, each party must achieve an understanding of what the other party values, even to the point of determining its BATNA.

For instance, at Corning the company's approach to labor relations is spelled out in an agreement, dubbed "A Partnership in the Workplace," that commits management to the goal of job security. Whereas Corning's goal is to prosper in the international business arena, it is grounded on the premise that nobody gets fired when tasks are consolidated. This allows unions to permit work rule changes and job consolidations.

▼ AVOIDING COMMON PITFALLS IN NEGOTIATION

The negotiation process is admittedly complex, and it is further characterized by all the possible confusions of sometimes volatile interpersonal and group dynamics. Accordingly, negotiators need to guard against some common mistakes.[31]

First, it is too easy in negotiation to stake out your position based on the assumption that in order to gain your way, something must be "subtracted" from the other party's way. This myth of the "fixed pie" is a purely distributive approach to negotiation. The whole concept of integrative negotiation is based on the premise that the "pie" can sometimes be expanded and/or utilized to the maximum advantage of all parties, not just one.

Second, because parties to negotiations often begin by stating extreme demands, the possibility of escalating commitment is high. That is, once "demands" have been stated, people become committed to them and are reluctant to back down. As a result, they may be prone to nonrational escalation of conflict. Concerns for "protecting one's ego" and "saving face" may enhance these tendencies. Self-discipline is needed to spot this tendency in one's own behavior as well as in others'.

Third, it is also common for negotiators to develop the belief that their positions are the only "correct" ones. This is characterized by overconfidence and the tendency to ignore other's needs. In some cases, negotiators completely fail to see merits in the other party's position—merits that an outside observer would be sure to spot. Such overconfidence makes it harder to reach a positive common agreement. It may even set the stage for disappointment if the negotiation is turned over to a neutral third party for resolution. In *arbitration,* such as the salary arbitration now common in professional sports, this third party acts as the "judge" and issues a binding decision after listening to the positions advanced by the parties involved in a dispute. Sometimes, a manager may be asked to serve as an arbitrator of disputes between subordinates, from matters as important as the distribution of task assignments to matters as seemingly trivial as access to a photocopy machine.

Fourth, it has been said that "negotiation is the process of communicating back and forth for the purpose of reaching a joint decision."[32] Two types of communication problems are especially likely to cause difficulties during a negotiation. The first is the *telling problem;* i.e., negotiation sometimes breaks down because the parties don't really "talk" to one another—at least not in the sense of making themselves truly understood. The second is the *hearing problem;* i.e., ne-

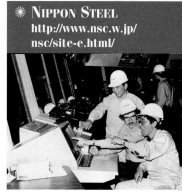

✳ NIPPON STEEL
http://www.nsc.w.jp/
nsc/site-e.html/

"Jishu Kenri" is the phrase used at Nippon Steel to describe how employees solve problems on the factory floor. First, each individual aims at self-realization by developing his or her capacity and displaying creativity. Second, all the employees respect one another and endeavor to create a lively, comfortable work area. Finally, through group activities, the employees contribute to the prosperity of the company and society.

gotiation sometimes breaks down because the parties are unable or unwilling to "listen" well enough to understand what each other is saying.

Fifth, it can also be said that positive negotiation occurs only when each party frequently asks questions to clarify what the other is saying, so that active listening is taking place. Each party occasionally needs to "stand in the other party's shoes" and to view the situation from the other's perspective.[33]

CHAPTER 18 STUDY GUIDE

SUMMARY

What is conflict?
- Conflict appears in a social situation as any disagreement over issues of substance or emotional antagonisms that creates friction between individuals or groups.
- Conflict can be either emotional—based on personal feelings, or substantive—based on work goals.
- When kept within tolerable limits, conflict can be a source of creativity and performance enhancement; it becomes destructive when these limits are exceeded.
- Conflict situations in organizations occur in vertical and lateral working relations and in line staff relations.
- Most typically, conflict develops through a series of stages, beginning with antecedent conditions and progressing into manifest conflict.
- Unresolved prior conflicts set the stage for future conflicts of a similar nature.

How can conflict be managed by indirect and direct approaches?
- Indirect forms of conflict management include appeal to common goals, hierarchical referral, organizational redesign, and the use of mythology and scripts.
- Direct conflict management proceeds with different combinations of assertiveness and cooperativeness on the part of conflicting parties.
- Win–win conflict resolution is preferred; it is achieved through collaboration and problem solving.
- Win-lose conflict resolution should be avoided; it is associated with competition and authoritative command.

What is negotiation?
- Negotiation occurs whenever two or more people with different preferences must make joint decisions.
- Managers may find themselves involved in various types of negotiation situations, including two-party, group, intergroup and constituency negotiation.
- Effective negotiation occurs when issues of substance are resolved and human relationships are maintained, or even improved, in the process.
- Ethical conduct is important to successful negotiations.

What are the different negotiation strategies?

- In distributive negotiation, the focus of each party is on staking out positions in the attempt to claim desired portions of a "fixed pie."
- In integrative negotiation, sometimes called principled negotiation, the focus is on determining the merits of the issues and finding ways to satisfy one another's needs.
- The success of the strategies depends upon avoiding common negotiating pitfalls and building good communications.

KEY TERMS

Accommodation (p. 387)
Authoritative command
   (p. 387)
Avoidance (p. 387)
Bargaining zone (p. 392)
BATNA (p. 394)
Collaboration (p. 387)
Competition (p. 387)
Compromise (p. 387)
Conflict (p. 378)

Conflict resolution
   (p. 382)
Constructive conflict
   (p. 381)
Destructive conflict (p. 381)
Distributive negotiation
   (p. 392)
Emotional conflicts (p. 379)
Integrative negotiation
   (p. 392)
Intergroup conflict (p. 380)

Interpersonal conflict
   (p. 380)
Interorganizational conflict
   (p. 380)
Intrapersonal conflict
   (p. 379)
Negotiation (p. 389)
Problem solving (p. 387)
Smoothing (p. 387)
Substantive conflicts
   (p. 379)

▼ MULTIPLE CHOICE

SELF-TEST 18

1. A conflict that occurs in the form of a fundamental disagreement over ends or goals to be pursued and the means for accomplishment is known specifically as a(n) ____ conflict. (a) relationship. (b) emotional (c) substantive (d) procedural

2. The indirect conflict management approach that uses chain of command for conflict resolution is known as ____ . (a) hierarchical referral (b) avoidance (c) organizational redesign (d) appeals to common goals

3. Which of the following is *not* a way in which conflict can be positive for a group or organization? (a) It can help identify otherwise neglected problems. (b) It can enhance creativity. (c) It can broaden the bargaining zone. (d) It can improve performance.

4. Lose–lose conflicts typically arise from each of the following *except* ____. (a) competition (b) compromise (c) accommodation (d) avoidance

5. When might a manager most effectively use accommodation? (a) When quick and decisive action is vital. (b) When she or he wants to build "credit" for use in later issues. (c) To let people cool down and gain perspective. (d) For temporary settlement to complex issues.

6. According to the conflict management grid, the ____ conflict management style is highly cooperative and assertive. (a) competition (b) compromise (c) accommodation (d) collaboration

7. The criteria for effective negotiation are ____. (a) harmony, efficiency, and quality (b) efficiency and effectiveness (c) ethical, practical, and cost effective (d) quality, practical, and productive

8. ____ are two goals that should be considered in any negotiation. (a) Performance and evaluation (b) Task and substance (c) Substance and relationship (d) Task and performance

9. Which of the following statements is true? (a) Principled negotiation leads to accommodation. (b) Hard distributive negotiation leads to collaboration (c) Soft distributive negotiation leads to accommodation or compromise. (d) Hard distributive negotiation leads to win–win conflicts.

10. Each of the following is a common negotiator pitfall, as identified by the text, *except* ____. (a) falling prey to the myth of the "fixed pie" (b) rational escalation to conflict (c) overconfidence (d) listening to other's needs (e) unethical behavior

▼ TRUE-FALSE

11. Intergroup conflict typically facilitates the coordination of task activities.   T F
12. Interpersonal conflicts can be substantive, emotional, or both.   T F
13. Moderate levels of conflict are constructive.   T F
14. When work-flow interdependency is high, conflicts often occur.   T F
15. The conflict management grid classifies management style along two dimensions: cooperativeness and assertiveness.   T F
16. Two goals are at stake in any negotiation: distributive and integrative.   T F
17. The most preferred approach to negotiation is distributive.   T F
18. In integrative negotiations, everyone tries to enlarge the "pie."   T F
19. BATNA requires that each party know what will be done if an agreement can't be reached.   T F
20. Two types of communication difficulties are common in negotiations: telling and hearing.   T F

▼ SHORT RESPONSE

21. List and discuss the four conflict situations faced by managers.
22. List and discuss the major indirect conflict management approaches.
23. Under what conditions might a manager use avoidance or accommodation?
24. Compare and contrast distributive and integrative negotiation. Which is more desirable? Why?

▼ APPLICATIONS ESSAY

25. Discuss the common pitfalls you would expect to encounter in negotiating your salary for your first job.

19

Change, Innovation, and Stress

When the School of Business at Georgetown University honored Robert Holland as its Business Leader of the Year, he responded by calling it "a vote of confidence" and saying "I won't let you down." There is little doubt about that: Since taking over as CEO of Ben & Jerry's Homemade, Holland has made a clear impact on the firm's operations. It all began when Holland, then running his own acquisitions firm, spotted an advertisement for a new Ben & Jerry's CEO. But there was a catch—you had to apply by writing a poem.

In a consulting career spanning international assignments and appointment as the first African-American associate and partner for McKinsey & Co., Holland believes his career benefited from affirmative action that helped "level the playing field." His move to Ben & Jerry's was motivated in part by his admiration for cofounder Ben Cohen's leadership in the area of what he calls "caring capitalism." But he also recognizes the need for change and development. Facing stiff competition in the gourmet ice-cream market, the trials of extending itself internationally, and the inevitable problems of growth, the company can't rest on past success. Says Holland, it "... must not lose touch with consumers and the fabric that is this off-beat company." (http://www.hoovers.com/masterlist/12673ml.html)[1]

"Turbulence" is a term used frequently these days when referring to the current environment of management. Robert Holland understands what it means at Ben & Jerry's; scholars and consultants know what it means to most people in the new workplace—they must be comfortable dealing with adaptation and continuous change.[2] Amidst the calls for greater productivity, willingness to learn from the successes of others, total quality, and continuous improvement, everyone is being called upon to achieve success while pursuing change and innovation, and experiencing inevitable stress. In the words of management consultant Tom Peters: "The turbulent marketplace demands that we make innovation a way of life for everyone. We must learn—individually and as organizations—to welcome change and innovation as vigorously as we have fought it in the past."[3]

This chapter addresses the important issues of change, innovation, and stress as they relate to developments in the modern workplace. As you read Chapter 19, keep in mind these questions.

- ◉ What is organizational change?
- ◉ What change strategies are used in organizations?
- ◉ Why can be done about resistance to change?
- ◉ How do organizations innovate?
- ◉ How does stress affect people at work?

CHANGE IN ORGANIZATIONS

"Change" is the watchword of the day for many, if not most, organizations. Some of this change may be described as *radical change,* or framebreaking change.[4] This is change that results in a major overhaul of the organization and/or its component systems. In today's business environments, such radical changes are often initiated by a critical event, such as a new CEO, a new ownership brought about by merger or takeover, or a dramatic failure in operating results. When it occurs in the life cycle of an organization, radical change is intense and all-encompassing.

Another common form of organizational change is *incremental change,* or frame-bending change. This type of change is frequent and less traumatic as part of an organization's natural evolution. Typical changes of this type include the introduction of new products, new technologies, and new systems and processes. Although the nature of the organization remains relatively the same, incremental change builds on the existing ways of operating to enhance or extend them in new directions. The capability of improving continuously through incremental change is an important asset in today's demanding environments.

The success of both radical and incremental change in organizations depends in part on **change agents**—the people who lead and support the change processes. These are individuals and groups who take responsibility for changing the existing patterns of behavior of another person or social system. Although change agents sometimes are hired as consultants from outside the organization, it is also true that managers, team leaders, and others working in today's dynamic times are expected to act as change agents.

> **Change agents** are people who take action to change the behavior of people and systems.

GLOBAL

The recent successes of Xerox in a highly competitive global marketplace are a real pleasure to many change agents, including former manufacturing chief Frank Pipp. A few years ago he led the first team of line managers on a "benchmarking" visit to their Japanese joint venture, Fuji-Xerox. They studied costs and processes to find ways of improving their own operations. When they came back and reported to top management, the response was, "We can't be that bad." Pipp replied, "We are." From that point on, the challenge to Pipp and others was to lead the processes of change to restore Xerox's reputation and success.[5]

▼ PLANNED AND UNPLANNED CHANGE

Not all change in organizations happens as a result of a change agent's direction. **Unplanned changes** occur spontaneously or randomly. They may be disruptive, such as a wildcat strike that results in a plant closure, or beneficial, such as an interpersonal conflict that results in a new procedure to smooth the flow of work between two departments. The appropriate goal when the forces of unplanned change begin to appear, is to act quickly to minimize any negative consequences and maximize any possible benefits. In many cases, unplanned changes can be turned into good advantage. A few years ago, for example, McDonalds' top management found their firm the target of environmental groups protesting the use of polystyrene "clamshell" food containers. A decision was made to change to a

> **Unplanned change** occurs spontaneously and without a change agent's direction.

401

quilted paper wrap. Although unplanned, this change helped the firm develop new environmental initiatives and improve its image with the public.[6]

Planned change, by contrast, comes about as a result of specific efforts on the part of a change agent. It is a direct response to someone's perception of a *performance gap*—a discrepancy between the desired and actual state of affairs. Performance gaps may represent problems to be resolved or opportunities to be explored. It is useful to think of most planned changes as efforts designed to deal with performance gaps in ways that benefit an organization and its members. Importantly, the processes of *continuous improvement* require constant vigilance to spot performance gaps—both problems and opportunities, and take action to resolve them. Facilitating ongoing change and developing commitments to continuous improvement are issues of special relevance in this chapter.

> **Planned change** is intentional and occurs with a change agent's direction.

▼ ORGANIZATIONAL FORCES AND TARGETS FOR CHANGE

The forces for change are ever present in and around today's dynamic work settings.[7] They are found in the *relationship between an organization and its environment*—mergers, strategic alliances, and divestitures are examples of organizational attempts to redefine their relationships with challenging environments. They are found in the *life cycle of the organization* as it passes from birth through growth and toward maturity—changes in culture and structures are examples of organizational attempts to adjust to these patterns of growth. They are found in the *political nature of organizations*—changes in internal control structures, including benefits and reward systems, are examples of organizational attempts to deal with shifting political currents.

Planned change based on any of these forces can be internally directed toward a wide variety of organization components, most of which have already been discussed in this book. As shown in Figure 19.1, these targets include organizational purpose, strategy, structure, and people, as well as objectives, culture, tasks, and technology. When considering these targets, however, it must be recognized that they are highly intertwined in the workplace. Changes in any one are likely to require or involve changes in others. For example, a change in the basic *tasks*—what it is that people do—is almost inevitably accompanied by a change in *technology*—the way in which tasks are accomplished. Changes in tasks and technology usually require alterations in *structures,* including changes in the patterns of authority and communication as well as in the roles of workers. These technological and structural changes can, in turn, necessitate changes in the knowledge, skills and behaviors of *people*—the members of the organization.[9]

Before leaving this discussion of organizational targets for change, a word of warning is in order. Managers sometimes fall prey to the latest "fads" for addressing these change targets. All too often, the results of costly programs are limited to superficial and temporary change. Tendencies toward accepting easy-to-implement, but questionable, "quick fixes" to problems should be avoided.[10] Planned organzational change, radical and incremental, should lead to substantive and long-lasting improvements. When change agents act with a solid understanding of change concepts and dynamics, this goal can often be achieved.

✹ BUCKMAN
LABORATORIES
INTERNATIONAL
http://www.buckman.
com/eng/namerica.
htm/

A new knowledge management system at Buckman Laboratories International uses internal electronic discussion groups to troubleshoot problems worldwide. Top management sets the example by actively using the system.[8]

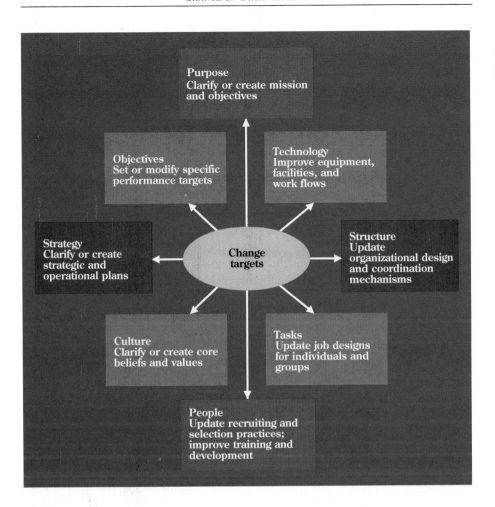

▼ PHASES OF PLANNED CHANGE

Psychologist Kurt Lewin recommends that any change effort be viewed as a process with three distinct phases—unfreezing, changing, and refreezing—all of which must be well handled for a change to be successful.[11]

Unfreezing **Unfreezing** is the managerial responsibility of preparing a situation for change. It involves disconfirming existing attitudes and behaviors to create a felt need for something new. Unfreezing is facilitated by environmental pressures, declining performance, recognition of a problem, or awareness that someone else has found a better way, among other things. Many changes are never tried or fail simply because situations are not properly unfrozen to begin with.

Large systems seem particularly susceptible to something called the *boiled frog phenomenon*.[12] This refers to a classic physiological experiment demonstrating that a live frog will immediately jump out when placed in a pan of hot water. When placed in cold water that is then heated very slowly, however, the frog will

> **Unfreezing** is the stage at which a situation is prepared for change.

403

stay in the water until the water boils the frog to death. Organizations, too, can fall victim to similar circumstances. When managers fail to monitor their environments, recognize the important trends, or sense the need to change, their organizations may slowly suffer and lose their competitive edge. Although the signals that change may be needed are available, they aren't noticed or given any special attention... until it is too late. The best organizations, by contrast, are led by people who are always on the alert and understand the importance of "unfreezing" in the change process.

To better meet the competitive challenges of change, General Motors is adding a new position to its corporate staff—Chief Learning Officer. The purpose is to coordinate information sharing around the firm's world-wide operations.[13]

Changing is the stage in which specific actions are taken to create change.

Changing   The **changing** stage involves taking action to actually modify a situation by changing things, such as the people, tasks, structure, and/or technology of the organization. Lewin believes that many change agents are prone to an *activity trap*. They bypass the unfreezing stage and start changing things prematurely or too quickly. Although their intentions may be correct, the situation has not been properly prepared for change. This often leads to failure. Changing something is hard enough in any situation, let alone having to do so without the proper foundations.

Refreezing is the stage where changes are reinforced and stabilized.

Refreezing   **Refreezing** is the final stage of the planned change process. Designed to maintain the momentum of a change and eventually institutionalize it as part of the normal routine, refreezing makes sure the full benefits of long-lasting change are secured. Refreezing involves positively reinforcing desired outcomes and providing extra support when difficulties are encountered. It involves evaluating progress and results, and assessing the costs and benefits of the change. And importantly, it allows for modifications to be made in the change to increase its success over time. When all of this is not done and refreezing is neglected, changes are often abandoned after a short time or incompletely implemented.

PLANNED CHANGE STRATEGIES

Managers and other change agents use various means for mobilizing power, exerting influence over others, and getting people to support planned change efforts. As described in Figure 19.2, each of these strategies builds from the various bases of social power discussed in Chapter 14. Note in particular that each power source has somewhat different implications for the planned change process.[14]

A **force–coercion strategy** uses authority, rewards, and punishments to create change.

▼ FORCE–COERCION

A **force–coercion strategy** uses legitimacy, rewards, and/or punishments as primary inducements to change. That is, the change agent acts unilaterally to try to

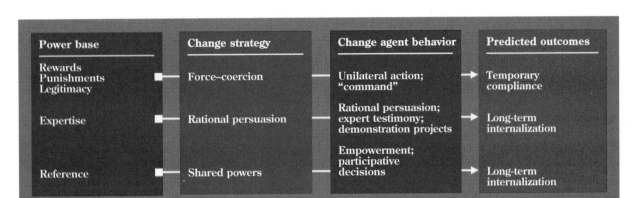

Power base	Change strategy	Change agent behavior	Predicted outcomes
Rewards Punishments Legitimacy	Force–coercion	Unilateral action; "command"	Temporary compliance
Expertise	Rational persuasion	Rational persuasion; expert testimony; demonstration projects	Long-term internalization
Reference	Shared powers	Empowerment; participative decisions	Long-term internalization

■ FIGURE 19.2

Power bases, change strategies, and predicted change outcomes.

"command" change through the formal authority of his or her position, to induce change via an offer of special rewards, or to bring about change via threats of punishment. People respond to this strategy mainly out of the fear of being punished if they do not comply with a change directive, or out of the desire for gaining a reward if they do. Compliance is usually temporary and continues only as long as the change agent and his or her legitimate authority are visible, or as long as the opportunities for rewards and punishments remain obvious.

Your actions as a change agent using the force–coercion strategy might match the following profile.[15]

> You believe that people who run things are basically motivated by self-interest and by what the situation offers in terms of potential personal gains or losses. Since you feel that people change only in response to such motives, you try to find out where their vested interests lie and then put the pressure on. If you have formal authority, you use it. If not, you resort to whatever possible rewards and punishments you have access to and do not hesitate to threaten others with these weapons. Once you find a weakness, you exploit it and are always wise to work "politically" by building supporting alliances wherever possible.

▼ RATIONAL PERSUASION

Change agents using a **rational persuasion strategy** attempt to bring about change through the use of special knowledge, empirical support, or rational arguments. This strategy assumes that rational people will be guided by reason and self-interest in deciding whether or not to support a change. Expert power is mobilized to convince others that the change will leave them better off than before. When successful, this strategy results in a longer lasting, more internalized change than does force–coercion.

As a change agent taking the rational persuasion approach to a change situation, you might behave as follows.

> You believe that people are inherently rational and are guided by reason in their actions and decision making. Once a specific course of action is demonstrated to be in

A **rational persuasion strategy** uses facts, special knowledge, and rational argument to create change.

a person's self-interest, you assume that reason and rationality will cause the person to adopt it. Thus, you approach change with the objective of communicating—through information and facts—the essential "desirability" of change from the perspective of the person whose behavior you seek to influence. If this logic is effectively communicated, you are sure of the person's adopting the proposed change.

▼ SHARED POWER

A **shared-power** strategy actively and sincerely involves the people who will be affected by a change in planning and making key decisions in respect to it. Sometimes called a *normative-reeducative approach,* this strategy tries to develop directions and support for change through involvement and empowerment. It builds essential foundations, such as personal values, group norms, and shared goals, so that support for a proposed change emerges naturally. Managers using normative-reeducative approaches draw upon the power of personal reference and also share power by allowing others to participate in planning and implementing the change. Given this high level of involvement, the strategy is likely to result in a longer lasting and internalized change.

As a change agent who shares power and adopts a normative-reeducative approach to change, you are likely to fit this profile:

> You believe that people have complex motivations. You feel that people behave as they do as a result of sociocultural norms and commitments to these norms. You also recognize that changes in these orientations involve changes in attitudes, values, skills, and significant relationships, not just changes in knowledge, information, or intellectual rationales for action and practice. Thus, when seeking to change others, you are sensitive to the supporting or inhibiting effects of any group pressures and norms that may be operating. In working with people, you try to find out their side of things and to identify their feelings and expectations.

> A **shared-power strategy** uses participative methods and emphasizes common values to create change.

▶ RESISTANCE TO CHANGE

> **Resistance to change** is an attitude or behavior that shows unwillingness to make or support a change.

Resistance to change is any attitude or behavior that reflects a person's unwillingness to make or support a desired change. Any such resistance is often viewed by change agents as something that must be "overcome" in order for change to be successful. This is not always the case, however. It is helpful to view resistance to change as feedback that can be used by the change agent to help better accomplish change objectives.[16] The essence of this constructive approach to resistance is to recognize that when people resist change, they are defending something important that appears threatened by the change attempt.

▼ WHY PEOPLE RESIST CHANGE

There are many reasons that people may resist change. Among them are fear of the unknown, insecurity, lack of a felt need to change, threat to vested interests, contrasting interpretations, and lack of resources. A work team's members, for example, may resist the introduction of advanced personal computers at their work stations because they have never before used the computer's operating system and are apprehensive that they cannot learn to use it successfully. They may wonder whether the new computers will be used as justification for "getting rid" of some of them eventually; or, they believe that they have been doing their jobs just fine, and do not need the new computers to improve things.

These and other viewpoints often create resistance to even the best and most well-intended planned changes. To deal better with these forces, managers find it useful to separate such responses into resistance that is directed toward (1) the change itself, (2) the change strategy, and (3) the change agent as a person.

Sometimes a change agent experiences *resistance to the change itself*. People may reject a change because they believe it is not worth their time, effort, or attention. To minimize resistance in such cases, the change agent should make sure that everyone who may be affected by a change knows specifically how it satisfies the following criteria.[17]

❶ *Benefit*—The change should have a clear relative advantage for the people being asked to change; it should be perceived as "a better way."

❷ *Compatibility*—The change should be as compatible as possible with the existing values and experiences of the people being asked to change.

❸ *Complexity*—The change should be no more complex than necessary; it must be as easy as possible for people to understand and use.

❹ *Triability*—The change should be something that people can try on a step-by-step basis and make adjustments as things progress.

■ Criteria for successful changes

Change agents must also be prepared to deal with *resistance to the change strategy*. Someone who attempts to bring about change via force–coercion, for example, may create resistance among individuals who resent management by "command" or the use of threatened punishment. People may resist rational persuasion strategy in which the data are suspect or the expertise of the advocates is not clearly demonstrated. They may similarly resist a shared power strategy that appears manipulative and insincere, rather than genuine.

Finally, *resistance to the change agent* can also occur. This form of resistance is directed at the person implementing the change and often involves personality and other differences. Change agents who are isolated and aloof from other persons in the change situation, who appear self-serving, and/or who have a high emotional involvement in the changes are especially prone to such problems. Research also indicates that change agents who differ from other persons in the change situation on such dimensions as age, education, and socioeconomic factors may encounter greater resistance to change.[18]

Take-A-Note 19.1

SEVEN REASONS FOR RESISTING CHANGE

1. Fear of the unknown
2. Lack of good information
3. Fear for loss of security
4. No reasons to change
5. Fear for loss of power
6. Lack of resources
7. Bad timing

▼ HOW TO DEAL WITH RESISTANCE

There are many things an informed change agent can do to deal positively with resistance to change, in any of its forms. Resistance will most often be managed best if it is recognized early in the change process. Among the possible ways for dealing with resistance to change, the following six approaches are common.[19]

One way to handle resistance to change is through *education and communication*. This can be accomplished by face-to-face discussions, group presentations, written or E-mail memos and reports, or use of experimental pilot programs. The objective is to educate people about a change before it is implemented and to help them understand the logic of the change. Education and communication seems to work best when resistance is based on inaccurate or incomplete information. A second way is the use of *participation and involvement*. With the goal of allowing others to help design and implement the changes, this approach asks people to contribute ideas and advice or to work on task forces or committees leading the change. This is a useful approach that offers special advantages when the change agent does not have all the information needed to successfully handle a problem situation.

Facilitation and support involves providing assistance—emotional and material—for people experiencing the hardships of change. A manager using this approach actively listens to problems and complaints, provides training in the new ways, and helps others to overcome performance pressures. Facilitation and sup-

Method	Use when	Advantages	Disadvantages
Education & communication	People lack information or have inaccurate information	Creates willingness to help with the change	Can be very time consuming
Participation & involvement	Other people have important information and/or power to resist	Adds information to change planning; builds commitment to the change	Can be very time consuming
Facilitation & support	Resistance traces to resource or adjustment problems	Satisfies directly specific resource or adjustment needs	Can be time consuming; can be expensive
Negotiation & agreement	A person or group will "lose" something because of the change	Helps avoid major resistance	Can be expensive; can cause others to seek similar "deals"
Manipulation & cooptation	Other methods don't work or are too expensive	Can be quick and inexpensive	Can create future problems if people sense manipulation
Explicit & implicit coercion	Speed important and change agent has power	Quick; overpowers resistance	Risky if people get "mad"

■ FIGURE 19.3

Methods for dealing with resistance to change.

port is highly recommended when people are frustrated by work constraints and difficulties encountered in the change process. A *negotiation and agreement* approach offers incentives to actual or potential change resistors. Tradeoffs are arranged to provide special benefits in exchange for assurances that the change will not be blocked. It is most useful when dealing with a person or group that will clearly lose something of value as a result of the planned change.

Manipulation and cooptation make use of covert attempts to influence others, selectively providing information and consciously structuring events so that the desired change occurs. In some cases, leaders of the resistance may be "bought off" with special side deals to gain their support. Manipulation and cooptation are common when other tactics just do not work or are too expensive. Finally, *explicit or implicit coercion* employs the force of authority to get people to accept change. Often, resistors are threatened with a variety of undesirable consequences if they do not go along as planned. This may be done, for example, in crisis situations when speed is of the essence.

Figure 19.3 summarizes additional insights into how and when each of these methods may be used for dealing with resistance to change. Regardless of the chosen strategy, it is always best to remember that the presence of resistance typically suggests that something can be done to achieve a better fit among the change, the situation, and the people affected. A good change agent deals with resistance to change by listening to feedback and acting accordingly.

QUALITY

Making change stick is not an easy challenge, but it can be mastered. One of the keys, as Dale Gambill, Vice President of Customer Care for Jaguar of North America, learned is dealing positively with resistance. During a meet-

ing with managers at which he started to speak about better customer service, they surprised him by complaining vocally that the company wasn't taking good enough care of them. Together with president Mike Dale, Gambill responded by putting the loudest complainers in charge of "egg groups" (*e*mployee *i*nvolvement *g*roups) to find solutions. The results have corrected many problems and the process has helped deal with the ongoing stress of continuous improvement and change.[20]

INNOVATION IN ORGANIZATIONS

> **Innovation** is the process of creating new ideas and putting them into practice.

The best organizations are able to "innovate" on an ongoing basis; the best managers and team leaders are able to help organization members utilize their "innovative" talents to the fullest. Formally stated, **innovation** is the process of creating new ideas and putting them into practice.[21] It is the means by

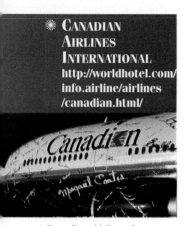

CANADIAN AIRLINES INTERNATIONAL
http://worldhotel.com/info.airline/airlines/canadian.html/

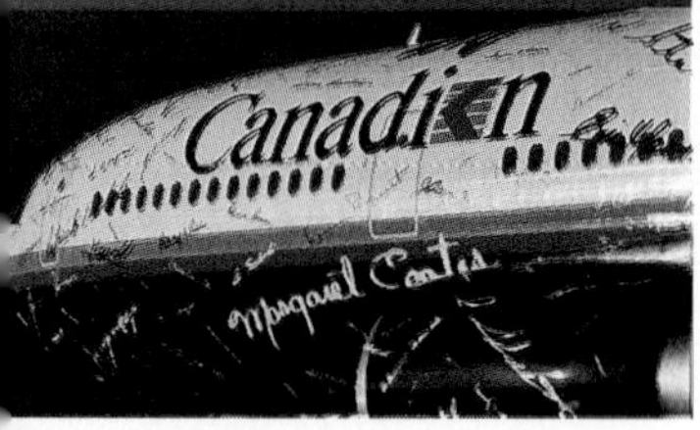
Canadian

Canadian Airlines International's "Service Quality" program involved changes in strategy, major processes, and systems. A training project for employees, contractors, and suppliers directly supported all aspects of the program.[22]

which creative ideas find their way into everyday practices, ideally those contributing to improved customer service and/or organizational productivity. *Product innovations* result in the introduction of new or improved goods or services to better meet customer needs; *process innovations* result in the introduction into operations of better ways of doing things.

THE INNOVATION PROCESS

The basic steps in a typical process of organizational innovation are shown in Figure 19.4. They include: (1) *idea creation* through spontaneous creativity, ingenuity, and information processing; (2) *initial experimentation* to establish the idea's potential value and application; (3) *feasibility determination* to identify anticipated costs and benefits; and (4) *final application* to producc and market a new product or service, or to implement a new approach to operations. Importantly, the innovation process is not complete until final application has been achieved. A new idea—even a great one—is not enough. In any organization, the idea must pass through all stages of innovation and reach the point of final application before its value can be realized.

FEATURES OF INNOVATIVE ORGANIZATIONS

The new workplace is placing great demands on organizations and their members to be innovative—and to be so continuously. Highly innovative organizations have *strategies and cultures* that are built around a commitment to innovation. This means, at the extreme, that the internal climate tolerates mistakes—well-intentioned ideas that just do not work out as expected. Highly innovative organizations, especially larger ones, have *structures* that support innovation. Newer organizational forms, in particular, emphasize creativity through teamwork and better cross-functional integration. They also try to utilize decentralization and empowerment to overcome the limitations of great size. A goal in "large" innovative organizations is to really act "small."

FIGURE 19.4
The innovation process: a case of new product development. [Source: John R. Schermerhorn, Jr., *Management for Productivity,* 4th ed. (New York: John Wiley & Sons, 1996), p. 661. Used by permission.]

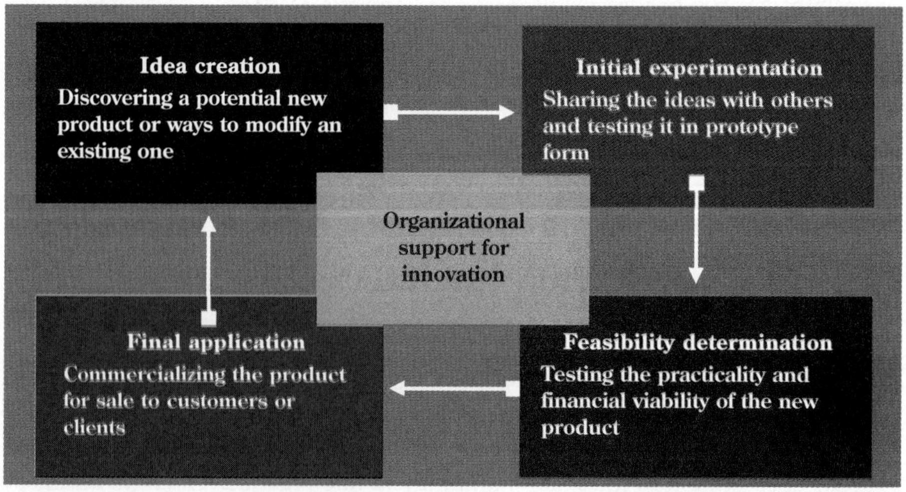
Idea creation
Discovering a potential new product or ways to modify an existing one
Initial experimentation
Sharing the ideas with others and testing it in prototype form
Organizational support for innovation
Final application
Commercializing the product for sale to customers or clients
Feasibility determination
Testing the practicality and financial viability of the new product

In highly innovative organizations, *staffing* is done with a clear commitment to innovation. These organizations actively support and encourage everyone to use their creative talents to the fullest. They also pay special attention to filling the critical innovation roles of idea generators, information gatekeepers, product champions, and project leaders. Finally, innovative organizations benefit from *top-management support*. Senior managers in the most innovative settings provide good examples for others to follow, eliminate obstacles to innovation, and try to get things done that make innovation easier. Former Johnson & Johnson CEO James Burke, for example, once said, "I try to give people the feeling that it's okay to fail." Quad Graphics founder Harry V. Quadrucci practices what has been dubbed "management by walking away." He believes that employees know what needs to be done, and management's job is to trust them to do their best, without a lot of rules or fear that they'll be punished if they make mistakes.[23]

THE DYNAMICS OF STRESS

As positive and necessary as the processes of change and innovation are in the new workplace, they are often accompanied by new and increased pressures on the people involved. To help ensure continuity of ideas and improvement, it is necessary to understand **stress** as a state of tension experienced by individuals facing extraordinary demands, constraints, or opportunities.[24] Any look toward your career future in today's dynamic times must include an awareness that stress is something you, as well as others, are sure to encounter.[25]

> **Stress** is tension from extraordinary demands, constraints, or opportunities.

▼ SOURCES OF STRESS

Simply put, **stressors** are the things that cause stress. Some trace directly to what people experience in the workplace, others trace to nonwork and personal factors.

> **Stressors** are things that cause stress.

Work-Related Stressors Work-related stress arises from many sources. It can result from excessively high or low task demands, role conflicts or ambiguities, poor interpersonal relations, or career progress that is either too slow or too fast. A list of common work-related stressors that anyone should be able to spot includes:[26]

- *Task demands*—being asked to do too much or being asked to do too little.
- *Role ambiguities*—not knowing what one is expected to do or how work performance is evaluated.
- *Role conflicts*—feeling unable to satisfy multiple, possibly conflicting, performance expectations.
- *Ethical dilemmas*—being asked to do things that violate the law and/or personal values.

> ■ Possible work-related stressors

- *Interpersonal problems*—experiencing bad relationships or working with others who do not get along.
- *Career developments*—moving too fast and feeling stretched; moving too slow and feeling plateaued.
- *Physical setting*—being bothered by noise, lack of privacy, pollution, or other unpleasant working conditions.

Nonwork and Personal Stressors   A possibly less obvious source of stress for people at work is the "spillover" effect from forces in their nonwork lives. Family events (e.g., the birth of a new child), economic difficulties (e.g., the sudden loss of a big investment), and personal affairs (e.g., a separation or divorce) can all be very stressful. Since it is often difficult to separate work and nonwork lives completely, stress of this nonwork sort can affect the way people feel and behave on the job as well as away from it.

Another set of stressors includes personal factors, such as individual needs, capabilities, and personality. These are properties of the individual that influence how he or she perceives and responds to stress emanating from work and nonwork sources. Stress can reach a destructive state more quickly, for example, when experienced by highly emotional people or by those with low self-esteem. People who perceive a good fit between job requirements and personal skills seem to have a higher tolerance for stress than do those who feel less competent as a result of a person–job mismatch.[28] Basic aspects of personality may also cause some people to experience more stress than others in similar situations. The achievement orientation, impatience, and perfectionism of individuals with Type A personalities, for example, often creates stress for them in work settings that others find relatively stress-free.[29]

▼ STRESS AND PERFORMANCE

It is easy to get the impression that stress always acts as a negative influence on our lives. There are actually two faces to stress—one positive and one negative.[30] Indeed, one of the most difficult tasks is to find optimum stress that allows for the potential advantages to be realized but not the disadvantages.

Constructive stress
has a positive impact on attitudes and/or performance.

Constructive stress, or *eustress,* acts in a positive way for the individual and/or the organization. Moderate levels of stress tend to act in this constructive or energizing way by prompting increased work effort, stimulating creativity, and encouraging greater diligence. You may know such stress as the tension that causes you to study hard before exams, pay attention, and complete assignments on time in a difficult class.

Destructive stress has a negative impact on attitudes and/or performance.

Destructive stress, or *distress,* is dysfunctional for the individual and/or the organization. Whereas moderate levels of stress can enhance performance, excessively high levels of stress can decrease it. Too much stress overloads and breaks down a person's physical and mental systems. They may react to high stress through absenteeism, turnover, errors, accidents, dissatisfaction, reduced performance, or even unethical behavior. Their performance can also suffer from illness brought on by stress and/or its consequences.

The Josephson Institute of Ethics is concerned about the risks of employers pushing people too hard. "Overtasking" involves asking employees to pursue unrealistic goals. One result can be unethical behavior or cheating. In the face of impossible performance standards, people may be led to falsify their "numbers" or engage in other questionable practices to make their performance look good. One example was the scandal at Sears auto repair shops in California. Store managers were demanding that shop managers meet very high sales goals; in some shops, these goals were met by customers being charged for services they had never received.[31]

▼ STRESS AND HEALTH

There is no doubt that stress can impact a person's health. It is a potential source of both anxiety and frustration, each of which can harm the body's physiological and/or psychological well-being over time.[32] Health problems associated with stress include heart attack, stroke, hypertension, migraine headache, ulcers, substance abuse, overeating, depression, and muscle aches, among others.

Managers should be alert to signs of excessive stress in themselves and their coworkers. The symptoms are multiple and varied. When it comes to observable work behaviors, the key things to look for are changes from normal patterns—a change from regular attendance to absenteeism, from punctuality to tardiness, from diligent work to careless work, from a positive attitude to a negative attitude, from openness to change to resistance to change, or from cooperation to hostility, for example. When it comes to personal habits and feelings, the warning signs of excessive stress are also observable.[33]

> ### Take-A-Note 19.2
> #### SIGNS OF EXCESSIVE STRESS
>
> - Change in eating habits
> - Change in alcohol consumption or smoking
> - Unhealthy feeling—aches and pains, upset stomach
> - Restlessness, inability to concentrate, sleeping problems
> - Feeling tense, uptight, fidgety, nervous
> - Feeling disoriented, overwhelmed, depressed, irritable

▼ EFFECTIVE STRESS MANAGEMENT

Stress prevention is the best first-line strategy for dealing with stress. It involves taking action to keep stress from reaching destructive levels in the first place—for yourself or for others. In particular, personal and nonwork stressors must be recognized so that action can be taken to prevent them from adversely affecting the work experience. Persons with Type A orientations, for example, may exercise self-discipline; supervisors of Type A employees may try to model a lower key, more relaxed approach to work. At another level, family problems may be partially relieved by a change of work schedule; the anxiety caused by pressing family concerns may be reduced by simply knowing that your supervisor understands. Organization and management practices in the new workplace can also help prevent stress from becoming excessive. These include empowerment

> **Stress prevention** involves minimizing the potential for stress to occur.

and participation, job redesign, goal setting, better communication, proper selection, and appropriate training.

Once stress has reached a destructive point, special techniques of *stress management* can be used to deal with it. This process begins with the recognition of stress symptoms and continues with actions being taken to maintain a positive performance edge. **Personal wellness** is important here. The term describes the pursuit of one's physical and mental potential through a personal health promotion program.[34] It recognizes individual responsibility to enhance and maintain wellness through a disciplined approach to physical and mental health. This requires attention to such things as smoking, weight, diet, alcohol use, and physical fitness.

The essence of personal wellness is a lifestyle that reflects a true and comprehensive commitment to health. It makes a great deal of sense as a preventive stress management strategy. Someone who aggressively maintains his or her health should be better prepared to deal with the inevitable stress of work in today's organizations. This person should also be able to take advantage of the constructive aspects of stress while avoiding its more destructive potential. Ultimately, a healthy personal life and a high quality of work life environment can help all of us handle successfully the stresses that inevitably accompany complex and fast-paced lives—both at home and at work.

> **Personal wellness** involves maintaining physical and mental health to better deal with stress when it occurs.

CHAPTER 19 STUDY GUIDE

SUMMARY

What is organizational change?
- Organizational change may be radical—frame breaking, or incremental—frame bending; both can be good for organizations seeking continuous improvement.
- Successful ongoing change is essential to organizations that must adapt to the shifting demands and opportunities of dynamic environments.
- Planned change takes place because change agents, individuals and groups, make it happen to resolve performance problems or take advantage of performance opportunities.
- Organizational targets for planned change include purpose, strategy, culture, structure, people, tasks, and technology.
- The planned change process requires attention to the three phases—unfreezing, changing, and refreezing.

What change strategies are used in organizations?
- Change strategies are the means used by change agents to bring about desired change in people and systems.
- Force–coercion change strategies use position power to bring about change by direct command or through rewards and punishments.

- Rational persuasion change strategies use logical arguments and appeals to knowledge and facts to convince people to change.
- Shared power change strategies involve other persons in planning and implementing change.

What can be done about resistance to change?

- Resistance to change should be expected and not feared; it is a source of feedback that can be used to improve a change effort.
- People usually resist change because they are defending something of value; they may focus their resistance on the change itself, the change strategy, and/or the change agent as a person.
- Successful change agents are open to resistance and respond to it in ways that create a better fit among the change, the situation, and all the people involved.
- Strategies for dealing with resistance to change include education and communication, participation and involvement, facilitation and support, negotiation and agreement, manipulation and cooptation, and explicit or implicit coercion.

How do organizations innovate?

- Innovation is the process of creating new ideas and then implementing them in practical applications.
- Product innovations result in improved goods or services; process innovations result in improved work methods and operations.
- Steps in the innovation process normally include idea generation, initial experimentation, feasibility determination, and final application.
- Common features of highly innovative organizations include supportive strategies, cultures, structures, staffing, and top management.

How does stress affect people at work?

- Stress emerges when people experience tensions caused by extraordinary demands, constraints, and/or opportunities in their jobs.
- Moderate levels of stress can be constructive and result in performance gains; too much stress can be destructive and result in performance losses.
- Stress can adversely affect a person's mental and/or physical health; we should be constantly alert for symptoms of excessive stress in our attitudes and behaviors, as well as in those of others.
- Work-related stressors arise from such things as excessive task demands, interpersonal problems, unclear roles, ethical dilemmas, and career disappointments.
- Nonwork stress can spill over to affect people at work; nonwork stressors may be traced to family situations, economic difficulties, and personal problems.
- Personal stressors derive from personality type, needs, and values, and can influence how stressful different situations become for different people.
- Stress can be managed by prevention—such as making adjustments in work and nonwork factors; it can also be dealt with through personal wellness—taking steps to maintain a healthy body and mind capable of better withstanding stressful situations.

KEY TERMS

Change agent (p. 401)
Changing (p. 404)
Constructive stress (p. 412)
Destructive stress (p. 412)
Force–coercion strategy
 (p. 404)
Innovation (p. 409)

Personal wellness (p. 414)
Planned change (p. 402)
Rational persuasion
 strategy (p. 405)
Refreezing (p. 404)
Resistance to change
 (p. 406)

Shared-power strategy
 (p. 406)
Stress (p. 411)
Stress prevention (p. 413)
Stressors (p. 411)
Unfreezing (p. 403)
Unplanned change (p. 401)

SELF-TEST 19

▼ MULTIPLE CHOICE

1. Performance gaps creating change situations include both problems to be resolved and _____. (a) costs to be avoided (b) people to be terminated (c) structures to be changed (d) opportunities to be explored
2. The presence or absence of a felt need for change is an issue in the _____ phase of planned change. (a) diagnostic (b) evaluative (c) unfreezing (d) changing
3. Which change strategy relies on empirical data, facts, and expert power to achieve its goals? (a) Force–coercion. (b) Rational persuasion. (c) Shared power. (d) Authoritative command.
4. Which change strategy is most associated with temporary compliance as a change outcome? (a) Force–coercion. (b) Rational persuasion. (c) Shared power. (d) Normative reeducation.
5. A good change agent _____ resistance to change in order to best achieve change objectives. (a) eliminates (b) ignores (c) listens to (d) retreats from
6. According to the criterion of _____, a good change is clearly perceived as a better way of doing things. (a) benefit (b) triability (c) complexity (d) compatibility
7. Training in use of a new computer technology is an example of managing resistance to change through _____. (a) participation and involvement (b) facilitation and support (c) negotiation and agreement (d) education and communication
8. The innovation process is not complete until _____ has occurred. (a) idea creation (b) invention (c) feasibility determination (d) final application
9. Task demands, ethical dilemmas, and career disappointments are examples of _____ stressors, while a Type A personality is an example of _____ stressors. (a) work-related, personal (b) work-related, nonwork (c) nonpersonal, personal (d) real, imagined
10. Which is an example of stress management by the personal wellness strategy? (a) role negotiation (b) management by objectives (c) regular physical exercise (d) flexible working hours

▼ TRUE–FALSE

11. The only significant change for today's organizations is radical or frame-breaking change.   T F
12. Change agents, formally defined, are outside consultants hired to help managers change their organizations.   T F
13. Changes in tasks, people, technology, and structures are often interrelated in organizations.   T F
14. Positive reinforcement of desired behaviors is part of the refreezing phase of planned change.   T F

15. The personality and style of the change agent may cause resistance to change. T F

16. The shared power change strategy is the same as the rational persuasion change strategy.   T F

17. A process innovation results in the creation of a new good or service for the organization.   T F

18. Product champions and information gatekeepers play important innovation roles in organizations.   T F

19. The only real way to deal with stress is to prevent its occurrence in the first place. T F

20. Stress from nonwork factors can spill over to affect a person's work activities.   T F

▼ SHORT RESPONSE

21. What should a manager do when forces for unplanned change appear?

22. What internal and external forces push for change in organizations?

23. What does the "boiled frog phenomenon" tell us about organizational change?

24. How might stress influence individual performance?

▼ APPLICATIONS ESSAY

25. When Jorge Maldanado became general manager of the local civic recreation center, he realized that many changes would be necessary to make the facility a true community resource. Having the benefit of a new bond issue, the center had the funds for new equipment and expanded programming. All he needed to do now was get the staff committed to new initiatives. Unfortunately, his first efforts to raise performance have been met with considerable resistance to change. A typcial staff comment is, "Why do all these extras? Everything is fine as it is." How may the strategies for dealing with resistance to change, as discussed in the chapter, be used by Jorge to move the change process along?

SUPPLEMENTARY MODULE

RESEARCH FOUNDATIONS OF ORGANIZATIONAL BEHAVIOR

This book is full of findings and conclusions about organizational behavior as a field of study. These findings and conclusions rely heavily on research foundations. For example, the different motivational approaches and recommendations discussed in Chapter 5 are based on such research foundations. Thus, one key reason that research foundations are so important to you is that they provide the base for the content of this course. A second reason is that you can use them to evaluate not only the findings in your text and course but also everyday findings that are reported. For example, you are likely to see arguments presented in the media concerning leadership, motivation, and many other OB topics. Those of you who become managers will encounter even more information about management and OB topics. Not all of this information has been developed systematically using research foundations and a scientific approach, however. This module will help you evaluate the strengths and weaknesses of the OB information you receive. For example, your boss may ask you to respond to a new article she has just read regarding improving work group performance. The information here can help you provide a knowledgeable response.

Finally, OB research foundations are important because they can guide you, as a manager, in asking the right questions and obtaining the right information to deal systematically with managerial and OB problems. For example, you may want to see whether the application of one of the leadership approaches in Chapter 15 works as predicted. This module can guide you in examining that question. The module alone will not make a scientist or an OB expert out of you, but it will help you think scientifically and use appropriate research foundations to deal with problems of concern to you.

THE SCIENTIFIC METHOD ◀

A key part of OB research foundations is the **scientific method,** which involves four steps. First, a *research question* or *problem* is specified. Then one or more *hypotheses* or explanations of what the research parties expect to find are formulated. These may come from many sources, including previous experience and careful review of the literature covering the problem area. The next step is the creation of a *research design*—an overall plan or strategy for conducting the research to test the hypothesis(es). Finally, *data gathering, analysis,* and *interpretation* are carried out.[1]

▼ THE VOCABULARY OF RESEARCH

The previous discussion conveyed a quick summary of the scientific method. It's important to go beyond that summation and further develop a number of aspects of the scientific method. Before doing that, we consider the vocabulary of research. Knowing that vocabulary can help you feel comfortable with several terms used in OB research as well as help in our later discussion.[2]

Variable   A **variable** is a measure used to describe a real-world phenomenon. For example, a researcher may count the number of parts produced by workers in a week's time as a measure of the workers' individual productivity.

Hypothesis   Building on our earlier use of the term, we can define a **hypothesis** as a tentative explanation about the relationship between two or more variables. For example, OB researchers have hypothesized that an increase in the number of rest pauses allowed workers in a workday will increase productivity. Hypotheses are "predictive" statements. Once supported through empirical research, a hypothesis can be a source of direct action implications. Confirmation of the above hypothesis would lead to the following implication: If you want to increase individual productivity in a work unit, give the subordinates more frequent rest pauses.

Dependent Variable   The **dependent variable** is the event or occurrence expressed in a hypothesis that indicates what the researcher is interested in explaining. In OB research, for example, individual performance is often the dependent variable of interest; that is, researchers try to determine what factors appear

The **scientific method** is a key part of the OB research foundations, which involves four steps: the research question or problem, hypothesis generation or formulation, the research design, and data gathering, analysis, and interpretation.

A **variable** is a measure used to describe a real-world phenomenon.

A **hypothesis** is a tentative explanation about the relationship between two or more variables.

A **dependent variable** is the event or occurrence expressed in a hypothesis that indicates what the researcher is interested in explaining.

419

An **independent variable** is the event or occurrence that is presumed by a hypothesis to affect one or more other events or occurrences as dependent variables.

An **intervening variable** is an event or occurrence that provides the linkage through which an independent variable is presumed to affect a dependent variable.

A **moderator variable** is an event or occurrence that, when systematically varied, changes the relationship between an independent variable and a dependent variable.

A **theory** is a set of systematically interrelated concepts, definitions, and hypotheses that are advanced to explain and predict phenomena.

Validity is the degree of confidence one can have in the results of a research study.

to predict increases in performance. One hypothesized relationship is that increased rest periods predict increased performance.

Independent Variable   An **independent variable** is the event or occurrence that is presumed by a hypothesis to affect one or more other events or occurrences as dependent variables. In the OB study on individual performance, increased rest periods is the independent variable.

Intervening Variable   An **intervening variable** is an event or occurrence that provides the linkage through which an independent variable is presumed to affect a dependent variable. It has been hypothesized, for instance, that participative supervisory practices—independent variable—improve worker satisfaction—intervening variable—and therefore increase performance—dependent variable.

Moderator Variable   A **moderator variable** is an event or occurrence that, when systematically varied, changes the relationship between an independent variable and a dependent variable. The relationship between these two variables differs depending on the level, for instance, high/low, young/old, male/female, of the moderator variable.[3] To illustrate, the previous example of individual performance hypothesizes that participative supervision leads to increased productivity. It may well be that this relationship holds true only when the employees feel that their participation is real and legitimate—a moderator variable. Likewise, it may be that participative supervision leads to increased performance for Canadian workers but not those from Brazil—here, country is a moderator variable.

Theory   A **theory** is a set of systematically interrelated concepts, definitions, and hypotheses that are advanced to explain and predict phenomena.[4] Theories tend to be abstract and to involve multiple variables. They usually include a number of hypotheses, each of which is based on clearly articulated arguments and definitions. Most, if not all, of the kinds of variables previously discussed would probably be involved in a theory. We should also note that many things we call "theories" in OB do not strictly meet the above definition. Rather, they represent viewpoints, explanations, or perspectives that have logical merit and that are in the process of being scientifically varified.

Validity   **Validity** is concerned with the degree of confidence one can have in the results of a research study. It is focused on limiting research errors so that results are accurate and usable.[5] There are two key types of validity: internal and external. *Internal validity* is the degree to which the results of a study can be relied upon to be correct. It is strongest when alternative interpretations of the study's findings can be ruled out.[6] To illustrate, if performance improves with more participative supervisory practices, these results have a higher degree of internal validity if we can rule out the effects of differences in old and new machines.

   External validity is the degree to which the study's results can be generalized across the entire population of people, settings, and other similar conditions.[7] We

420

cannot have external validity unless we first have internal validity; that is, we must have confidence that the results are caused by what the study says they are before we can generalize to a broader context.

Reliability   **Reliability** is the consistency and stability of a score from a measurement scale. There must be reliability for there to be validity or accuracy. Think of shooting at a bull's eye. If the shots land all over the target, there is neither reliability (consistency) or validity (accuracy). If the shots are clustered close together but outside the outer ring of the target, they are reliable but not valid. If they are grouped together within the bull's eye, they are both reliable and valid.[8]

> **Reliability** is the consistency and stability of a score from a measurement scale.

Causality   **Causality** is the assumption that change in the independent variable caused change in the dependent variable. This assumption is very difficult to prove in OB research. Three types of evidence are necessary to demonstrate causality: (1) the variables must show a linkage or association; (2) one variable must precede the other in time; and (3) there must be an absence of other causal factors.[9] For example, say we note that participation and performance increase together—there is an association. If we can then show that an increase in participation has preceded an increase in performance and that other factors, such as new machinery, haven't been responsible for the increased performance, we can say that participation probably has caused performance.

> **Causality** is the assumption that change in the independent variable has caused change in the dependent variable.

RESEARCH DESIGNS   ◀

As noted earlier, a **research design** is an overall plan or strategy for conducting the research to test the hypothesis(es). Four of the most popular research designs are laboratory experiments, field experiments, case studies, and field surveys.[10]

> A **research design** is an overall plan or strategy for conducting research to test a hypothesis.

▼ LABORATORY EXPERIMENTS

Laboratory experiments are conducted in an artificial setting in which the researcher intervenes and manipulates one or more independent variables in a highly controlled situation. Although there is a high degree of control, which, in turn, encourages internal validity, since these studies are done in an artificial setting, they may suffer from external validity.

To illustrate, assume we are interested in the impact of three different incentive systems on employee absenteeism: (1) a lottery with a monetary reward; (2) a lottery with a compensatory time off reward; and (3) a lottery with a large prize, such as a car. The researcher randomly selects individuals in an organization to come to an office to take part in the study. This randomization is important because it means that variables that are not measured are randomly distributed across the subjects so that unknown variables shouldn't be causing whatever is

> A **laboratory experiment** is conducted in an artificial setting in which the researcher intervenes and manipulates one or more independent variables in a highly controlled situation.

found. However, it often is not possible to obtain subjects randomly in organizations since they may be needed elsewhere by management.

The researcher is next able to select randomly each worker to one of the three incentive systems as well as a control group with no incentive system. The employees report to work in their new work stations under highly artificial but controlled conditions, and their absenteeism is measured both at the beginning and end of the experiment. Statistical comparisons are made across each group, considering before and after measures.

Ultimately, the researcher develops hypotheses about the effects of each of the lottery treatments on absenteeism. Given support for these hypotheses, the researcher could feel with a high degree of confidence that a given incentive condition caused less absenteeism than did the others since randomized subjects, pre- and posttest measures, and a comparison with a control group were used. However, since the work stations were artificial and the lottery conditions were highly simplified to provide control, external validity could be questioned. Ideally, the researcher would conduct a follow-up study with another design to check for external validity.

▼ FIELD EXPERIMENTS

Field experiments are research studies that are conducted in a realistic setting. Here, the researcher intervenes and manipulates one or more independent variables and controls the situation as carefully as the situation permits.

Applying the same research question as before, the researcher obtains management permission to assign one incentive treatment to each of three similar organizational departments, similar in terms of the various characteristics of people. A fourth control department keeps the current payment plan. The rest of the experiment is similar to the laboratory study except that the lottery treatments are more realistic but also less controlled. Also, it may be particularly difficult to obtain random assignment in this case since it may disrupt day-to-day work schedules, etc. When random assignment is not possible, the other manipulations may still be possible. An experimental research design without any randomization is called a *quasi-experimental design* and does not control for unmeasured variables as well as a randomized design.

▼ CASE STUDIES

Case studies are in-depth analyses of one or a small number of settings. Case studies often are used when little is known about a phenomenon and the researcher wants to examine relevant concepts intensely and thoroughly. They can sometimes be used to help develop theory that can then be tested with one of the other research designs. Returning to the incentive and absenteeism example, one might look at one or more organizations and intensely study organizational success or failure in designing or implementing the system(s). This information could provide insights to be investigated further with additional case studies or other research designs.

A major strength of case studies is their realism and the richness of data and insights they can provide. Some disadvantages are their lack of control by the re-

A **field experiment** is a research study that is conducted in a realistic setting, whereby the researcher intervenes and manipulates one or more independent variables and controls the situation as carefully as the situation permits.

A **case study** is an in-depth analysis of one or a small number of settings.

searcher, the difficulty of interpreting the results because of their richness, and the large amount of time and cost that may be involved.

▼ FIELD SURVEYS

Field surveys typically depend on the use of some form of questionnaire for the primary purpose of describing and/or predicting some phenomenon. Typically, they utilize a sample drawn from some large population. A key objective of field surveys is to look for relationships between or among variables. Two major advantages are their ability to examine and describe large populations quickly and inexpensively and their flexibility. They can be used to do many kinds of OB research, such as testing hypotheses and theories and evaluating programs. Field surveys assume that the researcher has enough knowledge of the problem area to know the kinds of questions to ask; sometimes, earlier case studies help provide this knowledge.

> A **field survey** is a research design that relies on the use of some form of questionnaire for the primary purpose of describing and/or predicting some phenomenon.

In terms of our incentive and absenteeism problem, assume the researcher knows about organizations that have used different kinds of incentive systems to reduce absenteeism and reviews the appropriate literature on the topic. The investigator then constructs a questionnaire and sends it to firms that have implemented such incentive systems. The goal here is to describe characteristics of those organizations and incentive systems that have been successful in reducing absenteeism.

A key disadvantage of this kind of study is the lack of control. The researcher does not manipulate variables; even such things as who completes the surveys and their timing may not be under the researcher's control. Another disadvantage is the lack of depth of the standardized responses; thus, sometimes the data obtained are superficial.

DATA GATHERING, ANALYSIS, AND INTERPRETATION

Once the research design has been established, we are ready for data gathering, analysis, and interpretation—the final step in the scientific method. Four common OB data-gathering approaches are interviews, observation, questionnaires, and nonreactive measures.[11]

▼ INTERVIEWS

Interviews involve face-to-face, telephone, or computer-assisted interactions to ask respondents questions of interest. Structured interviews ask the respondents the same questions in the same sequence. Unstructured interviews are more spontaneous and do not require the same format. Often a mixture of structured and unstructured formats is used. Interviews allow for in-depth responses and probing. They are generally time consuming, however, and require increasing amounts of training and skill, depending on their depth and amount of structure.

> An **interview** involves face-to-face, telephone, or computer-assisted interactions to ask respondents questions of interest.

▼ OBSERVATION

Observation involves watching an event, object, or person and recording what is seen.

Observation involves watching an event, object, or person and recording what is seen. Sometimes, the observer is separate from the participants and events and functions as an outside researcher. In other cases, the observer participates in the events as a member of a work unit. In the latter case, observations are summarized in some kind of diary or log. Sometimes, the observer is hidden and records observations behind one-way glass or by using hidden cameras and the like.

Two advantages of observation are that (1) behavior is observed as it occurs rather than being obtained by asking people after the fact, and (2) the observer can often obtain data that subjects can't or won't provide themselves. A couple of disadvantages are cost and the possible fallibility of observers who sometimes do not provide complete and accurate data.

▼ QUESTIONNAIRES

Questionnaires ask respondents for their opinions, attitudes, perceptions, and/or descriptions of work-related matters.

Questionnaires ask respondents for their opinions, attitudes, perceptions, and/or descriptions of work-related matters. They usually are based on previously developed instruments. Typically, a respondent completes the questionnaire and returns it to the researcher. Questions may be open ended, or they may be structured with true–false or multiple-choice responses.

Advantages of questionnaires include the relatively low cost and the fact that the anonymity that often accompanies them may lead to more open and truthful responses. Some disadvantages are the low response rates, which may threaten the generalizability of the results, and the lack of depth of the responses.

▼ NONREACTIVE MEASURES

Nonreactive measures are used to obtain data without disturbing the setting.

Nonreactive measures are used to obtain data without disturbing the setting being studied. Sometimes, these are termed *unobtrusive measures* since they are designed not to intrude in a research situation. Nonreactive measures can focus on such things as physical traces, archives, and hidden observation. A kind of physical trace occurred when John Fry at 3M distributed test batches of Post-It Notes to 3M employees and discovered that they were using them at higher rates than 3M's leading adhesive product—Scotch Tape.[12] Archives are records that an organization keeps as a part of its day-to-day activities, for example, minutes, daily production counts.

A major advantage of nonreactive measures is that they don't disturb the research setting and so avoid the reaction of a respondent to a researcher. One possible disadvantage is their indirectness; incorrect inferences may be drawn from nonreactive measures. They work best in combination with more direct measures.

▼ DATA ANALYSIS AND INTERPRETATION

Once the data have been gathered, they need to be *analyzed*. The most common means of analysis involves some kind of statistical approach, ranging from simple counting and categorizing to sophisticated multivariate statistical techniques.[13] It's beyond our scope to discuss this area beyond simply emphasizing its importance. However, various statistical tests often are used to examine support for hypotheses, to check for the reliability of various data-gathering approaches, and to provide information on causality and many other aspects of analysis.

After systematic analysis has been performed, the researcher *interprets* the results and prepares a report.[14] Sometimes, the report is used in-house by management; other times, the results are reported at various conferences and published in journals. Ultimately, many of the results in the OB area appear in textbooks like this one.

ETHICAL CONSIDERATIONS IN RESEARCH

Given our emphasis on ethical considerations throughout this book, it is appropriate to end our discussion of OB research with a look at its ethical considerations. These ethical considerations involve rights of four broad parties involved in research in general and in OB research in particular: society, subjects, clients, and researchers.[15]

In terms of *societal rights*—those of the broadest of the parties involved in OB research—three key areas exist: the right to be informed, the right to expect objective results, and the right to privacy or to be left alone. Subjects of research also have rights: the right to choose (to participate or not), to safety, and to be informed. The rights of the client involve two primary concerns: the right to expect high-quality research and the right of confidentiality. Finally, two rights of the researcher stand out: the right to expect ethical client behavior and the right to expect ethical subject behavior.

All of these rights need to be communicated and adhered to by all parties. Indeed, various organizations conducting research are increasingly endorsing codes of ethics to codify such rights. Two particular organizations that have codes of ethics for research covering OB and related areas are the American Psychological Association and the Academy of Management.[16]

THE
ORGANIZATIONAL BEHAVIOR
WORKBOOK

SUGGESTED APPLICATIONS OF WORKBOOK MATERIALS

 I. Cases for Critical Thinking

Case	Suggested Chapter	Cross-References and Integration
1. Drexler's Bar-B-Que	1 Organization Behavior and the New Workplace	organizational structure; design and culture; organizational change and innovation; decision making; leadership
2. Crossing Borders	2 International Dimensions of Organizational Behavior	new workplace and diversity; perception and attribution; performance management; job design; communication; conflict decision making
3. Never on a Sunday	3 Diversity and Individual Differences	new workplace; ethics and diversity; organizational structure, design, and culture; decision making; organizational change
4. Magrec, Inc.	4 Perception and Attribution	new workplace; ethics and diversity; organizational structure, design, and culture; decision making; organizational change
5. It isn't Fair	5 Motivation	perception and attribution; performance management and rewards; communication; ethics and decision making
6. Amoco's Global Human Resource Systems	6 Performance Management and Rewards	new workplace; culture; international; communication; decision making
7. Intergalactic Manufacturing	7 Learning and Reinforcement	motivation; culture; international; performance management and rewards; communication; ethics and decision making
8. I'm Not in Kansas Anymore	8 Job Design, Goal Setting, and Work Arrangements	organizational design; motivation; performance management and rewards; new workplace
9. The Forgotten Group Member	9 The Nature of Groups	teamwork; motivation; diversity and individual differences; perception and attribution; performance management and rewards; communication; conflict; leadership
10. Functional Diversity at IBM	10 Teamwork and Workgroup Design	diversity and individual differences; motivation; performance management and rewards; new workplace
11. First Community Financial	11 Basic Attributes of Organizations	new workplace; organizational structure and culture; performance management and rewards
12. Mission Management and Trust	12 Organizational Design and Learning	new workplace; organizational structure and culture; performance management and rewards
13. Craig Morancie	13 Organizational Culture	ethics and decision making; diversity and individual differences; perception and attribution; communication; conflict; leadership
14. Fidelity Insurance Company	14 Power and Politics	communication; conflict diversity and individual differences; motivation
15. Power or Empowerment at GM?	15 Leadership	communication; conflict; decision making; organizational change; job design; new workplace
16. The Poorly Informed Walrus	16 Communication	diversity and individual differences; perception and attribution; new workplace
17. I Still Do My Job, Don't I?	17 Decision Making	groups and teamwork; job design; decision making; communication; conflict; diversity and individual differences; leadership

Case	Suggested Chapter	Cross-References and Integration
18. *Theatre New Brunswick*	18 Conflict and Negotiation	perception and attribution; diversity and individual differences; job design; motivation; communication; ethics and decision making; groups and teamwork; power and influence; leadership
19. *The New Vice President*	19 Change, Innovation, and Stress	leadership; performance management and rewards; diversity and individual differences; communication; conflict and negotiation; power and influence

II. Experiential Exercises

Exercise	Suggested Chapter	Cross-References and Integration
1. *My Best Manager*	1 Organizational Behavior and the New Workplace	leadership
2. *My Best Job*	1 Organizational Behavior and the New Workplace	motivation; job design
3. *What Do You Value in Work?*	1 Organizational Behavior and the New Workplace	diversity and individual differences; performance management and rewards; motivation; job design; decision making
4. *My Asset Base*	1 Organizational Behavior and the New Workplace	perception and attribution; diversity and individual differences; groups and teamwork; decision making; new workplace
5. *Expatriate Assignments*	2 International Dimensions of Organizational Behavior	perception and attribution; diversity and individual differences; decision making
6. *Cultural Cues*	2 International Dimensions of Organizational Behavior	perception and attribution; diversity and individual differences; decision making; communication; conflict; groups and teamwork
7. *Prejudice in Our Lives*	3 Diversity and Individual Differences	perception and attribution; decision making; conflict; groups and teamwork; new workplace
8. *How We View Differences*	4 Perception and Attribution	culture; international; diversity and individual differences; decision making; communication; conflict; groups and teamwork; new workplace
9. *Alligator River Story*	4 Perception and Attribution	diversity and individual differences; decision making; communication; conflict; groups and teamwork
10. *Teamwork and Motivation*	5 Motivation	performance management and rewards; groups and teamwork
11. *Annual Pay Raises*	6 Performance Management and Rewards	motivation; learning and reinforcement; perception and attribution; decision making; groups and teamwork
12. *The Downside of Punishment*	7 Learning and Reinforcement	motivation; perception and attribution; performance management and rewards
13. *Tinker Toys*	8 Job Design, Goal Setting, and Work Arrangements	organizational structure; design and culture; groups and teamwork
14. *Eggsperiential Exercise*	9 The Nature of Groups	group dynamics and teamwork; diversity and individual differences; communication
15. *Scavenger Hunt—Team Building*	10 Teamwork and Workgroup Design	groups; leadership; diversity and individual differences; communication; leadership

Exercise	Suggested Chapter	Cross-References and Integration
16. *Identifying Group Norms*	10 Teamwork and Workgroup Design	groups; communication; perception and attribution
17. *Workgroup Culture*	10 Teamwork and Workgroup Design	groups; communication; perception and attribution; job design; organizational culture
18. *The Hot Seat*	10 Teamwork and Workgroup Design	groups; communication
19. *Jazz Ensembles*	10 Teamwork and Workgroup Design	groups; communication; job design; organizational structure; design and culture; new workplace
20. *Communication Networks*	10 Teamwork and Workgroup Design	groups; communication; organizational design
21. *Organizations Alive!*	11 Basic Attributes of Organizations	organizational design and culture; performance management and rewards; new workplace
22. *Fast Food Technology*	12 Organizational Design and Learning	organizations; organizational culture; job design; new workplace
23. *Rating Organizational Performance*	12 Organizational Design and Learning	organizations; performance management and rewards; new workplace
24. *Alien Invasion*	13 Organizational Culture	organizational structure and design; international; diversity and individual differences; perception and attribution
25. *My Best Manager: Revisited*	14 Power and Politics	new workplace; diversity and individual differences; perception and attribution
26. *Interview a Leader*	15 Leadership	performance management and rewards; group and teamwork; new workplace; organizational change and stress
27. *Leadership Skills Inventories*	15 Leadership	new workplace; decision making
28. *Active Listening*	16 Communication	group dynamics and teamwork; perception and attribution; new workplace
29. *Upward Appraisal*	16 Communication	perception and attribution; performance management and rewards
30. *"360" Feedback*	17 Decision Making	communication; perception and attribution; performance management and rewards
31. *Role Analysis Negotiation*	17 Decision Making	communication; group dynamics and teamwork; perception and attribution; communication; decision making
32. *The Ugli Orange*	17 Decision Making	communication; decision making
33. *Entering the Unknown*	17 Decision Making	communication; group dynamics and teamwork; perception and attribution
34. *Vacation Puzzle*	18 Conflict and Negotiation	conflict and negotiation; communication; power; leadership
35. *Who to Hire?*	18 Conflict and Negotiation	performance management and rewards; groups and teamwork; new workplace
36. *Gone Fishing*	18 Conflict and Negotiation	groups and teamwork; communication; conflict and negotiation
37. *Force-Field Analysis*	19 Change, Innovation, and Stress	decision making

III. Self-Assessment Inventories

Assessment	Suggested Chapter	Cross-References and Integration
1. A 21st Century Manager	1 Organization Behavior and the New Workplace	leadership; decision making; international
2. Turbulence Tolerance Test	1 Organization Behavior and the New Workplace	organizational change and stress
3. Global Work Orientation	2 International Dimensions of Organizational Behavior	diversity and individual differences; perception and attribution
4. Personal Values	3 Diversity and Individual Differences	new workplace; leadership
5. Managerial Assumptions	4 Perception and Attribution	new workplace; leadership
6. Intolerance for Ambiguity	4 Perception and Attribution	new workplace; leadership
7. Motivators or Hygienes?	5 Motivation 6 Performance Management and Rewards	performance management and rewards
8. Are You Cosmopolitan?	6 Performance Management and Rewards 8 Job Design, Goal Setting, and Work Arrangements	diversity and individual differences; organizational culture
9. Group Effectiveness	9 The Nature of Groups 10 Teamwork and Workgroup Design	organizations
10. Organizational Design Preference	11 Basic Attributes of Organization 12 Organizational Design and Learning	job design; diversity and individual differences
11. Which Culture Fits You?	13 Organizational Culture	diversity and individual differences
12. Empowering Others	14 Power and Politics	new workplace; leadership; perception and attribution
13. Machiavellianism	14 Power and Politics	leadership; diversity and individual differences
14. Personal Power Profile	14 Power and Politics	leadership; diversity and individual differences
15. Least Preferred Coworker Scale	15 Leadership	group dynamics and teamwork; new workplace
16. Leadership Style	15 Leadership	group dynamics and teamwork
17. "TT" Leadership Style	15 Leadership 16 Communication	new workplace; diversity and individual differences
18. Your Intuitive Ability	17 Decision Making	diversity and individual differences
19. Conflict Management Styles	18 Conflict and Negotiation	diversity and individual differences; communication
20. Your Personality Type	19 Change, Innovation, and Stress	diversity and individual differences; job design
21. Stress Inventory	19 Change, Innovation, and Stress	new workplace; diversity and individual differences

CASES FOR

CRITICAL
THINKING

CASE 1
Drexler's Bar-B-Que
....

Developed by Forrest F. Aven, Jr., University of Houston—
Downtown, and V. Jean Ramsey, Texas Southern University

Change seems to be a fact of life, yet in Texas some things remain the same—people's love for Texas-style barbecue. As you drive from Houston to Waco, for example, you will see many road-side stands asking you to stop by and sample different forms of bbq or bar b q (the tastes vary as much as the spellings and both are often inspired). In the cities, there are many restaurants, several of them large chains, that compete with smaller, neighborhood businesses for the barbecue portion of individuals' dining out budgets.

Survival can sometimes depend on the restaurant's ability to identify and capitalize on "windows of opportunity." Small businesses are presumed to be more flexible, having the ability to react more quickly to changes when they occur—but the risk is also greater for them than for large organizations, which can more easily absorb losses. But although there may be differences in scale, an important question for *all* organizations is whether they have the willingness and the ability to take advantage of opportunities as they arise. On February 14, 1995, Drexler's Bar-B-Que, a small "neighborhood" restaurant in Houston, the fourth largest city in the United States, had an opportunity to test whether it had what it took.

Drexler's Bar-B-Que is located at 2020 Dowling Street in an area of Houston called the Third Ward—an economically disadvantaged neighborhood not far from downtown—and has been in the family "almost forever." The more recent history, however, begins in the late 1940s, when a great uncle of the present owners operated the establishment as Burney's BBQ. He died in the late 1950s, and an uncle of the present owners took the restaurant over and, because of a leasing arrangement with another popular barbeque restaurant in Southwest Houston, changed the name of the restaurant to Green's Barbecue. In the 1970s, James Drexler, 12 years old, began working with his uncle and learned the secrets of the old family recipes for the barbecue beef, chicken, and sausage. He learned the business "from the ground up." In 1982, when his uncle died, James and his mother took over the business, ended the leasing arrangement, and, in 1985, renamed it Drexler's Bar-B-Que. To this day, it continues to be a "family affair," but there has been increased specialization in tasks as business has grown. James Drexler continues to do all the meat preparation, his mother, Mrs. Eunice Scott, handles the other food preparation (the "standard fare" is potato salid, cole slaw, barbeque beans, and slices of white bread), and his sister, Virginia Scott, manages the "front operations"—customer orders and the cash register. There are only two or three other full-time employees, although sometimes during the summer a couple of nephews work part time.

Drexler's is a family business with strong underlying values. It is in the neighborhood and is *of* the neighborhood. Despite the success of the business and the increased patronage of individuals from other parts of the city (many of whom previously had few occasions to do more than drive through the Third Ward), the Drexlers have never considered moving from their original location. The culture of the organization, and the values underpinning it, are influenced by the current head of the family, Mrs. Scott. Her values of honesty, hard work, and treating people fairly and with respect—and her faith in God—permeate the atmosphere and operations of Drexler's. She moves through the restaurant inquiring about individual needs—equally for long-time customers and new ones—and always with a smile and warm greeting for all. She is there every day the restaurant is open and holds the same set of high standards for herself as she does for others who work in the restaurant.

Values also get played out in the way in which Drexler's Bar-B-Que "gives back to" the surrounding African-American community. Drexler's has, for many years, sponsored a softball team and a local Boy Scout troop. Youths from the neighborhood have opportunities to go camping and visit a local amusement park because the family believes that a business should not just involve itself in the community but has the obligation to seek out aggressively opportunities to help others.

In some ways it would appear that Drexler's is not very flexible or adaptable. The restaurant is always closed at 6:00 P.M. and on Sundays and Mondays. The menu has remained the same for many years. Drexler's has always been well known in Houston's African-American community, especially in the southwest portion of the city. Regular customers have frequented the restaurant for many years, and a successful side business of catering social functions has also developed. Business has improved every year. During the early 1990s, the business had grown to a point where the small, somewhat ramshackle, restaurant could no longer service the demand—there simply were not enough tables or space. So the decision was made in 1994 to close the busienss for 6 months, completely raze the building, and rebuild a new and modern restaurant (with additional space attached for future expansion into related, and unrelated, businesses by other family members). It was a good decision—upon reopening, business doubled. But the biggest test of the restaurant's ability to adapt to changes came on February 14, 1995.

Mrs. Scott has two sons, James and Clyde Drexler. James is the co-owner of the restaurant, and Clyde is an NBA basketball player. In 1994, Clyde Drexler appeared at the restaurant to generate publicity for the reopening. But on February 14, 1995, he was traded from the Portland Trailblazers to the local NBA franchise, the Houston Rockets. Clyde had played his collegiate ball at the local university and was popular in the city of Houston. He and Hakeem Olajuwon, the "star" of the Rockets team, had played together in college and were part of the team known as the Phi Slamma Jamma. Clyde had been a very successful member of the Portland team; he had been selected to play on several all-star teams, had played for two NBA championships, and was a member of the original Dream Team that sent NBA players to the 1992 Summer Olympics.

The Houston Rockets, the defending NBA champions, were struggling during that winter of 1995. The acquisition of Clyde Drexler was seen as a "blockbuster" one and a key to helping the team repeat as NBA champions. The city was overjoyed with the idea that a local hero was returning home to assist the team in once more winning the championship.

The initial news of the trade brought many new customers to the restaurant. As the Rockets progressed through the playoffs during the spring of 1995, even more customers came. Some days, the restaurant had to close early because it ran out of food. During the semifinals with San Antonio and the finals with Orlando, there appeared to be as many newspaper articles and television reports originating from the restaurant as from the basketball arena. A radio station staged an event outside the restaurant for fans to earn tickets to the game. A major local newspaper gave the restaurant a favorble review in the food section. Many Rockets fans saw frequenting the restaurant as a way to "connect" to the ball team and came to hug Mrs. Scott or chat with her about her son, Clyde, or both. When the Rockets clinched their second NBA championship, everyone in the city knew about the Rockets, and many now knew of Drexler's Bar-B-Que.

The restaurant has since become the hub of several businesses located side by side. In addition to her two sons, Mrs. Scott has four daughters. Virginia Scott, who is heavily involved in the restaurant, is also co-owner of a beauty salon, with another sister, Charlotte Drexler. A bakery is owned and operated by a cousin, Barbara Wiltz. A bookstore with a sports emphasis is leased to a non-family member. In January 1996, a new addition was made to the building, and a significantly expanded catering business was begun. Meanwhile, the restaurant has increased its neighborhood involvement by offering free Thanksgiving and Christmas dinners to neighborhood residents in a neighborhood park.

Questions

1. Use the open systems model decribed in this chapter to show how Drexler's Bar-B-Que should operate as a learning organization.
2. How do the "values" of Drexler's Bar-B-Que relate to the ethics and social responsibility issues raised in this chapter?
3. What challenges of organization and managerial leadership face Drexler's in its current movement toward expansion? ∎

CASE 2
Crossing Borders
· ·

Developed by Bernardo M. Ferdman, California School of Professional Psychology, San Diego, CA and Plácida I. Gallegos, Southwest Communication Resources, Inc. and The Kaleel Jamison Consulting Group, Inc.

This case study is based on the experiences of Angelica Garza, a woman of Mexican-American heritage who worked for 10 years in the Human Resource (HR) function of a multinational medical products company. This maquiladora plant was in Tijuana, Baja California, a large city directly across the United States–Mexico border from San Diego, California. Maquiladoras are manufacturing plants owned by foreign capital in the regions of Mexico bordering the United States, which have been set up to take advantage of favorable laws and cheap labor.

The Tijuana plant was one of a number of operations for USMed. Six other U.S. facilities were located in the Northeast, the Midwest, and Florida. In addition to her work in the manufacturing plant, where Angelica spent most of her time, she was also responsible for human resources for the small, primarily

Source: This is an abridged version of a case appearing in the Field Guide of E. E. Kossek and S. Lobel, *Managing Diversity: Human Resource Strategies for Transforming the Workplace,* Oxford, England: Blackwell, 1996.

administrative facility in Chula Vista, on the U.S. side of the border. Eventually, there were 34 Americans—12 on the Mexican side and 22 on the United States side—and approximately 1100 Mexican nationals on the payroll.

There was little connection between Angelica and the HR managers at the other USMed plants, either in the United States or abroad. Angelica reported that USMed had no overall policy or strategy for dealing with human resources generally, and diversity specifically.

The transition in Mexico was not a smooth one for Angelica. Nothing in her U.S. experience had prepared her for what she encountered in Mexico. Her Anglo colleagues had only vague knowledge about the operation in Tijuana and had little interest in understanding or relating to the Mexican workforce. Given her Hispanic upbringing in the United States, Angelica had some understanding of the culture and values of the Mexican employees. Her Spanish-speaking skills also enabled her to understand and relate to the workers. Although she had some understanding of the workers, however, the assumption on the part of U.S. management that her knowledge and connection to the Mexican workers was seamless was false. There were many aspects of cultural differences between herself and the Mexican employees that the Anglo managers were unaware of:

In retrospect now, I can look back and [I'm] just amazed at what I was involved in at the time. I mean, I didn't have a clue. One of the things you find is that [people assume that Mexican Americans are most suited to work with Mexicans.] I guess just because I was of Mexican-American descent, it was like I would just know how to mingle with this total[ly] different culture.

As a result, Angelica experienced a great deal of frustration and misunderstanding. Her attempts to intercede between the management in Mexico and the United States often led to her disenfranchisement from her American colleagues, who did not value or appreciate her ideas or suggestions. Further complicating her experience in Mexico was the mixed reactions she engendered from the Mexican nationals. Because of her American status, Angelica was misunderstood and sometimes resented by Mexican employees and, at the same time, she lacked support from the U.S. organization.

I found that the Mexican women who were there [two women in accounting who were Mexican nationals, and had been there for about 5 years] were resentful. My saving grace was that I was an American because the Mexican women there looked at the Americans as being like a step above or whatever. And there was resentment of me coming in and taking away jobs. They perceived it as: They weren't doing a good job and we were coming in and taking responsibilities away from them. So me being a woman coming in, I was scrutinized by the two women who had been there. I couldn't get information from them. They gave me the least information or help they could and would be critical of anything I did once I took it from them.

You know, I look back and it was probably pretty frightening for them [the Mexican nationals] too, because we all came in and we knew what we had to do; [USMed was] very straightforward about, you know, you fail to do this and you can lose your job and you've got to do that or you could lose your job, so getting them to follow these protocols and these operating procedures was very difficult. Change is difficult anyway but getting them to follow some of those rules [was] real challenging.

Angelica understood the employees' approach to the work as stemming from local conditions and from Mexican cultural styles. The great expansion of maquiladoras brought a number of changes, including new expectations and different cultural styles on the part of the managers. At first, potential employees were unfamiliar with these new expectations; the employers needed to train the workers if they were to meet these expectations. This was happening in the context of the meeting of two cultures. In her role, Angelica saw herself as more American than Mexican, yet also as different from her Anglo colleagues. She saw herself as bringing American training, expectations, and styles:

Well, see I'm American. I mean I was an American manager, and that's where I was coming from. But I was forced to come up with systems that would eliminate future misunderstandings or problems. Being a Mexican American I thought it would be easier working in Mexico because I had some exposure to the culture, but it was a real culture shock for me. It was a different group of people socioeconomically. A lot of those people came from ranchitos, [from] out in the sticks, where there were no restrooms or showers. There weren't infrastructures in Tijuana at all. It's pretty good now compared to what it was 10 years ago. We used to go to work through people's backyards and dirt roads. Dead dogs were marks for how to get there! And I think now, that if you go to Tijuana now—it's been 10 years of maquiladoras there—you can find more qualified Mexican managers or supervisors or clerical people. [Finding] bilingual secretaries and engineers [was like] getting needles in a haystack back then.

I found myself being the only woman in an old-boy-network environment, and that was pretty tough. And it was also tough working in the Mexican environment. Because the Mexican men that I would deal with would look down on me because I was a woman. Again, my saving grace was because I was an American woman. If I had been a Mexican national woman then I would have really had probably more problems.

[For example] I had to work a lot, real close with the Mexican accounting manager, who was a male. And he would come to me and tell me how I had screwed up my numbers, or you didn't do this right, and stuff like that. I would go over the numbers and it was just a difference in terms of how things were calculated. Specifically, calculating an annual salary. He would do it by using 365 days, when I would do it by 52 weeks and you'd take your daily rate, it was different, it would always be off a little bit. But, I reported them the way the Americans would be expecting to see them.

Questions

1. What competencies are appropriate to ensure greater effectiveness of U.S. employees operating in a maquiladora or other non-U.S. organization?

2. What are some of the costs of not understanding diversity? What could the organization have gained by approaching the plant with greater cultural understanding?

3. From the HR perspective, what were the unique challenges that Angelica faced at various points in her work for USMed?

4. Angelica worked in a plant outside the United States. What do her experiences and perspectives tell us that applies to domestic operations? ∎

C A S E   3
Never on a Sunday

Developed by Anne C. Cowden, California State University, Sacramento

McCoy's Building Supply Centers of San Marcos, Texas, have been in continuous successful operation for almost 70 years in an increasingly competitive retail business. McCoy's is one of the nation's largest family-owned and -managed building-supply companies, with sales topping $400 million. The company serves 10 million customers a year in a regional area currently covering New Mexico, Texas, Oklahoma, Arkansas, Mississippi, and Louisiana in 103 stores employing 1600 employees. McCoy's strategy has been to occupy a niche in the market of small and medium-sized cities. McCoy's was originally a roofing business started by Frank McCoy in 1923; roofing remained the company's primary business until the 1960s, when it began to expand under the management of son, Emmett McCoy.

McCoy's grounding principle is acquiring and selling the finest quality products that can be found and providing quality service to customers. As an operations-oriented company, McCoy's has always managed without many layers of management. Managers are asked to concentrate on service-related issues in their stores: get the merchandise on the floor, price it, sell it, and help the customer carry it out. The majority of the administrative workload is handled through headquarters so that store employees can concentrate on customer service. The top management team (Emmett McCoy and his two sons, Brian and Mike, who serve as copresidents) has established 11 teams of managers drawn from the different regions McCoy's stores cover. The teams meet regularly to discuss new products, better ways for product delivery, and a host of items integral to maintaining customer satisfaction. Team leadership is rotated among the managers.

McCoy's has a workforce of 70 percent full-time and 30 percent part-time employees. McCoy's philosophy values loyal, adaptable, skilled employees as the most essential element of its overall success. To operationalize this philosophy the company offers extensive on-the-job training. The path to management involves starting at the store level and learning all facets of operations before advancing into a management program. All management trainees are required to relocate to a number of stores. Most promotions come from within. Managers are rarely recruited from the outside. This may begin to change as the business implements more technology requiring a greater reliance on college-educated personnel.

Permeating all that McCoy's does is a strong religious belief, including a strong commitment to community. In 1961 Emmett McCoy decided, in the wake of a devastating hurricane, to offer McCoy's goods to customers at everyday prices rather than charging what the market would bear. This decision helped establish McCoy's long-standing reputation of fair dealing, a source of pride for all employees, and allowed the company to begin its current expansion perspective. In 1989 McCoy's became a drug-free company. McCoy's takes part in the annual National Red Ribbon Campaign, "Choose to Be Drug Free." McCoy's also supports Habitat for Humanity in the United States and has provided support for low-income housing in Mexico.

Many McCoy family members are Evangelical Christians who believe in their faith through letting their "feet do it"; that is, showing their commitment to God through action, not just talk. Although their beliefs and values permeate the company's culture in countless ways, one very concrete way is reflected in the title of this case: Never on a Sunday. Even though Sundays are busy business days for retailers, all 103 McCoy's stores are closed on Sunday.

Questions

1. How do the beliefs of the McCoy family form the culture of this company?
2. Can a retailer guided by such strong beliefs compete and survive in the era of gigantic retailers such as Home Depot? If so, how?
3. Is such a strong commitment to social responsibility and ethical standards a help or a hindrance in managing a company?
4. How does a family-owned and -managed company differ from companies managed by outside professionals? ■

CASE 4
MAGREC, Inc.
....

Developed by Mary McGarry, Empire State College and Barry R. Armandi, SUNY-Old Westbury

Background

MagRec, Incorporated was started in the late 1960s by Mr. Leed, a brilliant engineers (he has several engineering patents), who was a group manager at Fairchild Republic. The company's product was magnetic recording heads, a crucial device used for reading, writing, and erasing data on tapes and disks. Need for the product and its future potential was great. The computer industry was in its embryonic stage, and *MagRec* had virtually no serious competition. In fact, almost all magnetic head manufacturers today use methods, techniques, processes, etc., that were developed and pioneered by *MagRec.*

Like any other startup, *MagRec* had a humble beginning. It struggled during the early years, facing cash-flow and technical problems. After a slow start, it began growing rapidly. In the mid-1970s it had captured 35% of the tape head market, making it the second largest supplier of MegaComputer computer tape heads in North America. Financially, the company suffered heavily in the early 1980s because of price erosions caused by Far East competition. Unlike all its competitors, the company resisted and never moved its manufacturing operations offshore. By the mid-1980s, the company had accumulated losses to a point of bankruptcy. Finally, plagued by a no-win situation, the company entered a major international joint venture, in which foreign governments agreed to participate as minority owners (20% equity). The company received blanket sales orders from Japanese firms (GME, Victor Data, Fijitsu, etc.). Things looked good once again. But . . .

Pat's Dilemma

When Fred Marsh promoted me to Sales Manager, I was in seventh heaven. Now, 6 months later, I feel I am in hell. This is the first time in my life that I am really on my own. I have been working with other people all my life. I tried my best and what I could not solve, I took upstairs. Now it's different because I am the boss (or am I?). Fred has taught me a lot. He was my mentor and gave me this job when he became Vice-President. I have always respected him and listened to his judgment. Now thinking back I wonder whether I should have listened to him at all on this problem.

It started one late Friday evening. I had planned to call my West Coast customer, Partco, to discuss certain contract clauses. I wanted to nail this one fast (Partco had just been acquired by Volks, Inc.). Partco was an old customer, in fact—through good and bad it had always stayed with us. It was also a *major* customer. I was about to call Partco when Dinah Coates walked in clutching a file. I had worked with Dinah for 3 years. She was good. I knew that my call to Partco would have to wait. Dinah had been cleaning out old files and came across a report about design and manufacturing defects in Partco heads. The report had been written 9 years ago. The cover memo read as follows:

To: Ken Smith, Director of Marketing
From: Rich Grillo, V.P. Operations
Sub: Partco Head Schedule

This is to inform you that due to pole-depth problems in design, the Partco heads (all 514 in test) have failed. They can't reliably meet the reading requirements.* The problem is basically a design error in calculations. It can be corrected. However, the fix will take at least six months. Meanwhile Ron Scott in production informs me that the entire 5,000 heads (the year's production) have aready been pole-slotted, thus they face the same problem.

Ken, I don't have to tell you how serious this is, but how can we o.k. and ship them to Partco knowing that they'll cause read error problems in the field? My engineering and manufacturing people realize this is the number one priority. By pushing the Systems Tech job back we will be back on track in less than six months. In the interim I can modify Global Widgets heads. This will enable us to at least continue shipping some product to Partco. As a possible alternate I would like to get six Partco drives. Michaels and his team feel that

---

*Authors' Note: Error signifies erroneous reading, not an error message. For example, instead of "$200" the head reads "$3005.42."

with quick and easy changes in the drives tape path they can get the head to work. If this is true we should be back on track within 6 to 8 weeks.

A separate section of the report read as follows:

Confidential
(Notes from meeting with Dom Updyke and Rich Grillo)

Solution to Partco heads problem
All Partco heads can be reworked (.8 hrs. ea.—cost insignificant) to solve Partco's read problems by grinding an extra three thousandths of an inch off the top of the head. This will reduce the overall pole depth to a point where no read errors occur. The heads will fully meet specifications in all respects except one, namely life. Dom estimates that due to the reduced chrome layer (used for wear) the heads useful life will be 2,500 hours instead of 6,000 hours of actual usage.

Our experience is that no customer keeps accurate records to tell actual usage and life. Moreover the cost is removed since Partco sells drives to MegaComputer who sells systems to end-users. The user at the site hardly knows or rarely complains about extra costs such as the replacement of a head 12 to 18 months down the line instead of the normal 2 years. Besides, the service technicians always innovatively believe in and offer plausible explanations—such as the temperature must be higher than average—or they really must be using the computer a lot.

I have directed that the heads be reworked and shipped to Partco. I also instructed John to tell Partco that due to inclement weather this week's shipment will be combined with next week's shipment.

Dinah was flabbergasted. The company planned to sell products deliberately that it knew would not meet life requirements, she said, "risking our reputation as a quality supplier. Partco and others buy our heads thinking they are the best. Didn't we commit fraud through outright misrepresentation?"

Dinah insisted I had to do something. I told her I would look into the matter and get back to her by the end of next week.

Over the weekend I kept thinking about the Partco issue. We had no customer complaints. Partco had always been extremely pleased with our products and technical support. In fact, we were their sole suppliers. MegaComputer had us placed on the preferred, approved ship to stock, vendors list. It was a fact that other vendors were judged against our standards. MegaComputer's Quality Control never saw our product or checked it.

Monday morning I showed the report to Fred. He immediately recollected it and began to explain the situation to me.

MagRec had been under tremendous pressure and was growing rapidly at the time. "That year we had moved into a new 50,000 sq. ft. building and went from 50 or 60 employees to over 300. Our sales were increasing dramatically." Fred was heading Purchasing at the time and every week the requirements for raw materials would change." "We'd started using B.O.A.s (Broad Order Agreements, used as annual purchasing contracts) guaranteeing us the right to increase our numbers by 100% each quarter. The goal was to maintain the numbers. If we had lost Partco then, it could have had a domino effect and we could have ended up having no customers left to worry about."

Fred went on to explain that it had only been a short-term problem that was corrected within the year and no one ever knew it existed. He told me to forget it and to move the file into the back storage room. I conceded. I thought of all the possible hassles. The thing was ancient history anyway. Why should I be concerned about it? I wasn't even here when it happened.

The next Friday Dinah asked me what I had found out. I told her Fred's feelings on the matter and that I felt he had some pretty good arguments regarding the matter. Dinah became angry. She said I had changed since my promotion and that I was just as guilty as the crooks who'd cheated the customers by selling low-life heads as long-life heads. I told her to calm down. The decision was made years ago. No one got hurt and the heads weren't defective. They weren't causing any errors.

I felt bad but figured there wasn't much to do. The matter was closed as far as I was concerned, so I returned to my afternoon chores. Little was I to know the matter was not really closed.

That night Fred called me at 10:00. He wanted me to come over to the office right away. I quickly changed, wondering what the emergency was. I walked into Fred's office. The coffee was going. Charlie (Personnel Manager) was there. Rich Grillo (V.P. Operations) was sitting on the far side of Fred's conference table. I instinctively headed there, for that was the designated smoking corner.

Ken (Director of Marketing) arrived 15 minutes later. We settled in. Fred began the meeting by thanking everyone for coming. He then told them about the discovery of the Partco file and filled them in on the background. The problem now was that Dinah had called Partco and gotten through to their new Vice President, Tim Rand. Rand had called Fred at 8 p.m. at home and said he was personally taking the Red Eye to find out what this was all about. He would be here in the morning.

We spent a grueling night followed by an extremely tense few weeks. Partco had a team of people going through our tests, quality con-trol, and manufacturing records. Our production slipped, and overall morale was affected.

Mr. Leed personally spent a week in California assuring Partco that this would never happen again. Though we weathered the storm, we had certain losses. We were never to be Partco's sole source again. We still retained 60% of their business, but had to agree to lower prices. The price reduction had a severe impact. Though Partco never disclosed to anyone what the issues were (since both companies had blanket nondisclosure agreements) word got around that Partco was paying a lower price. We were unable to explain to our other customers why Partco was paying this amount. Actually I felt the price word got out through Joe Byrne (an engineer who came to Partco from Systems Tech and told his colleagues back at Systems Tech that Partco really knew how to negotiate prices down). He was unaware, however, of the real issues. Faced with customers who perceived they were being treated unequitably, we experienced problems. Lowering prices meant incurring losses; not lowering them meant losing customers. The next two financial quarters saw sales dollars decline by 40%. As the Sales Manager, I felt pretty rotten presenting my figures to Fred.

With regard to Dinah, I now faced a monumental problem. The internal feeling was she should be avoided at all costs. Because of price erosions, we faced cutbacks. Employees blamed her for production layoffs. The internal friction kept mounting. Dinah's ability to interface effectively with her colleagues and other departments plummeted to a point where normal functioning was impossible.

Fred called me into his office 2 months after the Partco episode and suggested that I fire Dinah. He told me that he was worried about results. Although he had nothing personally against her, he felt that she must go because she was seriously affecting my department's overall performance. I defended Dinah by stating that the Partco matter would blow over and given time I could smooth things out. I pointed out Dinah's accomplishments and stated I really wanted her to stay. Fred dropped the issue, but my problem still persisted.

Things went from bad to worse. Finally, I decided to try to solve the problem myself. I had known Dinah well for many years and had a good relationship with her before the incident. I took her to lunch to address the issue. Over lunch, I acknowledged the stress the Partco situation had put on her and suggested that she move away for a while to the West Coast where she could handle that area independently.

Dinah was hurt and asked why I didn't just fire her already. I countered by accusing her of causing the problem in the first place by going to Partco.

Dinah came back at me, calling me a lackey for having taken her story to Fred and brought his management message back. She said I hadn't even attempted a solution and that I didn't have the guts to stand up for what was right. I was only interested in protecting my backside and keeping Fred happy. As her manager, I should have protected her and taken some of the heat off her back. Dinah refused to transfer or to quit. She told me to go ahead and fire her, and she walked out.

I sat in a daze as I watched Dinah leave the restaurant. What the hell went wrong? Had Dinah done the morally right thing? Was I right in defending *MagRec's* position? Should I have taken a stand with Fred? Should I have gone over Fred's head to Mr. Leed? Am I doing the right thing? Should I listen to Fred and fire Dinah? If not, how do I get my department back on track? What am I saying? If Dinah is right, shouldn't I be defending her rather than *MagRec*?

Questions

1. Place yourself in the role of the manager. What should you do now? After considering what happened, would you change any of your behaviors?

2. Do you think Dinah was right? Why or why not? If you were she and you had to do it all over again, would you do anything differently? If so, what and why?

3. Using cognitive dissonance theory, explain the actions of Pat, Dinah, and Fred. ∎

C A S E   5
It Isn't Fair
....

Developed by Barry R. Armandi, SUNY-Old Westbury

Mary Jones was in her senior year at Central University and interviewing for jobs. Mary was in the top 1 percent of her class, active in numerous extracurricular activities, and was highly respected by her professors. After the interviews, Mary was offered a number of positions with every company with which she interviewed. After much thought, she decided to take the offer from Universal Products, a multinational company. She felt that the salary was superb ($40,000), there were excellent benefits, and good potential for promotion.

Mary started work a few weeks after graduation and learned her job assignments and responsibilities thoroughly and quickly. Mary was asked on many occasions to work late because report deadlines were moved forward often. Without hesitation she said "Of course!" even though as an exempt employee she would receive no overtime. Frequently, she would take work home with her and use her personal computer to do further analyses. At other times, she would come into the office on weekends to monitor the progress of her projects or just to catch up on the ever-growing mountain of correspondence.

On one occasion her manager asked her to take on a difficult assignment. It seemed that the company's Costa Rican manufacturing facility was having production problems. The quality of one of the products was highly questionable, and the reports on the matter were confusing. Mary was asked to be part of a team to investigate the quality and reporting problems. The team stayed in poor accommodations for the entire 3 weeks they were there. This was because of the plant's location near its resources, which happened to be in the heart of the jungle. Within the 3-week period the team had located the source of the quality problem, corrected it, and altered the reporting documents and processes. The head of the team, a quality engineer, wrote a note to Mary's manager stating the following: "Just wanted to inform you of the superb job Mary Jones did down in Costa Rica. Her suggestions and insights into the reporting system were invaluable. Without her help we would have been down there for another 3 weeks, and I was getting tired of the mosquitos. Thanks for sending her."

Universal Products, like most companies, has a yearly performance review system. Since Mary had been with the Company for a little over 1 year, it was time for her review. Mary entered her manager's office nervous, since this was her first review ever and she didn't know what to expect. After closing the door and exchanging the usual pleasantries, her manager, Tom, got right to the point.

Tom: Well Mary, as I told you last week this meeting would be for your annual review. As you are aware, your performance and compensation are tied together. Since the philosophy of the company is to reward those who perform, we take these reviews very sincerely. I have spent a great deal of time thinking about your performance over the past year, but before I begin I would like to know your impressions of the company, your assignments, and me as a manager.

Mary: Honestly, Tom, I have no complaints. The company and my job are everything I was led to believe. I enjoy working here. The staff are all very helpful. I like the team atmosphere, and my job is very challenging. I really feel appreciated and that I'm making a contribution. You have been very helpful and patient with me. You got me involved right from the start and listened to my opinions. You taught me a lot and I'm very grateful. All in all I'm happy being here.

Tom: Great, Mary, I was hoping that's the way you felt because from my vantage point, most of

the people you worked with feel the same. But before I give you the qualitative side of the review, allow me to go through the quantitative appraisal first. As you know, the rankings go from 1 (lowest) to 5 (highest). Let's go down each category and I'll explain my reasoning for each.

Tom starts with category one (Quantity of Work) and ends with category ten (Teamwork). In each of the categories, Tom has either given Mary a five or a four. Indeed, only two categories have a four and Tom explains these are normal areas for improvement for most employees.

Tom: As you can see, Mary, I was very happy with your performance. You have received the highest rating I have ever given any of my subordinates. Your attitude, desire, and help are truly appreciated. The other people on the Costa Rican team gave you glowing reports and speaking with the plant manager, she felt that you helped her understand the reporting system better than anyone else. Since your performance has been stellar, I'm delighted to give you a 10 percent increase effective immediately!

Mary: (mouth agape, and eyes wide) Tom, frankly I'm flabbergasted! I don't know what to say, but thank you very much. I hope I can continue to do as fine a job as I have this last year. Thanks once again.

After exchanging some departing remarks and some more thank yous, Mary left Tom's office with a smile from ear to ear. She was floating on air! Not only did she feel the performance review process was uplifting, but her review was outstanding and so was her raise. She knew from other employees that the company was only giving out a 5 percent average increase. She figured

that if she got that, or perhaps 6 or 7, she would be happy. But to get 10 percent . . . wow!! Imagine . . .

Sue: Hi, Mary! Lost in thought? My, you look great. Looks like you got some great news. What's up?

Susan Stevens was a recent hire, working for Tom. She had graduated from Central University also, but a year after Mary. Sue had excelled while at Central, graduating in the top 1 percent of her class. She had laudatory letters of recommendations from her professors and was into many after school clubs and activities.

Mary: Oh, hi Sue! Sorry, but I was just thinking about Universal and the opportunities here.
Sue: Yes, it truly is . . .
Mary: Sue, I just came from my performance review and let me tell you, the process isn't that bad. As a matter of fact I found it quite rewarding, if you get my drift. I got a wonderful review, and can't wait till next year's. What a great company!
Sue: You can say that again! I couldn't believe them hiring me right out of college at such a good salary. Between you and me Mary they started me at $45,000. Imagine that? Wow, was I impressed. I just couldn't believe that they would . . . Where are you going, Mary? Mary? What's that you say "It isn't fair"? What do you mean? Mary? Mary . . .

Questions

1. Indicate Mary's attitudes before and after meeting Sue. If there was a change, why?
2. What do you think Mary will do now? Later?
3. What motivation theory applies best to this scenario? Explain.

■

C A S E 6
Amoco's Global Human Resource Systems

Developed by Ellen Ernst Kossek, Michigan State University

Headquartered in Chicago, Amoco, formerly Standard Oil of Indiana, began as a sleepy Midwestern U.S. refining company. Historically, Amoco has had a largely domestic focus in its human resources approach. "International human resources" primarily meant the personnel policies of U.S. expatriates—American citizens who work for Amoco abroad. Until several decades ago, most of Amoco's oil reserves were located in the United States; consequently, management had grown up with the view that most of the company's growth would come from within U.S. borders. Today, however, nearly 80 percent of new investment dollars are being targeted toward foreign operations.

Amoco mangement believes that developing a global approach necessitates transformation in attitudes, organizational processes, and human resource systems. Drivers of global mandates for change in HR practices are as follows:

Global competition: Competitors are increasingly outside the United States (British Petroleum, Royal Dutch Shell, ELF Acquitaine, BHP).

World Market Pressures

Major cash going overseas: Since most oil reserves and markets with most growth potential are now located overseas, operations will increasingly be done outside the United States.

Economic shift: The United States is no longer as dominant an economic base as it has been historically.

Global labor markets: A growing pool of talent will be hired beyond the U.S. labor market. There is also a need to manage cultural and political constraints on travel, work permits, type of assignments, and labor market conditions.

Excessive cost of expatriations: Because of the rising cost of expatriates, Amoco must use talent of local nationals to a greater extent. Yet, in some countries after the costs of social programs are entered into the analysis, staffing local nationals is not always necessarily cheaper.

Culture and value differences of global workforce: State-of-the-art U.S. practices may not favor applicants from non-U.S. cultures (e.g., targeted selection, individual reward and appraisal systems) or may have implementation problems. Expatriation of female employees is limited in some locations.

Increased pressures from foreign governments: Expectations have changed; foreign governments now demand that local nationals be employed.

Increasing need to have a global presence: In many cultures, a long relationship must be developed and evidence of *staying power* must be shown in order to get business; lack of presence may effect future bids in a country.

Ethics: Amoco's values will not permit it to engage in bribing or violating U.S. laws when abroad, even if it is the custom.

The number one competitive pressure shaping human resource activities is the changing competition of the oil industry. Increasingly, Amoco's competitors are foreign companies, such as British Petroleum and Royal Dutch Shell. Since most investment for new business will be spent overseas, it is essential that Amoco's human resource systems adapt accordingly. Management must also no longer view the United States as the premier economic base.

Because of the need for a global workforce, there will be significantly greater demand to integrate local nationals at all levels of an overseas subsidiary. Contributing to this view is the excessive cost of expatriations; that is, the high cost of moving U.S. employees abroad to run companies. Because of these financial pressures, Amoco must make greater use of the talent of local nationals. Yet, just hiring a great number of local nationals for managerial positions will not necessarily help a company globalize successfully; the ability to balance the parent company's view with local needs is a critical consideration. There is still a nagging (and some might say well-founded) fear in the minds of some Amoco executives that they must cautiously pick people who have allegiance to Amoco and not their local country's government. There is the tendency to be lean and mean in terms of placement of local nationals in key positions in developing countries. As a protective staffing strategy, even in developed countries, the vast majority of critical jobs are held by U.S. expatriates. In Norway, for example, some managers complain of a glass ceiling effect, a barrier that keeps

Source: This is an abridged version of a case appearing in the Field Guide of E. E. Kossek and S. Lobel, *Managing Diversity: Human Resource Strategies for Transforming the Workplace,* Oxford, England, Blackwell, 1996.

nationals from moving into key positions. And the trend seems to be spiraling downhill, despite the fact that the country's operations are extremely successful, are stable, and mix relatively well with the United States. Even in Northern European countries, cultural differences remain that are barriers to developing a global workforce. Work and family values are different in European countries compared to the U.S. workaholic corporate norm. It is not uncommon to see Norwegian male employees leave at 3:30 in the afternoon to go pick up their children from school, a practice that is still rare for male employees in the United States. Some U.S. managers have felt that if a lot of high-quality work needs to be done quickly in a short amount of time, U.S. managers are needed to get it done.

Developing worldwide human resource systems means analyzing cultural biases in "leading edge" practices developed with an American view. For example, targeted selection, whereby an interviewer asks questions that target the presence of key abilities found in successful U.S. managers, may not work well for individuals from countries that shun bragging excessively about one's strengths in an interview. Similarly, total quality management, which relies on self-empowerment, may require some modification before being applied abroad in cultures that value individualism less.

Over time, the amount of U.S. expatriation must decrease because of *de facto* cost pressures. Increasingly, a more cost-effective strategy might be to rely on the U.S. workforce more in the consultation role. Greater utilization of local nationals in running international operations might also better blend local laws and customs with Amoco's practices. Yet, typically,

when planning new ventures, the human resource plan is usually the last one put in place.

There is also an increasing need to have a presence in a country, in order to get a concession or a government approval to begin energy exploration. In many cultures, a long relationship must be developed and evidence of staying power must be shown to in order to get business. The lack of presence may affect future bids in a country. As one employee commented, "We're very good at managing the technical aspects of the exploration business—for instance we have led the industry in seismic techniques related to secondary tertiary recovery, but we're not very good at managing new cultures effectively to obtain entry." In Amoco's defense, some managers argue that, realistically, Amoco may not know whether it will be in a new country 6 more months or 6 or more years. This uncertainty is dependent on whether a discovery is made, an endeavor that can fail 90 percent of the time. Some managers contend that it makes more sense to use talent from the United States until a discovery is found. Yet a key to developing marketing strength in new markets is to open an office in a country even before a discovery is made. Typically, however, Amoco will not open an office in a new country until after a discovery is made and concessions are given. Because of this policy, Royal Dutch Shell has a 10-month jump on Amoco in Romania, since it was there long before a concession was made. Given the fact that the entitlement and social programs in many countries are very much more costly than in the United States, a counterargument can be made that it *does* make sense for a U.S. oil company to move slowly when hiring foreign employees. It would be extremely expensive to close a firm and pay off

the former workers if no oil were found. Because of these conditions, contract employees are often used heavily in the early stages of development.

Still, many believe that it is not possible for a company the size of Amoco to open as many offices worldwide as larger competitors, such as Royal Dutch Shell or Exxon. Rather, Amoco should focus its efforts on opening offices early in selected countries. Instead of using its technical strengths *after* a discovery is mde to gain business, Amoco should do a better job of making the world aware of its strength in applying technology well and leverage this capability to get new contracts.

Increasing pressures to hire locals are also being felt from foreign governments. Expectations today have changed. Foreign governments now demand greater employment of local nationals. This can be a problem in countries such as Trinidad, where lifetime employment is the norm. It is very difficult to be a low-cost operator when the biggest part of the costs come early; then, once the oil platforms are built and the growth is underway, the firm is left with a headcount that is not flexible.

An additional pressure stems from worldwide differences in ethics. Amoco values will not permit it to engage in bribing or violating U.S. laws when abroad, even if it is the custom and competitors are doing so. Ethics also affect the extent to which a multinational chooses to use techniques that minimize damage to the environment, even if there are no foreign environmental laws. Firms that are environmentally cautious may face much higher costs than their competitors. Yet some managers believe that Amoco's ethics could be turned into a competitive advantage to get new business, because many of Amoco's environmental approaches are leading edge. In Pakistan, for example, the government would not allow the import of beride, a chemical used in the drilling of wells. Amoco spent an extra quarter million dollars on its wells in lining pits and putting up a dustproof room for the lead, which can be hazardous to the environment, if mixed. Similarly, in Burma, where operations were in a jungle, Amoco cut a very narrow path around the area for the oil well and then reforested. In the United States, where environmental regulations are considered to be the most strict in the world, Amoco strives not only to meet but to exceed environmental regulations. As one manager states, "If you spend more now, you'll save a lot later, because you'll be ahead of regulatory changes." Some beleive that doing a better job marketing this record will increase global opportunities.

Questions

1. What is a global organization?
2. What are the key business pressures driving the globalization of human resource systems?
3. What are some HR practices that would help Amoco Production manage these tensions? ■

CASE 7
Intergalactic Manufacturing

Developed by Barry R. Armandi, SUNY-Old Westbury

Some time right before Christmas:

Laura: Oh no! Not another one of these crazy forms again. It seems every time I turn around Finance, Accounting, Personnel, or some other department wants me to fill out some dumb form. I swear those people don't know what the hell we do down here. They must think we just sit around waiting to hear from them so we can complete these lousy forms. I just don't have the time for this. (Throws the forms on her desk)

Tom: Let me see those. (Picks up the forms and scans them) Oh these. They're nothing more than those estimates the guys in Finance and Program Control want. Nothing important. Just give them the figures.

Laura: Tom, you don't understand. Do you know how long it would take for me to give them those figures? I've got to stop what I am doing and locate all the data, call my people in and have them stop what they are doing and get me the rest of the information. That will take days, if not weeks. As it is, we are already behind on the EKIM project.

Tom: Whoa! You mean to tell me you spend that much time getting those people the info? Are you nuts? You and I both don't have the time to do that, so why bother? I get mine in on time and never concern myself about it.

Laura: Yes, I've always wondered how you do it. Come on, let me in on the secret. I really need to learn some shortcuts so I can get the project done.

Tom: Sure, but there really is no big mystery. Most of us around here have been doing it for years and there have been no real major problems. After all, we still have our jobs and the company is still in business. Ha, Ha! In a nutshell, we fudge the figures! Of course, we try to give our best guess at them but there are some times and some figures we just pull out of the air. Some of the people even make a game out of it. Like Harry's section has a dart board with all these numbers on it and the supervisors take turns. Mary's area uses the random number generator in the computer. And then there's Fred. Good old enterprising Fred! That sly devil has started a pool. The person who comes close to the true figures gets the money. The only limitation is that his people are given 2 hours to give him the info, so no one really has an edge.

Laura: Tom, if I didn't know you better, I'd've thought you were kidding me. Do you know how important those figures are? Finance and Program Control are always screaming at us that they should be as precise as possible and that they use it to supply the guys at the top with current info. That's how we know how far off the plan we are.

Tom: LAURA, GET REAL! Let me give you a little lesson in organizational reality rather than all that textbook nonsense. First, we don't have the time, and even you admitted that. I'm not going to stay late every night and come in on weekends just to make Finance and Program Control look good. My family won't stand for it and I know yours won't either. Second, everybody does it. What are they going to do, fire us all? Fat chance! They need us and we all know it. So there's no punishment for handing in bad guesses. Third, you said that the figures should be as precise as possible. I think the operative term is *"as possible."* If anybody questions me, I always say that this is the best I can do under the circumstances. And don't our bosses always say that to us anyway? "Do the best that you can." Well, that's the best I can do and all I want to do. Fourth, and perhaps most importantly, what's the payoff? I mean, do we ever get rewarded for correct estimates? Once I nearly hit them on the head when I was first made a manager and my boss said "Thanks." That's all, nothing else. No pat on the back. No "Great Job! Keep up the good work!" Nothing more than a "Thanks." Well, after that I began thinking and talking to the oldtimers and decided not to waste my time anymore. Also, when we get our performance reviews every year, do you ever see the estimates mentioned? No way! So why bother? If they were that important, they would appear on our evaluations. Look, I probably could give you 10 more reasons for fudging, but the bottom line is that it is still your decision. Do what you want, only don't complain anymore.

Laura: Hmm! Maybe you're right, Tom. The estimates aren't on any evaluations I've seen and my boss hasn't discussed them with me. And besides you always get outstanding evaluations. I think I'll give it a try. After all, what could happen? Thanks a lot Tom! I really appreciate it. You've saved me a hell of a lot of time.

Company History

The Intergalactic Manufacturing Company (IMC) was created a number of years ago as a total global venture to marshall the planet's limited resources and to optimize the opportunity for continued interplane-

tary and interstellar exploration. IMC has plants, research and development locations, and regional offices around the world, with its central headquarters in New York.

The company is subdivided into a number of different subsidiaries whose responsibilities are to create prototypes and proposals, win government and United Nations' contracts, and produce and deliver products and services to be used for space travel and planetary exploration. Although the structure resembles the archaic matrix organizations of the twentieth century, IMC and most other large transnational organizations use the complex synergistic organization structure, or SOS. SOS requires, very simply that all organizational units work harmoniously together by having each subdivision specialize in component projects of the whole. Then one team, with a person from each subdivision, is responsible for the project's completion. Successes from using this approach abound, and IMC has always favored this structure.

Recently, IMC won a hotly contested competition for the United Nations' contract entitled the EKIM Project. In the early twenty-first century, after the cataclysm, earth's scientists found a remarkably new element in rock ore from samples obtained from moon base Alpha. This exciting new element, called EPAGA, permitted vegetation to grow from seed to fruition in a little less than 1 hour. When mixed with a glass of water, it reproduced and created 200 gallons of absolutely pure drinking and bathing water. Other tests and experiments have shown its potential for the manufacture of durable, comfortable, and inexpensive clothing; for the replacement of steel, concrete, and other building materials; as an aid to laser technology; for computer memories because

of its superconductivity at room temperatures; and for use in dematerialization, rematerialization, miniaturization, and enlargement. Other uses are also being contemplated. Obviously, EPAGA is the answer to many of earth's resource problems and has been termed the "everything element."

Unfortunately, only a small amount was located on the moon. Expeditions to planets within our solar system have uncovered no traces of the element. Probes to other galaxies have also turned up nothing, except for the small system called DANOM in the constellation Capricorn. There, a planet called OAT seems to be overly rich. In fact, all probes show the planet to be uninhabitable, and over 90% of it consists of EPAGA. Therefore, the United Nations' mandate, and ultimately its contract, calls for the mining of OAT. IMC is responsible for all the components of the mining armada. For the last 2 years, it has been busy trying to put the finishing touches on the EKIM Project. IMC has on occasion met its deadlines, but the biggest complaint from the U.N. is that completion dates are always pushed back. It is imperative that the completion of the armada occur no later than December of this year, since that is the last window for launch for another year.

Laura and Tom work in the TAGS (Tracking and Guidance Systems) Division of IMC. Their work is essential since a poor quality system would invalidate the precision needed by the hyperdrive units and throw the armada off by thousands of light years, if not another dimension. For the last 2 years, the system has gone through a number of revisions, tests, and reworks to fine tune it. Every 3 months, Finance and Program Control sends out the Job Finish Form (JFF). The JFF is used to determine how long it will take to complete the current jobs and tasks. It is important, not just so that upper management knows what's going on, but so that more resources can be diverted to complete the job on time. It is essential that the deadlines be met, and the JFF is the informational device that determines the reality of completion. Upper management relies on it extensively and believes that the estimates are correct. They use them to reposition various other projects and, using the synergistic organization structure, can move quickly both physical and human resources.

Amore's Problem

Mr. Daniel Amore is the CEO of IMC. He has come up through the organization and understands the trials and tribulations of operations management personnel. He is aware of the importance of EPAGA and the necessity of meeting the future deadlines of the EKIM project. His counterpart, spearheading the Project for the U.N., is General Steve "Skippy" Stillwater. The following phone conversation occurred between Amore and Stillwater two days after the JFFs had been compiled for the fourth quarter of last year.

Amore: General, how are you? Glad you called. I wanted to talk with you about that golf date and some other exciting research we have been working on that the U.N. may be interested in.

Stillwater: Dan, please call me "Skippy." We're old friends and shouldn't rest on formalities. Although I am always interested in what you guys are experimenting on, the reason for the call is much more urgent and timely. We need to know when EKIM will be completed. We are aware that IMC has had some trouble in the

past in meeting our time limits, but we must press you for a final completion date. As you know the project needs to be completed by December so we can launch on time. That means all preliminary testing and final tuning must be done by September so we can roll the armada to the launch pads by October. Phase One launch will take place in early November, with all armada units coordinated and positioned at our space station. The Phase Two launch will then take place in December. This is a very tight schedule and I know your people have been made aware of it by my people. So Dan, tell me what's going on.

Amore: Skippy, be assured that we are in good shape and will have no difficulty in meeting the deadline. As a matter of fact, I have just received the current completion estimates on EKIM. Every three months we get updates on every project and their completion times. Our people spend considerable time determining precisely the time remaining and the resources needed. Let me pull it out and tell you exactly. (Armore goes to his JFF summary file on this interactive computer display)

Ah, yes, here it is:

That's it Skippy! It looks good and I've been assured by my people that these dates are firm. I don't see any problem and feel pretty confident we will meet your deadline.

Stillwater: I'm a little concerned about the Processing Equipment and the Inertia Propulsion Drives dates. Isn't that cutting it close? What happens if there is some delay? Will you still be able to deliver by September?

Amore: Skip, I've already contacted those program managers and they know I'm on top of them and watching their areas very closely. Anyway with our Synergistic Structure I can switch resources from other areas that don't need as much, say Tracking and Guidance. And they have been pretty good about their estimates, so that is one area I am certain about. Everything is being monitored very carefully. Now come on Skip, let's talk about that golf date.

Stillwater: O.K. Dan. You know me, an old worry wart! I'll have to get back to you, however, on the date. Oh, if for some strange reason, you do get delayed, call me right away, O.K.?

Amore: Sure, talk to you soon. Take care. My best to Marge and the kids.

Component	Status	Completion Date
Hyperdrives	Completed and Tested	
Hulls	Completed and Tested	
Computers	Testing Underway	March
Environmentals	Final Construction	March
	Testing	April
Tracking and Guidance	Final Construction	May
	Testing	July
Defense Shields	Final Construction	May
	Testing	July
Mining Equipment	Testing Underway	June
Processing Equipment	Final Construction	June
	Testing	August
Inertia Propulsion Drives	Final Construction	June
	Testing	July

In April, Mr. Amore received the following memorandum from Al Shaw, manager of the Finance area. Upon reading the memo Mr. Amore shook his head, looked out the window for a moment, and picked up the phone.

Questions

1. Assume the role of Mr. Amore. What should you do immediately? What should you do for the long run?
2. Using expectancy theory, analyze why the situation of poor deadline reporting persists.
3. Discuss the communications process at IMC. Include in your discussion the emphasis on direction (downward, upward, lateral), the preferred network (formal, informal), and the barriers. ■

To: D. Amore
From: A. Shaw, Manager Finance Department
Date: April 25, 2025
Subject: JFF Update

This memo is to apprise you of the current status of the JFFs for the EKIM Project. The first quarter estimates are as follows:

Component	Status	Completion Date
Hyperdrives	Completed and Tested	
Hulls	Completed and Tested	
Computers	Completed and Tested	
Environmentals	Testing Underway	May
Tracking and	Final Construction	July
Guidance	Testing	September
Defense Shields	Final Construction	May
	Testing	July
Mining Equipment	Testing Underway	June
Processing Equipment	Final Construction	June
	Testing	August
Inertia Propulsion	Final Construction	June
Drives	Testing	July

As you can see from the above and in comparison to last quarter's estimates, we seem to be progressing according to the schedule contained in our strategy. The only obvious disconformity is in the Tracking and Guidance area. Frankly, I'm befuddled! This is the first real blatant variation we have had from them in a long time. I must stress concern, however, since if these figures are correct, we will not be able to meet our promised delivery date to the U.N.

Sorry to be the bearer of bad news! I would like to meet with you and discuss this matter more fully, as well as the entire JFF process.

CASE 8
I'm Not in Kansas Anymore

Developed by Anne C. Cowden, California State University, Sacramento

Telecommuting is defined as work done at home or in a remote location using technology as the link. Approximately 7.6 million people currently telecommute. The decision whether to allow employees to telecommute is controversial, owing to the number of managerial control questions raised by people working and/or managing off site.

For one manager of software projects (based in Los Angeles) who oversees 11 people in a 50-person office based in Dallas, the answer is that telecommuting is very effective, although not without drawbacks. Our manager, a veteran of 9 years of telecommuting, is in constant contact with her employees, software technical writers, and quality analysts–testers, through E-mail, with voice mailbox, phone, fax, and, at least once a month, face-to-face visits on site with each employee. One room in her home is fully outfitted as an office, one she can walk away from as a means of separating her personal and professional life. However, she is always connected to those whom she supervises. For example, on a weekend, if an employee has gone in to work, she can answer a question from home by merely walking into her home-based office.

To keep connected with her employees on a physical level, the manager meets individually with each employee on a monthly basis in Dallas. She spends an hour going over the priorities they have listed as activities for the month. Throughout the month the manager and the employees are in constant contact. Through both physical and electronic communication our manager is able to get to know her employees well. As she has noted, meeting with them in person allows her to "see" them over the phone, judging their psychological "space" by voice intonation when there is no physical face to communicate with. Our manager also interacts with other managers and line personnel through telecommuting. For example, she negotiates over the phone what goes into a product, the time line, the product budget, and all other factors necessary to managing a product effectively.

While our manager likes telecommuting and is able to manage effectively, there are both good points and drawbacks. The advantages include the freedom from commuting every day in full office dress, the complexity and challenge to stay well connected with employees, and the time gained by staying at home. The drawbacks can be the isolation that some initially feel when not having daily physical contact with others. Another drawback may be "workaholism" if one is unable to separate life from one's job. Burnout can be a factor if one works all the time.

If you are thinking of telecommuting, our manager would advise the following: get a good headset for talking on the phone; be prepared for the initial feelings of isolation; and keep in daily, close contact with your employees.

Questions

1. Is telecommuting the wave of the future, or does top management lose too much control when people are off site?
2. How would you like being a telecommuter, as either a manager or one being managed?
3. Do you think telecommuting is effective for both the employee and the organization? Why or why not? ■

CASE 9
The Forgotten Group Member

Developed by Franklin Ramsoomair, Wilfrid Laurier University

The Organizational Behavior course for the semester appeared to promise the opportunity to learn, enjoy, and practice some of the theories and principles in the textbook and class discussions. Christine Spencer was a devoted, hard working student, who had been maintaining an A- average to date. Although the skills and knowledge she had acquired through her courses were important, she was also very concerned about her grades. She felt that grades were paramount in giving her a competitive edge when looking for a job and, as a third-year student, she realized that she'd soon be doing just that.

Sunday afternoon. Two o'clock. Christine was working on an accounting assignment but didn't seem to be able to concentrate. Her courses were working out very well this semester, all but the OB. Much of the mark in that course was to be applied to the quality of groupwork, and so she felt somewhat out of control. She recollected the events of the past 5 weeks. Professor Sandra Thiel had divided the class into groups of five people and had given them a major group assignment worth 30 percent of the final grade. The task was to analyze a 7-page case and to come up with a written analysis. In addition, Sandra had asked the groups to present the case in class, with the idea in mind that the rest of the class members would be "members of the Board of Directors of the company" who would be listening to how the manager and her team dealt with the problem at hand.

Christine was elected "Team Coordinator" at the first group meeting. The other members of the group were Diane, Janet, Steve, and Mike. Diane was quiet and never volunteered suggestions, but when directly asked, she would come up with high-quality ideas. Mike was the clown. Christine remembered that she had suggested that the group should get together before

every class to discuss the day's case. Mike had balked, saying "No way!! This is an 8:30 class, and I barely make it on time anyway! Besides, I'll miss my 'Happy Harry' show on television!" The group couldn't help but laugh at his indignation. Steve was the businesslike individual, always wanting to ensure that group meetings were guided by an agenda and noting the tangible results achieved or not achieved at the end of every meeting. Janet was the reliable one who would always have more for the group than was expected of her. Christine saw herself as meticulous and organized and as a person who tried to give her best in whatever she did.

It was now week five into the semester, and Christine was now deep in thought about the OB assignment. She had called everyone to arrange a meeting for a time that would suit them all but seemed to be running into a roadblock. Mike couldn't make it, saying that he was working that night as a member of the campus security force. In fact, he seemed to miss most meetings and would send in brief notes to Christine, which she was supposed to discuss for him at the group meetings. She wondered how to deal with this. She also remembered the incident last week. Just before class started, Diane, Janet, Steve, and herself were joking with one another before class. They were laughing and enjoying themselves before Sandra came in. No one noticed that Mike had slipped in very quietly and had unobtrusively taken his seat.

She recalled the cafeteria incident. Two weeks ago, she had gone to the cafeteria to grab something to eat. She had rushed to her accounting class and had skipped breakfast. When she got her club sandwich and headed to the tables, she saw her OB group and joined them. The discussion was light and enjoyable as it always was when they met informally. Mike had come in. He'd approached their table. "You guys didn't say you were having a group meeting," he blurted. Christine was taken aback.

"We just happened to run into each other. Why not join us?"

Mike looked at them, with a noncommittal glance. "Yah . . . right," he muttered, and walked away.

Sandra Thiel had frequently told them that if there were problems in the group, the members should make an effort to deal with them first. If the problems could not be resolved, she had said that they should come to her. Mike seemed so distant, despite the apparent camaraderie of the first meeting.

An hour had passed, bringing the time to 3 p.m., and Christine found herself biting the tip of her pencil. The written case analysis was due next week. All the others had done their designated sections, but Mike had just handed in some rough handwritten notes. He had called Christine the week before, telling her that in addition to his course and his job, he was having problems with his girlfriend. Christine empathized with him. Yet, this was a group project! Besides, the final mark would be peer evaluated. This meant that whatever mark Sandra gave them could be lowered or raised, depending on the group's opinion about the value of the contribution of each member. She was definitely worried. She knew that Mike had creative ideas that could help to raise the overall mark. She was also concerned for him. As she listened to the music in the background, she wondered what she should do.

Questions

1. How could an understanding of the stages of group development assist Christine in leadership situations such as this one?
2. What should Christine understand about individual membership in groups in order to build group processes that are supportive of her work group's performance?
3. Is Christine an effective group leader in this case? Why or why not? ■

CASE 10
Functional Diversity at IBM
....
Developed by Toni A. Gregory, Private Consultant, and Ronald P. Lewis, IBM Consulting Group

Growing competition has forced the IBM Corporation to develop a new strategy that looks beyond the manufacturing, sale, and servicing of information systems to expand into new businesses. Sales and service of mainframes, once IBM's bread and butter, have taken a back seat to new ventures such as business consulting—designing business solutions for clients outside of IBM's traditional market segments.

IBM has taken the consulting business quite seriously and quite by storm. "Its consulting force practices in 30 countries and has hundreds of clients, ranging from corporate giants . . . to smaller companies." Beginning with an initial investment of $100 million in 1991, IBM's revenues from consulting had increased to $362 million by 1993.

Miles Smith, leader of IBM's Business Transformation Consulting Practice, has jumped on the consulting bandwagon. His previous experience had been in IBM's traditional hardware-related business, first as a technology specialist and later as a marketing executive. After initial training in consulting methodologies and approaches, Smith launched one of the 40 new consulting practices within IBM's new worldwide consulting operations.

I started with a very vague idea of what I wanted to do when I realized that the ultimate strength of my practice was going to be a function of the breadth and depth of the collective experiences of the team that we formed. Since our product line would be people, I realized that in order to have as wide a product line as possible, I would need to hire people different from me, different from each other and who brought a wide range of skills, backgrounds, interests and personalities.

Smith's 18 years of experience in a dozen different positions gave him a broad range of knowledge and the capability to assimilate clients' critical issues quickly. However, he

Source: This is an abridged version of a case from the Field Guide of E. E. Kossek and S. A. Lobel, *Managing Diversity: Human Resource Strategy for Transforming the Workplace,* Oxford, England, Blackwell, 1996.

lacked the depth of knowledge required to meet *specific* client needs, such as in the automotive vehicle development process or the banking mortgage lending process, increasing the need to leverage diversity to create a cross-functional team. To fulfill a wide range of client needs, Smith needed consultants who represented a diverse set of capabilities and experiences yet could work together as a team.

In the past, IBM had sought a certain profile of candidates from college campuses. All new hires into the marketing divisions went through the same training, and success was measured primarily on the individual's ability to sell IBM hardware and software to corporate America's data-processing organizations. The narrow "gene pool" that served IBM's traditional business fairly well was exactly what was *not* required in the consulting business. One of IBM's traditional strengths was the breadth of its product line. In the consulting business, the product line is the people and the different skills, experiences, and capabilities that they can bring to bear on clients' business problems.

Smith admitted he did not know what characteristics to look for in a consultant initially. Yet, he had under 2 months to hire six people who would make up the core of the consulting practice in order to get them into the required training classes. Smith confirms that there is something unique about each person he hired that gives him or her an edge that has made each invaluable to the consulting practice. "Each one brings a different set of skills to the table. This is what makes us truly cross-functional. Each person has a unique contribution to make to our success with clients. No one person represents all of the parts."

Smith's first hire was Sharon North. She seemed like a safe choice. She had been a top-performing salesperson and had recently helped start up another consulting practice. North wanted to join Smith's new group because its primary orientation toward business process reengineering was closer to her MBA area of concentration.

His next hire, Bob Hart, had never spent a day in IBM marketing. He had been hired into IBM product development after obtaining his engineering undergraduate degree. Hart progressed rapidly through the ranks, consistently getting responsibility for larger and more complex projects. After taking time out to earn a Master of Science degree in business administration, he joined the corporate staff to work on ways to improve IBM's processes in product development. Hart's depth of technical knowledge in engineering, combined with management and corporate experience, make him an extremely valuable asset to clients and the practice. He provides consulting services to businesses on process reengineering and business strategy and provides team members with expertise in project coordination and project management.

Susan Flannery, by contrast, had very little technical background but had significant experience in finance and planning. Eighteen months before joining the practice, Flannery had volunteered for an assignment to work on reengineering IBM's customer fulfillment process in the United States. As part of this assignment, Flannery not only developed the skills that the consultants in the practice would need, but she also worked under the mentorship of a consulting firm that was now a major competitor to IBM's own consulting business. Flannery had taken a chance with her career by taking an assignment that was "off the beaten track." Yet, it turned out that the experience was a key factor in her being selected to join the new practice.

Don Bend's career background was most like Smith's own. However, like Flannery, Bend had strayed from the normal route and spent 2 years teaching leadership development classes inside IBM. Much of the theory and many of the methods paralleled what the consultants would be doing for their clients. Bend's own leadership abilities also positioned him to be the informal team leader. In fact, over time, Smith recognized that Bend did as much of the mentoring and coaching as he did. In the past this would have made Smith uncomfortable, but the dynamics of the business were entirely different and, therefore, the roles needed to be as well. As a senior consultant for the practice, Bend is responsible for developing client relations, managing consulting engagements, and helping clients achieve desired results. He also acts as a behind-the-scenes coach for other team members.

Tom Boyd is the only team member who had any experience in consulting and services. His first 25 years with IBM were with the forerunner of the current consulting and services business. Boyd brought with him significant general management experience, strong project management skills, and the ability to facilitate communication and consensus building. He joined the practice in his twenty-ninth year in IBM, 12 years longer than the next most senior consultant on the team. Boyd is currently an engagement manager for a team of three consultants. His strengths are his skills in facilitating communication, his creative and analytical ability, and his ability to bring out the creativity in others.

Lisa Lee provides the team's systems and graphic support. She plays a pivotal role, even though she serves in a primarily administrative capacity and has less career experience than her peers. Lee's responsibility is to prepare proposals and final reports for clients. She was recruited because of her excellent reputation and proven skills in graphical report generation. Her ability to work with people and her writing skills complement her team members.

For companies like IBM, responding to new market opportunities means learning to manage these diverse individuals in cross-functional teams.

Questions

1. What was the main goal behind Smith's hiring plan?
2. Identify some key dimensions of diversity that might affect each team member's perspective.
3. How might Smith help the team wrestle with the following issues: tenure vs. performance; individual contributor vs. a team of peers; cross-functional interaction vs. collaborative interaction; management of self-directed teams, role of leadership in articulating desired values and behaviors? ■

C A S E   1 1
First Community Financial
....

Developed by Mark Osborn, Arizona Chamber of Commerce

First Community Financial is a small business lender that specializes in asset-based lending and factoring for a primarily small business clientele. First Community's business is generated by high-growth companies in diverse industries, whose capital needs will not be met by traditional banking institutions. First Community Financial will lend in amounts up to $1 million, so its focus is on small business. Since many of the loans that it administers are viewed by many banks as high-risk loans, it is important that the sales staff and loan processors have a solid working relationship. Since the loans and factoring deals that First Community finances are risky, the interest that it charges is at prime plus 6 percent or sometimes higher.

First Community is a credible player in the market because of its history and the human resource policies of the company. The company invests in its employees and works to assure that turnover is low. The goal of this strategy is to develop a consistent, professional team that has more expertise than its competitors.

Whereas Jim Adamany, President and CEO, has a strong history in the industry and is a recognized expert in asset-based lending and factoring, First Community has one of the youngest staff and management teams in the finance industry. In the banking industry, promotions are slow coming, because many banks employ conservative personnel programs. First Community, however, has recruited young, ambitious people who are specifically looking to grow with the company. As the company grows, so will the responsibility and rewards for these young executives. In his early thirties, for example, Matt Vincent is a Vice President; at only 28, Brian Zcray is Director of Marketing.

Since First Community has a diverse product line, it must compete in distinct markets. Its factoring products compete with small specialized factoring companies. Factoring is a way for businesses to improve their cash flow by selling their invoices at a discount. Factoring clients are traditionally the smallest clients finance companies must serve. Education about the nature of the product is crucial if the company is to be successful since this often is a new approach to financing for many companies. First Community's sales staff is well trained at understanding its product lines and acts as the client's representative as they work through the approval process.

To assure the loans or factoring deals fit within the risk profile of the company, First Community must ask many complex financial questions. Many small businesses are intimidated by credit officers, so First Community handles all of these inquiries through the business development officers. The business development officers, in turn, must understand the needs of their credit officers, who are attempting to minimize risk to the company while maintaining a friendly rapport with the client. By centralizing the client contract through educated sales representatives, First Community is able to ask the hard financial questions and still keep the clients interested in the process. A potential customer can easily be discouraged by a creditor administrator's strong questioning about financial background. Utilizing the business development officers as an intermediary reduces the fear of many applicants about the credit approval process. Thus, a sales focus is maintained throughout the recruitment and loan application process.

Internally at First Community Financial there is a continual pressure between the business development staff and the credit committee. The business development staff is focused on bringing in new clients. Their compensation in a large part is dependent on how many deals they can execute for the company. Like sales staff in any industry, they are aggressive and always look for new markets for business. The sales staff sells products from both the finance department and the factoring department, so they must interact with credit officers from each division. In each of these groups credit administrators are specifically responsible for ensuring that potential deals meet the lending criteria of the organization. While the business development officer's orientation is to bring in more and more deals, the credit administrator's primary goal is to limit bad loans.

The pressure develops when business development officers bring in potential loans that are rejected by the credit administrators. Since the business development officers have some experience understanding the credit risks of their clients, they often understand the policy reasoning for denying or approving a loan. The business development officers have additional concerns that their loans that have potential to be financed are approved because many of the referral sources of the sales staff will only refer deals to companies that are lending. If First Community fails to help many of a bank's referral clients, that source of business may dry up, as bankers refer deals to other lending institutions.

These structural differences are handled by focused attempts at improving communication. As noted before, the First Community staff experiences an extremely low turnover rate. This allows for the development of a cohesive team.

With a cohesive staff, the opportunity to maintain frank and open communication helps bridge the different orientations of the sales staff and the administration divisions. A simple philosophy that the opinions of all staff are to be respected is continually implemented.

Since approving a loan is often a policy decision, the sales staff and the loan administrators can have an open forum to discuss whether a loan will be approved. CEO Jim Adamany approves all loans, but since he values the opinions of all of his staff he provides them all an opportunity to communicate. Issues such as the loan history for an applicant's industry, current bank loan policies, and other factors can be openly discussed from multiple perspectives.

Questions

1. What coordinative mechanisms does First Community use to manage the potential conflict between its sales and finance/auditing functions?
2. What qualities should First Community emphasize in hiring new staff to ensure that its functional organizational structure will not yield too many problems?
3. What are the key types of information transfer that First Community needs to emphasize and how is this transmitted throughout the firm?
4. Why might a small finance company have such a simple structure while a larger firm might find this structure inappropriate? ■

CASE 12
Mission Management and Trust

Developed by Mark Osborn, Arizona Chamber of Commerce

With more than 500 business and political leaders in attendance from across the state of Arizona, CEO Carmen Bermudez of Mission Management and Trust accepted the prestigious ATHENA Award. The ATHENA, which is presented by the Arizona Chamber of Commerce, is annually awarded to companies that have a demonstrated track record in promoting women's issues within their company and the community. The 50-pound bronze statute that was presented to Mission Management and Trust was particularly special for the company's leadership because it was a tangible demonstration of their commitment to the community and to women's issues.

Mission Management and Trust is a small, newly formed company of just 8 employees that has already made great headway in an industry that is dominated by giant corpora-tions. Mission Management and Trust opened its doors just 2 years ago, and it already manages over $45 million in assets. What makes Mission's development even more impressive is that Mission is the first minority- and women-owned trust company in the nation.

The trust management industry provides services to individuals, organizations, and companies that want their assets managed and protected by specialized outside firms. Mission management provides personal service to its customers at a level of sophistication that is unusual for a firm of its small size. Understanding that the trust management business is highly competitive, Mission developed a unique strategy that highlighted socially conscious policies combined with good business relations.

When the company was formed in 1994, it was created with more than the goal of just making a profit. Founder Carmen Bermudez started Mission with three principal goals in mind. "1. To run a top quality trust company. 2. To promote within the company and, by example, increase opportunities for women and minorities. 3. To donate a portion of all revenue to charitable projects supported by clients and staff." As these statements demonstrate, Mission Management and Trust was created with a specific purpose in mind that was focused not just on the business of trust management but on the responsibility of being a good corporate citizen.

Even with these lofty goals, Mission faced the problem of finding clients who not only wanted quality services but were not hindered by some of the potential sacrifices a socially conscious investment company might make. Many investors want a high rate of return for their trusts, and social policy is of a much lesser concern. This was not the market Mission wanted to address, so it had to be selective in developing a client base.

Mission needed to find clients that fit its social philosophy about investing and corporate responsibility. The ideal customers would be individuals and organizations that were committed to socially conscious policies and wanted an investment strategy that reflected this commitment. Mission found a perfect niche in the market with religious institutions. Churches and other civic organizations across the nation have trusts that they use to fund special projects and maintain operating expenses. They need effective service, but in many cases these organizations must be mindful of investing in companies and other projects that do not refelct their ideals. For example, a trust company that invests in companies in the highly profitable liquor and cigarette industries would not be consistent with the philosophy of many religious organizations. Mission services this niche by developing an organization that is structurally designed to make socially conscious decisions.

Mission has already begun to meet one of its principal goals, which is to donate a portion of its profits to charities. By the end of 1994, Mission had already donated $4500 to causes ranging from Catholic Community Services to the Jewish Community Center scholarship program. These donations not only fulfill a goal of the organization but assist in the socially conscious client recruitment. Mission's target client base will find Mission a much more attractive trust company because of its charity programs. A religious organization can be comforted with the reality that some of the dollars it spends on trust management will be recycled into the causes it promotes itself. The mission policy makes good social policy, but it also makes good marketing sense. Understanding your clients is crucial to developing a small business, and Mission has mastered this principle.

Mission makes the most of its commitment to charitable causes by keeping its clients informed about the trust's activities and, more importantly, its community activities. *The Mission Bell,* a regular publication of Mission Management and Trust, details news and issues about the trust industry, company activities, and, most importantly, how Mission's social responsibility philosophy is being implemented. The name *Mission Bell* is more consistent with a religious publication than a corporate investing sheet, but it is consistent with its clients' needs. The name of the publication and its content clarify Mission's role and purpose. For example, the *Mission Bell Summer Issue* presented articles on new hires, breaking investment news, and an article about how Mission is working with other groups to support socially responsible corporate investing. Thus, the Mission philosophy is clearly defined in its marketing and communication strategies.

To be consistent with the goals of the organizations, Carmen Bremudez collected a small staff of highly experienced individuals whose backgrounds and principles fit Mission's ideals. She frequently comments that the best business decision she ever made was "giving preference to intelligent, talented, compatible people whose main attribute was extensive experience." Mission employees are not just experts in the field of finance but leaders in their communities. These dual qualifications fulfill three important requirements that are crucial for the company's success. With community involvement comes an appreciation of the investment sensitivities that are required by the organizations that Mission services. Secondly, individuals who are involved in the community have well-developed contacts that can be useful in business recruitment. Finally, socially active employees are committed to the purpose of the organization and help unify the corporate culture within Mission.

Claire B. Moore, Vice President of Mission Management and Trust, is a perfect example of how a corporate philosophy has been translated into practical personnel decisions. Claire was recruited because she had extensive banking experience, as demonstrated by her Vice President position in Bank of America (Arizona). Her professional qualifications are augmented by her extensive involvement in the community, which includes the University of Arizona Foundation Planned Giving Council, Tucson Symphony, and the Junior League, to name a few.

The Mission case is a clear example of how matching a philosophy with a market can bear solid results. Mission's commitment to its ideals is evident and reflected in all of their business practices. When human resources, investing, marketing, and strategic planning decisions are made with unified goals in mind, the chances are good that a strong successful corporate culture will develop.

Questions

1. How do the mission elements of Mission Management differ from most firms?
2. Does donating to charity before the firm is fully established mean that Mission is not demonstrating financial prudence?
3. Could Mission's unique mission contribute to effective coordination as well as adjustment to the market?
4. Would Mission's unique mission still yield success with more traditional investors? ■

CASE 13
Craig Morancie
....

Developed by John Seeger, Bentley College

Mike Brummer switched off the CNN headline news and turned toward the narrow motel desk, hoping to finish his week's reports for the headquarters office. Brummer, a Chapter Consultant for the Gamma Sigma fraternity, had driven four hours to reach the campus of Slidell State University, responding to a telephone call the Dean of Students had made to the fraternity's Executive Director the previous day.

Mike Brummer was one of five traveling consultants employed by the fraternity to assist its nearly 200 undergraduate chapters. As a college student himself the previous year, Brummer had been president of his own school's Gamma Sigma chapter, and his active role at the fraternity's International Conclave had led to an offer to join the headquarters staff for a 2-year assignment. As a Chapter Consultant, he visited some 40 campuses to help local chapters with whatever they most needed—planning new member recruitment, controlling finances, alumni relations, scholarship, ritual performance, etc. Gamma Sigma was intensely proud of its reputation and stature as an international fraternity and hoped every chapter would be recognized as "Number One" on its own campus.

Most chapter visits were scheduled ahead of time, so the local members and the consultant could plan for meetings with the college administration and the Alumnus Advisor. A few visits, however, took the form of firefighting or crisis intervention. Mike Brummer's trip to Slidell fell into this category.

This afternoon, Mike Brummer had met with the Dean of Students,

Source: Review copy for the *Case Research Journal.* Not for distribution or reproduction without written permission of the author. Copyright © 1996.

with several officers of this chapter, and then with Craig Morancie, a Slidell State freshman who had been, briefly, a Gamma Sigma pledge. Tomorrow, Brummer would meet with the chapter as a whole. He was concerned about what to say.

The Slidell chapter was unexceptional, Brummer thought, with few pressing problems other than housing, pledge retention, and a sharp dip in its GPA last semester. Only three students lived in the run-down, rented house; 26 other actives and 18 pledges lived at home or in the dorms. Rush was usually strong, but only 7 of last year's 24 pledges had been initiated (the lowest retention rate Mike had seen in his year and a half as a traveling consultant). Chapter morale was good and the men showed great pride, but the work schedules of most (at 25 hours a week or more) curtailed many of their activities. The chapter had a very experienced Alumnus Advisor and was well regarded by Dean Powell, but Greeks were little noticed by most students on this commuter-dominated campus.

Then, as Spring Rush ended, Craig Morancie accepted a membership invitation from the two G Sigs who had rushed him strongly; he signed the university's pledge form, affiliating with Gamma Sigma. A week later, however, when the other 18 new men were called by name for formal pledging, Craig Morancie was not called. After a long delay, Mark Medvene—one of the friends who invited him to join—came to say, "We're sorry, Craig, but the chapter just isn't ready for a black member."

He would have been an asset to the chapter, Craig had told Dean Powell the next day, and he was sure Mark and the others had wanted him as a real fraternity brother, not as a token. Four of the 12 fraternities at Slidell State had at least one black member, but Craig had not found other organizations he would want to join. Now, he wasn't sure he'd want to join Gamma Sigma either, even if the brothers there changed their minds. In his meeting with Mike Brummer, Morancie said:

If there were many against me, then I *shouldn't* have joined. It wouldn't have worked. But I want the chapter to see what they're doing, and to change. The Alumnus Advisor says he and the district officer will work with the chapter, but I don't see that as helping them changing anything. A lawsuit wouldn't help them change, either. It's too late for me, but who's going to be next? This should never happen again.

In their meeting with Brummer this afternoon, four members of the five-man chapter Executive Committee said they had favored pledging Morancie, but Jamie Todd, the chapter treasurer, had voiced a strong counteropinion in the crucial chapter meeting. Jamie acknowledged he had cast the negative vote that prevented Craig Morancie's pledging. But it wasn't bias on his part, he said; the vote expressed his responsibility to several members who weren't themselves at the meeting, and to many alumni brothers whose opinions on matters of race were well known.

Gamma Sigma Fraternity had eliminated its constitutional provision restricting membership in 1957,

when undergraduate delegates to its biennial Conclave voted decisively for the change. Hispanic, Asian and Jewish members had been common long before the constitutional change, and by the 1990s black members were also common, although many chapters had none. The fraternity was proud of its progress.

Gamma Sigma's international constitution, like that of most Greek societies, called for the unanimous vote of a chapter's brothers before a pledge could be initiated. To prevent isolated minorities from blocking the pledging or initiation of a new member, the constitution allowed any chapter to petition headquarters to override a "blackball" vote. Very few such petitions had ever been received at headquarters; many members were unaware of the override provision.

Mike Brummer knew that the Slidell State chapter customarily let its Rush Chairman decide which prospective new members should be invited to join. Because of the overlapping work schedules of most members, it was very difficult to schedule rush events so all the brothers could meet all the rushees. The Executive Committee told Mike Brummer this system had worked well over the years; pledges who caused conflict or couldn't fit in with the membership at large usually

dropped out long before the final ballot on initiation.

Mike Brummer was tired. His fraternity-supplied Chevrolet had turned 100,000 miles on the trip to Slidell, and he had driven every one of them. In the morning tomorrow he would call the Executive Director, and in the afternoon he would meet with the chapter's Alumnus Advisor. In the evening the chapter members would assemble for the special meeting he had called. Mike wondered what to aim for in that meeting: what would a "perfect" outcome be? How should he handle the arguments of Jamie Todd? How should he start the meeting? How could he get the men to quesiton their established ways of doing things?

Questions

1. You are Mike Brummer. How will you handle the chapter meeting tomorrow?
2. How can you tell which of these is the best way to go? How do you decide? Should we just take the majority vote? Is that necessarily the *best* approach?
3. What kind of outcome would you like to see, after this meeting? What would "perfect" be? What goal should you be looking for? What goal would make sense to the brothers? ■

Fidelity Insurance Company
. . . .

L eslie Jones, Supervisor, Benefits Administration at Fidelity Insurance Company was discouraged as she stared out her 20th-floor corner office window in downtown Toronto late one afternoon in August 1987. Her boss, Jack Miller, Manager of the Payroll and Benefits Department, had done it again. Leslie had just found out that Jack had given instructions to one of Leslie's staff members that directly contradicted what Leslie only the day before had asked.

454 THE ORGANIZATIONAL BEHAVIOR WORKBOOK ● ● ● ● ● ● ● ● ● ● ● ● ● ● ● ● ● ● ●

The latest incident was one in a series that Leslie had had to deal with during the year that she had held the position. Not only would she now have to sort out the problems caused by Jack's most recent interference, she was wondering if it really was worth staying.

Company History

Fidelity, a Toronto, Ontario based company, was one of over 50 insurance companies operating in Canada. Until the early 1970s it had been a relatively minor player in the Canadian insurance industry, serving primarily the Ontario market. In 1970 a change in senior management resulted in a new, aggressive strategy. Fidelity began to challenge its much larger competitors with innovative products and client services. By the early 1980s, Fidelity had expanded across Canada and had grown from 2000 to 5000 employees in under 10 years.

In June 1986, Fidelity doubled its asset base through the acquisition of its closest competitor, the Life Mutual Insurance Company, and became Canada's 9th largest insurance company. Fidelity's workforce

Source: Case material of the Western School of Business Administration is prepared as a basis for classroom discussion. This case was prepared by Janet Dibbs under the direction of Professor James A. Erskine.

also doubled, from preacquisition levels of 5000 employees to over 10,000. Fidelity's ambitious long-term objectives suggested that both the Company and its number of employees could be expected to increase in the future.

Benefits Administration

Employee benefits at Fidelity consisted of paid vacations, group insurance benefits (life, health, and disability insurance plans), a money purchase pension plan, an executive compensation plan, and a company stock purchase plan. The combined cost of these benefits totaled approximately 30% of the payroll.

The responsibilities of Benefits Administration included calculating and remitting tax on taxable benefits, administering the mechanics of the stock purchase plan (i.e., enrolling new entrants, making the monthly deductions from pay), and dealing with the numerous inquiries from staff and management about their benefit coverages. The Benefits group calculated the pension entitlements for every retiring employee. For employees considering early retirement, Benefits provided the estimated amount of pension they would be eligible to receive.

The Benefits Administration function had historically always been the responsibility of the Payroll and Benefits Department at Fidelity. As the company grew, so too did the size of the Payroll and Benefits department, from a staff of 6 in 1980, to over 30 by June 1986. With this growth in size it was becoming increasingly difficult to manage and control. Therefore, in June 1986 the Department was subdivided into three functional areas: Benefits Administration, Payroll Administration, and Payroll Control (see Exhibit 1). A new layer of management was established as a reuslt

of this reorganization, through the creation of supervisory positions heading each of the new areas.

Jack Miller

At 52 years old, Jack had spent his entire working life at Fidelity. The past 10 of his 33 years at the Company had been spent as Manager of the Payroll and Benefits Department. In 1980 he had been promoted to Assistant Vice-President (AVP) of Compensation and Benefits, but immediately thereafter was injured in a serious car accident. Realizing that he would be unable to perform the AVP function adequately, Jack had asked to be returned to his previous position. In his place, Desmond Smith was hired in 1981 from outside the Company to become AVP, Compensation and Benefits. Although he had not proposed the June 1986 department reorganization (this had come from Desmond Smith), at the time Jack had fully endorsed it. It was generally believed among his staff that Jack aspired to once again become AVP Compensation and Benefits. Many wondered if this was a realistic objective, and felt that it was much more likely that Jack would retire in his current position.

Jack seemed to have had a very good relationship with his staff in the Payroll and Benefits Department when it had consisted of only five people, all of whom were middle-aged women. It seemed that Jack's relationship with this initial core group of people continued to be better than with the newer and younger staff members who joined the Department between 1980 and 1987.

Leslie Jones

Now 30 years old, Leslie had worked at Fidelity for 7 years. She had started in an administrative position in

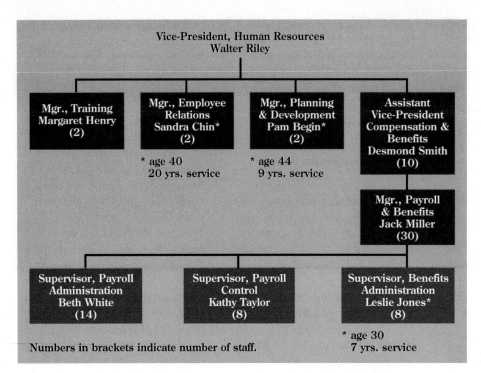

Vice-President, Human Resources
Walter Riley

| Mgr., Training Margaret Henry (2) | Mgr., Employee Relations Sandra Chin* (2) | Mgr., Planning & Development Pam Begin* (2) | Assistant Vice-President Compensation & Benefits Desmond Smith (10) |

* age 40
20 yrs. service

* age 44
9 yrs. service

Mgr., Payroll & Benefits
Jack Miller
(30)

| Supervisor, Payroll Administration Beth White (14) | Supervisor, Payroll Control Kathy Taylor (8) | Supervisor, Benefits Administration Leslie Jones* (8) |

* age 30
7 yrs. service

Numbers in brackets indicate number of staff.

Exhibit 1

the Customer Service Department as soon as she had finished university. The Customer Service Department gave her a broad understanding of the company's different products and services. After 3 1/2 years she was promoted to the Internal Audit department. This work involved visiting all the different branch offices and Head Office Departments to review and assess operating procedures. During her 2 years in Audit, Leslie was involved in reviews of almost all of the company's different functional areas.

Leslie had always been interested in working in the field of Human Resources. She felt the exposure gained from working in a Human Resources department would be very valuable for career advancement. Therefore, when a position for a Benefits Administrator in the Payroll and Benefits Department opened in April 1985, she eagerly pursued it. She was interviewed both by Personnel and Jack Miller and was subsequently transferred.

When Leslie joined the department, she was one of a team of four administrators, four clerks and a secretary reporting to Jack. As the Benefits Administrrator she was responsible for the entire range of Pension and Benefits Administration duties. From the outset Leslie found it very difficult to get support and direction from Jack. She decided that it must somehow be her fault; maybe she was slow to understand things because she was new to the department and unfamiliar with the work. Despite what she felt was a lack of guidance, Leslie soon developed proficiency and competence in the position.

When the position of Supervisor, Employee Benefits was created a year later, Leslie was interviewed by Jack and Desmond at their initiative and chosen for the promotion. Leslie felt that this promotion probably had more to do with the fact that she was really the only person in the department who had the skills in Employee Benefits

than with any confidence Jack might have had in her.

Leslie was responsible for managing a staff of seven employees. In addition to these supervisory responsibilities, she was to be responsible for preparing and managing the department's budget, liasing with senior management on benefits related issues, resolving disputes between employees and her staff, and ensuring that Fidelity continued to comply with the ever-changing federal and provincial governments' tax and benefits legislation.

The First Year

Leslie's problems with Jack began almost as soon as she assumed her new position. It quickly became apparent to her that he was unwilling to relinquish his former control. Instead of delegating routine matters to Leslie and her staff, Jack would handle them himself. In one instance, an employee considering early retirement had called Jack to ask for a pension calculation. He undertook the calculation himself, and without verifying the number or even notifying Leslie of what he had done, advised the employee of the amount. On the basis of this information, the employee decided to take early retirement. Only when the paperwork arrived in Leslie's area a month later was it discovered that Jack had provided the employee with a figure higher than warranted. Leslie went to discuss the problem with Jack, and he authorized her to pay the higher pension to the employee. The conversation was never documented.

Shortly after she had assumed the position her group became very busy processing and adding the Life Mutual employees to Fidelity's systems. Leslie had given instructions to her staff on the procedures to follow for processing this group. Jack had subsequently gone directly to her staff with different instructions. Unsure of whose orders to follow, one of the staff approached Leslie on behalf of the group to clarify what they should do. Leslie informed them that she was their immediate supervisor and it was therefore her instructions that they should follow. She also asked that they let her know if Jack ever again approached them with instructions different to those she had provided.

Leslie then went to Jack and "demanded" that in future if he disagreed with the instructions she had given to her staff, he should first discuss it with her rather than going directly to them. Jack denied ever having given differing instructions. Not wanting to involve her staff members in a one-on-one confrontation with Jack to determine who was telling the truth, Leslie dropped the issue with Jack. She reiterated to her employees, though, that they

were to advise her in the future of any such incidents.

Several times after this first incident Leslie had been told by her staff that Jack had contradicted her instructions. In response, sometimes Leslie would simply tell them to ignore Jack's instructions and wouldn't bother to advise Jack formally that she had "overruled" him. Other times, if the opportunity presented itself in conversation, Leslie would mention to Jack that she had maintained her position, and that unless he could provide her with evidence to support his approach, she would continue on her basis. Jack had consistently then let the issue drop.

After her first few months in the position she had asked for his evaluation of the work she had done so far. Instead of responding to her, Jack had expounded on managerial philosophies. She had sought feedback from him on several subsequent occasions on specific decisions that she had made. Each time, without saying so directly, Jack had made Leslie feel that her decisions were stupid ones.

In March 1987 Leslie had been invited by Desmond to attend a meeting with Jack, himself, and Walter Riley, the Vice-President of Human Resources, to discuss the strategy for implementing the planned changeover in the company pension plan from a defined benefit to a money purchase plan.* Walter had asked for Leslie's opinion on an

_____

*A defined benefit plan is one in which the company guarantees in advance the amount of pension that an employee will be eligible to receive upon retirement. Under a Money Purchase plan, the employee's pension is determined by the accumulated value of their pension contributions and the prevailing interest rates at the time of their retirement. The amount of pension under a Money Purchase plan therefore cannot be determined precisely until actual retirement.

issue, and before she was able to answer Jack interjected "Yes, cutie-pie, tell us what you think." Shocked and infuriated, Leslie looked over her shoulder and then back to Jack and responded, "Sorry, Jack, who were you talking to?" She then responded to Walter's question. Feeling that nothing would be gained by going to speak to Jack about his comments, she let the matter drop.

Leslie drew little comfort from the fact that both Beth White, the Supervisor of Payroll Administration and Kathy Taylor, the Supervisor of Payroll Control, both women in their early thirties, voiced almost identical complaints about Jack. Both of them had independently spoken with Desmond about the fact that they felt they weren't receiving adequate managerial direction and support in their positions. Desmond had responded to both women that he and Walter were both extremely satisfied with their work. He also suggested that from a career advancement prospective, it was his support, not Jack's that was critical.

Leslie had considered seeing Desmond about her own situation and, although she felt they had a good relationship, decided against it. She strongly felt that the problem was between herself and Jack, and that it was therefore up to her to resolve it. Instead, she decided to try to gain Jack's confidence and respect through working especially hard and being especially careful with every decision she made. It was therefore discouraging when she got the news from Pam Marin, one of her staff members, that Jack had again contradicted Leslie's instructions.

The Last Straw

Leslie was talking on the phone to a regional benefits manager when Pam Marin came into her office.

When Leslie hung up the phone Pam rather apologetically explained what had happened.

Leslie, I know that you told us that the Company policy for providing pension annuity quotations under the new Money Purchase pension plan is to provide the employee a preliminary quote only, and to make it clear to them that the actual amount of their pension could be either higher or lower, depending upon the interest rates on the date of their retirement. Well, Jack has just told me to give guaranteed, precalculated quotes to employees. He feels that employees have the right to know the exact amount of their pension well in advance of retirement.

"Oh, no, not again" thought Leslie. "Leave it to me" she responded, "but in the meantime, please continue to provide quotes on the preliminary estimate basis."

Despite the problems with Jack, Leslie found her position rewarding and challenging. It was because she enjoyed her job so much that she found these problems so frustrating. As she reflected on the endless series of incidents over the past year, and the dim prospects of any improvement in the situation over the future, she wondered if perhaps it was finally time to look for another job.

Questions

1. What type of power losses is Leslie experiencing as a result of Jack's actions?
2. Is this just a case of "good old boy" politics, or is it a clear case of discrimination against women? Explain.
3. What actions should be taken to correct Jack's behavior? ∎

CASE 15

Power or Empowerment at GM?
···
Developed by Aneil Mishra, Pennsylvania State University, Karen Mishra, Pennsylvania State University, and Kim Cameron, Brigham Young University

Introduction

Effective September 25, 1990, the management of the General Motors (GM) Parma, Ohio, stamping plant finalized another 3-year local agreement with the United Auto Workers' Union (UAW), Local 1005. It was the second local agreement they had negotiated together *on time* and *without intervention* from Detroit, since Parma's self-described revolutionary agreement 7 years previously. It was revolutionary because Parma's management and union had abandoned their old hostilities and incorporated a team-based approach to work, setting Parma in a new direction. The 1990 agreement formally documented their joint priorities of team-based work groups, extensive

employee training, and a supportive working environment. The Assistant Personnel Director for Hourly Employment, Bill Marsh, felt that, although this was another positive step in their ongoing relationship with Local 1005, the negotiating process seemed more "traditional" than the previous negotiation in 1987. Bob Lintz, the Plant Manager, agreed. Unexpectedly, the new Shop Committee Chairman, who is Local 1005's prime negotiator, had introduced over 600 demands at the start

of Parma's local contract negotiation. Even though management and the union were still able to finalize an agreement quickly, the tension created by the enormous list of demands still lingered. It could destroy the collaborative relationship that had been built over the past decade between management and the union leadership as well as the openness that Bob Lintz had managed to foster between himself and the hourly employees.

Background

In the early 1980s, Parma's corporate parent, GM, conducted a capacity rationalization study that concluded that almost 75 percent of Parma's operations should either be eliminated or tranferred to other GM facilities with 3 years. Despite a 1-year lapse in formal relations, and with no contract in effect, Parma's management and Local 1005 responded to this threat to plant survival by conducting a joint effort to bring in new business. This joint effort led to a number of competitive assessments of Parma's operations that identified several noncompetitive work practices. To acknowledge formally this new collaborative relationship, a new labor agreement was drafted and ratified in 1983 by Parma's rank and file that resulted in fewer work classifications and emphasized a team-based approach to managing work groups[1].

To implement this agreement, Parma's top management and Local 1005 created the Team Concept Implementation Group, or TCIG, to introduce this new Team Concept and spent $40 million on extensive training of the entire workforce in problem-solving, group dynamics, and effective communication skills. By 1990, the Team Concept had empowered hourly employees to assume more responsibility in their jobs and to focus on problem solving and work-related matters and to move beyond status differences exemplified by position titles or neckties.

Roger Montgomery, who had chaired the Shop Committee from 1981 until 1990, felt that he had been able to put aside his past doubts of management's sincerity and work with Bob to create an environment based on teamwork and trust. He credits Bob's sincerity and openness with their ability to respect each other and work together for the good of the plant and its jobs. Roger believed that Bob had to overcome significant obstacles in creating this collaborative relationship at Parma, especially in convincing members of management and supervision. After years of open hostility between management and labor, Roger knew that Bob had supervisors and managers who didn't want to change. After years of fighting for employees by getting doors on bathroom stalls and eliminating hall passes, Roger felt that his union team had achieved greater consensus about the need for change. He felt lucky because even though some of his shop committee might not have agreed with him about every detail, they did support his efforts out of loyalty to him and to his relationship with Bob. Bob Lintz also felt that his managers and Local 1005's leaders had worked hard to overcome decades-long hostilities and build a positive and collaborative relationship[2].

Current Situation

Bob and his managers are concerned about the tension that has been created by the new Shop Committee chairman's large number of demands, especially because there were only about 100 demands made by the union during the previous contract negotiations. Roger had

publicly endorsed this new chairman of the Shop Committee, yet management was not certain that he would continue Roger's strategy of collaboration within the union and between management and the union. With several new individuals in the union leadership, Parma's management also had to consider the possibility that the entire union leadership was actually becoming more adversarial, especially as the two political factions within the union continued to compete for support among members of Local 1005. Relations between hourly and salaried employees on the production floor could also suffer.

The list of demands from the new chairman of the Shop Committee could have resulted from the uncertainty that existed with the recent announcements of plant closings by GM. Since the mid-1980s, six GM stamping plants had been closed, and Parma's employment level had fallen. These plant closings and pressure from GM were the result of GM losing 10 percentage points of market share in under 10 years and corresponding deterioration in GM's bottom line. By the fall of 1990, GM was losing more than $1100 for every vehicle it produced in North America, in part because of GM's high fixed costs. With over $700 million in sales, Parma is an important plant to GM, but there is no guarantee that it will not be closed if demand for GM's products does not improve. Wall Street is criticizing GM for not being more aggressive in closing plants to remove excess capacity. The corporation is pressuring all of its facilities to reduce expenditures significantly and to eliminate all overtime. Parma has made substantial progress in maintaining revenues amidst declining demand, but it still needs to make significant improvements in productivity. For example, it has still

to better utilize the transfer presses that stamp automative doors and hoods. These presses were installed during the $600 million modernization in 1983, and in 1990 their uptime stands at 31 percent.[3]

Parma also needs to improve its quality and customer satisfaction. In 1989, Parma began supplying the metal frame for the minivan produced at GM's Tarrytown, New York, facility. Arthur Norelli, General Supervisor of Dimensional Control, remembers that in his first encounters with Parma, *"I found them initially, very defensive, almost adversarial. They were always right until we proved them wrong. If we had a part that wouldn't go together properly, they would say 'Well, you're not putting it together right.'"* Another customer, a transmission plant within GM's Powertrain Group, has concerns about Parma's ability to produce quality parts in a timely fashion. As recently as 1988, Parma was Powertrain's worst supplied for transmission components. Bill Hurles, a materials manager within the Powertrain Group, remembered Parma back then as "... *very dependable and very antagonistic.*"

In addition to pressures to improve costs, quality, and productivity, there are additional pressures on management from the union to bring stamping work in-house that has previously been outsourced. As Parma loses its prop shaft production to another GM facility, the union wants to bring back the production of sheet metal blankings, the first step in the stamping process. Blankings have been outsourced to a supplier, Medina Blanking, Inc., which produces an excellent quality product and has virtually become another department in Parma because of its highly responsive and capable delivery.

As GM closes plants and continues to downsize, Parma's salaried employees, too, are being affected significantly by efforts to reduce salaried employment and eliminate management layers throughout the organization. With fewer salaried employees, workloads are increasing even as promotional opportunities, compensation, and benefits stagnate. As is the case at most GM facilities, Parma's salaried employees are not unionized. As part of its efforts to cut costs, GM has eliminated the salaried year-end bonus, has sharply reduced merit raises, and is considering other benefit reductions. Profit sharing for both hourly and salaried employees has evaporated as losses in GM's North American operations have mounted to several billion dollars annually.

After 10 years of being a top manager at Parma and assuming responsibility for all of Parma's operations, Bob Lintz continues to fashion a top management team based on trust and openness. He also wants his managers to be committed toward eliminating hostilities that linger between the stamping and components operations within the plant, as well as between hourly and salaried employees. He is also looking for people who will support his informal and highly participative management style and who will work to increase the level of involvement among Parma's hourly employees. Although the TCIG has formally disbanded, its efforts are still ongoing. The weekly floor board meetings, where union officials and superintendents discuss plant floor issues, are still active and productive. The biweekly joint meeting of Bob and his staff, along with the Shop Committee chairman, the president of Local 1005, and the Shop Committee, are ongoing as well. These groups are representative of the Team Concept still at work at Parma.

Conclusion

Even though Bob's management team supports his desire to increase the level of involvement among Parma's hourly employees, Dean Baker commented, *"Sometimes I get frustrated, though, because I wish he'd have a little bit more confidence in the management organization."*

Parma's lead Training Coordinator, Pat Camarati, is concerned that many of Parma's managers and supervisors see the ongoing Team Concept training as more of a disruption than a necessity.

[1] *Harbour Report,* 1979–1989, p. 235.
[2] *Harbour Report,* 1989–1992, p. 69.
[3] It costs GM $795 more than Ford to produce a vehicle, $396 of which is attributed to GM's stamping plants. GM's current contract with the International UAW, to which Parma and all of GM's other facilities must adhere, provides union members 95% of their take-home pay for up to 3 years in the event they are laid off. This will cost the Corporation $4 billion over the 3-year agreement. In addition, UAW members received wage increases of 17%, bringing union wages and benefits to $36.60/hour.

Shop Committee member Ray Kopchak believes that, although they have made great strides, the biggest mistake the union and management can still make is to assume that their relationship can continue to improve without hard work. Seven years after beginning a new collaborative approach, he still feels that the easiest thing to do is *"to go back to the old traditional way. But I don't want to do that, it's not necessary. We've proven that management and the union can work together."*

Questions

1. How would you describe Parma's environment in terms of its level of uncertainty and complexity?
2. How would you characterize Bob Lintz's approach to communication, decision making, and the exercise of power to create change at Parma?
3. What are the most critical issues still facing Parma, and what should be done to address them?
4. How can resistance to change be overcome utilizing the existing workforce? ■

CASE 16
The Poorly Informed Walrus

Developed by Barbara McCain, Oklahoma City University

"How's it going down there?" barked the big walrus from his perch on the highest rock near the shore. He waited for the good word.

Down below, the smaller walruses conferred hastily among themselves. Things weren't going well at all, but none of them wanted to break the news to the Old Man. He was the biggest and wisest walrus in the herd, and he knew his business, but he had such a terrible temper that every walrus in the herd was terrified of his ferocious bark.

"What will we tell him?" whispered Basil, the second-ranking walrus. He well remembers how the

Old Man had raved and ranted at him the last time the herd had caught less than its quota of herring, and he had no desire to go through that experience again. Nevertheless, the walrus noticed for several weeks that the water level in the nearby Arctic bay had been falling constantly, and it had become necessary to travel much farther to catch the dwindling supply of herring. Someone should tell the Old Man; he would probably know what to do. But who? and how?

Finally Basil spoke up: "Things are going pretty well, Chief," he said. The thought of the receding water line made his heart grow heavy, but he went on: "As a matter of fact, the beach seems to be getting larger."

The Old Man grunted. "Fine, fine," he said. "That will give us a bit more elbow room." He closed his eyes and continued basking in the sun.

The next day brought more trouble. A new herd of walruses moved in down the beach and, with the supply of herring dwindling, this invasion could be dangerous. No one wanted to tell the Old Man, though only he could take the steps necessary to meet this new competition.

Reluctantly, Basil approached the big walrus, who was still sunning himself on the large rock. After some small talk, he said, "Oh by the way Chief, a new herd of walruses seems to have moved into our territory." The Old Man's eyes snapped open, and he filled his great lungs in preparation for a mighty bellow. But Basil added quickly, "Of course, we don't anticipate any trouble. They don't look like herring eaters to me. More likely interested in minnows. And as you know, we don't bother with minnows ourselves."

The Old Man let out the air with a long sigh. "Good, good," he said. "No point in our getting excited over nothing then is there?"

Things didn't get any better in the weeks that followed. One day,

peering down from the large rock, the Old Man noticed that part of the herd seemed to be missing. Summoning Basil, he grunted peevishly. "What's going on, Basil? Where is everyone?" Poor Basil didn't have the courage to tell the Old Man that many of the younger walruses were leaving every day to join the new herd. Clearing his throat nervously he said, "Well Chief, we've been tightening up things a bit. You know, getting rid of some of the dead wood. After all, a herd is only as good as walruses in it."

"Run a tight ship, I always say," the Old Man grunted. "Glad to hear that all is going so well."

Before long, everyone but Basil had left to join the new herd, and Basil realized that the time had come to tell the Old Man the facts. Terrified but determined, he flopped

up to the large rock. "Chief," he said, "I have bad news. The rest of the herd has left you." The old walrus was so astonished that he couldn't even work up a good bellow. "Left me?" he cried. "All of them? But why? How could this happen?"

Basil didn't have the heart to tell him so he merely shrugged helplessly.

"I can't understand it," the old walrus said. "And just when everything was going so well."

Questions

1. What barriers to communication are evident in this fable?
2. What communication "lessons" does this fable offer to those who are serious about careers in the new workplace? ∎

"I Still Do My Job, Don't I"

Developed by William T. Neese, Troy State University, and Daniel S. Cochran, Mississippi State University

The Parties Involved

William Booney had come to Yancey's Family Steakhouse of Nashville through a promotion. For the first time since he had come to work for the parent company, United Foods, he would have responsibility for an entire restaurant. As the General Manager, William would be in charge of the operation of his unit, which depended entirely on the performance of the employees and the management staff. He had a management staff of three; they were, in order of responsibility: John Aston, the Manager; Phillip Tate, the Assistant Manager, and Molly Houston, the Intern Trainee. In addition, there were 47 regular employees on the work schedule when William arrived.

The manager, John Aston, who had been transferred in a few months before William's arrival, had also come to Yancey's of Nashville with a promotion, but not much money in his bank account. As a

result, he was pleased when he learned about an affordable garage apartment for rent, and moved in quickly. His new landlords were the parents of three of the restaurant's teenage employees, and the apartment was located over the garage of their house.

The landlords, Mr. and Mrs. Dan Murphy, their two daughters Theresa and Lisa, and their son Dennis, had been living in this area of Nashville for years. All three of the Murphy teenagers worked part time for Yancey's, which was located a few miles from their neighborhood.

The Company

Yancey's Family Steakhouse chain was owned and operated by United Foods, a medium-sized restaurant corporation. In addition to Yancey's, United Foods had two other fast-food restaurant chains that were franchised from the original companies. In all, United owned approximately 700 restaurants, all located across the southeastern United States.

The Yancey's division, numbered at about 300 restaurants, was divided into several regions. Each region was the responsibility of a Regional Leader (RL), and consisted of 4 to 6 districts, with a District Leader (DL) responsible for an individual district. A district contained anywhere from 4 to 7 restaurants. Each restaurant was the responsibility of a General Manager (GM), who accomplished the various tasks necessary for operations through a management team (usually consisting of 3 managers in addition to the

Source: This case was prepared by William T. Neese of Troy State University and Daniel S. Cochran of Mississippi State University. The case was prepared for classroom discussion and was not intended to illustrate either effective or ineffective handling of administration situations. © 1988. All rights reserved to the authors and the North American Case Research Association. Permission to publish the case should be obtained from the authors and the North American Case Research Association.

GM) and 45 to 50 regular employees.

District Leaders rose through the management ranks and were delegated formal authority by the appropriate Regional Leader. The DL was responsible for recruiting and selecting managers to fill the open management positions in the district. Usually, operational input from GMs was relied on for internal employment decisions. In other words, DLs asked GMs who was ready for a promotion, because they were in the better position to know as front-line supervisors. General Managers and District Leaders often made joint disciplinary decisions concerning the lower level managers within the GM's restaurant, but formal authority for the final action taken rested with the DL.

General Managers were responsible for staffing regular employee positions in the restaurant. Formal authority rested with the GM for all employment-related decisions concerning the regular employees in his or her individual restaurant. The other three managers in the restaurant normally had the authority to report to the GM through a counseling procedure concerning employees in the unit. Ultimately, however, it was up to the GM to take formal action.

The management staff under a GM was formally a hierarchy. For example, when the GM was not at work in the restaurant, the Manager assumed responsibility for operations; the "good" Managers were eventually promoted to General Managers, "good" Assistant Managers were eventually promoted to Managers, and so forth.

The Restaurant

Not quite 4 years old when William took over, Yancey's of Nashville did not have the sales volume needed to

break even. Although the variable costs were always covered by monthly sales, the overhead assigned to the unit by the home office was almost never met. Many of the employees attributed lower sales to the location of the building, which was not near the interstate highway, where a mall and many of the other restaurants in the immediate area were located.

Bob Jackson, the District Leader for William's restaurant, had a different theory, however. Bob felt that the employees were the primary cause for the low sales. In his opinion, the place was a local teenager hangout, and that drove off the older customers that the restaurant needed as regulars.

"They're all buddies," Bob told William soon after William became General Manager. "They all go to the same high school and hang around with each other, and when a bunch of them have to work, the rest come visit. The first thing I want you to do," Bob told William, "is to turn this restaurant into an establishment which the more mature customer will want to patronize. We need their repeat business to turn sales volume around, and these kids just run them off."

Although food costs had been rising in the face of the low sales, what bothered William the most was the fact that the business was generally not being kept as clean as it should have been. When William was responsible for supervising the nightly cleanup, he noticed reluctance on the part of the teenagers to do a thorough job without being pushed. It aggravated William to have to interrupt his closing tasks to check and recheck their work, but eventually the job they did would be satisfactory. GMs usually only closed two nights a week, however, leaving five less-than-adequate cleanups. "Besides," he thought, "we shouldn't have to push so hard to get satisfactory work done around here."

William became determined to gain the cooperation of the management team to help him counter the restaurant's operational glitches. At the next weekly management meeting, he asked for their assistance in correcting a list of problems over the next few weeks. The problem William asked them to address immediately, however, was the state of the cleanliness throughout the restaurant. He had previously spoken to John or Phillip about their immediate need to improve the quality of the nightly cleanups, so he thought of this discussion as reinforcement. Intern Trainees never closed, so Molly was never responsible for nightly cleanups.

Feeling pretty good about the management meeting, William left the store in John's hands and went home for the night. The following morning, however, he was absolutely furious within 10 minutes after he came in to open the unit. Beside the fact that the restaurant was generally dirty because of a poor cleanup the previous night, he found a case of four 1-gallon containers of very expensive blue cheese salad dressing carelessly pushed under a shelf. Blue cheese dressing had to be refrigerated soon after arrival or it might be unsafe to consume. This case had been left out since the delivery, which was being unloaded about the time William left for home the night before. "There goes $30.00 down the drain!" he steamed. Thinking about the meeting of the day before, William just shook his head. It was then that the telephone rang.

The Telephone Call

"Why me?" William thought, as he hung up the telephone. The call had been from Mrs. Murphy, the mother of the three Murphy teenagers who worked for Yancey's, and also John's landlady. Fuming mad and seemingly on the verge of tears, she demanded to know what William was going to do "about this problem of ours!"

"Which one?" William thought, but responded, "I don't even know what the problem is, much less what I can do about it!"

"Well I'll just tell you!" exclaimed Mrs. Murphy. "That man John who works down there is corrupting my baby."

"Exactly what do you mean?" asked William.

"Your man John—he's a manager at your restaurant—has been taking advantage of my child. She's still a schoolgirl, and he's a grown man!" was her answer. "We opened our home to that man, and I trusted him! That hurts the most," she mumbled in a tone of despair.

"Mrs. Murphy, I just don't see how . . ." William was saying, when he was interrupted.

"How!? I'll tell you how!" Mrs. Murphy injected. "I caught the two of them in his room this morning!"

"Well I could . . ." attempted William.

"Well you better," said Mrs. Murphy, "because none of my children are going to be allowed to come to work again as long as that man is working there! I'm going to an attorney!" she said, then loudly hung up the phone.

"I Still Do My Job, Don't I?"

That night after the crowd had thinned out, William and his boss, Bob sat back in the office discussing the situation.

"Sir," William was saying to Bob, "the more I think about it the more obvious it becomes. I've been scheduling all four of them to work the same shifts as much as possible. John wanted me to so they could all ride together. . . . I asked him about Theresa as soon as he came in this afternoon."

"Well, what did he say?" asked Bob, in a somewhat disgusted tone of voice. "He knows he isn't supposed to become romantically involved with an employee. Heck, the guy wasn't born yesterday! Even if he hasn't paid attention to any of the horror stories he must have heard about this sort of thing, I told him about the policy when I transferred him into my district. Male managers just cannot be romancing around with female employees! He knows better!"

"He just said 'I still do my job don't I?' " replied William.

"What did you say then?" Bob asked.

"Well, I told him that I didn't think he was doing his job," William responded, and then continued: "I said that first, the nightly cleanups directly under his supervision simply were not acceptable, and that they indicated a gross lack of management direction, especially for a manager occupying a position with his level of responsibility. 'After all,' I told him, 'you are second in command, and your records show that you've never had this problem before.' I told him I knew it was hard to get a good cleanup late at night from some of the employees, but that it could be done if he tried hard enough. He seemed to agree. Then I told him I had found out about Phillip."

"You mean Phillip the Assistant Manager?" asked Bob, with concern in his voice. "What about him?"

"Phillip seems to think that if John can run around with the employees, he can too! I asked him at lunch today if he had known about John and Theresa, and he told me that everybody knew about them except their parents, me, and you—that is, at least until today. Then he told me that he had been out on a date with one of the servers, too!"

"Then what?" Bob moaned.

"After I told him that John was a bad example, and that dating an employee was against company policy, Phillip said he didn't see how it was any of Yancey's or my business what he and John did on their spare time! Do you know what John said when I told him about this little episode?"

"Tell me," said Bob.

"He told me that Phillip was right, that it wasn't any of our busi-

ness! What do you want to do about this mess?" asked William.

"Right now," replied Bob, "I really don't know!"

Questions

1. How can Bob use the behavioral decision model to make a decision in this situation?
2. Use the Vroom and Jago decision tree in Figure 17.2 to determine which type of decision method would be best in this situation.
3. What are the ethical issues involved in this case and how might Bob deal with them? ∎

CASE 18
Theatre New Brunswick
....

S hortly after 10:00 p.m. on April 12, 1990, Mary Hindle, Production Manager of Theatre New Brunswick in Fredericton, New Brunswick, heard the voices of Art and Jay, two stagehands coming back to do scheduled work. A few minutes later she heard the sound of furniture being moved. As she walked out of her office to the shop, Mary saw Art struggling on one end of a sofa. One glance and the reason was obvious. Art was completely inebriated.

Mary told Art that his drunken state was not acceptable and that everyone was tired of this type of behaviour. Mary told Art he had to either shape up or retire. Mary told him she expected his answer in the morning.

Art told Mary to "_ _," stomped away and slammed the stage door as he left. Jay and Mary stood in the middle of the shop, stunned.

Organization

Theatre New Brunswick (TNB) was founded as a professional theater by Walter Learning in 1968 in

Fredericton, N.B. Its home was the Playhouse located in downtown Fredericton, right across the street from the Provincial Legislature.

Originally, the Playhouse seated 1100 people, but the major renovations undertaken in 1975 to expand the backstage area reduced the seating to 763. The former stage floor area was now part of the backstage and was used as the carpentry shop.

TNB was unique among regional theaters in Canada. Every play produced toured on a regular circuit around New Brunswick. The tour generally took 2 weeks, and played to both subscribers and single-ticket patrons in each city of the tour.

TNB was a not-for-profit organization with an annual operating budget of about $1.8 million. Its revenues were generated from four main sources:

- Ticket sales (both subscription and single ticket)
- Government funding
- Donations (corporate sponsorships, individual donors) and fundraising events (auctions, sales of surplus prop furniture, special performances by celebrities such as Don Harron and Catherine MacKinnon)
- Rental of the Beaverbrook auditorium for touring performances such as the National Ballet Company and for local events ranging from travelogues to children's dance concerts.

The theater produced five mainstage plays annually, as well as two Young Company plays for grade school audiences, which toured throughout the school year. In the summer the only play usually produced was a small Young Company show. Rehearsals for the season generally began in September and the final mainstage tour was completed by mid-May.

The two senior positions at TNB, Artistic Director and General Manager, were hired by the Board of Directors. The Board was made up of volunteers chosen from communities from all over the province of New Brunswick. These volunteers were picked by the current board for their ability to help build the theatre's audience in their communities through ticket sales and its financial base through fundraising.

Martha MacDonald was General Manager. She had been at TNB for 10 seasons, working her way through the organization from receptionist to bookkeeper to accountant to business manager.

Her responsibilities as General Manager included submission of grant applications, supervision of the box office, marketing, subscriptions, finances, and coordination of all rentals of the building. All negotiations and contracting of the actors and directors of the plays were done by the General Manager. Securing the rights for plays to be produced and budgets created with the production manager were also responsibilities of the General Manager.

The Production Manager, Mary Hindle, reported to both the Artistic Director and the General Manager. All "artistic" decision making went through the Artistic Director. For example, design decisions, including deadlines and choice of designers, were discussed with the Artistic Director, whereas the budget for the design was discussed with the General Manager. This dual reporting and the fuzzy lines of responsibility were generally not a problem and were typical of theater organizations.

Source: This case was prepared by Heather Kitchen under the supervision of Professor James A. Erskine for the sole purpose of providing material for class discussion at the Western Business School. Certain names and other identifying information may have been disguised to protect confidentiality. It is not intended to illustrate either effective or ineffective handling of a managerial situation. Any reproduction, in any form, of the material in this case is prohibited except with the written consent of the School. Copyright 1992 © The University of Western Ontario. 11/05/92. Any form of reproduction, storage or transmittal of this material is prohibited without written permission from the Western Business School. This material is not covered under authorization from CanCopy or any Reproduction Rights Organization. Permission to reproduce or copies may be obtained by contacting Case and Publication Services, Western Business School, London, Ontario, N6A 3K7, or calling 519-661-3208.

In September 1989, Jill Armstrong began her position as the new Artistic Director of TNB. Jill had accepted the offer only after ascertaining that Martha MacDonald and Mary Hindle would both stay on in their current positions for her first season.

Theatre Company Operations

TNB, like most not-for-profit theaters in Canada, worked very hard to build and maintain its subscriber base. The base had grown from its first year numbers of 2000 to its present base of 5600.

Most production workers were hired on a seasonal or per production basis. The permanent staff base was very small, consisting of the Artistic Director, General Manager, Production Manager, Marketing Manager, Receptionist, and bookkeeping, maintenance, and box office staff.

The production staff fluctuated from a minimum of 15 to a maximum of about 35. Some of the production staff were hired on a seasonal contract, typically in the range of 30 weeks.

The touring element at TNB required special consideration when hiring actors, stage management, and the crew.

Touring required the ability for everyone involved to adapt to new surroundings quickly. The crew must help to make the actors feel comfortable with the new stage at every performance. A sense of camaraderie must quickly develop in a touring company. If it failed to develop, then the tour became incredibly difficult given the long hours and the high personal proximity. The theatre distributed a code of conduct to all employees and actors.

Theatre companies generally provided a per diem for the crew and it was up to each individual to choose whether to have shared accommodation and how much to spend on food, drink, and sundries. The hours on a one-night stand tour tended to be extremely long for the first several days until the crew moved along the learning curve. TNB's tours typically lasted 2 weeks.

Hours per week on tour often topped 85. Mary instituted a policy of giving the crew time off in lieu of overtime, which most crew members liked. The advantages of doing so were twofold. First, the morale of the crew while on tour was higher than in the past because they had a "paid vacation" to look forward to at the end of each tour. Second, the crew was too tired after a tour to work effectively and safely but, after 4 or 5 days off they were refreshed and eager to get back to the theatre. Several crew members had long-distance relationships and they traveled in the break.

The people most responsible for creating a good environment for work on tour were the stage management staff and the head stage carpenter and the head electrician. Their leadership ability and cooperation set the tone for the tour.

As Production Manager, Mary hired the people for those positions. Her criteria for hiring included those who:

- Cared about good production values
- Had a strong personality and could articulate their opinions
- Expressed a desire to work in the position
- Had the technical ability and endurance to do the job

The Production Staff generally looked for work with other professional theatre companies outside of the province during the off season. Some individuals applied for UIC benefits and some simply took the summer off and did not seek UIC benefits.

Mary Hindle

Mary Hindle was 32 years old and had been Production Manager of TNB for 3 ½ years. She held a Bachelor of Arts degree (Honours Drama and Theater Arts) and had worked for 10 years in professional theatre.

Mary spent her early career as a stage manager, working in theaters across Canada, including five seasons at the Neptune Theatre in Halifax, three seasons at the Stratford Festival, and seasons at the Charlottetown Festival, Festival Lennoxville, Theatre Plus in Toronto, New Play Centre in Vancouver, and The Citadel Theatre in Edmonton, Alberta.

Mary was generally regarded within the profession as one of the best stage managers in the country. She came to TNB in a roundabout manner. Mary was traveling to Ontario from Nova Scotia and stopped in Fredericton to visit some friends who were at TNB and to see a new Canadian play that was being presented. A snowstorm forced the closing of the Trans-Canada Highway and Mary had to stay in Fredericton for a few extra days.

TNB was midway through the season. The incumbent Production Manager was proving to be ineffectual. Malcolm Black was familiar with Mary's work as a Stage Manager and asked her to consider taking over the Production Manager position at TNB. After deliberation, Mary accepted the job.

Although Mary lacked formal management training, she under-

stood the theater well and enjoyed the challenge of running the production department. After finishing the rest of the current season, Mary undertook some changes in the off season. These included:

- Instituting a formal contract for all production personnel stating start and end dates, statutory holidays, salary, benefits and termination clauses that stipulated two weeks' written notice by either party
- Regulating the use of company vehicles and tools
- Creating a capital expenditure budget in order to improve equipment
- Establishing an accounting system that reported actual and projected production spending in the production department
- Instituting short weekly production meetings to keep all departments aware of production problems and achievements
- Traveling to at least one tour stop per tour to visit the crew and stage management staff and to discuss any problems that had developed.

The Production Staff was initially skeptical about the new Production Manager, but within a few months they began expressing appreciation for some of her techniques. By managing the Production Staff's time more efficiently, Mary cut overtime by 20 percent in her first full season. This allowed the staff to lead a more balanced life style and the quality of their work lives improved. The crew was more content, turnover decreased sharply, and accidents caused by exhausted workers were virtually eliminated.

Mary was viewed by the Production Staff as someone who was looking out for their best inter-

ests. They thought of her as being tough but fair. The production budget was balanced every season and production surpluses were spent on production items when possible. Each season, the various production departments submitted a "shopping list." Purchases were made based on need as ascertained by the Production Manager and the Technical Director. Morale was high. At the end of each season, Mary organized a garage sale of surplus props and costume pieces. The production and office staff volunteered their time to participate. Funds raised were used to purchase production equipment.

Art Langen

Art was born in Nova Scotia in 1963 and had first worked with Mary Hindle at the Neptune Theatre in Halifax. Mary was in her third season as Senior Stage Manager at the Neptune when 21-year-old Art got his first theater job as a stagehand on tour. Art and his friend Bill had been a problem on tour because they were habitually late for their morning call and were often hungover in the mornings. The rest of the production crew on the tour had worked together for some time and tended to get frustrated with Art and Bill's immature behavior. Art and Bill were particularly offensive to the women on tour; they posted Playboy magazine photographs in the van and used graphic language while doing their setups. Mary had to act as mediator on the tour, trying to sensitize all parties to each other.

Over the next 2 years at the Neptune, Art developed into an excellent craftsman, a quick worker and a more sensitive person. Although he was still hard living and known to drink heavily, he had matured and was no longer as adolescent in his behavior. Art was still petulant when he did not get his own way; however, he was generally well liked by actors, stage management crew and management at the Neptune.

In 1986, Art moved to Fredericton in order to live with his girlfriend, who was hired for the season at TNB. He worked outside of the theater as a craftsman and woodworker. The relationship disintegrated. The breakup happened just before Mary moved to Fredericton. Mary met Art a few times and they talked about the pain of his breakup.

Art's former girlfriend left the theater. At this time, Art approached Mary about coming back to work in theatre and specifically about working the TNB tour circuit. Mary discussed whether to hire Art with the Head Carpenter, Mark, and they decided to try Art in the position of Head Stage Carpenter.

Art was very pleased when he was hired at TNB in July 1987. He liked living in Fredericton, he enjoyed the nomadic life of touring, and he had friends in the city.

The 1990 Season

Mary Hindle felt after 3 ½ years as Production Manager that the theater had an excellent staff. She decided to leave TNB at the end of June 1990. Mary felt she had accomplished her goals and that it was time for someone with new and different ideas to take over.

Although Mary felt proud of the staff that she was leaving behind, she was worried about Art. Art had been the Head Stage Carpenter for two seasons at this point. Mark, the Head Carpenter, had come to Mary

several times about a change in Art's attitude. Mary had talked to Art about it but seemed to be making no headway with the talks.

Art had become increasingly disruptive over Jill's first season as Artistic Director and was openly hostile toward her. He had posted a notice on the call board which was critical of Jill and her artistic choices. He called on other production workers to voice their complaints about the choice of plays and the quality of the work.

As the season progressed, other crew members, such as Amy, the Stage Manager, and Gary, the Head Electrician, complained about Art crossing the boundary of "quick and dirty" to "sloppy and ineffective." Gary said that he was having to redo some of the work as it was not up to standard and Art was nowhere to be found. Adding further problems to this scenario were the two relationships that Art was having at the same time. He was involved with Caroline, Head of Wardrobe, and Sheila, the Assistant Stage Manager. The two women involved were friends and it was an interesting situation when they both went out on one of the larger tours, sharing a room.

Mary was becoming increasingly concerned with Art's behaviour and performance. Talking with him seemed to be doing no good. Since there were only 5 weeks left in the season, Mary did not want to disrupt the conclusion of the season. However, she was wondering whether Art should leave the theater at the end of the current season. Art had told Mary he wanted to return for another season. Mary talked to both Martha and Jill about the situation, and Martha was in agreement that the theatre would run more smoothly without Art.

The Incident

On Thursday, April 12, 1990, Mary had booked two stage carpenters to move furniture from the rehearsal hall to the stage after rehearsal finished at 10 p.m. This type of job occurred every 6 weeks. Mary made sure that different carpenters were called in to do the job each time, because it required returning to work 4 hours after finishing the regular day. Electrical setups and light focusing would be performed on the main stage at 8:00 a.m. the following morning, before the scheduled afternoon and evening rehearsals.

Art and Jay were called to do this particular move and Mary had returned that evening to supervise. She went out to the shop when she heard the work beginning. Art and Jay were moving the furniture. Art appeared to be completely intoxicated and Jay appeared sober.

Mary told Art that his drunken state was not acceptable and that everyone was tired of this type of behaviour. Mary told Art he had to either shape up or retire from TNB. Mary told him she expected his answer in the morning.

Art told Mary to "__ __," stomped away and slammed the stage door as he left. Jay and Mary stood in the middle of the shop, stunned.

Questions

1. Should Mary have anticipated Jack's behavior? Why or why not?
2. How would you assess Mary's comments to Jack when she said that Jack would need to "shape up or retire"?
3. Assume Mary does not want to upset the crew and decides to keep Art. What could she do? ∎

CASE 19
The New Vice President

[*Note:* Please read only those parts identified by your instructor. Do not read ahead.]

Part A

When the new President at Mid-West U took over, it was only a short time before the incumbent Vice President announced his resignation. Unfortunately, there was no one waiting in the wings, and a hiring freeze prevented a national search from commencing.

Many faculty leaders and former administrators suggested that the President appoint Jennifer Treeholm, the Associate Vice President for Academic Affairs, as interim. She was an extremely popular person on campus and had 10 years of experience in the role of Associate Vice President. She knew everyone and everything about the campus. Jennifer, they assured him, was the natural choice. Besides, Jennifer *deserved* the job. Her devotion to the school was unparalleled, and her energy knew no bounds. The new President, acting on advice from many campus leaders, appointed Jennifer Interim Vice President for a term of up to 3 years. He also agreed that she could be a candidate for the permanent position when the hiring freeze was lifted.

Jennifer and her friends were ecstatic. It was high time more women moved into important positions on campus. They went out for dinner to their every Friday night watering hole to celebrate and reflect on Jennifer's career.

Except for a brief stint outside of academe, Jennifer's entire career had been at Mid-West U. She started out teaching Introductory History,

then, realizing she wanted to get on the tenure track, went back to school and earned her Ph.D. at Metropolitan U. while continuing to teach at Mid-West. Upon completion of her degree, she was appointed as an Assistant Professor and, eventually, earned the rank of Associate based on her popularity and excellent teaching.

Not only was Jennifer well liked, but she devoted her entire life, it seemed, to Mid   West, helping to form the first union, getting grants, writing skits for the faculty club's annual follies, and going out of her way to befriend everyone who needed support.

Eventually, Jennifer was elected President of The Faculty Senate. After serving for 2 years, she was offered the position of Associate Vice President. During her 10 years as Associate Vice President, she handled most of the academic complaints, oversaw several committees, wrote almost all of the letters and reports for the Vice President, and was even known to run personal errands for the President. People just knew they could count on Jennifer.

Questions

1. At this point, what are your predictions about Jennifer as the Interim Vice President?

Source: Adapted from Donald D. Bowen, et al., *Experiences in Management and Organizational Behavior,* 4th ed. (New York: John Wiley & Sons, Inc.), 1997.

2. What do you predict will be her management/leadership style?
3. What are her strengths? Her weaknesses? What is the basis for your assessment?

After you have discussed Part A, please read Part B.

Part B

Jennifer's appointment as Interim Vice President was met with great enthusiasm. Finally, the school was getting someone who was "one of their own," a person who understood the culture, knew the faculty, and could get things done.

It was not long before the campus realized that things were not moving and that Jennifer, despite her long-standing popularity, had difficulty making tough decisions. Her desire to please people and to try to take care of everyone made it difficult for her to choose opposing alternatives. (To make matters worse, she had trouble planning, organizing, and managing her time.)

What was really a problem was that she did not understand her role as the Number Two person at the top of the organization. The President expected her to support him and his decisions without question. Over time the President also expected her to implement some of his decisions—to do his dirty work. This became particularly problematic when it involved firing people or saying no to old faculty cronies. Jennifer also found herself uncomfortable with the other members of the President's senior staff. Although she was not the only woman (the General Counsel, a very bright, analytical woman was part of the group), Jennifer found the behavior and decision-making style to be different from what she was used to.

Most of the men took their lead from the President and discussed very little in the meetings. Instead, they would try to influence decisions privately. Often a decision arrived in a meeting as a "fait accompli." Jennifer felt excluded and wondered why, as Vice President, she felt so powerless.

In time, she and the President spent less and less time together talking and discussing how to move the campus along. Although her relations with the men on the senior staff were cordial, she talked mostly to her female friends.

Jennifer's friends, especially her close-knit group of long-time female colleagues, all assured her that it was because she was "interim." "Just stay out of trouble," they told her. Of course this just added to her hesitancy when it came to making tough choices.

As the President's own image on campus shifted after his "honeymoon year," Jennifer decided to listen to her friends rather than follow the President's lead. After all, her reputation on campus was at stake.

Questions

1. What is the major problem facing Jennifer?
2. What would you do if you were in her position?
3. Would a man have the same experience as Jennifer?
4. Are any of your predictions about her management style holding up?

Part C

When the hiring freeze was lifted and Jennifer's position was able to be filled, the President insisted on a national search. Jennifer and her friends felt this was silly, given that she was going into her third year in the job. Nonetheless, she entered the search process.

After a year-long search, the Search Committee met with the President. The external candidates were not acceptable to the campus. Jennifer, they recommended, should only be appointed on a permanent basis if she agrees to change her management style.

The President mulled over his dilemma, then decided to give Jennifer the benefit of the doubt and the opportunity. He appointed her permanent Provost, while making the following, private agreement with her.

1. She will organize her office and staff and begin delegating more work to others.
2. She will "play" her Number Two position, backing the President and "echoing" his position on the University's vision statement.
3. She will provide greater direction for the Deans who report to her.

Jennifer agreed to take the position. She was now the University's first female Vice President and presided over a council of 11 Deans, 3 of whom were her best female friends. Once again, they sought out their every-Friday-night watering hole for an evening of dinner and celebration.

Questions

1. If you were Jennifer, would you have accepted the job?
2. What would you do as the new, permanent, Vice President?
3. Will Jennifer change her management style? If so, in what ways?
4. What are your predictions for the future?

Part D

Although people had predicted that things would be better once Jennifer was permanently in the job, they in fact became more problematic. People now expected Jennifer to be able to take decisive action. She did not feel she could.

Every time an issue came up, she would spend weeks, sometimes months, trying to get a sense of the campus. Nothing moved once it hit her office. After a while, people began referring to the Vice President's office as "the black hole" where things just went in and disappeared.

Her immediate staff were concerned and frustrated. Not only did she not delegate effectively, but her desire to make things better led her to try to do more and more herself.

The Vice President's job also carried social obligations and requests. Here again, she tried to please everyone and often ran from one evening obligation to another, trying to show her support and concern for every constituency on campus. She was exhausted, overwhelmed, and knowing the mandate under which she was appointed, anxious about the President's evaluation of her behavior.

The greatest deterioration occurred within her Dean's Council. Several of the male Deans, weary of waiting for direction from Jennifer regarding where she was taking some of the academic proposals of the President, had started making decisions without Jennifer's approval.

"Loose cannons," was how she described a couple of them. "They don't listen. They just march out there on their own."

One of the big problems with two of the Deans was that they just didn't take no for an answer when it came from Jennifer. Privately, each conceded that her "no" sounded like a "maybe." She always left room open to renegotiate.

Whatever the problem, and there were several by now, Jennifer's ability to lead was being questioned. Although her popularity was as high as ever, more and more people on campus were expressing their frustrations with what sometimes appeared as mixed signals from her and the President and sometimes was seen as virtually no direction. People wanted priorities. Instead, crisis management reigned.

Questions

1. If you were President, what would you do?
2. If you were Jennifer, what would you do?

Conclusion

Jennifer had a few "retreats" with her senior staff. Each time, she committed herself to delegate more, prioritize, and work on time management issues, but within 10 days or so, everything was back to business as usual.

The President decided to hire a person with extensive corporate experience to fill the vacant position of Vice President of Finance and Administration. The new man was an experienced team player who had survived mergers, been fired and bounced back, and had spent years in the Number Two position in sev-

eral companies. Within a few months he had earned the respect of the campus as well as the President and was in fact emerging as the person who really ran the place. Meanwhile, the President concentrated on external affairs and fund raising.

Jennifer felt relieved. Her role felt clearer. She could devote herself to academic and faculty issues and she was out from under the pressure to play "hatchet man."

As she neared the magic age for early retirement, she began to talk more and more about what she wanted to do next. ■

eXPERIENTIAL eXERCISES

My Best Manager

Procedure

1. Make a list of the attributes that describe the best manager you ever worked for. If you have trouble identifying an actual manager, make a list of attributes you would like the manager in your next job to have.
2. Form a group of four or five persons and share your lists.
3. Create one list that combines all the unique attributes of the "best" managers represented in your group. Make sure that you have all attributes listed, but list each only once. Place a check mark next to those that were reported by two or more members. Have one of your members prepared to present the list in general class dicussion.
4. After all groups have finished Step 3, spokespersons should report to the whole class. The instructor will make a running list of the "best" manager attributes as viewed by the class.
5. Feel free to ask questions and discuss the results.

My Best Job

Procedure

1. Make a list of the top five things you expect from your first (or next) full-time job.
2. Exchange lists with a nearby partner. Assign probabilities (or odds) to each goal on your partner's list to indicate how likely you feel it is that the goal can be accomplished. (*Note:* Your instructor may ask that everyone use the same probabilities format.)
3. Discuss your evaluations with your partner. Try to delete superficial goals or modify them to become more substantial. Try to restate any unrealistic goals

to make them more realistic. Help your partner do the same.
4. Form a group of four to six persons. Within the group have everyone share what they now consider to be the most "realistic" goals on their lists. Elect a spokesperson to share a sample of these items with the entire class.
5. Discuss what group members have individually learned from the exercise. Await further class discussion led by your instructor.

What Do You Value in Work?

Procedure

1. The following nine items are from a survey conducted by Nicholas J. Beutell and O. C. Brenner ("Sex Differences in Work Values," *Journal of Vocational Behavior,* Vol. 28, pp. 29–41, 1986). Rank order the nine items in terms of how important (9 = most important) they would be to you in a job.

   How important is it to you to have a job that:
   ____ Is respected by other people?
   ____ Encourages continued development of knowledge and skills?
   ____ Provides job security?
   ____ Provides a feeling of accomplishment?
   ____ Provides the opportunity to earn a high income?
   ____ Is intellectually stimulating?
   ____ Rewards good performance with recognition?
   ____ Provides comfortable working conditions?
   ____ Permits advancement to high administrative responsibility?

2. Form into groups as designated by your instructor. Within each group, the *men in the group* will meet to develop a consensus ranking of the items as they think the *women* in the Beutell and Brenner survey ranked them. The reasons for the rankings should be shared and discussed so they are clear to everyone. The *women in the group* should not participate in this ranking task. They should listen to the discussion and be prepared to comment later in class discussion. A spokesperson for the men in the group should share the group's rankings with the class.

Source: Adapted from Roy J. Lewicki, Donald D. Bowen, Douglas T. Hall, and Francine S. Hall, *Experiences in Management and Organizational Behavior,* 3rd ed. (New York: Wiley, 1988), pp. 23–26. Used by permission.

3. (*Optional*) Form into groups as designated by your instructor, but with each group consisting entirely of men or women. Each group should meet and decide which of the work values members of the *opposite* sex ranked first in the Beutell and Brenner survey. Do this again for the work value ranked last. The reasons should be discussed, along with reasons that each of the other values probably was not ranked first . . . or last. A spokesperson for each group should share group results with the rest of the class.

EXERCISE 4

My Asset Base

A business has an asset base or set of resources that it uses to produce a good or service of value to others. For a business, these are the assets of resources it uses to achieve results include capital, land, patented products or processes, buildings and equipment, raw materials, and the human resources or employees, among others.

Each of us has an asset base that supports our ability to accomplish the things we set out to do. We refer to our personal assets as *talents, strengths,* or *abilities.* We probably inherit our talents from our parents, but we acquire many of our abilities and strengths through learning. One thing is certain, we feel very proud of the talents and abilities we have.

Procedure

1. Printed here is a T chart that you are to fill out. On the right-hand side of the T, list four or five of your accomplishments—*things you have done of which you are most proud.* Your accomplishments should only include those things for which you can take credit, those *things for which you are primarily responsible.* If you are proud of the sorority to which you belong, you may be justifiably proud, but don't list it unless you can argue that the sorority's excellence is due primarily to your efforts. However, if you feel that having been invited to join the sorority is a major accomplishment for you, then you may include it.

When you have completed the right-hand side of the chart, fill in the left-hand side by listing *talents, strengths,* and *abilities* that you have that have enabled you to accomplish the outcomes listed on the right-hand side.

My Asset Base

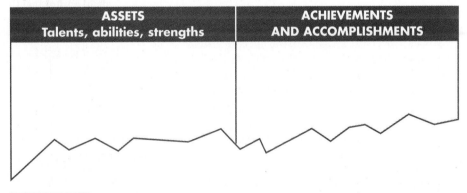

ASSETS Talents, abilities, strengths	ACHIEVEMENTS AND ACCOMPLISHMENTS

Source: Adapted from Donald D. Bowen, et al., *Experiences in Management and Organizational Behavior,* 4th ed. (New York: John Wiley & Sons, Inc.), 1997.

2. Share your lists with other team members. As each member takes turn sharing his or her list, pay close attention to your own perceptions and feelings. Notice the effect this has on your attitudes toward the other team members.
3. Discuss these questions in your group:
    (a) How did your attitudes and feelings toward other members of the team change as you pursued the activity? What does this tell you about the process whereby we come to get to know and care about people?
    (b) How did you feel about the instructions the instructor provided? What did you expect to happen? Were your expectations accurate?

• • • • EXERCISE 5 •

Expatriate Assignments

Contributed by Robert E. Ledman, Morehouse College

This exercise focuses on issues related to workers facing international assignments. It illustrates that those workers face a multitude of issues. It further demonstrates that managers who want employees to realize the maximum benefits of international assignments should be aware of, and prepared to deal with, those issues. Some of the topics that are easily addressed with this exercise include the need for culture and language training for the employees and their families and the impact that international assignments may have on an employee's family and how that may affect an employee's willingness to seek such assignments.

Procedure

1. Form into "families" of four or five. Since many students today have only one parent at home it is helpful if some groups do not have students to fill both parental roles in the exercise. Each student is assigned to play a family member and given a description of that person. Descriptions of family members are given below.
2. Enter into a 20-minute discussion to explore how a proposed overseas assignment will affect the family members. Your goal is to try to reach a decision about whether the assignment should be taken. You must also decide whether the entire family will relocate or only the family member being offered the assignmewnt. The assignment is for a minimum of 2 years, with possible annual extensions resulting in a total of

4 years, and your family, or the member offered the assignment will be provided, at company expense, one trip back to the states each year for a maximum period of 15 days. The member offered the assignment will not receive any additional housing or cost-of-living supplements described in the role assignment if he or she chooses to go overseas alone and can expect his or her living expenses to exceed substantially the living allowance being provided by the company. In your discussion, address the following questions:

(a) What are the most important concerns your family has about relocating to a foreign country?
(b) What information should you seek about the proposed host country to be able to make a more informed decision?
(c) What can the member offered the assignment do to make the transition easier if he or she goes overseas alone? If the whole family relocates?
(d) What should the member offered the assignment do to ensure that this proposed assignment will not create unnecessary stress for him or her and the rest of the family?
(e) What lessons for managers of expatriate assignees are presented by the situation in this exercise?

Try to reach some "family" consensus. If a consensus is not possible, however, resolve any differences in the manner you think the family in the role descriptions would ultimately resolve any differences.

3. Share your answers with the rest of the class. Explain the rationale for your answers and answer questions from the remainder of the class.

Source: Robert E. Ledman, Gannon University. Presented in the Experiential Exercise Track of the 1996 ABSEL Conference and published in the *Proceedings* of that conference.

4. (*Optional*) After each group has reported on a given question, the instructor may query the class about how their answers are consistent, or inconsistent, with the common practices of managers as described in the available literature.

Descriptions of Family Members
Person Being Offered Overseas Assignment

This person is a middle- to upper-level executive who is on a fast track to senior management. He or she has been offered the opportunity to manage an overseas operation, with the assurance of a promotion to a vice presidency upon return to the States. The company will pay all relocation expenses, including selling costs for the family home and the costs associated with finding a new home upon return. The employer will also provide language training for the employee and cultural awareness training for the entire family. The employee will receive a living allowance equal to 20% of salary. This should be adequate to provide the family a comparable standard of living to that which is possible on the employee's current salary.

Spouse of the Person Offered an Overseas Assignment (Optional)

This person is also a professional with highly transferrable skills and experience for the domestic market. It is unknown how easily he or she may be able to find employment in the foreign country. This person's income, although less than his or her spouse's, is necessary if the couple is to continue paying for their child's college tuition and to prepare for the next child to enter college in 2 years. This person has spent 15 years developing a career, including completing a degree at night.

Oldest Child

This child is a second semester junior in college and is on track to graduate in 16 months. Transferring at this time would probably mean adding at least one semester to complete the degree. He or she has been dating the same person for over a year; they have talked about getting married immediately after graduation, although they are not yet formally engaged.

Middle Child

This child is a junior in high school. He or she has already begun visiting college campuses in preparation for applying in the fall. This child is involved in a number of school activities; he or she is a photographer for the year book and plays a varsity sport. This child has a learning disability for which services are being provided by the school system.

Youngest Child

This child is a middle school student, age 13. He or she is actively involved in Scouting and takes piano lessons. This child has a history of medical conditions that have required regular visits to the family physician and specialists. This child has several very close friends who have attended the same school for several years.

EXERCISE 6

Cultural Cues

Contributed by Susan Rawson Zacur and W. Alan Randolph, University of Baltimore

Introduction

In the business context, culture involves shared beliefs and expectations that govern the behavior of people. In this exercise, *foreign culture* refers to a set of beliefs and expectations different from those of the participant's home culture (which has been invented by the participants).

Procedure

1. (10–15 minutes) Divide into two groups, each with color-coded badges. For example, the blue group could receive blue Post-it notes and the yellow group could receive yellow Post-it notes. Print your first name in bold letters on the badge and wear it throughout the exercise.

Source: Adapted by Susan Rawson Zacur and W. Alan Randolph from *Journal of Management Education,* Vol. 17, No. 4 (November, 1993) pp. 510–516.

Work with your group members to invent your own cultural cues. Think about the kinds of behaviors and words that will signify to all members that they belong together in one culture. For each category provided below, identify and record at least one important attribute for your culture.

Cultural Cues:	Your Culture:
Facial expression:	
Eye contact (note: you must have some eye contact in order to observe others!):	
Handshake:	
Body language (note: must be evident while standing):	
Key words or phrases:	

Once you have identified desirable cultrual aspects for your group, practice them. It is best to stand with your group and to engage one another in conversations involving two or three people at a time. Your aim in talking with one another is to learn as much as possible about each other—hobbies, interests, where you live, what your family is like, what courses you are taking; and so on, all the while practicing the behaviors and words identified above. It is not necessary for participants to answer questions of a personal nature truthfully. Invention is permissible because the conversation is only a means to the end of cultural observation. Your aim at this point is to become comfortable with the indicators of your particular culture. Practice until the indicators are second nature to you.

2. Now assume that you work for a business that has decided to explore the potential for doing business with companies in a different culture. You are to learn as much as possible about another culture. To do so, you will send from one to three representatives from your group on a "business trip" to the other culture. These representatives must, insofar as possible, behave in a manner that is consistent with your culture. At the same time, each representative must endeavor to learn as much as possible about the people in the other culture, while keeping eyes and ears open to cultural attributes that will be useful in future negotiations with foreign businesses. (*Note:* At no time will it be considered ethical behavior for the representative to ask direct questions about the foreign culture's attributes. These must be gleaned from firsthand experience.)

   While your representatives are away, you will receive one or more exchange visitors from the other culture, who will engage in conversation as they attempt to learn more about your organizational culture. You must strictly adhere to the cultural aspects of your own culture while you converse with the visitors.

3. (5–10 minutes) All travelers return to your home cultures. As a group, discuss and record what you have learned about the foreign culture based on the exchange of visitors. This information will serve as the basis for orienting the next representatives who will make a business trip.

4. (5–10 minutes) Select one to three different group members to make another trip to the other culture to check out the assumptions your group has made about the other culture. This "checking out" process will consist of actually practicing the other culture's cues to see whether they work.

5. (5–10 minutes) Once the traveler(s) have returned and reported on findings, as a group, prepare to report to the class what you have learned about the other culture.

Prejudice in Our Lives

Contributed by Susan Schor of Pace University and Annie McKee of The Wharton School,
University of Pennsylvania with the assistance of Ariel Fishman of The Wharton School

Procedure

1. As a large class group, generate a list of groups that tend to be targets of prejudice and stereotypes in our culture—such groups can include gender, race, ethnicity, sexual orientation, region, religion, etc. After generating a list, either as a class or in small groups, identify a few common positive and negative stereotypes associated with each group. Consider also relationships or patterns that exist between some of the lists. Discuss the implications for groups that have stereotypes that are valued in organizations versus groups whose stereotypes are viewed negatively in organizations.

2. As an individual, think about the lists you have now generated, and list those groups with which you identify. Write about an experience in which you were stereotyped as a member of a group. Ask yourself the following questions and write down your thoughts:

   (a) What group do I identify with?
   (b) What was the stereotype?
   (c) What happened? When and where did the incident occur? Who said what to whom?
   (d) What were my reactions? How did I feel? What did I think? What did I do?

(e) What were the consequences? How did the incident affect me and others?

3. Now, in small groups, discuss your experiences. Briefly describe the incident and focus on how the incident made you feel. Select one incident from the ones shared in your group to role play for the class. Then, as a class, discuss your reactions to each role play. Identify the prejudice or stereotype portrayed, the feelings the situation evoked, and the consequences that might result from such a situation.

4. Think about the prejudices and stereotypes you hold about other people. Ask yourself, "What groups do I feel prejudice toward? What stereotypes do I hold about members of each of these groups? How may such a prejudice have developed—did a family member or close friend or television influence you to stereotype a particular group in a certain way?

5. Now try to identify implications of prejudice in the workplace. How do prejudice and stereotypes affect workers, managers, relationships between people, and the organization as a whole? Consider how you might want to change erroneous beliefs as well as how you would encourage other people to change their own erroneous beliefs.

How We View Differences

Contributed by Barbara Walker

Introduction

Clearly, the workplace of the future will be much more diverse than it is today: more women, more peoples of color, more international representation, more diverse life-styles and ability profiles, etc. Managing a diverse

Source: Exercise developed by Barbara Walker, a pioneer on work on valuing differences. Adapted for this volume by Douglas T. Hall. Used by permission of Barbara Walker.

workforce and working across a range of differences is quickly becoming a "core competency" for effective managers.

Furthermore, it is also becoming clear that diversity in a work team can significantly enhance the creativity and quality of the team's output. In today's turbulent business environment, utilizing employee diversity will give the manager and the organization a competitive edge in tapping all of the available human resources more effectively. This exercise is an initial step in the examination of how we work with people whom we see as different from us. It is fairly simple, straightforward, and safe, but its implications are profound.

Procedure

1. Read the following:

Imagine that you are traveling in a rental car in a city you have never visited before. You have a 1-hour drive on an uncrowded highway before you reach your destination. You decide that you would like to spend the time listening to some of your favorite kind of music on the car radio.

The rental car has four selection buttons available, each with a preset station that plays a different type of music. One plays *country music,* one plays *rock,* one plays *classical,* and one plays *jazz.* Which type of music would you choose to listen to for the next hour as you drive along? (Assume you want to relax and just stick with one station; you don't want to bother switching around between stations.)

2. Form into groups based on the type of music that you have chosen. All who have chosen country will meet in an area designated by the instructor. Those who chose rock will meet in another area, etc. In your groups, answer the following question. Appoint one member to be the spokesperson to report your answers back to the total group.

Question

For each of the other groups, what words would you use to describe people who like to listen to that type of music?

3. Have each spokesperson report the responses of her or his group to the question in step 2. Follow with class discussion of these additional questions:
   (a) What do you think is the purpose or value of this exercise?
   (b) What did you notice about the words used to describe the other groups? Were there any *surprises* in this exercise for you?
   (c) Upon what sorts of data do you think these images were based?
   (d) What term do we normally use to describe these generalized perceptions of another group?
   (e) What could some of the consequences be?
   (f) How do the perceptual processes here relate to other kinds of intergroup differences, such as race, gender, culture, ability, ethnicity, health, age, nationality, etc.?
   (g) What does this exercise suggest about the ease with which intergroup stereotypes form?
   (h) What might be ways an organization might facilitate the valuing and utilizing of differences between people?

EXERCISE 9
Alligator River Story

The Alligator River Story
There lived a woman named Abigail who was in love with a man named Gregory. Gregory lived on the shore of a river. Abigail lived on the opposite shore of the same river. The river that separated the two lovers was teeming with dangerous alligators. Abigail wanted to cross the river to be with Gregory. Unfortunately, the bridge had been washed out by a heavy flood the previous week. So she went to ask Sinbad, a riverboat captain, to take her across. He said he would be glad to if she would consent to go to bed with him prior to the voyage. She promptly refused and went to a friend named Ivan to explain her plight. Ivan did not want to get involved at all in the situation. Abigail felt her only alternative was to accept

Sinbad's terms. Sinbad fulfilled his promise to Abigail and delivered her into the arms of Gregory.

When Abigail told Gregory about her amorous escape in order to cross the river, Gregory cast her aside with disdain. Heartsick and rejected, Abigail turned to Slug with her tail of woe. Slug, feeling compassion for Abigail, sought out Gregory and beat him brutally. Abigail was overjoyed at the sight of Gregory getting his due. As the sun set on the horizon, people heard Abigail laughing at Gregory.

Procedure
1. Read "The Alligator River Story."
2. After reading the story, rank the five characters in the story beginning with the one whom you consider the most offensive and end with the one whom you consider the least objectionable. That is, the character who seems to be the most reprehensible to you should be entered first in the list following the story,

Source: From Sidney B. Simon, Howard Kirschenbaum, and Leland Howe, *Values Clarification, The Handbook,* revised edition, copyright © 1991, Values Press, P.O. Box 450, Sunderland, MA. 01375. Send for a list of other strategy books from Value Press.

then the second most reprehensible, and so on, with the least reprehensible or objectionable being entered fifth. Of course, you will have your own reasons as to why you rank them in the order that you do. Very briefly note these too.

3. Form groups as assigned by your instructor (at least four persons per group with gender mixed).
4. Each group should:
   a. Elect a spokesperson for the group
   b. Compare how the group members have ranked the characters
   c. Examine the reasons used by each of the members for their rankings
   d. Seek consensus on a final group ranking
5. Following your group discussions, you will be asked to share your outcomes and reasons for agreement or nonagreement. A general class discussion will then be held.

EXERCISE 10

Teamwork and Motivation

Contributed by Dr. Barbara McCain, Oklahoma City University

Procedure

1. Read this situation.

You are the *owner* of a small manufacturing corporation. Your company manufactures widgets—a commodity. Your widget is a clone of nationally known widgets. Your widget, "WooWoo," is less expensive and more readily available than the nationally known brand. Presently, the sales are high. However, there are many rejects, which increases your cost and delays the delivery. You have 50 employees in the following departments: sales, assembly, technology, and administration.

2. In groups, discuss methods to motivate all of the employees in the organization—rank order them in terms of preference.

3. Design an organization motivation plan that encourages high job satisfaction, low turnover, high productivity, and high-quality work.

4. Is there anything special you can do about the minimum wage service worker? How do you motivate this individual? On what motivation theory do you base your decision?

5. Report to the class your motivation plan. Record your ideas on the board and allow all groups to build on the first plan. Discuss additions and corrections as the discussion proceeds.

Worksheet

Individual Worker	Team Member
Talks	
Me oriented	
Department focused	
Competitive	
Logical	
Written messages	
Image	
Secrecy	
Short-term sighted	
Immediate results	
Critical	
Tenure	

Directions: Fill in the right-hand column with descriptive terms. These terms should suggest a change in behavior from individual work to teamwork.

Annual Pay Raises

Procedure

1. Read the job descriptions below and decide on a percentage pay increase for each of the eight employees.

2. Make salary increase recommendations for each of the eight managers that you supervise. There are no formal company restrictions on the size of raises you give, but the total for everyone should not exceed the $7640 (a 4-percent increase in the salary pool) which has been budgeted for this purpose. You have a variety of information upon which to base the decisions, including a "productivity index" (PI), which Industrial Engineering computes as a quantitative measure of operating efficiency for each manager's work unit. This index ranges from a high of 10 to a low of 1. Indicate the percentage increase *you* would give each manager in the blank space next to each manager's name. Be prepared to explain why.

   ____ *A. Alvarez*   Alvarez is new this year and has a tough work group whose task is dirty and difficult. This is a hard position to fill, but you don't feel Alvarez is particularly good. The word around is that the other managers agree with you. PI = 3. Salary = $23,000.

   ____ *B. J. Cook*   Cook is single and a "swinger" who enjoys leisure time. Everyone laughs at the problems B.J. has getting the work out, and you feel it certainly is lacking. Cook has been in the job 2 years. PI = 3. Salary = $24,500.

   ____ *Z. Davis*   In the position 3 years, Davis is one of your best people even though some of the other managers don't agree. With a spouse who is independently wealthy, Davis doesn't need money but likes to work. PI = 7. Salary = $26,600.

   ____ *M. Frame*   Frame has personal problems and is hurting financially. Others gossip about Frame's performance, but you are quite satisfied with this second-year employee. PI = 7. Salary = $24,700.

   ____ *C.M. Liu*   Liu is just finishing a fine first year in a tough job. Highly respected by the others, Liu has a job offer in another company at a 15-percent increase in salary. You are impressed, and the word is that the money is important. PI = 9. Salary = $24,000.

   ____ *B. Ratin*   A first-year manager whom you and the others think is doing a good job. This is a bit surprising since Ratin turned out to be a "free spirit" who doesn't seem to care much about money or status. PI = 9. Salary = $23,800.

   ____ *H. Smith*   A first-year manager recently divorced and with two children to support as a single parent. The others like Smith a lot, but your evaluation is not very high. Smith could certainly use extra money. PI = 5. Salary = $23,000.

   ____ *G. White*   White is a big spender who always has the latest clothes and a new car. In the first year on what you would call an easy job, White doesn't seem to be doing very well. For some reason, though, the others talk about White as the "cream of the new crop." PI = 5. Salary = $23,000.

3. Convene in a group of four to seven persons and share your raise decision.

4. As a group, decide on a new set of raises and be prepared to report them to the rest of the class. Make sure that the group spokesperson can provide the rationale for each person's raise.

5. The instructor will call on each group to report its raise decisions. After discussion, an "expert's" decision will be given.

Source: Robert N. Lussier, *Human Relations in Organizations: A Skill Building Approach,* 2nd ed. (Homewood, IL: Richard D. Irwin, Inc., 1993).

The Downside of Punishment

Contributed by Dr. Barbara McCain, Oklahoma City University

Procedure

There are numerous problems associated with using punishment or discipline to change behavior. Punishment creates negative effects in the workplace. To better understand this, work in your group to give an example of each of the following situations:

1. Punishment may not be applied to the person whose behavior you want to change.

2. Punishment applied over time may suppress the occurrence of socially desirable behaviors.

3. Punishment creates a dislike of the person who is implementing the punishment.

4. Punishment results in undesirable emotions such as anxiety and aggressiveness.

5. Punishment increases the desire to avoid punishment.

6. Punishing one behavior does not guarantee that the desired behavior will occur.

7. Punishment follow-up requires allocation of additional resources.

8. Punishment may create a communication barrier and inhibit the flow of information.

Source: Adapted from class notes: Dr. Larry Michaelson, Oklahoma University.

Tinker Toys

Contributed by Bonnie McNeely, Murray State University

Materials Needed
Tinker toy sets.

Procedure

1. Form groups as assigned by the instructor. The mission of each group or temporary organization is to build the tallest possible tinker toy tower. Each group should determine worker roles: at least four students will be builders, some will be consultants who offer suggestions, and the remaining students will be observers who remain silent and complete the observation sheet provided below.

2. Rules for the exercise:
   a. Fifteen minutes allowed to plan the tower, but *only 60 seconds* to build.
   b. No more than two Tinker Toy pieces can be put together during the planning.
   c. All pieces must be put back in the box before the competition begins.
   d. The completed tower must stand alone.

Observation Sheet

1. What planning activities were observed?

   Did the group members adhere to the rules?

2. What organizing activities were observed?

   Was the task divided into subtasks? Division of labor?

3. Was the group motivated to succeed? Why or why not?

4. Were any control techniques observed?

   Was a time keeper assigned?

   Were backup plans discussed?

5. Did a clear leader emerge from the group?

   What behaviors indicated that this person was the leader?

   How did the leader establish credibility with the group?

6. Did any conflicts within the group appear?

   Was there a power struggle for the leadership position?

Source: Adapted from Bonnie McNeely, "Using the Tinker Toy Exercise to Teach the Four Functions of Management," *Journal of Management Educaiton,* Vol. 18, No. 4 (November 1994), pp. 468–472.

Eggsperiential Exercise

Contributed by Dr. Barbara McCain, Oklahoma City University

Materials Needed

1 raw egg per group

6 plastic straws per group

1 yd of plastic tape

1 large plastic jar

Procedure

1. Form into equal groups of five to seven people.
2. The task is to drop an egg from the chair onto the plastic without breaking the egg. Groups can evaluate the materials and plan their task for 10 minutes. During this period the materials may not be handled.
3. Groups have 10 minutes for construction.
4. One group member will drop the egg while standing on top of a chair in front of the class. One by one a representative from each group will drop their eggs.
5. Optional: Each group will name the egg.
6. Each group discusses their individual/group behaviors during this activity. Optional: This analysis may be summarized in written form. The following questions may be utilized in the analysis:
   (a) What kind of group is it? Explain.
   (b) Was the group cohesive? Explain.
   (c) How did the cohesiveness relate to performance? Explain.
   (d) Was there evidence of group think? Explain.
   (e) Were group norms established? Explain.
   (f) Was there evidence of conflict? Explain.
   (g) Was there any evidence of social loafing? Explain.

Scavenger Hunt—Team Building

Contributed by Michael R. Manning and Paula J. Schmidt, New Mexico State University

Introduction

Think about what it means to be a part of a team—a successful team. What makes one team more successful than another? What does each team member need to do in order for their team to be successful? What are the characteristics of an effective team?

Procedure

1. Form teams as assigned by your instructor. Locate the items on the list below while following these important rules:

   a. Your team *must stay together at all times*—that is, you cannot go in separate directions.
   b. Your team must return to the classroom in the time allotted by the instructor.

   The team with the most items on the list will be declared the most successful team.

2. Next, reflect on your team's experience. What did each team member do? What was your team's strategy? What made your team effective? Make a list of the most important things your team did to be successful. Nominate a spokesperson to summarize your team's discussion for the class. What items were similar between teams? That is, what helped each team to be effective?

Items for Scavenger Hunt

Each item is to be identified and brought back to the classroom.

1. A book with the word "team" in the title.
2. A joke about teams that you share with the class.

Source: Adapted from Michael R. Manning and Paula J. Schmidt, *Journal of Management Education,* Building Effective Work Teams: A Quick Exercise Based on a Scavenger Hunt. (Thousand Oaks, CA: Sage Publications, 1995), pp. 392–398. Used by permission. Reference for list of items for scavenger hunt from C. E. Larson and F. M. Lafas, *Team Work: What Must Go Right/What Can Go Wrong.* (Newbury Park, CA: Sage Publications, 1989).

3. A blade of grass from the university football field.
4. A souvenir from the state.
5. A picture of a team or group.
6. A newspaper article about a team.
7. Compose a team song and perform it for the class.
8. A leaf from an oak tree.
9. Stationery from the Dean's office.
10. A cup of sand.
11. A pine cone.
12. A live reptile. (*Note:* Sometimes a team member has one for a pet or the students are ingenious enough to visit a local pet store.)

13. A definition of group "cohesion" that you share with the class.
14. A set of chopsticks.
15. Bring back three cans of vegetables.
16. A branch of an elm tree.
17. Find and share three unusual items with the class.
18. A ball of cotton.
19. The ear from a prickly pear cactus.
20. A group name.

(*Note:* Items may be substituted as appropriate for your locale.)

EXERCISE 16

Identifying Group Norms

Procedure

1. Choose an organization you know quite a bit about.
2. Complete the questionnaire below, indicating your responses using one of the following:

> (a) Strongly agree or encourage it.
> (b) Agree with it or encourage it.
> (c) Consider it unimportant.
> (d) Disagree with or discourage it.
> (e) Strongly disagree with or discourage it.

If an employee in this organization were to . . . *Most other employees would:*

1. Show genuine concern for the problems that face the organization and make suggestions about solving them . . . ____
2. Set very high personal standards of performance . . . ____
3. Try to make the work group operate more like a team when dealing with issues or problems . . . ____
4. Think of going to a supervisor with a problem . . .
5. Evaluate expenditures in terms of the benefits they will provide for the organization . . . ____
6. Express concern for the well-being of other members of the organization . . . ____
7. Keep a customer or client waiting while looking after matters of personal convenience . . . ____
8. Criticize a fellow employee who is trying to improve things in the work situation . . . ____
9. Actively look for ways to expand his/her knowledge to be able to do a better job . . . ____
10. Be perfectly honest in answering this questionnaire . . . ____

Scoring

$$A = +2, B = +1, C = 0, D = -1, E = -2$$

1. Organizational/Personal Pride Score ____
2. Performance/Excellence Score ____

3. Teamwork/Communication
   Score ____
4. Leadership/Supervision
   Score ____
5. Profitability/Cost Effectiveness
   Score ____
6. Colleague/Associate Relations
   Score ____

7. Customer/Client Relations
   Score ____
8. Innovativeness/Creativity
   Score ____
9. Training/Development
   Score ____
10. Candor/Openness
    Score ____

Workgroup Culture

Contributed by Conrad N. Jackson, MPC, Inc.

Procedure

1. The bipolar scales on this instrument can be used to evaluate a group's process in a number of useful ways. Use it to measure where you see the group to be at present. To do this, *circle* the number that best represents *how you see the culture of the group*. You can also indicate how you think the group *should* function by using a different symbol, such as a square (□), or a caret (^) to indicate how you saw the group at some time in the past.
2. (a) If you are assessing your own group, have everyone fill in the instrument, summarize the scores, then discuss their bases (what members say and do that has led to these interpretations) and implications. This is often an extremely pro-

Source: Adapted from Donald D. Bowen, et al., *Experiences in Management and Organizational Behavior,* 4th ed. (New York: John Wiley & Sons, Inc.), 1997.

ductive intervention to improve group or team functioning.
   (b) If you are assessing another group, use the scores as the basis for your feedback. Be sure to provide specific feedback on behavior *you have observed,* in addition to the subjective interpretations of your ratings on the scales in this instrument.
   (c) The instrument can also be used to compare a group's self-assessment with the assessment provided by another group.

1. Trusting	1:2:3:4:5	Suspicious
2. Helping	1:2:3:4:5	Ignoring, blocking
3. Expressing feelings	1:2:3:4:5	Suppressing feelings
4. Risk taking	1:2:3:4:5	Cautious
5. Authenticity	1:2:3:4:5	Game playing
6. Confronting	1:2:3:4:5	Avoiding
7. Open	1:2:3:4:5	Hidden, diplomatic

The Hot Seat

Contributed by Barry R. Armandi, SUNY-Old Westbury

Procedure

1. Form into groups as assigned by your instructor.
2. Read the following situation.

A number of years ago, Professor Stevens was asked to attend a departmental meeting at a university. He had been on leave from the department, but a junior faculty member discreetly requested that he attend to protect the rights of the junior faculty. The Chair, or head of the department, was a typical Machiavellian, whose only concerns were self-serving. Professor Stevens had a number of previous disagreements with the Chair. The heart of the disagreements centered around the Chair's abrupt and domineering style and his poor relations with the junior faculty, many of whom felt mistreated and scared.

The department was a conglomeration of different professional types. Included in the mix were behavioralists, generalists, computer scientists, and quantitative analysts. The department was embedded in the School of Business, which had three other departments. There was much confusion and concern among the faculty, since this was a new organizational design. Many of the faculty were at odds with each other over the direction the school was now taking.

At the meeting, a number of proposals were to be presented that would seriously affect the performance and future of certain junior faculty, particularly those who were behavioral scientists. The Chair, a computer scientist, disliked the behavioralists, who he felt were "always analyzing the motives of people." Professor Stevens, who was a tenured full professor and a behavioralist, had an objective to protect the interests of the junior faculty and to counter the efforts of the Chair.

Including Professor Stevens, there were nine faculty present. The accompanying diagram shows the seating arrangement and the layout of the room. The **Xs** signify those faculty who were allies of the Chair. The **+s** are those opposed to the Chair and supportive of Professor Stevens, and the **?s** were undecided and could be swayed either way. The circled numbers represent empty seats. Both **?s** were behavioralists and the + next to them was a quantitative analyst. Near the door, the first **X** was a generalist, the two **+s** were behavioralists, and the second **X** was a quantitative analyst. The diagram shows the seating of everyone but Professor Stevens, who was the last one to enter the room. Standing at the door, Professor Stevens surveyed the room and within 10 seconds knew which seat was the most effective to achieve his objective.

3. Answer the following questions in your group.
   (a) Which seat did Professor Stevens select and why?
   (b) What is the likely pattern of communication and interaction in this group?
   (c) What can be done to get this group to work harmoniously?

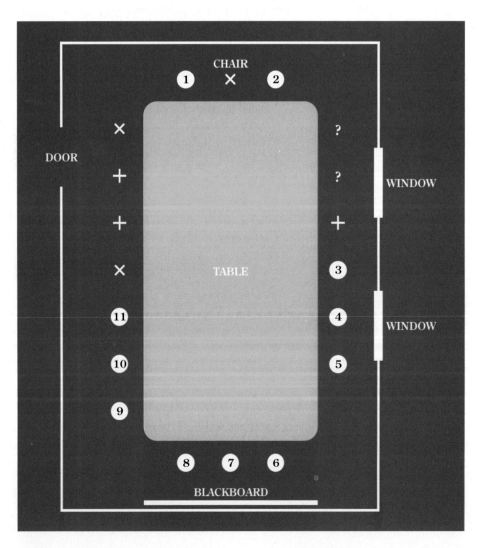

Jazz Ensembles

Contributed by Ronald E. Purser, Loyola University of Chicago, and Alfonso Montouri,
Saybrook Institute

Procedure

Listen carefully to the Miles Davis recording your instructor plays for you in class.

1. As you begin to listen to the music, try to identify and imagine you are one of the musicians in the Miles Davis band (Miles Davis on trumpet, Paul Chambers on bass, James Cobb on drums, Cannonball Adderly on alto saxophone, John Coltraine on tenor saxophone, and Wyn Kelly on piano). While you are listening to the band perform, make a list of the qualities, skills, attitudes, or conditions that you feel are conducive to the creative interactions among ensemble members. This list of qualities might take the form of action or process verbs, or descriptive adjectives. After the music is over, form into groups as assigned by the instructor.
2. Now share from your list of recorded observations and descriptive qualities of the jazz ensemble experience. As you share your findings with your group, try to actualize and enact the very qualities which you and others have identified as key to creative jazz performance. In other words, try to bring the spirit of the jazz ensemble performance into your own group. Afterwards, share your own reflections and observations of the dynamics and process that occurred within your group. Did the enactment of the "meta-task" have an influence on your group process? In what way? Did your group's enactment of jazz ensemble behaviors lead to interactions that are significantly different from experiences of previous group interactions in the course? Prepare and present a short summary of your group's findings for a report to the whole class. Be sure to discuss with the whole class the ensemble behaviors that your group found to be conducive to *team learning* and dialogue.

Source: Ronald E. Purser and Alfonso Montouri, *Journal of Management Education,* Vol. 18, No. 1, pp. 24–25. © 1994 by Sage Publications, Inc. Reprinted by permission of Sage Publications.

Communication Networks

Procedure

1. Set up three teams of five members each. The members should be seated in the network position shown in the accompanying diagrams. All other class members should form a circle around the three groups and observe them work.

    The arrows represent the communication flow. In **team 1, A** can talk only to B or D; **B** can talk only to A or C; **C** can talk only to B; **D** can talk to only A or or E; and **E** can talk only to D. In **team 2, A** can talk to B, C, D, or E individually but not as a group. **B, C, D,** and **E** cannot talk to one another, only to A. In **team 3,** anyone can talk to anyone.

Source: Robert N. Lussier, *Human Relations in Organizations: A Skill Building Approach,* 2nd ed. (Homewood, IL: Richard D. Irwin, Inc. 1993), p. 297. Used by permission.

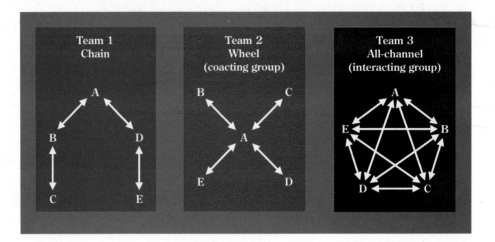

Team 1
Chain

Team 2
Wheel
(coacting group)

Team 3
All-channel
(interacting group)

The instructor gives each team member one of the 5" × 5" square puzzle pieces. Wait until told to start before making the puzzle.

2. Each team has up to 5 minutes to finish the puzzle following its communication network.

3. The instructor gives each team a copy of the completed puzzle to check its accuracy or to show the team how to do it.

4. Each team tells the class how it felt about following its communication network. How did the communication network affect the performance of the team?

5. The class as a whole discusses the results. Did any team finish? Which team was first? Which structure was most appropriate for this task?

• • • **EXERCISE 21** •

Organizations Alive!

Contributed by Bonnie L. McNeely, Murray State University

Procedure

1. Find a copy of the following items from actual organizations. These items can be obtained from the company where you now work, your parent's workplace, or from the university. Universities have mission statements, codes of conduct for students and faculty, organizational charts, job descriptions, performance appraisal forms, and control devices. Some student organizations also have these documents. All the items do not have to come from the same organization *Bring these items to class.*

(a) Mission Statement (d) Job Description
(b) Code of Ethics (e) Performance Appraisal Form
(c) Organizational Chart (f) Control Device

2. Form groups in class as assigned by your instructor. Share your items with the group, as well as what you learned while collecting these items. For example, did you find that some firms have a mission, but it is not written down? Did you find that job descriptions existed, but they were not really used or had not been updated in years?

Source: Adapted from Bonnie L. McNeely, "Make Your Principles of Management Class Come Alive," *Journal of Management Education,* Vol. 18, No. 2, May 1994, pp. 246–249.

Fast Food Technology

Contributed by D. T. Hall, Boston University, and F. S. Hall, University of New Hampshire

Introduction

A critical first step in improving or changing any organization is *diagnosing* or analyzing its present functioning. Many change and organization development efforts fall short of their objectives because this important step was not taken, or was conducted superficially. To illustrate this, imagine how you would feel if you went to your doctor complaining of stomach pains, and he recommended surgery without conducting any tests, without obtaining any further information, and without a careful physical examination. You would probably switch doctors! Yet, managers often attempt major changes with correspondingly little diagnostic work in advance. (It could be said that they undertake vast projects with half-vast ideas.)

In this exercise, you will be asked to conduct a group diagnosis of two different organizations in the fast food business. The exercise will provide an opportunity to integrate much of the knowledge you have gained in other exercises and in studying other topics. Your task will be to describe the organizations as carefully as you can in terms of several key organizational concepts. Although the organizations are probably very familiar to you, try to step back and look at them as though you were seeing them for the first time.

Procedure

1. In groups of four or six people, your assignment is described below.

One experience most people in this country have shared is that of dining in the hamburger establishment known as McDonald's. In fact, someone has claimed that 25th-century archeologists may dig into the ruins of our present civilization and conclude that 20-century religion was devoted to the worship of golden arches.

Your group, Fastalk Consultants, is known as the shrewdest, most insightful, and most overpaid management consulting firm in the country. You have been hired by the president of McDonald's to make recommendations for improving the motivation and performance of personnel in their franchise operations. Let us assume that the key job activities in franchise operations are food preparation, order-taking and dealing with customers, and routine clean-up operations.

Recently the president of McDonald's has come to suspect that his company's competitors such as Burger King, Wendy, Jack in the Box, Dunkin' Donuts, various pizza establishments, and others are making heavy inroads into McDonald's market.

He has also hired a market research firm to investigate and compare the relative merits of the sandwiches, french fries, and drinks served in McDonald's and the competitor, and has asked the market research firm to assess the advertising campaigns of the two organizations. Hence, you will not need to be concerned with marketing issues, except as they may have an impact on employee behavior. The president wants *you* to look into the *organization* of the franchises to determine the strengths and weaknesses of each. Select a competitor who gives McDonald's a good "run for its money" in your area.

The president has established an unusual contract with you. *He wants you to make your recommendations based upon your observations as a customer.* He does not want you to do a complete diagnosis with interviews, surveys, or behind-the-scenes observations. He wants your report in two parts. Remember, the president wants concrete, specific, and practical recommendations. Avoid vague generalizations such as "improve communications" or "increase trust." Say very clearly *how* management can improve organizational performance. Substantiate your recommendations by reference to one or more theories of motivation, leadership, small groups, or job design.

Part I

Given his organization's goals of profitability, sales volume, fast and courteous service, and cleanliness, the president of McDonald's wants an analysis that will *compare and contrast McDonald's and the competitor* in terms of the following concepts:

Organizational goals

Organizational structure

Technology

Environment

Employee motivation

Communication

Leadership style

Policies/procedures/rules/standards

Job design

Organizational climate

Part II

Given the corporate goals listed under Part I, what specific actions might McDonald's management and franchise owners take in the following areas to achieve these goals (profitability, sales volume, fast and courteous service, and cleanliness)?

Job design and workflow

Organizational structure (at the individual restaurant level)

Employee incentives

Leadership

Employee selection

How do McDonald's and the competition differ in these aspects? Which company has the best approach?

2. Complete the assignment by going as a group to one McDonald's and one competitor's restaurant. If possible, have a meal in each place. To get a more valid comparison, visit a McDonald's and a competitor located in the same area. After observing each restaurant, meet with your group and prepare your 10-minute report to the executive committee.

3. In class, each group will present its report to the rest of the class, who will act as the executive committee. The group leader will appoint a timekeeper to be sure that each group sticks to its 10-minute time limit. Possible discussion questions include:
   (a) What similarities are there between the two organizations?
   (b) What differences are there between the organizations?
   (c) Do you have any "hunches" about the reasons for the particular organizational characteristics you found? For example, can you try to explain why one organization might have a particular type of structure? Incentive system? Climate?
   (d) Can you try to explain one set of characteristics in terms of some other characteristics you found? For example, do the goals account for structure? Does the environment explain the structure?

EXERCISE 23

Rating Organizational Performance

Procedure
1. Select an organization (or unit of an organization) that you know quite a bit about.
2. Listed below are some statements that describe organizational performance. You should indicate how often you believe they occur in the organization you have selected. Using the scale below, place a number from 1 to 7 for each of the items to follow.

| Very infrequently | 1 | 2 | 3 | 4 | 5 | 6 | 7 | Very frequently |

____ 1. The work process is coordinated and under control.
____ 2. Participative decision making is widely and appropriately used.
____ 3. Rules, procedures, and formal methods guide the work.
____ 4. The goals are clearly understood by most members.
____ 5. The work effort is usually intense.
____ 6. There is a stable, predictable work environment.
____ 7. Innovation is stressed.
____ 8. There is a positive interpersonal climate.
____ 9. Quantification and measurement are key parts of the work climate.
____ 10. Consensual decision making is encouraged.
____ 11. Outsiders perceive it as a vibrant, high-potential unit.
____ 12. Creative insights, hunches, and innovative ideas are encouraged.
____ 13. It is easy to explain the overall objectives of the unit.
____ 14. There is a constant striving for greater accomplishment.
____ 15. Employees feel as though they really belong to the unit.
____ 16. The unit is clearly growing and improving over time.

Source: Adapted from Robert Quinn, *Beyond Rational Management* (San Francisco: Jossey-Bass, 1988). By permission.

3. Compute the rating for each performance dimension by summing scores as indicated below.

   #   2 + # 10 = ____ Participation, Openness
   #   8 + # 15 = ____ Commitment, Morale
   #   7 + # 12 = ____ Innovation, Adaptation
   # 11 + # 16 = ____ External Support, Growth
   #   5 + # 14 = ____ Productivity, Accomplishment
   #   4 + # 13 = ____ Direction, Goal Clarity
   #   1 + #   6 = ____ Stability, Control
   #   3 + #   9 = ____ Documentation, Information Management

   Form groups of four to six persons and share your organizational performance assessments.
4. Discuss the differences found and be prepared to share your findings with the rest of the class. Special consideration should be given to "why" such differences in organizations exist.

EXERCISE 24

Alien Invasion

Procedure

This is an exercise in organizational culture. You will be assigned to a team (if you are not already in one) and instructed to visit an organization by your instructor.

1. Visit the site assigned as a team working under conditions set forth in the "situation" below.
2. Take detailed notes on the cultural forms that you observe.
3. Prepare a presentation for the class that describes these forms and draw any inferences you can about the nature of the culture of the organization—its ideologies, values, and norms of behavior.
4. Be sure to explain the basis of your inferences in terms of the cultural forms observed.

You will have 20 minutes to report your findings, so plan your presentation carefully. Use visual aids to help your audience understand what you have found.

Situation

You are Martians who have just arrived on Earth in the first spaceship from your planet. Your superiors have ordered you to learn as much about Earthlings and the way they behave as you can without doing anything to make them aware that you are Martians. It is vital for the future plans of your superiors that you do nothing to disturb the Earthlings. Unfortunately, Martians communicate by emitting electromagnetic waves and are incapable of speech, so you cannot talk to the natives. Even if you did, it is reported by the usually reliable Bureau of Interplanetary Intelligence that Earthlings may become cannibalistic if annoyed. However, the crash course in Earth languages taught by the Bureau has enabled you to read the language.

Source: Adapted from Donald D. Bowen, et al., _Experiences in Management and Organizational Behavior,_ 4th ed. (New York: John Wiley & Sons, Inc.), 1997.

Remember, these instructions limit your data collection to observation and request that you *not* talk to the "natives." There are two reasons for this instruction. First, your objective is to learn what the organization does when it is simply going about its normal business and not responding to a group of students asking questions. Second, you are likely to be surprised at how much you can learn by simply observing if you put your mind to it. Many skilled managers employ this ability in sensing what is going on as they walk through their plant or office area.

Since you cannot talk to people, some of the cultural forms (legends, sagas, etc.) will be difficult to spot unless you are able to pick up copies of the organization's promotional literature (brochures, company reports, advertisements) during your visit. Do not be discouraged, because the visible forms such as artifacts, setting, symbols, and (sometimes) rituals can convey a great deal about the culture. Just keep your eyes, ears, and antennae open!

EXERCISE 25

My Best Manager: Revisited

Contributed by J. Marcus Maier, Chapman University

Procedure

1. Refer to the list of qualities—or profiles—the class generated earlier in the course for the "Best Manager."
2. Looking first at your Typical Managers profile, suppose you took this list to 100 average people on the street (or at the local mall) and asked them whether ____ (Trait X, quality Y) was "more typical of men or of women in our culture." What do you think *most* of them would say? That ____ (X, Y etc.) is more typical of *women*? or of *men*? Or of neither/both?[1] Do this for every trait on your list(s). (5 minutes)
3. Now do the same for the qualities we generated in our Best Manager profile. (5 minutes)
4. A straw vote is taken, one quality at a time, to determine the class's overall gender identification of each trait, focusing on the Typical Manager's profile (10–15 minutes). Then this is repeated for the Best Manager profile (10–15 minutes).[2]
5. Discussion. What do you see in the data this group has generated? How might you interpret these results? (15–20 minutes)

Source: Based on Dr. Maier's 1993 article, "The Gender Prism." *Journal of Management Education,* 17(3), 285–314. 1994 Fritz Roethlisberger Award Recipient for Best Paper (Updated, 1996).

[1] This gets the participants to move outside of their *own* conceptions to their awareness of *societal* definitions of masculinity and femininity.

[2] This is done by a rapid show of hands, looking for a clear majority vote. An "f" (for "feminine") is placed next to those qualities that a clear majority indicate are more typical of women, an "m" (for "masculine") next to those qualities a clear majority indicate would be more typical of men. (This procedure parallels the median-split method used in determining Bem Sex Role Inventory classifications.) If no clear majority emerges (i.e., if the vote is close), the trait or quality is classified as "both" (f/m). The designations "masculine" or "feminine" are used (rather than "men" or "women") to underscore the *socially constructed* nature of each dimension.

EXERCISE 26

Interview A Leader

Contributed by Bonnie McNeely, Murray State University

Procedure

1. Make an appointment to interview a leader. It can be a leader working in a business or nonprofit organization, such as a government agency, school, etc. Base the interview on the form provided here, but feel free to add your own questions.
2. Bring the results of your interview to class. Form into groups as assigned by your instructor. Share the responses from your interview with your group and compare answers. What issues were similar? Different? Were the stress levels of leaders working in nonprofit organizations as high as those working in for-profit firms? Were you surprised at the number of hours per week worked by leaders?
3. Be prepared to summarize the interviews done by your group as a formal written report, if asked to do so by the instructor.

Interview Questionnaire

Student's Name _____ Date _____

1. Position in the organization (title):
2. Number of years in current position:
   Number of years of managerial experience:
3. Number of people directly supervised:
4. Average number of hours worked a week
5. How did you get into leadership?
6. What is the most rewarding part of being a leader?
7. What is the most difficult part of your job?
8. What would you say are the *keys to success* for leaders?
9. What advice do you have for an aspiring leader?
10. What type of ethical issues have you faced as a leader?
11. If you were to enroll in a leadership seminar, what topics or issues would you want to learn more about?
12. (Student's question)

Sex: M_____ F_____ Years of formal education_____
Level of job stress: Very high_____ High_____ Average_____ Low_____
Profit organization_____ Nonprofit organization_____

_____

Source: Adapted from Bonnie McNeely, "Make Your Principles of Management Class come Alive," *Journal of Management Education,* Vol. 18, No. 2, May 1994, 246–249.

EXERCISE 27

Leadership Skills Inventories

Procedure

1. Look over the skills listed below and ask your instructor to clarify those you do not understand.
2. Complete each category by checking either the "Strong" or "Needs Development" category in relation to your own level with each skill.

3. After completing each category, briefly describe a situation in which each of the listed skills has been utilized.
4. Meet in your groups to share and discuss inventories. Prepare a report summarizing major development needs in your group.

Instrument

	Strong	Needs Development	Situation
Communication			
Conflict Management			
Delegation			
Ethical Behavior			
Listening			
Motivation			
Negotiation			
Performance Appraisal and Feedback			
Planning and Goal Setting			
Power and Influence			
Presentation and Persuasion			
Problem Solving and Decision Making			
Stress Management			
Team Building			
Time Management			

EXERCISE 28

Active Listening

Contributed by Robert Ledman, Morehouse College

Procedure

1. Review active listening skills and behaviors as described in the textbook and in class.
2. Form into groups of three. Each group will have a listener, a talker, and an observer (if the number of students is not evenly divisible by three, two observers are used for one or two groups).
3. The "talkers" should talk about any subject they wish, but only *if* they are being actively listened to. Talkers should stop speaking as soon as they sense active listening has stopped.

4. The "listeners" should use a list of active listening skills and behaviors as their guide, and practice as many of them as possible to be sure the talker is kept talking. Listeners should contribute nothing more than "active listening" to the communication.
5. The "observer" should note the behaviors and skills used by the listener and the effects they seemed to have on the communication process.
6. These roles are rotated until each student has played every role.
7. The instructor will lead a discussion of what was observed by the observers and what happened with the talkers and listeners. The discussion focuses on what behaviors from the posted list have been present, which have been absent, and how the communication has been affected by the listener's actions.

Source: Adapted from the presentation entitled "An Experiential Exercise to Teach Active Listening," presented at the Organizational Behavior Teaching Conference, Macomb, IL, 1995.

Upward Appraisal

Procedure

1. Form work groups as assigned by your instructor.
2. The instructor will leave the room.
3. Convene in your assigned work groups for a period of 10 minutes. Create a list of comments, problems, issues, and concerns you would like to have communicated to the instructor in regard to the course experience to date. *Remember,* your interest in the exercise is twofold: (a) to communicate your feelings to the instructor and (b) to learn more about the process of giving and receiving feedback.
4. Select one person from the group to act as spokesperson in communicating the group's feelings to the instructor.
5. The spokespersons should briefly convene to decide on what physical arrangement of chairs, tables, and so forth is most appropriate to conduct the feedback session. The classroom should then be rearranged to fit the desired specifications.
6. While the spokespersons convene, persons in the remaining groups should discuss how they expect the forthcoming communications event to develop. Will it be a good experience for all parties concerned? Be prepared to observe critically the actual communication process.
7. The instructor should be invited to return, and the feedback session will begin. Observers should make notes so that they may make constructive comments at the conclusion of the exercise.
8. Once the feedback session is complete, the instructor will call on the observers for comments, ask the spokespersons for their reactions, and open the session to general discussion.

"360" Feedback

Contributed by Timothy J. Serey, Northern Kentucky University

Introduction

The time of performance reviews is often a time of genuine anxiety for many organizational members. On one hand, it is an important organizational ritual and a key part of the Human Resource function. Organizations usually codify the process and provide a mechanism to appraise performance. On the other hand, it is rare for managers to feel comfortable with this process. Often, they feel discomfort over "playing God." One possible reason for this is that managers rarely receive formal training about how to provide feedback. From the manager's point of view, if done properly, giving feedback is at the very heart of his or her job as "coach" and "teacher." It is an investment in the professional development of another person, rather than the punitive element we so often associate with hearing from "the boss." From the subordinate's perspective, most people want to know where they stand, but this is usually tempered by a fear of "getting it in the

Source: Adapted from Timothy J. Serey, *Journal of Management Education,* Vol. 17, No. 2, May 1993. © 1993 by Sage Publications, Inc. Reprinted by permission of Sage Publications.

neck." In many organizations, it is rare to receive straight, non-sugar-coated feedback about where you stand.

Procedure

1. Review the section of the book dealing with feedback before you come to class. It is also helpful if individuals make notes about their perceptions and feelings about the course *before* they come to class.
2. Groups of students should discuss their experiences, both positive and negative, in this class. Each group should determine the dimensions of evaluating the class itself *and* the instructor. For example, students might select criteria that include the practicality of the course, the way the material is structured and presented (e.g., lecture or exercises), and the instructor's style (e.g., enthusiasm, fairness).
3. Groups select a member to represent them in a subgroup that next provides feedback to the instructor before the entire class.
4. The student-audience then provides the subgroup with feedback about their effectiveness in this exercise. That is, the larger class provides feedback to the subgroup about the extent to which students actually put the principles of effective feedback into practice (e.g., descriptive not evaluative; specific not general).

EXERCISE 31

Role Analysis Negotiation

Contributed by Paul Lyons, Frostburg State University

Introduction

A role is the set of various behaviors people expect from a person (or group) in a particular position. These role expectations occur in all types of organizations, such as one's place of work, school, family, clubs, and the like. Role ambiguity takes place when a person is confused about the expectations of the role. And, sometimes, a role will have expectations that are contradictory—for example, being loyal to the company when the company is breaking the law.

The Role Analysis Technique, or RAT, is a method for improving the effectiveness of a team or group. RAT helps to clarify role expectations, and all organization members have responsibilities that translate to expectations. Determination of role requirements, by consensus—involving all concerned—will ultimately result in more effective and mutually satisfactory behavior. Participation and collaboration in the definition and analysis of roles by group members should result in clarification regarding who is to do what as well as increase the level of commitment to the decisions made.

Procedure

Working alone, carefully read the course syllabus that your instructor has given you. Make a note of any questions you have about anything for which you need clarification or understanding. Pay particular attention to the performance requirements of the course. Make a list of any questions you have regarding what, specifically, is expected of you in order for you to be successful in the course. You will be sharing this information with others, in small groups.

Source: Adapted from Paul Lyons, "Developing Expectations with the Role Analysis Technique," *Journal of Management Education.* Vol. 17, No. 3, August 1993, pp. 386–389. © Sage Publications.

The Ugli Orange

Introduction

In most work settings, people need other people to do their job, benefit the organization, and forward their career. Getting things done in organizations requires us to work together in cooperation, even though the ultimate objectives of those other people may be different from our own. Your task in the present exercise is learning how to achieve this cooperation more effectively.

Procedure

1. The class will be divided into pairs. One student in each pair will read and prepare the role of Dr. Roland, and one will play the role of Dr. Jones (role descriptions to be distributed by instructor). Students should read their respective role descriptions and prepare to meet with their counterpart (see steps 2 and 3, below).
2. At this point the group leader will read a statement. The instructor will indicate that he or she is playing

---

Source: Adapted from D. T. Hall et al., *Experiences in Management and Organizational Behavior,* 3rd ed. (New York: John Wiley and Sons), 1988. Originally developed by Robert J. House. Adapted by D. T. Hall and R. J. Lewicki, with suggested modifications by H. Kolodny and T. Ruble.

the role of Mr. Cardoza, who owns the commodity in question. The instructor will tell you
   - (a) How long you have to meet with the other
   - (b) What information the instructor will require at the end of your meeting

   After the instructor has given you this information, you may meet with the other firm's representative and determine whether you have issues you can agree to.
3. Following the meetings (negotiations), the spokesperson for each pair will report any agreements reached to the entire class. The observer for any pair will report on negotiation dynamics and the process by which agreement was reached.
4. Questions to consider:
   - (a) Did you reach a solution? If so, what was critical to reaching that agreement?
   - (b) Did you and the other negotiator trust one another? Why or why not?
   - (c) Was there full disclosure by both sides in each group? How much information was shared?
   - (d) How creative and/or complex were the solutions? If solutions were very complex, why do you think this occurred?
   - (e) What was the impact of having an "audience" on your behavior? Did it make the problem harder or easier to solve?

Entering the Unknown

Contributed by Michael R. Manning, New Mexico State University; Conrad N. Jackson, MPC, Inc., Huntsville, Alabama; and Paula S. Weber, New Mexico Highlands University

Procedure

1. Form into groups of four or five members. In each group spend a few minutes reflecting on members' typical entry behaviors in new situations and their behaviors when they are in comfortable settings.
2. According to the instructor's directions, students count off to form new groups of four or five members each.
3. The new groups spend the next 15–20 minutes getting to know each other. There is no right or wrong way to proceed, but all members should become more aware of their entry behaviors. They should act in ways that can help them realize a goal of achieving comfortable behaviors with their group.

4. Students review what has occurred in the new groups, giving specific attention to the following questions:
   (a) What topics did your group discuss (content)? Did these topics involve the "here and now" or were they focused on "there and then"?
   (b) What approach did you and your group members take to the task (process)? Did you try to initiate or follow? How? Did you ask questions? Listen? Respond to others? Did you bring up topics?
   (c) Were you more concerned with how you came across or with how others came across to you? Did you play it safe? Were you open? Did you share things even though it seemed uncomfortable or risky? How was humor used in your group? Did it add or detract?
   (d) How do you feel about the approach you took or the behaviors you exhibited? Was this hard or easy? Did others respond the way you had anticipated? Is there some behavior you would like to do more of, do better, or do less of?
   (e) Were your behaviors the ones you had intended (goals)?
5. Responses to these questions are next discussed by the class as a whole. (*Note:* Responses will tend to be mixed within a group, but between groups there should be more similarity.) This discussion helps individuals become aware of and understand their entry behaviors.
6. Optional individuals have identified their entry behaviors. Each group can then spend 5–10 minutes discussing members' perceptions of each other:
   (a) What behaviors did they like or find particularly useful? What if anything did they dislike?
   (b) What were your reactions to others? What ways did they intend to come across? Did you see others in the way they had intended to come across?
   (Alternatively, if there is concern about the personal nature of this discussion, ask the groups to discuss what they liked/didn't like without referring to specific individuals.)

EXERCISE 34

Vacation Puzzle

Contributed by Barbara G. McCain and Mary Khalili, Oklahoma City University

Procedure

Can you solve this puzzle? Give it a try and then compare your answers with other classmates. Remember your communicative skills!

Puzzle

Khalili, McCain, Middleton, Porter, and Quintaro teach at Oklahoma City University. Each gets 2 weeks of vacation a year. Last year, each took his or her first week in the first 5 months of the year and his or her second week in the last 5 months. If each professor took each of his or her weeks in a different month from the other professors, in which months did each professor take his or her first and second week?

Here are the facts:

(a) McCain took her first week before Khalili, who took *hers* before Porter; for their second week, the order was reversed.

Source: Adapted to classroom activity by Dr. Mary Khalili.

(b) The professor who vacationed in March also vacationed in September.
(c) Quintaro did not take her first week in March or April.
(d) Neither Quintaro nor the professor who took his or her first week in January took his or her second week in August or December.
(e) Middleton took her second week before McCain but after Quintaro.

Month	Professor
January	
February	
March	
April	
May	
June	
July	
August	
September	
October	
November	
December	

• •

EXERCISE 35

Who to Hire?

Contributed by Janet W. Wohlberg, President, Hands-On Learning, Inc.

Introduction

As business becomes more global, managers are increasingly finding themselves dealing with national and cultural differences among employees and potential employees. Recruiting and developing a diverse work force, including managers and executives, has become a key to business competitiveness, both for obtaining the best talent and for being able to understand and relate to a diverse customer base. In making hiring decisions, individual managers and teams must learn to recognize the range of issues that arise when international and cross-cultural issues are part of the equation. This is a simulation of an executive selection decision that will allow you to practice the skills of utilizing these differences.

Background

You are a member of the management committee of a multinational company that does business in 23 coun-

tries. Whereas your company's headquarters are in Holland, your offices are scattered fairly evenly throughout the four hemispheres. Primary markets have been in Europe and North America; the strongest emerging market is the Pacific Rim. Company executives would like to develop what they see as a powerful potential market in the Middle East. Sales in all areas except the Pacific Rim have shown slow growth over the past 2 years.

At present, your company is seeking to restructure and revitalize its worldwide marketing efforts. To accomplish this, you have determined that you need to hire a key marketing person to introduce fresh ideas and a new perspective. There is no one currently in your company who is qualified to do this, and so you have decided to look outside. The job title is Vice-President for International Marketing; it carries with it a salary well into six figures ($US), plus elaborate benefits, an unlimited expense account, a car, and the use of the corporate jet. The person you hire will be based at the company's headquarters and will travel frequently.

A lengthy search has turned up five people with good potential. It is now up to you to decide whom to hire. Although all of the applicants have expressed a

Source: This exercise was written by Janet W. Wohlberg, President of Hands-On Learning, Inc. Copyright © Houghton Mifflin Company. Reprinted by permission of the author. Adapted for this volume by Douglas T. Hall.

sincere interest in the position, it is possible that they may change their minds once the job is offered. Therefore, you must rank them in order of preference so that if your first choice declines the position, you can go on to the second, and so on. Your instructor will provide you with the applicants' biographies.

Procedure

1. Read the background information and descriptions of each of the applicants. Consider the job and the cultures within which the individual to be hired will be operating. Rank the candidates from 1 to 5, with 1 being your first choice, and enter your rankings on a ranking sheet. Briefly, list the reasons for each of your rankings. Do not discuss your rankings with your classmates until told to do so.

2. Working with four to six of your classmates, discuss the applicants and rank them in the order of group preference. Do not vote. Rank the candidates from 1 to 5, with 1 being the group's first choice, and enter your group rankings on the ranking sheet in a column marked "Group Ranking." Briefly list the reasons for

each of the group's rankings. If your group represents more than one culture, explore the ways in which each person's cultural background may have influenced his or her individual decisions.

3. Report your rankings to the class, and discuss the areas of difference that emerged within your group while you were trying to reach concensus. Consider the following questions:

(a) Was your group able to explore openly any culturally based biases that came up—for example, feelings about homosexuality, religion, personality traits, politics?

(b) Did you make any comments or observations that you feel would have been fully acceptable in your own culture but were not accepted by the group? Explain.

(c) If the answer to (b) was yes, how did the reaction of the group make you feel about your membership in it? How did you handle the situation?

(d) What implications do you believe these cultural differences would have in business dealings?

EXERCISE 36

Gone Fishing

Procedure

1. Read the story "The Fishing Trip," which follows.
2. Assume you are a member of the group in the story, and rank the items in order of importance under column A.
3. Form groups of four to six people and rank the items again, this time placing your group rankings under column B.
4. Receive the ranking information of an experienced sea captain and follow further direction from your instructor.

The Fishing Trip

It was the first week in August when four friends set out on an overnight fishing trip in the Gulf of Mexico. Everything went well the first day—the sea was calm, they caught fish, and later they camped out on a lovely little island. However, during the night a very strong wind pulled the anchor free and drove their boat ashore, and the pounding waves broke the propeller. Although there were oars in the boat, the motor was useless.

A quick review of the previous day's journey showed that the group was about 60 miles from the nearest inhabited land. The small deserted island they were on had a few scrub trees and bushes but no fresh water. They knew from their portable AM–FM radio that the weather would be hot and dry, with daytime temperatures expected to be over 100°F the rest of the week. They all were dressed in light clothing, but each had a windbreaker for the cool evenings. They agreed that whatever happened they would stick together.

Source: Exercise developed from Charles Wales and Robert States, "The Fishing Trip," under an Exxon Guided Design IMPACT Grant. Used with permission.

The families back on shore expected the group to return from their trip that evening and would surely report them missing when they did not show up. They realized, however, that it might take time for someone to find them because they had gone out further than anyone might have expected.

Whereas some members of the group were quite concerned about this predicament, there was no panic. To help keep the group calm, one member—Jim—suggested that, just to be safe, they inventory the food and equipment available to them. "It might be several days before we are safe," Jim said, "and I think we should prepare for that." Kate, Tom, and Ann agreed, and their effort produced the list of items that follows.

After the list was complete, Jim suggested that every person independently rank each item according to its importance to the survival of the group. They all agreed to do this.

Items Available

Each person has:	A	B
(a) One windbreaker.	___	___
(b) One poncho.	___	___
(c) One sleeping bag.	___	___
(d) One pair of sunglasses.	___	___
The boat contains:		
(e) A cooler with two bottles of soda per person and some ice.	___	___
(f) One large flashlight.	___	___
(g) One first-aid kit.	___	___
(h) Fishing equipment.	___	___
(i) Matches, rope, and a few tools.	___	___
(j) One compass mounted on the boat.	___	___
(k) Two rear-view mirrors that can be removed from the boat.	___	___
(l) One "official" navigational map of the Gulf area where they were.	___	___
(m) One salt shaker (full).	___	___
(n) One bottle of liquor.	___	___

EXERCISE 37

Force-Field Analysis

Procedure

1. Choose a situation in which you have high personal stakes (for example: how to get a better grade in course X; how to get a promotion; how to obtain a position).
2. Using a version of the Sample Force-Field Analysis Form below, apply the technique to your situation.
   (a) Describe the situation as it now exists.
   (b) Describe the situation as you would like it to be.
   (c) Identify those "driving forces"—the factors that are presently helping to move things in the desired direction.

(d) Identify those "restraining forces"—the factors that are presently holding things back from moving in the desired direction.

3. Try to be as specific as possible in terms of the above in relation to your situation. You should attempt to be exhaustive in your listing of these forces. List them all!

4. Now go back and classify the strength of each force as weak, medium, or strong. Do this for both the driving and the restraining forces.

5. A this point you should rank the forces regarding their ability to influence or control the situation.

6. In groups of three to four persons share your analyses. Discuss the usefulness and drawbacks to using this method for personal situations and its application to organizations.

7. Be prepared to share the results of your group's discussion with the rest of the class.

Sample Force-Field Analysis Form

Current Situation:	Situation as You Would Like It To Be:
Driving Forces: ⟶ ⟵ Restraining Forces:	

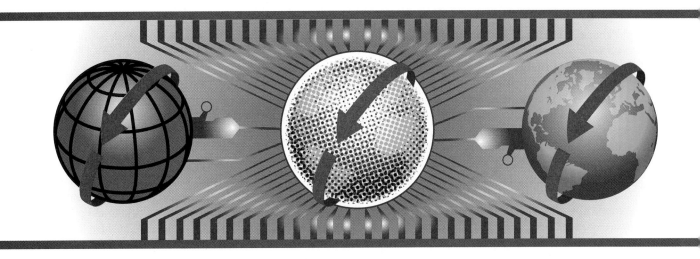

SELF-ASSESSMENT INVENTORIES

ASSESSMENT 1

A 21st-Century Manager

Instructions
Rate yourself on the following personal characteristics. Use this scale.

S	= Strong, I am very confident with this one.
G	= Good, but I still have room to grow.
W	= Weak, I really need work on this one.
?	= Unsure, I just don't know.

1. *Resistance to stress:* The ability to get work done even under stressful conditions.
2. *Tolerance for uncertainty:* The ability to get work done even under ambiguous and uncertain conditions.

Source: See *Outcome Management Project,* Phase I and Phase II Reports (St. Louis: American Assembly of Collegiate Schools of Business, 1986 & 1987).

3. *Social objectivity:* The ability to act free of racial, ethnic, gender, and other prejudices or biases.
4. *Inner work standards:* The ability to personally set and work to high-performance standards.
5. *Stamina:* The ability to sustain long work hours.
6. *Adaptability:* The ability to be flexible and adapt to changes.
7. *Self-confidence:* The ability to be consistently decisive and display one's personal presence.
8. *Self-objectivity:* The ability to evaluate personal strengths and weaknesses and to understand one's motives and skills relative to a job.
9. *Introspection:* The ability to learn from experience, awareness, and self-study.
10. *Entrepreneurism:* The ability to address problems and take advantage of opportunities for constructive change.

Scoring

Giving yourself 1 point for each S, and 1/2 point for each G. Do not give yourself points for W and ? responses. Total your points and enter the result here [PMF = _____].

Interpretation

This assessment offers a self-described *profile of your management foundations* (PMF). Are you a perfect 10, or is your PMF score something less than that? There shouldn't be too many 10s around. Ask someone who knows you to assess you on this instrument. You may be surprised at the differences between your PMF score as self-described and your PMF score as described by someone else. Most of us, realistically speaking, must work hard to grow and develop continually in these and related management foundations. This list is a good starting point as you consider where and how to further pursue the development of your managerial skills and competencies. The items on the list are recommended by the American Assembly of Collegiate Schools of Business (ΛΛCSB) as skills and personal characteristics that should be nurtured in college and university students of business administration. Their success—and yours—as 21st-century managers may well rest on (1) an initial awareness of the importance of these basic management foundations and (2) a willingness to strive continually to strengthen them throughout your work career.

Turbulence Tolerance Test

Instructions

The following statements were made by a 37-year-old manager in a large, successful corporation. How would you like to have a job with these characteristics? Using the following scale, write your response to the left of each statement.

> 4 = I would enjoy this very much; it's completely acceptable.
>
> 3 = This would be enjoyable and acceptable most of the time.
>
> 2 = I'd have no reaction to this feature one way or another, or it would be about equally enjoyable and unpleasant.
>
> 1 = This feature would be somewhat unpleasant for me.
>
> 0 = This feature would be very unpleasant for me.

_____ 1. I regularly spend 30 to 40 percent of my time in meetings.
_____ 2. Eighteen months ago my job did not exist, and I have been essentially inventing it as I go along.

Source: Peter B. Vail, *Managing as a Performance Art: New Ideas for a World of Chaotic Change* (San Francisco: Jossey-Bass, 1989), pp. 8–9. Used by permission.

_____ 3. The responsibilities I either assume or am assigned consistently exceed the authority I have for discharging them.

_____ 4. At any given moment in my job, I have on the average about a dozen phone calls to be returned.

_____ 5. There seems to be very little relation in my job between the quality of my performance and my actual pay and fringe benefits.

_____ 6. About 2 weeks a year of formal management training is needed in my job just to stay current.

_____ 7. Because we have very effective equal employment opportunity (EEO) in my company and because it is thoroughly multinational, my job consistently brings me into close working contact at a professional level with people of many races, ethnic groups and nationalities, and of both sexes.

_____ 8. There is no objective way to measure my effectiveness.

_____ 9. I report to three different bosses for different aspects of my job, and each has an equal say in my performance appraisal.

_____ 10. On average about a third of my time is spent dealing with unexpected emergencies that force all scheduled work to be postponed.

_____ 11. When I have to have a meeting of the people who report to me, it takes my secretary most of a day to find a time when we are all available, and even then, I have yet to have a meeting where everyone is present for the entire meeting.

_____ 12. The college degree I earned in preparation for this type of work is now obsolete, and I probably should go back for another degree.

_____ 13. My job requires that I absorb 100–200 pages of technical materials per week.

_____ 14. I am out of town overnight at least 1 night per week.

_____ 15. My department is so interdependent with several other departments in the company that all distinctions about which departments are responsible for which tasks are quite arbitrary.

_____ 16. In about a year I will probably get a promotion to a job in another division that has most of these same characteristics.

_____ 17. During the period of my employment here, either the entire company or the division I worked in has been reorganized every year or so.

_____ 18. While there are several possible promotions I can see ahead of me, I have no real career path in an objective sense.

_____ 19. While there are several possible promotions I can see ahead of me, I think I have no realistic chance of getting to the top levels of the company.

_____ 20. While I have many ideas about how to make things work better, I have no direct influence on either the business policies or the personnel policies that govern my division.

_____ 21. My company has recently put in an "assessment center" where I and all other managers will be required to go through an extensive battery of psychological tests to assess our potential.

_____ 22. My company is a defendant in an antitrust suit, and if the case comes to trial, I will probably have to testify about some decisions that were made a few years ago.

_____ 23. Advanced computer and other electronic office technology is continually being introduced into my division, necessitating constant learning on my part.

_____ 24. The computer terminal and screen I have in my office can be monitored in my bosses' offices without my knowledge.

Scoring

Total your responses and divide the sum by 24; enter the score here [TTT = _____].

Interpretation

This instrument gives an impression of your tolerance for managing in turbulent times—something likely to characterize the world of work well into the next century. In general, the higher your TTT score, the more comfortable you seem to be with turbulence and change—a positive sign. For comparison purposes, the average scores for some 500 MBA students and young managers was 1.5–1.6. The test's author suggests the TTT scores may be interpreted much like a grade point average in which 4.0 is a perfect A. On this basis, a 1.5 is below a C! How did you do?

• • • • • ASSESSMENT 3 •

Global Work Orientation

Instructions

Complete the following questionnaire

Are you prone to:	Definitely No				Definitely Yes
1. Impatience? Do you think "Time is money" or "Let's get straight to the point"?	1	2	3	4	5
2. Having a short attention span, bad listening habits, or being uncomfortable with silence?	1	2	3	4	5
3. Being somewhat argumentative, sometimes to the point of belligerence?	1	2	3	4	5
4. Ignorance about the world beyond your borders?	1	2	3	4	5
5. Weakness in foreign languages?	1	2	3	4	5
6. Placing emphasis on short-term success?	1	2	3	4	5
7. Believing that advance preparations are less important than negotiations themselves?	1	2	3	4	5
8. Being legalistic? Of believing "A deal is a deal," regardless of changing circumstances?	1	2	3	4	5
9. Having little interest in seminars on the subject of globalization, failing to browse through libraries or magazines on international topics, not interacting with foreign students or employees?	1	2	3	4	5

Scoring & Interpretation

Total your scores. A total of 27 or less suggests that you may have the temperament and foundations for success in global work. Anything less shows where personal development may be needed to prepare you for global career challenges.

Source: Reprinted by permission of the publisher from Cynthia Barmun and Natasha Wolninsky, "Why Americans Fail at Overseas Negotiations," *Management Review* (October 1989), 55–57, © 1989 American Management Association, New York. All rights reserved.

Personal Values

Instructions

Below are 16 items. Rate how important each one is to you on a scale of 0 (not important) to 100 (very important). Write the numbers 0–100 on the line to the left of each item.

Not important				Somewhat important				Very important		
0	10	20	30	40	50	60	70	80	90	100

____ 1. An enjoyable, satisfying job.
____ 2. A high-paying job.
____ 3. A good marriage.
____ 4. Meeting new people; social events.
____ 5. Involvement in community activities.
____ 6. My religion.
____ 7. Exercising, playing sports.
____ 8. Intellectual development.
____ 9. A career with challenging opportunities.
____ 10. Nice cars, clothes, home, etc.
____ 11. Spending time with family.
____ 12. Having several close friends.
____ 13. Volunteer work for not-for-profit organizations, such as the cancer society.
____ 14. Meditation, quiet time to think, pray, etc.
____ 15. A healthy, balanced diet.
____ 16. Educational reading, TV, self-improvement programs, etc.

Scoring

Transfer the numbers for each of the 16 items to the appropriate column below, then add the two numbers in each column.

	Professional	Financial	Family	Social
	1. ____	2. ____	3. ____	4. ____
	9. ____	10. ____	11. ____	12. ____
Totals	____	____	____	____

	Community	Spiritual	Physical	Intellectual
	5. ____	6. ____	7. ____	8. ____
	13. ____	14. ____	15. ____	16. ____
Totals	____	____	____	____

Interpretation

The higher the total in any area, the higher the value you place on that particular area. The closer the numbers are in all eight areas, the more well-rounded you are. Think about the time and effort you put forth in your top three values. Is it sufficient to allow you to achieve the level of success you want in each area? If not, what can you do to change? Is there any area in which you feel you should have a higher value total? If yes, which, and what can you do to change?

Source: Robert N. Lussier, *Human Relations in Organziations,* 2nd ed. (Homewood, IL.: Richard D. Irwin, 1993). By permission.

Managerial Assumptions

Instructions

Read the following statements. Use the space to the left to write "Yes" if you agree with the statement, or "No" if you disagree with it. Force yourself to take a "yes" or "no" position for every statement.

1. Are good pay and a secure job enough to satisfy most workers?
2. Should a manager help and coach subordinates in their work?
3. Do most people like real responsibility in their jobs?
4. Are most people afraid to learn new things in their jobs?
5. Should managers let subordinates control the quality of their work?
6. Do most people dislike work?
7. Are most people creative?
8. Should a manager closely supervise and direct work of subordinates?
9. Do most people tend to resist change?
10. Do most people work only as hard as they have to?

_____

Source: Schermerhorn, John R. Jr., *Management,* 5th ed. p. 51 (New York, Wiley, 1996). By permission.

11. Should workers be allowed to set their own job goals?
12. Are most people happiest off the job?
13. Do most workers really care about the organization they work for?
14. Should a manager help subordinates advance and grow in their jobs?

Scoring

Count the number of "yes" responses to items 1, 4, 6, 8, 9, 10, 12; write that number here as [X = ____]. Count the number of "yes" responses to items 2, 3, 5, 7, 11, 13, 14; write that score here [Y = ____].

Interpretation

This assessment sheds insight into your orientation toward Douglas McGregor's Theory X (your "X" score) and Theory Y (your "Y" score) assumptions. You should review the discussion of McGregor's thinking in Chapter 1 and consider further the ways in which you are likely to behave toward other people at work. Think, in particular, about the types of "self-fulfilling prophecies" you are likely to create.

Intolerance for Ambiguity

Instructions

To determine your level of tolerance (intolerance) for ambiguity, respond to the following items. PLEASE RATE EVERY ITEM; DO NOT LEAVE ANY ITEM BLANK. Rate each item on the following seven-point scale:

1	2	3	4	5	6	7
strongly disagree	moderately disagree	slightly disagree		slightly agree	moderately agree	strongly agree

Rating

____ 1. An expert who doesn't come up with a definite answer probably doesn't know too much.
____ 2. There is really no such thing as a problem that can't be solved.
____ 3. I would like to live in a foreign country for a while.

_____

Source: Based on Budner, S. (1962), "Intolerance of Ambiguity as a Personality Variable," *Journal of Personality,* Vol. 30, No. 1, pp. 29–50.

_____ 4. People who fit their lives to a schedule probably miss the joy of living.

_____ 5. A good job is one where what is to be done and how it is to be done is always clear.

_____ 6. In the long run it is possible to get more done by tackling small, simple problems rather than large, complicated ones.

_____ 7. It is more fun to tackle a complicated problem than it is to solve a simple one.

_____ 8. Often the most interesting and stimulating people are those who don't mind being different and original.

_____ 9. What we are used to is always preferable to what is unfamiliar.

_____ 10. A person who leads an even, regular life in which few surprises or unexpected happenings arise really has a lot to be grateful for.

_____ 11. People who insist upon a yes or no answer just don't know how complicated things really are.

_____ 12. Many of our most important decisions are based on insufficient information.

_____ 13. I like parties where I know most of the people more than ones where most of the people are complete strangers.

_____ 14. The sooner we all acquire ideals, the better.

_____ 15. Teachers or supervisors who hand out vague assignments give a chance for one to show initiative and originality.

_____ 16. A good teacher is one who makes you wonder about your way of looking at things.

_____ Total

Scoring

The scale was developed by S. Budner. Budner reports test–retest correlations of .85 with a variety of samples (mostly students and health care workers). Data, however, are more than 30 years old, so mean shifts may have occurred. Maximum ranges are 16–112, and score ranges were from 25 to 79, with a grand mean of approximately 49.

The test was designed to measure several different components of possible reactions to perceived threat in situations that are new, complex, or insoluble. Half of the items have been reversed.

To obtain a score, first *reverse* the scale score for the eight "reverse" items, 3, 4, 7, 8, 11, 12, 15, and 16 (i.e., a rating of 1 = 7, 2 = 6, 3 = 5, etc.). Then add up the rating scores for all 16 items.

Interpretation

Empirically, low tolerance for ambiguity (high intolerance) has been positively correlated with:

- Conventionality of religious beliefs
- High attendance at religious services
- More intense religious beliefs
- More positive views of censorship
- Higher authoritarianism
- Lower Machiavellianism

The application of this concept to management in the 1990s is clear and relatively self-evident. The world of work, and many organizations, are full of ambiguity and change. Individuals with a *higher* tolerance for ambiguity are far more likely to be able to function effectively in organizations and contexts in which there is a high turbulence, a high rate of change, and less certainty about expectations, performance standards, what needs to be done, etc. In contrast, individuals with a lower tolerance for ambiguity are far more likely to be unable to adapt or adjust quickly in turbulence, uncertainty, and change. These individuals are likely to become rigid, angry, stressed, and frustrated when there is a high level of uncertainty and ambiguity in the environment. High levels of tolerance for ambiguity, therefore, are associated with an ability to "roll with the punches" as organizations, environmental conditions, and demands change rapidly.

Motivators or Hygienes

Instructions

Most workers want job satisfaction. Below are 12 job factors that may contribute to job satisfaction. Rate each according to how important it is to you. Place a number on a scale of 1 to 5 on the line before each factor.

Very Important		Somewhat Important		Not Important
5	4	3	2	1

_____ 1. An interesting job
_____ 2. A good boss
_____ 3. Recognition and appreciation for the work I do
_____ 4. The opportunity for advancement
_____ 5. A satisfying personal life
_____ 6. A prestigious or status job
_____ 7. Job responsibility
_____ 8. Good working conditions (nice office)
_____ 9. Sensible company rules, regulations, procedures, and policies
_____ 10. The opportunity to grow through learning new things
_____ 11. A job I can do well and succeed at
_____ 12. Job security

Scoring

To determine if hygienes or motivators are important to you, place the numbers 1–5 that represent your answers below.

Hygiene Factors Score	Motivational Factors Score
2. _____	1. _____
5. _____	3. _____
6. _____	4. _____
8. _____	7. _____
9. _____	10. _____
12. _____	11. _____
Total points _____	Total points _____

Source: Robert N. Lussier, _Human Relations in Organziations,_ 2nd ed. (Homewood, IL.: Richard D. Irwin, 1993). By permission.

Are You Cosmopolitan?

Instructions

Answer the questions below using a scale of 1 to 5: 1 representing "strongly disagree"; 2, "somewhat disagree"; 3, "neutral"; 4, "somewhat agree"; and 5, "strongly agree."

____ 1. You believe it is the right of the professional to make his or her own decisions about what is to be done on the job.

____ 2. You believe a professional should stay in an individual staff role regardless of the income sacrifice.

____ 3. You have no interest in moving up to a top administrative post.

____ 4. You believe that professionals are better evaluated by professional colleagues than by management.

____ 5. Your friends tend to be members of your profession.

____ 6. You would rather be known or get credit for your work outside rather than inside the company.

____ 7. You would feel better making a contribution to society than to your organization.

____ 8. Managers have no right to place time and cost schedules on professional contributors.

Scoring and Interpretation

A "cosmopolitan" identifies with the career profession, and a "local" identifies with the employing organization. Total your scores. A score of 30–40 suggests a cosmopolitan work orientation, of 10–20 a "local" orientation, and 20–30 a mixed orientation.

Source: Developed from Joseph A. Raelin, *The Clash of Cultures, Managers and Professionals* (Harvard Business School Press, 1986).

Group Effectiveness

Instructions

For this assessment, select a specific group you work with or have worked with; it can be a college or work group. For each of the eight statements below, select how often each statement describes the group's behavior. Place the number 1, 2, 3, or 4 on the line next to each of the 8 numbers.

Usually	Frequently	Occasionally	Seldom
1	2	3	4

____ 1. The members are loyal to one another and to the group leader.

____ 2. The members and leader have a high degree of confidence and trust in each other.

____ 3. Group values and goals express relevant values and needs of members.

____ 4. Activities of the group occur in a supportive atmosphere.

____ 5. The group is eager to help members develop to their full potential.

____ 6. The group knows the value of constructive conformity and knows when to use it and for what purpose.

____ 7. The members communicate all information relevant to the group's activity fully and frankly.

____ 8. The members feel secure in making decisions that seem appropriate to them.

Scoring

____ Total. Add up the eight numbers and place an X on the continuum below that represents the score.

Effective group   8 . . . 16 . . . 24 . . . 32   Ineffective group

Interpretation

The lower the score, the more effective the group. What can you do to help the group become more effective? What can the group do to become more effective?

Organizational Design Preference

Instructions

To the left of each item, write the number from the following scale that shows the extent to which the statement accurately describes your views.

> 5 = strongly agree
>
> 4 = agree somewhat
>
> 3 = undecided
>
> 2 = disagree somewhat
>
> 1 = strongly disagree

I prefer to work in an organization where:

1. Goals are defined by those in higher levels.
2. Work methods and procedures are specified.
3. Top management makes important decisions.
4. My loyalty counts as much as my ability to do the job.
5. Clear lines of authority and responsibility are established.
6. Top management is decisive and firm.
7. My career is pretty well planned out for me.
8. I can specialize.
9. My length of service is almost as important as my level of performance.

10. Management is able to provide the information I need to do my job well.
11. A chain of command is well established.
12. Rules and procedures are adhered to equally by everyone.
13. People accept authority of a leader's position.
14. People are loyal to their boss.
15. People do as they have been instructed.
16. People clear things with their boss before going over his or her head.

Scoring

Total your scores for all questions. Enter the score here [____].

Interpretation

This assessment measures your preference for working in an organization designed along "organic" or "mechanistic" lines. The higher your score (above 64), the more comfortable you are with a mechanistic design; the lower your score (below 48), the more comfortable you are with an organic design. Scores between 48 and 64 can go either way. This organizational design preference represents an important issue in the new workplace. Indications are that today's organizations are taking on more and more organic characteristics. Presumably, those of us who work in them will need to be comfortable with such designs.

Source: John F. Veiga and John N. Yanouzas, *The Dynamics of Organization Theory: Gaining a Macro Perspective* (St. Paul, MN: West, 1979), pp. 158–160. Used by permission.

Which Culture Fits You?

Instructions

Check one of the following organization "cultures" in which you feel most comfortable working.

1. A culture that values talent, entrepreneurial activity, and performance over commitment; one that offers large financial rewards and individual recognition.
2. A culture that stresses loyalty, working for the good of the group, and getting to know the right people; one that believes in "generalists" and step-by-step career progress.
3. A culture that offers little job security; one that operates with a survival mentality, stresses that every individual can make a difference, and focuses attention on "turnaround" opportunities.
4. A culture that values long-term relationships; one that emphasizes systematic career development, regular

Source: Developed from Carol Hymowitz, "Which Corporate Culture Fits You?" *The Wall Street Journal* (July 17, 1989), p. B1.

training, and advancement based on gaining of functional expertise.

Scoring

These labels identify the four different cultures: 1 = "the baseball team," 2 = "the club," 3 = "the fortress," and 4 = "the academy."

Interpretation

To some extent, your future career success may depend on working for an organziation in which there is a good fit between you and the prevailing corporate culture. This assessment can help you learn how to recognize various cultures, evaluate how well they can serve your needs, and recognize how they may change with time. A risk taker, for example, may be out of place in a "club" but fit right in with a "baseball team." Someone who wants to seek opportunities wherever they may occur may be out of place in an "academy" but fit right in with a "fortress."

Empowering Others

Instructions

Think of times when you have been in charge of a group—this could be a full-time or part-time work situation, a student work group, or whatever. Complete the following questionnaire by recording how you feel about each statement according to this scale.

> 1 = Strongly disagree
> 2 = Disagree
> 3 = Neutral
> 4 = Agree
> 5 = Strongly agree

Source: Questionnaire adapted from L. Steinmetz and R. Todd, *First Line Management,* Fourth Edition (Homewood, IL: BPI/Irwin, 1986), pp. 64–67. Used by permission.

When in charge of a group I find:

_____ 1. Most of the time other people are too inexperienced to do things, so I prefer to do them myself.

_____ 2. It often takes more time to explain things to others than just to do them myself.

_____ 3. Mistakes made by others are costly, so I don't assign much work to them.

_____ 4. Some things simply should not be delegated to others.

_____ 5. I often get quicker action by doing a job myself.

_____ 6. Many people are good only at very specific tasks, and thus can't be assigned additional responsibilities.

_____ 7. Many people are too busy to take on additional work.

_____ 8. Most people just aren't ready to handle additional responsibilities.

_____ 9. In my position, I should be entitled to make my own decisions.

Scoring

Total your responses; enter the score here [_____].

Interpretation

This instrument gives an impression of your *willingness to delegate*. Possible scores range from 9 to 45. The lower your score, the more willing you appear to be to delegate to others. Willingness to delegate is an important managerial characteristic. It is essential if you—as a manager—are to "empower" others and give them opportunities to assume responsibility and exercise self-control in their work. With the growing importance of empowerment in the new workplace, your willingness to delegate is well worth thinking about seriously.

ASSESSMENT 13

Machiavellianism

Instructions

For each of the following statements, circle the number that most closely resembles your attitude.

Statement	Disagree A Lot	A Little	Neutral	Agree A Little	A Lot
1. The best way to handle people is to tell them what they want to hear.	1	2	3	4	5
2. When you ask someone to do something for you, it is best to give the real reason for wanting it rather than reasons that might carry more weight.	1	2	3	4	5
3. Anyone who completely trusts someone else is asking for trouble.	1	2	3	4	5
4. It is hard to get ahead without cutting corners here and there.	1	2	3	4	5
5. It is safest to assume that all people have a vicious streak, and it will come out when they are given a chance.	1	2	3	4	5
6. One should take action only when it is morally right.	1	2	3	4	5
7. Most people are basically good and kind.	1	2	3	4	5
8. There is no excuse for lying to someone else.	1	2	3	4	5
9. Most people forget more easily the death of their father than the loss of their property.	1	2	3	4	5
10. Generally speaking, people won't work hard unless forced to do so.	1	2	3	4	5

Source: From R. Christie and F. L. Geis, *Studies in Machiavellianism* (New York: Academic Press, 1970). By permission.

Scoring and Interpretation

This assessment is designed to compute your Machiavellianism (Mach) score. Mach is a personality characteristic that taps people's power orientation. The high-Mach personality is pragmatic, maintains emotional distance from others, and believes that ends can justify means. To obtain your Mach score, add up the numbers you checked for questions 1, 3, 4, 5, 9, and 10. For the other four questions, reverse the numbers you have checked, so that 5 becomes 1; 4 is 2; and 1 is 5. Then total both sets of numbers to find your score. A random sample of adults found the national average to be 25. Students in business and management typically score higher.

The results of research using the Mach test have found: (1) men are generally more Machiavellian than women; (2) older adults tend to have lower Mach scores than younger adults; (3) there is no significant difference between high Machs and low Machs on measures of intelligence or ability; (4) Machiavellianism is not significantly related to demographic characteristics such as educational level or marital status; and (5) high Machs tend to be in professions that emphasize the control and manipulation of people—for example, managers, lawyers, psychiatrists, and behavioral scientists.

ASSESSMENT 14

Personal Power Profile

Contributed by J. Marcus Maier, Chapman University

Instructions

Below is a list of statements that may be used in describing behaviors that supervisors (leaders) in work organizations can direct toward their subordinates (followers). First, carefully read each descriptive statement, thinking in terms of *how you prefer to influence others.* Mark the number that most closely represents how you feel. Use the following numbers for your answers.

> 5 = Strongly agree
>
> 4 = Agree
>
> 3 = Neither agree nor disagree
>
> 2 = Disagree
>
> 1 = Strongly disagree

Source: Modified version of T. R. Hinken and C. A. Schriesheim, "Development and Application of New Scales to Measure the French and Raven (1959) Bases of Social Power." *Journal of Applied Psychology,* Vol. 74, 1989, 561–567.

To influence others, I would prefer to:	Strongly Disagree	Disagree	Neither Agree nor Disagree	Agree	Strongly Agree
1. Increase their pay level	1	2	3	4	5
2. Make them feel valued	1	2	3	4	5
3. Give undesirable job assignments	1	2	3	4	5
4. Make them feel like I approve of them	1	2	3	4	5
5. Make them feel that they have commitments to meet	1	2	3	4	5
6. Make them feel personally accepted	1	2	3	4	5
7. Make them feel important	1	2	3	4	5
8. Give them good technical suggestions	1	2	3	4	5
9. Make the work difficult for them	1	2	3	4	5
10. Share my experience and/or training	1	2	3	4	5
11. Make things unpleasant here	1	2	3	4	5
12. Make being at work distasteful	1	2	3	4	5
13. Influence their getting a pay increase	1	2	3	4	5
14. Make them feel like they should satisfy their job requirements	1	2	3	4	5
15. Provide them with sound job-related advice	1	2	3	4	5
16. Provide them with special benefits	1	2	3	4	5
17. Influence their getting a promotion	1	2	3	4	5
18. Give them the feeling that they have responsibilities to fulfill	1	2	3	4	5
19. Provide them with needed technical knowledge	1	2	3	4	5
20. Make them recognize that they have tasks to accomplish	1	2	3	4	5

Scoring

Using the grid below, insert your scores from the 20 questions and proceed as follows: *Reward power*—sum your response to items 1, 13, 16, and 17 and divide by 4. *Coercive power*—sum your response to items 3, 9, 11, and 12 and divide by 4. *Legitimate power*—sum your response to questions 5, 14, 18, and 20 and divide by 4. *Referent power*—sum your response to questions 2, 4, 6, and 7 and divide by 4. *Expert power*—sum your response to questions 8, 10, 15, and 19 and divide by 4.

Reward	Coercive	Legitimate	Referent	Expert
1 ____	3 ____	5 ____	2 ____	8 ____
13 ____	9 ____	14 ____	4 ____	10 ____
16 ____	11 ____	18 ____	6 ____	15 ____
17 ____	12 ____	20 ____	7 ____	19 ____
Total ____	____	____	____	____
Divide by 4 ____	____	____	____	____

Interpretation

A high score (4 and greater) on any of the five dimensions of power implies that you prefer to influence others by employing that particular form of power. A low score (2 or less) implies that you prefer not to employ this particular form of power to influence others. This represents your power profile. Your overall power position is not reflected by the simple sum of the power derived from each of the five sources. Instead, some combinations of power are synergistic in nature—they are greater than the simple sum of their parts. For example, referent power tends to magnify the impact of other power sources because these other influence attempts are coming from a "respected" person. Reward power often increases the impact of referent power, because people generally tend to like those who give them things that they desire. Some power combinations tend to produce the opposite of synergistic effects, such that the total is less than the sum of the parts. Power dilution frequently accompanies the use of (or threatened use of) coercive power.

Least Preferred Coworker Scale

Instructions

Think of all the different people with whom you have ever worked—in jobs, in social clubs, in student projects, or whatever. Next think of the *one person* with whom you could work *least* well—that is, the person with whom you had the most difficulty getting a job done. This is the one person—a peer, boss, or subordinate—with whom you would least want to work. Describe this person by circling numbers at the appropriate points on each of the following pairs of bipolar adjectives. Work rapidly. There are no right or wrong answers.

Pleasant	8 7 6 5 4 3 2 1	Unpleasant
Friendly	8 7 6 5 4 3 2 1	Unfriendly
Rejecting	1 2 3 4 5 6 7 8	Accepting
Tense	1 2 3 4 5 6 7 8	Relaxed
Distant	1 2 3 4 5 6 7 8	Close
Cold	1 2 3 4 5 6 7 8	Warm
Supportive	8 7 6 5 4 3 2 1	Hostile
Boring	1 2 3 4 5 6 7 8	Interesting
Quarrelsome	1 2 3 4 5 6 7 8	Harmonious
Gloomy	1 2 3 4 5 6 7 8	Cheerful
Open	8 7 6 5 4 3 2 1	Guarded
Backbiting	1 2 3 4 5 6 7 8	Loyal
Untrustworthy	1 2 3 4 5 6 7 8	Trustworthy
Considerate	8 7 6 5 4 3 2 1	Inconsiderate
Nasty	1 2 3 4 5 6 7 8	Nice
Agreeable	8 7 6 5 4 3 2 1	Disagreeable
Insincere	1 2 3 4 5 6 7 8	Sincere
Kind	8 7 6 5 4 3 2 1	Unkind

Scoring

This is called the "least preferred coworker scale" (LPC). Compute your LPC score by totaling all the numbers you circled; enter that score here [LPC = ____].

Interpretation

The LPC scale is used by Fred Fiedler to identify a person's dominant leadership style. Fiedler believes that this style is a relatively fixed part of one's personality and is therefore difficult to change. This leads Fiedler to his contingency views, which suggest that the key to leadership success is finding (or creating) good "matches" between style and situation. If your score is 73 or above, Fiedler considers you a "relationship-motivated" leader; if your score is 64 and below, he considers you a "task-motivated" leader. If your score is between 65 and 72, Fiedler leaves it up to you to determine which leadership style is most like yours.

Source: Fred E. Fiedler and Martin M. Chemers. *Improving Leadership Effectiveness: The Leader Match Concept,* ed. 2 (New York: John Wiley & Sons, 1984). Used by permission.

Leadership Style

Instructions

The following statements describe leadership acts. Indicate the way you would most likely act if you were leader of a work group, by circling whether you would most likely behave in this way:

> always (A); frequently (F); occasionally (O); seldom (S); or never (N)

A F O S N	1. Act as group spokesperson.
A F O S N	2. Encourage overtime work.
A F O S N	3. Allow members complete freedom in their work.
A F O S N	4. Encourage the use of uniform procedures.
A F O S N	5. Permit members to solve their own problems.
A F O S N	6. Stress being ahead of competing groups.
A F O S N	7. Speak as a representative of the group.
A F O S N	8. Push members for greater effort.
A F O S N	9. Try out ideas in the group.
A F O S N	10. Let the members work the way they think best.
A F O S N	11. Work hard for a personal promotion.
A F O S N	12. Tolerate postponement and uncertainty.
A F O S N	13. Speak for the group when visitors are present.
A F O S N	14. Keep the work moving at a rapid pace.
A F O S N	15. Turn members loose on a job.
A F O S N	16. Settle conficts in the group.
A F O S N	17. Focus on work details.
A F O S N	18. Represent the group at outside meetings.
A F O S N	19. Avoid giving the members too much freedom.
A F O S N	20. Decide what should be done and how it should be done.
A F O S N	21. Push for increased production.
A F O S N	22. Give some members authority to act.
A F O S N	23. Expect things to turn out as predicted.
A F O S N	24. Allow the group to take the initiative.
A F O S N	25. Assign group members to particular tasks.
A F O S N	26. Be willing to make changes.
A F O S N	27. Ask members to work harder.
A F O S N	28. Trust members to exercise good judgement.
A F O S N	29. Schedule the work to be done.
A F O S N	30. Refuse to explain my actions.
A F O S N	31. Persuade others that my ideas are best.
A F O S N	32. Permit the group to set its own pace.
A F O S N	33. Urge the group to beat its previous record.
A F O S N	34. Act without consulting the group.
A F O S N	35. Ask members to follow standard rules.

T _____   P _____

Scoring

1. Circle items 8, 12, 17, 18, 19, 30, 34 and 35.
2. Write the number 1 in front of a *circled item number* if you responded S (seldom) or N (never) to that item.

3. Write a number 1 in front of *item numbers not circled* if you responded A (always) or F (frequently).
4. Circle the number 1's which you have written in front of items 3, 5, 8, 10, 15, 18, 19, 22, 24, 26, 28, 30, 32, 34, and 35.
5. *Count the circled number 1's.* This is your score for leadership *concern for people*. Record the score in the blank following the letter P at the end of the questionnaire.
6. *Count the uncircled number 1's.* This is your score for leadership *concern for task*. Record this number in the blank following the letter T.

● ● ● ● ● ● ASSESSMENT 17 ●

"TT" Leadership Style

Instructions

For each of the following 10 pairs of statements, divide 5 points between the two according to your beliefs, perceptions of yourself, or according to which of the two statements characterizes you better. The 5 points may be divided between the a and b statements in any one of the following ways: 5 for a, 0 for b; 4 for a, 1 for b; 3 for a, 2 for b; 1 for a, 4 for b; 0 for a, 5 for b, but not equally (2 ½) between the two. Weigh your choices between the two according to the one that characterizes you or your beliefs better.

1. (a) As leader I have a primary mission of maintaining stability.
   (b) As leader I have a primary mission of change.
2. (a) As leader I must cause events.
   (b) As leader I must facilitate events.
3. (a) I am concerned that my followers are rewarded equitably for their work.
   (b) I am concerned about what my followers want in life.
4. (a) My preference is to think long range: what might be.
   (b) My preference is to think short range: what is realistic.
5. (a) As a leader I spend considerable energy in managing separate but related goals.
   (b) As a leader I spend considerable energy in arousing hopes, expectations, and aspirations among my followers.
6. (a) Although not in a formal classroom sense, I believe that a significant part of my leadership is that of teacher.
   (b) I believe that a signifant part of my leadership is that of facilitator.
7. (a) As leader I must engage with followers at an equal level of morality.
   (b) As leader I must represent a higher morality.
8. (a) I enjoy stimulating followers to want to do more.
   (b) I enjoy rewarding followers for a job well done.
9. (a) Leadership should be practical.
   (b) Leadership should be inspirational.
10. (a) What power I have to influence others comes primarily from my ability to get people to identify with me and my ideas.
    (b) What power I have to influence others comes primarily from my status and position.

Scoring

Circle your points for items 1b, 2a, 3b, 4a, 5b, 6a, 7b, 8a, 9b, and 10a and add up the total points you allocated to these items; enter the score here [**T** = ____]. Next, add up the total points given to the uncircled items 1a, 2b, 3a, 4b, 5a, 6b, 7a, 8b, 9a, 10b; enter the score here [T = ____].

Interpretation

This instrument gives an impression of your tendencies toward "transformational" leadership (your **T** score) and "transactional" leadership (your T score). You may wnat to refer to the discussion of these concepts in Chapter 15. Today, a lot of attention is being given to the transformational aspects of leadership—those personal qualities that inspire a sense of vision and desire for extraordinary accomplishment in followers. The most successful leaders of the future will most likely be strong in both "T"s.

Source: Questionnaire by W. Warner Burke, Ph.D. Used by permission.

● THE ORGANIZATIONAL BEHAVIOR WORKBOOK **519**

Your Intuitive Ability

Instructions

Complete this survey as quickly as you can. Be honest with yourself. For each question, select the response that most appeals to you.

1. When working on a project, do you prefer to:
   (a) Be told what the problem is but be left free to decide how to solve it?
   (b) Get very clear instructions about how to go about solving the problem before you start?

2. When working on a project, do you prefer to work with colleagues who are:
   (a) Realistic?
   (b) Imaginative?

3. Do you most admire people who are:
   (a) Creative?
   (b) Careful?

4. Do the friends you choose tend to be:
   (a) Serious and hard working?
   (b) Exciting and often emotional?

5. When you ask a colleague for advice on a problem you have, do you:
   (a) Seldom or never get upset if he or she questions your basic assumptions?
   (b) Often get upset if he or she questions your basic assumptions?

6. When you start your day, do you:
   (a) Seldom make or follow a specific plan?
   (b) Usually first make a plan to follow?

7. When working with numbers do you find that you:
   (a) Seldom or never make factual errors?
   (b) Often make factual errors?

8. Do you find that you:
   (a) Seldom daydream during the day and really don't enjoy doing so when you do it?
   (b) Frequently daydream during the day and enjoy doing so?

9. When working on a problem, do you:
   (a) Prefer to follow the instructions or rules when they are given to you?

   (b) Often enjoy circumventing the instructions or rules when they are given to you?

10. When you are trying to put something together, do you prefer to have:
    (a) Step-by-step written instructions on how to assemble the item?
    (b) A picture of how the item is supposed to look once assembled?

11. Do you find that the person who irritates you *the most* is the one who appears to be:
    (a) Disorganized?
    (b) Organized?

12. When an expected crisis comes up that you have to deal with, do you:
    (a) Feel anxious about the situation?
    (b) Feel excited by the challenge of the situation?

Scoring

Total the number of "a" responses circled for questions 1, 3, 5, 6, 11; enter the score here [A = ____]. Total the number of "b" responses for questions 2, 4, 7, 8, 9, 10, 12; enter the score here [B = ____]. Add your "a" and "b" scores and enter the sum here [A + B = ____]. This is your *intuitive score*. The highest possible intuitive score is 12; the lowest is 0.

Interpretation

In his book *Intuition in Organizations* (Newbury Park, CA: Sage, 1989), pp. 10–11, Weston H. Agor states: "Traditional analytical techniques . . . are not as useful as they once were for guiding major decisions. . . . If you hope to be better prepared for tomorrow, then it only seems logical to pay some attention to the use and development of intuitive skills for decision making." Agor developed the prior survey to help people assess their tendencies to use intuition in decision making. Your score offers a general impression of your strength in this area. It may also suggest a need to further develop your skill and comfort with more intuitive decision approaches.

Source: AIM Survey (El Paso, TX: ENFP Enterprises, 1989). Copyright © 1989 by Weston H. Agor. Used by permission.

Conflict Management Styles

Instructions

Think of how you behave in conflict situations in which your wishes differ from those of one or more persons. In the space to the left of each statement below, write the number from the following scale that indicates how likely you are to respond that way in a conflict situation.

1 = very unlikely	2 = unlikely	3 = likely	4 = very likely

____ **1.** I am usually firm in pursuing my goals.

____ **2.** I try to win my position.

____ **3.** I give up some points in exchange for others.

____ **4.** I feel that differences are not always worth worrying about.

____ **5.** I try to find a position that is intermediate between the other person's and mine.

____ **6.** In approaching negotiations, I try to be considerate of the other person's wishes.

____ **7.** I try to show the logic and benefits of my positions.

____ **8.** I always lean toward a direct discussion of the problem.

____ **9.** I try to find a fair combination of gains and losses for both of us.

____ **10.** I attempt to work through our differences immediately.

____ **11.** I try to avoid creating unpleasantness for myself.

____ **12.** I try to soothe the other person's feelings and preserve our relationships.

____ **13.** I attempt to get all concerns and issues immediately out in the open.

____ **14.** I sometimes avoid taking positions that would create controversy.

____ **15.** I try not to hurt others' feelings.

Scoring

Total your scores for items 1, 2, 7; enter that score here [*Competing* = ____]. Total your scores for items 8, 10, 13; enter that score here [*Collaborating* = ____]. Total your scores for items 3, 5, 9; enter that score here [*Compromising* = ____]. Total your scores for items 4, 11, 14; enter that score here. [*Avoiding* = ____]. Total your scores for items 6, 12, 15; enter that score here [*Accommodating* = ____].

Interpretation

Each of the scores above corresponds to one of the conflict management styles discussed in Chapter 15. Research indicates that each style has a role to play in management but that the best overall conflict management approach is collaboration; only it can lead to problem solving and true conflict resolution. You should consider any patterns that may be evident in your scores and think about how to best handle conflict situations in which you become involved.

Source: Adapted from Thomas-Kilmann, *Conflict Mode Instrument,* Copyright © 1974, Xicom, Inc., Tuxedo, NY 10987. Used by permission.

Your Personality Type

Instructions

How true is each statement for you?

	Not True At All		Not True or Untrue		Very True
1. I hate giving up before I'm absolutely sure that I'm licked.	1	2	3	4	5
2. Sometimes I feel that I should not be working so hard, but something drives me on.	1	2	3	4	5
3. I thrive on challenging situations. The more challenges I have, the better.	1	2	3	4	5
4. In comparison to most people I know, I'm very involved in my work.	1	2	3	4	5
5. It seems as if I need 30 hours a day to finish all the things I'm faced with.	1	2	3	4	5
6. In general, I approach my work more seriously than most people I know.	1	2	3	4	5
7. I guess there are some people who can be nonchalant about their work, but I'm not one of them.	1	2	3	4	5
8. My achievements are considered to be significantly higher than those of most people I know.	1	2	3	4	5
9. I've often been asked to be an officer of some group or groups.	1	2	3	4	5

Scoring

Add all your scores to create a total score = ____.

Interpretation

Type A personalities (hurried and competitive) tend to score 36 and above. Type B personalities (relaxed) tend to score 22 and below. Scores of 23–35 indicate a balance or mix of Type A and Type B.

Source: From *Job Demands and Worker Health* (HEW Publication No. [NIOSH] 75–160), (Washington, DC: US Department of Health, Education and Welfare, 1975), pp. 253–54.

Stress Inventory

Procedure

1. Consider the events listed below, which you may have experienced during the past month or so and which you may feel to be emotionally unsettling. Then indicate your "Emotional Impact" score, using numbers from 1 to 10: 1 = little effect; 10 = significant effect. Place your score in Column A or Column B. You may divide the score for one event between the two columns, if appropriate. Score only events that you experienced; skip those which are not applicable to you.

2. Total your scores for each column and enter them on the appropriate lines. They highlight areas of your life that may act as ongoing sources of stress.

3. Form groups of two to three people and share any personal insights you have gained as a result of having completed the assessment.

4. Discuss the implications this information has for the future of such stressors in your life. What can you do to reduce the stress? To whom can you go for help? Be prepared to share your conclusions in an open class discussion.

Emotional Impact Assessment

Events beyond my power to change	Events within my power to change	
A	B	
_____	_____	(a) My course load or study requirements feel excessive.
_____	_____	(b) I find some instructors boring, or I feel inadequately challenged.
_____	_____	(c) I haven't enough quiet for study, or have too many distractions.
_____	_____	(d) My outside commitments conflict with school work.
_____	_____	(e) My class schedule creates problems.
_____	_____	(f) I feel too much peer or parent pressure.
_____	_____	(g) I question what value I get from going to school.
_____	_____	(h) My procrastination or cramming creates excessive pressure.
_____	_____	(i) I have continuing problems with one or more teachers or teaching assistants, or the administration.
_____	_____	(j) I am uncertain about my career objectives or future plans.
_____	_____	(k) I don't find school socially rewarding, or my standards and preferences conflict with other activities.
_____	_____	(l) I miss social support from a relationship, family, or roommate.
_____	_____	(m) I don't have adequate privacy.
_____	_____	(n) My budget is too tight.
_____	_____	(o) Transportation (e.g., parking, commuting, mobility) creates problems for me.
_____	_____	(p) I am concerned about security on or off campus.
_____	_____	(q) Getting the kind of food I prefer is a problem.
_____	_____	(r) I don't have easy access to my preferred forms of recreation.
_____	_____	(s) School facilities, such as the library, health care, or the computer center, are inadequate.
_____	_____	(t) I feel self-conscious about a personal problem (e.g., weight, complexion, social ease).
_____	_____	(u) other _____
_____	_____	(v) other _____
_____	_____	Totals

Source: Exercise created by Dorothy Hair, 1985. Used by permission.

ANSWERS TO SELF-TESTS

SELF-TEST 1 ANSWERS

▼ MULTIPLE CHOICE ▼ TRUE/FALSE

1. c	6. c	11. F	16. F
2. d	7. d	12. T	17. T
3. b	8. a	13. T	18. T
4. a	9. c	14. F	19. T
5. c	10. d	15. F	20. T

▼ SHORT RESPONSE

21. The term "valuing diversity" is used to describe behavior that respects individual differences. In the workplace this means respecting the talents and potential contributions of people from different races, and of different genders, ethnicities, and ages, for example. 22. An effective manager is one who is able to work with and support other people so that long-term high performance is achieved. This manager is able to create conditions for sustainable high performance by creating conditions for job satisfaction as well as high task performance. 23. Mintzberg would say that the executive would be very busy throughout the day and would work long hours. He would note that the day would be fragmented as the executive worked on many different tasks while subject to interruptions. He would point out that the day would be very communication intensive as the executive interacted with other people in a wide variety of scheduled and unscheduled meetings and through various telephone and other electronic media. 24. The treatment of an organization's workforce is part of workplace ethics and social responsibility. Although organizations today must be managed for performance success, they must also be managed to create a satisfied and capable workforce. As an indicator of the overall quality of human experience in the workplace, the quality of work life, or QWL, is an important organizational goal.

▼ APPLICATIONS ESSAY

25. The upside-down pyramid view of organizations puts customers at the top. This means that Petra and all of her employees must dedicate themselves to serving the store's customers in the best possible ways. The salespersons are the people who most immediately serve customer needs. They must be supported in these efforts by helpful assistant managers who coach and assist them in meeting customer needs all the time. The department heads and salespersons, in turn, must be supported by Petra as the owner–manager. She must always coach and assist them and work to keep the store's commitment to customer service foremost in their minds. In this sense, although Petra is the top manager, she stands at the bottom of the pyramid, supporting the efforts of everyone else in serving her customers.

SELF-TEST 2 ANSWERS

▼ MULTIPLE CHOICE ▼ TRUE/FALSE

1. c	6. c	11. F	16. T
2. b	7. a	12. F	17. T
3. d	8. b	13. F	18. F
4. a	9. c	14. T	19. F
5. c	10. a	15. T	20. T

▼ SHORT RESPONSE

21. OB is defined as the study of individuals and groups in organizations. The dimension of individualism–collectivism

reflects different cultural emphases on them and it appears in both the Hofstede and Trompenaars frameworks. As pointed out by Hofstede, for example, individualistic cultures tend to emphasize individual reward systems, whereas collectivist cultures emphasize teamwork. OB should help us become more aware of how cultural difference may affect the management of individuals and groups in various settings. 22. In high–power distance cultures managers are likely to be respected by subordinates and expected to exercise authority in their assigned roles. In low–power distance cultures the distinction between manager and subordinate may be more casual, and subordinates will expect to be more involved in decisions affecting them and their work. 23. A joint venture is a cooperative operation undertaken with the joint investment of two or more partner organizations, possibly from different countries, with the prospect of mutual gains. 24. An organization operating with Theory Z management principles will share many characteristics in common with traditional Japanese management practices. Such organizations will emphasize long-term employment relationships, participative decision making opportunities, and well-planned career development that includes a lot of lateral moves and cross-functional responsibilities.

▼ APPLICATIONS ESSAY

25. Any organization that wants to compete successfully in the global economy as a "world-class player" should embrace the concept of global organizational learning. By this I basically mean two things. First, the organization must have the systems, processes, and people in place to learn continuously from experience. This means that the organizational leadership builds a climate or culture in which change is viewed positively and adaptability and flexibility are important operating objectives. Second, in today's global economy this concept must be extended to include the ability to learn continuously from the best management and organizational practices that exist anywhere in the world. Thus, Mr. Bachand, you cannot be satisfied by being up to date on what the top Canadian and American firms are doing. You must broaden your scope and, importantly, you must broaden the scope of your entire organization to include awareness of what firms in other parts of the world are doing, and doing very well. In this case, you will not only be able to anticipate competition from foreign retailers such as Yaohan and Sainsbury's, you can also take advantage of their experience to update your practices and systems in appropriate ways. Global organizational learning means just what it says. It is the ability to utilize the world at large as the reference

point for continuously learning and adapting succesfully to changing environments.

▼ SELF-TEST 3 ANSWERS

▼ MULTIPLE CHOICE		▼ TRUE/FALSE	
1. c	6. c	11. F	16. T
2. b	7. d	12. F	17. T
3. c	8. a	13. T	18. F
4. c	9. c	14. F	19. T
5. b	10. a	15. T	20. F

▼ SHORT RESPONSE

21. Managing diversity and individual differences is concerned with matching organizational and job requirements with individual characteristics and with engaging in practices to utilize an increasingly diverse workforce in mutually constructive ways so as to enhance organizational competitiveness and provide individual development. 22. Diversity and individual differences are important because they have a strong impact on an organization's performance and competitiveness. 23. Demographic characteristics are important for a number of reasons: (1) they serve as the basis for managing diversity; (2) there are various nondiscrimination laws affecting them; (3) they are often erroneously used stereotypically to categorize individuals; and (4) they can form the basis of a biodata approach to help select employees. 24. Personality characteristics are important because of their predictable interplay with an individual's behavior

▼ APPLICATIONS ESSAY

25. Your boss needs to use selected demographic, aptitude and ability, personality, and value and attitude characteristics of individuals to help match specific job and organizational requirements. Along with this, your boss can use the kinds of accountability, development, and recruitment practices designed to manage a diverse, nontraditional workforce effectively.

▼ SELF-TEST 4 ANSWERS

▼ MULTIPLE CHOICE		▼ TRUE/FALSE	
1. b	6. a	11. F	16. F
2. c	7. c	12. T	17. F
3. b	8. d	13. T	18. T
4. b	9. b	14. T	19. T
5. c	10. b	15. F	20. T

▼ SHORT RESPONSE

21. A model similar to that in Figure 4.3 should be drawn, including a brief discussion of its components and the subcomponents discussed in the chapter. 22. There are six perceptual distortions listed and discussed; you may select any two and briefly note how they distort the perceptual process. 23. Attribution theory is most closely related to the interpretation stage of the perceptual process and is concerned with how individuals try to understand causes, assign responsibility, and evaluate personal characteristics of people involved in events. 24. Perceptual response categories can be divided into thinking and feeling and action. Thinking and feeling are related to such areas as attitudes and motivation, and motivation also crosses over into action. Decision making, negotiating, communication, and leadership are but some of the OB areas that may be mentioned.

▼ APPLICATIONS ESSAY

25. Attribution theory involves assigning causes and responsibility for various outcomes of events occurring at work and evaluating the personal characteristics of those involved, based on these assignments of cause and responsibility. These assignments can be divided into those under a person's control (internal) and those outside a person's control (external). These internal and external attributions are influenced by distinctiveness (behavioral consistency across situations), consensus (whether all people in a given situation perform similarly), and consistency (whether a person responds the same way across time). Then, you can briefly discuss the fundamental attribution error and the self-serving bias tendency and point out how these influence internal and external attributions. Finally, you can comment on some implications of these internal and external attributions in terms of dealing with employees and others in your boss's department.

▼ SELF-TEST 5 ANSWERS

▼ MULTIPLE CHOICE   ▼ TRUE/FALSE

1. d	6. b	11. F	16. F
2. c	7. a	12. F	17. F
3. b	8. b	13. F	18. T
4. a	9. b	14. T	19. T
5. a	10. c	15. T	20. F

▼ SHORT RESPONSE

21. The frustration–regression component in Alderfer's ERG theory allows for a lower level need to become acti-vated or reemphasized upon the frustration of a higher level one. For example, if a person is thwarted in satisfying growth needs on the job, such as by a lack of responsibility, the theory suggests they may focus instead on satisfying existence or social needs, such as asking for greater benefits in a labor contract. 22. A motivator factor is found in job content and involves such things as responsibility, recognition, and the opportunity for growth. It is a source of job satisfaction. A hygiene factor is found in the job context and involves such things as working conditions, technical quality of supervision, and base wage of salary. It is a source of dissatisfaction. Improving upon a motivator factor may eliminate dissatisfaction, but Herzberg believes this will not create satisfaction. To do that, the motivator factors must be separately addressed. 23. The multiplier effect links expectancy, instrumentality, and valence multi-plicatively together as determinants of motivation, that is $M = E \times I \times V$. This means that all three must be present and positive for motivation to occur. A theoretical zero for E, I, and/or V will create motivation equal to zero. 24. Although at first glance absenteeism and turnover are to be avoided in the workplace, they can have their positive or functional sides. Absenteeism may be functional, for example, when it allows an otherwise "burned-out" or "stressed-out" worker to psychologically regroup and thus return to work better prepared to meet expectations. Turnover is functional when it provides job openings that allow new persons with up-to-date skills and fresh ideas to be brought on board.

▼ APPLICATIONS ESSAY

25. Frankly, I can't agree totally with either Person A or Person B. The heart of the issue rests with something called the "satisfaction–performance controversy" in our textbook. The controversy involves a core issue in this conversation—whether or not satisfaction causes performance. It appears that satisfaction alone is no guarantee of high levels of job performance. Although a satisfied worker is likely not to quit and to have good attendance, his or her performance still remains uncertain. In the integrated model of motivation, performance is a function not only of motivation and effort, but also of individual attributes and organizational support. Thus I would be cautious in focusing only on creating satisfied or happy workers. I would try to create satisfied workers and high-performing ones. I would try to make sure that the rewards for performance create satisfaction. I would also try to make sure that the satisfied worker has the right abilities, training, and other support needed to perform a job really well. Assuming that satisfaction alone will always lead to high performance

seems risky at best; it leaves too many other important considerations left untouched.

▼ SELF-TEST 6 ANSWERS

▼ MULTIPLE CHOICE   ▼ TRUE/FALSE

1. d	6. d	11. F	16. F
2. c	7. b	12. F	17. T
3. c	8. a	13. T	18. F
4. b	9. d	14. T	19. F
5. d	10. a	15. T	20. F

▼ SHORT RESPONSE

21. HR strategic planning is the process of providing capable and motivated people to carry out the organization's mission. It incorporates HR staffing (recruitment, selection, and socialization) as well as training, career planning and development, performance appraisal, and the management of extrinsic and intrinsic rewards, especially pay. 22. Training helps enhance employee ability and other characteristics to provide a better match between job requirements and employee characteristics. Career planning and development recognizes that the match is dynamic and provides for work with managers and HR experts on long-term career concerns.   23. The linkage combines young adulthood and career entry/advancement; adulthood and career maintenance; and later adulthood and career withdrawal.   24. Evaluative aspects of performance appraisal involve such issues as promotions, transfers, terminations, and salary increases. Feedback and development aspects of performance appraisal involve their use to let ratees know where they stand in terms of the organization's expectations and performance objectives.

▼ APPLICATIONS ESSAY

25. HR management can contribute a number of skills to help managers in dealing with OB issues in the organization. HR management starts by looking at how HR strategic planning ties in with organizational strategic planning to provide capable and motivated people to carry out the organization's mission. More specifically, HR management starts with the staffing process, which involves recruitment, selection, and socialization of employees to provide a match between organization/job requirements and employee characteristics. The match is further enhanced through the HR training and career planning and development functions. To help determine how well the match is being achieved, performance appraisal is used. Finally, HR helps establish and maintain appropriate compensation

systems as part of the OB concern with extrinsic and intrinsic rewards.

▼ SELF-TEST 7 ANSWERS

▼ MULTIPLE CHOICE   ▼ TRUE/FALSE

1. c	6. b	11. F	16. F
2. a	7. a	12. F	17. F
3. c	8. b	13. F	18. F
4. c	9. a	14. T	19. F
5. b	10. c	15. T	20. T

▼ SHORT RESPONSE

21. In classical conditioning, learning occurs through a conditioned stimulus (a stimulus that was neutral but now draws forth a conditioned response), such as when dogs are taught to salivate (conditioned response) at the sound of a bell (conditioned stimulus). Such conditioned responses are involuntary or reflexive. Operant conditioning emphasizes learning that is achieved when the consequences of a behavior lead to changes in the probability of its occurrence. Unlike classical conditioning, the behavior resulting from operant conditioning is voluntary and not reflexive.   22. Reinforcement is linked to extrinsic rewards through the law of effect, which states that behavior resulting in a positive outcome (or extrinsic reward) is likely to be repeated and behavior resulting in an unpleasant outcome is not likely to be repeated.   23. Negative reinforcement involves the withdrawal of negative consequences when a desirable behavior occurs; it is designed to encourage desirable behavior. Punishment involves the administration of negative consequences or the withdrawal of positive consequences when an undesirable behavior occurs; it is designed to discourage undesirable behavior.   24. Behavioral self-management involves the social learning theory notion of tying together operant and cognitive learning approaches through the reciprocal interactions among people, behavior, and environment. Workers use numerous behavioral and cognitive strategies to enhance their self-efficacy and feeling of self-control.

▼ APPLICATIONS ESSAY

25. You are trying to use OB Mod to encourage student attendance and preparation for each class where the class is so large that it discourages a large amount of individual contact. One of numerous ways of using OB Mod in this situation is to establish an intermittent, positive reinforcement schedule. This could be done by using pop quizzes and/or requiring completion of homework, collected on an

intermittent basis. The quizzes or homework would count as enough of the total grade so that students will take them seriously. Given this, students will tend to be present for each class and to be prepared because they will not know when quizzes will be administered or homework collected. Note that this strategy is designed to encourage desirable (from your standpoint) behavior, rather than to try to eliminate undesirable behavior as would an emphasis on punishment.

▼ SELF-TEST 8 ANSWERS

▼ MULTIPLE CHOICE   ▼ TRUE/FALSE

1. c	6. b	11. T	16. F
2. d	7. a	12. T	17. T
3. d	8. a	13. F	18. F
4. a	9. d	14. F	19. T
5. a	10. c	15. T	20. F

▼ SHORT RESPONSE

21. Vertical loading adds to job responsibilities for planning and controlling that were previously performed by supervisors. This creates a job that is "bigger" and more motivational, not just in terms of the variety of tasks to be accomplished but also because of the self-management that planning and controlling involve. 22. Growth-need strength is a moderator variable in job characteristics theory. This means that it affects the extent to which a job that is enriched in the core characteristics will prove motivational for an individual. When growth-need strength is high, job enrichment is motivational; when growth-need strength is low, job enrichment may cause difficulties. 23. Commitment to task goals is largely tied to the degree of participation one is allowed in the goal-setting process. To increase commitment and acceptance of goals, the individual should be allowed to participate in goal-setting and influence the actual goals that are defined. When goals are imposed with discussion and involvement, people will be less committed to them. 24. Temporary part-time work is anything less than the normal full-time work week, for example, less than 40 hours, but performed on a temporary basis. Permanent part-time work, by contrast is the same reduced schedule but performed on a continuing basis. In this case the individual tends to be a "permanent" hire into a job that involves less than a full-time work week.

▼ APPLICATIONS ESSAY

25. The essence of the management by objectives concept is joint goal setting by supervisors and their subordinates.

In Jean-Paul's case, for example, I might expect to find him asking each associate to prepare a list of tentative sales goals for each month. Then I would expect to see the associate discussing these goals carefully with Jean-Paul, with the result that a final list of agreed-upon goals is documented. In the store setting, I would also expect to see these goals shared at a meeting between Jean-Paul and all associates. Given the understanding by everyone, Jean-Paul and the associates should be able to help and support one another as they work daily. Periodically, Jean-Paul should provide clear feedback on results so that the associates could take pride in their accomplishments and make adjustments. Finally, I would expect to see regular discussions between Jean-Paul and the associates about their progress during each month, as well as a formal review discussion at the end of the month.

▼ SELF-TEST 9 ANSWERS

▼ MULTIPLE CHOICE   ▼ TRUE/FALSE

1. b	6. a	11. T	16. T
2. b	7. a	12. F	17. F
3. a	8. c	13. T	18. F
4. c	9. d	14. T	19. T
5. b	10. c	15. F	20. F

▼ SHORT RESPONSE

21. Groups are potentially good for organizations for several reasons. Groups are good for people, they can improve creativity, they sometimes make the best decisions, they gain commitments to decisions, they help control the behavior of their members, and they can help to counterbalance the effects of large organization size. 22. Permanent formal groups appear on organization charts, serve an ongoing purpose, and may include departments, divisions, teams, and the like. Temporary groups are created to solve a specific problem or perform a defined task and then disband. Examples are committees, cross-functional task forces, and project teams. 23. Required behaviors are formally expected of group members. They are part of the group's formal structure and represent conditions of membership that are "required" to be exhibited. Emergent behaviors are not formally required of members. They "emerge" spontaneously as members work and relate together. They are part of the informal structure of the group. 24. Intergroup competition can create problems in the way groups work with one another. Ideally, an organization is a cooperative system in which groups are well integrated and help one another out as needed. When groups get competitive, there is a potential dys-

functional side. Instead of communicating with one another, they decrease communication; instead of viewing one another positively, they develop negative stereotypes of one another; instead of viewing each other as mutual partners in the organization, they become hostile and view one another more as enemies. Although intergroup competition can be good by adding creative tension and more focused efforts, this potential negative side should not be forgotten.

▼ APPLICATIONS ESSAY

25. I would tell Alejandro that consensus and unanimity are two different, but related, things. Consensus occurs through extensive discussion and much "give and take" where group members share ideas and listen carefully to one another. Eventually, one alternative emerges as preferred by most. Those who may disagree, however, know that they have been listened to and have had a fair chance to influence the decision outcome. Consensus, therefore, does not require unanimity. What it does require is the opportunity for any dissenting member to feel they have been able to speak and be sincerely listened to. A decision by unanimity that generates 100 percent agreement on an issue may be the ideal state of affairs, but it is not always possible to achieve. Thus, Alejandro should always try to help the QC members work intensively together, communicate well with one another, and sincerely share ideas and listen. However, he should not be concerned for complete unanimity on every issue. Rather, consensus should be the agreed-upon goal in most cases.

▼ SELF-TEST 10 ANSWERS

▼ MULTIPLE CHOICE   ▼ TRUE/FALSE

1. c	6. b	11. T	16. T
2. d	7. c	12. F	17. F
3. d	8. b	13. F	18. T
4. a	9. d	14. F	19. F
5. b	10. c	15. F	20. T

▼ SHORT RESPONSE

21. Team building usually begins when someone notices that a problem exists or may develop in the group. Members then work collaboratively to gather data, analyze the situation, plan for improvements, and implement the plans. Everyone is expected to participate in each step, and the group as a whole is expected to benefit from continuous improvement. 22. To help build positive norms, a team leader must first act as a positive role model. She or he should also hold meetings to review performance, provide feedback, and discuss and agree on goals. She or he should carefully select members for the team and be sure to reinforce and reward members for performing as desired. 23. A basic rule of group dynamics is that members of highly cohesive groups tend to conform to group norms. Thus, when group norms are positive for performance, the conformity is likely to create high-performance outcomes. When the norms are negative, however, the conformity is likely to create low-performance outcomes. 24. Self-managing teams take different forms. A common pattern, however, involves empowering team members to make decisions on the division of labor and scheduling, to develop and maintain the skills needed to perform several different jobs for the team, to help train one another to learn those jobs, and to help select new team members.

▼ APPLICATIONS ESSAY

25. My answer to the Internet call for "help" follows. *Dear Galahad. Greetings from Brighton. Saw your message and wanted to respond. Don't worry. There is no reason at all that a great design engineer can't run a high-performance project team. Go into the job with confidence, but try to follow some basic guidelines as you build and work with the team. First off, communicate high-performance standards right from the beginning. Set the tone in the first team meeting and even create a sense of urgency to get things going. Be sure that the members have the right skills, and find ways to create some early "successes" for them. Don't let them drift apart; make sure they spend a lot of time together. Give lots of positive feedback as the project develops and, perhaps most importantly, model the expected behaviors yourself. Go for it! /s/Elmoe.*

▼ SELF-TEST 11 ANSWERS

▼ MULTIPLE CHOICE   ▼ TRUE/FALSE

1. d	6. a	11. T	16. F
2. b	7. a	12. T	17. F
3. b	8. d	13. T	18. F
4. a	9. d	14. F	19. T
5. e	10. e	15. T	20. T

▼ SHORT RESPONSE

21. The first type of goal presented in the chapter is called an output goal. Output goals are designed to help an organization define its overall mission and to help define the

kind of business it is in. Output goals can often help define the types of products and the relationships the company has with its consumers. Output goals often help demonstrate how a company fits into society. The second kind of organizational goal is the systems goal. A systems goal helps the company realize what behaviors it needs to maintain for its survival. The systems goal provides the means for the ends. It is important to recognize the importance of systems goals for day-to-day operations. 22. Vertical integration is a hierarchy in which there is a clear separation of authority and duties. This separation represents a vertical specialization that demonstrates a hierarchical division of labor. A formal hierarchy is needed under this system to provide accountability to decision makers within the organization. A manager's scope of responsibilities increases as he or she moves up the organizational chart. In a flat organizational structure, decisions do not go through such a multilayered hierarchy. The decision-making authority and accountability are found in lower levels of the organization. The concept of specialization of authority at the low end of the organizational chart should also be recognized. 23. The first advantage is that functional specialization can yield clear task assignments that replicate an individual's training and experience. Functional specialization also provides the ability for departmental colleagues to build upon one another's knowledge and experience. The functional approach often helps facilitate communication among coworkers. This approach also provides an excellent training ground for new managers. Finally, this system is easy to explain because employees can understand the role of each group even though they do not understand a particular individual's functions. There are some major disadvantages to the system as well. The system may reinforce overspecialization. Many jobs within the system may become boring and too "routinized." The lines of communication within the organization may become overly complex. Top management is often overloaded with too many problems that should be addressed at a lower level. Many top managers spend too much time dealing with cross-functional issues. Finally, many individuals look up in the hierarchy for reinforcement instead of focusing their attention on products, services, and clients. 24. First, divisional specialization provides the organization with adaptability and flexibility to meet important demands of key external groups. Second, this system allows the organization the opportunity to spot external changes as they emerge. More importantly, the divisional approach provides for the integration of specialists deep within the hierarchy. Top management can create competition among divisions within the organization to promote efficiency and achievement. The negative aspects of divisional specialization are prevalent as well. There are often not enough highly trained specialists to deal with unique problems effectively. There can be duplication of effort as each division attempts to solve similar problems. Divisional goals are frequently given priority over organizational goals by divisional managers. Finally, an attempt to link resources through joint ventures often creates conflict among divisions.

▼ APPLICATIONS ESSAY

25. The notion that the Postal Service is a mechanistic bureaucracy is important because it suggests that there are already many controls built into the system by the division of labor. You should recognize several primary side effects that are exhibited when control mechanisms are placed on an individual in an organization such as the Postal Service. There is often a difficulty in balancing organizational controls. As one control is emphasized, others may be neglected. Controls often force managers to emphasize the "quick fix" instead of long-term planning. Often, controls lead to solutions that are not customized to specific problems (i.e., "across the board cuts"). Planning and documentation can become burdensome and limit the amount of action that actually occurs. Managers often become more concerned with internal paperwork than with problem solving or customers. And there are far too many supervisors and managers. Controls that are vaguely designed are often ineffective and unrealistic. As a result, the manager may interpret the control as he or she wants. The "do the best you can" goal that is commonly given to managers in the Postal Service is an example of this concept. Controls that are inserted drastically and harshly often cause panic among managers and administrators. A swift change in the territories of postal delivery clerks is an example. Finally, many goals and controls are inserted without the appropriate resources. This practice can make the attainment of goals difficult, if not impossible.

▼ SELF-TEST 12 ANSWERS

▼ MULTIPLE CHOICE   ▼ TRUE/FALSE

1. e	6. a	11. F	16. F
2. b	7. e	12. T	17. F
3. b	8. c	13. F	18. T
4. d	9. a	14. T	19. T
5. b	10. e	15. F	20. T

▼ SHORT RESPONSE

21. Weber believed that maintaining order and accountability was crucial to the success of the organization. He believed that an organization needed labor that was divided so that each worker was specialized. Every worker would have well-defined responsibilities and authorities. To complement this specialization, the organization should be arranged hierarchically. Authority should be arranged from the bottom up. A worker should be promoted only on the basis of merit and technical competence. Most importantly, employees were to work under rules and guidelines that were impersonal and applied to all staffers equally. The bureaucratic rules were to be enforced strictly. 22. Organic design is based on a decentralized hierarchy of authority. Decision-making power is spread horizontally across the organization. Workers are generally given few rules and regulations to govern their work. Management spends little time organizing and controlling staffers. If management needs to get involved, it is generally in an informal and personal manner. Thus, the organic structure provides its members with a high level of autonomy and low levels of control. Organic designs are generally better at problem solving than mechanistic designs. However, waste and inefficiencies are common in organic structures. These are the basic concepts behind an organic structure. Mechanistic designs are highly bureaucratized and organized. Where organic organizations stress autonomy and freedom, mechanistic design focuses on efficiency and formality. Decisions are made in a centralized command and control center. Control is maintained through elaborate systems of rules and regulations. Managers are heavily involved in employees' jobs. Unlike the manager in the organic system, a manager in a mechanistic system uses formal and impersonal communication channels to speak with employees. 23. James Thompson believed that technology could be divided into three categories—intensive, mediating, or long linked. An intensive technology occurs when uncertainty exists as to how to produce the desired outcomes. Teams of specialists are brought together to pool knowledge and resources to solve the problem. An interdependence among specialists develops because all parties need one another to fulfill the project successfully. This technology often occurs in the research and development portion of organizations. A mediating technology allows various parties to become interdependent. For example, the ATM network that most banks utilize allows customers to bank at other institutions and still be tied to their home bank, automatically. Without this technology, the banking industry would not be so well linked. The technology helps determine the nature of the banks' relationships with one another. Finally, Thompson believed that long-linked technologies had a unique effect on organizations as well. Long-linked technology is more commonly known as industrial technology. This type of knowledge allows organizations to produce goods in mass quantities. The assembly line designed by Henry Ford is one of the early examples of long-linked technology. Thompson uses these distinctions to highlight the various impacts that technology has on organizations. His approach differs greatly from Joan Woodward's approach, which focuses more on the mode of production. Woodward divides technology into three areas: small-batch manufacturing, mass production, and continuous process production. Small-batch technologies deal with producing small quantities of custom goods. Craftspersons are often characterized as small producers who must alter production to fit the needs of each client. Mass production technology deals with production of uniform goods to a mass market. The production design is altered to maximize speed while limiting product styles. The last type of technology deals with continuous-process technology. Oil refineries and chemical plants are classic examples of this type of technology. These industries are intensely automated and produce the same products without variation. 24. We define environmental complexity as an estimate of the magnitude of the problems and opportunities in an organization's environment as influenced by three main factors: degree of richness, degree of interdependence, and degree of uncertainty. Environmental richness is shown by an environment that is improving around the company. The economy is growing, and people are investing and spending money. Internally, the company may be growing, and its employees may be prospering as well. In a rich environment, organizations can succeed despite their poor organizational structure. An environment that is not rich allows only well-organized companies to survive in the long run. The second major factor in environmental complexity is the level of interdependence. This factor focuses on the relationships an organization needs to develop to compete in a certain setting. How free is that organization to conduct business? Uncertainty and volatility are the final factors that make up complexity. Organizations must decide how to deal with markets and environments that are continually changing and where the rate of change is changing.

▼ APPLICATIONS ESSAY

25. In the design and development of cars and trucks Ford must recognize both the voice of the customer and a whole

series of extremely complex technical requirements. If the company violates either the customer requirements or the technical requirements, it will not be able to develop a profitable vechicle. In the product and assemply plants these conflict forces are not as prominent, and the firm may opt for a simpler structure.

▼ SELF-TEST 13 ANSWERS

▼ MULTIPLE CHOICE   ▼ TRUE/FALSE

1. c	6. d	11. T	16. T
2. a	7. a	12. T	17. F
3. c	8. a	13. T	18. T
4. a	9. b	14. F	19. F
5. d	10. c	15. T	20. T

▼ SHORT RESPONSE

21. Cox's theory is designed for organizations that are located in the United States. His ideas may not be easily expanded to multinational corporations headquartered in other cultures. Cox believes that it is important for culturally divergent groups within an organization to communicate and educate one another. This helps subgroups become more tolerant and interactive with other portions of the organization. Second, the organization needs to make sure that one type of cultural group is not segregated into one type of position. When cultural subgroups are spread throughout the organization, the level of interaction increases as the stereotyping decreases. The company also needs to help restructure many of its informal lines of communication. By encouraging the integration of informal communication, subgroups become more involved with one another. The organization must also ensure that no one group is associated with the company's outside image. A company that is perceived to be uniform in its culture attracts individuals who are from a similar culture. Finally, Cox states that interpersonal conflict that is based on group identity needs to be controlled. 22. Groups first need to define who is in the group and who is not. Criteria for both formal and informal groups need to be established to provide a framework for membership. Second, the group needs to set standards of behavior. These standards should consist of a series of informal rules that describe proper behavior and activities for members. Finally, group members need to identify the friends and adversaries of the group. The identification process helps the group build alliances throughout the organization when they attempt to get pro-

jects and ideas completed. 23. If you have not had full-time employment, think seriously about this question because it is designed to help you appreciate the importance of organizational rules and roles. Formal rules should be covered to show that they help dictate procedures individuals use. Informal interaction should be discussed as well. Such questions as, "How are subgroups treated?" "Do different instructors have different rules?" and "Are Seniors treated differently from Sophomores in this system?" could all be potential subtopics. 24. The first element is the need for a widely shared philosophy. Although this first element seems vague, an effective company philosophy is anything but abstract. An organization member needs to be exposed to what the firm stands for. The firm's mission needs to be articulated often and throughout the organization. Organizations should put people ahead of rules and general policy mandates. When staffers feel included and important in a system they feel more loyal and accepting of the culture. Every company has heroes or individuals who have succeeded beyond expectations. Companies with strong company cultures allow the stories of these individuals to become well known throughout the organization. Through these stories, workers need to make sure that they understand the rituals and ceremonies that are important to the company's identity. Maintaining and enhancing these rituals helps many organizations keep a strong corporate culture. Informal rules and expectations must be evident so that workers understand what is expected of them and the organization. Finally, employees need to realize that their work is important; their work and knowledge should be networked throughout the company. The better the communication system in the company, the better the company's culture.

▼ APPLICATIONS ESSAY

25. Even in a small firm the OD process has three stages: (1) diagnosis —gather and analyze data to assess a situation and set appropriate change objectives; (2) intervention—change objectives pursued through a variety of specific activities; and (3) reinforcement—changes are monitored, reinforced, and evaluated. The diagnostic foundations of OD encompass three levels: (1) organizational—effectiveness understood with respect to external environment and major organizational aspects; (2) group —effectiveness viewed in a context of forces in the internal environment of the organization and major group aspects; and (3) individual—effectiveness considered in relation to the internal environment of the work group and individual aspects.

▼ SELF-TEST 14 ANSWERS

▼ MULTIPLE CHOICE   ▼ TRUE/FALSE

1. e	6. a	11. F	16. F
2. a	7. c	12. T	17. F
3. e	8. d	13. F	18. F
4. e	9. a	14. T	19. T
5. b	10. e	15. T	20. F

▼ SHORT RESPONSE

21. For the first part of the question, you should consider the notions of reward, coercive, legitimate, expert, and referent power. The response should recognize the difference between position sources and personal sources. The second part of the question concerns the power of lower level participants in organizational settings. Link the sources of power with Barnard's acceptance theory of authority. 22. The text introduces at least five basic guidelines for increasing position power. They are: (1) increase your centrality and criticality in the organization; (2) increase the personal discretion and flexibility of your job; (3) build into your job tasks that are difficult to evaluate; (4) increase the visibility of your job performance; (5) increase the relevance of your tasks to the organization. The text also identifies three basic guidelines for acquiring personal power. They are: (1) increase your knowledge and information as it relates to the job; (2) increase your personal attractiveness; (3) increase your effort in relationship to key organizational tasks. 23. The text identifies seven basic strategies of managerial influence: reason, friendliness, coalition, bargaining, assertiveness, higher authority, and sanctions. You should be able express them in everyday language along with an example. Each of these strategies is available to the manager in the downward influence attempt; however, the choices in upward influence attempts may be more limited. In the exercise of upward influence, influence attempts can be expected frequently to include assertiveness, friendliness, and reason. 24. Organizational politics is formally defined as "the management of influence to obtain ends not sanctioned by the organization or to obtain sanctioned ends through nonsanctioned influence means." You should be able to express this definition in everyday language that communicates a sense of understanding. It is important that politics not be viewed as an entirely dysfunctional phenomenon that can result in people becoming dissatisfied and feeling emotionally distraught or estranged from the organizational situation. In particular, the functional aspects of organizational politics include helping managers to overcome personal inadequacies, cope with change, channel personal contacts, and substitute for formal authority.

▼ APPLICATIONS ESSAY

25. Canadian Tire organization theorists recognize that strategic contingencies can govern the relative power of subunits. For a subunit to gain power vis-à-vis others, it must increase its control over such strategic contingencies as scarce resources, the ability to cope with uncertainty, controlling centrality in the work flow, and substitution of work activities according to abilities.

▼ SELF-TEST 15 ANSWERS

▼ MULTIPLE CHOICE   ▼ TRUE/FALSE

1. a	6. c	11. F	16. F
2. b	7. c	12. F	17. T
3. b	8. a	13. T	18. T
4. b	9. b	14. T	19. F
5. b	10. b	15. F	20. F

▼ SHORT RESPONSE

21. Leadership is a special case of influence that gets an individual or group to do what the leader wants done. Leadership tends to emphasize adaptive or useful change, whereas management is designed to promote stability or to enable the organization to run smoothly. 22. Leader trait and behavior approaches assume that, in a given setting, leadership (as opposed to other variables) is central to task performance and human resource maintenance outcomes. 23. Situational contingency approaches to leadership assume that leader traits and/or behaviors act in conjunction with situational contingencies (other important aspects of the leadership situation) to determine outcomes. 24. Traditional leadership assumes that leadership and its substantive effects can be easily identified and measured. The new leadership consists of charismatic, visionary, transformational, and related perspectives, according to which followers tend to attribute extraordinary leadership abilities to a leader when they observe certain behaviors. These attributions help transform followers to achieve goals that transcend their own self-interests and help transform the organization.

▼ APPLICATIONS ESSAY

25. In Dick Grove's virtual corporation, most of the interaction between Grove and those working for him takes place

via telephone and the Internet—there is very little face-to-face interaction. This contrasts with what has traditionally been the more typical leadership setting, in which there is lots of face-to-face contact. Thus, most of the influence takes place without face-to-face contact.

Given this situation, Grove can think especially in terms of leadership substitutes—his influence is unnecessary and redundant—and neutralizers—he is prevented from behaving in a certain way or his influence is nullified. His subordinates appear to have the experience, ability, and training so that substitutes for supportive and task-oriented leadership are operating. The job characteristics seem to be intrinsically satisfying enough to substitute for supportive leadership, and Grove's physical separation may neutralize task-oriented and supportive leadership and encourage the use of modems and the Internet to help overcome this. If he is astute, Grove should be able to take advantage of some of the at-a-distance notions, such as ideological orientation, persistence, and social courage, to promote some aspects of the new leadership. If he reinforces these with expertise, originality, and other close-up behaviors in periodic headquarters face-to-face meetings, he may be able to build on traditional leadership and the use of neutralizers and substitutes to provide the necessary influence.

▼ SELF-TEST 16 ANSWERS

▼ MULTIPLE CHOICE ▼ TRUE/FALSE

1. c	6. c	11. F	16. T
2. d	7. a	12. F	17. T
3. a	8. c	13. F	18. F
4. b	9. b	14. T	19. T
5. a	10. a	15. T	20. F

▼ SHORT RESPONSE

21. Channel richness is a useful concept for managers because it describes the capacity of a communication channel to convey and move information. For example, if a manager wants to convey basic and routine information to a lot of people, a lean channel such as the electronic bulletin or written memorandum may be sufficient. However, if the manager needs to convey a complicated message and one that may involve some uncertainty, a richer channel such as the face-to-face meeting may be necessary. Simply put, the choice of channel may have a lot of impact on the effectiveness of a communication attempt. 22. Informal communication channels are very important in today's organizations. The modern workplace places great emphasis on cross-functional relationships and communication. It places

great emphasis on employee involvement and participation in decision making. All this requires that people know and talk with one another, often across departmental lines. Progressive organizations make it easy for people to interact and meet outside of formal work assignments and relationships. When people know one another, they can more easily and frequently communicate with one another. 23. Status effects can interfere with the effectiveness of communication between lower and high levels in an organization. Lower level members are concerned about how the higher level will respond, especially if the information being communicated is negative or unfavorable. In such cases, a tendency exists to filter or modify the information to make it as attractive as possible to the recepient. The result is that high-level decision makers in organizations sometimes act on innaccurate or incomplete information. Although their intentions are good, they just aren't getting good information from their subordinates. 24. There may be a gender difference in communication styles. Some research suggests that the socialization of women makes them more sensitive to others, whereas men are socialized to be more aggressive and individualistic. The impact on communication styles may be that women are more inclined to behave in ways that make them perceived as interested in others, willing to communicate with others, and willing to work with others in empowering ways. Questions have also been raised regarding how well women and men communicate with one another. It is suggested men may communicate to advance their positions, whereas women communicate to make connections. As these possibilities are considered, however, the tendency to use inappropriate gender stereotypes should be avoided.

▼ APPLICATIONS ESSAY

25. Organizations depend upon communication flowing upward, downward, and laterally. Rapid developments in technology have brought a heavy reliance upon computers to assist in the movement of this information. E-mail is one part of an electronic organizational communication system. Research does suggest that people may fall prey to the "impersonality" of computer-based operations and that the personal or face-to-face side of communication may suffer. Rather than eliminate E-mail and other forms of computer-mediated communication, however, the managing director should work hard to establish proper E-mail protocols and provide many other avenues for communication. The managing director can serve as a role model in his or her use of E-mail, in being regularly available for face-to-face interactions, by holding regular meetings, and by "wandering around" frequently to meet and talk with people from all

levels. In addition, the director can make sure that facility designs and office arrangements support interaction and make it less easy for people to disappear behind computer screens. Finally, the director must actively encourage communication of all types and not allow himself or herself to get trapped into serving as a classic example of the "E-mail boss."

▼ SELF-TEST 17 ANSWERS

▼ MULTIPLE CHOICE   ▼ TRUE/FALSE

1. c	6. a	11. F	16. F
2. b	7. c	12. F	17. T
3. c	8. b	13. F	18. F
4. b	9. a	14. T	19. T
5. d	10. a	15. F	20. F

▼ SHORT RESPONSE

21. Heuristics are simplifying strategies or "rules of thumb" that people use to make decisions. They make it easier for individuals to deal with uncertainty and limited information, but they can also lead to biased results. Common heuristics include availability—making decisions based on recent events; representativeness—making decisions based on similar events; and anchoring and adjustment—making decisions based on historical precedents. 22. Individual or authority decisions are made by the manager or team leader acting alone based on information that he or she possesses. Consultative decisions are made by the manager or team leader after soliciting inputs from other persons. Group decisions are made when the manager or team leader asks others to participate actively in problem solving. The ideal form of the group decision is true consensus. 23. Escalating commitment is the tendency to continue with a previously chosen course of action even though feedback indicates that it is not working. This can easily lead to waste of time, money, and other resources, and the sacrificing of opportunity to pursue a course of action offering more valuable results. Escalating commitment is encouraged by the popular adage, "If at first you don't succeed, try, try, again." Another way to look at it is "throwing good money after bad." 24. Most people are too busy to respond personally to every problem that comes their way. The effective manager and team leader knows when to delegate decisions to others, how to set priorities, and when to abstain from acting altogether. Questions to ask include: *Is the problem easy to deal with? Might the problem resolve itself? Is this my deci-*

sion to make? Is this a solvable problem within the context of the organization?

25. British author and consultant Charles Handy believes that everyone today must take charge of their own career and career development. They must do so to meet the demands of a very challenging and continuously changing work environment. Success in this environment, he believes, is best achieved by people who build "portfolios" of personal skills. These portfolios include specific competencies that can be used by employers; they are capabilities that keep one marketable as a valuable "product" that many employers might want. The goal is to find ways to differentiate yourself from other potential job candidates and always make yourself attractive to alternative employers. Thus the "portfolio" concept requires that we are always adding to our skills and capabilities, and are always keeping up with a changing environment to make ourselves desirable job candidates. This portfolio must be subject to continuous development; each new job assignment must be well selected and rigorously pursued as a learning opportunity. Most importantly, Handy points out that this is a personal responsibility. He states: "The future is not guaranteed . . . education in those circumstances becomes an investment, wide experience is an asset provided that it is wide and not shallow."

▼ SELF-TEST 18 ANSWERS

1. c	6. e	11. F	16. F
2. a	7. a	12. T	17. F
3. c	8. c	13. T	18. T
4. a	9. c	14. T	19. T
5. b	10. e	15. T	20. T

▼ SHORT RESPONSE

21. Managers are faced with the following conflict situations: vertical conflict—conflict that occurs between hierarchical levels; horizontal conflict—conflict that occurs between those at the same hierarchical level; line-staff conflict—conflict that occurs between line and staff representatives; role conflict—conflict that occurs when the communication of task expectations is inadequate or upsetting. 22. The major indirect conflict management approaches are: appeals to common goals—involves focusing the attention of potentially conflicting parties on one mutually desirable conclusion; hierarchical referral—using the chain of command for conflict resolution; organizational redesign—including decoupling, buffering, linking pins, and liaison groups; use of myths and scripts—managing super-

ficially through behavioral routines (scripts) or to hide conflict by denying the necessity to make a tradeoff in conflict resolution. 23. You should acknowledge that different styles may be appropriate under different conditions. Avoidance is the extreme form of nonattention and is most commonly used when the issue is trivial, more important issues are pressing, or to let individuals cool off. An accommodation strategy is used when an issue is more important to the other party than it is to you, or to build social credits. 24. Distributive negotiation focuses on staking out positions and claiming portions of the available "pie." It usually takes the form of hard negotiation—the parties maximize their self-interests and hold out to get their own way—or soft negotiation—one party is willing to make concessions in order to reach an agreement. Distributive negotiation can lead to competition, compromise, or accommodation, but it tends to be win–lose oriented in all cases. Integrative negotiation focuses on the merits of an issue and attempts to enlarge the available "pie." It may lead to avoidance, compromise, or collaboration. It tends to be more win–win oriented and seeks to satisfy the needs and interests of all parties.

▼ APPLICATIONS ESSAY

25. When negotiating the salary for your first job, you should attempt to avoid the common pitfalls of negotiation. They include: falling prey to the myth of the "fixed pie"; nonrational escalation of conflict, such as trying to compare the proposed salary to the highest offer you have heard; overconfidence; and ignoring other's needs (the personnel officer probably has a fixed limit). While the initial salary may be very important to you, you should also recognize that the initial salary may not be as important as what type of job you will have and whether you will have an opportunity to move up in the firm.

▼ SELF-TEST 19 ANSWERS

▼ MULTIPLE CHOICE ▼ TRUE/FALSE

1. d	6. a	11. F	16. F
2. c	7. b	12. F	17. F
3. b	8. d	13. T	18. T
4. a	9. a	14. T	19. F
5. c	10. c	15. T	20. T

▼ SHORT RESPONSE

21. Not all change in organizations is planned. Unplanned change—that which occurs spontaneously or by surprise—

can be useful. The appropriate goal in managing unplanned change is to act immediately once the change is recognized to minimize any negative consequences and maximize any possible benefits. The goal is to take best advantage of the change situation by learning from the experience. 22. External forces for change are found in the relationship between an organization and its environment. Examples are the pressures of mergers, strategic alliances, and divestitures. Internal forces for change include those found in different lifecycle demands as the organization passes from birth through growth and toward maturity. Internal forces also include the political nature of organizations as reflected in authority and reward systems. 23. The basic point of the boiled frog phenomenon is that organizations may suffer disastrous outcomes if they fail to monitor changing environments properly and to change with them actively. The phenomenon traces to a classic physiology experiment that demonstrated that a live frog will immediately jump out when placed in a pan of hot water. When placed in cold water that is then heated very slowly, however, the frog will stay in the water until the water boils the frog to death. Organizations can fall victim to similar circumstances; managers must be ever alert to help avoid this fate. 24. There are two sides to stress—constructive and destructive. Up to a certain point, stress is beneficial to performance because it helps to stimulate effort and even creativity. Beyond that point, stress becomes harmful because anxiety and other problems detract from performance. Thus the relationship between stress and performance is curvilinear; too little or too much stress is negative on performance, whereas moderate stress is positive on performance. The problem is finding the "friction" point where stress can be maintained for any given individual at the moderate level.

▼ APPLICATIONS ESSAY

25. Jorge may begin his attempts to deal with resistance to change by using education and communication. Through one-on-one discussions, group presentations, and even visits to other centers he can better inform his staff about the nature and logic of the changes. He should also utilize participation and involvement by allowing others, for example in a series of task forces, to help choose the new equipment and design the new programs. In all this he should offer enough facilitation and support to help everyone deal with any hardships the changes may cause. He should be especially alert to listen to any problems and complaints that may arise. On certain matters, Jorge might use negotiation and agreement to exchange benefits for staff support. In

the extreme case, manipulation and cooperation through covert attempts to influence others might be used to achieve needed support, although this is not advisable. Similarly, explicit or implicit coercion would use force to get people to accept change at any cost. My advice would be to stick with the first four strategies as much as possible and avoid the latter two.

GLOSSARY

Ability   The capacity to perform the various tasks needed for a given job.

Accommodation   Occurs when one party involved in a conflict gives in to the other.

Achievement-oriented leadership   Emphasizes setting challenging goals, stressing excellence and high standards of performance.

Action research   The process of systematically collecting data on an organization, feeding it back for action planning, and evaluating results by collecting and reflecting on more data.

Active listening   Restating and paraphrasing the source's words to help the source better say what he or she really means.

Active management by exception   Intervening with subordinates only if standards are not met.

Activities   The verbal and nonverbal things group members say and do.

Activity measures   Performance appraisal criteria based on behavior or actions.

Adhocracy   An organizational structure that emphasizes shared, decentralized decision making, and the virtual absence of formal controls.

Adjourning stage   Stage of group development at which the group is prepared to disband when its task is accomplished.

Adult transitions   The series of life stages relevant to personality development (early adulthood, midlife, and later adulthood).

Affective components   The components of an attitude that are the specific feelings regarding the personal impact of the antecedents.

Affirmative action   Emphasizes achieving equality of opportunity in the work setting through the changing of organizational demographics (sex, age, racioethnicity mixes, and the like).

Anchoring and adjustment heuristic   Bases a decision on incremental adjustments to an initial value determined by historical precedent or some reference point.

Appeal to common goals   Focusing of the attention of potentially conflicting parties on one mutually desirable conclusion.

Aptitude   The capability of learning something.

Arbitration   When a neutral third party acts as judge and issues a binding decision affecting those parties at a negotiation impasse.

Artificial intelligence (AI)   Studies how computers can be made to think like the human brain.

Asia Pacific Economic Cooperation Forum (APEC)   A grouping of Asia-Pacific basin countries seeking to develop trade agreements.

Assessment center   A selection technique designed to provide a comprehensive view of a job candidate by evaluating the candidate's performance across many situations.

Attitudes   Predispositions to respond in a positive or negative way to someone or something in one's environment.

Attribution theory   The attempt to understand the

cause of an event, assess responsibility for outcomes of the event, and assess the personal qualities of the people involved.

Authoritarianism A personality trait that focuses on the rigidity of a person's beliefs.

Authoritative command A direct conflict management technique whereby a formal authority dictates a solution and specifies what is gained and lost by whom.

Automation Allows machines to do work previously accomplished by people.

Availability heuristic Bases a decision on recent events relating to the situation at hand.

Avoidance In conflict management involves pretending the conflict does not really exist and hoping that it will simply go away.

Avoidance learning In reinforcement involves the withdrawal of negative consequences that tend to increase the likelihood of repeating the behavior in similar settings; also known as negative reinforcement.

Bargaining zone The zone between one party's minimum reservation point and the other party's maximum reservation point in a negotiating situation.

BATNA The best alternative to a negotiated agreement, or each party's position on what he or she must do if an agreement can't be reached.

Behavioral components Components of an attitude that are the intentions to behave in a certain way based on a person's specific feelings or attitudes.

Behavioral decision theory Views decision makers as acting only in terms of what they perceive about a given situation.

Behaviorally anchored rating scales (BARS) A performance appraisal approach that describes observable job behaviors, each of which is evaluated to determine good versus bad performance.

Beliefs Ideas about someone or something and the conclusions people draw about them.

Benefit cycle A pattern of successful adjustment followed by further improvements.

Biodata Biographical data; that is, the specific values of background variables such as gender, age, race, ethnicity, and able-bodiedness.

Biographic characteristics Background characteristics of variables that help shape what a person has become, such as gender, age, race, ethnicity, and able-bodiedness; sometimes called demographic characteristics.

Brainstorming Generating ideas through "freewheeling" discussion and without criticism.

Buffering Setting up inventories to reduce conflicts when the inputs of one group are the outputs of another.

Bureaucracy An ideal form of organization whose characteristics were defined by the German sociologist Max Weber.

Career planning An OD intervention that creates opportunities for achieving long-term congruence between individual goals and organizational career opportunities.

Career planning and development Working with managers and/or HR experts on career issues.

Career plateau A position from which someone is unlikely to move to advance to a higher level of responsibility.

Career stages Different points of work responsibility and achievement through which people pass during the course of their work lives.

Case study An in-depth analysis of one or a small number of settings.

Causality The assumption that change in the independent variable caused change in the dependent variable.

Central tendency error Occurs when managers lump everyone together around the average, or middle, category.

Centralization The degree to which the authority to make decisions is restricted to higher levels of management.

Centralized communication networks Networks that route all communication in a group through a central person or "hub."

Certain environments Provide full information on the expected results for decision-making alternatives.

Change agents People with responsibility for changing the behavior of a person or social system.

Changing The stage of the change process in which specific actions are taken to change a situation.

Channel richness The capacity of a communication channel to convey information effectively.

Channels The pathways through which messages are communicated.

Charisma A dimension of leadership that provides vision and a sense of mission and instills pride, respect, and trust.

Charismatic leaders Those leaders who, by force of their personal abilities, are capable of having a profound and extraordinary effect on followers.

Classical conditioning A form of learning through association that involves the manipulation of stimuli to influence behavior.

Classical decision theory Views decision makers as acting in a world of complete certainty.

Coacting networks Networks found in groups whose members work independently on common tasks.

Coercive power The extent to which a manager can deny desired rewards or administer punishment to control other people.

Cognitive components The components of an attitude that are the beliefs, opinions, knowledge, or information a person possesses.

Cognitive dissonance A state of perceived inconsistency between a person's expressed attitudes and his or her actual behavior.

Cognitive learning A form of learning achieved by thinking about the perceived relationship between events and individual goals and expectations.

Cognitive resource theory A contingency theory where leadership depends on the leader's or subordinate group member's ability/competency; stress; experience; and group support of the leader.

Cohesiveness The degree to which members are attracted to and motivated to remain a part of a group.

Collaboration A direct and positive approach to conflict management that involves a recognition by all the conflicting parties that something is wrong and needs attention through problem solving.

Collateral organization An OD intervention designed to improve creative problem solving by pulling a representative set of members out of the formal organization structure to engage in periodic small-group, problem-solving sessions.

Communication The process of sending and receiving symbols with attached meanings.

Competition A conflict management technique whereby a victory is achieved through force, superior skill, or domination.

Compressed work week A work schedule that allows a full-time job to be completed in four 10-hour workdays.

Compromise Occurs when each party involved in a conflict gives up something to the other.

Conceptual skill The ability to analyze and solve complex problems.

Conditioned response The behavior that results from a conditioned stimulus.

Conditioned stimulus Something that incites action as a result of having been learned.

Confirmation trap The tendency to seek confirmation for what is already thought to be true, and to not search for disconfirming information.

Conflict Occurs when parties disagree over substantive issues or when emotional antagonisms create friction between them.

Conflict resolution Occurs when the reasons for a conflict are eliminated.

Confrontation meeting An OD intervention designed to help determine how an organization might be improved and to start action toward such improvement.

Confucian dynamism A cultural tendency with emphasis on persistence, the ordering of relationships, thrift, a sense of shame, personal steadiness, reciprocity, protecting "face," and respect for tradition.

Conglomerates Firms that own several different unrelated businesses.

Consensus A group decision that has the expressed support of most members.

Consistency A measure of whether an individual responds the same way across time.

Constructive conflict Conflict that results in positive benefits to the group.

Constructive stress Stress that has a positive impact on attitudes and/or performance.

Consultative decisions Decisions made by one

individual after seeking input from or consulting with members of a group.

Content theories Profile different needs that may motivate individual behavior.

Contingency approach Seeks ways to meet the needs of different management situations.

Contingent rewards Rewards given in exchange for mutually agreed upon goal accomplishments.

Continuous improvement The belief that anything and everything done in the workplace should be continually improved.

Continuous reinforcement A reinforcement schedule that administers a reward each time a desired behavior occurs.

Contrast effects Occur when an individual's characteristics are contrasted with those of others recently encountered who rank higher or lower on the same characteristics.

Control The set of mechanisms used to keep actions and outputs within predetermined limits.

Controlling Monitoring performance and taking any needed corrective action.

Coordination The set of mechanisms used in an organization to link the actions of its subunits into a consistent pattern.

Counteracting networks Networks found where subgroups disagree on some aspect of overall group operations.

Countercultures Patterns of values and philosophies that outwardly reject those of the larger organization or social system.

Crafted decisions Decisions created to deal uniquely with a problem at hand.

Creativity Generates unique and novel responses to problems.

Critical incident diary A method of performance appraisal that records incidents of unusual success or failure in a given performance aspect.

Cultural symbol Any object, act, or event that serves to transmit cultural meaning.

Culture The learned and shared ways of thinking and acting among a group of people or society.

Culture shock A feeling of frustration and confusion resulting from time spent in an unfamiliar culture.

Decentralization The degree to which the authority to make decisions is given to lower levels in an organization's hierarchy.

Decentralized communication networks Networks that link all group members directly with one another.

Decision making The process of choosing among alternative courses of action; involves identifying a problem and choosing a course of action to deal with it.

Decision Support System (DSS) Combines advances in computer hardware and software with the development of extensive information bases to aid line managers in decision making.

Decoding The interpretation of the symbols sent from the sender to the receiver.

Decoupling Separating or reducing the contact between two conflicting groups.

Deficit cycle A pattern of deteriorating performance that is followed by even further deterioration.

Delphi technique Generating decision-making alternatives through a series of survey questionnaires.

Demographic characteristics Background variables (e.g., age, gender) that help shape what a person becomes over time.

Departmentation by customer Grouping of individuals and resources by client.

Departmentation by geography Grouping of individuals and resources by geographical territory.

Dependent variable The event or occurrence expressed in a hypothesis that indicates what the researcher is interested in explaining.

Destructive conflict Conflict that works to the group's or organization's disadvantage.

Destructive stress Stress that has a negative impact on attitudes and/or performance.

Directive leadership Leadership that spells out the "what" and "how" of subordinates' tasks.

Disruptive behavior Any behavior that harms group process.

Distinctiveness A measure of how consistent a person's behavior is across different situations.

Distributed leadership The sharing of responsibility for meeting group task and maintenance needs.

Distributive justice The degree to which all people are treated the same under a policy regardless of individual differences.

Distributive negotiation Negotiation in which the focus is on "positions" staked out or declared by the parties involved who are each trying to claim certain portions of the available "pie."

Divisional departmentation The grouping of individuals and resources by product, service, client, or legal entity.

Divisionalized design An organization design that establishes a separate structure for each business or division.

Dogmatism A personality trait that regards legitimate authority as absolute and accepts or rejects others based on their acceptance of authority.

Domestic multiculturalism Cultural diversity within a given national population.

Dual-career couple A couple that has both adult partners employed.

Effective communication Communication that results in the intended meaning of the source and the perceived meaning of the receiver being one and the same.

Effective groups Groups that achieve high levels of both task performance and human resource maintenance.

Effective manager A manager who helps others achieve sustainable long-term high levels of task performance.

Effective negotiation Occurs when issues of substance are resolved without any harm to the working relationships among the parties involved.

Efficient communication Communication that is low cost in its use of resources.

Electronic brainstorming Computer-mediated brainstorming wherein special software facilitates idea generation and evaluation.

Emergent behaviors Those things that group members do in addition to, or in place of, what is formally asked of them by the organization.

Emotional conflict Conflict that involves interpersonal difficulties that arise over feelings of anger, mistrust, dislike, fear, resentment, and the like.

Empathy The ability to view a situation as others see it.

Employee involvement groups Members of such groups meet regularly to examine work-related problems and opportunities.

Empowerment Allowing individuals or groups to make decisions that affect them or their work.

Encoding The process of translating an idea or thought into meaningful symbols.

Environmental complexity The magnitude of the problems and opportunities in the organization's environment as evidenced by the degree of richness, interdependence, and uncertainty.

Equity theory Adams' theory, which posits that people will act to eliminate any felt inequity in the rewards received for their work in comparison with others.

ERG theory Alderfer's theory, which identifies existence, relatedness, and growth needs.

Escalating commitment The tendency to continue a previously chosen course of action even when feedback suggests that it is failing.

Ethical behavior Behavior that is morally accepted as "good" and "right" as opposed to "bad" and "wrong."

Ethical dilemmas Situations that require a person to choose among actions that offer possible benefits while also violating ethical standards.

Ethnocentrism A belief that assumes that the ways of one's own culture are the *best* ways of doing things.

European Union (EU) An agreement linking European member countries with its goal of political, economic, and monetary union.

Existence needs Desires for physiological and material wellbeing.

Expatriate A person who works and lives in a foreign country for an extended time.

Expectancy effect The tendency to create or find in another situation or individual that which one has expected to find in the first place.

Expectancy The probability that work effort will be

followed by a given level of performance accomplishment.

Experiential learning A personal commitment to pursue all available day-to-day learning opportunities and to experiment with new behaviors.

Expert power The ability to control another's behavior because of the possession of knowledge, experience, or judgment that the other person does not have but needs.

External adaptation The process of reaching goals and dealing with outsiders.

External recruitment The process of attracting the best qualified individuals from outside the firm to apply for a given job.

External validity The degree to which the study's results can be generalized across the entire population of people, settings, and other similar conditions.

Externals People who have an external locus or control; they believe that what happens to them is beyond their control.

Extinction The withdrawal of the reinforcing consequences for a given behavior.

Extrinsic rewards Rewards given to the individual by some other person in the work setting.

Feedback The process of communicating how one feels about something another person has done or said.

Feeling-type individuals People who are oriented toward conformity and try to accommodate themselves to other people.

Felt negative inequity Exists when someone feels they have received relatively less than others in proportion to work inputs.

Felt positive inequity Exists when someone feels he or she has received relatively more than others in proportion to work inputs.

Field experiment A research study that is conducted in a realistic setting, whereby the researcher intervenes and manipulates one or more independent variables and controls the situation as carefully as the situation permits.

Field survey A research design that relies on the use of some form of questionnaire for the primary purpose of describing and/or predicting some phenomenon.

FIRO-B Theory The fundamental interpersonal relations theory of membership compatibilities in groups.

Fixed interval schedule A reward schedule that provides rewards at the first appearance of a behavior after a given time has elapsed.

Fixed ratio schedule A reward schedule that provides rewards each time a certain number of behaviors occur.

Flexible benefit plans Pay systems that allow workers to select benefits according to their individual needs.

Flexible manufacturing Uses adaptive technology and integrated job designs to shift production among alternative products.

Flexible working hours Work schedules that give employees some daily choice in scheduling arrival and departure times from work.

Force–coercion strategy Uses authority, rewards, and punishments to create change.

Forced distribution A method of performance appraisal that uses a small number of performance categories, such as "very good," "good," "adequate," and "very poor."

Formal communication channels Communication pathways that follow the official organization structure and chain of command.

Formal groups Officially designated groups for a specific organizational purpose.

Formal leadership The process of exercising influence from a position of formal authority in an organization.

Formal structure The intended configuration of positions, job duties, and lines of authority among the component parts of an organization.

Formalization The written documentation of work rules, policies, and procedures.

Forming stage The stage of group development that is concerned with the initial entry of members to a group; the members initially enter and begin to identify with each other.

Founding story The tale of the lessons learned and the efforts of the founder of the organization.

Functional absenteeism A failure of people to attend work on a given day, which leads to positive results for the people and/or the organization.

Functional departmentation The grouping of individuals and resources by skill, knowledge, and action.

Functional turnover A decision by people to terminate their employment, which leads to positive results for the people and/or the organization.

Fundamental attribution error The tendency to underestimate the influence of situational factors and to overestimate the influence of personal factors in evaluating someone else's behavior.

Future shock The discomfort people experience in times of continual and uncertain change.

Gain sharing A pay system that links pay and performance by giving the workers the opportunity to share in productivity gains through increased earnings.

General Agreement on Trade and Tariffs (GATT) An agreement among most countries of the world to cooperate in reducing trade barriers and restrictions.

General environment The set of cultural, economic, educational, and legal–political forces common to organizations operating within a given geographical area.

Glass ceiling A hidden barrier limiting advancement of women and minorities in organizations.

Global corporation A firm that operates in many countries, with a total world view, and without allegiance to any one national "home."

Global economy The worldwide interdependence of resource suppliers, product markets, and business competition.

Global manager A manager who has the international awareness and cultural sensitivity needed to work well across national borders.

Global organizational learning The ability to gather from the world at large the knowledge required for long-term organizational adaptation.

Goal setting The process of developing and setting motivational performance objectives for people in their jobs.

Grafting The process of acquiring individuals, units, and/or firms to bring in useful knowledge to the organization.

Grapevine The network of friendships and acquaintances through which rumors and other unofficial information are passed among an organization's informal groups.

Graphic rating scale A scale that lists a variety of dimensions thought to be related to high-performance outcomes in a given job and that the individual is expected to exhibit.

Great man/trait theory States that certain traits, e.g., height, integrity, intelligence, are related to success and that, once identified, these traits can be used to select leaders.

Group Two or more people working together regularly to achieve common goals.

Group decisions Decisions that are made by all members of the group.

Group dynamics The forces operating in groups that affect the ways members work together.

Groupware Software that allows for computer-mediated meetings and group decision making.

Growth needs Desires for continued personal growth and development.

Halo effect Occurs when one attribute of a person or situation is used to develop an overall impression of the person or situation.

Halo error Results when one person rates another person on several different dimensions and gives a similar rating for each one.

Heterogeneous groups Groups that have members with diverse backgrounds, interests, values, and attitudes.

Heuristics Simplifying strategies or "rules of thumb" used in decision making.

Hierarchical referral Uses the chain of command for conflict resolution; problems are referred up the hierarchy for more senior managers to reconcile.

Hierarchy of needs theory Maslow's theory that offers a pyramid of physiological, safety, social, esteem, and self-actualization needs.

High-context cultures Cultures in which messages are expressed only partially by the spoken and written word, and supported by body language and other situational factors.

High-Mach personalities   People who tend to behave in ways consistent with Machiavelli's basic principles and who are skilled at influencing others.

Higher order needs   Esteem and self-actualization in Maslow's hierarchy.

Hindsight trap   A tendency to overestimate the degree to which an event that has already taken place could have been predicted.

Homogeneous groups   Groups that have members with similar backgrounds, interests, values, and attitudes.

Horizontal loading   Increases job breadth by adding task variety without changing task difficulty.

Horizontal specialization   A division of labor through the formation of work units or groups within an organization.

Human resource strategic planning   Hiring capable, motivated people to carry out the organization's mission and strategy.

Human resources   The people who do the work and make the contributions of organizations possible.

Human skill   The ability to work well with other people.

Hygiene factors   In a job context, the external work setting; they are sources of job *dis*satisfaction.

Hypothesis   A tentative explanation about the relationship between two or more variables.

Impression management   The systematic attempt to behave in ways that create and maintain desired impressions of oneself in the eyes of others.

Incremental change   Frame-bending change that occurs as part of an organization's natural evolution.

Independent variable   The event or occurrence that is presumed by a hypothesis to affect one or more other events or occurrences as dependent variables.

Individual consideration   A leadership dimension whereby the leader provides personal attention,

treats each employee individually, and coaches and advises subordinates.

Individual decisions   Decisions that are made by one individual in behalf of a group.

Individualism view   Considers ethical behavior to be that which is best for an individual's long-term self-interests.

Individualism–collectivism   The tendency of a culture's members to emphasize individual self-interests or group relationships.

Influence   A behavioral response to the exercise of power.

Informal communication channels   Channels that do not follow the official organization structure or chain of command.

Informal groups   Unofficial groups that emerge to serve special interests.

Informal leadership   The process of exercising influence through special skills or resources that meet the needs of others.

Innovation   The process of creating new ideas and putting them in practice.

Inspiration   The communication of high expectations, the use of symbols to focus efforts, and the expression of important purposes in simple ways.

Instrumental values   Values that reflect a person's beliefs about the means for achieving desired ends.

Instrumentality   The probability that a given level of performance will lead to various work outcomes.

Integrative negotiation   Negotiation in which the focus is on the merits of the issues, and the parties involved try to enlarge the available "pie" rather than stake claims to certain portions of it.

Intellectual stimulation   Promotes intelligence, rationality, and careful problem solving.

Interacting networks   Networks that are found in groups with high interdependence among members.

Interactions   Interpersonal acts occurring among group members.

Interfirm alliances   Announced cooperative agreements or joint ventures between two independent firms.

Intergroup conflict Occurs among groups in an organization.

Intergroup dynamics Relationship between groups cooperating and competing with one another.

Intergroup team building A form of team building and organization development designed to help two or more groups improve their working relationships with one another and experience improved group effectiveness.

Intermittent reinforcement A reinforcement schedule that rewards behavior only periodically.

Internal integration The creation of a collective identity and the means of matching methods of working and living together.

Internal recruitment The process of attracting the best qualified individuals from within the firm to apply for a given job.

Internal validity The degree to which the results of a study can be relied upon as being correct.

Internals People who have an internal locus of control; they believe that they control their own fate or destiny.

International management Management in organizations whose activities span more than one country.

International organizational behavior The study of individuals and groups in organizations that operate internationally and with multicultural workforces.

Interorganizational conflict Conflict that occurs between organizations.

Interpersonal conflict Occurs between two or more individuals in opposition to each other.

Interrole conflict Incompatible expectations from two or more roles.

Intersender role conflict Incompatible role expectations from two or more people.

Intervening variable An event or occurrence that provides the linkage through which an independent variable is presumed to affect a dependent variable.

Interview Face-to-face, telephone, or computer-assisted interactions to ask respondents questions of interest.

Intrapersonal conflict Occurs within the individual because of actual or perceived pressures from incompatible goals or expectations.

Intrasender role conflict Incompatible role expectations from the same person.

Intrinsic rewards Rewards received by the individual directly through task performance.

Intuition The ability to know or recognize quickly the possibilities of a situation.

Intuitive-type individuals People who prefer the big picture and like solving new problems, dislike routine, and prefer to look for possibilities rather than work with facts.

ISO 9000 Identifies quality standards set by the International Standards Organization as a universal framework for quality assurance.

Job analysis The procedure used to collect and classify information about tasks the organization needs to complete.

Job characteristics theory Identifies five core job characteristics of special importance to job design—skill variety, task identity, task significance, autonomy, and feedback.

Job content Factors in a person's specific tasks and responsibilities.

Job context Factors in a person's external work setting.

Job description A written description of job duties/responsibilities, relationship with other jobs, and related matters.

Job design The process of defining job tasks and the work setting to accomplish them.

Job enlargement Increases job breadth and task variety by adding new tasks of similar difficulty to a job.

Job involvement The willingness of a person to work hard and to apply effort beyond normal job expectations.

Job redesign An OD intervention that creates opportunities for achieving long-term congruence between individual goals and organizational career opportunities.

Job rotation Increases job breadth task variety by

shifting workers among jobs involving tasks of similar difficulty.

Job satisfaction   The degree to which individuals feel positively or negatively about their jobs.

Job sharing   Allows one full-time job to be divided among two or more persons.

Job simplification   Standardizes tasks and employs people in very routine jobs.

Job specification   A statement of the qualifications required for a person to perform a given job.

Joint venture   A form of strategic alliance whereby two or more firms, often from different countries, make joint investments to establish a new operation.

Judgment   The use of intellect in making decisions.

Justice view   Considers ethical behavior to be that which is fair and impartial in its treatment of people.

Kinesics   The study of gestures and body postures.

Laboratory experiment   An experiment conducted in an artificial setting in which the researcher intervenes and manipulates one or more independent variables in a highly controlled situation.

Laissez-faire   Abdicating responsibilities and avoiding decisions.

Law of contingent reinforcement   The view that, for a reward to have maximum reinforcing value, it must be delivered only if the desired behavior is exhibited.

Law of effect   The observation that behavior which results in a pleasing outcome will be likely to be repeated; behavior that results in an unpleasant outcome is not likely to be repeated.

Law of immediate reinforcement   The more immediate the delivery of a reward after the occurrence of a desirable behavior, the greater the reinforcing effect on behavior.

Leader match training   Training leaders to diagnose a situation to match their high and low LPC scores with situational control, as measured by leader–member relations, task structure, and leader position power.

Leader–member relations   A measure of member support for the leader.

Leadership   A special case of interpersonal influence that gets an individual or group to do what the leader wants done.

Leadership prototype   The picture people have in their minds of what the image of a model leader should look like.

Leading   Creates enthusiasm to work hard to accomplish tasks successfully.

Learning   A relatively permanent change in behavior that occurs as a result of experience.

Least preferred coworker (LPC) scale   A measure of a person's leadership style based on a description of the person with whom respondents have been able to work least well.

Legitimate power   The extent to which a manager can use the internalized values of a subordinate that the "boss" has a "right of command" to control other people; also called formal authority.

Leniency error   The tendency to give relatively high ratings to virtually everyone.

Liaison groups   Groups that coordinate the activities of certain units to prevent destructive conflicts between them.

Life-long learning   Continuous learning from work and life experiences.

Line units   Work groups that conduct the major business of the organization.

Linking pins   Persons who are assigned to manage conflict between groups that are prone to conflict.

Locus of control   The internal–external orientation—the extent to which people feel able to affect their lives.

Long term–short term orientation   The degree to which a culture emphasizes values associated with the future versus the past or present.

Lose–lose conflict   Occurs when nobody really gets what he or she wants.

Low-context cultures   Cultures in which words convey the main parts of a message.

Lower order needs   Physiological, safety, and social needs in Maslow's hierarchy.

Lump-sum increase   A pay system in which people elect to receive their annual wage or salary increases in one or more "lump-sum" payments.

Lump-sum payment   A one-time payment, often based on a gain-sharing formula, given by an employer instead of yearly percentage wage or salary increase.

Mach scales   A series of instruments developed by psychologists to measure a person's Machiavellian orientation.

Machiavellians   People who view and manipulate others purely as objects or for personal gain.

Machine bureaucracy   An entire organization characterized by the mechanistic design.

Maintenance activities   Activities that support the emotional life of the group as an ongoing social system.

Management by objectives (MBO)   A process of joint goal setting between a supervisor and a subordinate.

Management philosophy   A philosophy that links key goal-related issues with key collaboration issues to come up with general ways by which the firm will manage its affairs.

Managerial script   A series of well-known routines for problem identification and alternative generation and analysis common to managers within the firm.

Managers   People who are formally responsible for supporting the work efforts of other people.

Maquiladoras   Foreign-owned plants that operate on the Mexican side of the border but ship the finished products to the United States for sale and distribution.

Masculinity–femininity   The degree to which a society values so-called masculine traits such as assertiveness and independence or feminine traits such as concern for relationships.

Matrix departmentation   A combination of functional and divisional patterns wherein an individual is assigned to more than one type of unit.

Mechanistic design   A highly bureaucratic organization that emphasizes vertical specialization and control, impersonal coordination and control, and reliance on rules, policies, and procedures.

Merit pay   A compensation system that bases an individual's salary or wage increase on a measure of the person's performance accomplishments during a specific time period.

Mimicry   Copying the successful practices of others.

Mission statement   Identifies the purpose of an organization and the domain in which an organization intends to operate; often written statements.

Mixed messages   Misunderstandings that occur when a person's words communicate one thing while his or her nonverbal cues communicate another.

Moderator variable   An event or occurrence that, when systematically varied, changes the relationship between an independent variable and a dependent variable.

Monochronic culture   Cultures in which people tend to do one thing at a time.

Moral-rights view   Considers ethical behavior to be that which respects fundamental rights shared by all human beings.

Motivator factors   In job content, the tasks people actually do; they are sources of job satisfaction.

Motivator–hygiene theory   Identifies job context as sources of job _dis_satisfaction and job content as the source of job satisfaction; also called the two-factor theory.

Multinational corporation   A business firm with extensive international operations in more than one country.

Multinational organizations (MNOs)   Firms that pursue nonprofit missions and operations around the globe.

Multiskilling   Team members are trained in skills to perform different jobs.

Myers–Briggs Type Indicator   A paper and pencil test used to measure a person's problem-solving style, personal conceptions, and other aspects of personality.

Myths   Proclamations or beliefs about a situation that deny the necessity to make tradeoffs in conflict resolution.

Nature/nurture controversy   One argument states that personality is determined by heredity or genetic endowment (nature); the other maintains that personality is determined by environment and experience (nurture).

Need for achievement The desire to do better, solve problems, or master complex tasks.

Need for affiliation The desire for friendly and warm relations with others.

Need for power The desire to control others and influence their behavior.

Negative reinforcement The withdrawal of negative consequences that tend to increase the likelihood of repeating the behavior in similar settings; also known as avoidance.

Negotiation The process of making joint decisions when the parties involved have different preferences.

Noise Anything that interferes with the effectiveness of communication.

Nominal group technique Using structured rules for generating and prioritizing ideas.

Nonreactive measures Used to obtain data without disturbing the setting.

Nonroutine problems Problems that are unique and must be addressed through creative problem solving, or crafted decisions.

Nonverbal communication Communication that takes place through facial expressions, body movements, eye contact, and other physical gestures.

Norming stage Stage of group development, also called the initial integration stage, in which the group begins to come together as a coordinated unit and strives to maintain balance.

Norms Rules or standards for the behavior of group members.

Observation Watching an event, object, or person and recording what is seen.

Off-the-job training Instruction received away from the actual workplace; involves lectures, videos, and simulations.

On-the-job training Instruction received while performing the job in the actual workplace, e.g., internships, apprenticeships, job rotation.

Open systems Systems that transform human and material resources from the environment into finished goods and services.

Operant conditioning The process of controlling behavior by manipulating, or "operating" on, its consequences.

Organic design An organizational structure that emphasizes horizontal specialization, an extensive use of personal coordination, and loose rules, policies, and procedures.

Organization charts Diagrams that depict the formal structures of organizations.

Organization development (OD) The application of behavioral science knowledge in a long-range effort to improve an organization's ability to cope with change in its external environment and increase its problem-solving capabilities.

Organization development interventions Activities initiated in support of an OD program and designed to improve the work effectiveness of individuals, groups, or the organization as a whole.

Organization myth An unproven and often unstated belief that is accepted uncritically.

Organizational behavior (OB) The study of individuals and groups in organizations.

Organizational behavior modification (OB Mod) The systematic reinforcement of desirable work behavior and the nonreinforcement or punishment of unwanted work behavior.

Organizational commitment The degree to which a person strongly identifies with and feels a part of the organization.

Organizational communication The process by which information is exchanged in the organizational setting.

Organizational (or corporate) **culture** The system of shared actions, values, and beliefs that develops within an organization and guides the behavior of its members.

Organizational design The process of choosing and implementing a structural configuration for an organization.

Organizational ecology The study of how facility design influences performance and communication.

Organizational governance The pattern of authority, influence, and acceptable managerial behavior established at the top of the organization.

Organizational learning The process of an organization's acquiring knowledge and using information to adapt to changing circumstances.

Organizational myth A commonly held cause–effect relationship or assertion that cannot be empirically supported.

Organizational politics The management of influence to obtain ends not sanctioned by the organization or to obtain sanctioned ends through non-sanctioned means of influence.

Organizational strategy The process of positioning the organization in the competitive environment and implementing actions to compete successfully.

Organizations Collections of people working together in a division of labor to achieve a common purpose.

Organizing The process of dividing up tasks and arranging resources to accomplish them.

Output controls Controls that focus on desired targets and allow managers to use their own methods for reaching defined targets.

Output goals The goals that define the type of business an organization is in.

Output measures Performance appraisal criteria based on actual work output.

Paired comparison A comparative method of performance appraisal whereby each person is directly compared with every other person.

Parochialism The tendency to assume that the values and characteristics of one's culture are the only correct ones.

Participative leadership Focuses on consulting with subordinates and seeking and taking their suggestions into account.

Passive management by exception Intervening with subordinates only if standards are not met.

Perception The process through which people receive, organize, and interpret information from their environment.

Performance appraisal A process of systematically evaluating performance and providing feedback on which performance adjustments can be made.

Performance gap A discrepancy between an actual and a desired state of affairs.

Performing stage The stage of group development when the group performs in a mature, organized fashion; also called the total integration stage.

Permanent groups Formal groups that perform on a continuing basis.

Permanent part-time work A work schedule in which someone works less than the standard 40 hours in one week on a permanent basis.

Permanent work groups Also called command groups, these groups often appear on organization charts as departments, divisions, or teams and are officially created to perform a specific, ongoing function.

Person schemas The way individuals sort others into categories.

Person-in-situation schemas Combined schemas built around persons and events.

Person–role conflict Incompatibility of role expectations with personal values.

Personal bias error Occurs when a rater allows specific biases, such as racial, age, or gender, to enter into performance appraisal.

Personal conceptions The ways individuals tend to think about their social and physical environment and their major beliefs and personal perspectives concerning a range of issues.

Personal wellness The pursuit of one's physical and mental potential through a personal health promotion program.

Personality The overall profile or combination of traits that characterize the unique nature of a person.

Personality dynamics The ways in which an individual integrates and organizes social traits, values and motives, personal conceptions, and emotional adjustment.

Planned change Change that occurs by a change agent's intentional direction.

Planning The process of setting objectives and identifying the actions needed to achieve them.

Policies Guidelines for actions that outline important objectives and indicate how activities are to be performed.

Polychronic culture A culture in which people tend to do more than one thing at a time.

Position power A measure of the leader's task expertise and reward/punishment authority.

Positive reinforcement The administration of positive consequences that tend to increase the likelihood of repeating the behavior in similar settings.

Power The ability to get someone else to do something you want done, or the ability to make things happen or get things done the way you want.

Power distance   The willingness of a culture to accept status and power differences among its members.

Primary beneficiaries   Particular groups expected to benefit from the efforts of specific organizations.

Problem solving   Gathering and evaluating information in solving problems and making decisions.

Procedural justice   The degree to which policies and procedures are properly followed in all cases to which they apply.

Process consultation   An OD intervention concerned with helping a group improve on such things as norms, cohesiveness, decision-making methods, communication, conflict, and task and maintenance activities.

Process controls   Controls that attempt to specify the manner in which tasks are to be accomplished.

Process reengineering   The total rethinking and redesign of organizational processes to improve performance and innovation; involves analyzing, streamlining, and reconfiguring actions and tasks to achieve work goals.

Process theories   Theories that seek to understand the thought processes determining behavior.

Professional bureaucracy   An entire organization that relies on organic features in its design.

Programmed decisions   Decisions that are determined by past experience as appropriate for a problem at hand.

Projection   The assignment of personal attributes to other individuals.

Punishment   The administration of negative consequences that tend to reduce the likelihood of repeating the behavior in similar settings.

Quality circle   Members of a quality circle meet regularly to find ways for continuous improvement of quality operations.

Quality performance   When the customers' needs are being met and all tasks are done right the first time.

Quality of work life (QWL)   The overall quality of human experiences in the workplace.

Quasi-experimental design   An experimental research design without random assignment of individuals to experimental research conditions or without random assignment of experimental treatment to individuals.

Questionnaires   Forms that ask respondents for their opinions, attitudes, perceptions, and/or descriptions of work-related matters.

Racioethnicity   A term used to reflect the broad spectrum of employees of differing ethnicities or races who are providing an ever-increasing portion of the new workforce.

Radical change   Frame-breaking change that results in a major makeover of the organization.

Ranking   A comparative technique of performance appraisal that involves rank ordering of each individual from best to worst on each performance dimension.

Rational persuasion strategy   Uses facts, special knowledge, and rational argument to create change.

Realistic job preview (RJP)   A recruitment technique whereby applicants are provided with an objective description of the organization and the job.

Recency error   A biased rating that develops by allowing the individual's most recent behavior to speak for his or her overall performance on a particular dimension.

Recruitment   The process of attracting the best qualified individuals to apply for a job.

Referent power   The ability to control another's behavior because of the individual's wanting to identify with the power source.

Refreezing   The stage of the change process where changes are reinforced and stabilized.

Reinforcement   The administration of a consequence as a result of behavior.

Relatedness needs   Desires for satisfying interpersonal relationships.

Relationship goals   Goals that take into account how well people involved in a negotiation, and their constituencies, will be able to work with one another once the process is concluded.

Reliability   The consistency and stability of a score from a measurement scale.

Representative heuristic   A "rule of thumb" that bases a decision on similarities between the situation at hand and stereotypes of similar occurrences.

Required behaviors   Those contributions the organization formally requests from group members as a basis for continued affiliation and support.

Research design   An overall plan or strategy for conducting research to test a hypothesis.

Resistance to change   An attitude or behavior that shows unwillingness to make or support a change.

Restricted communication networks   Networks that involve polarized subgroups who contest one another's positions in sometimes antagonistic relations.

Reward power   The extent to which a manager can use extrinsic and intrinsic rewards to control other people.

Risk environments   Business environments that provide only probabilities regarding expected results for decision-making alternatives.

Rites   Standardized and recurring activities used at special times to influence the behaviors and understanding of organizational members.

Rituals   Systems of rites.

Role   A set of expectations for a team member or person in a job.

Role ambiguity   Occurs when someone is uncertain about what is expected of him or her.

Role conflict   The inability of a person in a role to respond to the expectations of one or more members of the role set; *also,* when someone is unable to respond to role expectations that conflict with one another.

Role negotiation   Negotiation that takes place when people share expectations to clarify what each should be doing in a job or as group members.

Role overload   Occurs when someone is expected to do too much in a role.

Role underload   When someone is expected to do too little in a role.

Routine problems   Problems that can be addressed through standardized responses or programmed decisions.

Rules and procedures   Written documents that verify in detail how tasks are to be performed and/or decisions made in various circumstances.

Sagas   Embellished heroic accounts of the story of the founding of an organization.

Satisficing   Decision making that chooses the first satisfactory decision alternative.

Scanning   Looking outside the firm and bringing back useful solutions to problems.

Schemas   Cognitive frameworks that represent organized knowledge about a given concept or stimulus developed through experience.

Scientific method   Research guided by four steps: the research question or problem, hypothesis generation or formulation, the research design, and data gathering, analysis, and interpretation.

Script schemas   Knowledge frameworks that describe the appropriate sequence of events in a given situation.

Scripts   Behavioral routines that become part of the organization's culture.

Selection   The series of steps from initial applicant screening to hiring.

Selective perception   The tendency to single out for attention those aspects of a situation or person that reinforce or emerge and are consistent with existing beliefs, values, and needs.

Self-concept   The view individuals have of themselves as physical, social, and spiritual or moral beings.

Self-efficacy   An individual's belief about the likelihood of successfully completing a specific task; it is sometimes called the "effectance motive"; a person's belief that he or she can perform adequately in a situation.

Self-esteem   A belief about one's own worth based on overall self-evaluation.

Self-fulfilling prophecy   The confirmation of one's initial expectations by creating in the work situation that which one has expected to find.

Self-managing teams   Teams that are empowered to make decisions about planning, doing, and evaluating their daily work.

Self-monitoring   A person's ability to adjust his or her behavior to external, situational factors.

Self schemas Cognitive frameworks that represent organized knowledge and information about one's own appearance, behavior, and personality.

Self-serving bias The tendency to deny personal responsibility for performance problems but to accept personal responsibility for performance success.

Sensation-type individuals People who prefer routine and order, and emphasize well-defined details in gathering information.

Sensitivity training An OD intervention designed to increase the self-awareness of individuals and their "sensitivity" toward other people.

Sentiments The feelings, attitudes, beliefs, or values held by group members.

Shamrock organizations Firms that operate with a core group of permanent workers supplemented by outside contracts and part-time workers.

Shaping The creation of a new behavior by the positive reinforcement of successive approximations to the desired behavior.

Shared meaning A sense of broader purpose workers infuse into their tasks as a result of interaction with one another and reinforcement by the rest of the organization.

Shared-power strategy Uses participative methods and emphasizes common values to create change.

Simple design An organization configuration involving one or two ways of specializing individuals and units.

Situational control The extent to which leaders can determine what their group is going to do and what the outcomes of their actions and decisions are going to be.

Skill-based pay A system that rewards people for acquiring and developing job-relevant skills in number and variety relevant to the organization's need.

Smoothing Playing down differences among conflicting parties and highlighting similarities and areas of agreement; also known as accommodation.

Social information–processing approach Believes that individual needs and task perceptions result from socially constructed realities.

Social learning Learning that is achieved through the reciprocal interaction between people and their environment.

Social loafing Occurs when people work less hard in groups than they would individually.

Social responsibility The obligation of organizations to behave in ethical and moral ways.

Social traits Surface-level traits that reflect the way one appears to others through interactions.

Socialization Orienting new employees to the firm and its work units.

Societal goals Goals reflecting the intended contributions of an organization to the broader society.

Sociotechnical systems Organizational systems that integrate people and technology into high-performance work settings.

Span of control The number of individuals reporting to a supervisor.

Specific environment The set of suppliers, distributors, competition, and government agencies with which a particular organization must interact to survive and grow.

Staff units Groups that assist the line units by performing specialized services to the organization.

Standardization The degree to which the range of actions in a job or series of jobs is limited.

Status A person's relative rank, prestige, or standing in a group.

Status congruence The consistency between a person's status within and outside of a group.

Stereotyping The assignment of an individual to a group or category (e.g., old person) and ascribing the attributes commonly associated with the group or category to the person in question.

Stimulus Something that incites action.

Storming stage Stage of group development that is concerned with sorting out member expectations; there is high emotionality and tension among group members; conflict may develop over leadership and authority.

Strategic alliance An alliance of two or more firms to work together cooperatively to accomplish limited or continuing performance objectives.

Stress Tension from extraordinary demands, constraints, or opportunities.

Stress prevention Taking action to minimize the occurrence of destructive stress.

Stressors Things that cause stress.

Strictness error   Occurs when a rater tends to give everyone a low rating.

Structural redesign   An OD intervention that involves realigning the structure of the organization or major subsystem in order to improve performance.

Subcultures   Unique patterns of values and philosophies within a group that are not consistent with the dominant culture of the larger organization or social system.

Substance goals   Goals that take into account outcomes tied to the "content" issues at hand in a negotiation.

Substantive conflict   Fundamental disagreement over ends or goals to be pursued and the means for their accomplishment.

Substitutes for leadership   Organizational-, individual-, or task-situational variables that substitute for leadership in causing performance/human resource maintenance.

Supportive leadership   Focuses on subordinate needs and well-being and promoting a friendly work climate.

Survey feedback   An OD intervention that begins with the collection of data via questionnaires from organization members or a representative sample of them.

Synergy   The creation of a whole that is greater than the sum of its parts.

Systems goals   Goals concerned with conditions within the organization that are expected to increase its survival potential.

T-groups   Small training groups whose members work together with a professional trainer to share feelings and concerns during sensitivity training.

Task activities   Actions that directly contribute to the performance of important group tasks.

Task performance   The quality and quantity of the work produced or the services provided by a person or group.

Task structure   The degree to which a leader's task goals, procedures, and guidelines are spelled out in the group.

Team building   A collaborative way to gather and analyze data to improve teamwork and implement change; involves a sequence of planned action steps.

Teams   People working together to achieve a common purpose for which they are all accountable.

Teamwork   Occurs when group members work together in ways that well utilize their skills to accomplish a purpose.

Technical skill   An ability to perform specialized tasks.

Technology   The combination of resources, knowledge, and techniques that create a product or service output for an organization.

Telecommuting   Working at home or in remote location that uses computer and other electronic communication linkages with the corporate office.

Temporary groups   Formal groups that perform for a designated time or task only.

Temporary part-time work   A work schedule in which someone works less than the standard 40 hours in one week on a temporary basis.

Temporary work groups   Also called task groups, these groups are created to solve a specific problem or perform a defined task and typically disband once the purpose is accomplished.

Terminal values   Values that reflect a person's beliefs about ends to be achieved.

Theory   A set of systematically interrelated concepts, definitions, and hypotheses that are advanced to explain and predict phenomena.

Theory Z management   The use by organizations anywhere of management and organization practices often identified with the Japanese.

Thinking-type individuals   People who use reason and intellect to deal with problems.

360-degree evaluations   Performance evaluations that are based on feedback from all of the contacts a person may have on the job.

Total quality management (TQM)   A total commitment to high-quality results, continuous improvement, and meeting customer needs.

Total service management   A term used to emphasize the customer commitment that underlies true total quality management.

Training   Provides the opportunity to acquire and improve job-related skills.

Transactional leadership   A leadership style whereby the leader exerts influence during daily leader–subordinate exchanges without much emotion.

Transformational leadership A leadership style whereby the followers' goals are broadened and elevated and confidence is gained to go beyond expectation.

Turnover Decisions by people to terminate their employment.

Two-factor theory Herzberg's theory that identifies job context as a source of job *dis*satisfaction and job content as the source of job satisfaction.

Type A orientation A personality orientation characterized by impatience, desire for achievement, and perfectionism.

Type B orientation A personality characterized by an easygoing and less competitive nature than Type A.

Uncertain environments Business environments that provide no information to predict expected results for decision-making alternatives.

Uncertainty avoidance The cultural tendency to be uncomfortable with uncertainty and risk in everyday life.

Unfreezing The stage of the change process at which a situation is prepared for change.

Unplanned change Change that occurs spontaneously and without a change agent's direction.

Upside-down pyramid An organizational structure that puts customers first and views the job of managers as supporting customer service workers.

Utilitarian view Considers ethical behavior to be that which delivers the greatest good to the greatest number of people.

Valence The value to the individual of various work outcomes.

Validity The degree of confidence one can have in the results of a research study.

Value congruence Occurs when individuals express positive feelings upon encountering others who exhibit values similar to their own.

Values Global beliefs that guide actions and judgments across a variety of situations.

Valuing diversity Managing and working with others in full respect for their individual differences.

Variable A measure used to describe a real-world phenomenon.

Variable interval schedule A reinforcement schedule that provides rewards for a behavior at random times.

Variable ratio schedule A reinforcement schedule that provides rewards after a behavior has occurred a random number of times.

Vertical loading Increases job depth by adding supervisory task responsibilities for planning and evaluating work.

Vertical specialization A hierarchical division of labor that distributes formal authority and establishes how critical decisions will be made.

Vicarious learning Involves capturing the lessons of others' experiences.

Virtual corporation A temporary network or alliance of otherwise independent companies pursuing a joint business interest.

Virtual team A work team that convenes and operates with its members linked together electronically via networked computers.

Whistleblower A person who exposes wrongdoing in organizations in order to preserve ethical standards.

Win–lose conflict Conflict that occurs when one party achieves its desires at the expense of and to the exclusion of the other party's desires.

Win–win conflict A result achieved by collaboration to address the real issues in a conflict situation and the use of problem solving to reconcile differences.

Workforce diversity A broad mix of workers from different racial and ethnic backgrounds, of different ages and genders, of different degrees of able-bodiedness, and of different domestic and national cultures.

Zone of indifference The range of authoritative requests to which a subordinate is willing to respond without subjecting the directives to critical evaluation or judgement, hence to which the subordinate is indifferent.

ENDNOTES

▼ CHAPTER 1 ENDNOTES

[1]Information from "Shattering the AFL-CIO's Glass Ceiling," *Business Week* (November 13, 1995), p. 46.

[2]See Alvin Toffler, *Powershift: Knowledge, Wealth, and Violence at the Edge of the 21st Century* (New York: Bantam Books, 1990).

[3]John Huey, "Managing in the Midst of Chaos," *Fortune* (April 5, 1993), pp. 38–48. See also Tom Peters, *Thriving on Chaos* (New York: Knopf, 1991).

[4]The foundation report on diversity in the American workplace is *Workforce 2000: Work and Workers in the 21st Century* (Indianapolis: The Hudson Institute, 1987). For comprehensive discussions see Martin M. Chemers, Stuart Oskamp, and Mark A. Costanzo, *Diversity in Organizations: New Perspectives for a Changing Workplace* (Beverly Hills, CA.: Sage, 1995); and, Robert T. Golembiewski, *Managing Diversity in Organizations* (Tuscaloosa, AL: The University of Alabama Press, 1995).

[5]Information from *Business Week,* (August 24, 1995).

[6]Information from Francine Schwadel, "Sears Sets Model for Employing Disabled," *The Wall Street Journal* (March 4, 1996), p. B6.

[7]See "Diversity: Beyond the Numbers Game," *Business Week* (August 14, 1995), pp. 60–61; Special Section: "Women in Business," *The Wall Street Journal* (July 26, 1995); "Blacks in America: The Other Half," *The Economist* (November 4, 1995), p. 35; and the Associated Press reports on women's salary surveys, January 16, 1996.

[8]Ross Howard, "Minority Males Fare Worst, Wage Disparity Study Says," *The Globe and Mail* (October 23, 1995).

[9]Carol A. McKeen and Merridee L. Bujaki, "Taking Women into Account," *CA Magazine,* Vol. 127 (March 1994), pp. 29-35.

[10]Information on Europe from "Out of the Typing Pool, Into Career Limbo," *Business Week* (April 15, 1996), pp. 92-94.

[11]Gilbert Fuchsberg, "Total Quality Is Termed Only Partial Success," *The Wall Street Journal* (October 1, 1993), p. B1.

[12]Information from Robert Heller, "TQM — Not a Panacea but a Pilgrimage," *Management Today* (January 1993); William Armbruster, "Honeywell Has Edge in the European Market," *Journal of Commerce* (January 17, 1990); and Richard Ringer, "Honeywell Names New Top Officers," *The New York Times* (January 17, 1993).

[13]See, for example, Jay R. Galbraith, Edward E. Lawler III, and Associates, *Organizing for the Future: The New Logic for Managing Organizations* (San Francisco: Jossey-Bass, 1993); and, Peter Drucker, *Managing in a Time of Great Change* (New York: Truman Talley, 1995).

[14]Michael Hammer and James Champy, *Reengineering the Corporation* (New York: Harper-Collins, 1993).

[15]See Thomas A. Stewart, "Planning a Career Without Managers," *Fortune* (March 20, 1995), pp. 72–80.

[16]William H. Davidow and Michael S. Malone, *The Virtual Corporation: Structuring and Revitalizing the Corporation of the 21st Century* (New York: Harper Business, 1993).

[17]See Andrew Kupfer, "Along Together: Will Being Wired Set us Free?" *Fortune* (March 20, 1995), pp. 94–104.

[18]Charles Handy, *The Age of Unreason* (Boston: Harvard Business School Press, 1990). See also his later book, *The Age of Paradox* (Boston: Harvard Business School Press, 1994).

[19]See Stewart, op. cit., 1995; Brian Dumaine, "The New Non-Manager Managers," *Fortune* (February 22, 1993), pp. 80–84; and Walter Kiechel III, "How We Will Work in the Year 2000," *Fortune* (May 17, 1993), pp. 38–52.

[20]See George Huber, "Organizational Learning: The Contributing Process and the Literature," *Organizational Science,* Vol. 2 (1991), pp. 88–115; D. A. Garvin, "Building a Learning Organization," *Harvard Business Review* (November/December, 1991), pp. 78–91; and, Peter Senge, *The Fifth Discipline* (New York: Harper, 1990).

[21]Information from "It's Not Easy Making Pixie Dust," *Business Week* (September 18, 1995), p. 134.

[22]Tom Peters, "Managing in a World Gone Bonkers," *World Executive Digest* (February 1993), pp. 26–29. See also Tom Peters, *Liberation Management* (New York: Knopf, 1992).

[23]David A. Kolb, "On Management and the Learning Process," in David A. Kolb, Irwin M. Rubin, and James M. McIntyre, eds., *Organizational Psychology: A Book of Readings,* 2nd ed. (Englewood Cliffs, NJ: Prentice Hall, 1974), pp. 27–42.

[24]See Jay W. Lorsch (ed.), *Handbook of Organizational Behavior* (Englewood Cliffs, N.J.: Prentice-Hall, 1987), for a general overview. For specific details on the Hawthorne studies see Ronald G. Greenwood and Charles D. Wrege, "The Hawthorne Studies," in Daviel A. Wren and John A. Pearce, II (eds.), *Papers Dedicated to the Development of Modern Management: Celebrating 100 Years of Modern Management* (Academy of Management 1986); and Ronald G. Greenwood, A. Bolton and R.A. Greenwood, "Hawthorne Half a Century Later: Relay Assembly Participants Remember," *Journal of Management,* (Fall/Winter, 1983), pp. 217–231.

[25]Geert Hofstede, "Cultural Constraints in Management Theories," *Academy of Management Executive,* Vol. 7 (1993), pp. 81–94. See also his book *Culture's Consequences* (Beverly Hills, CA: Sage Publications, 1980).

[26]Two recent books on mission statements are Patricia Jones and Larry Kahaner, *Say It and Live It: The 50 Corporate Mission Statements that Hit the Mark* (New York: Currency/Doubleday, 1995) and John Graham and Wendy Havlick, *Mission Statements: A Guide to the Corporate and Nonprofit Sectors* (New York: Garland Publishers, 1995).

[27]For a report see Fred "Chico" Lager, *Ben & Jerry's: The Inside Scoop* (New York: Crown, 1994).

[28]See Henry Mintzberg, *The Nature of Managerial Work* (New York: Harper & Row, 1973); Morgan W. McCall, Jr., Ann M. Morrison, and Robert L. Hannan, *Studies of Managerial Work: Results and Methods,* Tech-

nical Report No. 9 (Greensboro, N.C.: Center for Creative Leadership, 1978); John P. Kotter, *The General Managers* (New York: Free Press, 1982); Robert E. Kaplan, *The Warp and Woof of the General Manager's Job,* Technical Report No. 27 (Greensboro, NC: Center for Creative Leadership, 1986).

[29]Kotter, op. cit., 1982; John P. Kotter, "What Effective General Managers Really Do," *Harvard Business Review,* Vol. 60 (November/December 1982), p. 161. See Kaplan, op. cit., 1984.

[30]Herminia Ibarra, "Managerial Networks," Teaching Note #9-495-039, Harvard Business School Publishing, Boston, MA.

[31]See also Fred Luthans, Richard M. Hodgetts, and Stuart A. Rosenkrantz, *Real Managers* (New York: Harper Collins, 1988); Fred Luthans, Stuart Rosenkrantz, and Harry Hennessey, "What Do Successful Managers Really Do?" *The Journal of Applied Behavioral Science,* Vol. 21 (No. 2), 1985, pp. 255–270.

[32]Robert L. Katz, "Skills of an Effective Administrator," *Harvard Business Review,* Vol. 52 (September/October 1974), p. 94. See also Richard E. Boyatzis, *The Competent Manager: A Model for Effective Performance* (New York: John Wiley, 1982).

[33]See Blair Sheppard, Roy J. Lewicki, and John Minton, *Organizational Justice: The Search for Fairness in the Workplace* (New York: Lexington Books, 1992); and Jerald Greenberg, *The Quest for Justice on the Job: Essays and Experiments* (Thousand Oaks, CA: Sage Publications, 1995).

[34]See Steven N. Brenner and Earl A. Mollander, "Is the Ethics of Business Changing," *Harvard Business Review,* Vol. 55 (January/February 1977), pp. 50–57; Saul W. Gellerman, "Why 'Good' Managers Make Bad Ethical Choices," *Harvard Business Review,* Vol. 64 (July/August 1986), pp. 85–90; Barbara Ley Toffler, *Tough Choices: Managers Talk Ethics* (New York: John Wiley, 1986); Justin G. Longnecker, Joseph A. McKinney, and Carlos W. Moore, "The Generation Gap in Business Ethics," *Business Horizons,* Vol. 32 (September/October 1989), pp. 9–14; John B. Cullen, Vart Victor, and Carroll Stephens, "An Ethical Weather Report: Assessing the Organization's Ethical Climate," *Organizational Dynamics,* (Winter 1990), pp. 50–62; Dawn Blalock, "Study Shows Many Execs Are Quick to Write Off Ethics," *The Wall Street Journal* (March 26, 1996), p. C1.

[35]Developed in part from Alan L. Otten, "Ethics on the Job: Companies Alert Employees to Potential Dilemmas," *The Wall Street Journal* (July 14, 1986), p. 17.

[36]Based on Gellerman, op. cit., 1986.

[37]For research on whistleblowers see Paula M. Miceli and Janet P. Near, *Blowing the Whistle* (New York: Lexington, 1992).

[38]Information from Susan Gaines, "The Home Depot," *Business Ethics* (November/December 1995), p. 36.

[39]David A. Nadler and Edward E. Lawler III, "Quality of Work Life: Perspectives and Directions," *Organizational Dynamics,* Vol. 11 (1983), pp. 22–36; the discussion of "QWL" in Thomas G. Cummings and Edgar F. Huse, *Organizational Development and Change* (St. Paul, MN: West, 1990).

▼ CHAPTER 2 ENDNOTES

[1]Information from John Lorinc, "Road Warriors," *Canadian Business* (October, 1995), pp. 26–43; and Arthur Johnson, "Editor's Note," *Canadian Business* (October, 1995), p. 11.

[2]See Kenichi Ohmae, *The Borderless World* (New York: Harper Business, 1989).

[3]See Kenichi Ohmae, *The Evolving Global Economy* (Cambridge, Mass.: Harvard Business School Press, 1995); and, *World Investment Report 1995: Transnational Corporations and Competitiveness* (New York: United Nations Conference on Trade and Development, 1995).

[4]William B. Johnston, "Global Workforce 2000: The New World Labor Market," *Harvard Business Review* (March-April, 1991), pp. 115-127.

[5]Data from *Fortune* (August 7, 1995), p. 136 and *The Wall Street Journal* (October 2, 1995), p. R33. For up-to-date statistics see annual reports by *The Wall Street Journal, Fortune, Business Week, and The Economist,* among other business periodicals.

[6]See Kenichi Ohmae *The End of the Nation State: The Rise of Regional Economies* (New York: The Free Press, 1995).

[7]Information from "American Workers Watch as Best Jobs Go Overseas," *The International Herald Tribune* (August 29, 1995), p. 1.

[8]Information on Canadian investment from Johanna Powell, "The U.S.A.'s Irresistible Pull," *The Financial Post* (September 30, 1995), p. 30.

[9]"The South Korean Economy Goes Global at Last," *The New York Times* (October 24, 1995), pp. C6, C7.

[10]"Just a Wee Bit of Life in Slicon Glen," *World Business* (March/April 1996), p. 13.

[11]Brian O'Reilly, "Your New Global Workforce," *Fortune* (December 14, 1992), pp. 52–66.

[12]See "Clinging to the Safety Net: Most Nations Want to Streamline Their Economies Slowly," *Business Week* (March 11, 1996), cover story.

[13]Information from "Europe: A Convoy in Distress," *The Economist* (March 16th, 1996), pp. 49-50; and, "Europe: Ever More Complicated Union," *The Economist* (March 30th, 1996), pp. 47-48.

[14]Sarita Kendall and Nancy Dunne, "Business Spurs All-America Free Trade Accord," *Financial Times* (March 22, 1996), p.3.

[15]Udayan Gupta, "African-American Firms Gain Foothold in South Africa," *The Wall Street Journal* (October 6, 1994), p. B2.Other parts of the world are active in regional economic alliances as well.

[16]"Don't Be An Ugly-American Manager," *Fortune* (October 16, 1995), p. 225; Shawn Tully, "The Hunt for the Global Manager," *Fortune* (May 21, 1990), pp. 140–144; and Robert T. Moran and John R. Riesenberger, *Making Globalization Work: Solutions for Implementation* (New York: McGraw-Hill, 1993).

[17]"Working Overseas—Rule No.1: Don't Miss the Locals," *Business Week* (May 15, 1995), p. 8.

[18]"Don't Be An Ugly-American Manager," *Fortune* (October 16, 1995), p. 225.

[19]Vanessa Houlder, "Foreign Culture Shocks," *Financial Times* (March 22, 1996), p. 12.

[20]Information from Brian O'Reilly, "How Execs Learn," *Fortune* (April 5, 1993), pp. 52–58.

[21]Two well-regarded works on culture are Gert Hofstede, *Culture's Consequences* (Beverly Hills, CA: Sage Publications, 1980); and, Fons Trompenaars, *Riding the Waves of Culture: Understanding Cultural Diversity in Business* (London: Nicholas Brealey Publishing, 1993). For an excellent discussion of the concept, see also Chapter 3, "Culture: The Neglected Concept," in Peter B. Smith and Michael Harris Bond, *Social Psychology Across Cultures* (Boston: Allyn and Bacon, 1994).

[22]A classic work is Benjamin Lee Whorf, *Language, Thought and Reality* (New York: John Wiley, 1956), p. 116.

[23]Edward T. Hall, *Beyond Culture* (New York: Doubleday, 1976).

[24]A classic work and the source of our examples is Edward T. Hall, *The Silent Language* (New York: Anchor Books, 1959).

[25]Allen C. Bluedorn, Carol Felker Kaufman, and Paul M. Lane, "How Many Things Do You Like to Do at Once?" *Academy of Management Executive,* Vol. 6 (November 1992), pp. 17–26.

[26]Edward T. Hall's book *The Hidden Dimension* (New York: Anchor Books, 1969; Magnolia, MI: Peter Smith, 1990) is a classic reference and the source of our examples. See also Edward T. Hall, *Hidden Differences* (New York: Doubleday, 1990).

[27]The classic work is Max Weber, *The Protestant Ethic and the Spirit of Capitalism* (New York: Scribner, 1930). For a description of religious influences in Asian cultures, see S. Gordon Redding, *The Spirit of Chinese Capitalism* (New York: Walter de Gruyter, 1990).

[28]Geert Hofstede, *Culture's Consequences: International Differences in Work-Related Values,* (Beverly Hills, CA: Sage Publications, 1980).

[29]Hofstede, op. cit. (1980); Geert Hofstede and Michael H. Bond, "The Confucius Connection: From Culture Roots to Economic Growth," *Organizational Dynamics,* Vol. 16 (1988), pp. 4–21.

[30]Chinese Culture Connection, "Chinese Values and the Search for Culture-Free Dimensions of Culture," *Journal of Cross-Cultural Psychology,* vol. 18 (1987), pp. 143–164.

[31]Hofstede and Bond, "The Confucious Connection: From Culture Roots to Economic Growth," (1988); and, Geert Hofstede, "Cultural Constraints in Management Theories," *Academy of Management Executive,* Vol. 7 (February 1993), pp. 81–94. See also Jim Rohwer, *Asia Rising: Why America Will Prosper as Asia's Economies Boom* (New York: Simon & Schuster, 1995).

[32]See John R. Schermerhorn, Jr., "Implications of the Likely Interaction of Individualism-Collectivism and Power Distance," *Proceedings of the Eastern Academy of Management Conference, "The Changing Role of the Pacific Rim Economies: Cooperation and Competition,"* Nanyang Technological University, Singapore, June 11-15, 1995.

[33]Nancy J. Adler, *International Dimensions of Organizational Behavior,* 2nd ed. (Boston: PWS-Kent, 1991).

[34]Fons Trompenaars, *Riding the Waves of Culture,* op cit.

[35]Adler, op. cit. (1991).

[36]Alvin Toffler, *The Third Wave* (New York: William Morrow, 1980).

[37]See two articles by Sam Quinones: "A Job is a Dream" and "Maquila Economics" in *Mexico Business* (October 1995), pp. 55–56 and 45–50.

[38]Information from Mary Scott, "Interview with Howard Schultz," *Business Ethics* (November/December, 1995), pp. 26–29; and, Pascal Zachary, "Starbucks Asks Foreign Suppliers to Improve Working Conditions," *The Wall Street Journal* (October 23, 1995), p. B4.

[39]See Hofstede, op. cit. (1980) and op. cit. (1993); Adler, op. cit. (1991).

[40]Adler, op. cit. (1991).

[41]See Rosalie Tung, "Expatriate Assignments: Enhancing Success and Minimizing Failure," *Academy of Management Executive* (May 1987), pp. 117–126; and Adler, op. cit. (1991).

[42]Nancy J. Adler, "Reentry: Managing Cross-Cultural Transitions," *Group and Organization Studies,* Vol. 6, No. 3 (1981), pp. 341–356; and Adler, 1991, op. cit.

[43]Information from Shari Caudron, "Preparing Managers for Overseas Assignments," *World Executive's Digest* (November 1992), pp. 72–73.

[44]William Ouchi, *Theory Z: How American Businesses Can Meet the Japanese Challenge* (Reading, MA: Addison-Wesley, 1981); Richard Tanner and Anthony Athos, *The Art of Japanese Management* (New York: Simon & Schuster, 1981).

[45]See Eamonn Fingleton, *Blindside: Why Japan is Still on Track to Overtake the U.S. by the Year 2000* (New York: Houghton Mifflin, 1995).

[46]See Chapter 13, "Japanese and Korean Management Systems," in Min Chen, *Asian Management Systems* (New York: Routledge, 1995); and J. Bernard Keys, Luther Tray Denton, and Thomas R. Miller, "The Japanese Management Theory Jungle—Revisited," *Journal of Management,* Vol. 20 (1994), pp. 373–402.

[47]Eamonn Fingleton, "Jobs for Life: Why Japan Won't Give Them Up," *Fortune* (March 20, 1995), pp. 119–125.

[48]"In Faint Praise of the Blue Suit," *The Economist* (January 13, 1996), pp. 59–60.

[49]Chen, op. cit., 1995; Jerry Sullivan and Richard B. Peterson, "Japanese Management Theories: A Research Agenda," in Benjamin A. Prasad, ed., *Advances in International Comparative Management,* Vol. 4 (Greenwich, CT: JAI Press, 1989), pp. 255–275.

[50]Timothy Aeppel, "Suzuki Trips Translating its Style into Hungarian," *The Asian Wall Street Journal* (May 7 and 8, 1993), pp. 1, 22.

[51]Information from "Staying Ahead: Samsung Leads Chaebol in Management Reforms," *Far Eastern Economic Review* (May 13, 1993), pp. 68–69.

▼ CHAPTER 3 ENDNOTES

[1]Information from Michelle N. Martinez, "Equality Effort Sharpens Bank's Edge," *HR Magazine* (January 1995), pp. 38–43.

[2]J. Laabs, "Interest in Diversity Training Continues to Grow," *Personnel Journal* (October 1993), p. 18.

[3]L. R. Gomez-Mejia, D. B. Balkin, and R. L. Cardy, *Managing Human Resources* (Englewood Cliffs, NJ: Prentice-Hall, 1995), p. 154.

[4]John P. Fernandez, *Managing a Diverse Workforce* (Lexington, MA: D. C. Heath, 1991); D. Jamieson and Julia   O'Mara, *Managing Workplace 2000* (San Francisco: Jossey-Boss, 1991).

[5]T. G. Exner, "In and Out of Work," *American Demographics* (June, 1992), p. 63, and A. N. Fullerton, "Another Look at the Labor Force," *Monthly Labor Review* (November 1993), p. 34; M. K. Foster and B. J. Orser, "A Marketing Perspective on Women in Management," *Canadian Journal of Administrative Sciences* (Vol. 11, No. 4, 1994), pp. 339–345.

[6]Robert Howard, "Values Make the Company: An Interview with Robert Haas," *Harvard Business Review* (September/October 1990).

[7]The following discussion is based on L. Gardenswartz and A. Rowe, *Managing Diversity: A Complete Desk Reference and Planning Guide* (Homewood, IL: Business One Irwin, 1993), p. 405.

[8]Michelle N. Martinez, op. cit. (1995), p. 40.

[9]Information from Sharon Johnson, "Hospitals Prepare for the International Marketplace," *New York Times Advertising Supplement* (November 12, 1995), p. WF7.

[10]L. R. Gomez-Mejia, D. B. Balkin, and R. L. Cardy, op. cit. (1995).

[11]See G. N. Powell, *Women and Men in Management* (Beverly Hills, CA: Sage Publications, 1988); T. W. Mangione, "Turnover—Some Psychological and Demographic Correlates," in R. P. Quinn and T. W. Mangione, eds., *The 1969-70 Survey of Working Conditions* (Ann Arbor: University of Michigan Survey Research Center, 1973); R. Marsh and H. Mannari, "Organizational Commitment and Turnover: A Predictive Study," *Administrative Science Quarterly* (March 1977), pp. 57–75; R. J. Flanagan, G. Strauss, and L. Ulman, "Worker Discontent and Work Discontent and Work Place Behavior," *Industrial Relations* (May 1974), pp. 101–23; K. R. Garrison and P. M. Muchinsky, "Attitudinal and Biographical Predictions of Incidental Absenteeism," *Journal of Vocational Behavior* (April 1977), pp. 221–230; G. Johns, "Attitudinal and Nonattitudinal Predictions of Two Forms of Absence from Work," *Organizational Behavior and Human Performance* (December 1978), pp. 431–44; R. T. Keller, "Predicting Absenteeism from Prior Absenteeism, Attitudinal Factors, and Nonattitudinal Factors," *Journal of Applied Psychology* (August 1983), pp. 536–540.

[12]M. K. Foster and B. J. Orser, op. cit. (1994), pp. 339–345; and J. P. Fernandez, op. cit. (1991).

[13]American Association of Retired Persons, *The Aging Work Force* (Washington, DC:AARP, 1995), p. 3.

[14]Paul Mayrand, "Older Workers: A Problem or the Solution?" *AARP Textbook Authors Conference Presentation* (October 1992), p. 29; G. M. McEvoy and W. F. Cascio, "Cumulative Evidence of the Relationship Between Employee Age and Job Performance," *Journal of Applied Psychology* (February 1989), pp. 11–17.

[15]K. M. Kacmar and G. R. Ferris, "Theoretical and Methodological Considerations in the Age-Job Satisfaction Relationship," *Journal of Applied Psychology* (April 1989), pp. 201–207.

[16]See John P. Fernandez, op. cit. (1991), p. 236.

[17]See Taylor H. Co and Stacy Blake, "Managing Cultural Diversity: Implications for Organizational Competitiveness," *Academy of Management Executive* (Vol. 5, No. 3, 1991), p. 45.

[18]Literature covering this topic is reviewed in Stephen P. Robbins, *Organi-*

zational Behavior, 7th ed. (Englewood Cliffs, NJ: Prentice-Hall, 1995), Ch. 3.

19Larry L. Cummings and Donald P. Schwab, *Performance in Organizations: Determinants and Appraisal* (Glenview, IL: Scott, Foresman, 1973), p. 8.

20See J. E. Hunter and R. F. Hunter, "Validity and Utility of Alternative Predictors of Job Performance," *Psychological Bulletin* (January 1984), pp. 72–98.

21See J. Hogan "Structure of Physical Performance in Occupational Tasks," *Journal of Applied Psychology* (Vol. 76, 1991) pp. 495–507.

22Information from Sharon Johnson, "The Global Marketplace," *New York Times Advertising Supplement* (November 12, 1995), pp. WF16–WF17.

23See B. Dumaine, "America's Toughest Bosses," *Fortune* (October 18, 1993), pp. 39–48.

24See N. Brody, *Personality: In Search of Individuality* (San Diego, CA: Academic Press, 1988), pp. 68–101; C. Holden, "The Genetics of Personality," *Science* (August 7, 1987), pp. 598–601.

25See Geert Hofstede, *Culture's Consequences: International Differences in Work-Related Values,* abridged ed. (Beverly Hills: Sage Publications, 1984).

26Chris Argyris, *Personality and Organization* (New York: Harper & Row, 1957).

27Daniel J. Levinson, *The Seasons of a Man's Life* (New York: Alfred A. Knopf, 1978).

28M. R. Barrick and M. K. Mount, "The Big Personality Dimensions and Job Performance: A Meta Analysis," *Personnel Psychology* (Vol. 44, 1991), pp. 1–26, and "Autonomy As a Moderator of the Relationships Between the Big Five Personality Dimensions and Job Performance," *Journal of Applied Psychology* (February, 1993), pp. 111–118.

29See Jim C. Nunnally, *Psychometric Theory,* 2nd ed. (New York: McGraw Hill, 1878), Ch. 14.

30 See David A. Whetten and Kim S. Cameron, *Developing Management Skills,* 2nd ed. (New York: Harper Collins), p. 66.

31Raymond G. Hunt, Frank J. Krzystofiak, James R. Meindl, and Abdalla M. Yousry, "Cognitive Style and Decision Making," *Organizational Behavior and Human Decision Processes,* (Vol. 44, No. 3, 1989), pp. 436–453. For additional work on problem-solving styles, see Ferdinand A. Gul, "The Joint and Moderating Role of Personality and Cognitive Style on Decison Making," *The Accounting Review* (April 1984), pp. 264–277; Brian H. Kleiner, "The Interrelationship of Junigian Modes of Mental Functioning with Organizational Factors: Implications for Management Development," *Human Relations* (November 1983), pp. 997–1012; James L. McKenney and Peter G. W. Keen, "How Managers' Minds Work," *Harvard Business Review* (May/June 1974), pp. 79–90.

32Some examples of firms using the Myers-Briggs Indicators are J. M. Kunimerow and L. W. McAllister, "Team Building with the Myers-Briggs Type Indicator: Case Studies," *Journal of Psychological Type* (Vol. 15, 1988), pp. 26–32; G. H. Rice, Jr., and D. P. Lindecamp, "Personality Types and Business Success of Small Retailers," *Journal of Occupational Psychology,* (Vol. 62, 1989), pp. 177–182; and B. Roach, *Strategy Styles and Management Types: A Resource Book for Organizational Management Consultants* (Stanford, CA: Balestrand Press, 1989).

33Kunimerow and McAllister, op. cit. (1988); Rice and Lindecamp, op. cit (1989); Roach, op. cit, (1989).

34J. B. Rotter, "Generalized Expectancies for Internal versus External Control of Reinforcement," *Psychological Monographs* (Vol. 80, 1966), pp. 1–28.

35Don Hellriegel, John W. Slocum, Jr., and Richard W. Woodman, *Organizational Behavior,* 5th ed. (St. Paul, MN: West, 1989), p. 46.

36See John A. Wagner III and John R. Hollenbeck, *Management of Organizational Behavior* (Englewood Cliffs, NJ: Prentice-Hall, 1992), Ch. 4.

37Niccolo Machiavelli, *The Prince,* George Bull, transl. (Middlesex U.K. Penguin, 1961).

38Richard Christie and Florence L. Geis, *Studies in Machiavellianism* (New York: Academic Press, 1970).

39See M. Synder, *Public Appearances/Private Realities: The Psychology of Self-Monitoring* (New York: W. H. Freeman, 1987).

40Ibid.

41Adapted from R. W. Bortner, "A Short Scale: A Potential Measure of Pattern A Behavior," *Journal of Chronic Diseases* (Vol. 22, 1969). Used by permission.

42See Meyer Friedman and Ray Roseman, *Type A Behavior and Your Heart* (New York: Alfred A. Knopf, 1974). For another view, see Walter Kiechel III, "Attack of the Obsessive Managers," *Fortune* (February 16, 1987), pp. 127–128.

43Viktor Gecas, "The self-concept," in Ralph H. Turner and James F. Short, Jr., eds. Vol. 8 *Annual Review of Sociology,* (Palo Alto, CA: Annual Review, Inc., 1982), p. 3. Also see Arthur P. Brief and Ramon J. Aldag, "The 'Self' in Work Organizations: A Conceptual Review," *Academy of Management Review* (January 1981), pp. 75–88; and Jerry J. Sullivan, "Self Theories and Employee Motivation," *Journal of Management* (June 1989), pp. 345–363.

44Compare Philip Cushman, "Why the Self Is Empty," *American Psychologist* (May 1990), pp. 599–611.

45Based in part on a definition in Viktor Gecas, op. cit. (1982), p. 3.

46Suggested by J. Brockner, *Self-Esteem at Work* (Lexington, MA: Lexington Books, 1988) p. 144; and Wagner and Hollenbeck, op. cit. (1992), pp. 100–101.

47See P. E. Jacob, J. J. Flink, and H. L. Schuchman, "Values and Their Function in Decisionmaking," *American Behavioral Scientist* (Vol. 5, Suppl. 9 1962), pp. 6–38.

48See M. Rokeach and S. J. Ball Rokeach, "Stability and Change in American Value Priorities, 1968–1981," *American Psychologist* (May 1989), pp. 775–784.

49Milton Rokeach, *The Nature of Human Values* (New York: Free Press, 1973).

50See W. C. Frederick and J. Weber, "The Values of Corporate Managers and Their Critics: An Empirical Description and Normative Implications," in W. C. Frederick and L. E. Preston, eds., *Business Ethics: Research Issues and Empirical Studies* (Greenwich, CT: JAI Press, 1990), pp. 123–144.

51Gordon Allport, Philip E. Vernon, and Gardner Lindzey, *Study of Values* (Boston: Houghton Mifflin, 1931).

52Adapted from R. Tagiuri, "Purchasing Executive: General Manager or Specialist?" *Journal of Purchasing* (August 1967), pp. 16–21.

53Bruce M. Meglino, Elizabeth C. Ravlin, and Cheryl L. Adkins, "Value Congruence and Satisfaction with a Leader: An Examination of the Role of Interaction," unpublished manuscript (Columbia, SC: University of South Carolina, 1990), pp. 8–9.

54Ibid.

55Daniel Yankelovich, *New Rules! Searching for Self-Fulfillment in a World Turned Upside Down* (New York: Random House, 1981); Daniel Yankelovich, Hans Zetterberg, Burkhard Strumpel, and Michael Shanks, *Work and Human Values: An International Report on Jobs in the 1980s and 1990s* (Aspen, CO: Aspen Institute for Humanistic Studies, 1983).

56See Jamieson and O'Mara, op. cit. (1991), pp. 28–29.

57See Sang M. Lee, Sangjim Yoo, and Tosca M. Lee, "Korean Chaebol: Corporate Values and strategies," *Organizational Dynamics* (Spring 1991), p. 40.

58Compare Martin Fishbein and Icek Ajzen, *Belief, Attitude, Intention and Behavior: An Introduction to Theory and Research* (Reading, MA: Addison-Wesley, 1975).

59See A. W. Wicker, "Attitude Versus Action: The Relationship of Verbal and Overt Behavioral Responses to Attitude Objects," *Journal of Social Issues* (Autumn 1969), pp. 41–78.

60Leon Festinger, *A Theory of Cognitive Dissonance* (Palo Alto, CA: Stanford University Press, 1957).

[61]H. W. Lane and J. J. DiStefano, eds., *International Management Behavior* (Scarborough, Ontario: Nelson Canada, 1988), pp. 4–5; Z. Abdoolcarim, "How Women Are Winning at Work," *Asian Business* (November 1993), pp. 24–29.

[62]Sharon Johnson, "Diversity Training Now More Comprehensive," *New York Times Advertising Supplement* (November 12, 1995), p. WF6.

[63]Sharon Johnson, "NYNEX Establishes Awards Program" *New York Times Advertising Supplement* (November 12, 1995), p. WF9.

[64]See "Managing Diversity," *Black Enterprise* (July 1993), p. 84.

▼ CHAPTER 4 ENDNOTES

[1]"Vormawah Holds Unique Position as Africa's First Female Sea Captain," *Lubbock Avalanche-Journal* (January 3 1996), p. 4B.

[2]H. R. Schiffmann, *Sensation and Perception: An Integrated Approach,* 3rd ed. (New York: Wiley, 1990).

[3]"Clark's Catch Engraved in NFL Lore." *Lubbock Avalanche-Journal* (January 11, 1992), p. D5.

[4]See M. W. Levine and J. M. Shefner, *Fundamentals of Sensation and Perception;* Georgia T. Chao and Steve W. J. Kozlowski, "Employee Perceptions on the Implementation of Robotic Manufacturing Technology," *Journal of Applied Psychology* (Vol. 71, 1986), pp. 70–76; Steven F. Cronshaw and Robert G. Lord, "Effects of Categorization, Attribution, and Encoding Processes in Leadership Perceptions," *Journal of Applied Psychology* (Vol. 72, 1987), pp. 97–106.

[5]Based on Kevin Rubens, "Changes in Russia Challenge HR," *HR Magazine* (November 1995), p. 72.

[6]See Robert Lord, "An Information Processing Approach to Social Perception's, Leadership, and Behavioral Measurement in Organizations," in B. M. Staw and L. L. Cummings, eds., *Research in Organizational Behavior,* Vol. 7 (Greenwich, CT: AI Press, 1985), pp. 87–128; T. K. Srull and R. S. Wyer, *Advances in Social Cognition* (Hillsdale, NJ: Erlbaum, 1988); U. Neisser, *Cognition and Reality* (San Francisco: W. HJ. Freeman, 1976), p. 112.

[7]See J. G. Hunt, *Leadership: A New Synthesis* (Newbury Park, CA: Sage Publications, 1991), Ch. 7; R. G. Lord and R. J. Foti, "Schema Theories, Information Processing, and Organizational Behavior," in H. P. Sims, Jr., and D. A. Gioia, eds., *The Thinking Organization* (San Francisco: Jossey-Bass, 1986), pp. 20–48; S. T. Fiske and S. E. Taylor, *Social Cognition* (Reading, MA: Addison-Wesley, 1984).

[8]See J. S. Phillips, "The Accuracy of Leadership Ratings: A Categorization Perspective," *Organizational Behavior and Human Performance* (Vol. 33, 1984), pp. 125–138; J. G. Hunt, B. R. Baliga, and M. F. Peterson, "Strategic Apex Leader Scripts and an Organizational Life Cycle Approach to Leadership and Excellence," *Journal of Management Development* (Vol. 7, 1988), pp. 61–83.

[9]D. Bilimoria and S. K. Piderit, "Board Committee Membership Effects of Sex-Biased Bias," *Academy of Management Journal* (Vol. 37, 1994), pp. 1453–1477.

[10]C. Pasternak, "Diversity Uncommon Among Executives," *HR Magazine* (November 1994), p. 20.

[11]Dewitt C. Dearborn and Herbert A. Simon, "Selective Perception: A Note on the Departmental Indentification of Executives," *Sociometry* (Vol. 21, 1958), pp. 140–144.

[12]J. P. Walsh, "Selectivity and Selective Perception: An Investigation of Managers' Belief Structures and Information Processing," *Academy of Management Journal* (Vol. 24, 1988), pp. 453–470.

[13]Based on "Marketing Excellence Ontario Award Recipient, 1995 Entrepreneur of the Year," *Canadian Business* (November 1995), pp. 11–12.

[14]J. Sterling Livingston, "Pygmalion in Management," *Harvard Business Review* (July/August 1969).

[15]D. Eden and A. B. Shani, "Pygmalian Goes to Boot Camp," *Journal of Applied Psychology* (Vol. 67, 1982), pp. 194–199.

[16]See B. R. Schlenker, *Impression Management: The Self-Concept, Social Identity, and Interpersonal Relations* (Monterey, CA: Brooks/Cole, 1980); W. L. Gardner and M. J. Martinko, "Impression Management in Organizations," *Journal of Management* (June 1988), p. 332; R. B. Cioldini, "Indirect Tactics of Image Management: Beyond Banking," in R. A. Giacolini and P. Rosenfeld, eds., *Impression Management in the Organization* (Hillsdale, NJ: Erlbaum, 1989), pp. 45–71.

[17]"How Gillette Is Honing Its Edge," *Business Week* (September 28, 1992), p. 60; "Training Program Assures Supply of Global Talent," *Personnel Journal* (January 1993), p. 56; "We Had To Change the Playing Field," *Forbes* (February 4, 1991), pp. 84–86.

[18]See H. H. Kelley, "Attributon in Social Interaction," in E. Jones, et al., eds., *Attribution: Perceiving the Causes of Behavior* (Morristown, NJ: General Learning Press, 1972).

[19]See Terence R. Mitchell, S. G. Green, and R. E. Wood, "An Attribution Model of Leadership and the Poor Performing Subordinate," in Barry Staw and Larry L. Cummings, eds., *Research in Organizational Behavior* (New York: JAI Press, 1981) pp. 197–234; John H. Harvey and Gifford Weary, "Current Issues in Attribution Theory and Research," *Annual Review of Psychology* (Vol. 35, 1984), pp. 427–459.

[20]Data reported in John R. Schermerhorn, Jr., "Team Development for High Performance Management," *Training & Development Journal* (Vol. 40, November 1986), pp. 38–41.

[21]R. M. Steers, S. J. Bischoff, and L. H. Higgins, "Cross Cultural Management Research," *Journal of Management Inquiry* (December 1992), pp. 325–326; J. G. Miller, "Culture and the Development of Everyday Causal Explanation," *Journal of Personality and Social Psychology* (Vol. 46, 1984), pp. 961–978.

[22]A. Maass and C. Volpato, "Gender Differences in Self-Serving Attributions About Sexual Experiences," *Journal of Applied Psychology* (Vol. 19, 1989), pp. 517–542.

[23]See J. M. Crant and T. S. Bateman, "Assignment of Credit and Blame for Performance Outcomes," *Academy of Management Journal* (February 1993), pp. 7–27; E. C. Pence, W. E. Pendelton, G. H. Dobbins, and J. A. Sgro, "Effects of Causal Explanations and Sex Variables on Recommendations for Corrective Actions Following Employee Failure," *Organizational Behavior and Human Performance* (April 1982), pp. 227–240.

[24]See F. Forsterling, "Attributional Retraining: A Review," *Psychological Bulletin* (November 1985), pp. 496–512.

▼ CHAPTER 5 ENDNOTES

[1]Information from Greg Southam, "Unusual Approach Builds a Winner; Company Owner Rejects Traditional Management Teachings," *The Edmonton Journal* (November 30, 1994), p. D6.

[2]See John P. Campbell, Marvin D. Dunnette, Edward E. Lawler III, and Karl E. Weick, Jr., *Managerial Behavior Performance and Effectiveness* (New York: McGraw-Hill, 1970), Chapter 15.

[3]For a review article that identifies a still relevant need for more integration among motivation theories, see Terrence R. Mitchell, "Motivation—New Directions for Theory, Research and Practice," *Academy of Management Review,* Vol. 7 (January 1982), pp. 80–88.

[4]Geert Hofstede, "Cultural Constraints in Management Theories," *Academy of Management Executive,* Vol. 7 (February 1993), pp. 81–94.

[5]Geert Hofstede, *Culture's Consequences: International Differences in Work-Related Values,* abridged ed.(Beverly Hills, CA: Sage Publications, 1984).

[6]Abraham Maslow, *Eupsychian Management* (Homewood, IL: Irwin, 1965), and *Motivation and Personality,* 2nd ed. (New York: Harper & Row, 1970).

[7]Lyman W. Porter, "Job Attitudes in Management: II. Perceived Importance of Needs as a Function of Job Level," *Journal of Applied Psychology,* Vol. 47 (April 1963), pp. 141–148.

[8]Douglas T. Hall and Khalil E. Nougaim, "An Examination of Maslow's Need Hierarchy in an Organizational Setting," *Organizational Behavior and Human Performance,* Vol. 3 (1968), pp. 12–35; Porter, op. cit. (1963); John M. Ivancevich, "Perceived Need Satisfactions of Domestic Versus Overseas Managers," Vol. 54 (August 1969), pp. 274–278.

[9]Mahmoud A. Wahba and Lawrence G. Bridwell, "Maslow Reconsidered: A Review of Research on the Need Hierarchy Theory," *Academy of Management Proceedings* (1974), pp. 514–520; Edward E. Lawler III and J. Lloyd Shuttle, "A Causal Correlation Test of the Need Hierarchy Concept," *Organizational Behavior and Human Performance,* Vol. 7 (1973), pp. 265–287.

[10]Nancy J. Adler, *International Dimensions of Organizational Behavior,* 2nd ed. (Boston: PWS-Kent, 1991), p. 153.

[11]Ibid.; Richard M. Hodgetts and Fred Luthans, *International Management* (New York: McGraw Hill, 1991), Chapter 11.

[12]Information from Sinclair Hugh, "A Business Education Partnership." *HR Magazine* (January 1991); Sinclair Hugh and Edward Quesada, "Everyone Wins in this Partnership;" Weber Metals, Inc., the Paramount School District, "Workplace Literacy," *Personnel Journal* (October 1990).

[13]Clayton P. Alderfer, "An Empirical Test of a New Theory of Human Needs," *Organizational Behavior and Human Performance,* Vol. 4 (1969), pp. 142–175; Clayton P. Alderfer, *Existence, Relatedness, and Growth* (New York: Free Press, 1972); Benjamin Schneider and Clayton P. Alderfer, "Three Studies of Need Satisfaction in Organization," *Administrative Science Quarterly,* Vol. 18 (1973), pp. 489–505.

[14]Lane Tracy, "A Dynamic Living Systems Model of Work Motivation," *Systems Research,* Vol. 1 (1984), pp. 191–203; John Rauschenberger, Neal Schmidt, and John E. Hunter, "A Test of the Need Hierarchy Concept by a Markov Model of Change in Need Strength," *Administrative Science Quarterly,* Vol. 25 (1980) pp. 654–670.

[15]Sources pertinent to this discussion are David C. McClelland, *The Achieving Society* (New York: Van Nostrand, 1961); David C. McClelland, "Business, Drive and National Achievement," *Harvard Business Review,* Vol. 40 (July/August 1962), pp. 99–112; David C. McClelland, "That Urge to Achieve," *Think* (November/December 1966), pp. 19–32; G. H. Litwin and R. A. Stringer, *Motivation and Organizational Climate* (Boston: Division of Research, Harvard Business School, 1966); pp. 18–25.

[16]George Harris, "To Know Why Men Do What They Do: A Conversation with David C. McClelland," *Psychology Today,* Vol. 4 (January 1971), pp. 35–39.

[17]David C. McClelland and David H. Burnham, "Power Is the Great Motivator," *Harvard Business Review,* Vol. 54 (March/April 1976), pp. 100–110; David C. McClelland and Richard E. Boyatzis, "Leadership Motive Pattern and Long-Term Success in Management," *Journal of Applied Psychology,* Vol. 67 (1982), pp. 737–743.

[18]P. Miron and D. C. McClelland, "The Impact of Achievement Motivation Training in Small Businesses," *California Management Review* (Summer 1979), pp. 13–28.

[19]See J. J. Miller and J. A. Kilpatrick, *Issues for Managers: An International Perspective* (Homewood, IL: Irwin, 1987).

[20]The complete two-factor theory is well explained by Herzberg and his associates in Frederick Herzberg, Bernard Mausner, and Barbara Bloch Synderman, *The Motivation to Work,* 2nd ed.(New York: John Wiley, 1967); and Frederick Herzberg, "One More Time: How Do You Motivate Employees?" *Harvard Business Review,* Vol. 46 (January/February 1968), pp. 53–62.

[21]From Herzberg, op. cit. (1968), pp. 53–62.

[22]See Robert J. House and Lawrence A. Wigdor, "Herzberg's Dual-Factor Theory of Job Satisfaction and Motivation: A Review of the Evidence and a Criticism," *Personnel Psychology,* Vol. 20 (Winter 1967), pp. 369–389; and Steven Kerr, Anne Harlan, and Ralph Stogdill, "Preference for Motivator and Hygiene Factors in a Hypothetical Interview Situation," *Personnel Psychology,* Vol. 27 (Winter 1974), pp. 109–124.

[23]Nathan King, "A Clarification and Evaluation of the Two-Factor Theory of Job Satisfaction," *Psychological Bulletin* (July 1970) pp. 18–31; Marvin Dunnette, John Campbell, and Milton Hakel, "Factors Contributing to Job Satisfaction and Job Dissatisfaction in Six Occupational Groups," *Organizational Behavior and Human Performance* (May 1967), pp. 143–174; R. J. House and L. Wigdor, "Herzberg's Dual Factor Theory of Job Satisfaction and Motivation: A Review of the Evidence and a Criticism," *Personnel Psychology* (Summer 1967), pp. 369–389.

[24]Adler, op. cit. (1991), Ch 6; Nancy J. Adler and J. T. Graham, "Cross Cultural Interaction: The International Comparison Fallacy," *Journal of International Business Studies* (Fall 1989), pp. 515–537; Frederick Herzberg, "Workers Needs: The Same around the World," *Industry Week* (Sept 27, 1987), pp. 29–32.

[25]See Adler, op. cit. (1991) and Hofstede, op. cit. (1980).

[26]See, for example, J. Stacy Adams, "Toward an Understanding of Inequality," *Journal of Abnormal and Social Psychology,* Vol. 67 (1963), pp. 422–436; and J. Stacy Adams, "Inequity in Social Exchange," in L. Berkowitz, ed., *Advances in Experimental Social Psychology,* Vol. 2 (New York: Academic Press, 1965), pp. 267–300.

[27]Adams, op. cit. (1965).

[28]These issues are discussed in C. Kagitcibasi and J.W. Berry, "Cross-Cultural Psychology: Current Research and Trends," *Annual Review of Psychology,* Vol. 40 (1989), pp. 493–531.

[29]Victor H. Vroom, *Work and Motivation* (New York: John Wiley, 1964).

[30]See Richard T. Mowday, "Equity Theory Predictions of Behavior in Organizations," in Richard M. Steers and Lyman W. Porter, eds., *Motivation and Work Behavior,* 4th ed. (New York: McGraw-Hill, 1987), pp. 89–110.

[31]Gerald R. Salancik and Jeffrey Pfeffer, "A Social Information Processing Approach to Job Attitudes and Task Design," *Administrative Science Quarterly,* Vol. 23 (June 1978), pp. 224–253.

[32]See Terence R. Mitchell, "Expectancy Models of Job Satisfaction, Occupational Preference and Effort: A Theoretical, Methodological, and Empirical Appraisal," *Psychological Bulletin,* Vol. 81 (1974), pp. 1053–1077; Mahmoud A. Wahba and Robert J. House, "Expectancy Theory in Work and Motivation: Some Logical and Methodological Issues," *Human Relations,* Vol. 27 (January 1974), pp. 121–147; Terry Connolly, "Some Conceptual and Methodological Issues in Expectancy Models of Work Performance Motivation," *Academy of Management Review,* Vol. 1 (October 1976), pp. 37–47; Terrence Mitchell, "Expectancy-Value Models in Organizational Psychology," in N. Feather, ed., *Expectancy, Incentive and Action* (New York: Erlbaum and Associates, 1980).

[33]Examples from Adler, op. cit. (1991), p. 159.

[34]Information from Andrew Server "Patagonia CEO Reels Company," *Fortune* (December 14, 1992).

[35]See William E. Wymer and Jeanne M. Carsten, "Alternative Ways to Gather Opinions," *HR Magazine,* Vol. 37, 4 (April 1992), pp. 71–78.

[36]The Job Descriptive Index (JDI) is available from Dr. Patricia C. Smith, Department of Psychology, Bowling Green State University; the Minnesota Satisfaction Questionnaire (MSQ) is available from the Industrial Relations Center and Vocational Psychology Research Center, University of Minnesota.

[37]Barry M. Staw, "The Consequences of Turnover," *Journal of Occupational Behavior,* Vol. 1 (1980), pp. 253–273.

[38]John P. Wanous, *Organizational Entry* (Reading, MA: Addison-Wesley, 1980).

[39]Charles N. Greene, "The Satisfaction-Performance Controversy," *Business Horizons,* Vol. 15 (1972), p. 31; Michelle T. Iaffaldano and Paul M. Muchinsky, "Job Satisfaction and Job Performance: A Meta-Analysis," *Psychological Bulletin,* Vol. 97 (1985), pp. 251–273; Greene, op. cit. (1972), pp. 31–41; Dennis Organ, "A Reappraisal and Reinterpretation of the Satisfaction-Causes- Performance Hypothesis," *Academy of Management Review,* Vol. 2 (1977), pp. 46–53; Peter Lorenzi, "A Comment on Organ's Reap-

praisal of the Satisfaction-Causes-Performance Hypothesis," *Academy of Management Review,* Vol. 3 (1978), pp. 380–382.

[40]Lyman W. Porter and Edward E. Lawler III, *Managerial Attitudes and Performance* (Homewood, IL: Irwin, 1968).

[41]This integrated model is consistent with the comprehensive approach suggested by Martin G. Evans, "Organizational Behavior: The Central Role of Motivation," in J. G. Hunt and J. D. Blair, eds., *1986 Yearly Review of Management of the Journal of Management,* Vol 12 (1986), pp. 203–222.

▼ CHAPTER 6 ENDNOTES

[1]Based on T. Nhan, "Turning a Problem into Profit," *Charlotte Observer* (March 7, 1994), p. D1 as described in L. R. Gómez-Mejía, D. B. Balkin, and R. L. Cardy, *Managing Human Resources* (Englewood Cliffs, NJ: Prentice-Hall, 1995), p. 223.

[2]For a good discussion of human resource management strategy and its linkage to overall management strategy see A. J. Templer and R. J. Cattaneo, "A Model of Human Resources Management Effectiveness," *Canadian Journal of Administrative Sciences* (Vol. 12, No. 1, 1995) pp. 77–88.

[3]See J. R. Schermerhorn, Jr., *Management,* 5th ed., (New York: Wiley, 1996), Ch. 12; G. M. Bounds, G. H. Dobbins, and O. S. Fowler, *Management: A Total Quality Perspective* (Cincinnati: South-Western, 1995), Ch. 9; Gómez-Mejía, op. cit. 1995), Chs. 2, 6.

[4]Bounds, Dobbins, and Fowler, op. cit. (1995), p. 313–318.

[5]Bounds, Dobbins, and Fowler, op. cit. (1995), p. 315.

[6]Bounds, Dobbins, and Fowler, op. cit. (1995), p. 317.

[7]Summarized from Bounds, Dobbins, and Fowler, op. cit. (1995), pp. 319–321; Gómez-Mejí, Balkin, and Cardy, op. cit. (1995), Ch. 6; Schermerhorn, op. cit. (1966), pp. 290–293.

[8]See "Blueprints for Service Quality: The Federal Express Approach," *AMA Management Briefing* (New York: AMA Publications, 1991).

[9]Based on A. Uris, *Eighty-eight Mistakes Interviewers Make and How To Avoid Them (New York: AMA Publications, 1988).*

[10]G. C. Thornton, *Assessment Centers in Human Resource Management* (Reading, MA: Addison-Wesley, 1992).

[11]B. B. Gaugler, D. B. Rosenthal, G. C. Thornton, and C. Bentson, "Meta-Analysis of Assessment Center Validity," *Journal of Applied Psychology* (Vol. 72, 1987), pp. 493–511; G. M. McEvoy and R. W. Beatty, "Assessment Centers and Subordinate Appraisals of Managers: A Seven-Year Study of Predictive Validity," *Personnel Psychology* (Vol. 42, 1989), pp. 37–52.

[12]P. M. Muchinsky, "The Use of Reference Reports in Personnel Selection: A Review and Evaluaton," *Journal of Occupational Psychology* (Vol. 52, 1979), pp. 287–297.

[13]See "The Revenge of the Fired," *Newsweek* (February 16, 1987), pp. 46–47.

[14]This training discussion based on Bounds, Dobbins, and Fowler, op. cit. (1995), pp. 326–329; Schermerhorn, op. cit. (1996), pp. 294–295; S. R. Robbins, *Organization Behavior* (Englewood Cliffs, NJ: Prentice-Hall, 1996), pp. 641–644.

[15]See Rob Muller, "Training for Change," *Canadian Business Review* (Spring 1995), pp. 16–19.

[16]Much of the discussion in this section is based on Daniel C. Feldman, "Careers in Organizations: Recent Trends and Future Directions," *Journal of Management* (Vol. 15, June 1989), pp. 135–156; Irving Janis and Dan Wheeler, "Thinking Clearly about Career Choices," *Psychology Today* (May 1978), p. 67; Walter Kiechel III, "How We Will Work in the Year 2000," *Fortune* (May 17, 1993), pp. 38–52.

[17]Based on A. Arkin, "The Lucas Approach to Ethics," *People Management* (October 5, 1995), p. 32.

[18]Charles Handy, *The Age of Unreason* (Boston: Harvard Business School Press, 1991).

[19]"The New Professionals," *World Executive's Digest* (May 1993), pp. 14–16.

[20]Based on Janis and Wheeler, op. cit. (1978), p. 67.

[21]Daniel J. Levinson, *The Seasons of a Man's Life* (New York: Alfred A. Knopf, 1978). See also Douglas T. Hall, *Careers in Organizations* (Santa Monica, CA: Goodyear, 1975).

[22]See Lloyd Baird and Kathy Kram, "Career Dynamics: Managing the Superior-Subordinate Relationship," *Organizational Dynamics* (Spring 1983), p. 47; Paul H. Thompson, Robin Zenger Baker, and Norman Smallwood, "Improving Professional Development by Applying the Four-Stage Career Model," *Organizational Dynamics* (Autumn 1986), pp. 49–62.

[23]Thomas P. Ference, James A. F. Stoner, and E. Kirby Warren, "Managing the Career Plateau," *Academy of Management Review* (Vol. 2, October 1977), pp. 602–612.

[24]We especially thank Dr. Lawrence Peters, Texas Christian University, for his fine critique of an earlier version of this section and the many useful suggestions provided.

[25]Discussion in this section based on Charles J. Fombrun and Robert L. Laud, "Strategic Issues in Performance Appraisal, Theory and Practice," *Personnel* (Vol. 60, November/December 1983), p. 24; Gómez-Mejía, Balkin, and Cardy, op. cit. (1995), Ch. 8; "Performance Appraisal: Current Practices and Techniques," *Personnel* (May/June, 1984), p. 57.

[26]J. Stuller, "Why Not 'Implacement'?" *Training Magazine* (June 1993), pp. 37–40.

[27]See G. P. Latham and K. N. Wexley, *Increasing Productivity Through Performance Appraisal* (Reading, MA: Addison-Wesley, 1981), p. 80.

[28]R. J. Newman, "Job Reviews Go Full Circle," *U.S. News and World Report* (November 1, 1993), pp. 42–43; J. A. Lopez. "A Better Way?" *Wall Street Journal* (April 13, 1994), p. R6; M. S. Hirsch, "360 Degrees of Evaluation," *Working Woman* (August 1994), pp. 20–21; B. O'Reilly, "360 Degree Feedback Can Change Your Life," *Fortune* (October 17, 1994), pp. 93–100.

[29]Ivan Maisel and Steve Richardson, "The Price of Glory," *Dallas Morning News* (June 6, 1993), p. 16B.

[30]For more detail, see Latham and Wexley, op. cit. (1981); Stephen J. Carroll and Craig E. Schneier, *Performance Appriaisal and Review Systems* (Glenview, IL: Scott, Foresman, 1982).

[31]Adaptive from J. P. Campbell, M. D. Dunnette, R. D. Arvey, and L. V. Hellervik, "The Development Evaluation of Behaviorally Based Rating Scales," *Journal of Applied Psychology,* (Vol. 57, 1973), pp. 15–22. Copyright 1973 by the American Psychological Association. Reprinted by permission of the publisher and author.

[32]See George T. Milkovich and John W. Boudreau, *Personnel/Human Resource Management: A Diagnostic Approach,* 5th ed. (Plano, TX: Business Publications, 1988).

[33]For pro and con discussons of BARS, see R. Jacobs, D. Kafry, and S. Zedeck, "Expectations of Behaviorally Anchored Ratings Scales," *Personnel Psychology* (Vol. 33, Autumn 1980), pp. 595–640; Frank J. Landy and James L Farr, "Performance Rating," *Psychological Bulletin* (Vol. 87, 1980), pp. 72–102; David L. Devries, Ann M. Morrison, Sandra L. Shullman, and Michael L. Gerlach, *Performance Appraisal on the Line* (Greensboro, NC: Center for Creative Leadership, 1986), Ch. 3.

[34]For a detailed discussion see S. J. Carroll and H. L. Tosi, Jr., *Management of Objectives: Application and Research* (New York: Macmillan, 1976); A. P. Raia, *Managing by Objectives* (Glenview, IL: Scott, Foresman, 1974).

[35]For discussion of a number of these errors, see Devries, Morrison, Shullman, and Gerlach, op. cit (1986), Ch. 3.

[36]E. G. Olson, "The Workplace Is High on the High Court's Docket," *Business Week* (October 10, 1988), pp. 88–89.

[37]Based on J. J. Bernardin and C. S. Walter, "The Effects of Rater Training and Diary Keeping on Psychometric Error in Ratings," *Journal of Applied Psychology* (Vol. 61, 1977), pp. 64–69; see also R. G. Burnask and T. D. Hollman, "An Empirical Comparison of the Relative Effects of Sorter Re-

sponse Bias on Three Rating Scale Formats," *Journal of Applied Psychology* (Vol. 59, 1974), pp. 307–312.

38Based on W. F. Cascio and H. J. Bernardin, "Implication of Performance Appraisal Litigation for Personnel Decisions," *Personnel Psychology* (Vol. 34, 1981), pp. 211–212. See also see Devries, Morrison, Shullman, and Gerlach, op. cit. (1986), for a discussion.

39See Paul Slattery, "A New Way to Appraise," *HR Magazine* (Vol. 36, October 1991), pp. 27–32.

40J. Zignon, "Making Performance Appraisal Work for Teams," *Training* (June, 1994), pp. 58–63.

41See H. L. Angle, C. C. Manz, and A. H. Van de Ven, "Integrating Human Resource Management and Corporate Strategy: A Preview of the 3M Story," *Human Resource Management* (Vol. 24, 1985), pp. 51–68.

42For complete reviews of theory, research, and practice, see Edward E. Lawler III, *Pay and Organizational Effectiveness* (New York: McGraw-Hill, 1971); Edward E. Lawler III, *Pay and Organization Development* (Reading MA: Addison-Wesley, 1981); Edward E. Lawler III, "The Design of Effective Reward Systems," in Jay W. Lorsch, ed., *Handbook of Organizational Behavior* (Englewood Cliffs, NJ: Prentice-Hall, 1987) pp. 255–271.

43As an example, see D. B. Balkin and L. R. Gómez-Mejía, eds., *New Perspectives on Compensation* (Englewood Cliffs, NJ: Prentice-Hall, 1987).

44Jone L. Pearce, "Why Merit Pay Doesn't Work: Implications from Organization Theory," in David B. Balkin and Luis R. Gómez-Mejía, eds. *New Perspectives on Compensation* (Englewood Cliffs, NJ: Prentice-Hall, 1987), pp. 169–178; Jerry M. Newman, "Selecting Incentive Plans To Complement Organizational Strategy," in David B. Balkin and Luis R. Gómez-Mejía, eds., *New Perspectives on Compensation* (Englewood Cliffs, NJ: Prentice-Hall, 1987), pp. 214–224; Edward E. Lawler III, "Pay for Performance: Making It Work," *Compensation and Benefits Review* (Vol. 21, 1989), pp. 55–60.

45See Daniel C. Boyle, "Employee Motivation that Works," *HR Magazine* (October 1992), pp. 83–89. Kathleen A. McNally, "Compensation as a Strategic Tool," *HR Magazine* (July 1992), pp. 59–66.

46M. Philip, "Flexible Benefit Plans Let Employees Pick and Choose Their Extra Goodies," *The [Toronto] Globe and Mail* (August 1, 1988), p. B13.

47C. O'Dell, *People, Performance and Pay* (Scottsdale, AZ and Houston, TX: American Compensation Association and American Productivity Center, 1987).

48S. Caudron, "Master the Compensation Maze," *Personnel Journal* (June 1993), pp. 640–648.

49N. Gupta, G. E. Ledford, G. D. Jenkins, and D. H. Doty, "Survey Based Prescriptions for Skill-Based Pay," *American Compensation Association Journal* (Vol. 1, No. 1, 1992), pp. 48–59; L. W. Ledford, "The Effectiveness of Skill-Based Pay," *Perspectives in Total Compensation* (Vol. 1, No. 1, 1991), pp. 1–4.

50See Brian Graham-Moore, "Review of the Literature," in Brian Graham-Moore and Timothy L. Ross, eds., *Gainsharing* (Washington, DC: The Bureau of National Affairs, 1990), p. 20.

51S. E. Markham, K. D. Scott, and B. L. Little, "National Gainsharing Study: The Importance of Industry Differences," *Compensation and Benefits Review* (January/February 1992), pp. 34–45.

52C. O'Dell and J. McAdams, "The Revolution in Employee Benefits," *Compensation and Benefits Review* (May/June, 1987), pp. 68–73.

▼ CHAPTER 7 ENDNOTES

1Based on Linda Thornburg, "Money Is Still the Best Reward," *HR Magazine* (August 1994), pp. 58–59.

2For good overviews, see W. E. Scott, Jr., and P. M. Podsakoff, *Behavioral Principles in the Practice of Management* (New York: John Wiley, 1985); Fred Luthans and Robert Kreitner, *Organizational Behavior Modification and Beyond* (Glenview, IL: Scott, Foresman, 1985).

3For some of B. F. Skinner's work, see *Walden Two* (New York: Macmillan, 1948), *Science and Human Behavior* (New York: Macmillan, 1953), and *Contingencies of Reinforcement* (New York: Appleton-Century-Crofts, 1969).

4A Bandura, *Social Learning Theory* (Englewood Cliffs, NJ: Prentice-Hall, 1977).

5See, for example, A. M. Morrison, R. P. White, and E. Van Velsor, *Breaking the Glass Ceiling* (Reading, MA: Addison-Wesley, 1987).

6See J. D. Zalesny and J. K. Ford, "Extending the Social Information Processing Perspective: New Links to Attitudes, Behaviors and Perceptions," *Organizational Behavior and Human Decision Processes* (Vol. 47, 1990), pp. 205–246; M. E. Gist, C. Schwoerer, and B. Rosen, "Effects of Alternative Training Methods of Self-Efficacy and Performance in Computer Software Training," *Journal of Applied Psychology* (Vol. 74, 1989), p. 884–891; D. D. Sutton and R. W. Woodman, "Pygmalion Goes to Work: The Effects of Supervisor Expectations in a Retail Setting," *Journal of Applied Psychology* (Vol. 74, 1989), pp. 943–950; M. E. Gist, "The Influence of Training Method on Self-Efficacy and Idea Generation Among Managers," *Personnel Psychology* (Vol. 42, 1989), pp. 787–805.

7See M. E. Gist, "Self Efficacy: Implications in Organizational Behavior and Human Resource Management," *Academy of Management Review* (Vol. 12, 1987), pp. 472–485; A Bandura, "Self Efficacy Mechanisms in Human Agency," *American Psychologist* (Vol. 37, 1987), pp. 122–147.

8E. L. Thorndike, *Animal Intelligence* (New York: Macmillan, 1911), p. 244.

9Adapted from Luthans and Kreitner, op. cit. (1985).

10This discussion is based on Luthans and Kreitner, op. cit. (1985).

11Both laws are stated in Keith L. Miller, *Principles of Everyday Behavior Analysis* (Monterey, CA: Brooks/Cole, 1975), p. 122.

12See Christine M. Harris, "A Celebration of Scientific Achievement," *HR Magazine* (Vol. 20, 1988), pp. 63–74.

13"Paying Employees Not To Go to the Doctor," *Business Week* (March 21, 1983), p. 150; "Giving Goodies to the Good," *Time* (November 21, 1985), p. 98; "Incentive Plans Spur Safe Work Habits, Reducing Accidents at Some Plants," *The Wall Street Journal* (January 27, 1987), p. 1.

14See John Putzier and Frank T. Novak, "Attendance Management and Control," *Personnel Administrator* (August 1989), pp. 59–60.

15Robert Kreitner and Angelo Kiniki, *Organization Behavior,* 2nd ed. (Homewood, IL: Irwin, 1992).

16K. M. Evans, "On-the Job Lotteries: A Low-Cost Incentive that Sparks Higher Productivity," *Compensation and Benefits Review* (Vol. 20, No. 4, 1988), pp. 63–74; A. Halcrow, "Incentive! How Three Companies Cut Costs," *Personnel Journal* (February 1986), p. 12.

17A. R. Korukonda and James G. Hunt, "Pat on the Back Versus Kick in the Pants: An Application of Cognitive Inference to the Study of Leader Reward and Punishment Behavior," *Group and Organization Studies* (Vol. 14, 1989), pp. 299–234.

18See Carrie A. Miles and Jean M. McCloskey, "People: The Key to Productivity," *HR Magazine* (Vol. 38, February 1993), p. 42.

19Based on an example in Luthans and Kreitner, op. cit. (1985), pp. 125–126.

20Developed in part from Hamner, "Using Reinforcement Theory in Organizational Settings," in Henry L. Tosi and W. Clay Hamner, eds., *Organizational Behavior and Management: A Contingency Approach* (Chicago: St. Clair Press, 1977), pp. 388–395.

21Based on an example in Luthans and Kreitner, op. cit. (1985), pp. 125–126.

22See "Janitorial Firm Success Story Started with Cleaning Couple," *Lubbock Avalanche-Journal* (August 25, 1991), p. E7.

23Rudy M. Yandrick, "Helping Supervisors Solve People Problems," *HR Magazine* (October 1995), pp. 52–53.

24Edwin A. Locke, "The Myths of Behavior Mod in Organizations," *Acad-*

emy of Management Review (Vol. 2, October 1977), pp. 543–553. For a counterpoint see Jerry L. Gray, "The Myths of the Myths about Behavior Mod in Organizations: A Reply to Locke's Criticisms of Behavior Modification," *Academy of Management Review* (Vol. 4, January 1979), pp. 121–129.

25Robert Kreitner, "Controversy in OBM: History, Misconceptions, and Ethics," in Lee Frederiksen ed., *Handbook of Organizational Behavior Management* (New York: Wiley, 1982), pp. 71–91.

26W. E. Scott, Jr., and P. M. Podsakoff, *Behavioral Principles in the Practice of Management* (New York: Wiley, 1985).

27Also see W. Clay Hamner, "Reinforcement Theory and Contingency Management in Organizational Settings," in Richard M. Steers and Lyman W Porters, eds., *Motivation and Work Behavior,* 4th ed. (New York: McGraw-Hill, 1987), pp. 139–165; Luthans and Kreitner, op. cit. (1985).

28Charles C. Manz and Henry P. Sims, Jr. *Superleadership* (New York: Berkley, 1990).

▼ CHAPTER 8 ENDNOTES

1Information from Thomas A. Stewart, "How a Little Company Won Big by Betting on Brainpower," *Fortune* (September 4, 1995), pp. 121–122.

2Ibid., p. 122.

3Frederick W. Taylor, *The Principles of Scientific Management* (New York: W.W. Norton, 1967).

4Frederick Herzberg, "One More Time: How Do You Motivate Employees?" *Harvard Business Review,* Vol. 46 (January/February 1968), pp. 53–62.

5Paul J. Champagne and Curt Tausky, "When Job Enrichment Doesn't Pay," *Personnel,* Vol. 3 (January/February 1978), pp. 30–40.

6William W. Winpisinger, "Job Enrichment: A Union View," in Karl O. Magnusen, ed., *Organizational Design, Development and Behavior: A Situational View* (Glenview, IL: Scott, Foresman, 1977), p. 222.

7For a complete description and review of the research, see J. Richard Hackman and Greg R. Oldham, *Work Redesign* (Reading, MA: Addison-Wesley, 1980). For forerunner research see Charles L. Hulin and Milton R. Blood, "Job Enlargement Individual Differences, and Worker Responses," *Psychological Bulletin,* Vol. 69 (1968), pp. 41–55; Milton R. Blood and Charles L. Hulin, "Alienation, Environmental Characteristics and Worker Responses," *Journal of Applied Psychology,* Vol. 51 (1967), pp. 284–290.

8Information from Kerry Shapansky, "How Fact-Based Management Works for Xerox," *CMA Magazine,* Vol. 68 (December 1994/January 1995), pp. 20–22.

9See J. Richard Hackman and Greg Oldham, "Development of the Job Diagnostic Survey," *Journal of Applied Psychology,* Vol. 60 (1975), pp. 159–170.

10Gerald Salancik and Jeffrey Pfeffer "An Examination of Need—Satisfaction Models of Job Attitudes," *Administrative Science Quarterly,* Vol. 22 (1977), pp. 427–456; Gerald Salancik and Jeffrey Pfeffer, "A Social Information Processing Approach to Job Attitude and Task Design," *Administrative Science Quarterly,* Vol. 23 (1978), pp. 224–253.

11Information from Robert Frank, "Efficient UPS tries to Increase Efficiency," *The Wall Street Journal* (May 24, 1995), pp. B1, B4.

12William A. Pasmore, "Overcoming the Roadblocks to Work—Restructuring Efforts," *Organizational Dynamics,* Vol. 10 (1982), pp. 54–67; Hackman and Oldham, op. cit. (1975).

13George W. England and Itzhak Harpaz, "How Working Is Defined: National Contexts and Demographic and Organizational Role Influences," *Journal of Organizational Behavior* (July 1990), pp. 253–266.

14See William A. Pasmore, *Designing Effective Organizations: A Sociotechnical Systems Perspective* (New York: Wiley, 1988).

15See "The Kindergarten That Will Change the World," *The Economist*

16(March 4, 1995), p. 63, for a report on how sociotechnical systems are used by Toyota in Japan.

16See Malcolm S. Salter and Wayne A. Edesis, "Wolfsburg at the Center," *Harvard Business Review* (July/August 1991).

17Peter Senker, *Towards the Automatic Factory: The Need for Training* (New York: Springer-Verlag, 1986).

18See Ramchandran Jaikumar, "Postindustrial Manufacturing," *Harvard Business Review,* Vol. 44 (1986), pp. 69–76.

19C. Begole, "How to Get the Productivity Edge," *Working Woman* (May 1991), pp. 47–60.

20Michael Hammer, "Reengineering Work: Don't Automate, Obliterate," *Harvard Business Review* (July/August 1990), pp. 104–112.

21Denis D. Umstot, Terence R. Mitchell, and Cecil H. Bell, Jr., "Goal Setting and Job Enrichment: An Integrated Approach to Job Design," *Academy of Management Review,* Vol. 3 (October 1978), p. 868.

22See Thomas M. Koulopoulos, *The Workflow Imperative: Building Real World Business Solutions* (New York: Van Nostrand Reinhold, 1995).

23Information from "The Business Imperative for Workflow & Business Process Reengineering," *Fortune* (November 27, 1995), special advertising supplement.

24Edwin A. Locke, Karyll N. Shaw, Lise M. Saari, and Gary P. Latham, "Goal Setting and Task Performance: 1969–1980," *Psychological Bulletin,* Vol. 90 (July/November 1981), pp. 125–152; Edwin A. Locke and Gary P. Latham, "Work Motivation and Satisfaction: Light at the End of the Tunnel," *Psychological Science,* Vol. 1, No. 4 (July 1990), pp. 240–246; and Edwin A. Locke and Gary P. Latham, *A Theory of Goal Setting and Task Performance* (Englewood Cliffs, NJ: Prentice-Hall, 1990).

25Gary P. Latham and Edwin A. Locke, "Goal Setting—A Motivational Technique That Works," *Organizational Dynamics,* Vol. 8 (Autumn 1979), pp. 68–80; Gary P. Latham and Timothy P. Steele, "The Motivational Effects of Participation versus Goal-Setting on Performance," *Academy of Management Journal,* Vol. 26 (1983), pp. 406–417; Miriam Erez and Frederick H. Kanfer, "The Role of Goal Acceptance in Goal Setting and Task Performance," *Academy of Management Review,* Vol. 8 (1983), pp. 454–463; and R. E. Wood and E. A. Locke, "Goal Setting and Strategy Effects on Complex Tasks," in B. Staw and L. L. Cummings, eds., *Research in Organizational Behavior* (Greenwich, CT: JAI Press, 1990).

26See E. A. Locke and G. P. Latham, "Work Motivation and Satisfaction," *Psychological Science* Vol. 1, No. 4 (July 1990), p. 241.

27Locke and Latham, op. cit. (1990).

28Information from Harvey Enchin, "High-Tech Heart, Lots of Sole," *The Globe and Mail* (July 14, 1992), p. B24 and "From Tech to Trends," *The Globe and Mail* (June 15, 1993), p. B1.

29Information from Strat Sherman, "Stretch Goals: The Dark Side of Asking for Miracles," *Fortune* (November 13, 1995), pp. 231–232.

30For a good review of MBO, see Anthony P. Raia, *Managing by Objectives* (Glenview IL: Scott, Foresman, 1974); Steven Kerr summarizes the criticisms well in "Overcoming the Dysfunctions of MBO," *Management by Objectives,* Vol. 5, No. 1 (1976).

31Craig C. Pinder, *Work Motivation Theory, Issues, and Applications* (Dallas, TX: Scott, Foresman, 1984), p. 169.

32For overviews see Allan R. Cohen and Herman Gadon, *Alternative Work Schedules: Integrating Individual and Organizational Needs* (Reading, MA: Addison-Wesley, 1978); and Jon L. Pearce, John W. Newstrom, Randall B. Dunham, and Alison E. Barber, *Alternative Work Schedules* (Boston: Allyn and Bacon, 1989).

33See, for example, Sue Shellenbarger, "Work & Family," *The Wall Street Journal* (September 6, 1995), p. B1.

34C. Latack and L. W. Foster, "Implementation of Compressed Work Schedules: Participation and Job Redesign as Critical Factors for Employee Acceptance," *Personnel Psychology,* Vol. 38 (1985), pp. 75–92.

35Cohen and Gadon, op. cit. (1978).

36C. Trost and C. Hymowitz, "Careers Start Giving in to Family Needs,"

The Wall Street Journal (June 18, 1990), p. B1; Robert N. Lussier, "Should Your Organization Use Flextime?" *Supervision* (September 1990), pp. 14–16; and Table No. 643 in the U.S. Bureau of Labor Statistics, USDL News Release, Annual Pay Levels in Metropolitan Areas (1988), p. 388.

[37]J. A. Hollingsworth and F. A. Wrebe, "Flextime: An International Innovation With Limited U.S. Acceptance," *Industrial Management,* Vol. 31 (March/April, 1989), pp. 22–26.

[38]"Aetna Life & Casualty Company," *The Wall Street Journal* (June 4, 1990), p. R35; (June 18, 1990), p. B1.

[39]Getsy M. Selirio, "Job Sharing Gains Favor as Corporation Embrace Alternative Work Schedule," *Lubbock Avalanche-Journal* (December 13, 1992), p. 2E.

[40]Ibid.

[41]"Bell Job Plan Gets Careful Look," *The Globe and Mail* (November 17, 1993), pp. B1, B12.

[42]Daniel C. Feldman and Helen I. Doerpinghaus "Missing Persons No Longer: Managing Part-Time Workers in the '90s," *Organizational Dynamics* (Summer 1992), pp. 59–72.

[43]"'Flexiplace' at IBM," *Canadian Business Review* (Spring 1993), p. 22.

[44]See Jonathan N. Goodrich, "Telecommuting in America," *Business Horizons* (July/August 1990), pp. 31–37; Michael Alexander, "Travel-Free Commuting," *Nation's Business* (December 1990), pp. 33–37.

[45]Information from Ibid.

[46]Joyce Lain Kennedy, *The Dallas Morning News* (December 20, 1992), p. 43D.

▼ CHAPTER 9 ENDNOTES

[1]See Harold J. Leavitt, *Managerial Psychology* (Chicago: University of Chicago Press, 1972); Harold J. Leavitt, "Suppose We Took Groups Seriously," in Eugene L. Cass and Frederick G. Zimmer, eds., *Man and Work in Society* (New York: Van Nostrand Reinhold, 1975), pp. 67–77; and Harold J. Leavitt and Jean Lipman-Blumen, "Hot Groups," *Harvard Business Review* (July/August, 1995), pp. 109–116.

[2]For a good discussion of groups and teams in the workplace see Jon R. Katzenbach and Douglas K. Smith, "The Discipline of Teams," *Harvard Business Review* (March/April, 1993), pp. 111–120.

[3]Leavitt, op. cit. (1975); Leavitt and Lipman-Blumen, op cit. (1995).

[4]See, for example, Edward E. Lawler, III, *High-Involvement Management* (San Francisco: Jossey-Bass, 1986).

[5]Information from "Empowerment That Pays Off," *Fortune* (March 20, 1995), pp. 145–146.

[6]Marvin E. Shaw, *Group Dynamics: The Psychology of Small Group Behavior,* 2nd ed. (New York: McGraw-Hill, 1976).

[7]Bib Latane, Kipling Williams, and Stephen Harkins, "Many Hands Make Light the Work: The Causes and Consequences of Social Loafing," *Journal of Personality and Social Psychology,* Vol. 37 (1978), pp. 822–832; E. Weldon and G. M. Gargano, "Cognitive Effort in Additive Task Groups: The Effects of Shared Responsibility on the Quality of Multiattribute Judgments," *Organizational Behavior and Human Decision Processes,* Vol. 36 (1985), pp. 348–361; John M. George, "Extrinsic and Intrinsic Origins of Perceived Social Loafing in Organizations," *Academy of Management Journal* (March 1992), pp. 191–202.

[8]David M. Herold, "The Effectiveness of Work Groups," in Steven Kerr, ed., *Organizational Behavior* (New York, John Wiley, 1979), p. 95.

[9]Rensis Likert, *New Patterns of Management* (New York: McGraw-Hill, 1961).

[10]For a good discussion of task forces, see James Ware, "Managing a Task Force," Note 478-002, Harvard Business School, 1977.

[11]See "The Corporate Jungle Spawns a New Species: The Project Manager," *Fortune* (July 10, 1995), pp. 179–180.

[12]Information from Frank Muller, "A New Engine of Change in Employee Relations," *Personnel Management* (July 1991); and Jack Semple, "The Rover Revolution," *Management Today* (May 1992).

[13]J. Steven Heinen and Eugene Jacobson, "A Model of Task Group Development in Complex Organization and a Strategy of Implementation," *Academy of Management Review,* Vol. 1 (October 1976), pp. 98–111; Bruce W. Tuckman, "Developmental Sequence in Small Groups," *Psychological Bulletin,* Vol. 63 (1965), pp. 384–399; and Bruce W. Tuckman and Mary Ann C. Jensen, "Stages of Small Group Development Revisited," *Group & Organization Studies,* Vol. 2 (1977), pp. 419–427.

[14]See J. Richard Hackman, "The Design of Work Teams," in Jay W. Lorsch, ed., *Handbook of Organizational Behavior* (Englewood Cliffs, NJ: Prentice Hall, 1987), pp. 343–357.

[15]Herold, op. cit. (1979).

[16]Information from Anne B. Fisher, "Making Change Stick," *Fortune* (April 17, 1995), pp. 121–131.

[17]Warren Watson, "Cultural Diversity's Impact on Interaction Process and Performance," *Academy of Management Journal,* Vol. 16 (1993).

[18]William C. Schutz, *FIRO: A Three-Dimensional Theory of Interpersonal Behavior* (New York: Rinehart & Co., 1958).

[19]William C. Schutz, "The Interpersonal Underworld," *Harvard Business Review,* Vol. 36, No. 4 (July/August, 1958), p. 130.

[20]Katzenbach and Smith, op. cit. (1993).

[21]E. J. Thomas and C. F. Fink, "Effects of Group Size," in Larry L. Cummings and William E. Scott, eds., *Readings in Organizational and Human Performance* (Homewood, IL: Irwin, 1969), pp. 394–408.

[22]Shaw, op. cit. (1976).

[23]George C. Homans, *The Human Group* (New York: Harcourt Brace, 1950).

[24]Information from James S. Hirsch, "U.S. Hotels Allow Staff Serving on Front Lines to Soothe Riled Guests," *The Asian Wall Street Journal* (March 10, 1993), p. 20.

[25]For a discussion of intergroup dynamics see, Schein, op. cit. (1988), pp. 106–115.

[26]"Producer Power," *The Economist* (March 4, 1995), p. 70.

[27]Ibid.

[28]This discussion is developed from Schein, op cit. (1988), pp. 69–75.

[29]Information from Jeffrey A. Mello, "A Strategized Approach Toward AIDS in the Workplace: Experience at Sun Life," *Employment Relations Today (EEO),* Vol. 21 (Autumn 1994), pp. 329–338.

[30]Ibid., p. 73.

[31]Developed from guidelines presented in the classic article by Jay Hall, "Decisions, Decisions, Decisions," *Psychology Today* (November 1971), pp. 55, 56.

[32]This and subsequent treatment of liabilities developed from the classic article by Norman R. F. Maier, "Assets and Liabilities in Group Problem Solving," *Psychological Review,* Vol. 74 (1967), pp. 239–249.

[33]Irving L. Janis, "Groupthink," *Psychology Today* (November 1971), pp. 43–46; Irving L. Janis, *Groupthink,* 2nd ed. (Boston: Houghton Mifflin, 1982). See also J. Longley and D. G. Pruitt, "Groupthink: A Critique of Janis' Theory," in L. Wheeler, ed., *Review of Personality and Social Psychology* (Beverly Hills, CA: Sage Publications, 1980); Carrie R. Leana, "A Partial Test of Janis's Groupthink Model: The Effects of Group Cohesiveness and Leader Behavior on Decision Processes," *Journal of Management,* Vol. 11, No. 1 (1985), pp. 5–18. See also Jerry Harvey, "Managing Agreement in Organizations: The Abilene Paradox," *Organizational Dynamics* (Summer, 1974), pp. 63–80.

[34]Janis, op. cit. (1982).

[35]Gayle W. Hill, "Group versus Individual Performance: Are N1 1 Heads Better Than One?" *Psychological Bulletin,* Vol. 91 (1982), pp. 517–539.

[36]These techniques are well described in George P. Huber, *Managerial*

Decision Making (Glenview, IL: Scott, Foresman, 1980): Andre L. Delbecq, Andrew L. Van de Ven, and David H. Gustafson, *Group Techniques for Program Planning: A Guide to Nominal Groups and Delphi Techniques* (Glenview, IL: Scott, Foresman, 1975); and William M. Fox, "Anonymity and Other Keys to Successful Problem-Solving Meetings," *National Productivity Review,* Vol. 8 (Spring 1989), pp. 145–156.

[37]Delbecq et al., op. cit. (1975); Fox, op. cit. (1989).

▼ CHAPTER 10 ENDNOTES

[1]Information from "What a Zoo Can Teach You," *Fortune* (May 18, 1992); Thomas Stewart, "The Search for the Organization of Tomorrow," *Fortune* (May 18, 1992); and Nancy Austin, "Making Team Work," *Working Woman* (January 1993).

[2]*Fortune* (May 7, 1990), pp. 52–60.

[3]Jon R. Katzenbach and Douglas K. Smith, "The Discipline of Teams," *Harvard Business Review,* (March/April, 1993a), pp. 111–120; and Jon R. Katzenbach and Douglas K. Smith, *The Wisdom of Teams: Creating the High-Performance Organization* (Boston: Harvard Business School Press, 1993b).

[4] Ibid, 1993a and 1993b.

[5]"Should the CEO Be One Person?" *World Executive Digest* (February 1993), pp. 22–24.

[6]Information from "The New Workplace," *Business Week* (April 29, 1996), pp. 107-117.

[7]Katzenbach and Smith, op. cit. (1993a), p. 112.

[8]Developed from Katzenbach and Smith, op. cit. (1993a), pp. 118–119.

[9]For a good discussion of team building, see William D. Dyer, *Team Building,* 2nd ed. (Reading, MA: Addison-Wesley, 1987).

[10]Chuah Bee Hwa, "Leadership Training Via Outdoor Activities," *The New Straits Times* (April 19, 1993), p. 1.

[11]Developed from a discussion by Edgar H. Schein, *Process Consultation* (Reading, MA: Addison-Wesley, 1969), pp. 32–37; Edgar H. Schein, *Process Consultation: Volume I* (1988), pp. 40–49.

[12]Robert F. Bales, "Task Roles and Social Roles in Problem-Solving Groups," in Eleanor E. Maccoby, Theodore M. Newcomb, and E. L. Hartley, eds., *Readings in Social Psychology* (New York: Holt, Rinehart & Winston, 1958).

[13]For a good description of task and maintenance functions see John J. Gabarro and Anne Harlan, "Note on Process Observation," Note 9-477-029, Harvard Business School, 1976.

[14]This and the subsequent discussion of maintenance activities are developed from Schein, *Process Consultation: Volume I,* 2nd ed. (Reading, MA: Addison-Wesley, 1988), pp. 49–53; Rensis Likert, *New Patterns of Management* (New York: McGraw-Hill, 1961), pp. 166–169.

[15]This example is from Roger Harrison, "When Power Conflicts Trigger Team Spirit," *European Business* (Spring 1972), pp. 57–65.

[16]Information courtesy of Memphis Center for Cosmetic Dentistry.

[17]See Daniel C. Feldman, "The Development and Enforcement of Group Norms," *Academy of Management Review,* Vol. 9 (1984), pp. 47–53.

[18]Developed from Allen and Pilnick, op. cit. (1973).

[19]See Robert F. Allen and Saul Pilnick, "Confronting the Shadow Organization: How To Select and Defeat Negative Norms," *Organizational Dynamics* (Spring 1973), pp. 13–17; Alvin Zander, *Making Groups Effective* (San Francisco: Jossey-Bass, 1982), Ch. 4; Daniel C. Feldman, "The Development and Enforcement of Group Norms," *Academy of Management Review,* Vol. 9 (1984), pp. 47–53.

[20]For a summary of research on group cohesiveness, see Marvin E. Shaw, *Group Dynamics* (New York: McGraw-Hill, 1971), pp. 110–112, 192.

[21]Information from Stratford Sherman, "Secrets of HP's 'Muddled' Team," *Fortune* (March 18, 1996), pp. 116-120.

[22]See Kenichi Ohmae, "Quality Control Circles: They Work and Don't Work," *The Wall Street Journal* (March 29, 1982), p. 16; Robert P. Steel, Anthony J. Mento, Benjamin L. Dilla, Nestor K. Ovalle, and Russell F. Lloyd, "Factors Influencing the Success and Failure of Two Quality Circles Programs," *Journal of Management,* Vol. 11, No. 1 (1985), pp. 99–119; Edward E. Lawler, III, and Susan A. Mohrman, "Quality Circles: After the Honeymoon," *Organizational Dynamics,* Vol. 15, No. 4 (1987), pp. 42–54.

[23]For early research on related team concepts see Richard E. Walton, "How To Counter Alienation in the Plant," *Harvard Business Review* (November/December 1972), pp. 70–81; Richard E. Walton, "Work Innovations at Topeka: After Six Years," *Journal of Applied Behavior Science,* Vol. 13 (1977), pp. 422–431; Richard E. Walton, "The Topeka Work System: Optimistic Visions, Pessimistic Hypotheses, and Reality," in Zager and Rosow, eds., *The Innovative Organization,* Ch. 11.

[24]Information from Vanaja Dhanan and Cecille Austria, "Where Workers Manage Themselves," *World Executive's Digest* (October 1992), pp. 14–16.

[25]Example from "Rounding Up Quality at USAA," *AIDE Magazine* (Fall 1983), p. 24. See also "Management Meccas," *Business Week* (September 18, 1995), pp. 122–132.

[26]See Andrew Kupfer, "Along Together: Will Being Wired Set Us Free?" *Fortune* (March 20, 1995), pp. 94–104.

[27]R. Brent Gallupe and William H. Cooper, "Brainstorming Electronically," *Sloan Management Review* (Fall 1993), pp. 27–36.

[28]William M. Bulkeley, "Computerizing Dull Meetings Is Touted as an Antidote to the Mouth That Bored," *The Wall Street Journal* (January 28, 1992), pp. B1, B2.

[29]See Gallupe and Cooper, op. cit. (1993).

[30]See Kenneth Labich, "Rethinking Almost Everything," *Fortune* (May 13, 1996), p. 6; and, Richard Farson, *Management of the Absurd* (New York: Simon and Schuster, 1996).

[31]Information from Myron Maget, Who's Winning the Information Revolution?" *Fortune* (November 30, 1992), pp. 110–117.

▼ CHAPTER 11 ENDNOTES

[1]Marcus B. Osborn, "Organizational Structure at First Community Financial," Working paper, Department of Public Administration, Arizona State University, Tempe, AZ, 1996.

[2]See Richard M. Cyert and James G. March, *A Behavioral Theory of the Firm* (Englewood Cliffs, NJ: Prentice Hall, 1963). A good discussion of organizational goals is also found in Charles Perrow, *Organizational Analysis: A Sociological View* (Belmont, CA: Wadsworth, 1970) and in Richard H. Hall, "Organizational Behavior: A Sociological Perspective," in Jay W. Lorsch, ed., *Handbook of Organizational Behavior* (Englewood Cliffs, NJ: Prentice Hall, 1987), pp. 84–95.

[3]See Richard N. Osborn, James G. Hunt, and Lawrence R. Jauch, *Organization Theory: Integrated Text and Cases* (Melbourne, FL: Krieger, 1985).

[4]H. Talcott Parsons, *Structure and Processes in Modern Societies* (New York: Free Press, 1960).

[5]See, for instance, Thomas J. Peters and Richard Waterman, Jr., *Search of Excellence: Lessons from America's Best-Run Companies* (New York: Harper & Row, 1982).

[6]Adapted from Terri Lammers, "The Effective and Indispensable Mission Statement," *Inc.* (August 1992), pp. 1, 7, 23.

[7]See, for instance, I. C. MacMillan and A. Meshulack, "Replacement versus Expansion: Dilemma for Mature U.S. Businesses," *Academy of Management Journal,* Vol. 26 (1983), pp. 708–726.

[8]William H. Starbuck and Paul C. Nystrom, "Designing and Understanding Organizations," in P. C. Nystrom and W. H. Starbuck, eds., *Handbook of Organizational Design: Adapting Organizations to Their Environments* (New York: Oxford University Press, 1981).

[9]Laura Didio, "How Data General Is Turning Itself Around," *LAN Times* (January 6, 1992), pp. 26–29.

[10]See Osborn, Hunt, and Jauch, op. cit. (1985).

[11]See Paul R. Lawrence and Jay W. Lorsch, *Organization and Environment* (Homewood, IL: Irwin, 1969).

[12]For a review, see Osborn, Hunt, and Jauch, op. cit. (1985).

[13]James B. Quinn, *Intelligent Enterprise: A Knowledge and Service Based Paradigm for Industry* (New York: The Free Press, 1992).

[14]See Osborn, Hunt, and Jauch, op. cit. (1985).

[15]For further discussion, see J. Ivancevich, J. Donnelley, and J. Gibson, *Managing for Performance* (Plano, TX: Business Publications, 1986); Herbert Simon, "Making Management Decisions, The Role of Intuition and Emotion." Academy of Management Executives, Vol. 1 (1987), pp. 57–64.

[16]William G. Ouchi and M. A. McGuire, "Organization Control: Two Functions," *Administrative Science Quarterly,* Vol. 20 (1977), pp. 559–569.

[17]Adapted from W. Edwards Deming, "Improvement of Quality and Productivity Through Action by Management," *Productivity Review* (Winter 1982), pp. 12 22; and W. Edwards Deming, *Quality, Productivity and Competitive Position* (Cambridge, MA: MIT Center for Advanced Engineering, 1982).

[18]*Reimer Express Corporate Annual Report* (1994); J. Lorinc, "Dr. Deming's Traveling Quality Show," *Canadian Business,* Vol. 63 (September 1990), pp. 38–42.

[19]For a discussion, see Stephen P. Robbins, *Organization Theory: Structure, Design and Applications,* 3rd ed. (Englewood Cliffs, NJ: Prentice Hall, 1990), pp. 420–458.

[20]Ibid.

[21]This section is based on Osborn, Hunt, and Jauch, op. cit. (1985), pp. 273–303.

[22]For a good discussion of matrix structures, see Stanley Davis, Paul Lawrence, Harvey Kolodny, and Michael Beer, *Matrix* (Reading, MA: Addison-Wesley, 1977).

[23]Adapted from P. R. Lawrence and J. W. Lorsch, *Organization and Environment: Managing Differentiation and Integration* (Homewood, IL: Richard D. Irwin, 1967).

▼ CHAPTER 12 ENDNOTES

[1]P. Ingrassia and B. A. Stertz, "With Chrysler Ailing, Lee Iacocca Concedes Mistakes in Managing," *The Wall Street Journal* (September 17, 1990), pp. 1, 12; A. A. Marcus, *Business and Society: Ethics, Government, and the world economy* (Homewood, IL: Irwin.1993). pp. 352–359; William McWhirter, "Chrysler's Second Amazing Comeback," *Time* (November 9, 1992), p. 51.

[2]R. N. Osborn, J. G. Hunt, and L. Jauch, *Organization Theory: Integrated Text and Cases* (Melbourne, FL: Krieger, 1984), pp. 123–215.

[3]See Henry Mintzberg, *Structure in Fives: Designing Effective Organizations* (Englewood Cliffs, NJ: Prentice Hall, 1983).

[4]For a comprehensive review, see W. Richard Scott, *Organizations: Rational, Natural, and Open Systems,* 2nd ed. (Englewood Cliffs, NJ: Prentice Hall, 1987).

[5]Max Weber, *The Theory of Social and Economic Organization,* translated by A. M. Henderson and H. T. Parsons (New York: Free Press, 1947).

[6]Mintzberg, op. cit. (1983).

[7]Mintzberg, op. cit. (1983).

[8]See Osborn, Hunt, and Jauch, op. cit. (1984) for an extended discussion.

[9]See Peter Clark and Ken Starkey, *Organization Transitions and Innovation —Design* (London: Pinter Publications, 1988).

[10]Osborn, op. cit. (1984)

[11]Ibid.

[12]Marcus B. Osborn, *The Case of Sony and Columbia,* Working Paper, Department of Public Administration, Arizona State University, Tempe, 1996;

Charles Flemming, "Super Soiree at SPE," *Variety* (September 7, 1992), p. 5; Ronald Grove, "Is Sony Finally Getting the Hang of Hollywood?" *Business Week* (September 7, 1992), p. 76; Peter Hart, "Sony's Twins Hit the Terrible Twos: Two Years Later," *Variety* (September 9, 1991), p. 1.

[13]See Peter M. Blau and Richard A. Schoenner, *The Structure of Organizations* (New York: Basic Books, 1971).

[14]Joan Woodward, *Industrial Organization: Theory and Practice* (London: Oxford University Press, 1965).

[15]James D. Thompson, *Organization In Action* (New York: McGraw-Hill, 1967).

[16]Woodward, op. cit. (1965).

[17]For reviews, see Osborn, Hunt, and Jauch, op. cit. (1984; and Louis Fry, "Technology-Structure Research: Three Critical Issues," *Academy of Management Journal,* Vol. 25 (1982), pp. 532–552.

[18]Mintzberg, op. cit. (1983).

[19]Charles Perrow, *Complex Organizations: A Critical Essay,* 3rd ed. (New York: Random House, 1986).

[20]Mintzberg, op. cit. (1983).

[21]This section is based on R. N. Osborn and J. G. Hunt, "The Environment and Organization Effectiveness," *Administrative Science Quarterly,* Vol. 19 (1974), pp. 231–246; and Osborn, Hunt, and Jauch, op. cit. (1984).

[22]Douglas G. Shaw and Vincent C. Perro, "Beating the Odds: Five Reasons Why Companies Excel," *Management Review* (August 1992); P&G Annual Report, 1992, 1995.

[23]See R. N. Osborn and C. C. Baughn, "New Patterns in the Formation of U.S./Japanese Cooperative Ventures," *Columbia Journal of World Business,* Vol. 22 (1988), pp. 57–65.

[24]R.N. Osborn, *The Evolution of Strategic Alliances in High Technology,* Working Paper, Department of Management, Wayne State University, Detroit, MI, 1993; and Shawn Tully, "The Modular Corporation," *Fortune* (February 8, 1993).

[25]Adapted from "Another Lap for Mercedes Chief," *Fortune* (April 30, 1992), p. 185; "Daimler's Drive to Become a High-Tech Speedster," *Business Week* (February 12, 1990), p. 55; "Downshift at Daimler," *Business Week* (November 6, 1992), p. 88; "The Flawed Vision of Edzard Reuter," *Economist* (April 27, 1991), p. 65.

[26]*Nike Annual Report,* 1995.

[27]L. R. Jauch and R. N. Osborn, "Toward an Integrated Theory of Strategy," *Academy of Management Review,* Vol. 6 (1981), pp. 491–498; Alfred D. Chandler, *The Visible Hand: The Managerial Revolution in America* (Cambridge, MA: Bellknap, 1977); Karen Bantel and R. N. Osborn, *The Influence of Performance, Environment, and Size on Firm Strategic Clarity,* Working Paper, Department of Management, Wayne State University, Detroit, MI, 1990.

[28]M. E. Porter, *Competitive Strategy,* New York: The Free Press, 1980.

[29]Based on information in Vaune Davis, "Crash Diet," *Canadian Business* (June 1989), pp. 183–186.

[30]G. Huber, "Organizational Learning: The Contributing Process and the Literature," *Organization Science,* Vol. 2, No. 1 (1991), pp. 88–115.

[31]J. W. Myer and B. Rowan, "Institutionalized Organizations: Formal Structure as Myth and Ceremony," *American Journal of Sociology,* Vol. 83 (1977), pp. 340–363.

[32]J. March, Decisions and Organizations, Oxford: Basil and Blackwell, 1988.

[33]J. M. Wexler, "Videoconferences Give Life to Team Approaches," *Computerworld* (September 14, 1992), pp. 37, 67.

[34]Osborn, R. N. and D. H. Jackson, Leaders, "Riverboat Gamblers on Purposeful Unintended Consequences in the Management of Complex Technologies," *Academy of Management Journal* Vol. 31 (1988) pp. 924–947.

[35]See Stinchcombe, A. L. 1983 *Economic Sociology* New York: Academic Press.

[36]Ibid.

37Osborn and Jackson, op. cit. (1988).

38O. P. Walsch and G. R. Ungson, "Organization Memory," *The Academy of Management Review,* Vol. 16, No. 1 (1991), pp. 57–91.

39Marcus, A. A. 1993 *Business and Society: Ethics Government and the World of Economy.* Homewood Jelinoes, Richard N. Irwin.

40Ibid.

▼ CHAPTER 13 ENDNOTES

1Edgar Schein, "Organizational Culture," *American Psychologist,* Vol. 45 (1990), pp. 109–119.

2Schein, op. cit. (1990).

3This example was reported in an interview with Edgar Schein, "Corporate Culture is the Real Key to Creativity," *Business Month* (May 1989), pp. 73–74.

4See T. Deal and A. Kennedy, *Corporate Culture* (Reading, MA: Addison-Wesley, 1982); and Peters and R. Waterman, *In Search of Excellence* (New York: Harper & Row, 1982).

5Based on work by Jeffrey Sonnenfeld, as reported by Carol Hymowitz, "Which Corporate Culture Fits You?" *The Wall Street Journal* (July 17, 1989), p. B1.

6A. Cooke and D. M. Rousseau, "Behavioral Norms and Expectations: A Quantitative Approach to the Assessment of Organizational Culture," *Group and Organizational Studies,* Vol. 13 (1988), pp. 245–273.

7Martin and C. Siehl, "Organization Culture and Counterculture," *Organizational Dynamics,* Vol. 12 (1983), pp. 52–64.

8Martin and Siehl, op. cit. (1983).

9"Is Sony Finally Getting the Hang of Hollywood," *Business Week* (September 7, 1992), p. 76.

10Taylor Cox, Jr., "The Multicultural Organization," *The Academy of Management Executive,* Vol. 2, No. 2 (May 1991), pp. 34–47.

11Schein, op. cit. (1990); and E. Schein, *Organizational Culture and Leadership* (San Francisco: Jossey-Bass, 1985), pp. 52–57.

12Peters and Waterman, op. cit. (1982).

13Schein, op. cit. (1990) and (1985).

14H. Gertz, *The Interpretation of Culture* (New York: Basic Books, 1973).

15J. M. Byer and H. M. Trice, "How an Organization's Rites Reveal Its Culture," *Organizational Dynamics* (Spring 1987), pp. 27–41.

16*Business Week* (November 23, 1992), p. 117.

17H. M. Trice and J. M. Beyer, "Studying Organizational Cultures Through Rites and Ceremonials," *Academy of Management Review,* Vol. 3 (1984), pp. 633–669.

18J. Martin, M. S. Feldman, M. J. Hatch, and S. B. Sitkin, "The Uniqueness Paradox in Organizational Stories," *Administrative Science Quarterly,* Vol. 28 (1983), pp. 438–453.

19Deal and Kennedy, op. cit. (1982).

20R. N. Osborn and C. C. Baughn, *An Assessment of the State of the Field of Organizational Design* (Alexandria, VA: U.S. Army Research Institute, 1994).

21R. N. Osborn and D. Jackson, "Leaders, River Boat Gamblers or Purposeful Unintended Consequences," *Academy of Management Journal,* Vol. 31 (1988), pp. 924–947.

22G. Hofstede and M.H. Bond, "The Confucius Connection: From Cultural Roots to Economic Growth," *Organizational Dynamics,* 16 (1991), pp. 4–21.

23Adapted from Annette Miller, "Reach Out and Prod Someone," *Newsweek* (October 14, 1991); Connie Wallace, "Lessons in Marketing—From a Maverick," *Working Woman* (October 1990); Laura Zinn, "Whales, Human Rights, and Rain Forests," *Business Week* (July 15, 1991).

24Warner Burke, *Organization Development* (Reading, MA: Addison-Wesley, 1987); Wendell L. French and Cecil H. Bell, Jr., *Organization Develop-ment,* 4th ed. (Englewood Cliffs, NJ: Prentice Hall, 1990); Edgar F. Huse and Thomas G. Cummings, *Organization Development and Change,* 4th ed. (St. Paul, MN: West, 1989).

25Warren Bennis, "Using Our Knowledge of Organizational Behavior," in Lorsch, pp. 29–49.

26Huse and Cummings, op. cit. (1989), pp. 8–9.

27George M. Fodor, "Atlantic-Tracy Image Reflects Quality," *Industrial Distribution* (October 1991).

28Excellent overviews are found in Cummings and Huse, op. cit. (1989), pp. 32–36, 45; and French and Bell, op. cit. (1990).

29Richard Beckhard, "The Confrontation Meeting," *Harvard Business Review,* Vol. 45 (March/April 1967), pp. 149–155.

30See Dale Zand, "Collateral Organization: A New Change Strategy," *Journal of Applied Behavioral Science,* Vol. 10 (1974), pp. 63–89; Barry A. Stein and Rosabeth Moss Kanter, "Building the Parallel Organization," *Journal of Applied Behavioral Science,* Vol. 16 (1980), pp. 371–386.

31J. Richard Hackman and Greg R. Oldham, *Work Redesign* (Reading, MA: Addison-Wesley, 1980).

▼ CHAPTER 14 ENDNOTES

1Adapted from "ASAP Interview with Bill Gates, *Forbes ASAP* (1992), p. 84; "Identity Crises," *Forbes Magazine* (May 25, 1992), p. 82; "Microsoft Aims Its Arsenal at Networking," *Business Week* (October 12, 1992), pp. 88–89; "The PTC and Microsoft," *Business Week* (December 28, 1992), p. 30; "The PC Wars Are Sweeping into Software," *Business Week* (July 13, 1992), p. 132.

2Rosabeth Moss Kanter, "Power Failure in Management Circuit," *Harvard Business Review* (July/August 1979),   pp. 65–75.

3John R. P. French and Bertram Raven, "The Bases of Social Power," in Dorwin Cartwright, ed., *Group Dynamics: Research and Theory* (Evanston, IL: Row, Peterson, 1962), pp. 607–623.

4See French and Raven, op. cit. (1962).

5Stanley Milgram, "Behavioral Study of Obedience," in Dennis W. Organ, ed., *The Applied Psychology of Work Behavior* (Dallas: Business Publications, Inc., 1978), pp. 384–398. Also see Stanley Milgram, "Behavioral Study of Obedience," *Journal of Abnormal and Social Psychology,* Vol. 67 (1963), pp. 371–378; Stanley Milgram, "Group Pressure and Action Against a Person," *Journal of Abnormal and Social Psychology,* Vol. 69 (1964), pp. 137–143; "Some Conditions of Obedience and Disobedience to Authority," *Human Relations,* Vol. 1 (1965), pp. 57–76; Stanley Milgrim, *Obedience to Authority* (New York: Harper and Row, 1974).

6Based on information in John Lornic, "Managing When There Is No Middle," *Canadian Business* (June 1991), pp. 86–89, 94.

7Chester Barnard, *The Functions of the Executive* (Cambridge, MA: Harvard University Press, 1938).

8Barnard, *The Functions of the Executive.* Cambridge, MA: Harvard University Press.

9See Steven N. Brenner and Earl A. Mollander, "Is the Ethics of Business Changing?" *Harvard Business Review,* Vol. 55 (February 1977), pp. 57–71; Barry Z. Posner and Warren H. Schmidt, "Values and the American Manager: An Update," *California Management Review,* Vol. XXVI (Spring 1984), pp. 202–216.

10John P. Kotter, "Power, Success, and Organizational Effectiveness," *Organizational Dynamics,* Vol. 6 (Winter 1978), p. 27.

11David A. Whetten and Kim S. Cameron, *Developing Managerial Skills* (Glenview, IL: Scott, Foresman, 1984), pp. 250–259.

12Ibid., pp. 260–266.

13David Kipinis, Stuart M. Schmidt, Chris Swaffin-Smith, and Ian Wilkinson, "Patterns of Managerial Influence: Shotgun Managers, Tacticians, and Bystanders," *Organizational Dynamics,* Vol. 12 (Winter 1984), pp. 60, 61.

[14]Ibid., pp. 58–67; David Kipinis, Stuart M. Schmidt, and Ian Wilkinson, "Intraorganizational Influence Tactics: Explorations in Getting One's Way," *Journal of Applied Psychology,* Vol. 65 (1980), pp. 440–452.

[15]Warren K. Schilit and Edwin A. Locke, "A Study of Upward Influence in Organizations," *Administrative Science Quarterly,* Vol. 27 (1982), pp. 304–316.

[16]Ibid.

[17]Thomas A. Stewart, "New Ways to Exercise Power," *Fortune* (November 6, 1989), pp. 52–64.

[18]Although the work on organizational politics is not extensive, useful reviews include a chapter in Robert H. Miles, *Macro Organizational Behavior* (Santa Monica, CA: Goodyear, 1980); Bronston T. Mayes and Robert W. Allen, "Toward a Definition of Organizational Politics," *Academy of Management Review,* Vol. 2 (1977), pp. 672–677; Gerald F. Cavanagh, Dennis J. Moberg, and Manuel Velasquez, "The Ethics of Organizational Politics," *Academy of Management Review,* Vol. 6 (July 1981), pp. 363–374; Dan Farrell and James C. Petersen, "Patterns of Political Behavior in Organizations," *Academy of Management Review,* Vol. 7 (July 1982), pp. 403–412; D. L. Madison, R. W. Allen, L. W. Porter, and B. T. Mayes, "Organizational Politics: An Exploration of Managers' Perceptions," *Human Relations,* Vol. 33 (1980), pp. 92–107.

[19]Mayes and Allen, "Toward a Definition of Organizational Politics," p. 675.

[20]Jeffrey Pfeffer, *Power in Organizations* (Marshfield, MA: Pitman, 1981), p. 7.

[21]Excerpted by Marcus Osborn, "Empowerment and Politics among Caterpillar and the UAW: Should Firms Be Permitted To Hire Permanent Replacement Workers," Working Paper, Department of Political Science, Arizona State University, Tempe, 1996

[22]B. E. Ashforth and R. T. Lee, "Defensive Behavior in Organizations: A Preliminary Model," *Human Relations* (July 1990), pp. 621–648; personal communication with Blake Ashforth, December 1992.

[23]See Pfeffer, op. cit. (1981); M. M. Harmon and R. T. Mayer, *Organization Theory for Public Administration* (Boston: Little Brown, 1986); W. Richard Scott, *Organizations: Rational, Natural and Open Systems* (Englewood Cliffs, NJ: Prentice Hall, 1987).

[24]Developed from James L. Hall and Joel L. Leldecker, "A Review of Vertical and Lateral Relations: A New Perspective for Managers," in Patrick Connor, ed., *Dimensions in Modern Management,* 3rd ed. (Boston: Houghton Mifflin, 1982), pp. 138–146, which was based in part on Leonard Sayles, *Managerial Behavior* (New York: McGraw-Hill, 1964).

[25]See Jeffrey Pfeffer, *Organizations and Organization Theory* (Boston: Pitman, 1983); Jeffrey Pfeffer and Gerald R. Salancik, *The External Control of Organizations* (Englewood Cliffs, NJ: Prentice Hall, 1978).

[26]R. N. Osborn "A Comparison of CEO Pay in Western Europe, Japan and the U.S.," Working Paper, Department of Management, Wayne State University, Detroit, MI, 1995.

[27]James D. Thompson, *Organizations in Action* (New York: McGraw-Hill, 1967); R. N. Osborn and D. H. Jackson, "Leaders, Riverboat Gamblers, or Purposeful Unintended Consequences in Management of Complex Technologies," *Academy of Management Journal,* Vol. 31 (1988), pp. 924–947; M. Hector, "When Actors Comply: Monitoring Costs and the Production of Social Order," *Acta Sociologica,* Vol. 27 (1984), pp. 161–183; T. Mitchell and W. G. Scott, "Leadership Failures, the Distrusting Public and Prospects for the Administrative State," *Public Administration Review,* Vol. 47 (1987), pp. 445–452.

[28]J.J. Jones, *The Downsizing of American Potential* (New York, Raymond Press, 1996).

[29]Mark Alpert, "The Ghetto's Hidden Wealth," Fortune (July 29, 1991), pp. 167–174.

[30]This discussion is based on Cavanagh, Moberg, and Velasquez, op. cit. (1981); and Manuel Velasquez, Dennis J. Moberg, and Gerald Cavanagh,

"Organizational Statesmanship and Dirty Politics: Ethical Guidelines for the Organizational Politician," *Organizational Dynamics,* Vol. 11 (1983), pp. 65–79, both of which offer a fine treatment of the ethics of power and politics.

▼ CHAPTER 15 ENDNOTES

[1]Niklas Van Daehne, "The New CEO: Easy Rider," *Success* (January/February, 1996), pp. 55–56.

[2]See J. P. Kotter, *A Force for Change: How Leadership Differs from Management* (New York: Free Press, 1990).

[3]See Bernard M. Bass, *Bass and Stogdill's Handbook of Leadership,* 3rd ed. (New York: The Free Press, 1990).

[4]See Alan Bryman, *Charisma and Leadership in Organizations* (London: Sage Publications, 1992), Ch. 5.

[5]Ralph M. Stogdill, *Handbook of Leadership* (New York: Free Press, 1974).

[6]Bass, op. cit. (1990).

[7]Rensis Likert, *New Patterns of Management* (New York: McGraw-Hill, 1961).

[8]Bass, op. cit (1990), Ch. 24.

[9]Robert R. Blake and Jane S. Mouton, *The New Managerial Grid* (Houston: Gulf, 1978).

[10]Compare C. A. Schriesheim and S. L. Castro, "Leader-Member Exchange (LMX) and Mentoring as Complementary Concepts in Leadership Research: A Closer Examination," unpublished manuscript, School of Business Administration, University of Miami, Coral Gables, FL, November, 1995; G. B. Graen and M. Uhl-Bien, "Relationship-Based Approach to Leadership: Development of Leader-Member Exchange (LMX) Theory of Leadership Over 25 Years: Applying a Multi-Level Multi-Domain Perspective," *Leadership Quarterly,* Vol. 6 (Summer 1995), pp. 219–247.

[11]Schriesheim and Castro, op. cit. (1995).

[12]G. Yukl, *Leadership in Organizations,* 3rd ed. (Englewood Cliffs, NJ: Prentice-Hall, 1994), p. 240.

[13]See M. F. Peterson, "PM Theory in Japan and China: What's in It for the United States?" *Organizational Dynamics* (Spring 1988) pp. 22–39; J. Misumi and M. F. Peterson, "The Performance-Maintenance Theory of Leadership: Review of a Japanese Research Program," *Administrative Science Quarterly,* Vol. 30 (1985), pp. 198–223; P. B. Smith, J. Misumi, M. Tayeb, M. F. Peterson, and M. Bond, "On the Generality of Leadership Style Measures Across Cultures," paper presented at the International Congress of Applied Psychology, Jerusalem, July 1986.

[14]Graen and Uhl-Bien, op. cit. (1995).

[15]This section is based on Fred E. Fiedler and Martin M. Chemers, *The Leader Match Concept,* 2nd ed. (New York: John Wiley, 1984).

[16]This section is based on Fred E. Fiedler and Joseph E. Garcia, *New Approaches to Effective Leadership* (New York: John Wiley, 1987).

[17]See L. H. Peters, D. D. Harke, J. T. Pohlmann, "Fiedler's Contingency Theory of Leadership: An Application of the Meta-analysis Procedures of Schmidt and Hunter," *Psychological Bulletin,* Vol. 97 (1985), pp. 274–285.

[18]Yukl, op. cit. (1994), op. 309.

[19]F. E. Fiedler, M. M. Chemers, and L. Mahar, *Improving Leadership Effectiveness: The Leader Match Concept* (New York: John Wiley, 1977).

[20]For documentation, see Fred E. Fiedler and Linda Mahar, "The Effectiveness of Contingency Model Training: A Review of the Validation of Leader Match," *Personnel Psychology* (Spring 1979), pp. 45–62; Fred E. Garcia, Cecil H. Bell, Martin M. Chemers, and Dennis Patrick, "Increasing Mine Productivity and Safety through Management Training and Organization Development: A Comparative Study," *Basic and Applied Social Psychology* (March 1984), pp. 1–18; Arthur G. Jago and James W. Ragan, "The Trouble with Leader Match Is that It Doesn't Match Fiedler's Con-

tingency Model," *Journal of Applied Psychology* (November 1986), pp. 555–559.

[21]See Yukl, op. cit. (1994); R. Ayman, M. M. Chemers, and F. E. Fiedler, "The Contingency Model of Leadership Effectiveness: Its Levels of Analysis," *Leadership Quarterly,* Vol. 6 (Summer 1995), pp. 147–168.

[22]This section is based on Robert J. House and Terence R. Mitchell, "Path-Goal Theory of Leadership," *Journal of Contemporary Business* (Autumn 1977), pp. 81–97.

[23]Ibid.

[24]C. A. Schriesheim and L. L. Neider, "Path-Goal Theory: The Long and Winding Road," *Leadership Quarterly* (In press, 1996); M. G. Evans, "Commentary on R. J. House's a Path-Goal Theory of Leader Effectiveness," *Leadership Quarterly* (In press, 1996).

[25]R. J. House, "Path-Goal Theory of Leadership: Lessons, Legacy, and a Reformulated Theory," *Leadership Quarterly* (In press, 1996).

[26]See the discussion of this approach in Paul Hersey and Kenneth H. Blanchard, *Management of Organizational Behavior* (Englewood Cliffs, NJ: Prentice-Hall, 1988).

[27]R.P. Vecchio and C. Fernandez, "Situational Leadership Theory Revisited," in M. Schnake, ed., *1995 Southern Management Association Proceedings* (Valdosta, GA: Georgia Southern University 1995), pp. 137–139.

[28]The discussion in this section is based on Steven Kerr and John Jermier, "Substitutes for Leadership: Their Meaning and Measurement," *Organizational Behavior and Human Performance,* Vol. 22 (1978), pp. 375–403. Jon P. Howell, David E. Bowen, Peter W. Dorfman, Steven Kerr, and Phillip M. Podsakoff, "Substitutes for Leadership: Effective Alternatives to Ineffective Leadership," *Organization Dynamics* (Summer 1990), pp. 21–38.

[29]Phillip M. Posakoff, Peter W. Dorfman, Jon P. Howell, and William D. Todor, "Leader Reward and Punishment Behaviors: A Preliminary Test of a Culture-Free Style of Leadership Effectiveness," *Advances in Comparative Management,* Vol. 2 (1989), pp. 95–138; T. K. Peng, "Substitutes for Leadership in an International Setting," unpublished manuscript, College of Business Administration, Texas Tech University (1990). See P. M. Podsakoff and S. B. MacKenzie, "Kerr and Jermier's Substitutes for Leadership Model: Background, Empirical Assessment, and Suggestions for Future Research, *Leadership Quarterly* (In press. 1996).

[30]See T. R. Mitchell, S. G. Green, and R. E. Wood, "An Attributional Model of Leadership and the Poor Performing Subordinate: Development and Validation." In. L. L. Cummings and B. M. Staw, eds., *Research in Organizational Behavior,* Vol. 3 (Greenwich, CT: JAI Press, 1981), pp. 197–234.

[31]James G. Hunt, Kimberly B. Boal, and Ritch L. Sorenson, "Top Management Leadership: Inside the Black Box," *Leadership Quarterly,* Vol. 1 (1990), pp. 41–65.

[32]Based on Geert Hofstede, *Cultures Consequences: International Differences in Work Related Values* (Beverly Hills, CA: Sage Publications, 1984).

[33]Hunt, Boal, and Sorenson, op. cit. (1990).

[34]See J. Pfeffer, "Management as Symbolic Action: The Creation and Maintenance of Organizational Paradigms," in L. L. Cummings and B. M. Staw, eds., *Research in Organizational Behavior,* Vol. 3 (Greenwich, CT: JAI Press, 1981), pp. 1–52.

[35]James R. Meindl, "On Leadership: An Alternative to the Conventional Wisdom," in B. M. Staw and L. L. Cummings, eds., *Research in Organizational Behavior,* Vol. 12 (Greenwich, CT: JAI Press, 1990), pp. 159–203.

[36]Compare with Bryman, op. cit. (1992).

[37]Bass, op. cit. (1990), Ch. 12.

[38]See R. J. House, "A 1976 Theory of Charismatic Leadership," in J. G. Hunt and L. L. Larson, eds., *Leadership: The Cutting Edge* (Carbondale, IL: Southern Illinois Press, 1977), pp. 189–207; R. J. House, W. D. Spangler and J. Woycke, "Personality and Charisma in the U.S. Presidency," *Administrative Science Quarterly,* Vol. 36 (1991), pp. 364–396.

[39]See Jane M. Howell and Bruce J. Avolio, "The Ethics of Charismatic

Leadership: Submission or Liberation," *Academy of Management Executive,* Vol. 6 (May 1992) pp. 43–54.

[40]Jay A. Conger and R. N. Kanungo, eds., *Charismatic Leadership: The Elusive Factor in Organizational Effectiveness* (San Francisco: Jossey-Bass, 1988).

[41]Conger and Kanungo, op. cit. (1988).

[42]B. Shamir, "Social Distance and Charisma: Theoretical Notes and an Exploratory Study," *Leadership Quarterly,* Vol. 6 (Spring 1995), pp. 19–48.

[43]See B. M. Bass, *Leadership and Performance Beyond Expectations* (New York: Free Press, 1985); A. Bryman, *Charisma and Leadership in Organizations* (London: Sage Publications, 1992), pp. 98–99.

[44]Adapted from Warren Bennis, "Managing the Dream: Leadership in the 21st Century," *Training: The Magazine of Human Resource Development* (May 1990); Henry Lelfer, "Serving Up Seminars for 'Strokers,'" *Air Transport World* (April 1990); Martin Nobel, "Europe's Airlines: The View from Carlzan," *Interavia Aerospace World* (January 1993); and Arthur Reed, "SAS Opens New Training Facility," *Air Transport World* (April 1989).

[45]Bryman, op. cit. (1992), Ch. 6; B. M. Bass and B. J. Avolio, "Transformational Leadership: A Response to Critics," in M. M. Chemers and R. Ayman, eds., *Leadership Theory and Practicie: Perspectives and Directions* (San Diego), CA: Academic Press, 1993), pp. 49–80.

[46]See B. M. Bass and B. J. Avolio, "The Implications of Transactional and Transformation Leadership for Individual Team and Organizational Development," *Research in Organization Change and Development,* Vol. 4 (1990), pp. 231–272.

[47]See Jay A. Conger and Rabindra N. Kanungo, "Training Charismatic Leadership: A Risky and Critical Task," in Jay A. Conger, Rabindra N. Kanungo, and Associates eds., *Charismatic Leadership: The Elusive Factor in Organizational Effectiveness* (San Francisco: Jossey-Bass, 1988), Ch. 11.

[48]See J. R. Kouzes and B. F. Posner, *The Leadership Challenge: How to Get Extraordinary Things Done in Organizations* (San Francisco: Jossey-Bass, 1991).

[49]Marshall Sashkin, "The Visionary Leader," in Conger and Kanungo, eds., *Charismatic Leadership: The Elusive Factor in Organizational Effectiveness* (San Francisco, Jossey-Bass, 1988), Ch. 5.

[50]J. G. Hunt, 1991. *Leadership: A New Synthesis* Beverly Hills, CA: Sage.

[51]J. G. Hunt and A. Ropo, "Multi-Level Leadership: Grounded Theory and Mainstream Theory Applied to the Case of General Motors," *Leadership Quarterly,* Vol. 6 (Fall 1995), pp. 379–412.

[52]See Charles C. Manz and Henry P. Sims, Jr., *Super Leadership* (New York: Berkley Books, 1989), pp. 201–202.

[53]Peter Larson, "Winning Strategies," *Canadian Business Review* (Summer 1989), p. 41.

▼ CHAPTER 16 ENDNOTES

[1]Information from Jan Norman, "Free Flow of Ideas from Employees Can Help Boost Small Businesses," *The Columbus Dispatch* (October 2, 1995), p. 18.

[2]See Henry Mintzberg, *The Nature of Managerial Work* (New York: Harper & Row, 1973); Morgan W. McCall, Jr., Ann M. Morrison, and Robert L. Hannan, *Studies of Managerial Work: Results and Methods,* Technical Report No. 9 (Greensboro, NC: Center for Creative Leadership, 1978); and John P. Kotter, *The General Managers* (New York: Free Press, 1982).

[3]Steve Axley, author of *Communication at Work: Management and the Communication-Intensive Organization* (Westport, CT.: Quorum Books, 1996), points out that ultimate meaning in any communication is created by the receiver or perceiver of the message.

[4]Developed from J. Stephen Morris, "How to Make Criticism Sessions Productive," *The Wall Street Journal* (October 12, 1981), p. 24.

[5]See Axelrod, *Communication at Work: Management and the Communication Intensive Organization*, op cit.

[6]Information from "Management Meccas," *Business Week* (September 18, 1995), pp. 122–132.

[7]See Richard L. Birdwhistell, *Kinesics and Context* (Philadelphia: University of Pennsylvania Press, 1970).

[8]Edward T. Hall, *The Hidden Dimension* (Garden City, NY: Doubleday, 1966).

[9]See D. E. Campbell, "Interior Office Design and Visitor Response," *Journal of Applied Psychology,* Vol. 64 (1979), pp. 648–653; P. C. Morrow and J. C. McElroy, "Interior Office Design and Visitor Response: A Constructive Replication," *Journal of Applied Psychology,* Vol. 66 (1981), pp. 646–650.

[10]M. P. Rowe and M. Baker, "Are You Hearing Enough Employee Concerns?" *Harvard Business Review,* Vol. 62 (May/June 1984), pp. 127–135.

[11]This discussion is based on Carl R. Rogers and Richard E. Farson, *Active Listening* (Chicago: Relations Center of the University of Chicago).

[12]See Richard L. Daft and R. H. Lengel, "Information Richness: A New Approach to Managerial Behavior and Organization Design," in Barry M. Staw and Larry L. Cummings, eds., *Research in Organizational Behavior,* Vol. 6 (Greenwich, CT: JAI Press, 1984), pp. 191–233.

[13]Networking is considered an essential managerial activity by Kotter, op. cit. (1982).

[14]Thomas J. Peters and Robert H. Waterman, Jr., *In Search of Excellence* (New York: Harper & Row, 1983).

[15]Richard V. Farace, Peter R. Monge, and Hamish M. Russell, *Communicating and Organizing* (Reading, MA: Addison-Wesley, 1977), pp. 97–98.

[16]The statements are from *Business Week* (July 6, 1981), p. 107.

[17]See A. Mehrabian, *Silent Messages* (Belmont, CA: Wadsworth, 1981).

[18]See C. Barnum and N. Woliansky, "Taking Cues from Body Language," *Management Review,* Vol. 78 (1989), p. 59; S. Bochner, ed., *Cultures in Contact: Studies in Cross-Cultural Interaction* (London: Pergamon, 1982); A. Furnham and S. Bocher, *Culture Shock: Psychological Reactions to Unfamiliar Environments* (London: Methuen, 1986).

[19]This research is reviewed by John C. Athanassiades, "The Distortion of Upward Communication in Hierarchical Organizations," *Academy of Management Journal,* Vol. 16 (June 1973), pp. 207–226.

[20]See Peters and Waterman, op. cit. (1983).

[21]Portions of this section are adapted from John R. Schermerhorn, Jr., Management, 5th ed. (New York: John Wiley & Sons, 1996), pp. 375–378. Used by permission.

[22]Information from "Oh, What an Untabled Web," *Business Week* (February 26, 1996), p. 82.

[23]C. Reuss and D. Silvis, eds., *Inside Organizational Communication* (New York: Longmans, 1985).

[24]*Business Week* (May 16, 1994), p. 8.

[25]Information from Tina Lassen, "Miles of Fun," *WorldTraveler Magazine* (November 1995), pp. 64–68, 103.

[26]The concept of interacting, coacting, and counteracting groups is presented in Fred E. Fiedler, *A Theory of Leadership Productivity* (New York: McGraw-Hill, 1967).

[27]Research on communication networks is found in Alex Bavelas, "Communication Patterns in Task-Oriented Groups," *Journal of the Accoustical Society of America,* Vol. 22 (1950), pp. 725–730. See also "Research on Communication Networks," as summarized in Marvin E. Shaw, *Group Dynamics: The Psychology of Small Group Behavior* (New York: McGraw-Hill, 1976), pp. 137–153.

[28]Information from "Honda's Civic Lesson," *Business Week* (September 18, 1995), pp. 71–76.

[29]See, for example, Arno Penzias, "New Paths to Success," *Fortune* (June 12, 1995), pp. 90–94.

[30]See C. Brod, *Technostress: The Human Cost of the Computer Revolution* (Reading, MA: Addison-Wesley, 1984); and G. Brockhouse, "I Have Seen the Future...," *Canadian Business* (August 1993), pp. 43–45.

[31]Arno Penzias, "New Paths to Success," *Fortune* (June 21, 1995), pp. 90–94.

[32]Reported by *Working Woman* (November 1995), p. 14.

[33]Ibid.

[34]Deborah Tannen, *You Just Don't Understand: Women and Men in Conversation* (New York: Ballantine Books, 1991).

[35]For an editorial opinion see Jayne Tear, "They Just Don't Understand Gender Dynamics," *The Wall Street Journal* (November 20, 1995), p. A14.

[36]See "My Boss, Big Brother," *Business Week* (January 22, 1996), p. 56.

[37]Thomas Petzinger, Jr., "The Front Lines," *The Wall Street Journal* (November 10, 1995), p. B1.

▼ CHAPTER 17 ENDNOTES

[1]Information from Seth Lubove, "Salad in a Bag," *Forbes* (October 23, 1995), pp. 201–203.

[2]For a concise overview see George P. Huber, *Managerial Decision Making* (Glenview, IL: Scott, Foresman, 1980).

[3]Subsequent discussion adapted with permission from John R. Schermerhorn, Jr., *Management for Productivity,* (New York: John Wiley, 1989), pp. 70–71. Copyright © 1989 John Wiley & Sons. Reprinted by permission of John Wiley & Sons, Inc.

[4]This discussion is based on James G. March and Herbert A. Simon, *Organizations* (New York: John Wiley, 1958), pp. 137–142.

[5]Ibid.

[6]Herbert A. Simon, *Administrative Behavior* (New York: Free Press, 1947).

[7]Mary Zey, ed., *Decision Making: Alternatives to Rational Choice Models* (Thousand Oaks, CA: Sage Publications, 1992).

[8]Simon, *Administrative Behavior,* op cit.

[9]Weston H. Agor, *Intuition in Organizations* (Newbury Park, CA: Sage Publications, 1989).

[10]Henry Mintzberg, "Planning on the Left Side and Managing on the Right," *Harvard Business Review,* Vol. 54 (July/August 1976), pp. 51–63.

[11]Developed from Weston H. Agor, "How Top Executives Use Their Intuition To Make Important Decisions," *Business Horizons,* Vol. 29 (January/February, 1986, pp. 49–53; see also Agor, op. cit. (1989).

[12]The classic work in this area is found in a series of articles by D. Kahneman and A. Tversky: "Subjective Probability: A Judgement of Representativeness," *Cognitive Psychology,* Vol. 3 (1972), pp. 430–454; "On the Psychology of Prediction," *Psychological Review,* Vol. 80 (1973), pp. 237–251; "Prospect Theory: An Analysis of Decision Under Risk," *Econometrica,* Vol. 47 (1979), pp. 263–291; "Psychology of Preferences," *Scientific American* (1982), pp. 161–173; "Choices, Values, Frames," *American Psychologist,* Vol. 39 (1984), pp. 341–350.

[13]Definition and subsequent discussion based on Max H. Bazerman, *Judgement in Managerial Decision Making,* 3rd ed. (New York: John Wiley, 1994).

[14]See Cameron M. Ford and Dennis A. Gioia, *Creative Action in Organizations* (Thousand Oaks, CA: Sage Publications, 1995).

[15]G. Wallas, *The Art of Thought* (New York: Harcourt, 1926). Cited in Bazerman, op. cit. (1994).

[16]E. Glassman, "Creative Problem Solving," *Supervisory Management* (January, 1989), pp. 21–26; and B. Kabanoff and J.R. Rossiter, "Recent Developments in Applied Creativity," *International Review of Industrial and Organizational Psychology,* Vol. 9 (1994), pp. 283–324.

[17]Information from Kenneth Labich, "Nike vs. Reebok," *Fortune* (September 18, 1995), pp. 90–106.

[18]James A. F. Stoner, *Management,* 2nd ed. (Englewood Cliffs, NJ: Prentice Hall, 1982), pp. 167–168.

[19]Victor H. Vroom and Philip W. Yetton, *Leadership and Decision Making* (Pittsburgh: University of Pittsburgh Press, 1973); Victor H. Vroom and Arthur G. Jago, *The New Leadership* (Englewood Cliffs, NJ: Prentice Hall, 1988).

[20]Information from "Artificial Imagination," *Business Week* (March 18, 1996), p. 60.

[20]Adapted from Ellyn E. Spagins, "Reverse Review," *Inc.* (October 1992).

[21]Barry M. Staw, "The Escalation of Commitment to a Course of Action," *Academy of Management Review,* Vol. 6 (1981), pp. 577–587; Barry M. Staw and Jerry Ross, "Knowing When to Pull the Plug," *Harvard Business Review,* Vol. 65 (March/April 1987), pp. 68–74. See also Glen Whyte, "Escalating Commitment to a Course of Action: A Reinterpretation," *Academy of Management Review,* Vol. 11 (1986), pp. 311–321.

[22]Bazerman, op. cit. (1994), pp. 79–83.

[23]J. Z. Rubin, "Negotiation: An Introduction to Some Issues and Themes," *American Behavioral Scientist,* Vol. 27 (1983), pp. 135–147.

[24]J. Lorinc, "Power Failure," *Canadian Business* (November 1992), pp. 50–58; and, "The Politics of Power," *Canadian Business* (March 1993), pp. 41–42.

[25]Alan L. Otten, "Ethics on the Job: Companies Alert Employees to Potential Dilemmas," *The Wall Street Journal* (July 14, 1986), p. 17.

[26]For an expanded discussion of such ethical frameworks for decision making, see Linda A. Travino and Katherine A. Nelson, *Managing Business Ethics* (New York: Wiley, 1995).

[27]Saul W. Gellerman, "Why `Good' Managers Make Bad Ethical Choices," *Harvard Business Review,* Vol. 64 (July/August 1986), pp. 85–90. See also Barbara Ley Toffler, *Tough Choices: Managers Talk Ethics* (New York: Wiley, 1986).

[28]Information from Mary Scott, "Odwalla, Inc.," *Business Ethics* (November/December, 1995), p. 35.

[29]Fons Trompenaars, *Riding the Waves of Culture: Understanding Cultural Diversity in Business* (London: Nicholas Brealey Publishing, 1993), p. 6.

[30]Information from "The Real Fast Track is Overseas," *Fortune* (August 21, 1995), p. 129.

[31]See Trompenaars, *Riding the Waves of Culture,* op cit., pp. 58–59.

[32]For a good discussion of decision making in Japanese organizations see Min Chen, *Asian Management Systems* (New York: Routledge, 1995).

[33]Nancy J. Adler, *International Dimensions of Organizational Behavior,* 2nd ed. (Boston: PWS-Kent, 1991).

[34]Trompenaars, *Riding the Waves of Culture,* op cit., p. 10.

[35]See "Computers That Think Are Almost Here," *Business Week* (July 17, 1995), pp. 68–73.

[36]Information from "The Brain Behind the Brain," *Business Week* (July 17, 1995), p. 71.

[37]A. R. Dinnis and J.S. Valacich, "Computer Brainstorms: Two Heads are Better Than One," *Journal of Applied Psychology* (February 1994), pp. 77–86.

[38]B. Kabanoff and J. R. Rossiter, "Recent Developments in Applied Creativity," *International Review of Industrial and Organizational Psychology,* Vol. 9 (1994), pp. 283–324.

[39]Adapted from Walter Kiechel III, "How We Will Work in the Year 2000," *Fortune* (May 17, 1993), pp. 38–52.

[40]Charles Handy, *The Age of Unreason* (Boston: Harvard Business School Press, 1991).

[41]Quote from "The New Professionals," *World Executive's Digest* (May 1993), p. 14.

[42]Ibid.

▼ CHAPTER 18 ENDNOTES

[1]See Henry Mintzberg, *The Nature of Managerial Work* (New York: Harper & Row, 1973); and John R. P. Kotter, *The General Managers* (New York: The Free Press, 1982).

[2]Richard E. Walton, *Interpersonal Peacemaking: Confrontations and Third-Party Consultation* (Reading, MA: Addison-Wesley, 1969).

[3]Kenneth W. Thomas and Warren H. Schmidt, "A Survey of Managerial Interests with Respect to Conflict," *Academy of Management Journal,* Vol. 19 (1976), pp. 315–318.

[4]Walton, op. cit. (1969).

[5]Ibid.

[6]Richard E. Walton and John M. Dutton, "The Management of Interdepartmental Conflict: A Model and Review," *Administrative Science Quarterly,* Vol. 14 (1969), pp. 73–84.

[7]For a discussion, see A. Priddle, "CAMI Has a Coming Out Party," *The Windsor Star* (May 12, 1990), p. A17; and A. Blankenshift, "CAMI One of Canada's Best," *Detroit Free Press* (December 10, 1995), p. C1.

[8]Douglas Lavin, "Chrysler's Stallkamp Gets Suppliers to Help Cut Costs," *The Asian Wall Street Journal* (May 17, 1993), p. 9.

[9]Developed from Don Hellriegel, John W. Slocum, Jr., and Richard W. Woodman, *Organizational Behavior,* 3rd ed. (St. Paul: West, 1983), pp. 471–474.

[10]See Gary Johns, *Organizational Behavior* (Glenview, IL: Scott, Foresman, 1983), pp. 415–417; and Walton and Dutton, op. cit. (1969).

[11]These stages are consistent with the conflict models described by Alan C. Filley, *Interpersonal Conflict Resolution* (Glenview, IL: Scott, Foresman, 1975); and Louis R. Pondy, "Organizational Conflict: Concepts and Models," *Administrative Science Quarterly,* Vol. 12 (September 1967), pp. 269–320.

[12] See D.J. McAllister, "The Affect and Cognition Based Trust as Foundations for Interpersonal Cooperation in Organizations," *Academy of Management Journal,* Vol. 38 (1995), pp. 24–59.

[13]Rensis Likert and Jane B. Likert, *New Ways of Managing Conflict* (New York: McGraw-Hill, 1976).

[14]See Jay Galbraith, *Designing Complex Organizations* (Reading, MA: Addison-Wesley, 1973).

[15]David Nadler and Michael Tushman, *Strategic Organizational Design* (Glenview, IL: Scott, Foresman, 1988).

[16]E. M. Eisenberg and M. G. Witten, "Reconsidering Openness in Organizational Communication," *Academy of Management Review,* Vol. 12 (1987), pp. 418–426.

[17]R. G. Lord and M. C. Kernan, "Scripts as Determinants of Purposeful Behavior in Organizations," *Academy of Management Review,* Vol. 12 (1987), pp. 265–277.

[18]See Filley, op. cit. (1975); and L. David Brown, *Managing Conflict at Organizational Interfaces* (Reading, MA: Addison-Wesley, 1983).

[19]Ibid., pp. 27, 29.

[20] J. Osborn, "A Study of Conflict Resolution in Dominant and Counter Cultures." Master of Education Thesis, Wayne State University, Detroit, MI, 1996.

[21]Developed from John Schermerhorn, Jr., *Managing for Productivity* (New York: John Wiley, 1994).

[22]For discussions, see Robert R. Blake and Jane Strygley Mouton, "The Fifth Achievement," *Journal of Applied Behavioral Science,* Vol. 6 (1970), pp. 413–427; Kenneth Thomas, "Conflict and Conflict Management," in M. D. Dunnett, ed., *Handbook of Industrial and Organizational Behavior* (Chicago: Rand McNally, 1976), pp. 889–935; and Kenneth W. Thomas, "Toward Multi-Dimensional Values in Teaching: The Examples of Conflict Behaviors," *Academy of Management Review,* Vol. 2 (1977), pp. 484–490.

[23]For an excellent overview, see Roger Fisher and William Ury, *Getting to*

Yes: Negotiating Agreement Without Giving In (New York: Penguin, 1983). See also James A. Wall, Jr., *Negotiation: Theory and Practice* (Glenview, IL: Scott, Foresman, 1985).

24Mintzberg, op. cit. (1973).

25Roy J. Lewicki and Joseph A. Litterer, *Negotiation* (Homewood, IL: Irwin, 1985), pp. 315–319.

26Ibid., pp. 328–329.

27Following discussion based on Fisher and Ury, op. cit. (1983); and Lewicki and Litterer, op. cit. (1985).

28This example is developed from Bazerman, pp. 106–108.

29For a discussion of Xerox's labor relations practices, see March and Levin and *Xerox Annual Report,* 1995.

30For a detailed discussions see Fisher and Ury, op. cit., and Lewicki and Litterer, op. cit. (1985).

31Developed from Max H. Bazerman, Judgement in Managerial Decision Making, 2nd ed. (New York: John Wiley & Sons, 1991), pp. 127–141.

32Fisher and Ury, op. cit. (1983), p. 33.

33Lewicki and Litterer, op. cit. (1985), pp. 177–181.

▼ CHAPTER 19 ENDNOTES

1Information from *Georgetown Business,* Vol. VIII (Fall, 1995), pp. 1, 2.

2See Peter F. Drucker, *Managing for the Future: The 1990s and Beyond* (New York: Truman Talley Books/Dutton, 1992).

3Tom Peters, *Thriving on Chaos* (New York: Random Huuse ,1987); and Tom Peters, "Managing in a World Gone Bonkers," *World Executive Digest* (February 1993), pp. 26–29.

4See David Nadler and Michael Tushman, *Strategic Organizational Design* (Glenview, IL: Scott, Foresman, 1988); and Noel M. Tichy, "Revolutionize Your Company," *Fortune* (December 13, 1993), pp. 114–118.

5Information from Jeremy Main, "How to Steal the Best Ideas Around," *Fortune* (October 19, 1992), pp. 102–106.

6"Food for Thought," *The Economist* (August 29, 1992), pp. 62–63. See also John F. Love, *McDonald's: Beyond the Arches,* rev. ed. (New York: Bantam Doubleday Bell, 1996).

7Rosabeth Moss Kanter, Barry A. Stein, and Todd D. Jick, "Meeting the Challenges of Change," *World Executive's Digest* (May 1993), pp. 22–27.

8Information from Alex Markels, "It's Time You Became a Manager of Change, The Consultants Say," *The Wall Street Journal* (October 31, 1995), p. B1.

9Robert A. Cooke, "Managing Change in Organizations," in Gerald Zaltman, ed., *Management Principles for Nonprofit Organizations* (New York: American Management Association, 1979). See also David A. Nadler, "The Effective Management of Organizational Change," in Jay W. Lorsch, ed., *Handbook of Organizational Behavior* (Englewood Cliffs, NJ: Prentice Hall, 1987), pp. 358–369.

10See, for example, Ralph H. Kilmann, *Beyond the Quick Fix* (San Francisco: Jossey-Bass, 1984); Noel M. Tichy and Mary Anne Devanna, *The Transformational Leader* (New York: John Wiley, 1986); and Peter M. Senge, *The Fifth Discipline: The Art & Practice of the Learning Organization* (New York: Doubleday, 1990).

11Kurt Lewin, "Group Decision and Social Change," in G. E. Swanson, T. M. Newcomb, and E. L. Hartley, eds., *Readings in Social Psychology* (New York: Holt, Rinehart and Winston, 1952), pp. 459–473.

12Tichy and Devanna, op. cit. (1986), p. 44.

13Information from Robyn Meredith, "G.M. Considers Executive to Manage Learning," *The New York Times* (March 19, 1996), p. C5.

14The change strategies are described in Robert Chin and Kenneth D. Benne, "General Strategies for Effecting Changes in Human Systems," in Warren G. Bennis, Kenneth D. Benne, Robert Chin, and Kenneth E.

Corey, eds., *The Planning of Change,* 3rd ed. (New York: Holt, Rinehart and Winston, 1969), pp. 22–45.

15The change strategy examples in this part are developed from an exercise reported in J. William Pfeiffer and John E. Jones, *A Handbook of Structured Experiences for Human Relations Training,* Vol. II (La Jolla, CA: University Associates, 1973).

16Donald Klein, "Some Notes on the Dynamics of Resistance to Change: The Defender Role," in Warren G, Bennis, et al., eds., *The Planning of Change,* 3rd ed., op cit., pp. 117–124.

17See Everett M. Rogers, *Communication of Innovations,* 3rd ed. (New York: Free Press, 1993).

18Ibid.

19John P. Kotter and Leonard A. Schlesinger, "Choosing Strategies for Change," *Harvard Business Review,* Vol. 57 (March/April 1979), pp. 109–112.

20Information from Anne B. Fisher, "Making Change Stick," *Fortune* (April 17, 1995), pp. 121–130.

21Edward B. Roberts, "Managing Invention and Innovation," *Research Technology Management* (January/February 1988), pp. 1–19. For an extensive case study see John Clark, *Managing Innovation and Change* (Thousand Oaks, CA: Sage Publications, 1995).

22Information from Rob Muller, "Training for Change," *Canadian Business Review* (Spring, 1995), pp. 16–19.

23Quote from Kenneth Labich, "The Innovators," *Fortune* (June 6, 1988), pp. 49–64.

24Arthur P. Brief, Randall S. Schuler, and Mary Van Sell, *Managing Job Stress* (Boston: Little Brown, 1981).

25Portions of this treatment of stress have been developed by permission from John R. Schermerhorn, Jr., *Management for Productivity,* 3rd ed. (New York: John Wiley, 1989), pp. 647–652.

26For career implications and stress of whistleblowing see Hal Lancaster, "Workers Who Blow the Whistle on Bosses Often Pay High Prices," *The Wall Street Journal* (July 18, 1995), p. B1.

27Information from Hillary Chura, "Even Away from the Office, CEO Connected to Business," *The Columbus Dispatch* (October 23, 1995), p. 8.

28See Orlando Behling and Arthur L. Darrow, *Managing Work-Related Stress* (Chicago: Science Research Associates, 1984).

29Meyer Friedman and Ray Roseman, *Type A Behavior and Your Heart* (New York: Alfred A. Knopf, 1974).

30See H. Selye, *The Stress of Life,* rev. ed. (New York: McGraw-Hill, 1976).

31Information from Anne B. Fisher, "Welcome to the Age of Overwork," *Fortune* (November 30, 1992), pp. 64–71.

32Ibid.

33See John D. Adams, "Health, Stress, and the Manager's Life Style," *Group and Organization Studies,* Vol. 6 (September 1981), pp. 291–301.

34Robert Kreitner, "Personal Wellness: It's Just Good Business," *Business Horizons,* Vol. 25 (May/June 1982), pp. 28–35.

▼ ENDNOTES: SUPPLEMENTAL MODULE

1See Richard L. Daft, "Learning the Craft of Organizational Research," *Academy of Management Review* Vol. 8 (October 1983), pp. 539–546; Eugene Stone, *Research Methods in Organizational Behavior* (Santa Monica, CA: Goodyear, 1978), p. 21.

2Stone, op. cit. (1978), p. 26.

3Stone, op. cit. (1978).

4C. William Emory, *Business Research Methods,* rev. ed. (Homewood, IL: Irwin, 1980).

5Duane Davis and Robert M. Casenza, *Business Research for Decision Making* (Belmont, CA: Wadsworth, 1993), p. 134.

[6]Davis and Casenza, op. cit. (1993), Ch. 5.

[7]Davis and Casenza, op. cit. (1993).

[8]Davis and Casenza, op. cit. (1993), p. 174.

[9]Davis and Casenza, op. cit. (1993), p. 125.

[10]This section based on Davis and Casenza, op. cit. (1993), Ch. 5.

[11]This section based on Stone, op. cit. (1978).

[12]See G. Pinchot, *Intrapreneuring* (New York: Harper, 1985).

[13]See A. D. Aczel, *Complete Business Statistics* (Homewood, IL: Irwin, 1989) for further discussion.

[14]Davis and Casenza, op. cit. (1993).

[15]Davis and Casenza, op. cit. (1993), Ch. 14.

[16]Unreferenced.

PHOTO CREDITS

COMPANY INDEX

NAME INDEX

SUBJECT INDEX